Y0-CAO-963

SOVIET POLITICS AND SOCIETY IN THE 1970's

Studies of the Russian Institute Columbia University

The Russian Institute of Columbia University sponsors the *Studies of the Russian Institute* in the belief that their publication contributes to scholarly research and public understanding. In this way the Institute, while not necessarily endorsing their conclusions, is pleased to make available the results of some of the research conducted under its auspices.

SOVIET POLITICS AND SOCIETY IN THE 1970's

EDITED BY

Henry W. Morton
and Rudolf L. Tőkés

THE FREE PRESS
A Division of Macmillan Publishing Co., Inc.
NEW YORK

Collier Macmillan Publishers
LONDON

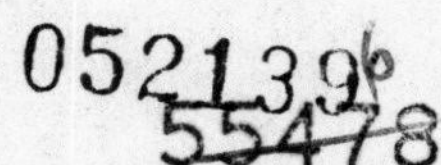

The Free Press
A Division of Macmillan Publishing Co., Inc.
866 Third Avenue, New York, N.Y. 10022

Collier–Macmillan Canada Ltd.

Library of Congress Catalog Card Number: 73-10575

Printed in the United States of America

printing number
2 3 4 5 6 7 8 9 10

Library of Congress Cataloging in Publication Data
Main entry under title:

Soviet politics and society in the 1970's.

Dedicated to John N. Hazard on the occasion of his 65th birthday.
Includes bibliographical references.
CONTENTS: Tőkés, R. L. Dissent: the politics for change in the USSR.—Hodnett, G. Technology and social change in Soviet Central Asia; the politics of cotton growing.—Jančar, B. W. Women and Soviet politics. [etc.]
1. Russia—Politics and government—1953– Addresses, essays, lectures. 2. Russia—Social conditions—Addresses, essays, lectures. I. Morton, Henry W., 1929– ed. II. Tőkés, Rudolf L., 1935– ed. III. Hazard, John Newbold, 1909–
DK274.S6517 309.1'47'085 73-10575
ISBN 0-02-922090-4

Affectionately dedicated to
John N. Hazard
Scholar, Teacher, Friend
on the occasion of his
Sixty-fifth Birthday

Contents

Preface

The volume is a collective effort by ten former students of John N. Hazard to honor our good friend and teacher on his 65th birthday and in the 28th year of his association with the Russian Institute of Columbia University.

The contributors to this volume represent different generations of Russian Institute alumni. Some were there in the early years (Cattell), and some are recent graduates (Taubman and Friedgut). Most of us represent the "middle generation," who listened to Hazard's lectures on Soviet political institutions in Fayerweather Hall in the 1950's and early 1960's. We all benefited greatly from John Hazard's teaching and scholarship; from his warm, friendly, and congenial personality; and from his constant encouragement and wise counsel.

Because of the great number of potential contributors who would have wished to honor him, the editors' criterion for selection was to ask only those who are political scientists and past students of John N. Hazard. Therefore, we were, regretfully, forced to exclude great numbers of eminently qualified historians, economists, scholars of Soviet literature, lawyers and others who had formed a close association with him over the years.

The editors believed that the best way to pay our respects to our former teacher was for our authors to present their chapters in a form that could benefit students, specialists, and laymen alike, so that this book would be both used and useful and would not be a disparate, unfocused collection of essays which would gather dust on library shelves. The project needed coherence, structure, and direction in order to become an anti-Festschrift, so to speak.

The themes we chose reflect two major, interlocking interests of John Hazard's distinguished career: first, his overarching and sustained concern with politics and social change in the USSR, and second, his more recent interest in the influence and application of the Soviet model in

Communist-party–dominated and Third-World countries. The scheme of the book is explained in the Introduction.

Acknowledgments

There are many who made this project possible and to whom thanks are due. First and foremost we wish to thank our contributors for their cooperative spirit and punctuality in delivery of their first drafts and revisions. This greatly eased the work of the editors and made it a model symposium for us. Our work was greatly assisted by a two-day workshop which we held at the American Political Science Association meeting in Washington, D.C., in September, 1973, at which time these chapters were first read and critiqued. We particularly wish to thank our workshop discussants—Seweryn Bialer, Jonathan Harris, Henry Krisch, Jane Shapiro, and Robert Sharlet—for the incisive written and oral comments which they so conscientiously prepared and Robert Wesson for his participation. We thank Professor Loren Graham of the Russian Institute and Professor Marshall Shulman, the institute director, for their encouragement and assistance, and we commend the R.I. staff for their helpfulness and courtesy. We also wish to express our appreciation for the editorial assistance of Elaine Ulman and the help of Mary P. Tőkés and Minnie Meyers, Norma Sileo and Ann Pelner in retyping, editing, and assembling the manuscript. Lastly, we are grateful to our respective institutions—Queens College of the City University of New York and the Graduate Research Foundation of the University of Connecticut—for their supportive services, which greatly eased the editors' burden. On a personal note Henry W. Morton wishes to give credit to Rudolf L. Tőkés for the genesis of this volume and to thank his colleague for asking him to become a partner in a rewarding intellectual enterprise.

A Biographical Note

John N. Hazard was born in Syracuse, New York, on January 5, 1909. Like his father before him he attended the Hill School (1921–1926) and Yale University, from which he received his B.A. in 1930. His first visit to the USSR took place in that same year, when he traveled around the world in the company of several classmates.

Upon his return, Hazard entered the Harvard Law School, where he received the LL.B. and the Addison Brown Prize in International Law in 1934. At this point John Hazard's career took a different turn from those of his coevals. Instead of practicing law in the United States, he accepted a fellowship from the Institute of Current World Affairs to study Soviet law at the Moscow Juridical Institute.

The three-and-one-half years that Hazard spent at the institute (fall, 1934, through December, 1937) were the formative years in his development into an internationally renowned authority on Soviet law and government. It was a singular experience to be the first American to study at the Moscow Juridical Institute and to receive from it a certificate. Hazard arrived a novice in his knowledge of Soviet society and of the Russian language, but he was eager to learn. He could not prepare himself for the task in the United States by attending a Russian area program or by taking specialized courses on Soviet society, because these did not exist at that time. Of his first months at the institute he wrote:

> There are Ukrainians, White Russians, Armenians, Jews, Georgians, Azerbaijanians and numerous representatives from more remote regions of Asia. It is the young man or woman from Buriat-Mongolia, from Uzbekistan, from Tajikistan and from the Afghan and Iranian borders who adds the international touch to this institute, dedicated to the training of judges, prosecutors and practising attorneys. . . . In this tower of Babel, with its many races, languages and points of view, I found myself quite unembarrassed being a foreigner. Men and women from the non Russian areas of the Union spoke just as haltingly as I and the huge Soviet capital was even more startling to many of them than to me, who had been reared in American cities.[1]

During Hazard's stay the USSR was in the midst of an economic, social, and political upheaval. Under Stalin's single-minded direction the country was rapidly being transformed into an industrial power. This took place at the expense of the consumer, who suffered severe hardships, because his basic needs for food, shelter, and clothing went unrequited. These were also the Soviet "times of trouble," when Stalin concentrated absolute power in his own hands and unleashed a mass purge through the security police.

Hazard lived through these eventful times that shaped the destiny of the USSR. In an atmosphere of contradictory political events, which he tried to comprehend without being privy to essential facts and without the benefit of historical hindsight, he of necessity devoted his time to learning Russian, studying Soviet law, attending court sessions, and

1. John N. Hazard, "In the Soviet Law School," *Asia* (October, 1939), 565.

battling the cold and the bed bugs which had taken up permanent residence in his spartan quarters.

The year 1934 saw the building of the Moscow subway and the baffling assassination of Kirov, party secretary of Leningrad and second in command to Stalin. In 1936 a new constitution, which stressed democratic practices and guaranteed basic civil rights of all citizens, was promulgated with much fanfare. At the same time leading opponents of Stalin were publicly confessing to crimes of counterrevolutionary conspiracy and espionage. The Moscow Institute of Law was directly affected by these developments. E. B. Pashukanis, the country's leading legal authority, was one who fell victim to the purge, because, in Hazard's words, "he advocated the withering of the state and law (civil law courses were to be terminated) at a time when Stalin sharply increased the powers of the state, the coercive forces in particular." [2]

The removal of Pashukanis threw the law institute into complete confusion. His influence, once pervasive among teachers and students, suddenly became subversive. His numerous disciples were removed, "their books . . . withdrawn from libraries and bookstalls, and their doctrine . . . branded as the teaching of enemies of the people." [3] Hazard decided to stay an additional semester, the fall of 1937, to see what new directions Soviet law would take in the wake of Pashukanis' purge.

By the end of his stay Hazard had become a sophisticated student of Soviet law and society, at a time when this country had only a few. The basic principle that he took with him, a principle which he has applied ever since in his teaching and writing, is that Soviet law, despite arbitrary and illegal acts carried out by coercive agencies of the state, has an important function in regulating the activities of citizens and public enterprises and in adjudicating disputes that arise among them; that, in fact, no society can function without such legal rules and regulations. Furthermore, the promulgating of laws and the reporting of civil and criminal court cases serve as valuable sources of information and are indicators of the direction of societal development and change. Hazard applied these precepts in his first book, *Soviet Housing Law* (1939), which also served as his dissertation for the J.S.D. which he received from the University of Chicago in 1939.

Upon his return to the United States Hazard wished to specialize in problems of public and private international law, particularly in cases

2. John N. Hazard, "Housecleaning in Soviet Law," *The American Quarterly on the Soviet Union,* I, no. 1 (April, 1938), 1–2.
3. *Ibid.*

relating to the USSR. With this in mind he joined a New York law firm in 1939.

When the Second World War broke out Hazard was appointed deputy director of the lend-lease program to the USSR and remained in that position until 1946, although he was given various leaves from time to time to perform special assignments. Thus he served as special assistant to Vice-President Henry Wallace on his mission to the USSR and China in 1944; as adviser on Soviet law to the U.S. prosecutor in preparation of the Nuremberg trials of Nazi war criminals in 1945; and as the adviser on state trading in the Commercial Policy Division of the Department of State during his last six months in Washington.

Hazard left government service permanently in 1946 to accept the position of professor of public law and government at Columbia University. In doing so he joined four distinguished colleagues, Geroid T. Robinson (history), Philip Mosely (international relations), Abram Bergson (economics), and Ernest Simmons (literature) as charter professors of the first Russian institute operating under the auspices of a major university. The reason for establishing a Russian area program was to satisfy a need to familiarize Americans with the USSR, which had been a major ally during the war but which had evolved into a cold-war opponent soon thereafter; to generate scholarly inquiry into many aspects of Soviet politics, economics, and society, which up to that time had not been studied; and to satisfy the demand of universities and government agencies for young men and women who had received systematic training in the Soviet area. Of the original quintet, only John Hazard is still active in teaching and research at Columbia University.

As teacher and scholar Hazard has left an indelible mark. He has taught his many students, of whom the contributors represent but a small sample, that political analysis can only be developed from a firm basis of empirical data; he has consistently rejected impressionistic interpretations of politics and society, of model building with little relevance to real-world situation. "Like the Dutch painters of several centuries ago," he frequently remarked, "I like to see the leaves on the geraniums."

After leaving the USSR John Hazard rapidly established himself as a leading authority on Soviet law and government. His scholarly output has been prodigious. Between 1939 and 1972 he published five major books, the aforementioned *Soviet Housing Law, Law and Social Change in the USSR* (1953), *The Soviet System of Government* (1957 and now in its fourth edition), *Settling Disputes in Soviet Society: The Formative Years of Legal Institutions* (1960), and *Communists and Their Law: A*

Search for the Common Core of the Legal Systems of the Marxian Socialist States (1969). In addition he contributed 33 chapters on various topics to other books and published more than 115 articles in scholarly journals. This list does not include his contributions to encyclopedias, bibliographies, and books that he edited or coedited.

Besides his teaching and scholarly activities he has served as officer of numerous professional associations. Those which elected him to the presidency were the International Association of Legal Sciences in 1968, the American Branch of the International Law Association in 1973, and the American Foreign Law Association in 1973. He has also served on the editorial boards of political science, Slavic, and international and comparative law journals and gave meritorious service as managing editor of the *American Slavic and East European Review* from 1951 to 1959.

John Hazard's esteemed place as the doyen of American scholarship specializing in Soviet law was duly recognized by Freiburg University of Germany and Lehigh University, which conferred honorary doctorates upon him in 1969 and 1970, respectively, and by his election as a titular member of the International Academy of Comparative Law in 1959 and as a corresponding member of the British Academy in 1973.

This brief biographical sketch would be far from complete if we did not record that on March 8, 1941, John Hazard married Miss Susan Lawrence. They have four children: John Gibson and William Lawrence, Nancy and Barbara Peace.

H. W. Morton

Contributors

David E. Albright received his certificate from the Russian Institute and his Ph.D. from Columbia University in 1971. He was awarded a Ford Foundation Foreign Area Fellowship, from 1959 to 1961 and a research fellowship from the Center for International Studies, M.I.T. in 1966–67. He is associate editor of *Problems of Communism* and author of the forthcoming *The Dilemma of Courtship: The Soviet Union, China and Ghana.*

David T. Cattell received his certificate from the Russian Institute in 1949 and his Ph.D. from Columbia University in 1953. He was awarded a Social Science Research Fellowship in 1950–51 and a Rockefeller Grant in International Relations in 1963. He spent 1962 and 1966 in the USSR as an exchange scholar under the auspices of the Soviet-American Academic Exchange. He is professor of political science at the University of California at Los Angeles and author of *Leningrad: A Case Study of Soviet Urban Government* (1968), *Soviet Diplomacy and the Spanish Civil War* (1957), and *Communism and the Spanish Civil War* (1955).

Theodore Friedgut is director of the Soviet and East European Research Centre at the Hebrew University of Jerusalem. Dr. Friedgut received his B.A. and M.A. degrees at the Hebrew University and his doctorate in political science from Columbia University. He was an exchange fellow at Moscow State University and traveled widely in the USSR, particularly in Georgia. His publications include a contribution to *Columbia Essays on International Affairs* (1970), a chapter, "The Democratic Movement: Dimensions and Perspectives," in R. L. Tőkés' (ed.), *The Politics and Ideologies of Dissent in the USSR* (1974), and articles in scholarly journals. Dr. Friedgut is presently at work on a book on Soviet local and community politics.

Grey Hodnett is an associate professor of political science at York University. He received his A.B. degree from Harvard and his M.A., Ph.D. and the Russian Institute Certificate from Columbia University. Professor Hodnett taught at Columbia (1964–1967) and has been on the York political science faculty since 1967. Between 1969 and 1971 he held an appointment as senior research fellow at the Institute of Advanced Studies of the Australian National University. His publications include *The Ukraine and the Czechoslovak Crisis* (with Peter J. Potichnjy (1970), *Leaders of the Soviet Republics 1955–1972* (with Val Ogareff) (1973), and articles in *Problems of Communism, Slavic Review, Soviet Studies,* and the forthcoming *Documents on the History of the CPSU, vol. IV* (1974).

Barbara Wolfe Jančar is an assistant professor of political science at Union College and the executive director of International Science Exchange, a private consulting firm. She was formerly on the faculty of Skidmore College and has also taught at the George Washington University Center at Newport, R.I. Dr. Jančar graduated from Smith College and did her graduate work at Columbia University (M.A., Ph.D., and certificate, Institute on East Central Europe). Her publications include *The Philosophy of Aristotle* (1963, 1966), *Czechoslovakia 1971* (1970), *Czechoslovakia and the Absolute Monopoly of Power* (1971), two major monographs on problems of mental health and regional development in upstate New York, and several articles in *Orbis*, *East Europe*, and other scholarly journals. Presently she is completing a book tentatively entitled *Women Under Communism: A Comparative Analysis.*

Peter H. Juviler is associate professor of political science at Barnard College and an associate of the Russian Institute of Columbia University. He received his certificate from the Russian Institute in 1954 and his Ph.D. in 1960. He is the author of numerous articles which have appeared in *Survey*, *Soviet Studies*, the *American Slavic and East European Review*, *Problems of Communism*, and other journals. He is coeditor of and contributor to *Soviet Policy-Making* (1967). He was a member of the first US/USSR educational exchange program in 1958–1959 and went again under its auspices in the spring semester of 1964. He is the author of the forthcoming *Revolutionary Law and Order: Delinquency, Crime and Soviet Policy.*

Henry W. Morton is professor of political science at Queens College of the City University of New York. He received his certificate from the Russian Institute of Columbia University in 1954 and his Ph.D. in 1959.

He is the author of *Soviet Sport: Mirror of Soviet Society* (1963), *The Soviet Union and Eastern Europe* (1971), and coeditor of and contributor to *Soviet Policy-Making* (1967). He spent the spring semester, 1964, in the USSR as a member of the US/USSR educational exchange and was a senior research fellow of the Russian Institute of Columbia University in 1967–1968.

Paul Shoup is an associate professor of political science at the University of Virginia. He received his B.A. from Swarthmore and Ph.D. from Columbia. Professor Shoup also spent a year at the University of Belgrade. His publications include *Communism and the Yugoslav National Question* (1968), "National Question in the Political Systems of Eastern Europe," in I. Deak *et al.*, eds., *Eastern Europe in the 1970s* (1972), and articles in *The American Political Science Review*, *Slavic Review*, and *Problems of Communism.*

William C. Taubman received his certificate from the Russian Institute of Columbia University in 1965 and his Ph.D. in 1969. He was awarded a Foreign Area Fellowship from 1963 to 1967, a Fulbright-Hays Fellowship in 1965–66, and spent the academic year 1965–66 at Moscow State University under the auspices of the Soviet-American Academic Exchange. He is an associate professor of political science at Amherst and author of *Views from Lenin Hills* (New York, 1967) and *Governing Soviet Cities* (New York, 1973) and editor of *Globalism and Its Critics* (Lexington, Mass., 1973).

Rudolf L. Tőkés is an associate professor of political science at the University of Connecticut. He received his higher education at the Law School, University of Budapest, Western Reserve University (B.A.), Columbia University (M.A., Ph.D., and certificate, Institute on East Central Europe). Formerly on the faculty of Wesleyan University (1964–1970), he held a visiting appointment at Yale University (1968, 1972) and was a senior fellow at the Research Institute on Communist Affairs, Columbia University (1969–1971). He is also the associate editor of *Studies in Comparative Communism.* His publications include *Béla Kun and the Hungarian Soviet Republic* (1967), *The Politics and Ideologies of Dissent in the USSR* (1974), which he edited and contributed to, chapters in collective volumes, articles and reviews in *Problems of Communism*, *Slavic Review*, *Studies in Comparative Communism*, *East Europe*, *Etudes*, and other scholarly journals. Professor Tőkés is presently completing the second volume of his history of the Communist party of Hungary.

Introduction

The central theme of this volume is change and the consequences of political and societal change in the USSR in the 1960's and the 1970's. The way we understand this term, change denotes various manifestations of transition from one stage of socioeconomic development to another. The Soviet system's evolution from a Stalinist totalitarian, rapidly industrializing and still semiegalitarian society into an authoritarian polity with a developing modern economy and an increasingly rigidly structured society has been a complex and multifaceted process.

The authors of the ten essays that comprise this book sought to focus on three general areas and, within these, several specific areas of inquiry. The general themes are: (1) the dynamics of political institutions with emphasis on elements of conflict and change; (2) the relationship of politics, society, and welfare with particular attention to the shifting and often overlapping patterns of stability and reform; and (3) the international developmental and ideological impact of the "Soviet example," supplemented by a critique of some currently fashionable theories of "change" in communist systems.

Pursuant to our shared concern with the broad problem of change in the USSR, each contributor endeavored to transcend the limitations of a "before and after" framework and focused on a specific body of empirical evidence with which to measure and analyze some new and salient aspect of change in Soviet society and politics and to hypothesize about that aspect.

In the first part there are three essays dealing with the dimensions, ideologies, and future policy-making potentials of dissent, with the economics and politics of a key agricultural commodity (cotton), and with the social position and political role of Soviet women.

Tőkés suggests that contemporary literary, scientific, religious, and nationality dissent are symptoms of a newly evolving relationship between the rulers and the ruled in the USSR. The former are no longer absolute wielders of power, and the latter are no longer obedient and uncritical subjects of their political masters. Both the people and the regime are groping for a new political equilibrium (one that might include a partial redistribution of power), as well as for new forms of political and ideological legitimacy that are acceptable to both.

Hodnett seeks to demonstrate that the study of the politics, administration, and the ideological tensions arising out of central and regional planning, resource allocation, and mobilization efforts aimed at increasing cotton production in Soviet Central Asia offers significant clues to many still imperfectly understood problems of politics and economics, centralization and regional autonomy, Russian and Central Asian nationalism, and so on. Proceeding from Bickford's models of "plantation economy" and "plantation society," Hodnett establishes a comparative framework concerning the similarities and differences between the modernization processes of the American South and Soviet Central Asia and offers a critical evaluation of the Soviet economic performance in that hitherto backward section of the USSR.

Jančar, in her study "Women and Soviet Politics," argues that, in terms of full political equality, economic opportunity, and social position, the promise of the October Revolution is still not fulfilled for most Soviet women. Despite the Soviet system's remarkable achievements in health, education, and cultural modernization, in virtually all respects the USSR is still a male-dominated, traditional society whose leaders, while paying lip service to the classical Marxist principles of total equality between men and women under socialism, do, in effect, consciously discriminate against women—especially within the ruling Communist party. In conclusion, Jančar suggests that the day of the Soviet women's liberation is still far away—notwithstanding the remarkable growth in the number of highly educated professional, hence economically indispensable, women in the Soviet Union.

The second part of the volume focuses on four related aspects of change in Soviet social and welfare policies. These are housing construction, crime control and prevention, consumer-welfare planning, and the workings of a city soviet in the Georgian Union Republic.

Morton's study analyzes the Soviet government's impressive housing construction program that has provided more than one-half of the Soviet population with new dwelling units in the last 15 years. This achievement, perhaps historically unparalleled in its scope, has also produced new problems. New housing has not been equally distributed among the 15 republics. Particularly favored in receiving new apartment units are those citizens who live in large industrial cities in the European part of the Soviet Union. Despite the tempo of government housing construction, the minimum housing standard set by the regime in the early 1920's has not been widely achieved, and severe shortages still exist. Because of this fact, Soviet leaders still rely heavily on privately and cooperatively built housing to help satisfy the public's demand for shelter.

The study of crime as a social, political, and scholarly research problem by Soviet party and government officials and academic criminologists is the subject of Juviler's essay. The role of the consulting experts in the policy-making process, unlike in the lawyer-studded American and European legislatures and executive branches, is essentially limited to the Ministry of Justice and to the party Central Committee's Department of Administrative Organs. Crime fighting is greatly hampered by ingrained habits of secrecy, poor record-keeping practices, and by the authorities' reluctance to confront the underlying socioeconomic causes of lawbreaking. From these Juviler analyzes Soviet criminal statistics over extended periods of time and outlines certain trends in several specific areas of unlawful behavior and indicates the law enforcement agencies' responses thereto.

Consumer-welfare services have succeeded, according to Cattell, in substantially raising the quality of urban life. The problem with them has been that they were slow to materialize, that the approach did not rest on comprehensive planning, and that they were insufficiently financed. Three stages of development are noted. The first, commenced by Stalin, concerned itself primarily with health, education, and social security. The second, initiated by his successors in the mid-1950's, concentrated its energies primarily on housing construction and only belatedly paid attention to essential ancillary sectors—such as transportation, roads, sewers, retail stores, schools, and day-care centers—which the new tenants could not do without. The third, begun in the early 1970's, saw Soviet planners turning their attention to dramatically improving retail services and trade. No consumer-welfare planning, according to the author, can succeed unless decision making is decentralized and local authorities are given a participatory role in the planning and execution processes.

Theodore Friedgut's concern is with "Who Governs" Kutaisi, the Georgian Republic's second largest city. In this community power study he describes how local leadership rules, penetrates, and mobilizes the community; analyzes the role of elected deputies; notes the extent to which the Georgian cultural tradition affects the city's governance; points to the limited authority of local officials vis-à-vis republic-controlled enterprises (for example, the chemical plant owns most of the city's housing); and comments on the heavy reliance on volunteer units that have been created to assist the administrators in checking services in stores, policing the streets, processing citizens complaints and applications, and maintaining proper passport control in places of residency. The author gathered much of his information from interviews of Kutaisi officials and from conversations with former citizens of Kutaisi who have since emigrated.

Studies in the concluding part are concerned with the external impact, regional developmental comparability, and scientific research implications of what we, for want of a better term, call the *Soviet example*.

Albright proposes a tentative Soviet model, or a "set of fundamentals," consisting of methods of acquiring political power and techniques employed to achieve the modernization of a backward society. In testing the appeals of this model for the 62 nonruling Communist parties of the Third World, Albright analyses the domestic platforms, modernization programs, and positions taken in the Sino-Soviet conflict by these parties. He concludes that the "influence of the Soviet model of development in the Third World has gone down in recent years," as has the attractiveness of the once-revolutionary Soviet ideology as a source of inspiration and intellectual guidance for national liberation wars.

Shoup's essay explores the developmental similarities and differences between the Soviet Union and the countries that make up today's communist Eastern Europe since the turn of the century. Apart from the shared conditions of socioeconomic backwardness that the two areas have displayed over time, there have been consistent and significant differences in the realm of cultural traditions, political ideologies, and religious belief systems. Contrary to expectations, these differences have become more pronounced since the Second World War and have been reinforced by other, equally unexpected, mainly economic and ideological factors (such as nationalism).

Taubman's concluding essay offers a critical "guided tour" to some of the leading contemporary "convergence," "developmental," "modernization," "revisionist" and "pluralist" theories of change in communist systems. In attempting to clear up the semantic ambiguities and to identify the latent ideological biases of several leading proponents of these models and other social-science explanations concerning the phenomenon of change, Taubman develops an "extended revisionist scheme" in which he attempts to reconcile some of the more obvious differences between such theories and Soviet realities.

In our capacity as editors of a volume of original studies on Soviet politics and society in the 1970's, we have sought to encourage the identification of topics and the development of research strategies that held the promise of substantially improving the state of our knowledge about some aspects of today's Soviet Union. In doing so, we have deliberately refrained from inviting contributors on such subjects as foreign affairs, military, cultural, and educational policies, Marxist-Leninist ideology, party propaganda, and the like. Instead, we focused on matters that permitted our contributors to draw upon a wide range of fresh and reasonably accurate empirical evidence, as well as to employ new, in some instances yet untested (at least in Soviet field situations), methodological tools of inquiry with which to order, conceptualize, and present their findings to the readers of this book.

The results, we hope, justify both the choice of problem areas to which the authors of this volume have addressed themselves and the methodologies they have utilized in developing their cases and reporting their results. Concerning methodologies, we wish to point out the deliberately eclectic nature of research methods with which the contributors approached their subject matter. It will be apparent from the following studies that the editors and the contributors have, on the whole, been rather underwhelmed by the results and remain somewhat skeptical about the so-called "behavioral revolution" in political science. We believe that the introduction into Soviet studies of semantic, culture-bound neologisms and intellectually barren model-building exercises have thus far produced neither the kind of new evidence nor original insight that their proponents have claimed.

Our doubts about the usefulness, intellectual validity and applicability to the study of communist politics of much of what the contemporary American behavioral theorists have to offer have led most of us to highly selective borrowing from such authorities and compelled us to delve deeper—through content analysis, personal interviews, and more extensive perusal of available evidence—into the live stuff of verifiable data on Soviet society and politics. It may be noted in this connection that most essays in this volume are based on extensive field research and interviews, while the rest are based on the utilization of unpublished and not widely used Soviet source material. From a combination of new evidence and selective use of modern social science techniques, we sought to provide serious students of contemporary Soviet society and politics with a body of reliable data, as well as with some fresh insights into the subject of our collective inquiry.

Although we cannot and do not wish to attribute all the following conclusions to all contributors, in our judgment the essential findings of the ten studies may be summarized under five headings.

1. The Soviet system's continued capacity for evolutionary change has been perhaps the most important finding of this volume. Capability for change without major systemic crises, it seems to us, represents a new level of developmental maturity that the Soviet Union has achieved after five decades of existence. From this we surmise that this ability will remain unimpaired and, barring a major war or international conflict of similar magnitude, might well improve in the coming decades. In any event, we have found no compelling reason to believe that either the continued influence of Marxist-Leninist ideology or that of the senior party bureaucracy (most of them holdovers from the Stalin era) could or would significantly hamper the system's inherent flexibility and responsiveness to challenges posed by social and political change.

2. We have also found that, on the whole, the regime *has* been successful in surmounting the difficulties posed by the social and political consequences of modernization. Our evidence relates that the party and the government have been able to manipulate, though not necessarily fully control, these consequences and to prevent them from developing into debilitating societal and political crises that might threaten the incumbents' political survival. To be sure, some of the structural faults of the economic system—such as the intractable problems of the mechanization, incentives, and productivity of collective and state farms, outdated planning methods, and excessive centralization of economic decision making—are likely to persist and continue to impair the leadership's responsiveness to demands for change.

3. The studies have also found that along with the growth of the system's overall legitimacy there have been many unfulfilled demands by several groups and social entities for meaningful political participation, equal protection under the laws, and improved distribution of goods and services that the party and government have not been able and are not likely to be able or willing to satisfy in the near future. Just as in the past, the regime's legitimacy deficiencies will continue to be defended by the authorities by means of coercion, interference with the daily lives of the population and other forms of restrictions on the free expression of public opinion. While it seems quite unrealistic to expect significant changes on this score, there is reason to believe—if the post-Khrushchev collective leadership's record to date is any indication of future performance—that coercive policies, in the traditional Stalinist sense, *have* changed. Specifically, the scope of the state's coercive activity, the manner of its deploy-

ment, and, most importantly, signs of the Soviet people's growing civil courage in response to acts of official lawlessness must be considered as signs of change, indicating perhaps a beginning of a shift in the balance of power between the rulers and their subjects—and tomorrow's citizens.

4. In terms of broad stages of socioeconomic development, we think that the Soviet Union has, by and large, completed the transition from a Stalinist-type totalitarian system based on coercion and mobilization of societal and economic resources and has entered a new phase that will be characterized by a set of internal policy problems appreciably different from those that prevailed in an earlier period. Specifically, we think that domestic policy dilemmas of the Soviet leadership during the next decade will be focused more on issues such as housing, social justice, equal educational and welfare opportunities, sexual equality, religious freedoms, and freedom of the press, than on "metaproblems" such as the dilemmas over investment priorities ("sector A and B"), national-defense–related expenditures, and Sino-Soviet and Soviet-American relations. In any event, to the extent these new policy dilemmas may be regarded as representative of group demands (that is, those of urban dwellers, peasants, nationalities, religious minorities, intellectuals, women, the youth, and so on), we would submit that a *new kind of politics*, that of the interaction of the Communist party and several increasingly vocal interest groups or interest-group–like formations, will constitute the most important element of change in Soviet politics in the next two decades.

5. In sum, we feel that the *general characteristics* of the system—that is, its internal balance of power, the quality of its leadership, the overall levels of its socioeconomic development, and the nature of its political legitimacy—will all be subject to incremental or evolutionary changes in the years to come. These are not likely to change very significantly—unlike what we might call the *operational characteristics* of the system, which include the likely scenarios of political succession, specific patterns of resolution of intraparty conflict, style of policy making, the nature of group politics, and also the relevance and viability of Marxist-Leninist ideology for the regime's developmental tasks and its survival. These aspects, it seems to us, are more likely to be influenced by the above indicated consequences and manifestations of change in Soviet politics and could, quite conceivably, develop into various kinds of subsystemic crises.

Lest they be misunderstood, the above arguments do not represent our, let alone our contributors', endorsement of the guiding philosophies and governing policies of the Soviet party and government. What we actually sought to accomplish was to provide an up-to-date, possibly controversial, synthesis of what we believe the essays in this volume portend for those interested in the present state and future prospects of Soviet society and politics. Moreover, we hope that our efforts to transcend labels of "anti-behavioral" or "revisionist" to characterize the results of this volume and our approach to the matter has given us the necessary freedom to take a fresh view of the Soviet scene and provide answers to questions that have been posed but not satisfactorily resolved by adherents of other ideologies and methods when studying the theory and practice of Soviet politics.

Rudolf L. Tőkés

PART ONE

The Dynamics of Political Institutions: Conflict and Change

CHAPTER 1

Dissent: The Politics for Change in the USSR

Rudolf L. Tőkés

Legitimacy and Authority

Alienation and dissent are inevitable results of any exercise of political power. Power may be defined as the ability of an individual, organization, political party, or government to cause individuals or groups to act or refrain from acting in a certain way.[1] Power thus evokes images of compulsion, punishment, and/or the withholding of rewards as means of securing compliance with authoritative commands. Although the exercise of power is inseparable from the politics of any human relationship and is indispensable to the maintenance of an organized community of men, the nature of power relationships and the quality of compliance-producing methods tend to be different in every political system.

If we conceive of the USSR as a "mobilization system" committed to the realization of Marxist-Leninist goals of nation building, modernization, and psychological transformation of citizens into "new socialist men," we are describing a kind of power relationship between the rulers and the ruled that is qualitatively different from those prevailing in noncommunist systems. In fact it may be argued that rightful authority and political legitimacy in communist systems are based not on the Weberian triad—"rational-legal," "traditional," and "charismatic"—but on a functionally more appropriate mixture of "coercion, organization, persuasion, and rewards." [2]

It is the Communist party's commitment to the achievement of a utopian end-state of political development (that is, communism) that distinguishes the system's legitimacy from that of the noncommunist polities. When the stage of communism is attained, the dialectical tensions and contradictions between the polity's developmental base and the superstructure of its values, beliefs, and ideologies reach an equilibrium. The state withers away, and with it its coercive apparatus and other legitimacy-building devices. Thus, the use of coercion to eliminate coercion, the maintenance of a highly structured state and party bureaucracy to liquidate all forms of organization, and the delayed gratification of material and cultural wants to provide for "everyone according to his needs" are the salient components of what may be termed the "legitimacy paradox" of the building of socialism and communism.

The Soviet system, whose legitimacy is founded on an ultimately self-liquidating dialectical disequilibrium between its ideological superstructure and the lagging level of its actual developmental base, tends to create, of necessity, alienation and dissent in the form of latent or manifest opposition—critical of its leaders, its ruling hierarchy, and its policies.[3] Therefore, if communist nation building is perceived as a sustained effort to realize the regime's ideological goals while attempting to mitigate the contradictions between the Communist party's stated and feasible developmental objectives,[4] it may be assumed that the potential for dissent and opposition is always present. Their influence is determined both by the efficacy of the party's exercise of power and by the intensity of these dichotomies at any given period of time.[5]

These general observations on legitimacy and authority indicate that dissent in Soviet politics is as old as the regime itself.[6] Yet, with some notable exceptions, the literature on contemporary Soviet politics is generally unhelpful for the understanding of this important aspect of political, social, and ideological change in the USSR. The dissident movement in post-Stalin Russia—its participants, ideologies, programs, strategies, and systemic implications—is a complex phenomenon that is not readily amenable to conventional explanations in the form of either historical-institutional or empirical survey research analysis. As a result, the matter has been ignored by and large by adherents of historical, institutional, and behavioral schools of methodological persuasion in Soviet studies.

The traditional analysts, or, for want of a better term, "Kremlinologists," have been accustomed to studying specific issues, personalities, and policy debates from a content analysis of censored material. When confronted with self-published, or *samizdat*, writings of Soviet dissidents from all walks of life criticizing the regime without necessarily advocating its overthrow, most academic Kremlinologists tended to react with skepticism and often ignored the matter altogether. They were deeply involved in the apocalyptic yet paradoxically policy-oriented world of cold-war scholarship, and had no faith in the power of ideas, even though the

October Revolution that gave birth to the Soviet system had been the result of an idea whose time came in 1917.

Those of the behavioral persuasion, though ostensibly concerned with "systemic change" in communist politics, have also overlooked the importance of dissent and with it a whole series of dissident demands and policy inputs aimed at *changing* the system. Preoccupied with empirical and often culture-bound techniques of measuring and accounting for political behavior in the Soviet Union, virtually all behaviorally oriented investigators have tended to discount the influence of the unorganized masses, as well as that of the alienated intellectuals, on the political life of the USSR.

Political dissent is real and is alive in the USSR. The evidence is quite conclusive.[7] It takes the form of over 1,200 samizdat documents, ranging from one-page letters to book-length studies by Soviet dissidents, the publication of more than a dozen underground journals and newsletters that have reached the West in recent years, and, generally, the record of the regime's domestic opponents. It indicates that dissent and other forms of unorthodox and unauthorized political activity in the USSR may have become a new, and, in the long run, possibly significant dimension of that country's politics. This new dimension, if it may be described as such, warrants careful scrutiny by everyone seriously interested in the study of political, social, and ideological change in posttotalitarian communist systems.[8]

Dissent: Evidence and Conceptualization

The limitations on research into Soviet political developments in general and dissent in particular are considerable. At the top, pervasive secrecy surrounds the important substantive and procedural details of policy making, elite interaction, and competition for power. Below, the nonelites' activities are equally difficult to trace. Apart from the officially authorized channels of communication, such as letters to the editor and onesided reportage on the daily life of the Soviet people, there is not much that can be said with certainty about the private beliefs and political values of the average citizens for whom most dissidents claim to speak.[9] On the other hand, there is a great deal of information available about the politically relevant behavior of various functional elites, such as party bureaucrats, factory managers, and military officers, as well as cultural, educational, and scientific groups. Since Soviet dissidents seem to fall into both the (articulate) elite and the (inarticulate) nonelite categories, most dissent studies have tended to focus on the more visible, though not necessarily more important activities of the elites rather than the masses.[10]

Before proceeding further we should identify some problems of data verification and the limits of permissible inferences that we may draw from the documentable aspects of Soviet dissent. First of all, there are many things that we simply do *not* know and are unlikely to learn in the near future about unorthodox political, literary, and scientific activities in Russia. Among these unknowns we may mention the exact number of people involved in such activities, their educational and social background, and their previous professional and political careers.[11] Do they have a record of previous deviant behavior? Have they had prison or labor-camp experience? In the case of nine-tenths of those whom we can identify by name as having participated in unorthodox political activities or as having been signers, distributors, or possessors of dissident literature, we have no information beyond the fact of their arrest.[12]

Besides the problem of insufficient data to answer the "who" part of our inquiry, there are significant semantic and analytic difficulties in classifying the "what," or the content of dissident writings. While most samizdat documents are quite explicit concerning the grievances their authors describe and the remedies they propose, we, in a sense, share the problem of the Soviet courts in trying, and finally failing, to isolate the "political" from the apolitical or "artistic" aspects of such writings as Josif Brodsky's personalist poetry, some of Yuli Daniel's and Andrei Sinyavsky's novels and fantastic tales, the contents of Aleksandr Ginzburg's and Yuri Galanskov's underground literary journals, and so on.[13]

Apart from semantic ambiguities, the Western reader, with few exceptions (for instance, Zhores Medvedev's lucid account of the Lysenko case),[14] is also uninformed about the internal politics—expecially personality clashes, delayed settling of old ideological or professional disputes, and the like—behind samizdat platforms, programmatic statements, manifestos, open letters, and collective and individual petitions that make up the stuff of self-published dissident writing in the USSR.[15]

The authenticity of unsigned underground polemical literature is often doubtful. In Russia, with its long tradition of diversionary plots and counterplots between antiregime conspiratorial societies and the secret police—both the Zubatov and the Andropov variety[16]—one must question the authenticity not only of the Khrushchev memoirs,[17] but of many unsigned and even some signed samizdat writings that have been accepted as genuine documents by the understandably sympathetic Russian emigre press and by the Soviet dissidents' Western well-wishers, too. Also, the possibility that some samizdat authors might have succumbed to the psychological pressures of their hostile environment and hence may *not* be in complete possession of their mental faculties and actually might belong to "ward seven," should not be discounted when judging the intellectual quality and general representativeness of a given samizdat item.

There are many methodological and substantive ambiguities surrounding the phenomenon of dissent that place definite limitations on the scope of inquiry into this area of Soviet politics. One must be careful not to overestimate the influence of dissent on the regime and its policies. Indeed, one should be extremely wary of predicting rapid changes in a country that is run by the world's most durable and stable bureaucracy. A government, in which a cabinet minister can serve under three party leaders and six prime ministers for 31 years in the same post may be called many things but not unstable or weak.[18] Similarly, any attempt to envisage fundamental reforms by the ruling-party elite must reckon with the remarkable longevity of the personnel serving in the higher party organs. Jerry Hough in his study "The Soviet System—Petrification or Pluralism?" pointed out that between 1965 and 1971, as distinct from earlier periods of CPSU history, the Politburo's membership remained essentially the same, and the makeup of the Central Committee changed very little over these years.[19] Should we call these developments, or perhaps nonevents, signs of petrification and decay or manifestations of institutional maturity and great political strength or both?

Therefore, the interaction of authority and dissent in the Soviet Union must be understood as taking place not in a political vacuum but in a still fundamentally Stalinist institutional framework resting on the Soviet "silent majority's" conservative neonationalistic consensus, which in turn is effectively maintained and adroitly manipulated by the Communist party bureaucracy.

The thesis of this essay is that since the mid-1950's two significant trends have been at work in Soviet politics. The first is characterized by institutional entropy, the withering away of Marxist-Leninist-Stalinist ideology as a doctrine of modernization and as an effective tool of political socialization and legitimacy building. The other is characterized by signs of incipient pluralism in the realm of policy-making and administrative practices. This process has been marked by political stability at the top and by the emergence of an internal political reform movement from below. The latter has been led by liberal members of cultural, scientific, and key developmental elites seeking to counteract the causes and manifestations of what they perceive as the Soviet system's degeneration and decay and the threat of a return to Stalinism.

This thesis, when conceptualized in terms of authority and legitimacy, suggests that since 1953 there has been a gradual growth in the regime's political legitimacy in the eyes of the great majority of Soviet citizens. This grass-roots support is based on the popular approval of party- and government-sponsored measures of economic and political relaxation in the areas of living standards, housing, welfare, and education, and the elimination of the most objectionable aspect of Stalinist terror and massive official interference with the lives of average citizens. On the other hand, as the regime's authority has grown, there has been a concomitant amelioration of its political legitimacy in the eyes of certain identifiable groups of Soviet citizens who constitute the social base of the contemporary Soviet dissident movement.

The following arguments will seek to introduce evidence in support of this thesis by offering (1) a brief description of the origins and development of the postwar dissident movement in the USSR, (2) an analysis of the ideologies and stated positions of the three main groups of Soviet dissenters, (3) a tentative evaluation of the policy-making potential of dissent (that is, its serviceability as a positive and usable input into the top level decision-making process articulated by each of these groups, and (4) a concluding hypothesis concerning the place of dissent in a modified scheme of contemporary Soviet politics.

Opposition and Dissent

After Stalin's death and with the receding of terror in public life, a vacuum of authority and legitimacy developed in the political orientations of four groups of Soviet citizens. These were the postwar generation of educated young men and women; the recently released—though not necessarily rehabilitated—surviving victims of the Stalinist purges; the cultural and technical intelligentsia; and members of certain national minority groups who had survived the Stalinist genocide in Siberian exile. The nature of this void, as perceived by these groups, is difficult to define, yet it seems certain that many of these physical and psychological victims of the personality cult considered Stalinism criminally illegitimate and yearned for the creation of rational and predictable patterns of authority through the restoration of "socialist legality" and the (generally dimly understood) "Leninist norms of party life."

The odds were formidable against any kind of thorough restructuring of Soviet policy and politics in the mid-1950's. These included the CPSU leadership's apprehensions (based on Hungary's and Poland's experiences in 1956) of the likely consequences of uncontrolled or unduly rapid de-Stalinization, and the party bureaucracy's reluctance to support more than the slightest lessening of the Communist party's authority in the eyes of the Soviet people. This attitude was further reinforced by the apparent willingness of the people to settle for considerably less than genuine political freedom, strict legality, or higher living standards that were well within the capabilities of Soviet polity and economy by that time. The post-totalitarian Soviet society was not and still is not prepared to support fundamental changes in the status quo beyond those promised by the 20th CPSU Congress and subsequently introduced by Khrushchev's reforms between 1957 and 1963.

The Soviet system or some of its significant aspects have been judged as illegitimate by two segments of post-totalitarian Soviet society: educated young people and alienated intellectuals who had been imperfectly socialized into the values of the system and whose idealistic commitment to the regime's legitimacy had been shattered earlier by Krushchev's secret speech and more recently by the ideological trauma of the Sino-Soviet conflict and the Czechoslovakian invasion of 1968. Those who were former victims of Stalinism had been more than sufficiently sensitized to the regime's still visible Stalinist features and had good reason to doubt Khrushchev's sincerity and commitment to a meaningful program of liberalization.[20]

In order to understand the specific meaning of the critical posture taken by members of these groups, it may be helpful to distinguish between the concepts of "opposition" and "dissent." [21] In the Soviet context, these terms have different meanings.

For the purposes of this essay it will be argued that in the USSR both the opposition and the dissenters may have programs and platforms critical of the ruling elite: both tend to perceive its authority as deficient in terms of legitimacy and demand that the incumbents make general or specific structural and policy changes. However, the opposition proper—that is, those presently not occupying seats of power (if they are, their activities should be labeled as intraparty factionalism and not opposition)

—must have the "will to power" and must be prepared to *act* on their convictions, whether or not such beliefs and actions can be accommodated within the framework of legal and extralegal norms and practices that the party leadership has traditionally defended when confronted with challenges of this kind.

To illustrate the difference between opposition and dissent, we would consider a Chinese-sponsored conspiratorial society, made up of unreformed Stalinists in the CPSU apparat, the government, army, and police bureaucracy—an opposition group whose platform must, by definition, include revolution, or, at any rate, the forcible overthrow of the incumbent CPSU leadership and the establishment of a new one in its stead.[22] An army-sponsored "Bonapartist" military coup would also fall into this category, as would a separatist movement broadly supported by the elites of a significant national minority, such as the Ukrainians.

"Dissenters" proper as far as may be surmised from the available documentary evidence have no *direct* designs on power.[23] From a closer analysis of ideological positions that one may infer from the relevant published and accessible samizdat literature, it may be argued that two basic intellectual tendencies prevail among the Soviet dissenters. These may be classified as representing either "competing conceptions of rationality," [24] utilized to "criticize, to exhort, to persuade" in hopes of being listened to by the authorities[25] or competing conceptions of morality and ethical validity with which dissenters hope to resocialize those segments of the population and the elites (especially the youth and intellectuals) most susceptible to attempts to undermine the regime's authority on ethical, religious, cultural, or philosophical grounds.

From a combination of these two tendencies, dissent in contemporary Soviet politics is defined as a culturally conditioned political reform movement seeking to ameliorate and ultimately to eliminate the perceived illegitimacy of the posttotalitarian Communist-party leadership's authoritarian rule into authoritative domination[26] through (1) structural, administrative, and political reforms; (2) ideological purification and cultural modernization; and (3) the replacement of scientifically unverifiable normative referents with empirical (nonideological) criteria as political guidelines and developmental success indicators.

In developing the various components of this definition we shall attempt to show that there are, in fact, at least two discernible tendencies among contemporary dissenters; that both tendencies are culturally conditioned and are rooted in classical patterns of orientation and behavior toward political authority on the part of the Russian intelligentsia; and that the three postulated goals of the reform movement actually conform to the dissenters' stated objectives.

Dissent: Stages of Development

The postwar history of dissent in the Soviet Union may be divided into four phases: The first, the "subversive-militant" phase between 1946 and 1954; the second, the "political counterculture" phase between 1956 and 1964; the third, the "national movement" phase between 1965 and early 1971; and the last, the "retrenchment and polarization" phase which began in late 1971. Although we intend to focus on the last two, brief summaries of the highlights of the preceding periods seem to be in order at this point.

The first, or "subversive-militant," phase, between 1946 and 1953, was characterized by confrontations between the central authority and militant nationalists in the Ukraine and Baltic states (escalating at times into open guerilla warfare and large-scale military operations) and by the activities of radical leftist and religious opposition groups in major Soviet cities and in Siberian concentration camps.[27] The platforms of the "Lenin Group" (1946–1948), "Workers' Opposition" (1947), "Democratic Movement of Northern Russia" (1947) formed by illegally arrested Red Army officers in Vorkuta, and the *Istina Truda Lenina* group (1948) founded by Moscow University students, while defending the Communist party's leading position in Soviet society, advocated a return to Leninist norms of party life and, somewhat paradoxically also demanded the restoration of the right of intraparty opposition that had been denied to their ideological predecessors by Lenin at the 10th Congress of the Communist party in 1921. Members of such camp study circles, much against the intentions of the regime that had sent them there, made extensive use of the holdings of the sometimes excellent camp libraries for their own purposes.[28]

At the other end of the ideological spectrum and, in a way, complementing Stalin's radical orthodox opponents, were the religious dissenters. They were imprisoned members of religious minorities and fundamentalist sects. The latter, especially the "Monachki," who advocated an ideology of Christian utopian communism, developed novel methods of nonviolent resistance and achieved a record of success against the notoriously illiberal camp administrators and NKVD officials.[29] Their dignified demeanor and insistence on moral criteria for judging the legitimacy of political authority established a significant precedent for all camp inmates—Marxist, believers, and old and young alike. These former inmates, sometimes several years after their release, took advantage of their relative immunity from rearrest and employed similar methods and criteria to press their case for rehabilitation with the always reluctant and often openly hostile authorities.[30]

The second, or "politicized counterculture," phase of postwar dissent began shortly after the 20th Congress of the CPSU in 1956 and lasted, with a few interruptions, until the arrest of Yuli Daniel and Andrei Sinyavsky in the fall of 1965. This phase was characterized by the broadening of the dissidents' popular base, especially among students and young intellectuals and by the emergence of new literary culture heroes whose personal example in both creative and political activities galvanized the young generation into formulating their own frequently very much politicized platforms of opposition to the regime and its official ideology.

This is how Vladimir Osipov, a young Komsomol official who later became an organizer of a dissident student group and in the late 1960's editor of the conservative, nationalist-Slavophile underground journal *Veche* described his and his contemporaries' reaction to Khrushchev's "secret speech" on Stalin:

> Overthrown was the man who had personified the existing system and ideology to such an extent that the very words "the Soviet power" and "Stalin" seemed to have been synonymous. We all, the future rebels, at the dawn of our youth had been fanatical Stalinists (and) had believed with a truly religious fervor. . . .
>
> Khrushchev's speech and the 20th Congress destroyed our faith, having extracted from it its very core; the core was Joseph Stalin, for such had been the propaganda of the preceding two and one half decades. It was easier for the old communists: for them Stalin had not been the nail on which the whole of socialism was hanging. With the full force of hatred of fanatics we attacked our "werewolf." [31]

The events of the Polish October Revolution and the Hungarian Revolution of 1956 made a profound impact upon the university students of Moscow and Leningrad, two thousand of whom were disciplined or expelled from the universities in the latter city. Among these suddenly radicalized students, as many as seven political-literary groups were formed and all but one published samizdat journals of their own.[32] According to another account, antiparty activism, prompted by ideologies of "true Marxism-Leninism" was not confined to students alone. This source tells of "several dozens" of groups, among which the most prominent were the "Leningrad Faculty of Philosophy group led by Molostov; the Pimenov group in Leningrad with small cells at other university centers as well; the Krasnopevtsev-Khaibulin-Rendel group at the University of Moscow; the Moscow right-wing nationalist-Bolshevik group of Polenov; and the Union of Leninist Revolutionaries led by Trofimov, with main groups at the universities of Moscow and Leningrad and small branches at several provincial universities." [33]

Although the officials' ruthless suppression of student activism did succeed in temporarily silencing dissent among the youth, the cumulative effects of the Pasternak affair and the growing number of clandestinely published and circulated anti-Stalinist writings led to the revival of the youth movement in the early 1960's.[34]

We may surmise from the relevant court testimonies of Yosif Brodsky, Yuri Galanskov, Alexander Ginzburg, Viktor Khaustov, Vladimir Bukovsky, Evgenii Kushev, V. N. Delaunay, Natalia Gorbanevskaia, and Olga Iofe, and from the published dialogues between Pavel Litvinov and the police authorities that their cultural preferences and political outlook had been conditioned by three factors:[35]

First, they regarded themselves as the first "guilt-free" generation in Soviet history; as such, they explicitly disclaimed any moral responsibility for the regime's past crimes against the Soviet people and the older generation's moral cowardice in failing to stand up against Stalinist injustices.

Second, with the tapering off of the regime's mobilizing momentum, they, like many young Soviet men and women, found it difficult if not impossible to identify with the intellectually uninspiring, emotionally shallow, and bureaucratically promoted developmental and political challenges offered to them by the party and government gerontarchy.

Third, thus alienated from their morally unacceptable family and political environment, the young generation sought intellectual fulfillment and political leadership from those not contaminated by the sins of the past.[36] The culture heroes of their peer group, many of whom had been driven by similar motives, accepted their new role as spokesmen for the young seekers of artistic truth, moral integrity, and generational purpose. However, in an authoritarian political system such as the Soviet Union, literary heroes have limited opportunities and few incentives to become leading representatives of the culturally significant but politically powerless constituency of the young generation. Although under these circumstances a nonconformist may gain indirect political influence, it can only be acquired through adverse publicity and notoriety bestowed upon him in the form of official disapproval, possible arrest, a closed trial, and a term in a prison or labor camp. The awareness of these risks in politically imprudent behavior, therefore, has compelled many would-be dissenters to refrain from fully satisfying their followers' expectations.

In the summer of 1964 the Yugoslav writer Mihajlo Mihajlov interviewed several liberal Soviet intellectuals, including Bella Akhmadulina, Ilya Ehrenburg, and Vladimir Tendryakov. He found them to be very reluctant to explore the uncharted "gray" zone that lies between permissible and forbidden areas of politically relevant literacy and artistic activity.[37]

Besides these internationally known and socially prominent rebels, there were others who did have the courage to break through the officially tolerated liberal half-truths that have become a new form of literary *lakirovka* and to address themselves to the fundamental existential problems of Soviet society regardless of the consequences. The numerous contributors to Alexander Ginzburg's underground literary journal *Syntaxis* (1959), the Moscow student Vladimir Osipov's *Spiral* (1960), and Yuri Galanskov's *Phoenix 61* (1962), as well as Yosif Brodsky, Yuli Daniel, Andrei Sinyavsky, Aleksandr Solzhenitsyn, and a host of other dissident writers have been on the whole, if perhaps not better writers and poets, certainly more faithful and intellectually more consistent chroniclers of Soviet society than their politically well-connected brethren in the Moscow or Leningrad literary establishment.[38]

However, the dilemma between speaking up against injustice and remaining silent is more complex than the above analysis seems to indicate. Mihajlov's essay, "Why are We Silent?" offers a compelling explanation of this matter:

> The socialist intellectual who expresses himself freely before the Western public begins to feel, somehow, like a traitor. I believe this feeling has been experienced even by writers who, thanks to unusual circumstances, have succeeded in speaking the truth about their society in their own country. Pasternak, Dudinstev, and Solzhenitsyn must have felt this uneasiness. And this sense of treachery is a much more decisive factor in inhibiting free expression than fear of the reprisals to which socialist intellectuals submit themselves. For socialist criticism is employed not only as a weapon against the socialist states but also against socialism, and against all those oppressed by poverty and racial prejudice in the Western world. So we intellectuals in socialist societies feel like traitors when we speak the truth—traitors both to our countries and to all who

fight for freedom in capitalist society. And this is why the majority of us are silent.[39]

Issue Areas and Demands

The third, or "national movement," phase of organized dissent began with the arrest of Andrei Sinyavsky and Yuli Daniel in September 1965. The works of these writers had been smuggled to the West and published there under the pseudonyms of Abram Tertz and Nikolai Arzhak. They were detained under Section I of Article 70 of the Criminal Code of the RSFSR for "agitation and propaganda carried out with the purpose of subverting or weakening the Soviet State." In early February, 1966 Sinyavsky and Daniel were tried, found guilty, and sentenced to five and seven years at hard labor, respectively.[40]

In retrospect it is clear that it was this trial and a combination of circumstances surrounding it—including the specifics of the indictment, the conduct of the accused, the exclusion of the public, and the authorities' heavy-handed methods of handling the case—that should be considered the turning point in the history of postwar dissent.[41]

The wave of protest initially triggered by this trial grew between 1965 and 1971 into a nationwide movement. Its platforms and ideological postures may be summarized under seven headings. These were (1) *political democracy*: demands concerning governmental processes and policies at the All-Union Republic and local-soviet level, critical opinions on foreign policies, the CPSU and its ideology; (2) *nationality rights*: Ukrainian, Baltic, and Central Asian nationality demands for political, cultural, economic, and educational equality and autonomy, as well as petitions demanding full rehabilitation for nationality victims of Stalinism; (3) *human rights-socialist legality*: demands, reports, petitions, open letters, and memoranda concerning official violations of civil rights, conditions in jails, penal colonies, and psychiatric hospitals, as well as women's rights; (4) *developmental rationality*: demands, recommendations, and critical suggestions concerning economic policies; agricultural problems, especially those of the collective and state farms; the efficacy of educational policies and practices at the elementary, high-school, and university levels; and the working conditions of those involved in planning, scientific research, and experimentation; (5) *religious autonomy*: petitions, open letters, and appeals concerning church-state relations, religious persecution, religious education and facilities, and specific

Jewish demands regarding freedom of worship and the right of unhindered departure for Israel; (6) *quality of life*: critical declarations, essays, petitions concerning labor policies, welfare, pensions, the quality of public services, and so on; and (7) *artistic freedoms*: demands concerning the abolition of censorship, publishing controls, and greater autonomy for literary and artistic associations.

For the sake of conceptual clarity these demands will be regarded as issue areas,[42] that, taken as a whole, represent the *programmatic content* of the contemporary Soviet political-reform movement. From this it may be inferred that these seven issue areas in effect amount to the dissidents' definition of the dimensions of the systems' illegitimacy, which, if successfully overcome by the regime, is expected to result in "a relationship which is perceived as legitimate by all actors concerned," that is to say in authoritative, rather than authoritarian, domination.[43]

Table 1-1 is based on the recalculated results of a survey of "proposals

TABLE 1–1 Dissent in the USSR–Issue Areas and Demands in Samizdat Documents (1968–1970)[44]

Issue Area	Demands
Political Democracy (Governmental processes, legislative, executive, judicial policies; Union Republics and local soviets; elections, foreign policy—general, relations with capitalist and socialist countries; the CPSU, Stalinism in government, ideology, Marxism-Leninism)	99 (25.5%)
Nationality Rights (Specific Ukrainian political, economic, cultural, and educational demands; miscellaneous demands by Baltic nationalities, Tatars, Volga Germans, and other smaller nationality groups)	89 (22.7%)
Human Rights-Socialist Legality (Human rights in general; specific civil rights; criminal code; trials; conditions in penal colonies, jails, and psychiatric hospitals; women's rights)	69 (17.6%)
Developmental Rationality (General economic problems, agricultural policies, collective and state farms, planning, research and experimentation; education—general, primary, secondary, higher)	54 (13.6%)
Religious Autonomy (Church-state relations, religious persecution, religious education and facilities, specific Jewish demands)	30 (7.6%)
Quality of Life (Labor policies, welfare, pensions, public services, miscellaneous social demands)	26 (6.6%)
Artistic Freedoms (Censorship, publishing controls, literary associations, creative independence)	25 (6.4%)
Total Number of Demands	392 (100.0%)

for systemic change in the USSR by Soviet citizens" on the basis of the first 538 samizdat documents catalogued by the Radio Liberty Research Department. The original survey made in August, 1971 found that over 50 percent (274) of the documents in the sample contained specific demands. These, with due allowance for certain documents containing several kinds of demands, were classified under seven issue areas. The sample is unsystematic, and probably not fully representative of the import of the total samizdat literature. Therefore, conclusions drawn from the ranking and weight distribution of issue areas listed here must be considered tentative at this time. Other surveys focusing on special subcategories of samizdat publications (that is, petitions, open letters, memoranda, polemical essays, samizdat journal reportage, major literary, historical, philosophical, scientific, and other special-interest studies and monographs) could, in all probability, produce appreciably different results. The present survey, therefore, is merely indicative of the approximate dimensions of documentable dissident interest articulation.

With these caveats in mind it still seems possible to make some general inferences from this data. Perhaps the most striking fact is that the greatest percentage of demands was concerned with politics, policy making, and ideology, rather than, say, religious autonomy or artistic freedoms. The predominance of political issue-oriented thinking among the dissidents attests to their preoccupation with the *fundamental* systemic legitimacy defects of the Soviet system. The priority accorded to politics made good strategic sense as it emphasized the movement's consensus concerning its priorities and the tasks it had to perform *before* focusing on related procedural matters such as human rights and socialist legality. The relative prominence of nationality demands seems to suggest that the still unresolved problem of national, cultural, linguistic, and political autonomy for the non-Russian peoples of the USSR is the greatest single source of illegitimacy of the Soviet federal system. The extreme urgency attached by dissenters to problems of the quality of citizenship and apprehensions toward the officially promoted policies of "cultural convergence of all peoples of the USSR" (that is, Russification) are well reflected in demands advanced in this issue area.

Although the question of human rights has been the most visible aspect of the dissident movement, the number of samizdat items addressed to this matter seems to indicate that the role of law is seen by most people, though certainly not the articulate elites, as secondary to political considerations that, in the final analysis, determine the way the law is applied in the USSR. Since most people, conditioned by Russian traditions in this matter, expect the conditions in jails and penal colonies to be harsh, demands and protest letters of this kind are generally issued by intellectuals rather than by nonelite dissenters. From this sample it seems clear that religious persecution is distinctly minority concern in the USSR. Although this issue, due mainly to the large-scale involvement of Jews in the movement and to more recent resurgence of Catholic resistance in the Baltic republics, has improved its relative standing among the rest of the dissident demands since 1970, it is still secondary to some other issue areas in the mainstream of the political-reform movement.

Apart from a score of documents of a comprehensive and polemical nature,[45] most samizdat literature is addressed to one or two—possibly three—related issue areas. It is usually prompted by: (1) the emergence of an issue of general concern, such as the expectation of the revival of Stalinism in some context; (2) specific acts of official lawlessness, such as someone's illegal arrest and trial; (3) instances of police violations of constitutional guarantees; and (4) highly publicized cases (often through Western radio broadcasts, hence the neologism "radizdat) involving official interference with artistic, scientific, or literary activities.

Ideologies of Dissent

Proceeding from our earlier scheme of differentiating between dissenting intellectuals representing "competing conceptions of rationality" and "competing conceptions of morality and ethical validity," we propose a corresponding classification of dissenting philosophies into "instrumental-pragmatic" and "moral-absolutist" ideologies.[46]

For the purposes of the following arguments, moral-absolutist dissenters are defined as modern heirs of the classical Russian literary, artistic, and philosophical traditions and corresponding libertarian political postures.[47]

From the idea that the moral-absolutist dissenters' commitment to reshaping Soviet political culture is rooted in specific traditions of the Russian intelligentsia, it may be inferred that the ideological ingredients of this particular dissident posture include the following.[48]

1. A set of self-regarding views which attribute spiritual and moral leadership to creative intellectuals who are considered to be superior to the political establishment—especially the party bureaucracy. The latter is viewed as wholly devoid of such qualities and is judged as a usurper of power over the people and their "natural leaders"; or, as Solzhenitsyn wrote in *The First Circle,* "a great

writer is, so to speak, a second government. That's why no regime anywhere has ever loved its great writers, only its minor ones.[49]

2. A politically unproductive but psychologically satisfying preoccupation with problems of moral rectitude, of the clash of "inner truth" and conventional wisdom (*istina* versus *pravda*), of questions of man's destiny in the modern world, and of ambivalent, or expressly negative attitudes toward the materialistic ethical foundations of Marxism-Leninism.[50]
3. Efforts to create a new counterelite moral philosophy with which to repair the ravages of Stalinism in the realm of interpersonal relations and lay the foundations for a national, as well as a generational, reconciliation between the victims and the opponents of the party and police dictatorship.[51]
4. Deeply divided orientations toward ideologies of technical progress (Marxist and capitalist alike) and the values of industrial civilization and growing concern about the destructive potential of modern science and military technology.[52]

The physical and moral courage that Sinyavsky and Daniel and scores of other defendants displayed before the Soviet courts was an important and novel feature of the "national movement" phase of postwar Soviet dissent. The refusal to be intimidated by hostile judges, menacing prosecutors, hapless defense lawyers, packed courtrooms, prearranged sentences, and the prospect of a long term in a forced-labor camp must be contrasted with the behavior of accused political criminals of the Stalin era.

Unlike the psychologically and physically broken defendants before the Stalinist courts, many of whom sincerely believed that their false testimony and death would serve the cause of socialism, none of the young dissidents (agents provocateurs and police informers excepted) were inhibited by the "Rubashov-complex" of the intellectual ambivalence toward unjust charges.

The Soviet dissidents' conduct, however courageous and high principled, has also been based on rational calculations concerning the authorities' political capabilities at the time of their trial. As members of a traditionally highly politicized counterelite, Russian intellectuals have, over the last hundred years, developed remarkably acute survival instincts, a kind of "calculus of dissent" with which to predict and act upon opportunities provided by legitimacy crises, leadership conflicts, and similar signs of impending political change.[53]

In sum, although lacking the resources in terms of direct access to the leadership and influence over the masses to translate their protest into specific policy outputs or direct political action, the moral-absolutist dissenters were indispensable to creating an atmosphere in which others —the technical-scientific elites, the nationalities, and the Jewish advocates of religious freedom—with greater leverage over Soviet policy-making processes could advance their "constituency-specific" interests and general civil-rights demands.

Most instrumental-pragmatic dissenters are liberal members of the scientific, technical, educational, and academic elites, but many unattached Soviet urban intellectuals also belong to this group.[54] Of these we shall focus on members of the scientific community. While it is extremely difficult to make valid generalizations about the philosophical postures of such dissimilar people as Peter Kapitsa, Zhores Medvedev, Andrei Sakharov, Lev Landau, Igor Tamm, and Mikhail Leontovich, not to mention the hundreds of physicists, chemists, biologists, mathematicians, and other scientific research workers who have written and openly endorsed manifestos, appeals, and similar documents, this much seems to be warranted by the available evidence:[55]

As scientists and empirical investigators of physical phenomena, these men have, over the years, developed a wide range of problem-solving tools, methodologies, and philosophies of scientific inquiry that by the 1960's have become totally incongruous with the Communist party's coercively maintained standards of scientific validity and political relevance.

Zhores Medvedev's letter to the Central Committee's Ideological Commission is addressed to this very problem:

> If ideology is a science, if communism is a science, if Marxism-Leninism is a science, then any criticism of any proposition in these sciences is also a science and not a "deviation." In any science, if it is not a collection of empty dogmas, certain propositions are continually going out of date and need to be replaced. New ideas, new propositions are always appearing in connection with new circumstances, new conditions, new relationships. If the ideology of society in its broad sense is science and not merely a weapon of political power, then the organ of power whether state or political, should not regulate the permissible limits of discussion. . . . if the organ of power itself takes part in the discussion and use force and breaks its own laws, which it established by roughly meddling with the constitutional rights of those taking part in the discussion, in that case it turns ideology not into science, but into a pseudo-science, a dogma, a collection of subjective rules.[56]

Because of the scientists' privileged position in society and crucial importance to the country's economic modernization and military strength, they have been relatively free from political harrassment. Their growing disinclination to accept unreasonable policy directives from the party's scientific bureaucrats has developed into a kind of collective self-assertion on behalf of intellectual autonomy, cultural nonconformity and ideological eclecticism.

In the beginning, Kapitsa, Tamm, Sakharov, and their colleagues seemed generally unconcerned with the system's defective ideological foundations and merely objected to bureaucratic intreference with scientific and academic activities. Peter Kapitsa's speech at the International Symposium on the Planning of Science in Prague in late 1959 illustrates this point: "Organizers are indeed needed to guide collective work in science. But scientists themselves, not administrators, should be such organizers." [57]

In the early 1960's it became clear that repeated reorganization of the scientific establishment had failed to produce the desired results in terms of research productivity and improved cooperation between industry and science.[58] It was also apparent that reforms were no more conducive to unhindered experimentation and unorthodox inquiry than had been similar measures in the past. As T. H. Rigby noted in a similar context: "The USSR cannot import foreign technical ideas wholesale without risking some ideological contraband." [59] As a consequence, a new constituency favoring a science-modernization policy developed among those most adversely affected by the party's inept reforms. The consensus of this new science lobby was succinctly expressed by Zhores Medvedev in his epitaph for the recently terminated Lysenko era.

> False doctrines, being an extreme product of the normal background of science, and having been created by extremist, fanatical representatives of the world of science, can achieve a monopolistic position only in state systems that are extremist in nature, as a particular manifestation of many other deviations from the reasonable norms of organized human society.[60]

The Soviet scientific community's intellectual transformation began with the dismissal of Stalinist pseudoscience and eventually reached the point of formulating comprehensive counterideologies containing political programs—a complex process indeed. Soviet scientists have instinctively rejected the Communist party's authority in nonpolitical, particularly scientific, matters, but as privileged members of an elite explicitly committed to a "scientific" world view and program of modernization, they have found it difficult to work out a counterideology which is both elitist in upholding the technical and scientific intellectuals' traditional social standing and academic prerogatives, and democratic in the sense of contributing to the restoration of constitutional guarantees, artistic freedoms, and fundamental civil rights for everyone—including nonelites and non-Russians—in the Soviet Union.

The scientists' vacillation between their traditional elitist and newly born egalitarian inclinations may be illustrated by citing Andrei Sakharov on the position of intellectuals in socialist society:

> Recognition by the working class and the intelligentsia of their common interests has been a striking phenomenon of the present day. The most progressive, internationalist, and dedicated element of the intelligentsia is, in essence, *a part of the working class*, and the most advanced, educated internationalist and broadminded part of the working class is part of the intelligentsia. (Emphasis added.)[61]

This, even as a tactical ruse to preserve the appearences of ideological orthodoxy was, of course, nonsense, and every educated Soviet reader must have considered it as such. Sakharov, however, was neither naive nor disingenuous in attempting to disguise himself and his fellow scientists as bona fide proletarians. Rather, his arguments seem to have been motivated by the modern Soviet intellectuals' collective insecurity as a marginal class in Soviet society and by their fear of isolation from the people—whom Sakharov knew to be neither "internationalist" nor "broadminded," but chauvinistic and intolerant of intellectualism of any kind.

Under these circumstances the scientists' search for allies against the "party's central apparatus and its officials," as Sakharov defined his target, led them to link up with the young people and the literary intelligentsia whose struggle for democracy the scientists, with few exceptions, ignored until the late 1960's.

Dissident Demands: Trends of Articulation

The available evidence suggests that the moral-absolutist and instrumental-pragmatic tendencies of dissent, though never far from one another in terms of issue areas, gradually converged in the late 1960's and crystallized into a set of commonly endorsed intellectual postures and policy demands.

The findings in Table 1–2 are based on my analysis of 10 samizdat documents that appeared in 1966 and 9 in 1970 that were later identified

TABLE 1–2 Soviet Dissent: Issue areas and Ideological Trends, 1966–1970

Issue Area	Moral-Absolutist		Instrumental-Pragmatic	
	1966	1970	1966	1970
Political Democracy	High[a]	High	Medium[b]	High
Nationality Rights	Medium	High	———	Medium
Human Rights-Socialist Legality	High	High	Medium	High
Developmental Rationality	Low[c]	Low	High	High
Quality of Life	High	High	———	Medium
Religious Autonomy	Medium	High	———	Medium
Artistic Freedoms	High	High	Low	Medium

a. "High" means clear priority accorded to a given issue area by samizdat documents in this period.
b. "Medium means prominent place but no overriding importance attached to the issue area.
c. "Low" means passing reference.

as "milestone events" in a comprehensive bibliographic survey of samizdat material that appeared in this period.[62]

The evidence (summarized in Table 1–2), despite its obvious limitations, permits us to make some general observations about trends in Soviet dissident interest articulation in each issue area: (1) At the end of the "national movement" phase there were only two issue areas (political democracy and human rights-socialist legality) out of the possible seven where the intensity of demands articulated by both groups coincided in full. (2) The instrumental-pragmatic group's radicalization tended to lag behind that of the other by at least one or two years between 1966 and 1970. (3) Each group initially had certain "blind spots"—nationality rights, religious autonomy, and developmental rationality, respectively—that gradually disappeared.

Although it was not feasible to take a frequency count of the number of demands advanced in each issue area in either sample, it was apparent that literary documents tended to emphasize the issue areas of political democracy, human rights, artistic freedoms, and quality of life, while the more analytical and legalistic writings stressed political democracy, developmental rationality, and socialist legality.

The partial coalescence of these two comparable, yet in some ways incompatible, ideologies, when placed in the context of Soviet political developments between 1966 and 1970, suggests that the convergence of dissident ideologies in this period was facilitated by two sets of factors. The first may be described as the Brezhnev-Kosygin-Podgorny leadership's attempts at re-Stalinization in various spheres of Soviet political, social, and cultural life. The second factor may be conceptualized as the emergence, in the second half of the 1960's, of four related crises of the regime that the dissenters perceived as manifestations of its illegitimacy.

Briefly, these crises involved (1) the Communist party's authority stemming from the unresolved succession struggle among Khrushchev's heirs, factional infighting over resource allocation priorities, and the leadership's mismanagement of conflicts within the socialist camp—the Sino-Soviet schism and the Czechoslovak crisis in particular.[63] (2) the Communist party's power and self-confidence as manifested in its policies of re-Stalinization, yet its paradoxical inability or unwillingness to control effectively the spreading dissident movement;[64] (3) the relevance of the regime's doctrinal foundations to the developmental dilemmas facing the USSR, especially in areas of technology and scientific progress where the United States further increased its lead over the Communist party-directed Soviet science and economy;[65] and (4) the regime's legitimacy-building processes and political socialization efforts in particular, as shown by the indifferent elite and mass participation in the hollow rituals of the 50th anniversary celebrations (1967) and those of the Lenin centenary in 1970.[66]

These crises of the system's political legitimacy, which the dissenters chose to interpret as signs of weakness, have not been sufficient in themselves to bring about the convergence of the two schools of dissent. However, what must have made the joining of forces not only possible but inevitable was the discovery by many scientists and prominent intellectuals who used to imagine themselves immune to police harrassment that, with the recent resurgence of Stalinism in many fields of Soviet life, they were just as vulnerable to arrest and detention for an unspecified terms (usually in one of the KGB's psychiatric institutions) as an illiterate Tatar peasant who was caught by the police when trying to return to his native village from Siberian exile without a resettlement permit.

Dissent: Nationality and Religious

The foregoing discussion focused on members of elite groups and on the political, moral, and ethical motivations of their dissident activities. These men and women belong to the broadly defined stratum of "intelligentsia" and, with such exceptions as the traditionally impecunious students, enjoy much higher living standards than an average factory worker, collective-farm peasant or an old-age pensioner. In any event, it is *not* the lack of admittedly modest economic privileges or a pervasive sense of insecurity but intellectual and cultural-traditional considerations that drove members of both moral-absolutist and instrumental-pragmatic ideological persuasion into open dissent.

Unlike these ideologically motivated critics of the regime, the mass of average Soviet citizens have neither the opportunity, nor the ability and the disposition to articulate their alienation from the system. Yet, dissent does exist among several identifiable groups of average Russians and non-Russians, as well. Since there are few alternatives to expressing opposition in ways other than overt action (public demonstrations, sit-ins, strikes, and so forth) for Soviet nonelites, their dissent represents an extreme case of alienation (anomie) and is often expressed in a militant fashion.

Thus, in the broadest sense, by "militant-anomic" dissenters we mean all nonelites, economic have-nots, and groups with low social status in Soviet society who have been denied the economic, social, cultural, and political benefits which the system has bestowed on most Great Russians, urban dwellers, and members of privileged groups. From this *potential* reservoir of militant-anomic dissent, the following clearly identifiable groups have made a contribution to dissident activities: (1) Major non-Russian nationalities of the Soviet Union—especially the Ukrainians and other groups with histories of independent nationhood and/or a record of armed resistance to Russian and Soviet domestic imperialism, such as the Latvians, Lithuanians, Estonians, Georgians, and Armenians.[67] (2) Survivors of national minority groups where were uprooted, decimated, and exiled to Siberia under Stalin, especially the Tatar and the Chechen Ingush.[68] (3) Politically active Orthodox clergymen and laymen, members of persecuted religious minorities, particularly the Jews, Ukrainian and Baltic Catholics, and several small Protestant denominations and fundamentalist sects.[69]

Like the last three groups, peoples of the Siberian and northern Russian subculture—including present and former inmates of labor camps, political exiles, survivors of forcibly resettled national and religious groups, and, on the western borders, ethnic groups adjacent to their former homelands (Rumanians, Slovaks, Hungarians, Poles, and so forth)—are all *potential* dissenters but have not been heard from in samizdat publications.[70]

Each anomic-militant group represents a set of challenges to the regime's political legitimacy. In the case of the major nationalities and the religious groups—especially the Jews—it is the intellectuals who articulate their respective constituencies' demands for nationality rights, political democracy, religious autonomy, human rights, and socialist legality and for the resolution of their grievances peculiar to their specific groups.[71]

The intellectuals of the various nationalities—unlike their Russian counterparts in Moscow, Leningrad, and other urban centers of dissent—derive their influence from being regarded as bearers of their nations' cultural traditions and true political consciousness. These ascribed attributes of moral and ideological leadership serve as unifying bonds between the indigenous elites and the people for whom they speak. It is this element of nationality consciousness and cultural cohesiveness that "colors, intensifies, and makes . . . more volatile all other conflicts" that exist between the regime and the people.[72]

Because of this sense of close unity within the national group and its close relationship with their "natural leaders," it may be supposed that dissident Ukrainian and Baltic intellectuals and those of the various other minority groups represent a far greater threat to the Russian-dominated Union-Republic Communist party's political power than do most Russian intellectuals to the CPSU. For most Russian intellectuals, "the people" tends to be more of an abstract neopopulist concept than a source of political support against the party bureaucracy. Since it is the non-Russian cultural and scientific elites who transmit and apply the party's modernization program to the particular conditions of their native land, ideological disloyalty among these elites could upset the regime's political stability and military security, as well.

Regardless of the issue area, inherent in all demands of national groups is the right of self-determination and, by implication, the right of secession from the USSR.[73] Since the latter is a constitutionally guaranteed right (Article 17), the Russian dissidents' slogan "Respect your own Constitution" has altogether different implications in Kiev, Riga, Kaunas, Reval, Tbilisi, or Erevan than it does in Pushkin Square in Moscow. Similarly, a large number of nationality grievances—cultural Russification; large-scale transfer of native technical and administrative experts to other Union Republics and their replacement with comparably- or less-skilled Russians; political, economic, and educational discrimination based on national origin; and instances of officially condoned wanton destruction of cultural objects and the burning of libraries—generally do not affect Russians wherever they may live in the Soviet Union.[74] All this contributes to the nationality elites' heightened sense of ethnic and cultural identity and political awareness.

The available data on the cases of Valentyn Moroz, Svyatoslav Karavansky, and Vyacheslav Chornovil seem to support this contention.[75] These men were loyal communists in their early 20's when they first encountered the secret police in the course of their respective professional activities as historian, linguist, and journalist. When confronted by the police they were made aware of the realities of second-class citizenship. Their "cases" developed from unfounded insinuations into equally unfounded but severely punishable charges of antistate activities and "bourgeois-nationalist" deviations, and they were forced to reexamine their beliefs and rediscover their true national and cultural identity. Samizdat statements and petitions written by these men and subsequently circulated by their supporters are similar in many respects to comparable Russian dissident documents. However, in the authorities' judgment, as suspected Ukrainian nationalists, their offenses transcended the limits of semilegitimacy and were deemed to represent a distinct threat to the stability of the USSR.[76] For example, Andrei Amalrik, a Russian and son of a prominent scholar, was sentenced in October, 1970 to a three-year term in a labor camp for his dissident activities. A month later, Valentyn Moroz, a Ukrainian and son of a peasant, received a nine-year sentence on similar, and indeed less-publicized charges.[77]

The predicament of the religious minorities, especially the Jews, is in many ways comparable to the situation of the intellectuals of the various national groups. In addition to the burden of official, ideological, antireligious biases and the legacy of related discriminatory policies against all believers, Jews have also been victims of traditional Russian, Ukrainian, and Baltic anti-Semitism which the party leadership has often utilized to divert popular attention from the regime's domestic or foreign difficulties.[78]

The position of intellectuals and religious leaders from economically and culturally less-developed areas—especially Soviet Central Asia, the Soviet Far East, and Moldavia—is further complicated by their communities' visible, and by all standards very impressive, educational and economic progress under Russian communist rule. A Kazakh, an Uzbek, a Tadzhik, a Moldavian intellectual, or a Moslem religious leader, although very likely profoundly alienated from the theory and practice of forced Russification and ideological secularization, has few if any alternatives to cooperating with Moscow's representatives in most matters involving his native land or religious constituency.[79]

The ideological spectrum of anomic-militant dissent also includes at least two identifiable groups from the majority nation, the Great Russians. The recent appearance of a pamphlet *Slovo Natsii (A Nation Speaks)* and the samizdat journal *Veche (Diet)* provides us with documentary evidence that the hitherto "missing link" of Russian nationalism and orthodox Slavophile ideologies from the current revival of traditional political beliefs does exist after all. D. Pospielovsky's perceptive analysis reveals that *A Nation Speaks* "represents extreme nationalist views with an admixture of racism," while *Veche* offers a "modernized version of traditional Russian Slavophilism."[80] The former, speaking on behalf of "Russian Patriots," maintains that of "all peoples of the USSR," it is the Russians who bear the greatest burden, including that of the modernization, education, and protection of the non-Russian nationalities. These right-wing dissidents also advocate the formation of a "racially pure" (that is, non-Jewish or "cosmopolitan") unified and undivided Russia and propose to do away with democracy as a decadent and unworkable theory of statecraft.

Although *Veche*'s initial position was far more moderate in these matters, in recent issues of the journal there seems to be a marked shift toward a more conservative, authoritarian "religio-racist" position. This latest trend may be viewed as a delayed conservative reaction to the same legitimacy crises that led to the radicalization and eventual convergence of the moral-absolutist and the instrumental-pragmatic groups at the end of the "national movement" phase of the postwar dissent movement. This new trend is nourished by Great Russian, lower-class authoritarian, nationalistic frustrations, and if it succeeds in enlisting the support of urban and small-town working-class elements, which is not at all unlikely, it may become a significant force for the Soviet party and government to reckon with.[81]

The fourth, "retrenchment and polarization," phase of Soviet dissent began in 1971. This new, perhaps final, phase of organized dissent is marked by the disintegration of the temporary national unity of the Democratic Movement; by a return to individual, uncoordinated, and intermittent group activities; and by the ideological polarization of the anti-regime forces. These developments came about as a result of the changed political, social, and economic context in which the interaction between the regime and its opponents had been taking place.[82]

By 1970 it became clear that the gradual convergence of issue areas of unauthorized interest articulation and the dissidents' growing emphasis on illegitimate, mainly political and nonelite, concerns presented a potentially serious security problem to the regime. The rapid politization of dissident demands and the radicalization of the form and substance of nationality and religious-interest articulation persuaded the leadership that, on balance, the usefulness, even as a safety valve, of such demands was outweighed by their subversive and politically destabilizing potential.

Once the CPSU elite had concluded, to paraphrase Dahl, that the cost of continued toleration of organized dissent exceeded the likely cost of its repression, they proceeded on several fronts to put an end to it. On the basis of reports in the 1971–2 issues of the *Chronicle of Current Events*, we might reconstruct the regime's strategy as follows: a determined effort to stamp out the samizdat journals, primarily the *Chronicle*, to apprehend their provincial correspondents, and to harass their editors.[83] Tactics such as intensified surveillance, deprivation of private telephones, restrictions on contacts with foreign journalists, repeated summonses to appear before secret-police examiners, and threats to invoke the notorious "anti-parasite" laws against those dismissed from their jobs were employed against the more prominent leaders of the movement.

In contrast to petty harassment of this kind, low-status dissenters were dealt with swiftly and ruthlessly. With the partial exception of prospective Jewish emigrants to Israel, all suspected Ukrainian and Baltic nationalistic and religious dissenters who were apprehended during the police campaigns of 1971–2 received unusually harsh sentences, often in the form of more than one kind of punishment (prison plus exile, strict regime labor camp plus exile, and so forth).[84]

After successfully dividing the protest movement into isolated intellectual leaders and incarcerated followers, the regime went on to reduce the ranks of prominent dissenters. They imprisoned some (P. Yakir); in the case of Yuri Galanskov, they withheld medical treatment, thus murdering him;[85] they let some leave the USSR (J. Brodsky, Esenin-Volpin, P. Litvinov, B. Tsukerman, Y. Glazov, V. Chalidze, Z. Medvedev; and they compelled the rest to remain silent or, in the case of Sakharov and Shafarevich, to accept new, severely restrictive guidelines for their continued activity in the USSR.

Although the nature of these new arrangements is still ambiguous, the fact that the *only* collective statement by dissident Soviet intellectuals in 1972 was an appeal to the authorities to extend he scope of the impending amnesty law to include political prisoners in connection with the fiftieth anniversary of the USSR, indicated a retreat from the illegitimate issue area of political democracy to the less objectionable matter of human rights-socialist legality.[86] All this, of course, did not preclude the circulation of individual appeals made on behalf of other persecuted individuals.

Rather it signaled the end of organized actions seeking to promote political reforms in the USSR.

The resignation of V. Chalidze from the Moscow Human Rights Committee in the summer of 1972 and the subsequent departure of A. Tverdokhlebov from that group in an apparent dispute over the committee's insufficiently critical reaction to Chalidze's loss of his Soviet citizenship while on an officially sanctioned lecture tour in the United States suggest that in the winter of 1972 the last viable center of organized dissent was about to disappear from the Soviet political scene.[87]

Dissent: Impact on Policy Making

The foregoing arguments sought to describe and analyze the social bases, the ideological positions, and the first stages of development of the postwar political reform movement in the Soviet Union. Next we shall seek to establish the place and significance of the Democratic Movement in the Soviet political process and offer a series of tentative propositions concerning the policy-making potentials of the two main schools of dissent (instrumental-pragmatic and moral-absolutist) and the newly emerging third branch of dissent (anomic-militant).

In the broadest sense, dissent may be viewed as a form of interest articulation with a normative content. Although the movement, on the whole, seems to meet the sociological requirements of a "group," that is, "group self-consciousness, ascribed group status, and a set of shared values," [88] it shall not be regarded as an "interest group" either in the classical or the modern sense of the term. The conspicuous failure of interest-group theories to account for the *motivation* of unorthodox interest articulation in communist systems in terms other than social status and material gain renders them largely useless as rigorous analytic devices for the study of the contemporary Soviet dissident movement.[89] Instead, we would be inclined to view the movement as a new, amorphous dimension of Communist-party functional-elite[90] interaction and an extension of posttotalitarian group politics into traditionally illegitimate or semi-legitimate areas of political activity.

The dynamics of this new dimension of Soviet politics may best be analyzed by tentatively defining the conditions under which the ideas of dissenters might influence the political decisions made by the Communist party.[91] As a general proposition we would suggest that, for the purpose

TABLE 1–3 Factors of Legitimacy-Illegitimacy of Interest Articulation in Posttotalitarian Soviet Politics

	Legitimate	Semilegitimate	Illegitimate
Issue Area	Developmental rationality	Human rights-socialist legality Quality of life Artistic freedoms religious autonomy	Political democracy Nationality rights The "Stalin issue" "Cult of personality"
Target	Only to proper authorities and authorized grievance-managing institutions and agencies	Proper authorities plus leaks to unauthorized persons	Others—"the people," "public opinion," foreign correspondents, etc.
Affective Content	Legitimacy-supportive—"constructive," in "party" or "patriotic" spirit	Policy-legitimacy—critical	Anti regime—"anti-Soviet," "anti party," "illegal," etc.
Style of Articulation	Pragmatic-bargaining	Absolute-value oriented (traditional intelligentsia posture)	Militant-activist
Mode of Aggregation	Unorganized individuals	Ad hoc group organized to promote one issue (intermittent interaction)	Multi purpose organization (frequent and routinized interaction)
Agent	High status in party or in a developmentally or politically crucial functional interest group—scientists, military technocrats, economists, etc.	High-medium status—most scientists, very prominent writers, rehabilitated CPSU officials, or surviving family members, well-connected intellectuals, etc.	Low status—unattached intellectuals, students, national minorities, former camp inmates, religious minorities, fringe groups, etc.

of evaluating its *policy-making potential,* dissent in a Communist polity be defined as a form of unauthorized interest articulation involving demands on the political system for action or inaction that the Communist party leadership may deem legitimate, semilegitimate, or illegitimate, depending on the (1) issue area, (2) the target (intended recipient), (3) the affective content (mobilizing potential), (4) the style of articulation, (5) the mode of aggregation and (6) the agent's (articulator's) ascribed political and social status. Hence, it would tend to *respond* to it in a favorable, ambivalent, or repressive manner.

This schematic chart is built on a set of a priori assumptions about the nature of Soviet political processes and official perceptions concerning the legitimacy of unauthorized interest articulation in the post-Khrushchev period. Robert Dahl's study of the conditions, characteristics, and developmental variables that determine the relationship between a political regime and its opponents offers two axioms that help explain that Soviet situation in a cogent fashion.[92] Dahl proposed that (1) "the likelihood that a government will tolerate an opposition increases as the expected costs of toleration decrease," and (2) "the likelihood that a government will tolerate an opposition increases as the expected costs of suppression increase."

If we accept these propositions as self-evident, we may assume that contributions to policy which are designed to encourage the system's successful development are considered legitimate and are therefore viewed favorably by the party but that demands for political self-determination by militant national minorities are deemed inherently subversive and hence are suppressed by the regime. In a similar fashion, from the Communist party's viewpoint, grievances addressed to the proper authorities (police, procuracy, party officials, newspapers, and so forth) are preferable to those aimed at nonelites or foreigners; "constructive" suggestions are preferable to bitter denunciations; compromise to militant intransigence; an isolated individual to an established multipurpose organization; and a trusted or eminent member of the elite to a marginal—presumably alienated—member of society.

If we further assume that these perceptual biases represent typical patterns of party-elite orientations toward various forms of dissent, we may be able to offer a series of tentative propositions concerning the policy-making potential of each school of dissent.

The *moral-absolutists'* contributions to the Communist party's policy dilemmas tend to fall into the "legitimate" category only in terms of interest aggregation techniques and occasionally that of the "agent" who, as often as not, comes from a low-status—hence politically potentially subversive—social background.[93]

The moral-absolutists' conspicuous failure to concern themselves with problems of economic modernization and their lack of the necessary economic and scientific background for the articulation of their own basic economic demands in politically acceptable terms seems to be the literary community's greatest liabilities for policy-making purposes. That is, as long as the party and the economic bureaucracy feel free to dismiss moral-absolutist demands for higher living standards, better housing, and improved rural living conditions as possibly well-intentioned but amateurish and developmentally irrelevant demogogy, the literary community can have little influence on policy making in this crucial area of the regime's developmental legitimacy.

The moral-absolutists, as conscious heirs to the traditions of the radical libertarian Russian intelligentsia, are also handicapped by the style and content of their interest articulation. The authorities—whose orientations toward unorthodox political activities are steeped in equally traditional authoritarian Russian bureaucratic beliefs and patterns of behavior—find their suggestions, as a rule, inadmissible as legitimate contributions to the policy-making process. Moreover, the intellectuals' preoccupation with the past history and present dangers of Stalinism—the most vulnerable aspect of the incumbents' legitimate political authority—has introduced an apocalyptic and politically irreconcilable element of conflict into Soviet politics that not only affects the regime's ongoing political socialization efforts but tends to disrupt the collective party leadership's precarious internal balance of power, as well.

From this we may conclude that the moral-absolutists' influence on the policy-making process can be, at best, only indirect in one or more of three possible ways. The demands of the intelligentsia for, say, continued de-Stalinization may be manipulated to advance the interests of a certain party leadership faction (for example, Khrushchev's role in consenting to the publication of Yevtushenko's "Stalin's Heirs" and Solzhenitsyn's *One Day in the Life of Ivan Denisovich*) or may be used in either a negative or a positive context as debating points in the party's highest deliberative bodies. The appeal, on the eve of the 23rd CPSU Congress, by Soviet intellectuals warning the party about the dangers of continued re-Stalinization might be illustrative of this contingency[94] and could be utilized by the leadership as post facto justification of policies independently arrived at (especially in the field of foreign policies toward China, Yugoslavia, and other socialist countries where esoteric communication of this type may seem politically prudent at a given stage of policy deliberations). The publication of a provocative article by Ernst Henry, on Mao Tse-tung's alleged plans for world conquest and his rejoinder to his Chinese critics, when placed in the context of Sino-Soviet negotiations in the winter of 1967–1968, seems to be a good example of this kind of unofficial esoteric communication.[95] Or did Ernst Henry have Leonid Brezhnev rather than Mao Tse-tung in mind?

Unlike the literary intelligentsia and members of the younger generation, most, if not all, *instrumental-pragmatic* dissenters are members of established, politically significant, and developmentally indispensible elites who are in a position to influence policy making in several legitimate ways and a variety of semilegitimate ones. Also, unlike the moral-absolutists, Soviet scientists and technical intellectuals have tended to become involved in politics only with the greatest reluctance—and even then essentially as a means of individual or collective self-defense against the return of Stalinism.

The dialogue between the arrested mathematician Revol't Pimenov and the Leningrad city party committee's ideological specialist V. S. Medvedev illustrates this point.

> Medvedev: "You are not living right. A whole collection of anti-Soviet literature was taken away from you."
>
> Pimenov: "There was not one line that called for an overthrow, a weakening, or anything detrimental to Soviet authority. . . ."
>
> Medvedev: "I am not concerned with legal niceties. In essence I am discussing with you . . . Where did you get such an interest in that kind of literature?"
>
> Pimenov: "The reason for all this is that for some time we scientists have lost our sense of personal security. It has been roughly from the end of 1966. Until then somehow there was no fear. But we have been forced to experience fear. Why? It is necessary to examine the social reasons for this fear.
>
> To work in science, there must be faith in the future. When there is no such faith, there can be only narrow specialists who are busy with their discipline and who are not interested in public issues. The threat to personal security explains the studying of politics. All this began with the writers. The most important element in the trials was how they were conducted. The violation of legal rights drew attention to them and aroused public concern.[96]

Pimenov's calm rebuttal of the apparatchik's menacing questions suggests a posture of self-confidence and inner strength that has become a characteristic feature of interest articulation by dissident Soviet scientists.

In an age when success in global ideological contests is measured in terms of economic development and scientific progress, distinguished scholars such as Andrei Sakharov, Mikhail Leontovich, Igor Shafarevich, and their colleagues cannot be dealt with in the same way as the imprisoned—and notoriously unproductive—Soviet scientists used to be treated by Beria's men in Stalinist times. Unlike the politically impotent denizens of Solzhenitsyn's *First Circle*, contemporary Soviet scientists, as a result of the effective reduction in the range of party and government decision-making monopoly in fields of science policy, basic research, and its applications in industry, agriculture, and military technology, until early 1972 enjoyed a considerable degree of personal immunity from administrative interference and ideological harassment.[97]

From this it follows that even allowing for delays due to inefficiency, bureaucratic infighting, and ideological confusion, constructive policy suggestions sooner or later receive a hearing by an appropriate nonspecialist decision-making body or a responsible party official.

The scientists' position in nonideological areas rest on a "more modern form of authority" than that of the party.[98] Therefore, they tend to present their case in a manner that the political leadership cannot find objectionable on any but general ideological—hence, in the short run developmentally very likely irrelevant—grounds.[99]

Moreover, as far as it is possible to establish from the published evidence (at least until March, 1971), members of the scientific community have not confronted the party leadership with nonnegotiable demands of any kind. Rather, as it may be surmised from the Sakharov-Medvedev-Turchin memorandum to Brezhnev, Kosygin, and Podgorny, the dissident scientists tended to regard themselves as loyal, expert advisors to a political leadership that was assumed to be open-minded in scientific and economic matters. One would never guess from the scientists' impeccably orthodox language that they privately might consider these political leaders as fit only to run a penal colony, or as "bandits in the guise of state officials," as a recent samizdat statement written by "A Group of Scientists from the USSR Academy of Sciences" put it.[100] Indeed, one might not see that they are involved in a high-stakes game of matching wits with respected intellectual equals.

In any case, it seems clear that the instrumental-pragmatists' message, ostensibly concerned with developmental rationality is, in reality, about political power. That is, the scientists' arguments concerning the necessity of "further democratization of public life . . . under the aegis of the CPSU" for the sake of more rapid economic modernization might be considered as a tentative opening move in a proposed bargaining relationship between two partners, at least within the context of the relationship between the party and the scientific intellectuals at that time. They might be interpreted as an attempt to facilitate the exchange of the scientific community's "quid" of political loyalty and continued cooperation with the party for the "quo" of a larger share of policy-making influence and guaranteed civil rights for the instrumental-pragmatist cluster of functional elites.[101] Indeed, as David Holloway noted in this context, "the scientists' gain is not necessarily the politicians' loss." [102] Judging from the scientists' success in obtaining the release of Zhores Medvedev from a KGB psychiatric hospital in June, 1970, following weeks of intensive negotiations with party and police authorities, there is reason to believe that at least on an experimental and case-by-case basis *some* aspects of this proposed new modus vivendi may have gone into effect in the summer of 1970.[103]

However, as 31 scientists and academic intellectuals pointed out in an open letter on June 30, 1970, the benefits of such trade-offs should be extended to nonscientists, as well.[104]

> A professional group of scholars defends Zhores Medvedev. We welcome such collective efforts. This is a wonderful thing. It would not be a bad idea for example if writers would follow this initiative and defend their colleagues. We are only emphasizing that those who do not belong to any professional group are in need of the same total and fervent support by society.

We can only speculate whether this letter represents the consensus of the entire instrumental-pragmatic group or only the sentiment of its radical or egalitarian faction. In any case, apart from Andrei Sakharov and his 1972 memoranda (of which more will be said in the concluding part of this essay), the scientists have studiously refrained from commenting on the issues of religious freedom and nationality rights. Since these are matters which primarily concern the older, rural, and uneducated segments of the population, it is not surprising that few Soviet scientists care to become involved in such nonelite causes. Although this noncommittal posture might be tactically advantageous for the instrumental-pragmatists in the short run, it is inconceivable that the temporary bargaining leverage thus gained can be maintained in a political system in which one-half the population consists of non-Russians, many of whom, especially the Baltic and Central Asian peoples, consider religious freedom as their fundamental right and paramount political objective.

The instrumental-pragmatic dissenters' influence on the policy-making process is potentially considerable. Under optimum conditions—defined as "Evolution" or "Adaption" in Brzezinski's program of possible futures for the Soviet political system in the 1970's[105]—they might make significant contributions in one or more of the following ways:

1. By openly endorsing the developmental rationality of positions taken by members of specific CPSU leadership factions, the scientists can influence the outcome of policy disputes stemming from dilemmas within the party apparat about the allocation of resources. In this context, the scientists may play an important role in developing ways of implementing domestic and foreign scientific innovation under Soviet circumstances. The Liberman proposals and the Soviet economists' role in evaluating the potential usefulness of economic innovations in Eastern Europe, such as the Hungarian New Economic Mechanism, seem to be relevant at this juncture.[106]

2. Through the routinization of ad hoc bargaining relationships (see the Medvedev case) scientists might acquire significant political leverage in the science policy-making process, including a decisive voice in resolving problems of "basic versus applied research," and the funding, structure, and personnel policies of research institutes and university science departments.[107]

3. Upon recognizing the mutually beneficial nature of this relationship, it will be in the interests of both sides to channel the scientific community's contributions to policy through representative, quasi-institutional, advisory bodies based on the common interests of two autonomous partners.[108]

4. In the long run, this process of intense instrumental interaction could lead to the development of non-Marxist methods of problem solving and philosophies of scientific inquiry and to a corresponding erosion of the party's normative criteria-based ideological legitimacy.[109]

Under unfavorable or extreme conditions—defined by Brzezinski as "Petrification," "Fundamentalism," and "Disintegration"[110]—most of this program would probably become irrelevant. However, short of predicting the doom of the USSR as a going political concern with a given and a rapidly proliferating set of developmental needs, it is hard to envisage any future Soviet policy-making arrangements that would fail to provide an important role for leading members of the scientific community—political dissenters and conformists alike.

Concerning the *anomic-militant* group's policy-making capabilities, it may be argued that the nationalities' and the religious minorities' greatest assets are their sheer numbers, rising birthrates, and strategic location along the western, Central Asian, and eastern boundaries of the USSR.[111] Even though in a numerical majority in the USSR, the national groups, with the possible exception of the Ukrainians, (1) are underrepresented both in the Communist party and in the highest party and government decision-making bodies;[112] (2) tend on a per capita basis to benefit less from resource allocations earmarked for economic modernization, improvement of rural working conditions, and the preservation of indigenous cultural traditions than do the Russians;[113] and (3) in terms of socioeconomic mobility are handicapped by the system's Russian-based *nomenklatura*, or cadre policies.

On the basis of the foregoing and from demands advanced in relevant dissident documents, it may be inferred that the nationalities' and the religious minorities' policy-making capabilities, though potentially considerable, are relevant only in the following areas:

1. National groups may play an ambiguous role and could exercise indirect influence on the ethnic-political balance of various CPSU and government decision-making bodies. This could be accomplished by spokesmen who use the national issue to advocate or oppose policies which might affect regional supporters or opponents of party and government leadership factions, decisions on granting or denying resource allocations for specific areas, and a host of related issues that concern the economic development and political stability of a given Union or Autonomous Republic.[114]

2. Nationality problems must exercise a significant influence on the drafting of a new Soviet constitution—in progress since early 1962[115]—in terms of laying the legal foundations for a new modus vivendi for the Russians and the non-Russian peoples of the Soviet Union.

3. In the realm of Soviet foreign policies we can identify three examples of the *indirect* influence of a nationality group or religious minority on specific foreign or domestic policy decisions:

a. From early 1969 on—as one of the unexpected by-products of the Sino-Soviet schism—the nationality issue became a focal point of contention between the Chinese leaders and Khrushchev's successors. To Chinese accusations that "Soviet revisionist new Tsars" exercise "fascist bourgeois" dictatorship over the "oppressed nationalities" of the USSR,[116] the Soviet government might be compelled to respond and to review some aspects of its cultural policies, especially in Union Republics whose elites were thought to be vulnerable to Chinese propaganda of this kind. (A Soviet-Rumanian dispute over the cultural and political rights of

Rumanians living in Bessarabia may also be mentioned in this connection.)[117]

b. Among several possible reasons behind the Soviet decision to invade Czechoslovakia, the impact of the Prague Spring on the Ukrainian intellectuals might have been regarded as significant by the Soviet leadership. Alarmed reports about the sudden upsurge of nationalist and Marxist revisionist ideologies among the youth and the intellectuals were issued by the Ukrainian First Secretary Shelest and his non-Russian fellow apparatchiki who made up the majority of speakers at the July 1968 Plenum of the CPSU Central Committee. These could have contributed to the Russian leaders' (probably false) perceptions concerning the threat that the "Czechoslovak model" posed to the political stability of the USSR.[118]

c. In a similar fashion, it may be argued that Soviet foreign policy reverses in the Middle East have been great morale boosters for the entire Jewish community in the USSR.[119] The resulting growth of ethnic identity/national consciousness and political assertiveness among Soviet Jews and the world sympathy—fostered by U.S. government pressure—generated by officially condoned acts of anti-Semitism have forced the Soviet leadership to reconsider its restrictive emigration policies and allow increasing numbers of Jews to leave for Israel.[120]

Dissent: Politics for Change in the USSR

As the foregoing discussion on the policy-making potential of dissident interest articulation has suggested, we still do not have enough empirically sound evidence to go much beyond low-level theorizing on this matter. We know that political dissent has been, and will probably continue to be, a recognizable factor in Soviet politics. We also know that until now dissent has not made a significant—either positive or negative—impact on the regime and its policies.

In the larger perspective of postwar Soviet politics, however, dissent tends to acquire an altogether different meaning. With the benefit of hindsight it may be argued that the emergence of public contestation and unorthodox interest articulation have been unintended but inevitable by-products of a planned process of liberalization or "postmobilization decompression" that developed a momentum of its own during the "national movement" phase.

Temporary legitimacy crises, internal political readjustments, unresolved succession problems, and economic difficulties were, to a great extent, responsible for the remarkable spread of dissent in the late 1960's. From this it may be argued that some of these factors, such as the problem of political succession—itself a proven source of indecision and vacillation at the top—were merely temporary difficulties that, once resolved, would be followed by the reassertion of central control and, with it, the eradication of political dissent.

However, as the preceding analysis of the sources of dissent indicated, the underlying causes of all three schools of dissent are *systemic* in origin and are therefore not susceptible to remedies that fail to alleviate substantially or indeed eliminate completely the fundamental political and ideological sources of alienation. Although the regime's congenital legitimacy defects are not and need not be conducive to internal crisis and instability in the short run, the system's long-term cohesion, economic development, and overall prosperity are inconceivable without significant ideological revisions, structural alterations, and substantial improvements in the policy-making processes.

The logic of this hypothesis, when applied to Brzezinski's adaptation-evolution model of future Soviet political development, which is the only Soviet future that is worth contemplating in this context, presumes continued *contestation,* as well as a growing degree of *interdependence* between the regime and its domestic, particularly instrumental-pragmatic, critics. The reasons for the likelihood of future contestation seem self-evident and require no future explanations at this point. The question of interdependence is more speculative and calls for a more explicit kind of reasoning.

It may be argued at the outset that the presently available explanations concerning the nature of postmobilization Soviet politics are not satisfactory because they fail to account for the paradox posed by the coexistence of an internal political reform movement with an increasingly stable political system in the USSR. The relationship and the contradictions between the regime and its non-anomic-militant critics has been, to use the Chinese phrase, "nonantagonistic," hence generally amenable to noncoercive solutions, such as bargaining, compromise, and other instrumental means of resolving conflict. All this suggests an abstract, and, within the foreseeable future, a very real possibility of a two-player gaming situation between the party and those presently alienated technical, scientific, and cultural elites without whose active cooperation the regime cannot survive, let alone realize its ambitious developmental objectives.

It is patently inaccurate to maintain, as Fleron does, that in a "monocratic political system" such as the USSR, if the political elite "does not possess . . . the skills necessary to running the society . . . it can obtain them *at no cost* from various specialized elites . . . without having to exchange for it a voice in the policy-making process."[121] (Emphasis added.) This kind of reasoning assumes that the use of coercion does not involve an expenditure of resources and is therefore "cost free." Moreover, it greatly underestimates the resources available to the regime and the dissidents to influence each other. It also overstates the importance of the cooptation process as a device to defuse conflicts between the CPSU and specialized groups; and it entirely ignores the possibility of future expansion of the boundaries of the political decision-making process in the USSR.

In support of this contention it must be pointed out that the Communist party's leadership has never had and is not likely to have an opportunity to make a "rational choice" aimed at the maximization of its own power to the total exclusion of all others.[122] To view traditional boundaries of policy-making prerogatives as given and not subject to the system's changing political, developmental, security, and social needs is tantamount to labeling Soviet politicians either dull clerks or superhuman manipulators of power and influence. To be sure, they are neither. Rather, if the regime's past policy-making performance is any indication of its leaders' skill, flexibility, and resourcefulness, there is reason to believe that they will be able to adjust to new political realities and, in this case, to the continued existence of dissent during the coming decades.

Although the specific patterns of accommodation to new realities are impossible to predict at this time, there are several salient aspects of this kind of interaction that can be identified on the basis of the data introduced in the earlier part of this study.

First we shall postulate that the Marxist-Leninist ideology which has legitimated the Communist party's monopoly of power in the USSR has become ritualized to the point that it has lost most if not all of its instrumental meaning.[123] In the long run, this permits the leadership to adjust the system's laws, institutions, and political processes with less and less regard to the precepts of the founding myths of the Soviet party and state. Ritualized ideology and political flexibility thus achieved will be complemented by the routinization of interest articulation by the regime's critics. The latter, in turn, will be less and less constrained by the Russian intelligentsia's tradition of politically unproductive confrontations based on absolute values and more inclined to develop a kind of "cost-benefit consciousness" or a new "calculus of dissent" when advancing their claims on the regime. Once this happens, dissent will lose its ideologically subversive meaning, and hence the threat it poses to the incumbents' political legitimacy.

The validity of this hypothesis depends, to some extent, on the definition of the *conditions* under which this kind of interaction might take place. Specifically, what could be the *point of entry* for dissident interest articulation in Soviet policy-making processes in the 1970's and the 1980's?

A partial, but generally persuasive, answer to this question may be obtained by adopting Darrell Hammer's model on the hierarchy of decision making in Soviet politics.[124] According to Hammer's scheme, there are three kinds of decisions ("Political," "Policy," and "Administrative") that correspond to the distribution of power in the USSR. Political decisions involve primarily elite maintenance functions such as party organizational and cadre policies, as well as the *ultimate sanctioning of directives* in areas of resource allocation, ideological work, national defense, and foreign policy. Decisions of this kind are the prerogative of the CPSU Politburo. Policy decisions involve the *implementation* of political decisions (save internal party matters) in consultation with groups and individuals from the government bureaucracy and specialist groups such as the military, the scientific community, the economists, and so forth. Administrative decisions involve the *execution* of policy directives by low-level decision-making units, such as regional and local soviets.

The separation of politics and administration (or party and state) that this scheme implies does not, as Hammer has correctly observed, guarantee a corresponding growth in autonomy to the bureaucratic and specialist groups which participate in the decision-making process. Nor, we must add, does it confer unlimited power on the party to make political, let alone policy, decisions. The case in point, apart from our earlier arguments concerning the long-term inevitability of specialist involvement in decision making in the USSR, is another potentially equally significant process that may be called "postmobilization etatism." This term denotes a recurring trend in Soviet history characterized by the emergence of *incipient bipolarity* in party-state relations (1939–1954, 1962, and since 1966) and by the ascendancy of the state and its encroachment on some of the party's decision-making prerogatives, particularly in economics, science, and national defense. The evidence begins with Stalin's virtual disbanding of the highest-level party bodies and continues through

Malenkov's *choice* (in March, 1953) of premiership instead of party leadership—a gross miscalculation, but, under the circumstances an understandable one. It includes Khrushchev's abortive party reorganization scheme in 1962 and the record of the Brezhnev-Kosygin-Podgorny triumvirate, particularly the continued influence and possibly even veto power of the last two. All of this is highly suggestive and requires no additional elaboration at this point.

The stipulated erosion of the party's power and the state's proportionate gain does not in itself benefit the dissenters or necessarily enhance their influence over all three types of decision-making processes in the USSR. What does seem more probable is that the continued bifurcation of political power could tip the balance, to cite the classic Soviet dichotomy, in favor of economics over politics. Once that happens, the traditional boundaries of political participation will expand, most likely in the areas of policy and possibly administrative decisions. From this it follows that the point of entry for dissident interest articulation, especially the instrumental-pragmatic variety, is more likely to be located in areas where traditions of a consultative relationship between the party and specialist groups have already been established: that is, on the policy decision level.

A case for a growing, and eventually routinized, specialist involvement in making policy decisions may be further buttressed by a tentative listing of the benefits and costs accruing to both sides from this kind of relationship.

The issuing by both sides of "effective mutual guarantees,"[125] based on shared beliefs concerning the regime's long-term systemic goals, is an indispensable condition for the transformation of specialist-elite-party *interaction* into mutually binding political *interdependence* of all participants involved in decision-making processes. Such guarantees have already been offered by the instrumental-pragmatic cluster of would-be policy-making partners. A favorable response from the party, in the form of extending sweeping guarantees and immunity from persecution to all legitimate and semilegitimate interest articulators, will not be forthcoming in the near future. Yet, the past cannot and will not indefinitely encroach upon the present, and the system's developmental needs will compel the party to devise a strategy of liberalization that, by definition, must include additional incentives (such as the selective enlargement of the scope of personal freedoms) to constructive elite participation in decision-making processes. In doing so the party has nothing to lose but the burden of its conservative middle-echelon bureaucracy and stands to gain the active cooperation of an educationally highly qualified new constituency committed to the orderly development and modernization of the Soviet system. What are the *present* demands of this constituency on Soviet policy matters?

When analyzing the evolution of Sakharov's arguments between 1968 and 1972, we are struck by the instrumental-pragmatists' growing concern for Soviet middle-class problems such as the shortage of well-trained and adequately paid doctors and teachers, the quality of educational, cultural, and social services, the endemic rise of alcoholism, and the general deterioration of the quality of Soviet life.[126] These widely shared concerns and other aspects of Soviet middle-class discontent, when skillfully articulated and publicized through legitimate and samizdat channels, are the most likely issues to receive a hearing and be acted upon by the authorities.

The Soviet middle class that has come into being since the war has had no spokesmen thus far. This group, long taken for granted, is now beginning to assert its collective interests. Its emancipation from an ideological defined status of "stratum" into a social class coequal with the workers and the peasants is long overdue. The pervasive insecurity and the unfulfilled ambitions of this class seem to offer the best opportunities for the realization of dissident demands in Soviet politics. Sakharov's suggestions concerning the establishment of a "public watchdog agency" and an "International Committee of Experts" to safeguard human rights in the USSR may be regarded as the articulation of these concerns and perhaps a step toward the creation of Soviet ombudsmen and public control over policy and especially administrative decisions. "Interest aggregation by impartial sympathetic third parties" [127] in the USSR may not be as farfetched as most Western observers seem to believe.

The foregoing general observations now may be amended by a set of more specific considerations concerning the cost-benefit aspects of future Soviet dissent.

Instrumental-pragmatic interest articulation, including recent middle-class demands, may be regarded as reaffirmation of those aspects of the system's legitimacy that stem from its ideological commitment to "distributive justice" [128] in welfare, health, education, and equal opportunity within the framework of a politically enlightened socialist society. Therefore, to the extent that related dissident demands are supportive of the essential elements of the institutional status quo, they, though not necessarily their present advocates, qualify as legitimate inputs into the policy-making process.

The introduction of a controlled, within-system adversary relationship to replace the ersatz dialectics of "criticism-self-criticism" could open up much needed political safety valves and facilitate orderly and noncoercive resolutions of systemic tensions. Whether we term the benefits of the institutionalization of party-specialist group dialogues as conducive to "political decompression" or liken the phenomenon to the deicing function of forced air bubbles piped into winter harbors ("aeration effect"), the results are likely to contribute to a new political *decision-making style* and, with it, to *policy-making interdependence*.

If we assume that the three levels of Soviet decision making are essentially inseparable and that the instrumental-pragmatic interest articulation tends to enrich "the flow of problems, values and data that are the raw material processed by policy-making," to enhance the decision makers' "policy-issue knowledge," and to improve the "net output," [129] we may postulate that dissident demands that are processed at the policy decision level tend to enhance the *overall quality* of Soviet decision making on all three levels.

Another beneficial aspect of dissent from the viewpoint of long-term systemic development lies in its potential for *"reconstructive leadership."* [130] To the extent that dissent of whatever kind, does, in fact, entail the active participation of groups otherwise unrepresented or underrepresented in the political process, the leadership is presented with a more balanced set of contributions to policy-problems under consideration. Thus, the decision makers are in an improved position to act in a purposeful, politically prudent, and developmentally functional manner.[131]

Although the above arguments may appear to have described the interaction and the respective calculations of rational cost-benefit-conscious political actors without regard to their possibly nonrational ideological and other culturally conditioned biases, it is axiomatic that within the parameters of the evolution-adaptation model the foreseeable objective circumstances will leave both sides with few, if any, realistic alternatives to constructive cooperation and eventual interdependence in the realm of policy making and perhaps in other areas of politics, as well.

In sum, this study has tried to show that a political reform movement does, in fact, exist in the USSR and to suggest that imaginative borrowing of innovative ideas and co-optation of dissenters into the policy-making process by the regime offer a realistic way out of its chronic difficulties at a very low political cost. Even from the viewpoint of the hardened apparatchiki of the CPSU Politburo the system's eventual democratization is preferable to anarchy, civil war, and the kind of apocalyptic climax that Amalrik predicted in his *Will the Soviet Union Survive Until 1984?*

Chances are good that the USSR will survive until 1984 and well beyond, but they will be much greater if the regime finds a way, as it must, to accommodate the forces of change in the Soviet Union. What seems less certain is whether Western academic Sovietologists will be adequately prepared to analyze accurately *changes* in the USSR when they actually materialize in that country. I hope that this study has made a contribution to that end.

Notes

I wish to thank Professor Zbigniew Brzezinski, director of the Research Institute on Communist Affairs, Columbia University and the Graduate Research Foundation, University of Connecticut for their generous support and other forms of assistance given to me for the research, writing, and preparation of this study. I also wish to thank Professor Grey Hodnett of York University for his helpful comments on an earlier draft of this study and Dr. Gene Sosin for his kind advice and assistance with samizdat documents.

1. For other definitions see Herbert Goldhamer and Edward Shils, "The Types of Power and Status," *The American Journal of Sociology, XLV* (1939), 171–82 and Robert A. Dahl, "The Concept of Power," *Behavioral Science II* (July, 1957), 201–15. Reprinted in S. Sidney Ulmer, ed., *Introductory Readings in Political Behavior* (Chicago, 1961), 334–42 and 342–63 respectively.

2. Alfred G. Meyer, "Authority in Communist Political Systems," in Lewis J. Edinger, ed., *Political Leadership in Industrialized Societies* (New York, 1967), 92.

3. As Clement Moore pointed out: "Leninism, as a practical ideology imposes the obligation upon those who would use it as a legitimating principle to relate their actions to the abstract goals posited by their pure ideology," adding however, that "there is never a final 'proof' of the meetings of means and ends." Clement H. Moore, "The Single Party as a Source of Legitimacy," in Samuel P. Huntington and Clement H. Moore, eds., *Authoritarian Politics in Modern Society* (New York, 1970), 55. See also Barrington Moore, Jr., *Soviet Politics—The Dilemma of Power* (New York, 1965), 38–58.

4. For a systematic statement on the nature of this dichotomy, see Chalmers Johnson, "Comparing Communist Nations," in Chalmers Johnson, ed., *Change in Communist Systems* (Stanford, 1970), 1–32. See also Richard Lowenthal, "Development vs. Utopia in Communist Policy," *Ibid.*, 33–116.

5. For a seminal study on the balance of forces between the regime and its opponents, see Harry Eckstein, "On the Etiology of Internal Wars," *History and Theory*, IV, 2 (1965), 133–63. See also Ted Robert Gurr, "A Causal Model of Civil Strife: A Comparative Analysis Using New Indices," *The American Political Science*

Review, LXII (December, 1968), 1104–24 and Ted Robert Gurr, *Why Men Rebel* (Princeton, 1971), especially Chaps. 8–9.

6. The best study on this subject is Robert V. Daniels, *The Conscience of the Revolution* (Cambridge, Mass., 1960). For an important empirical study on the various components of estrangements from the values of the system, see Ada W. Finifter, "Dimensions of Political Alienation," in Ada W. Finifter, ed., *Alienation and the Social System* (New York, 1972), 189–212.

7. The following categories of samizdat sources, all originating from the Soviet dissident movement, have been utilized for this study:

a. Samizdat documents that have or will have appeared in volumes I–XXIII of *Sobranie Dokumentov Samizdata (Collection of Samizdat Documents*, hereafter *SDS*) and catalogued under individual *Arkhiv Samizdata (Samizdat Archive, AS* hereafter) numbers by the Research Department of Radio Liberty (Munich). These are being distributed to subscribers by one of the four U.S. repositories: The Library of Congress, The Hoover Institution, Ohio State University, and MIT.

b. Russian language samizdat books and monographs published by the Alexander Herzen Foundation (Amsterdam).

c. Russian language reproduction of samizdat material by the Russian emigre press including *Grani* and *Posev* (Frankfurt) and *Novoe Russkoe Slovo* (New York).

d. Western language translations of samizdat books, articles, letters, etc. Such book-length monographs and collections of miscellaneous material include:

Andrei Amalrik, *Involuntary Journey to Siberia* (New York, 1970) and *Will the Soviet Union Survive Until 1984?* (New York, 1970); Abraham Brumberg, ed., *In Quest of Justice* (New York, 1970); Vladimir Boukovsky, *Une nouvelle maladie mentale en URSS, l'Opposition* (Paris, 1971); Vyacheslav Chornovil, *The Chornovil Papers* (New York, 1968); Ivan Dzyuba, *Internationalism or Russification?* (2nd rev. ed.) (London, 1970); Roger Garaudy, ed., *Le testament de Varga* (Paris, 1970); Evgenia Ginzburg, *Into the Whirlwind* (Harmondsworth, England, 1968); Piotr Grigorenko, *Staline et la deuxieme guerre mondiale* (Paris, 1969); Natalia Gorbanevskaya, *Red Square at Noon* (New York, 1972); A. Guinzbourg, *Le livre blanc de l'affaire Siniavsky-Daniel* (Paris, 1969); Pavel Litvinov, ed., *The Demonstration on Pushkin Square* (Boston, 1969); Anatoly Marchenko, *My Testimony* (New York, 1969); J. J. Marie and Carol Head, eds., *L'affaire Guinzbourg-Galanskov* (Paris, 1969); Roy Medvedev, *Let History Judge* (New York, 1971), *Faut-il rehabiliter Staline?* (Paris, 1969) and *De la democratie socialiste* (Paris, 1972); Roy Medvedev and Zhores A. Medvedev, *A Question of Madness* (New York, 1971); Zhores A. Medvedev, *The Rise and Fall of T. D. Lysenko* (New York, 1969) and *The Medvedev Papers* (New York, 1971); V. Moroz, *A Report from the Beria Preserve* (Philadelphia, 1969); Peter Reddaway, ed., *The Trial of the Four* (New York, 1972), *Uncensored Russia* (New York, 1972); Karel van het Reve, *Dear Comrade—Pavel Litvinov and the Voices of Soviet Citizens in Dissent* (Toronto, 1969).

8. Recent scholarly studies on dissent and dissent-related political changes in the USSR include: Heinz Brahm, ed., *Opposition in der Sowjetunion* (Dusseldorf, 1972); Kurt Marko, *Dogmatismus und Emanzipation in der Sowjetunion* (Stuttgart, 1972); Zev Katz, *Soviet Dissent and the Social Structure in the USSR* (Cambridge, Mass., 1971); Peter Potichnyj, ed., *Dissent in the Soviet Union* (Hamilton, Ont., 1971); Walter D. Connor, "Societal Complexity and Political Dissent: Five Soviet

Themes," paper delivered at the Fifth National Meeting of the American Association for the Advancement of Slavic Studies (Dallas, March 15, 1972); Howard L. Biddulph, "Soviet Intellectual Dissent as a Political Counter-Culture," *Western Political Science Quarterly*, XXV, 3 (September, 1972), 522–33; Frederick C. Barghoorn, "Some Hypotheses Regarding Sources of Political Dissent in the USSR," paper delivered at the Fifth National Meeting of the American Association for the Advancement of Slavic Studies (Dallas, March 15, 1972); Erik P. Hoffman, Political Opposition in the Soviet Union," in Barbara N. McLennan, ed., *Political Opposition and Dissent* (forthcoming); and Rudolf L. Tőkés, ed., *The Politics and Ideologies of Dissent in the USSR* (forthcoming). See also volumes of *Problems of Communism, Survey, Soviet Jewish Affairs, Studies in Comparative Communism, Ukrainian Review, Estonian Events for 1965–72* and Radio Free Europe *Research*, Radio Liberty *Research*, and *Dispatch* for this period.

9. Frederic J. Fleron "Soviet Area Studies and the Social Sciences: Some Methodological Problems," in Frederic J. Fleron, ed., *Communist Studies and the Social Sciences* (Chicago, 1969), 1–36. See also Robert C. Tucker, "On the Comparative Study of Communism," *World Politics*, XIX, 2 (January, 1967), 246–47 and Alex Inkeles, "Models and Issues in the Analysis of Soviet Society," *Survey*, 60 (July, 1966), 3–17.

10. By "dissent studies" we mean works on Soviet dissent written for nonspecialists. Some of these include: Abraham Rothberg, *The Heirs of Stalin* (Ithaca, 1972); Anatole Shub, *The New Russian Tragedy* (New York, 1969); *An Empire Loses Hope* (London, 1971); An Observer, *Message from Moscow* (New York, 1969); Sergius Yakobson and R. V. Allen, *Aspects of Intellectual Ferment and Dissent in the Soviet Union,* prepared for the Committee on the Judiciary, United States Senate (Washington, 1968); Julius Jacobson, ed., *Soviet Communism and the Socialist Vision* (New Brunswick, N.J., 1972); D. Richard Little, ed., *Liberalization in the USSR: Facade or Reality?* (Lexington, 1968); Cornelia Gerstenmaier, *The Voices of the Silent* (New York, 1972); David Burg and George Feifer, *Solzhenitsyn* (London, 1972).

11. On the social background and occupation of Soviet dissidents, see Amalrik, *Will the Soviet Union Survive*. . . .

12. On the quantifiable aspects of Soviet dissent see Theodore Friedgut, "The Democratic Movement: Dimensions and Perspectives," in Rudolf L. Tőkés, ed., *The Politics and Ideologies of Dissent in the USSR*.

13. Attempts to decipher the "political" meaning in contemporary Soviet belles lettres include the introductory essays written to the following collections: George Lichtheim and Walter Laqueur, eds., *The Soviet Cultural Scene 1956–1957* (New York, 1958); Hugh McLean and Walter N. Vickery, eds., *The Year of Protest 1956* (New York, 1961); Patricia Blake and Max Hayward, eds., *Dissonant Voices in Soviet Literature* (New York, 1962); Patricia Blake and Max Hayward, eds., *Half-Way to the Moon: New Writings from Russia* (New York, 1964); Priscilla Johnson and Leopold Labedz, eds., *Khruschev and the Arts* (Cambridge, 1965); Max Hayward, ed., *On Trial* (New York, 1966); Michael Scammel, ed., *Russia's Other Writers* (London, 1970); R. G. Davis-Poynter, ed., *For Freedom: Theirs and Ours* (New York, 1969).

14. Z. A. Medvedev, *The Rise and Fall*. . . .

15. Peter Reddaway's editorial comments in *Uncensored Russia* are most helpful in clarifying many previously unknown details of the personalities and politics of many samizdat authors. Also, annotated biographical directories by the Research Department, Radio Liberty appended to issues of *Khronika Tekuschikh Sobytii (Chronicle of Current Events, Chronicle* hereafter), could, when checked against

other sources, elucidate the identity and careers of individuals mentioned in these issues. See *SDS,* X, for issues 1–24 and see *Materialy Samizdata (Samizdat Materials*) (Radio Liberty) issue No. 26/72 (July 10, 1972) for *Chronicle*, no. 25, no. 34/72 (August 18, 1972), for No. 26 and No. 47/12 (December 6, 1972), and for issue No. 27. For an informed discussion on the phenomenon of samizdat, particularly the *Chronicle*, see "The Future of Samizdat: Significance and Prospects," (London, 1971), mimeo. See also Martin Dewhirst and Robert Farrel, *Soviet Censorship* (Metuchen, N.J., 1973).

16. This point is made in Zbigniew Brzezinski and Samuel P. Huntington, *Political Power, USA/USSR* (New York, 1964), 111. See also D. Pospielovsky, "The Zubatov Experiment and Its Relevance to Today's Soviet Union," paper delivered at the Annual Meeting of the Northeast Chapter of the American Association for the Advancement of Slavic Studies (Montreal, May 5, 1971). Also "KGB Samizdat," RFE *Research*, Communist Area, 1015 (May 18, 1972).

17. For two contrasting opinions on the authenticity of the Khrushchev memoirs, see George F. Kennan, "Khrushchev Remembers," *The New York Review of Books*, XVI, 3 (February 25, 1971), 3–4 and Victor Zorza, "The Khrushchev Memoirs," *The Manchester Guardian Weekly*, 104 (February 6, 1971), 11–13.

18. Tibor Szamuely's contribution to the symposium "Five Years After Khrushchev," *Survey*, 72 (Summer, 1969), 61.

19. Jerry F. Hough, "The Soviet System: Petrification or Pluralism," *Problems of Communism*, XXII, 2 (March–April, 1972), 25–45. See also Philip D. Stewart, "Towards More Adequate Models of Elite Mobility in Communist Politics," paper delivered at the International Studies Association meeting (Dallas, March 17, 1972).

20. On the evolution of intelligentsia attitudes toward legitimate authority and Stalinism, see K. Volny, "Intelligentsia i demokraticheskoe dvizhenie" [Intellectuals and the democratic movement] (1970) in *SDS*, XI, *AS* 607; and R. Medvedev, *La democratie*, . . . 346–57.

21. Opposition is defined by Barghoorn as "the persistent—and from the official point of view—objectionable advocacy of policies differing from or contrary to those which the dominant group in the supreme CPSU control and decision-making bodies . . . adopt." (Frederick C. Barghoorn, "Soviet Political Doctrine and the Problem of Opposition," *Bucknell Review*, XII, 2 [May, 1964], 1–29). Skilling has identified four types ("integral," "functional," "fundamental," and "specific") of opposition in communist political systems in Eastern Europe. (H. Gordon Skilling, "Background to the Study of Opposition in Communist Eastern Europe," *Government and Opposition*, III, 3 [Summer, 1968], 237–39). See also D. J. R. Scott, "Resistance and Opposition," *Survey*, 64 (July, 1967), 35–40; Conquest, *Russia After Khrushchev*, especially Chap. 7, "The Logic of Faction," 68–76; and Frederick C. Barghoorn, "The General Pattern of Soviet Dissent," in Potichnyj, ed., *Dissent in the Soviet Union*, 1–3.

22. Suggestions concerning the desirability of this kind of radical change in the Soviet Union were advanced by the Chinese-sponsored "Fighters' Committee for the Reestablishment of a Marxist-Leninist Party in the Soviet Union." Cf. *Hung Ch'i*, 1 (1969); *Peking Review*, 21 (May 17, 1968) and 43 (October 25, 1968), as republished in *Studies in Comparative Communism*, II, 1 (January, 1969), 125–34.

23. This characterization of dissident intentions therefore excludes those underground groups whose platforms advocate the forcible overthrow of the regime.

24. Cf. Meyer, in Edinger, *Political Leadership*, . . . 105.

25. Leonard Schapiro, quoted in Skilling, "Background . . ." 300, n.4.

26. By "authoritative domination" we mean "a relationship of inequality between two or more actors measured by unquestioning acceptance of communications

or compliance with decisions issued by one actor, a relationship which is perceived as *legitimate* by all actors involved." (Emphasis added.) (Meyer, in Edinger, ed., *Political Leadership,* . . . 84).

27. The following is based on *Samizdat 1*, la voix de l'opposition communiste en U.R.S.S. (Paris [Seuil], 1969), 25–32.

28. Marchenko, *My Testimony*, 256ff.

29. *Samizdat 1*, 108–11.

30. According to Billington many of these former inmates are "revered as saints in the intellectual community," and, as "righteous remnants from the past" wield "enormous moral authority" especially among the youth. (James H. Billington, "Beneath the Panoply of Power, the Intelligentsia Hits at the Old Order," *Life* [November 10, 1967], 70ff.

31. Vladimir Osipov, "Ploschad' Mayakovskogo, stat'ia 70" [Mayakovsky Square, article 70], in "Samizdat," *Grani*, 80 (September, 1971). Also in *SDS,* VII, *AS* 527; quoted in D. Pospielovsky, "Some Aspects of the History and Ideational Development of the Dissident Movement in the Post-Stalin Soviet Union," paper delivered at the Eleventh Annual Central Slavic Conference at William Jewell College (Liberty, Mo., November 17, 1972), 4, 6.

32. *Samizdat 1*, 38ff.

33. This information was made available in unpublished reports by Messrs. Tel'nikov (March 28, 1972) and Krivoshein (June 2, 1972). Cited in D. Pospielovsky, "Some Aspects . . .", p. 8.

34. For a concise analysis of the events of this period, see Robert Conquest, *Courage of Genius: The Pasternak Affair* (Philadelphia, 1962).

35. Cf. "The Trial of Josif Brodsky: A Transcript," *New Leader*, XLVII, 18 (August 31, 1964); Marie and Head, *L'Affaire* . . . ; Reddaway, *The Trial of the Four*; Pavel Litvinov, open letter, *The New York Times* (December 27, 1967); *Chronicle* 15 (August 30, 1971), in *SDS, XI, AS,* 415. See also Pyotr Yakir, *A Childhood in Prison* (London, 1972).

36. The process of loyalty transference from traditional authority figures (the political leader or the head of the family) to culture heroes is, of course, far more complex than the narrative suggests. Anthony Wallace's "Principle of Conservation of Cognitive Structure" offers a three-step program for the authority-erosion process: "(1) The individual will not abandon any particular conception of reality . . . even in the face of direct evidence of its current inutility, without having had an opportunity to construct a new mazeway . . . in which the invalid conception is not a functionally necessary component; (2) . . . initial confrontation of the individual with the evident inutility will arouse an anxiety-denial syndrome and this anxiety-denial response may continue for a considerable period of time. (3) . . . it is easier for the individual to abandon a conception if substitutes are offered and models of new mazeways are presented." (Anthony Wallace, *Culture and Personality* [New York, 1961], 161). See also, John Kosa, *Two Generations of Soviet Man* (Chapel Hill, 1962), 185–97.

37. Mihajlo Mihajlov, *Moscow Summer* (New York, 1965). For a more optimistic interpretation see Merle Fainsod, "The Role of the Intellectual in the Soviet Union," in H. Malcolm Macdonald, ed., *The Intellectual in Politics* (Austin, 1966), 74–89.

38. Text of *Syntaxis*, nos. 1–3 reproduced in *Grani*, 58 (1965), 97–193. Text of *Phoenix 61* in *Grani*, 52 (1962), 86–190.

39. Mihajlo Mihajlov, *Russian Themes* (New York, 1968), 329–30.

40. Text of trial proceedings and related materials in Hayward, *On Trial.*

41. Between December, 1965 and late 1969 there were 30 separate appeals,

memoranda, and letters of protest concerning the Daniel-Siniavsky case. These are listed in Albert Boiter, ed., *Five Years of Samizdat: A Bibliography* (Munich, 1971), 52–3.

42. This term has been adopted from James N. Rosenau, "Pre-Theories and Theories of Foreign Policy." In conformity with Rosenau's caveat concerning the use of this term, "a typology of issue-areas must be cast in sufficiently abstract terms to encompass past and future values as well as present ones." In R. Barry Farrell, ed., *Approaches to Comparative and International Politics* (Evanston, 1966).

43. Meyer, in Edinger, *Political Leadership*, . . . 84.

44. Gerd R. von Doemming, "A Guide to Proposals for Systemic Change in the USSR offered by Soviet Citizens," *Reference Handbook*, 82, Research Department, Radio Liberty, (Munich, August, 1971). In the original survey, "demand" as a unit of analysis is defined as "clearly stated . . . alternative" to the status quo. With access to no more than 20 percent of documents analyzed in this survey it was not possible to obtain complete verification of the accuracy of von Doemming's sampling methods. The 20 percent (about 50 documents) checked for this purpose show that von Doemming's analysis was sound and possibly too conservative in not identifying dissident statements as "demands" when these failed to offer a "clearly stated alternative."

45. There are four basic types of samizdat writings: (1) programmatic statements complete with platforms, systematized ideologies, and action programs; (2) monographic studies addressed to a historical, philosophical, political, or economic problems from an unorthodox viewpoint; (3) self-published journals and newsletters that have appeared with a degree of regularity; (4) "special interest" or personal statements of dissident opinion. The following partial list will emphasize some typical documents in each category:

a. "Memorandum Demokratov Verkhovnomu Sovetu SSSR o nezakonnom zakhvate vlasti rukovodstvom KPSS i ego antikonstitutsionnoi deiatel'nosti" [Memorandum of the Democratic Movement to the USSR Supreme Soviet concerning the illegal seizure of power by the CPSU leadership and its anticonstitutional actions], *SDS*, XI, *AS*, 602; Demokraty Rossii, Ukrainy i Pribaltiki "Programma demokraticheskogo dvizheniia Sovetskogo Soiuza" [The Democrats of Russia, the Ukraine and the Baltic States], "The Program of the Democratic Movement of the Soviet Union," *SDS*, V, *AS*, 340; S. Zorin and N. Alekseev, "Vremia ne zhdat" [Time does not wait], *SDS*, V, *AS*, 368; "Vserossiiskii sotsial-khristianskii soiuz osvobozhdeniia naroda: sostav, programma, metody raboty, ideologicheskie pozitsii, prichiny porazheniia" [The All-Russian Social-Christian Union for the Emancipation of the People: Its structure, program, working methods, ideological positions, and causes of its defeat], (1969), *Posev*, 1 (1971), 38–43; and Andrei Sakharov, "Thoughts on Progress, Peaceful Coexistence and Intellectual Freedom," *The New York Times* (July 22, 1968).

b. R. Medvedev, *Let History Judge*; Garaudy, *Le testament* . . . ; R. Medvedev, "Blizhnevostochnyi konflikt i evreiskii vopros v SSSR" [The Middle Eastern conflict and the Jewish question in the USSR], (1970), *SDS*, VIII, *AS*, 496; S. Razumnyi, "Rasstanovka politicheskikh sil v KPSS" (The distribution of political power in the CPSU), (1969), *SDS*, IX, *AS*, 570; B. I. Tsukerman, "Rassuzhdeniia o prave" (Speaking about the law), (1968–1969), *SDS*, VII, *AS*, 483; A. Kazakov, "K voprosu sravneniia zhizhnennogo urovnia trudiashchchikhsiia Rossii, SSSR i kapitalisticheskikh stran" [On the question of comparison of living standards of workers in (Tsarist) Russia, the USSR, and the capitalist countries], (1971), in *Svobodnaia Mysl'* [Free Thought], (December 20, 1971); *SDS*, XXIV(?), *AS*, 1180.

c. *Khronika Tekushchikh Sobytii* [The Chronicle of Current Events], (1968), ed.

by a group of Moscow intellectuals; *Iskhod* [Exodus], (1970), by Jewish dissidents; *Informatsiia* [Information], (196?), by Crimean Tatars; *Obshchestvennye Problemy* [Social Problems], (1969–1971), by V. Chalidze; *Vestnik Spaseniia* [Herald of Salvation], (1960–), by Baptist believers; *Bratsky Listok* [Fraternal Leaflet], (196?–), by Baptist believers; *Politicheski Dnevnik* [Political Diary], (196?–), by a group of Moscow (?) intellectuals; *Ukrainski Visnyk* [Ukrainian Herald], 1968?–), by a group of Ukrainian intellectuals; *Seyatel'* [The Sower], 1971–), by a group of social democrats (?); *Svobodny Mysl'* [Free Thought], (1971–), by a group of socialist intellectuals (?); *Kolokol'* [The Bell], (196?–); and *Veche* [Diet–Forum], (1970–), by V. Osipov.

d. About 80 percent of samizdat writings belong to this category, therefore no attempt will be made to list a representative sample.

46. This taxonomy has been prompted by the following passage by Goldhamer and Shils: "Attempted domination may meet with obedience or disobedience. The motivation for obedience and disobedience is *instrumental* to the extent that it is based on an anticipation of losses and gains, and *noninstrumental* to the extent that it is based on ethical or affective imperative of conduct dictating obedience or disobedience to the command." (Goldhamer and Shils, Ulmer, "Introductory Readings, . . .", 355). Comparable taxonomies have been proposed by L. Feuer, "Scientific Opposition—Literary Opposition," in "The Intelligentsia in Opposition," *Problems of Communism*, XIX, 6 (November–December, 1970), 4–10; by D. Pospielovsky, "Neo-Marxist," "Pragmatic Liberal," and "Social Christian Personalist," in "The Monk: A New Samizdat Manuscript," Radio Liberty *Dispatch* (January 22, 1970); by Andrei Amalrik, "Genuine Marxism-Leninism," "Christian ideology," and "Liberal ideology," in *Will the Soviet Union* . . . ; by Howard Biddulph, "Fundamental," "Integral," and "Specific Policy," in Soviet Intellectual Dissent . . ." 523; and most recently by Yuri Glazov, who identified as many as eight ideological trends in the Democratic Movement: "Neo-Communist," "Constitutionalist," "Neo-Slavist," "Christian Socialist," "Liberal," "Christian Democratic," "Civil Rights Advocates," and the "Jewish Activists." Cf. "Embryo of a Social Democratic Party?" RFE *Research*, Communist Area, 1516 (August 21, 1972), 1–2.

47. Their chief function in the political reform movement is to redefine the legitimacy of the posttotalitarian Soviet political culture that consists of "existential beliefs, general values that set goals of behavior, norms that regulate the means to achieve goals [and] emotional attachments" in order to "reshape the situation in which political action takes place." (Sidney Verba, "Comparative Political Culture," in Lucian Pye and Sidney Verba, eds., *Political Culture and Political Development* [Princeton, 1965], 513, 517.) For a systematic analysis of the dynamics and specific properties of Russian and Soviet political culture, see Frederick C. Barghoorn, "Soviet Russia: Orthodoxy and Adaptiveness," in *ibid.*, 450–511.

48. For helpful analyses on aspects of cultural continuity and change among Soviet literary intellectuals, see James H. Billington, "The Intellectuals," in Kassof, *Prospects for Soviet Society*, 449–72; Timothy McClure, "The Politics of Soviet Culture, 1964–1967," *Problems of Communism*, XVI, 2 (March–April, 1967), 30–31; and Leopold Labedz, "The Destiny of Writers in Revolutionary Movements," *Survey, 18*, 1 (82) (Winter, 1972), 8–46.

49. Alexander Solzhenitsyn, *The First Circle* (New York, 1968), 358.

50. The following passage from Solzhenitsyn's Nobel lecture on Literature illustrates this point: "Anyone who has once taken up the Word can never again evade it, a writer is not a detached judge of his compatriots and contemporaries, he is an accomplice to all the evil committed in his native land by his countrymen. And if the tanks of his fatherland have flooded the asphalt of a foreign capital with blood

then the brown spots have slapped against the face of the writer forever. And if one fatal night they suffocated his sleeping, trusting friend, then the palms of the writer bear the bruises from that rope." In *Le Prix Nobel en 1971* (Stockholm, 1972), 172.

51. Cf. A Antipov, "Ot brozheniia umov—k umstvennomu dvizheniiu" (From the ferment of minds to intellectual movement), *SDS*, VI, *AS*, 388.

52. Solzhenitsyn is worth citing on this point: "What then is the place and role of the writer in this cruel, dynamic, split world on the brink of its ten destructions? After all we have nothing to do with letting off rockets, we do not even push the lowliest of hand carts, we are quite scorned by those who respect only material power. [Yet] it is not natural for us to step back, to lose faith in the steadfastness of goodness, in the indivisibility of truth and to just impart to the world our bitter, detached observations: how mankind has become hopelessly corrupt, how men have degenerated, and how difficult it is for the few beautiful and refined souls to live amongst them?" In *Le Prix Nobel. . . .*

53. A systematic comparison of speeches and statements by the defendants of the 15 most important political trials in the late 1960's could reveal a more definite pattern of dissident strategies and perceptions of political trends and ideological shifts within the CPSU. A samizdat collection containing texts of 14 closing statements by defendants at trials held between 1966 and 1970 was published in 1970. Cf. *Chronicle*, 17 (December 31, 1970), in *SDS*, X, *AS*, 555.

54. The circle of the Moscow Human Rights Committee and signers of letters protesting the unlawful detainment of Soviet scientists such as Zhores Medvedev, Revol't Pimenoy, and several others who have been arrested since 1970 seem to belong to this category of dissenters. Cf. *Dokumenty Komitety Prav Cheloveka* (Documents of the Moscow Human Rights Committee), (New York, 1972).

55. The following is based in part on "Report on Soviet Science," *Survey*, 52 (July, 1964), 3–165; Nicholas de Witt, "The Politics of Soviet Science," *The American Behavioral Scientist*, VI, 4 (December, 1962), 7–11; Loren Graham, "Reorganization of the U.S.S.R. Academy of Science," in Peter H. Juviler and Henry W. Morton, eds., *Soviet Policy-Making* (New York, 1967), 136–61; George Fischer, *Science and Politics: The New Sociology in the Soviet Union* (Ithaca, 1964); Eugene Zaleski *et al.*, *Science Policy in the USSR* (Paris, 1969); Zhores A. Medvedev, "The Closed Circuit: A Record of Soviet Scientific Life," *Nature*, 5264 (September 19, 1970), 1197—1202; S. P. Pisarev, "Memorandum to the Presidium of the USSR Academy of Sciences" (April 20, 1970), *Survey*, 77 (Autumn, 1970), 179–89; "The State of the Soviet Basic Sciences," Radio Liberty *Dispatch* (September 16, 1970); Kenneth Sherrill, "The Attitudes of Modernity," *Comparative Politics*, I, 2 (January, 1969), especially 209–211; and John Turkevich, "Soviet Science Appraised," in William R. Nelson, ed., *The Politics of Science* (New York, 1968), 396–406. See also Rudolf L. Tőkés, "A Question of Science," *Problems of Communism*, XXII, 1 (January—February, 1973), 44–48.

56. Zhores A. Medvedev, *The Medvedev Papers.*

57. Albert Parry, ed., *Peter Kapitsa on Life and Science* (New York, 1968), 192. On the general problem of the scientists' relationship to the science bureaucracy, see Norman Kaplan, "Research Administration and the Administrator: USSR and US," *Administrative Science Quarterly*, XI, 2 (1961), 51–72.

58. Nicholas De Witt, "Soviet Science: the Institutional Debate," *Bulletin of Atomic Scientists*, XVI, 6 (June, 1960), 208–11; Graham, "U.S.S.R. Academy of Science," and Linda I. Greenberg, "The Impact of Soviet Science Policy on the Scientific Establishment," paper delivered at the Fourth National Convention of the AAASS (Denver, March 26, 1971).

59. T. H. Rigby, "Security and Modernisation," *Survey*, 64 (July, 1967), 25ff.

60. Z. A. Medvedev, *The Rise and Fall, . . .* 247.

61. A. Sakharov, "Thoughts on Progress . . ." and K. Volny, "Intelligentsia, . . ." 39ff.

62. Albert Boiter, *Five Years of Samizdat: A Bibliography*, Reference Handbook, 77, (Munich, 1971), 5–6, 10. The sample for 1966 includes two book-length monographs: Andrei Amalrik, *Nezhelannoe puteshestvie v Sibir* [Involuntary Journey to Siberia], (New York, 1970) and Nadezhda Mandelshtam, *Vospominaniia* [Hope Against Hope], (New York, 1970); three open letters: by 25 intellectuals to Brezhnev, by Vyacheslav Chornovil to the Ukrainian Procuracy, and by Lidia Chukovskaya to N. Solokhov, in *SDS*, IV, *AS*, 273; *SDS*, II, *AS*, 167; and *SDS*, IV, *AS*, 221; one issue each of two underground literary journals: that of *Russkoe Slovo* and the SMOG poets in *Grani*, 66 (1967), 34 and *Grani*, 65 (1966), 3—24; a trial transcript: A. Guinzbourg, *Le livre blanc de l'affaire Siniavsky-Daniel* (Paris, 1969); and a transcript of a debate on Soviet historiography: on the book of A. M. Nekrich, *1941–21 June*, in *SDS*, VII, *AS*, 466. The sample for 1970 includes three open letters: by Sakharov, Turchin, and Medvedev to Brezhnev, Kosygin, and Podgorny, by M. Rostropovich to the Soviet press (on Solzhenitsyn's behalf), and by the Initiative Group for Defense of Civil Rights in the USSR to the United Nations, in *Survey*, 76 (Summer, 1970, 169–70, *SDS*, VII, 447, and *ibid*., 433; a protest note: by Solzhenitsyn on the arrest of Zhores Medvedev, in *SDS*, VI, *AS*, 386; the text of a television interview: "Three Voices of Dissent," (CBS television interview with Amalrik, Yakir, and Bukovsky), in *Survey*, 77 (Autumn, 1970), 128–45; a religious appeal: to members of the Baptist (EKhB) Church in *SDS*, VII, *AS*, 442; a statement about the formation of a committee of human rights: *Dokumenty Komiteta Prav Cheloveka*; a study on the persecution of the Hutsul minority in the western Ukraine: by Valentin Moroz in *SDS*, VI, *AS*, 411; and two issues of the Jewish samizdat journal, *Iskhod* [*Exodus*]: *Soviet Jewish Affairs*, I, 1 (June, 1971).

63. Cf. Zbigniew Brzezinski, "The Soviet Past and Future," *Encounter* (March, 1970), 3—16; Sidney Ploss, "Politics in the Kremlin, *Problems of Communism*, XIX, 3 (May–June, 1970), 1–14; and Dan C. Heldman, "The Sino-Soviet Split and Party Legitimacy," *Survey*, 77 (Autumn, 1970), 70–85.

64. As Amalrik suggested, "in reality, the regime is losing more and more control in the country. . . . for a totalitarian regime, the degree of control is already insufficient ." ("Three Voices," 134). Eckstein's formulation is more specific on this point: "repression can be a two-edged sword. Unless it is based upon extremely good intelligence, and unless its application is sensible, ruthless, and continuous, its effects may be quite opposite to those intended. Incompetent repression leads to a combination of disaffection and contempt for the elite." (Harry Eckstein, "On the Etiology, . . ." 154).

65. Cf. Zbigniew Brzezinski, "Dysfunctional Totalitarianism," in Klaus von Beyme, ed. *Theory and Politics* (The Hague, 1972), 380–2.

66. An Observer, *Message . . .*, 81.

67. Frederick C. Barghoorn, *Soviet Russian Nationalism* (New York, 1956); John A. Armstrong, *Ukrainian Nationalism*, 2nd ed. (New York, 1963); V. Stanley Vardys, *Lithuania under the Soviets* (New York, 1965); "Nationalities and Nationalism in the USSR," *Problems of Communism*, XVII, 5 (September–October, 1967), 2–107; Hugh Seton-Watson, "Nationalism and Imperialism," in *The Impact of the Russian Revolution 1917–1967* (New York, 1967), especially 147–60; and John A. Armstrong, "The Ethnic Scene in the Soviet Union: The View of the Dictatorship," in Erich Goldhagen, ed., *Ethnic Minorities in the Soviet Union* (New York, 1968), 3–49.

68. Robert Conquest, *The Soviet Deportation of the Nationalities* (New York, 1960). See also Allen Hetmanek, "The Crimean Tatars in Central Asian Exile," Radio Liberty *Dispatch* (January 24, 1969).

69. Michael Bourdeaux, *Patriarchs and Prophets* (New York, 1970); Lionel Kochan, ed., *The Jews in Soviet Russia Since 1917* (London, 1970); and Walter Kolarz, *Religion in the USSR* (New York, 1962).

70. Elizabeth Bacon, *Central Asians Under Russian Rule* (Ithaca, 1966); Edward Allworth, ed., *Central Asia: A Century of Russian Rule* (New York, 1967); Walter Kolarz, *Peoples of the Soviet Far East* (New York, 1954); and Olaf Caroe, *Soviet Empire*, 2nd ed. (New York, 1967).

71. Our emphasis on the intellectuals does not imply a negative judgment concerning the existence of widespread discontent among the masses belonging to the various nationalities. However, verifiable evidence about strikes in labor camps and at Siberian construction sites, food riots, local uprisings in remote areas, etc., is very difficult to obtain from published sources; therefore, these alleged instances of anomic behavior will not be discussed in this study.

72. Grey Hodnett and Peter Potichnyj, *The Ukraine and the Czechoslovak Crisis,* Occasional Paper 6, Department of Political Science, Australian National University (Canberra, 1970), 5.

73. Samuel Bloembergen, "The Union Republics: How Much Autonomy?" *Problems of Communism,* XVI, 5 (September–October, 1967), 27–35; and Grey Hodnett, "Debate over Soviet Federalism," *Soviet Studies,* XVIII, 4 (April, 1967), 458–81.

74. On the Ukranian situation, see Hodnett and Potichnyij, *The Ukraine,* 5–26. On the general impact of Russian rule on the nationalities see "Soviet Colonialism: Does it exist?" *Problems of Communism,* XIII, 1 (January–February, 1964), especially Michael Rywkin's "Central Asia and the Price of Sovietization," 7–15.

75. Vyacheslav Chornovil, *The Chornovil Papers,* 1–77, 150–52, and 166–266; Ivan Dzyuba, *Internationalism or Russification?; Voices of Human Courage: Appeals from Two Ukrainian Intellectuals to Soviet Authorities* (New York, 1968); Michael Browne, ed., *Turmoil in the Ukraine* (London, 1971), 119–174. See also Ukrainian Intellectuals Tried by the KGB, Excerpts from *Ukrainska intelligentsiya pid sudom KGB* (Munich, 1970), RFE *Research,* Communist Area, 0680 (August 4, 1970).

76. Yaroslav Bilinsky, "Assimilation and Ethnic Assertiveness among Ukrainians of the Soviet Union," in Goldhagen, ed., *Ethnic Minorities,* 147–84.

77. *The New York Times* (November 13, 1970), and "The Accused Hits Back: The Moroz Case," RFE *Research,* Communist Area, 0813 (December 1, 1970). For excerpts from the transcribed proceedings of both trials, see *Chronicle,* 17 (December 31, 1970), *SDS,* X, *AS* 555. See also "Valentin Moroz' Final Testimony," RFE *Research* Communist Area, No. 1276 (January 26, 1972).

78. B. D. Weinryb, "Anti-Semitism in Soviet Russia," in Kochan, ed., *Jews in Soviet Russia,* 288–320. On nationality enmities evoked by the sociopolitical position of Jews as one of the "mobilized diasporas," see John A. Armstrong, *Ideology, Politics and Government in the Soviet Union,* rev. ed. (New York, 1967), 131–32. See also Mikhail Agurski, "Selling Anti-Semitism in Moscow," *The New York Review of Books,* XIX, 8 (November 16, 1972), 19–23.

79. Edward Allworth, "The Changing Intellectual and Literary Community," in Allworth, ed., *Central Asia,* 349–96 and A. Nove, "History, Hierarchy and the Nationalities: Some Observations on Soviet Social Structure," *Soviet Studies,* XXI, 1 (July, 1969), 70–92, especially 84–89. See also "The Intellectual Potential of

Soviet Asians," RFE *Research*, Communist Area, 1506 (August 1, 1972).

80. Dimitry Pospielovsky, "The Resurgence of Russian Nationalism in Samizdat," *Survey*, XIX, 86 (1973 Winter), 51–74. The program of the semi-Fascist A. Fetisov and his group goes well beyond both of the conservative nationalist platforms. See *Chronicle*, 7 (April 30, 1969); *SDS*, X, *AS*, 196.

81. Samizdat articles such as A. Kazakov, "K voprosu o sravnenii zhiznennogo urovnia trudiashchikhsiia Rossii, SSSR i drugikh kapitalistichekikh stran" [On the question of the workers' living standards in Russia, in the USSR, and in other capitalist countries], in *Svobodnaia Mysl*, 1 (December 20, 1971), in *SDS*, XXIV (?), *AS*, 1180; and clandestinely circulating handbills in Moscow working-class districts (May 1972). This may well find a receptive audience among the low-paid industrial workers and collective-farm peasants. Cf. Paige Bryan, "Concerning Economic Grievances from Samizdat," Radio Liberty *Research*, CRD, 162/72, (July 7, 1972). See also "Soviet Underground Urges Strikes to Raise Standards," *The New York Times* (June 20, 1972).

82. For a concise summary of the highlights of Soviet dissident activities since 1971, see Anatole Shub, "The Escalation of Soviet Dissent—and of Soviet Repression," *The New York Times Sunday Magazine* (September 10, 1972), 31, 92–4.

83. Cf. "Civil Rights Journal Frightens the Central Committee into Action," RFE *Research*, Communist Area, 1283 (February 4, 1972).

84. Cf. "Dissidents Among National Minorities in the USSR," Radio Liberty *Dispatch* (August 29, 1972) and "Current Events in the Ukraine," RFE *Research*, Communist Area, 1585 (October 31, 1972).

85. *The New York Times* (November 28, 1972).

86. *The New York Times* (November 19, 1972).

87. *The New York Times* (January 18, 1973).

88. Milton Lodge, "Groupism in the Soviet Union," in Fleron, ed., *Communist Studies*, 255.

89. Cf. John C. Harsanyi, "Rational-Choice Models of Political Behavior vs. Functionalist and Conformist Theories," *World Politics*, XXI, 4 (July, 1969), 517ff. See also Franklyn Griffiths, "A Tendency-Analysis of Soviet Policy-Making," in H. Gordon Skilling and Franklyn Griffiths, eds., *Interest Groups in Soviet Politics* (Princeton, 1970), 335–77; Michael P. Gehlen, "Group Theory and the Study of Soviet Politics," and Isaac Deutscher, "Pressure Groups," in Sidney I. Ploss, ed., *The Soviet Political Process* (Waltham, Mass., 1971), 35–54, 265–71; and David E. Langsam and David W. Paul, "Soviet Politics and the Group Approach: A Conceptual Note," *Slavic Review*, XXXI, 1 (March, 1972), 136–41.

90. By "functional elites," we mean members of specialized (non-party) bureaucracies and former "transmission belts"—i.e., the staffs of the state administration, planning agencies, the military, the trade unions, the Komsomol, and the educational, cultural, and scientific establishments. The term therefore includes both "specific interest groups" and "policy groups" as these are defined in Brzezinski and Huntington, *Political Power USA/USSR*, 191–234.

91. On the differences between "political" and "policy" decisions in the USSR, see Darrel P. Hammer, "Towards a Theoretical Model of Non-Competitive Political Systems: Conflict and Decision-Making in the USSR," paper prepared for delivery at the 1967 Annual Meeting of the American Political Science Association (Chicago, September, 1967), 29–33.

92. Robert A. Dahl, *Polyarchy* (New Haven, 1971), 15.

93. Socially prominent creative intellectuals of the stature of the poet Tvardovsky and the cellist Rostropovich appear to be exceptions to this generalization.

94. Cf. *SDS*, IV, *AS*, 273.

95. Cf. Ernst Henry, "The View from the Pamirs," *Literaturnaia Gazeta*, 39, 40 (September 27, October 4, 1967) in the *Current Digest of the Soviet Press (CDSP)*, XX, 1 (January 28, 1968, 1–6; and "Politics and Entomology," *Literaturnaia Gazeta*, 8 (February 21, 1968), in *CDSP*, XX, 9 (March 21, 1968). See also William E. Griffith, "On Esoteric Communication," *Studies in Comparative Communism*, III, 1 (January, 1970), 47–54.

96. *The New York Times* (October 8, 1970). Subsequently the Kaluga district court sentenced Pimenov to five years in exile. Cf. *Chronicle*, 16 (October 31, 1970) in *SDS*, X, *AS*, 500.

97. For examples of renewed party efforts to restore ideological conformity among dissident scientists in the early 1970's, see R. Ianovsky, "The Scientists' Ideological Convictions," *Sovetskaia Rossiia* (August 28, 1970), in *CDSP*, XXII, 46 (December 15, 1970); "O Rabote partiinogo komiteta fizicheskogo instituta imeni P. N. Lebedeva Akademii Nauk SSSR" [On the work of the party committee of the Lebedev Physics Institute of the USSR Academy of Sciences], *Partiinaia Zhizn'* 23 (1970), 3ff; V. Yagodkin, "Party Life in Scientific Collectives," *Kommunist*, 11 July, 1972), in *CDSP*, XXVI, 41 (November 8, 1972), 9–11; and G. Petrov, "Facing One's Comrades" (The Communists at a Research Institute Discuss Their Tasks in Connection with the Forthcoming Exchange of Patry Documents), *Pravda* (July 31, 1972), in *CDSP*, XXIV, 32 (September 6, 1972), 14–15.

98. "The truly modern form of authority is that of the specialist." (Alexander Mitscherlich, "Changing Patterns of Political Authority: A Psychiatric Interpretation," in Edinger, *Political Leadership* . . . , 33).

99. Kurt Marko, "Soviet Ideology and Sovietology," *Soviet Studies*, XIX, 4 (April, 1968), 473ff.

100. Cf. *SDS*, VII, *AS*, 434. Also in *Posev*, 11 (1970), 61–2.

101. Cf. A. D. Sakharov, V. F. Turchin, and R. A. Medvedev, "Open Letter to L. I. Brezhnev, A. N. Kosygin and N. V. Podgorny," *Survey*, 76 (Summer, 1970), 165.

102. David Holloway, "Scientific Truth and Political Authority in the Soviet Union," *Government and Opposition*, V, 3 (Summer, 1970), 356.

103. Cf. "Pis'mo dvadsati uchenykh" [Letter of twenty scholars], (June 4, 1970), *SDS*, VI, *AS*, 417 and "Pis'mo A. D. Sakharova, L. I. Brezhnevu v zashchitu Zh. A. Medvedeva" [Sakharov's letter to Brezhnev in defense of Medvedev], (June 6, 1970), *SDS*, VII, *AS*, 471. In this instance the scientists' bargaining tactics may be characterized as "persuasion through partisan analysis." Cf. Charles E. Lindblom, *The Policy Making Process* (Englewood Cliffs, 1968), 118.

104. G. vD., "Soviet Scientists in Defense of Human Rights," RFE *Research*, Communist Area, 0797 (November 18, 1970).

105. "Pluralist evolution would involve the transformation of the party into a more pluralist body. . . . Its role would be more that of a moral-ideological stimulant than that of a ruler; the state, as well as the society itself would become the more important source of innovation and change."

"Technological Adaptation would involve the transformation of the bureaucratic-dogmatic party into a technologically expert party. . . . Nationalism would replace ideological dogmas as the basic integrative principle linking society with the state [dominated by] a wider coalition of Party-State-Military-Economic leaderships." Zbigniew Brzezinski, *Between Two Ages* (New York, 1970), 165–6.

106. Cf. Vladimir G. Treml, "Interaction of Economic Thought and Economic Policy in the Soviet Union," *The History of Political Economy*, I, 1 (Spring, 1969),

187–216; "The Politics of Libermanism," *Soviet Studies*, XIX, 4 (April, 1968), 567–72; Richard W. Judy, "The Economists," in Skilling and Griffiths, *Interest Groups . . .*, especially 245–51; Zvi Y. Gitelman, "The Diffusion of Political Innovation from Eastern Europe to the Soviet Union," SAGE *Professional Papers*, Comparative Politics Series, 01–027, III, 1972, especially 49–52.

107. Here the main area of contention still seems to be at the research institute level between the party organization seeking to enforce central directives and groups of senior scientists trying to protect the integrity of their ongoing research programs. Cf. G. Petrov, "Facing One's Comrades," 15.

108. Brzezinski calls this an "institutionalized process of mediation," "The Soviet Political System," *ibid.*

109. In this connection it might not be too far fetched to propose that the wholesale granting of exit visas to dissident Jewish and Russian scientists in 1971 and 1972 was designed to physically remove from the scene those prominent scholars whose continued presence could have jeopardized the party's leading position in matters of ideology and science policy.

110. "Oligarchic petrification would involve the maintenance of the dominant role of the party and the retention of the essentially dogmatic character of its ideology. In effect, 'more of the same.' "

"Militant fundamentalism would involve a revivalist effort to rekindle ideological fervor . . . that would necessitate the application of force . . . something along the lines of Mao Tse-tung's Cultural Revolution to shake up the rigidly bureaucratized structure of the Soviet system."

"Political disintegration would involve internal paralysis in the ruling elite . . . splits in the armed forces, restiveness among the youth and the intellectuals and open disaffection among the nationalities." (Brzezinski, *Between Two Ages*).

For an incisive critique of Brzezinski's scenarios, see Jerry F. Hough, "The Soviet System."

111. On demographic changes see Rein Taagepera, "National Differences Within Soviet Demographic Trends," *Soviet Studies*, XX, 4 (April, 1969), 478–89; Garip Sultan, "Demographic and Cultural Trends Among Turkic Peoples in the Soviet Union," in Goldhagen, ed., *Ethnic Minorities*, 251–73; and R. A. French, "Recent Population Trends in the USSR," *Soviet Affairs*, St. Antony's Papers, 10 (London, 1966), 68–95. On the strategic implications of the Central Asian and Far Eastern border areas, see W. A. Douglas Jackson, *Russo-Chinese Borderlands* (New York, 1962), 98–110; Harrison E. Salisbury, *War Between Russia and China* (New York, 1969), 13–38; Peter S. H. Tang, "Sino-Soviet Border Regions: Their Changing Character," in Kurt London, ed., *Unity and Contradiction* (New York, 1962), 265–94; and Dennis Doolin, *Territorial Claims in the Sino-Soviet Conflict: Documents and Analysis* (Stanford, 1965).

112. Yaroslav Bilinsky, "The Rulers and the Ruled," in "Nationalities and Nationalism," 16–26; George Fischer, *Science and Politics*, 73–91; and T. H. Rigby, *Communist Party Membership in the USSR 1917–1967* (Princeton, 1968), 364–69.

113. Vsevolod Holubnychny, "Some Economic Aspects of Relations among the Soviet Republics," in Goldhagen, ed., *Ethnic Minorities*, 50–120; Violet Conolly, *Beyond the Urals* (London, 1967), especially Pt. 3; and N. Teodorovich, "The Preservation of Ancient Relics in the USSR," *Bulletin*, XIV, 5 (May, 1967), 31–37.

114. Unexpected personnel changes within the hitherto stable CPSU Politburo, most notably the dismissal of the Ukrainian party First Secretary Piotr Shelest in May, 1972 and drastic personnel shifts in Central Asian Union Republics during 1972 may be connected with the local party leaders' handling of nationality dissent,

as well as with Brezhnev's attempts to create a new, politically more favorable ethnic balance within the top CPSU bureaucracy. Cf. *The New York Times* (June 10, 1972); "Dissent and the Nationality Problem," RFE *Research*, Communist Area, 1309 (March 3, 1972; "Ukrainian Minister on Russification of Higher Education," RFE *Research*, Communist Area, 1565 (October 9, 1972), and Ia. A. Churianov, "Georgia and her Party Leaders," Radio Liberty *Dispatch* (November 27, 1972).

115. Jerome M. Gilison, "Khrushchev, Brezhnev and Constitutional Reform," *Problems of Communism*, XXI, 5 (September–October, 1972), 69–78.

116. Hung Chuan-yu, "The New Tsars—Common Enemy of the People of all Nationalities in the Soviet Union," *Peking Review*, XII, 27 (July 4, 1969), 25–27. See also James Chritchlow, "Soviet Writers Link Polycentrism Abroad to Separatism at Home," Radio Liberty *Dispatch* (May 20, 1969) and "Kiev Attacks Ukrainian 'Pro-Chinese' Group," RFE *Research*, Communist Area, 1327 (March 10, 1972).

117. Fritz Ermarth, "Bodyul Again Attacks Anti-Russian Feeling in Moldavia," RFE *Research*, (March 17, 1967); and A. Kashin, "Rumania and Polycentrism," *Bulletin*, XIII, 10 (October, 1966), 43–49.

118. Fritz Ermarth, *Internationalism, Security and Legitimacy: The Challenge to Soviet Interests in East Europe 1964–1968*, Rand Corporation Memorandum, RM-5909-PR (March, 1969), 90–117.

119. Zev Katz, "After the Six-Day War," in Kochan, ed., *Jews in Soviet Russia*, 321–36.

120. The results of a worldwide press campaign against the threatened summary trial and capital punishment of Russian Jews for the attempted hijacking of a Soviet airplane seem to support this contention.

The imposition of the so-called education tax compelling prospective emigrants to reimburse the state for the cost of their education might be a face-saving device for the CPSU leadership against conservative criticism of its relaxed emigration policies toward Jews. Cf. "The Unpublished 'Education Tax' Law," Radio Liberty *Dispatch* (September 21, 1972).

121. Frederic J. Fleron, "Toward a Reconceptualization of Political Change in the Soviet Union," *Comparative Politics*, I, 2 (January, 1969), 256–7.

122. John C. Harsanyi, "Rational-Choice Models of Political Behavior vs Functionalist and Conformist Theories," *World Politics*, XXI, 4 (July, 1969), 523.

123. C. H. Moore, "The Single Party . . . ," in Huntington-Moore, *Authoritarian Politics*, 66ff.

124. Hammer, "Towards a Theoretical Model . . . ," 22ff.

125. Cf. Dahl, *Polyarchy*, 217–8.

126. For an excellent analysis of the development of Sakharov's demand and policy recommendations, see Peter Dornan, "Academician Sakharov–Despairing Optimist of the Human Rights Movement, June 1968–June 1972," Radio Liberty *Research* (July 31, 1972).

127. Harsanyi, "Rational-Choice Models, . . ." 522.

128. Robert C. Tucker, *The Marxian Revolutionary Idea* (New York, 1969), Chap. 2 and Robert J. Osborn, *Soviet Social Policies: Welfare, Equality and Community* (Homewood, Ill., 1970), 17–53.

129. Yehezkel Dror, *Public Policymaking Reexamined* (Scranton, Pa., 1968), 43–48.

130. Charles E. Lindbolm, *The Policy-Making Process* (Englewood Cliffs, 1968), 105–6.

131. Francis G. Castles, "Interest Articulation: A Totalitarian Paradox," *Survey*, 73 (Autumn, 1969).

CHAPTER 2

Technology and Social Change in Soviet Central Asia: The Politics of Cotton Growing

Grey Hodnett

In the early 1950's a revolution took place in American cotton growing.[1] The first region to experience its full force was the Southwest, but the Black Belt did not long escape its effects. The plantation system, based on mass unskilled black labor, gave way—more rapidly toward the West, less rapidly in the East—to a capital-intensive, highly mechanized form of agriculture conducted by a new group of technically trained and profit-minded rural entrepreneurs.[2] The key to this historic breakthrough in cotton cultivation was the marketing, after years of unsuccessful experimentation, of an effective mechanical cotton picker in 1948.[3] Throughout the world cotton growing has been, and largely still remains, one of the most labor-intensive of all forms of agriculture. Historically, it has called for the presence of large numbers of unskilled laborers. Half or more of the labor expenditure occurs at the harvesting stage, and consequently vast economic and social stakes have been involved in the invention and successful deployment of mechanical harvesters: a single machine can replace up to 100 hand pickers.[4]

When it first became apparent in the United States that the technical problems of mechanization had been solved, some observers argued that the limitations imposed upon southern industrialization by the presence of the plantation-sharecropping system and the monopolistic economic and political power of northern capitalism would seriously retard mechanical harvesting.[5] In fact, however, despite delays and continuing use of substantial numbers of field workers, the machines were adopted.[6] Greatly amplifying the earlier impact of tractor mechanization, the harvesters played a key role in pushing hundreds of thousands of poorly educated, unskilled and totally unprepared blacks out of southern agriculture.[7] The inability of local or metropolitan southern industry to absorb redundant cotton growers did not force them to remain in rural areas; the absence of restraints upon movement permitted them to seek employment in the modern competitive economy of the urban North. In northern big cities their vulnerability to new forms of racial discrimination, lack of compensating political power, growing economic superfluousness, and changing expectations helped produce the crisis of the 1960's.

The present chapter deals with a similar revolution which—with a lag of approximately 15 years—has been underway in Soviet Central Asia.[8] As in the United States, technological and economic problems have programmed the main phases of the transformation of cotton growing in the USSR: major difficulties encountered in introducing mechanization have arisen first; then local problems of labor redundancy; and finally broader dilemmas of structural adjustment of the entire regional economy. These topics are treated below in sequential order, following a brief summary of Soviet cotton policy objectives and strategies of implementation.

Before launching into the analysis, however, I should point out briefly why cotton picking in Central Asia *is* a serious political question. Although Slavs are numerous in Central Asian cities, the area is inhabited predominantly by racially distinct Turkic national groups (whose members have mainly dwelt in rural localities). Cotton growing has provided the matrix for the economic life of a majority of these people, and hence whatever affects cotton in turn affects the mass of the population. Deep-rooted Muslim cultural patterns have made this a difficult population for the Russians to assimilate. Furthermore, the 1970 Census shows that it is multiplying far more rapidly than that of the Slav nationalities and will, over the course of 20 to 30 years, undoubtedly come to constitute a sizably larger—perhaps disturbingly larger—proportion of the total Soviet population. The territory that it inhabits occupies a strategic flank of the USSR, running from China in the east to Iran in the west. The main city, Tashkent, is a bastion of Russian military, economic, administive, and cultural might in Asia. Hence, the external significance of Central Asia is by no means limited to its assigned role of showcase to the Third World of how capitalism can be "bypassed." Apart from the geopolitical stakes involved in the region, it is growing in importance to metropolitan Russia as a raw materials and energy base (nonferrous metals, natural gas, oil, and hydroelectricity) and as a prime center of irrigated farming (grains and subtropical fruits and vegetables, in addition to cotton). Like the Ukraine already, it is becoming a fundamental component of Soviet power lying outside the Russian heartland.

"Plantation Economies"

Soviet Central Asia has often been pictured by Soviet and Western authorities as a "developing area" and favorable comparisons are correctly drawn with neighboring countries in terms of literacy and general education, improved standards of public health, greater availability of public services, emancipation of women, and overall higher standards of living.[9] These fruits of modernization under Soviet rule cannot be gainsaid, nor can the role played by Russians in helping to bring them about. Yet, modernization in Central Asia has taken place under specific conditions which have also circumscribed and limited development. One *might* argue that the most obvious socioeconomic fact about Soviet Central Asia is that it is, in a technical sense, a plantation region or subeconomy. About three-quarters of the natives living in the countryside are engaged in cotton growing; the institution which organizes their lives, whether a collective or state farm, could be called a "plantation"; and the network of economic relationships to which the farm is linked could be identified as a type of "plantation agriculture." The present study asks: To what extent *can* Central Asia be classed as a plantation region and to what extent have features characteristic of plantation agriculture influenced the ongoing transformations associated with cotton mechanization? In order to answer these questions, we need a dynamic model of a plantation economy. The most appropriate model available is that elaborated by George L. Beckford in *Persistent Poverty: Underdevelopment in Plantation Economies of the Third World*.[10]

Beckford analyses the *economic* and *sociopolitical* dimensions of plantation *production units* and the *overall environment* in which these units are located. He attempts to explain how "plantation economies," which arose as instruments of political colonization based on the exploitation of immigrant non-white labor, have their own "dynamics of underdevelopment" despite "constitutional" decolonization and to suggest how the plantation pattern can be broken. As an economic unit a "plantation" produces a single main field or horticultural crop for sale in an export market.[11] It discourages production of food crops and livestock. It employs large numbers of year-round unskilled workers, who perform under the close supervision of overseers. Ordinarily, however, it has difficulty enlisting sufficient labor by means of monetary incentives. Ownership of the plantation may be lodged with limited liability companies, private individuals, or the state. Regardless of the type of ownership, ultimate decision making about prices and wages, production schedules, capital investment, and other key matters is exercised at a distance, from a metropolitan country or region. In the broader "plantation economy," the plantation is merely the bottom rung of a vertically integrated structure that peaks in an outside metropolitan industrial center. Within the plantation region, plantations occupy most of the good land, holding onto it successfully in the face of attempted piecemeal encroachment by land-hungry peasants, who perforce depend upon the plantations for supplementary employment. Apart from land ownership, the dominant position of the plantation sector is guaranteed by its monopoly access to capital and credit, command of the region's agricultural research, and utilization of the only well-developed infrastructure for processing and distribution. This one-sided concentration on the plantation crop is made possible by means of the import of cheap foodstuffs produced by subsidized farmers abroad.

The plantation is also the basic building block of "plantation society." It is a "total" institution which not only monopolizes the means of livelihood of its resident laborers but also determines their cultural horizons. Socially and occupationally the plantation is stratified by race. Family structure and social solidarity among plantation workers are weak, while birth rates are high. Plantation dwellers collectively lack dignity, security and self-respect. As individuals they compete with each other in trying to "beat the system." As a group they adopt an imitative attitude toward the life-style of the white plantation bosses. "Plantation society" at large can be conceptualized as a "plural society," in the sense in which this notion has been employed by J. S. Furnivall and M. G. Smith.[12] It is marked by a high level of ethnic tension. Social integration arises primarily from common involvement by most members of the community in production of the plantation crop. Politically, integration is achieved by a concentration of effective power in the hands of a small planter class; a situation facilitated by the existence of a de facto alliance between the dominant white group and decultured natives, who feel contempt for the "backwardness" of their own people. Domination is implemented through highly centralized bureaucratic rule, a by-product of which is weak and unresponsive local government.

Beckford's essential point is that this system entails high economic and human costs *for the plantation country or region* and stifles the potentially most dynamic source of growth; namely, the *peasant* sector. "The structure of the system is such that many of the proximate economic, social and political variables that contribute to development do not come into effective play."[13] Apart from the anomic propensities of "plantation societies," with their poor education, low levels of achievement motivation, and exploitative human relationships, there are fundamental economic obstacles to development imposed by plantation agriculture. Beckford views the following as the most significant:

1. A fracturing of resource supply and demand;
2. Inequality in the distribution of wealth and income;
3. Foreign ownership of producing units that drains the supply of investable funds from the income stream;
4. The export orientation of plantation production that results in accumulation of backwash effects from terms of trade adjustments;
5. The low-skill content of plantation work that inhibits the diffusion of skills and improvement in the quality of labor inputs;
6. Resource-use distortions that prevent the flexible deployment of resource services to high-income producing activities;
7. The canalization of linkages and associated development potential by metropolitan plantation enterprises;
8. The multinational character of investment allocation by metropolitan enterprise that further reduces the flow of investable funds;
9. Limited technical knowledge of production possibilities apart from the particular plantation crop which results from the excessive concentration of research by company plantations and which prevents a rational pattern of agricultural development.[14]

Are there sources of evolutionary change built into the plantation system itself which will remove these obstacles? Beckford's answer is a qualified no. Four trends are characteristic of plantation economies: concentration of land ownership, rising nonplantation unemployment *and* an increasing plantation labor shortage, expansion of mechanization, and high rates of emigration from plantation areas or countries to the metropolis.[15] By themselves, these trends produce no fundamental alteration in the system; they are either not strong enough to upset the "dynamic equilibrium of underdevelopment" or merely help to reinforce it—as in the case of emigration of potential revolutionaries. The key to change lies in political action: action which imparts an awareness of the true economic situation to the mass of the native population, wins a commitment to change, and then—with the help of indigenous scholarship—uses state power to effect *closure* of the economy and a restructuring of economic institutions. To what extent, we may now ask, does Beckford's model help to illuminate problems of modernization in Soviet Central Asia?

The Russian Quest for Cotton

The need for cotton

Over the past hundred years there has been great continuity in Russian cotton policy. The three main objectives have been: (1) to obtain as much cotton as possible, (2) to be independent of foreign sources of supply, and (3) given these first two aims, to pay as little as possible. While cotton had been grown by Central Asians for millennia, it was through Russian initiative after the conquest of the region in the 19th century that old unproductive native methods of cultivation were eliminated, high-yield American upland seed introduced, model plantations established, land tenure rights restructured, large-scale new irrigation works undertaken, and modern ginning mills set up. A policy initially concerned with attaining low-cost supplies for the Russian textile industry regardless of the source was gradually superseded by one intended to secure Russia's "cotton independence" through protective tariffs, tax incentives and subsidized freight rates.[16] The drive to expand domestic cotton production was harshly intensified after the Revolution, and the pursuit of "cotton independence" crowned with success following collectivization.[17]

Yet when Stalin died, he left the peoples of the Soviet Union and Eastern Europe not only underfed but also poorly clothed. Shabby dress was the universal badge of Stalinism. Basic clothing has been and continues to be a much more important part of the Soviet standard of living than it is in more affluent Western countries. In 1953 and after, political decompression and awareness of repressed public needs compelled the Soviet leaders to think seriously about expanding clothing production in Eastern Europe, as well as the USSR.[18] During the present century a radical shift has been taking place in the locus of world cotton production and the production and marketing of cotton textiles. Both have been shifting from the developed to the developing areas of the world.[19] However, the European communist countries have constituted an exception to the rule, following the "developing" rather than the "developed" pattern of cotton consumption. This "institutional" (in Beckford's terminology) feature of the bloc economy has had great implications for Central Asia. The Soviet (and East European) strategy of dealing with the clothing problem remained firmly geared to cotton. "People will be wearing short pants," said Khrushchev, "if we don't have cotton." During most of the period covered by the present study, the artificial fiber revolution bypassed the Soviet bloc. In a consumer sense the Soviet Union *was* a developing society; there was an unwillingness to invest in and disrupt the existing textile plants; and, most importantly, the political decision to modernize the chemical industry still lay in the future.

Soviet cotton requirements have been accentuated by foreign trade considerations. Even in the absence of the historical drive for "cotton independence," which has continued unabated, the Soviet Union would probably have been discouraged from making large foreign purchases of ordinary medium-staple cotton in the 1950's by its high price on the international market—a by-product of American domestic price supports.[20] Cotton also plays an important—indeed expanding—role in the Soviet Union's own exports. With the exception of grain it is the largest agricultural export commodity. Roughly 5 percent of the crop is annually shipped to the East European bloc countries. The East European standard of living is thus materially supported by Soviet cotton, and East European claims for larger deliveries have been keenly felt—especially in the post-1956 period.[21] The textile industry in Eastern Europe has been partly equipped to handle Soviet grades of cotton fiber—making it harder for these countries to shift their source of supply but at the same time increasing their leverage on the USSR to maintain and expand exports.[22] Adding to the supply needs has been the fact that in recent years the Soviet Union has emerged as an important exporter of cotton to Western Europe, for which it is paid in hard currency, and to other countries such as India.

The Central Asian farming system

Standard Soviet institutions have provided the organizational framework within which the relentless quest for cotton has taken place. The Tsarist cotton economy was not based upon large Russian-owned plantations. By discouraging land ownership on the part of Russians, while encouraging commercialization, Tsarist policy helped to bring into existence an intermediate social stratum that performed the role of linking native growers (many of them tenant farmers for native landowners) and Russian consumers.[23] Essentially the same social formation exists today, operating within a bureaucratic rather than commercial framework and responding to wage and career rather than profit cues. The political calculations which led to the creation of large "absentee-owned" collective farms and their subsequent amalgamation into even larger production units (1950–53), together with the acceptance of hundreds of thousands of tiny private plots, laid the foundations—as Theodore Schultz has argued—for great economic inefficiency in the use of labor and farm machinery. This inefficiency was compounded by the suppression of rent and of farm product and factor prices.[24] The administrative and ideological controls maintaining the integrity of the production unit have effectively prevented attempts by peasants to reform the system from within by expressing their grievances (Albert Hirschman's "Voice");[25] but given the grudging toleration of a parallel "free" agricultural market, the same political controls have only partly contained the ever-present tendency of collective farmers to work half-heartedly or to withdraw their labor ("Exit") from collective cotton farming and put it to better use on their small but remunerative private plots. This tendency, present generally throughout Soviet agriculture, is especially pronounced in cotton farming where none of the crop is distributed in kind to the kolkhozniki. It significantly softens the "total" character of the collective or state farm.

Of all the means to increase cotton output, the extension of irrigated land has appealed most to the Muscovite imagination, from Tsarist officials to Brezhnev—perhaps because of its compatibility with the bureaucratic instrumentalities at hand.[26] Thus, Lenin had his famous decrees on irrigation; Stalin his Great Fergana Canal; Khrushchev his Kara-Kum Canal, Golodnaia Steppe, and Twenty-Year Plan; and Brezhnev his May (1966) Plenum.[27] Even more important in practise as a means of expanding cotton output has been the imposition on Central Asia of crop structures severely weighted toward cotton. From the native standpoint, Russian policy has long been characterized by an unnatural and undesirable monocrop emphasis. Evidence supporting this conclusion is provided by the spontaneous revision of plantings toward food crop production at times of crisis (World Wars I and II);[28] by the chronic political sensitivity of the subject (purge accusations in the 1930's and 1940's, tireless public reiteration ever after that supplying cotton is the "internationalist obligation" of Central Asia); and by the implications of the writings of contemporary reformers (see below).

The cotton-based crop structure has been extended and maintained to a significant degree by a combination of monetary and material incentives, and this is one of the areas in which the parallels with Beckford's model of the "plantation economy" are most striking. Generally speaking the procurement prices paid to the farms have discriminated markedly in favor of cotton, sometimes being set for other crops and livestock products below the level of production costs—a policy carried to self-defeating extremes during the Seven-Year Plan (1959–65) and even later.[29] A long-standing measure introduced in 1935 to stimulate cotton production, which accentuated the effect of procurement prices, was the *premii-nadbavok* (premium) system that rewarded procurements above those set by the planned contractual agreement (*kontraktsionnyi dogovor*).[30] The food deficit created by the cotton-first strategy has been covered since Tsarist times by grain and other food imports from outside Central Asia (a characteristic feature of plantation economies), while self-corrective market tendencies in Central Asia itself have been kept in check by administrative measures (obligatory procurement targets, restraints on private plots, prevention of "speculation" in the kolkhoz markets, and so forth). A most important means of connecting these imports directly with cotton production was the *vstrechnaia prodazha* (matching sale) system, introduced in 1932, which linked assured delivery to the farms of grain and other basic items with cotton production.[31] This arrangement fulfilled the same function performed in capitalist plantation economies by the "furnish" and credit system, symbolized by the plantation store.

Whether in overall terms there has been a fair relationship between the cost of foodstuffs and other goods supplied to the cotton growers of Central Asia and the price paid for cotton—a basic component of the terms of trade between the Russian industrial metropolis and the Muslim agrarian dependency—is an unresolved question.[32] It appears, however, that many Russians—including Khrushchev—have *believed* in stereotypical fashion that the cotton farmers of Central Asia have been getting rich on the procurement prices, and that the reason why Central Asia has not been more self-sufficient in grain, meat, and other foodstuffs is that the natives have preferred to live off the back of the hard-working Slavs. It would be interesting to know whether such an image of the relationship has been stimulated by a simple-minded juxtaposition of the ruble/ton procurement prices of cotton and—let us say—wheat. I suspect that it has, on the grounds that accurate and *inclusive cost* data have probably been scarce and not widely circulated.

Postwar procurement policy

Perhaps for this reason, and certainly because of competing priorities and the claims of other crop growers in different regions, Soviet postwar cotton procurement policy has consisted of cycles of ambitious plans combined with inadequate incentives, campaigns of coercive mobilization, failure followed by purges,[33] and then belated price increases followed by success. In 1945 a series of joint party-state resolutions inaugurated a campaign to restore cotton output, which had sagged during the war. Nonfulfillment of these resolutions was one of the motives behind the first wave of postwar purges in the cotton-growing republics.[34] Subsequently a joint Central Committee and Council of Ministers resolution of February 4, 1949 *doubled* the purchase price of cotton and released cotton farms from compulsory delivery to the state of livestock products and grain.[35] Within a short time "voluntarism" reasserted itself. At the 19th Party Congress in 1952 such visionary targets were approved for the Fifth Five-Year Plan that one cannot be sure how seriously they were taken at that time.[36] Exhortation and pressure failed to lift output, and the most prominent offenders—the Uzbek leaders—were purged in 1955, following Khrushchev's unfortunate intervention into cottongrowing at the Tashkent cotton meeting of November 1954. At that meeting —indeed at all the cotton meetings he ever attended—Khrushchev complained that procurement prices were too high and output targets too low. However, cotton output did not significantly increase until after the next hike in procurement prices in 1956.[37]

Stagnation of production at the level achieved after the 1956 rise lasted through 1962. During this period the advancing of bold new plans in cotton growing[38] and the repeated jacking-up of "socialist obligations" was accompanied by a deliberate *reduction* of incentives. At the Moscow All-Union Meeting of Cotton Growers in February 1958 Khrushchev urged that deductions into farm indivisible funds be increased in order to support greater self-investment by cotton-growing kolkhozes; at the June, 1958 Plenum of the Central Committee both the *premii-nadbavok* and *vstrechnaia prodazha* systems were liquidated; at the December, 1958 Plenum of the Central Committee, which ratified the Seven-Year Plan in agriculture, cotton targets and "obligations" were cranked up once again; and at the December, 1959 Plenum of the Central Committee Khrushchev endorsed the "proposal" (which he himself had surely solicited beforehand) of the first secretaries of Uzbekistan and Tadzhikistan, Rashidov and Ul'dzhabaev, that the wage rates of cotton growers be reduced, while at the same time calling for higher "obligations."[39]

These decisions, which are now admitted to have had a baneful influence on cotton growing, did make sense within the context of the assumptions underlying the fateful Seven-Year Plan targets for agriculture.[40] At the December, 1958 Plenum of the Central Committee, which confirmed the agricultural Seven-Year Plan, Khrushchev asserted that a qualitatively higher stage had been achieved in Soviet agriculture since the September 1953 Plenum of the Central Committee. He claimed in effect that the success which *had* been achieved demonstrated that such problems as the "restoration of the principle of material interestedness," the recruitment of new farm leaders, the investment of "enormous" funds in agriculture, the acquisition of farm machinery by the kolkhozes, the elimination of inadequacies in the planning and procurement system, and —not least—the attainment of adequate grain production had all been *solved*. It followed from this assumption that a more radical regional specialization of agriculture (for example, cotton growing in Central Asia) could be pursued, while at the same time increasing meat and milk production everywhere; that private farming activity could be cut back; and that farm financing could be put on a new basis. Farm incomes in the future were to rise solely through increases in productivity and expanded output, as procurement prices fell; and a large percentage of new investment was to come from the peasant in the form of lower rates of income distribution to farm members and higher rates of deduction into farm indivisible funds.[41]

The colossal miscalculation of the self-financing capacity of the farms implicit in Khrushchev's thinking and in the Seven-Year Plan was the source of many of the problems that plagued Soviet agriculture throughout the rest of the Khrushchev era, not least in cotton growing.[42] As the shortfalls below the Seven-Year Plan targets for cotton production and new land development increased from year to year, the demands to raise cotton output became more and more strident, compelling farm officials to put still greater acreage under cotton. Yet the rapid failure of his *grain* policy forced Khrushchev to demand at the January 1961 Plenum of the Central Committee that the Central Asian republics cover more of their own grain requirements and become more self-sufficient in meat and milk production.[43] The mixed success at best of this endeavor is suggested by Table 2-1. Furthermore, as average *yields* sagged (because of soil depletion, inadequate fertilizer supply, and reduced wages), it was necessary for Khrushchev to insist in November 1961 that cotton growers reintroduce the long-neglected cotton-alfalfa crop rotation—leaving it to the cotton farmers themselves to reconcile the gaping contradiction in his demands.[44] Relative success in the Golodnaia Steppe irrigation project program encouraged Khrushchev to begin to consider land development as the key to the cotton riddle, but the supporting investment program did not materialize until the May 1966 Plenum of the Central Committee.

TABLE 2–1 Per Capita Production of Food Products in Uzbekistan, 1959–1965
(kilograms)

	Year						
	1959	1960	1961	1962	1963	1964	1965
Meat	18.1	20.6	16.7	16.4	15.9	16.5	14.5
Milk	95.0	98.7	89.6	87.7	86.9	87.8	89.7
Eggs	53.2	53.0	53.7	56.9	59.4	44.1	53.5
Grains	62.2	60.9	52.3	70.7	93.8	129.7	59.3
Potatoes	24.8	18.7	16.4	17.2	16.8	19.0	16.1
Vegetables	41.4	43.5	40.7	46.1	52.6	48.2	45.6
Fruits	23.4	11.5	16.6	14.0	15.1	14.8	19.0
Grapes	14.1	22.1	24.4	18.1	14.9	19.1	21.1

Source: V. S. Nekhai, "Proizvodstvo prodovol' stennykh tovarov i uroven' udovletvoreniia v nikh naseleniia," in A. M. Aminov, ed., *Razvitie i sovershenstvovanie sotsialisticheskikh proizvodstvennykh otnoshenii v period stroitelstva kommunizma* (Tashkent: 1968), 177.

The decisive turn toward "subjectivism" accompanying the Seven-Year Plan inaugurated a six-year (1958–63) period of intensified coercive mobilization in cotton growing, as in agriculture generally. "Demandingness" toward subordinates became the watchword, as wage, machinery, and fertilizer inputs were held back. "If you don't weed out the weak ones," Khrushchev told the leaders in cotton growing, "the weak ones may drag you out of your republic, oblast and other seats. This can happen, comrades!" [45] This was no idle threat. The Seven-Year Plan period had begun with purges in Turkmenistan (December, 1958), Uzbekistan (March, 1959), and Azerbaidzhan (July, 1959), and was later punctuated by purges in Tadzhikistan (April, 1961), Kirgizia (May, 1961) and Turkmenistan (December, 1962–March, 1963) among the cotton plantation republics. The agricultural issues in each of the purges were not completely identical: the Turkmens had failed to promote square-cluster planting, high yields, and machine harvesting; the Uzbeks and the Azerbaidzhanis had followed suit and had also failed to fulfill their plans; the Kirgiz had not succeeded in lifting livestock production, were not mechanizing harvesting, and also failed to meet the cotton target; the Tadzhiks committed all of these mistakes in cotton growing and were falsifying production figures on a massive scale to boot; and the Turkmens' "primitive" performance in opening up new land by the Kara-Kum Canal cast a dark shadow on the prospects for Khrushchev's desired expansion of cotton output through new irrigation construction. The purges also differed in the extent to which the republic leaders publicly opposed elements of Khrushchev's cotton policy. What united most of the purged leaders was their toleration of adjustments to Khrushchev's policy that emerged "below" and promised to have the least unfavorable immediate impact upon cotton deliveries. By implication this "deal" with the growers involved recognition of de facto supply relationships and concessions to the interests of all involved in cotton growing, including—above all—the bulk of the native peasantry.

By 1963 the truth could no longer be ignored that more incentives, not just more pressure and administrative centralization, were necessary to bring cotton production up to plan levels. Thus, the last major act in cotton policy under Khrushchev was a joint resolution of March 15, 1963 that raised cotton procurement prices on the average by 20 percent, provided more recognition for geographical variations in costs, specifically instructed that the increased income be passed on to the kolkhozniki in the form of higher wages, restored the system of *vstrechnaia prodazha* of grain to cotton-growing kolkhozes, and released the kolkhozes (as of 1964) from paying for state-planned irrigation construction.[46] This repudiation of the basic financial assumptions of Khrushchev's cotton policy rapidly brought gratifying results.

Khrushchev's successors moved slowly in providing further incentives specifically earmarked for cotton growers, although in August 1965 they did raise procurement prices 50 percent for that portion of each year's harvest which exceeded the average level attained over the three previous years—a cautious restoration of the premium system.[47] The main assistance to cotton growing came from the general agricultural reform measures inaugurated by the March 1965 Plenum of the Central Committee and from a series of subsequent measures in 1965 and 1966 that further released kolkhozes from irrigation expenses, extended their short-term borrowing ability, wrote off old MTS debts, and introduced a new system of amortization.[48] While the attention of the new Soviet leadership was fixed upon land development plans,[49] the production targets set by the 23rd Congress remained unfulfilled, as procurements and yields declined for three consecutive years after rising to a new high in 1966. The situation was particularly grim in Azerbaidzhan, whose cotton fields by this time suffered from acute salinization; and failures in cotton growing were a contributory factor in the purge of the Azerbaidzhani leadership in 1969. Brezhnev acknowledged at the October 1968 Plenum of the Central Committee that a new look had to be taken at cotton prices, and a joint resolution of February 13, 1969 raised the average procurement price by 15 percent.[50] The cycle was completed with the outstanding harvest of 1970.

What were the results of this great effort, of the permanent campaign from year to year following the cotton cultivation cycle, of the demotions and promotions of thousands of officials, of the constriction and relaxation of financial pressure? In a purely quantitative sense the results were good—they represent one of the main success stories in recent Soviet agricultural history. Both the Seven-Year Plan and the subsequent Five-Year Plan (1966–70) were fulfilled, although not by much. The Soviet Union became in 1971 the world's largest cotton producer, with the highest average yield per land unit among the major producers.[51] Although problems abound in land development, with delays in settlement and serious salinization over hundreds of thousands of hectares, the overall achievements are physically impressive, and some irrigation projects —such as the Kara-Kum Canal—are remarkable indeed. (This canal promises in the future significantly to expand the life-space of the Turkmen people.) The road to high output, however, has not been one smoothly ascending path. Cotton has been one of the more acutely price sensitive of Soviet crops. Especially as a commercial monocrop, its cultivation offers nothing immediately in kind (for example, food or fodder) to the peasant, who—with his irrigated private plot to fall back on—has thus probably been more selectively responsive to wage rates than plantation workers elsewhere. As Table 2-2 shows production has been boosted from plateau to plateau (1949–55, 1956–62, 1963–65, 1966–69) by reluctantly granted price concessions.

These price rises are symptomatic of the failure of Soviet cotton growing to achieve a breakthrough in cost and productivity. Khrushchev was right in thinking that the Soviet government *ought* to be paying progressively less—not more—for cotton, because productivity *ought* to be rising; his mistake lay in calculating how this could be achieved. What the real cost is of Soviet cotton is hard to determine. At the time of Stalin's death in 1953, expenditures in man-days per centner in Soviet cotton growing were far above the targets set in 1925, above the prerevolutionary norm, and probably even above the Egyptian norm.[52] They dropped from about 9.0 in 1953 to 5.6 in 1965 and 5.2 in 1970. Yet, in the most recent period at least, the ruble/ton cost has risen from 325 in 1965 to 404 in 1970. How much the Soviets are really paying if such factors are taken into account as salinated land, freight costs on food, and opportunities forgone through the cultivation of other crops and larger imports of cotton is probably not known to anyone. Foreign

TABLE 2–2 Cotton Production in the USSR, 1951–1970

Year	**1951**	**1952**	**1953**	**1954**	**1955**	**1956**	**1957**	**1958**	**1959**	**1960**
Planned production (million tons)	155–165% in 1955 over 1951					156% in 1960 over 1955			increase to	
Actual production	3.73	3.78	3.85	4.20	3.89	4.33	4.21	4.34	4.65	4.29
Actual yield (centners/hectare)	13.7	13.3	20.5	19.1	17.7	21.0	20.1	20.2	21.6	19.6
Year	**1961**	**1962**	**1963**	**1964**	**1965**	**1966**	**1967**	**1968**	**1969**	**1970**
Planned production	5.70–6.10 in in 1965 from 1959					5.60–6.00 yearly average 1966–70				
Actual production	4.52	4.30	5.21	5.29	5.66	5.98	5.97	5.95	5.71	6.89
Actual yield	19.3	18.0	21.0	21.5	23.2	24.3	24.5	24.3	22.5	25.1

Sources: *Sel'skoe khoziaistvo SSSR* (Moscow: 1971), 194; *Current Soviet Policies* (New York: 1953); XX *s'ezd kommunisticheskoi partii sovetskogo soiuza, stenograficheskii otchet* (Moscow: 1956), 459; *Vneocherednoi XXI s'ezd kommunisticheskoi partii sovetskogo soiuza, stenograficheskii otchet* (Moscow: 1959), 492; and XXIII *s'ezd kommunisticheskoi partii sovetskogo soiuza, stenograficheskii otchet* (Moscow: 1966), 31.

specialists think that Soviet cotton growing has been a costly proposition, and Soviet leaders have obviously agreed.[53] This is the reason why they have sought for many years to mechanize cotton harvesting.

The Drive for Mechanization

Official attitudes toward machine harvesting

When mechanical harvesters first threatened to invade the state of Tennessee, Boss Crump proposed that they be outlawed as a menace to employment and established rural life. Not a trace of this attitude can be detected in the public statements of top Soviet leaders, whether Russian or native. An analysis of the speeches and articles of purged leaders in the cotton-growing republics—Babaev (Turkmenistan), Kamalov (Uzbekistan), Mustafaev (Azerbaidzhan), Razzakov (Kirgizia), Ul'dzhabaev (Tadzhikistan), as well as lesser lights—strongly suggests that any opposition to mechanization at *this* level of the republic elite has been based on doubts about the adequacy of the machines and related technical considerations, not upon sociopolitical fears of labor redundancy. In short, mechanization has been seen as an entirely positive phenomenon. The arguments explicitly or implicitly advanced are as follows. First, mechanization promises to reduce the cost of cotton, and thus the cost of clothing, dramatically. Second, it makes possible the cultivation of vast new irrigated lands. Third, it releases labor which can be used more productively in settling new lands, serving in other branches of agriculture (for example, livestock raising or fruit and vegetable growing), or working in industry. And fourth, it promotes highly desired social changes in the Central Asian village: the upgrading of education and occupational skills; the emancipation of women from heavy labor in the fields, their training in modern jobs (for example, as harvester operators), and indirectly the recruitment of their assistance in dismantling obstructive "remnants" of Muslim social life;[54] the elimination of rural overpopulation; physical reconstruction of the villages;[55] incorporation of Central Asians in the urban "internationalist" and "proletarian" environment; reduction in the birthrate, and so on. Thus, throughout the 1950's and 1960's, but especially since the Moscow All-Union Meeting of Cotton Growers in February, 1958, the Soviet leadership has tirelessly pushed machine harvesting, setting ambitious (and unfulfilled) targets and exerting constant pressure down through the party and agricultural bureaucracies. Implementation of this general policy aim, however, has been decisively affected by difficulties encountered in designing and manufacturing effective machinery; winning wholehearted support from republic-level leaders; mobilizing the efforts of intermediate agricultural and political officials; and creating conditions at the farm level conducive to mechanization.

The mechanization campaign

The Soviet government has sponsored research on mechanical harvesting since the 1920's and showed great interest in American experiments in the prewar period. The Amtorg Trading Corporation purchased 2 of the 10 machines built by the Rust brothers in 1936, and the American inventors were themselves invited to Uzbekistan that same year for consultations.[56] Since the war Soviet experts have kept well abreast of developments in U.S. cotton-growing technology. The first mass-produced Soviet harvester appeared in 1949—the vertical spindle SkhM-48. It worked but had serious design flaws. These were somewhat rectified in a new model, the SkhM-48M. In the meantime, however, partisans of horizontal spindles began to press their case. For several years well-placed vertical-spindle advocates were able to keep the SkhM-48M rolling off the assembly line:

> The Deputy Minister of Agriculture of the Uzbek SSR comrade Volkov (former chief of the State Special Design Bureau for Cotton), the Deputy Director for Research of the Central Asian Institute for the Mechanization and Electrification of Irrigated Agriculture comrade Zenin, the Chief of the laboratory for vertical-spindle machines of the SSDBC comrade Prikhod'ko through their actions attempted to keep the horizontal-spindle machines out of serial production. They wouldn't listen to the voice of scientists, designers and operators who, on the basis of experimental data, considered the horizontal-spindle machine more progressive. When anyone spoke in favor of a healthy competition between the vertical-spindle and the horizontal-spindle machines, comrades Volkov, Prikhod'ko and others labelled them "anti-mechanizers."[57]

So later said the deputy head of the Heavy Industry Department of the Uzbek CC, a horizontal-spindle man.

At the same time the spindle controversy—which had arisen from "below" within the agricultural R and D complex in Uzbekistan—became enmeshed in a running fight between the top leadership of Uzbekistan, supported by the USSR Ministry of Cotton Growing and the All-Union

Research Institute of Cotton Growing (located in Uzbekistan), and the leaders of Tadzhikistan, over quite a different issue. In 1950 the Tadzhiks had begun experimentally to reduce the width of rows from 70 to 50 and even 45 centimeters and to sow cotton in square clusters. This procedure permitted two-directional tractor cultivation and weeding and was said by its proponents to have many other virtues, as well: cotton bolls were denser, water was distributed more evenly and economically, heat was better retained, the system was applicable everywhere regardless of rainfall or slope, full mechanization was facilitated, and so forth. Moreover, the new method promised revolutionary yields: the Tadzhik Party First Secretary Bobodzhan Gafurov (an historian by profession), publicly claimed that "in the near future" yields of 50 to 60 centners could be anticipated.[58] The Tadzhiks were resisted by cotton-growing officials in Uzbekistan and Moscow for respectable technical reasons *and* in order to maintain investment momentum behind new irrigation construction; but in 1952 a special investigatory commission chaired by the then secretary of the All-Union CC, Pantaleimon Ponomarenko, grudgingly allowed the Tadzhiks to continue. The intrinsic merits of square clusters were overshadowed, perhaps, by the fact that Tadzhikistan was the only republic which regularly fulfilled its cotton procurement plan.

The issue of square clusters and narrow rows was decided, in principle at least, at the Tashkent All-Union Cotton-Growing Meeting in November, 1954. Khrushchev was confronted here with a choice between plan fulfillers who said cotton output could be quickly raised through a simple change in cultivation, and plan nonfulfillers like the chairman of the Uzbek Council of Ministers, Usman Iusupov, who—in Khrushchev's words—were demanding "enormous sums, millions in investment, and a large number of machines" for land development. Khrushchev opted for square clusters with narrow rows and against the Uzbek leaders—who were soon purged. As his questions to participants at the meeting indicated, Khrushchev personally was unsure about the issue of horizontal versus vertical spindles.[59] Iusupov, under heavy attack, defended the SkhM-48M and tried to argue that he had shown a "certain reserve" toward narrow rows and square clusters "not because I did not understand the significance of these progressive methods, but because I feared that the shift to narrow rows would complicate the broad introduction of mechanization." [60] But Gafurov proclaimed: "Cotton harvesting machines with vertical spindles, it seems to us, must be replaced by two-row machines with horizontal spindles." [61] It was this view, not surprisingly, that carried the day: political support for vertical-spindle machines had been undermined, and the policy shift in row width rendered their continued production indefensible anyway. As one design official later bitterly observed: "In 1954 a transition was begun to rows of 45 centimeters. This meant that the entire twenty-years' labor of the designers was wasted." [62]

With the cessation of production of the SkhM-48M in 1954, work intensified on perfecting horizontal-spindle models amidst continuing professional controversy and simmering resentment over the 1954 decisions. Speaking in 1957 to an audience of cotton specialists, the designer just quoted declared:

> Three years have passed since then—and we do not have machines for the 45 centimeter row. We also do not have machines for the 50 centimeter row. I have heard that this year a machine has been created which works more or less well on the 50 centimeter row, but I am convinced that two to three years will be required for this machine to work more or less satisfactorily.
>
> I think that the work of designers has been channeled along the wrong groove. In my opinion a crude mistake was committed when we shifted to the 45 centimeter row. We hobbled our "steel horse" in this way. . . . A crude mistake was committed in stopping production of the SkhM-48 cotton harvesting machine.[63]

Although the proponents of vertical spindles remained in positions of power,[64] from which they made a partial comeback after Khrushchev's departure, the introduction of horizontal-spindle machines slowly began. In 1955 the SkhS-1,2 appeared in limited numbers and in 1958 another model, the KhVS-1,2 was set for mass production. An important joint CC-Council of Ministers resolution of July 2, 1959 on cotton mechanization called for radical improvements in the design of harvesters and a sharp expansion in their manufacture.[65] In 1961 design work began on a new, more efficient two-row machine, the KhT-1,2, and it went into serial production in 1964. The main developments after 1964 were the perfection of a four-row harvester (the 14KhB-2,4) and the very gradual introduction of scrapping machines, which gather loose cotton on the ground. Design work on these and other machines had to accommodate itself to a shift back to even wider rows (90 centimeters) than had existed before 1954.[66] An important footnote to this sketch of harvester development is that even by 1970, after long years of experimentation, a machine had still not been perfected that would pick the long-staple cotton of Turkmenistan and Tadzhikistan. Throughout the period studied this strategically important part of the crop (about 20 percent in these republics) could only be harvested by hand.

Changes in row width, bureaucratic infighting, and malcoordination of production braked the manufacture of harvesters in the 1950's and hence limited their use. As Table 2-3 shows, the supply of harvesters began to increase sharply only in 1962, levelling out in 1967. Although complaints have been raised by republic officials about insufficient supply of harvesters, the important question has been whether the harvesters on hand have been used. As a matter of fact the number employed at any time has always been substantially lower than the number available, and targets for machine harvesting have rarely been met. At the real beginning of the mechanization campaign in 1958, for example, the harvesters on hand in Uzbekistan were considered capable of picking 30 to 35 percent of the crop, whereas the percentage actually machine harvested was 2 percent or less. At the end of the period under consideration, to take another example at random, over 800 harvesting machines were standing idle during the 1970 harvest in Turkmenistan. Even the most casual reading of the Central Asian press suggests that failure to send the harvesters into the fields has been endemic for many years.

Nevertheless, the degree of machine harvesting has increased, reaching a respectable 33 percent for the entire Soviet cotton crop by the end of the 1960's. (The Seven-Year Plan target for 1965 was 70 percent of medium-staple cotton.) In Uzbekistan the figures have risen as follows: 1955—1.7%; 1958—2%; 1962—11%; 1965—24%; 1969—29%; 1970—34%. The level of machine harvest is roughly 10 percent higher on state farms than on collective farms. There are also significant differences among republics and among districts within republics. Thus, 39 percent of the crop was machine harvested in Kirgizia in 1970; 33 percent in Turkmenistan in 1970; but only 21 percent in Tadzhikistan in 1969. Where the figure was about 35 percent for Kirgizia in 1966, it was only 9 percent for Azerbaidzhan. In some oblasts of Uzbekistan that same year farmers were machine-picking 50 to 70 percent of the crop, while individual collective and state farms were reaching 80 to 95 percent. The pattern, in other words, bears some resemblance to that of the United States 15 years earlier.

Reasons for slow mechanization

The reason why machine harvesting has consistently lagged behind expectations tell us much about economic and social relations in the Central Asian countryside. Where the machines have not been available

TABLE 2–3 Cotton Harvesting Machines in the USSR, 1950–1970
(thousands)

Year	'50	'51	'52	'53	'54	'55	'56	'57	'58	'59	'60	'61	'62	'63	'64	'65	'66	'67	'68	'69	'70
Manufactured	4.6	–	–	–	–	.6	.9	.1	.0	.5	3.2	4.3	6.1	7.1	7.0	8.0	7.0	6.4	5.7	5.7	5.9
In use	4.8	4.8	–	–	21.7	24.8	25.7	–	10.0[a]	10.0	11.0	11.0	15.0[b]	20.0	27.0	33.5	38.6	40.4	41.9	41.0	37.0

Sources: *Sel'skoe khoziaistvo SSSR,* 378, 400; *Narodnoe khoziaistvo uzbekskoi SSSR v 1965 godu* (Tashkent: 1966), 43; *Narodnoe khoziaistvo srednei azii v 1963 godu* (Tashkent: 1964), 79; *Narodnoe khoziaistvo SSSR v 1965 g.* (Moscow: 1966), 339; and *Ezhegodnik bol'shoi sovetskoi entsiklopedii: 1957* (Moscow: 1957), 57.

a. 22.0 at beginning of year.
b. Does not include Azerbaidzhan.

in sufficient numbers or have not been designed to pick the specific (long-staple) kind of cotton being harvested, no further explanation is required. For the most part, however, the reasons have been more complex. Until at least the mid-1960's, it was probably the case that a substantial number of farm officials—perhaps a majority—felt that the machines being manufactured still suffered from serious unresolved design difficulties. Despite polemical assertions since 1957 that Soviet models were already better than American models, there was often an implicit argument in speeches by top leaders that the machines were not really all *that* bad. When the present author suggested in 1971 to a leading cotton-growing administrator in Uzbekistan that the frequently voiced charge of "conservatism" really explained nothing, he agreed and offered the opinion that the basic reason for slow progress in harvest mechanization had been mechanical defects in the harvesters.[67]

Regardless of the original condition of the machines, a significant factor affecting mechanization has obviously been a frequent absence of adequate harvester maintenance and repair facilities.[68] Every year as harvest time nears repair work runs far behind schedule, and many harvesters do not make it to the gate or do so only "on paper." [69] In this respect, as well as financially, the liquidation of the MTS was poorly timed and hurt Central Asian agriculture. As one writer has observed: "The repair base of agriculture was seriously undermined in the period of the MTS reorganization. In Uzbekistan many kolkhozes, sovkhozes and sovkhoz divisions do not have their own repair shops." He argued that raion branches of "Sel'khoztekhnika" should take over the maintenance of kolkhoz harvesters on a contractual basis.[70] Others have gone further and wondered whether the time has not come to "create an organization of the MTS type." [71]

Agronomic problems have been another source of slow mechanization. Cotton growing is one of the most complicated forms of farming, involving some 60 to 70 separate operations. The shift from hand to machine harvesting requires a qualitatively more accurate and punctual performance of each of these steps. With hand picking it is possible, up to a point, to let some operations slide or to make up later for earlier negligence. If planting is dragged out, for example, and the bolls ripen later in the fall, when the fields may be muddy, it does not matter as long as people rather than machines are sent out to do the picking. Machine harvesting requires that a high percentage of the bolls ripen at a certain time and at a precise distance from the ground and from other bolls, in a weedless and leafless space. For this to occur, all operations must be closely synchronized: the land must be planed flat at the start; the soil must be watered earlier; fertilizer must be spread more evenly; furrows must be plowed absolutely straight and deeper; weeding cannot be haphazard; defoliation must work; the seeds must perform as specified, and so on. Inability to put all of these pieces together at once has been a most important factor retarding mechanization. This failure has been caused partly by input problems: insufficient land planing equipment, underpowered tractors, inadequate herbicides, undependable defoliants, unperfected seed, and so on. But equally it has been caused by the inability of the farm officials fully to control and direct labor in a sustained fashion throughout the year—as Beckford shows, a root problem of plantation agriculture.

The overall mechanization of cotton growing has posed a general problem of how labor should be organized in Central Asian collective farms. Traditionally, before and after the MTS reorganization, machine work and field cultivation were handled by separately organized groups. Weeding, hoeing and picking were performed by numerically large field brigades which were assigned relatively small sections of the sown area. These brigades tended simply to be populated points mobilized for labor, and were intimately implicated in a symbiotic fashion with the particularistic interests of extended families and the private-plot economy. Mechanization has been accompanied by an official attempt to combine machine operators and field workers in a single labor unit ("tractor-field brigades" first, then "complex-mechanization brigades"). These brigades have fewer members, whose average skill level is higher, and they are responsible for much larger sown areas surrounding several populated points. Not surprisingly, progress has been slow in organizing these brigades, for they represent the dismantling of the long-established Soviet cotton production unit and the socioeconomic compromises built into it. It has taken much time and effort to raise the skill levels of an expanding percentage of the rural labor force, although this is being accomplished. Probably the most serious obstacle preventing a restructuring of work units, however, has been the rural labor surplus.

The four republics composing the Central Asian "economic region" are the *only* republics in the USSR in which the number of kolkhoz households increased between 1960 and 1970.[72] As Table 2-4 shows, the percentage of collective farms in Central Asia having over 500 households vastly exceeds the percentage for the USSR as a whole and for the RSFSR. Within the Central Asian economic region, however, there are significant territorial differences in the distribution of household numbers

TABLE 2–4 Distribution of Kolkhozes by Number of Households in 1971 (percent)

Number of Households	1–100	101–200	201–300	301–500	501–750	750+	Total
USSR	3.0	17.8	19.8	29.0	17.8	12.6	100
RSFSR	3.6	21.8	24.4	30.0	12.9	7.3	100
Azerbaidzhan SSR	8.2	34.0	22.9	25.2	7.3	2.4	100
Central Asian economic region	0.6	3.6	7.3	22.4	28.3	37.8	100
Uzbek SSR	0.1	1.6	4.7	19.8	31.2	42.6	100
Kirgiz SSR	–	2.0	5.3	27.4	28.6	36.7	100
Tadzhik SSR	2.5	8.9	7.1	14.9	20.2	46.4	100
Turkmen SSR	0.9	6.7	17.4	33.7	25.7	15.6	100

Source: *Sel'skoe khoziaistvo SSSR*, 491.

among and within republics. These differences in kolkhoz population density reflect marked regional variations in the quality of soil, climatic conditions, and water availability. They have been accentuated by the distorting effect on the relative profitability and wage levels of farms produced by inadequate recognition of economic rent[73] and by the *premii-nadbavok* system of procurement prices.[74]

In view of the large number of households living on Central Asian collective farms, it is hardly surprising that mechanization has been slower where there has been an oversupply of labor, or that mechanized harvesting has proceeded more rapidly on state farms—which tend to be located in newly developed and underpopulated areas; the same problem has occurred in the United States. As Uzbek Minister of Agriculture K. Khanazarov once stated:

> The great availability of laborers on many farms of various zones has already become an unfavorable factor, and has essentially turned into a serious obstacle in the path of the broad introduction of mechanization and growth of labor productivity. Is it possible successfully to introduce mechanization and raise labor productivity in farms where there is one able-bodied worker per hectare? . . . High labor expenditures as a rule occur in most brigades and farms to which many people are attached. This is fully understandable. Each person has to be provided with work even if it is useless, superfluous for getting a big harvest.[75]

What is paradoxical, but in accord with Beckford's analysis of plantations, is that farms fully or even over-supplied with their own labor force have chronically relied upon the assistance of outsiders to handpick their crop. "Every year hundreds of thousands of city dwellers are brought in for the harvest, which causes enormous harm to the economy, retarding the development of other branches of agriculture and industry." [76] The number of outsiders dragooned into this yearly operation has depended upon the rate at which kolkhozniki opt out of harvest work. In October, 1962 in Uzbekistan 186,000 outsiders put in an average 26 days' labor in cotton, for example, while 400,000 kolkhozniki did not participate. Over that entire year 73.6 percent of the Uzbek kolkhoz labor resources were in fact used, as against 85.1 percent in Turkmenistan but only 56.9 percent in Tadzhikistan, which provides some indication of the varying dependence of the farms on outside pickers.[77] What nonparticipation means in concrete terms may be illustrated by data for October, 1967 on the Akhunbabaev Kolkhoz of Namangan Raion, Uzbekistan. Here, at the height of the harvest season, 1,561 people picked cotton, including 291 outsiders; yet 718 kolkhozniki could not be enticed into the fields.[78] This apparent paradox may be explained as one of a set of "role bargains" that the leaders of cotton farms are compelled to make.

Cotton farm managers, like other Soviet economic officials, operate in a setting of great pressure from above to achieve multiple targets—pressure that is not matched by appropriate supplies or by opportunities at hand. The key target by which they are judged and largely rewarded has been the *val,* gross output plan fulfillment, and not cost reduction, the introduction of harvesting machines, and so on. On the other hand, cotton farm managers have had to be more attuned, perhaps, to the interests of their labor force than Soviet economic leaders. Khrushchev himself best described the "antimechanizing" attitude of cotton-farm officials:

> The philosophical defense of the *ketmen*, if one could call it that, is as follows: the labor-day (wage unit—G. H.) in the kolkhozes is dear so let the kolkhozniki work with the *ketmen* and earn more labor-days. Without the *ketmen*, so it is said, not all kolkhozniki will be employed, the kolkhozniki's number of labor-days will be reduced, and, consequently, their wages will decline.[79]

Other evidence can be found corroborating the assertion that a desire to protect the employment and incomes of kolkhozniki has been a significant motive of managers. For example:

> Insufficient mechanization in cotton growing is not explained by the lack of machinery on the part of kolkhozes. The cause of retarded tempos in raising labor productivity and lowering the cost of output lies in the surplus labor force created by the growth in mechanization of production processes. The kolkhozes strive to utilize surplus labor by broadening the

front of manual cotton cultivation, of harvesting, and by the slow introduction of agricultural machinery.[80]

> In many kolkhozes as a result of the growth of mechanization of cotton growing labor is being released that does not always find a place in other branches of the economy. As a result the number of kolkhozniki is growing who are not employed in communal production, a surplus labor force is being formed which is becoming a serious obstacle in the path of growth of labor productivity. When there is a surplus labor force the introduction of mechanization is artificially held back, many manual operations are retained, a considerably larger labor force is employed in work than is required.[81]

In attempting to understand the behavior of farm leaders, we may first assume that it is highly unlikely that they are psychologically insensitive to the income needs of their "own" people. To some extent, it also appears, the formally democratic structure of the collective farm has compelled them to respond to the membership—particularly in such crucial matters as decisions on how many harvesting machines the farm should purchase (a decision made by the MTS and higher authorities before 1958).[82] Soviet farm officials, like their American counterparts on southern plantations, have required very substantial numbers of laborers to perform nonharvest operations which for a variety of reasons have not been mechanized (for example, weeding in the absence of effective herbicides). Reciprocally, they have had to recognize the members' interest in their private plots—an interest threatened by the projected restructuring of the labor unit and introduction of crop rotation,[83] but intensified by Khrushchev's price and wage policy (especially between 1958–1962).

In Uzbekistan, for example, *farm* income rose by 20 percent between 1957 and 1961, while production expenses increased by 43 percent. Relative cost increases occurred in land development, irrigation maintenance, machinery, fertilizer, defoliants, pesticides and aerial spraying. Hence, "the wage fund for kolkhozniki stayed at the original level, or in a number of kolkhozes even declined." [84] Another author comments:

> The procurement price established [in 1958] on the basis of average branch expenditures deprived an overwhelming percentage of cotton-growing kolkhozes of the possibility of earning additional income. . . . The sharpness of the question of the procurement price level showed itself in these years with special force because the kolkhozes had to mobilize greater sums to obtain the machinery which earlier had belonged to the MTS and also to acquire the latest new machinery. . . . They had to construct new production buildings, achieve intensive assimilation of uncultivated sectors of land, and create an independent repair base.

> These circumstances were not fully taken into account in the procurement price, which led to an increase in the share of gross income deducted into the indivisible fund with a simultaneous decline in the share of the consumption fund.[85]

In Turkmenistan kolkhoz income from cotton dropped by 10 percent between 1958 and 1961, and wages paid out must have dropped even further.[86] Figures on the percentage of household income derived from private plots in Central Asia are hard to come by. In Uzbekistan in 1960 private plots accounted for about 54 percent of milk, 48 percent of vegetables, 47 percent of melons, 34 percent of meat, and 29 percent of grain produced in the collective-farm sector, and 64 percent of all kolkhoz cows were privately owned. The average working kolkhoznik was said to receive 1,800 rubles per year from his private plot, out of a total income of 6,100 rubles.[87] In 1965 in Tadzhikistan private plots contributed 58.1 percent of milk, 55.9 percent of vegetables, 54.3 percent of eggs, 52.9 percent of potatoes, 51.0 percent of fruit, 41.9 percent of meat, 23.5 percent of wool, and 17.4 percent of grapes produced in kolkhozes. Over the years 1960 to 1965 money income received from the sale of private plot produce averaged 30.7 percent of the total money income of kolkhozniki.[88]

It is within this overall context that farm leaders must take account of cost factors. The compromise they are able to effect among the official demand to reduce labor costs while increasing output, the unofficial demand to fulfill the *val* whatever the cost, and the inarticulate demand of collective farmers to provide a basic livelihood plus an opportunity to earn outside income—the "role bargain," in other words—depends upon the possibility of bringing in outside workers. These students, city dwellers, office workers, and soldiers are the "migrant laborers" of Central Asia. As in the United States, their cost to the *farm* does not appear to have been excessive.[89] The main expenses involved in the yearly exodus to the cotton fields are those of interrupted education and disorganized schedules in urban work places; and these are borne—with vexation but probably without calculation—by the state.[90] In contrast, the cost to the farms of machines has been high; especially during the Khrushchev-inspired cost-price squeeze.[91] As one chairman declared: "A kolkhoz will willingly buy one to three, or even five machines; but when it comes to creating a fleet that will handle the machine harvesting of all the cotton, farm leaders shy away from such a step. And this is understandable. A kolkhoz, as a rule, uses the cotton harvesting machines for just a short period." [92] Central Asian farm managers have also had to contend, as have their American counterparts, with reduced procurement prices for machine-harvested cotton, which is graded lower.[93] Equally important has been the failure to adjust the procurement planning system to the machine age. In 1958, for example, when Khrushchev was lambasting cotton growers for not using mechanical pickers, the procurement contract in force demanded that the farms deliver not less than 50 percent of the harvest to the procurement centers by the end of September, making hand picking obligatory since "normal machine work can begin only when 50 to 60 percent of the bolls have opened, which usually occurs at the beginning of October."[94] This arbitrary deadline defined "plan fulfillment," to which the personal income and career prospects of the farm leaders themselves were closely geared.

Ultimately, the delay in harvesting mechanization was greatly affected by poor decisions at the top. There is much to recommend separate features of Khrushchev's program. What Khrushchev failed to recognize was that the revolution he sought to achieve in cotton growing necessitated the most carefully planned integration of concurrent changes in a variety of areas of science, applied technology, and agronomy. He pushed mechanization before the machines were really effective, and his decision in favor of narrow rows got the campaign off to a very bad start. The malcoordination of measures necessary to implement the mechanization policy arose not least from Khrushchev's solicitation of misleading information about what could be achieved on the average farm under average conditions. Probably the greatest weakness of all at the top has been an impatience and inability to deal effectively with the micro-economics of cotton production—poor plantation management in the metropolitan office. The problems of cotton mechanization are technically akin to the problems of raising labor productivity in industry and have responded poorly to coercive mobilization.

The Impact of Mechanization

Released labor

High-level Soviet thinking about the effect of cotton mechanization has been confined largely to the labor-saving (labor-releasing) aspect of the problem, yet there has been a certain reticence in publishing precise figures on the gains realized or anticipated. In the technical literature one frequently finds such comments as: "The reduction of labor requirements in this or that economic region of the country and in separate branches of the economy sometimes raises serious problems";[95] "In evaluating prospective labor resources one must take into account that along with the high natural growth rate of the population labor resources will be released as a result of measures for the complex mechanization of agriculture, especially such labor-intensive branches as cotton growing";[96] and "The organization of complex-mechanization tractor-field brigades would permit tens of thousands of workers to be released from cotton growing [in Tadzhikistan]." [97] At the start of the mechanization campaign a leading expert on cotton-growing mechanization estimated that it should be possible to release 600,000 to 700,000 of the 1,060,000 laborers then in cotton brigades, leaving a residual force of from 200,000 to 250,000 in the spring to 300,000 to 350,000 at the peak of the harvest.[98] In 1969 the first deputy chairman of the Turkmen Council of Ministers provided some idea of the actual scale of labor release when he stated that the machine harvest level achieved in 1968 (approximately 30 percent) had freed 70,000 kolkhozniki from harvesting, with others having been replaced by machine cultivators.[99] If one assumes that 50 percent of their labor was expended on harvesting, then it would appear that the de facto labor-releasing effect of a 30 percent mechanized harvest was roughly 35,000 kolkhozniki in Turkmenistan, or a somewhat higher percentage of those actually participating in collective work. Turkmenistan has the highest rate of participation among Central Asian republics and in many regions a labor shortage, which suggests that the labor-releasing impact of mechanization is higher in Uzbekistan and higher still in Tadzhikistan, where participation drops off and featherbedding is greater.

Alternative modes of labor redistribution

It was noted above that Soviet spokesmen have mentioned four possible modes of redistributing labor released by cotton mechanization: resettlement on new cotton farms, transfer to other branches of agriculture, employment in local rural industry, and migration to the towns. The large land development projects approved by the Soviet government since 1954 have called for substantial population resettlement in Central Asia, although details of precise goals have appeared only infrequently in the press. The 1954 resolution on cotton growing in Uzbekistan, for example, called for the resettlement of 40,000 kolkhoz *households* between 1954 and 1958;[100] and the resolution on Tadzhikistan called for the resettlement of 20,000 households ("primarily from the mountainous grain-growing districts") between 1954 and 1959.[101] In a speech in 1959 the Chairman of the Uzbek Council of Ministers observed that in order to meet the Seven-Year Plan target of irrigating 450,000 to 500,000 hectares of new land it would be necessary to resettle "tens of thousands of families from old regions." [102] And writing in 1967, the head of the Uzbek State Planning Committee stated that future plans for developing the Golodnaia Steppe alone required the resettlement there of "hundreds of thousands of able-bodied people" and that plans for new irrigation in the Karshi Steppe and the lower Amu-Daria necessitated "great work in the territorial redistribution of the republic's labor resources." [103]

Incentives have been offered to kolkhozniki willing to move and in some cases they have been effective.[104] The present author was impressed by the new houses, school, club, paved roads, and other amenities that had been constructed on the new Karl Marx Kolkhoz outside of Margelan in the Fergana Valley, which he was able to visit in 1971. Without wishing to minimize the achievement of the 480 families on the farm and their capable chairman, one must nevertheless note that the virgin land to which they moved was no more than 15 to 20 miles from their old homes and was situated next to the Great Fergana Canal in a generally hospitable environment. Many new farms in Central Asia have not been as fortunate. Accounts in the press are legion of farms in newly irrigated regions which lack decent housing, minimum consumer services, schools, and leisure facilities; and which therefore suffer serious labor shortages and rapid labor turnover. It has not been easy to uproot large numbers of Central Asians and set them down again in the treeless wastes of the Golodnaia Steppe, Kara-Kum Canal, and other newly irrigated areas. An additional factor that should be noted in this connection is that the group best suited for resettlement—those aged 20 to 40 with skills—is precisely the group most needed to carry out mechanization on existing farms.

The shifting of redundant labor to other sectors of agriculture has been held back so far by the same forces which have encouraged monocrop tendencies and inhibited crop rotation. Unrealistic cotton procurement targets for republics have been divided up into unrealistic plans for raions. Raion leaders have thus been forced to restrain diversification of the crop structure by farm leaders. The watchword of raion leaders is

"Never lower the *val*!" complained three kolkhoz chairmen. "So we're caught in a vicious circle: we haven't delivered the *val* because we don't have crop rotation, because the land has been misused; but we can't introduce crop rotation because we are afraid to fall down on the *val*." [105] As new lands have not come into operation as scheduled nor with anticipated yields, and as old lands have succumbed to salinization,[106] it has been correspondingly harder to move to crop rotation. This difficulty has been greatly increased by one of the most unfortunate legacies of Khrushchev's cotton policy—the emergence in the mid-1960's of widespread wilt; a dangerous consequence of monocropping predicted by experts a decade earlier. As Ziiadullaev observes:

> As a result of the reduction of alfalfa sowings and non-fulfillment of the plan for developing new lands the weight of cotton in the total sown area on irrigated lands has reached 80 percent, in the Andizhan and Fergana oblasts—over 86 percent, on individual farms—95 percent, and on sovkhozes in the Golodnaia Steppe—up to 98 percent. This has led to considerable weed infestation of fields, and massive spread of agricultural pests and cotton diseases, especially wilt. For example, in 1964 30 percent of all the cotton sowings, and in Andizhan Oblast 60 percent, were infected by wilt. The harvest losses from wilt infection reached 10–15 percent. Kolkhozes and sovkhozes are spending enormous sums on the struggle with wilt.[107]

In 1971 an Uzbek author stated that "Until recently crop rotation as a fundamental measure in the struggle with cotton wilt has not been materially rewarded." [108] But the more basic financial problem has obviously been the structure of procurement prices for many years. Not only has it discriminated harshly against many other branches of agriculture (see footnote 29), but its internal inconsistency and irrationality has worked against even that level of diversification which would have been compatible with regime cotton goals. The results of Soviet procurement policy on the crop structure of Uzbekistan are shown in Table 2-5. Seven-Year Plan food production targets in Uzbekistan were badly underfulfilled,[109] and between 1959 and 1965 "the production of all types of food products in the republic as a whole did not keep up with the population and in 1965 was almost at the level of 1940." [110] It is doubtful whether the successful introduction of crop rotation and a more balanced crop structure will open up greater numbers of jobs *in the future*. Most other branches of agriculture have a lower labor-land ratio than cotton growing and are even more susceptible to mechanization. The experience in the American South has been that "though most of the acreage released from cotton

TABLE 2–5 Sown Areas in Uzbekistan, 1940–1970

		40	50	53	55	56	57	58	59	60	61	62	63	64	65	66	67	68	69	70
Total sown area (thousand hectares)		3099	2804	2912	2972	3022	3036	3165	3098	3149	3174	3230	3335	3545	3447	3353	3315	3495	3480	3589
Total sown irrigated		na	na	na	na	na	na	na	na	2293	na	2236	2318	2350	2308	2346	2373	2412	2445	2464
Cotton	% of sown area	31	40	40	46	43	44	46	47	46	48	49	49	46	47	48	48	46	48	50
	% of irrigated	na	na	na	na	na	na	na	na	63	na	70	70	69	70	69	68	67	68	74[a]
Grain	% of sown area	48	41	33	33	34	33	32	31	29	33	34	34	40	37	34	32	36	34	33
	% of irrigated	na	na	na	na	na	na	na	na	8	na	12	9	12	9	8	8	11	9	7
Vegetables, potatoes	% of sown area	3	2	na	3	na	na	3	3	4	3	3	3	3	3	3	4	4	4	na
and melons	% of irrigated	na	na	na	na	na	na	na	na	5	na	3	4	4	4	3	5	5	5	3
Fodder	% of sown area	15	15	15	18	16	17	18	18	18	15	13	10	11	12	14	15	13	13	13
	% of irrigated	na	na	na	na	na	na	na	na	23	na	14	16	14	15	17	18	16	16	16

Sources: *Narodnoe khoziaistvo srednei azii v 1963 godu,* 136, 133, 141, 142; *Narodnoe khoziaistvo uzbekskoi SSR v 1965 godu,* 107–110; *Narodnoe khoziaistvo uzbekskoi SSR v 1969 godu* (Tashkent: 1970), 95–97; *Sel'skoe khoziaistvo SSSR,* 114, 115, 130, 241; and *Narodnoe khoziaistvo SSSR v 1959 godu,* 334, 347.

a. Includes all technical crops.

cultivation may have been employed in other uses, these have not been such as to absorb fully the released farm labor." [111]

The third alternative mode of labor redistribution is employment in rural nonagricultural jobs: rural industrial enterprises processing agricultural products and local raw materials, interkolkhoz organizations, kolkhoz enterprises, and rural service and cultural establishments. For years there has been much general talk of these forms of employment as a bridge between town and countryside. As of 1970 the only interkolkhoz organizations which had reached *any* significant level of development in Central Asia were in the fields of construction and fodder provision. Among kolkhoz enterprises proper (*podsobnye predpriiatiia*) only lumber and grain mills stood out in reasonably substantial numbers.[112] In Tadzhikistan:

> at the present time [1969] only a small fraction of kolkhozes in the republic have subsidiary enterprises. Their role in raising the level of employment among kolkhozniki is negligible. In 1965, for example, 0.4 percent of the total number of working kolkhozniki were employed in subsidiary enterprises. Only one kolkhoz in the republic had an enterprise for processing vegetables and fruits and only one a brick factory. In 1965 the volume of industrial output of the kolkhozes made up 1.9 percent of the republic's total industrial output.[113]

It seems fair to say that at the present time the Soviet Government has scarcely begun to promote rural nonagricultural employment in Central Asia.

The last officially sanctioned outlet for released agricultural labor is, of course, migration to urban industrial employment. That there is an ever-expanding pool of potential migrants hardly seems in doubt. Calculations by Shatskikh and Khadzhibaev indicate, for example, that 179 out of 310 kolkhozes in Tadzhistan in 1964 had a surplus labor force, and that the overall excess was 17 percent even at the given level of mechanization and labor productivity.[114] Yet, as they show elsewhere, migration to the towns has been very slow, in sharp contrast with the pattern outside of Central Asia. Between 1960 and 1965 only 10 percent of the natural population increase in rural areas was lost to the cities; the rest remained on the land.[115] In 1969 another writer observed: "In the Uzbek SSR, out of 100 able-bodied kolkhozniki released from rural production, only a little over 10 percent transferred to other branches or resettled in other regions; the remainder settled back into private farming. This is also characteristic for the other republics of Central Asia." [116] In short, migration has lagged behind mechanization.

Reasons for delayed migration

There are several reasons why the migratory effects of mechanization have been delayed. The majority of those who have been released by mechanization so far have been women, who constitute a majority of the cotton pickers and form the base of the rural class of unskilled plantation laborers. Especially in Muslim Central Asia, their undereducation and subordinate status in the family make them least likely to migrate. The second factor which has contained the "push" from the village has been the overall lower level of education acquired by kolkhozniki (including poor Russian language training), and thus the difficulty they have encountered or foreseen in adjusting to an urban industrial way of life. A third factor which has offset the "pull" from the city has been the possibility of surviving fairly comfortably on the private plot. This is the meaning of data indicating that the percentage of able-bodied kolkhozniki who could but do not wish to participate in collective work has increased in the past 15 years.[117] When Khrushchev proclaimed the slogan "Give the green light to cotton!" he was in fact inviting kolkhozniki to produce food on their private plots for the kolkhoz market. Political leaders in Central Asia appear to have tolerated a healthy amount of "speculation" on the free market; a "role bargain" probably imposed upon them by calculations of how best to avoid displays of nonnative discontent in urban areas and industrial settlements. For reasons discussed at length above, kolkhoz leaders have also accommodated themselves to a substantial amount of private plot activity. This is indicated by the elasticity of field boundaries, failure to enforce restrictions on the number and pasturing of private cattle, and toleration of "households" contributing few laborers to the farm.

The last factor affecting migration has been the relative desirability of living and working in the city. This is a topic on which conflicting opinions exist. It has been implied by some authors that the native kolkhozniki in Central Asia prefer to stay in the countryside because they enjoy a higher standard of living there than Russian city dwellers.[118] Soviet observers frequently suggest, on the contrary, that kolkhozniki—especially young people—gravitate naturally to the towns.[119] Some objective economic facts which shed light on the matter have been set forth in a useful article by Popadiuk on incomes of different groups in Uzbekistan.[120] Popadiuk divides income into three main streams: wages, social consumption, and private plots. He shows that while the average daily wage of a working kolkhoznik in 1968 had risen to 78.4 percent of that of an industrial worker (83.6 percent in 1965), his average *yearly* wage was 62.8 percent and the average per capita *family* income from wages was 36.3 percent (p. 21). However, the combined per capita income of kolkhozniki was 87.4 percent of that of "workers and employees" in 1968, as against 73.1 percent in 1963 (p. 25). Private plots made the difference, contributing 22.8 percent of the kolkhoznik's income in 1968 (p. 27). The income spread between town and country, Popadiuk argues, is now narrower in Uzbekistan than in the RSFSR. One must also include in the equation "life-style" considerations: "modern convenience" in a small flat versus separate dwellings, shaded gardens, fresh vegetables and fruit, space, and so forth. The increasingly prevalent phenomenon of natives who hold full-time state jobs but live on kolkhozes suggests that the advantage *now* may well lie with country living combined with employment in nearby small towns.

However, it does not appear—least of all to concerned Central Asians—that the present pattern of cotton mechanization, labor release, absorption by the private plots, and very gradual migration can last indefinitely. "Calculations show," wrote one group of authors about Uzbekistan, "that the average yearly growth in rural labor resources in the future will be 45,000–50,000 persons. In addition, complex mechanization will release an ever greater quantity of labor; the increased supply of machinery to agriculture will increase labor resource reserves and the problem of employment will become still more complex." [121] The dynamic factor operating alongside mechanization is the changing birthrate. What the 1970 Census reveals is that between 1959 and 1970 the natural rate of increase of the indigenous Muslim peoples of Central Asia rapidly accelerated to a level approximately three times that of the Russians themselves.[122] Thus, the rural population has begun to expand with impressive speed. As I have already noted, the four republics of Uzbekistan, Kirgizia, Tadzhikistan and Turkmenistan were the only republics in the Soviet Union in which the number of kolkhoz households did not decrease but increased between 1960 and 1970. Figures for Tadzhikistan show that between 1939 and 1959 the number of people actually living on kolkhozes remained the same, whereas between 1959 and 1964 the number rose by 24 percent.[123] Demographically the situation resembles that described by Street in the 20th century Black Belt and by Beckford for other plantation societies. It poses important choices for the Soviet leadership, whether or not the latter wishes to face them.

The Dilemmas of Development

The official response

What will the future effect of declining agricultural employment and mounting rural population pressure be? The answer to this question depends greatly upon the economic policy choices that must be made in the 1970's. There is little evidence that the Soviet leadership has yet adopted any basically new policy with respect to the Central Asian *economy* intended to meet the challenge created by the gradual transformation of cotton *production units* and the high birthrate. As late as 1964, it was possible for the following remarkable interpretation of Soviet policy to be printed in Isupov's important work on nationality demography:

> The climatic conditions and specific features of agricultural production in the republics of Central Asia and the Caucasus . . . demand workers with the necessary knowledge and labor habits of farming in these areas. Such workers are, above all, the native peoples of these republics. The mass recruitment of this population into industry, transport, construction, etc., might weaken the development of quite important sectors of agriculture. In planning the development of the economy, the specific features of such regions are taken into account. For example, in the Seven-Year Plan of developing the economy of the U.S.S.R. for 1959–1965, it is indicated that the Uzbek SSR will continue in the future to be the main cotton base of the country. Therefore, basic attention in Uzbekistan will continue to be devoted to the development of cotton growing.[124]

The implications of Isupov's statement are, perhaps, somewhat misleading. Since he articulated this rationale for a plantation economy there *has* been an attempt to diversify the Central Asian crop structure, even if this new emphasis was largely forced upon the Soviet leadership by soil exhaustion, the spread of wilt, and food supply shortages. Nevertheless, there has been no abandonment of the cotton *kompleks* in agriculture. In the nonagricultural sector, industrial development is an observable fact. But much of this industry is strictly cotton related: ginning, the textile industry, agricultural machine building, and so forth. Some newer and much-publicized high priority industry is not cotton related but what is *its* nature? This is the question which Central Asian economists, inferentially, are asking. Does it contribute to well-rounded regional growth and employment, or does it simply feed resources to metropolitan industrial centers? A great deal of the newer development that breaks away from cotton belongs either to one or another branch of extractive industry or to power production or both. In Turkmenistan, for example, by far the most important industry is now oil mining. It is located away from the main indigenous populated areas and has provided only modest employment opportunities to Turkmens. In Uzbekistan the most important post-Stalin growth industry has been natural-gas extraction, which has been oriented through pipeline construction to the further economic development of the Urals and the Moscow region. And in Tadzhikistan, hydroelectric-dam construction has been the high priority sector, in combination with the expansion here and elsewhere in Central Asia of nonferrous metallurgy. The latter (for example, aluminum production) is a highly energy-intensive form of industry that employs relatively small numbers of workers, mostly skilled. Thus, what appears to be happening is the creation of some new branches of primary industry which do not affect the cotton base of the regional economy and do not provide new large-scale employment opportunities.

Criticism of the Central Asian economic pattern

Since the Second World War there has been a running debate behind the scenes over what the profile of economic development ought to be in Central Asia. Focusing initially on the question of crop structures, the discussion has become broader in scope, taking in the rural economy generally, and the pattern of industrialization. The nature of the debate is indicated by Mukhitdinov's remarks about agriculture in 1957:

> In developing the agriculture of Uzbekistan, we need a *kompleks* not just in general, as individual comrades understand this in the sense that each may have a little of everything for himself, may strive to create a closed economy like a feudal economy; we need an agricultural *kompleks on a cotton basis*.[125]

The arguments which have been expressed can be assigned to two "tendencies of articulation," to use Franklyn Griffiths' phrase. The first looks at Central Asian economic development from an ostensibly "all-union" and urban point of view, insists that all-union and local interests are best promoted by narrow specialization in a limited number of fields, is concerned most with vertical and interregional integration, and defines subsidiary development that supports fields of specialization in a restrictive manner. This first tendency is one that would easily be comprehended by Beckford's London- or New York-based plantation directors. The second looks at Central Asian development from the standpoint of rural Central Asia, argues that rounded development best promotes all-union, as well as local interests, and focuses upon horizontal intrarepublic and intra-regional intergration. Since 1953, authorities holding views of the first type have ordinarily avoided charging their enemies—publicly at least—with "bourgeois nationalism." Instead, we find references to "localism," "national narrow-mindedness," and the like. Proponents of the second type (not all of whom are natives) have been happy to avoid head-on ideological clashes with their adversaries, and have customarily argued their case in terms of declared regime ideals and real cost factors. It is they who have been trying, in recent years, to come to grips with the problems posed by agricultural mechanization and rural overpopulation.

One of the paradoxes of the *current* job market in Central Asia confronting them is that an industrial labor *shortage* exists in the larger cities and on large construction sites despite the surplus rural population. The existence of these jobs, together with the temperate climate and relatively favorable urban conditions, has produced an in-migration of Russians and other non-Central Asians that has been a source of anxiety to demographers such as Perevedentsev, and Central Asians concerned with preserving the national identity and economic status of their peoples. These immigrants are mainly peasants from the Volga region, the Urals, and Siberia.[126] In the specialist literature, it is argued that this influx of Russians is irrational, both in terms of the overexpansion of the large cities in which they settle and the labor shortages in areas from which they may come or to which they might go—such as Siberia and the Soviet Far East. And, apparently, some attempts have even been made by administrative decree to prevent the external recruitment of industrial workers.[127] However, to this observer, the basic problem appears *not* to be politically motivated encouragement of Slavic immigration (although separate enterprise leaders are, from time to time, accused of favoring or even seeking workers from outside the region), but the absence of sufficient qualified native job applicants. Despite impressions to the contrary, the native industrial working class in Central Asia is still relatively small; in 1965, for example, there were only about 200,000 Uzbek industrial workers in Uzbekistan.[128] This situation is partly a consequence of difficulties encountered in recruiting native women for jobs in large factories in the cities. Equally, it is a consequence of inadequate technical training.

In past years, the provision of tertiary technical education for particular industries being developed in Central Asia has sometimes been a bone of contention, with native officials arguing that Moscow planning and educational authorities have prevented the creation of facilities needed to train native cadres. More recently, the question of effective terminal vocational secondary education has been much debated in Central Asia, as elsewhere in the Soviet Union. With the rapidly expanding number of high-school graduates, a smaller percentage can be admitted to tertiary technical institutes and the overall key to ethnic group advance has shifted from the acquisition of general secondary education to attainment of technical secondary education. Central Asian leaders do complain that their republics have not received their fair share of vocational schools and facilities. Thus, for example, Ziiadullaev remarks: "The average yearly contingent of workers and employees in the Uzbek SSR in 1965 represented 2.7 percent of the all-union total, yet the share of qualified workers prepared in the system of professional-technical education was only 2 percent of the number of workers prepared in the system of instruction for the Soviet Union as a whole." [129]

However, not all the blame for lower levels of technical secondary education among natives can be assigned to the central authorities. Once again, traditional attitudes toward the role of women put the Central Asian nationalities in a disadvantageous position. In this connection, the chairman of the Tadzhik Gosplan, Makhkamov, recently observed:

> Native girls are drawn into vocational schools quite feebly. Despite the keen shortage of workers in the textile industry, where, as is well-known, female labor predominates, there are very few girls from the local nationality studying in the two vocational schools preparing textile workers.[130]

Another important factor affecting vocational secondary education is a strong prejudice against blue-collar work among parents and students. An official responsible for vocational education in Tadzhikistan describes this attitude as follows:

> In life we frequently encounter the fact that schoolleavers, who, for various reasons, cannot matriculate to establishments of higher education, look upon the labor of a qualified worker as not befitting them. . . . A majority of children in the higher grades connect their future with the mental labor professions (doctor, teacher, scholar, jurist, etc.) or with managerial functions in industry. However, these intentions run at cross purposes with the factual division of social labor and the requirements of the economy for cadres.[131]

While technical education is recognized by Central Asian leaders to be of great importance to their future, even greater significance is attached to relating industry to the capacities and needs of the native people and of the Central Asian republics. In practical terms, this objective means altering prevailing *structural* features of the economy and changing *location* policy. It is a noteworthy fact that Central Asian leaders specifically chosen for their political reliability and lacking any experience in agricultural management have nonetheless come—sooner or later—to express deep dissatisfaction with the pace of rural development. Thus, seven years after the purge of the Azerbaidzhan leadership, the new first secretary and former health official, Akhundov, complained before the Central Committee:

> There are now about one thousand kolkhozes [in Azerbaidzhan—G. H.], but four thousand populated points. In 50 percent of these populated points, there are 25 to 100 residents. Naturally, there are no public facilities there, no water, schools, hospitals, polyclinics, clubs, heating. . . .
>
> Twenty-six percent of our able-bodied population is engaged in housework and private farming. Yet a process of releasing people is taking place as a result of the expansion of mechanization. Thus we have cotton brigades with 12 people, 25 people and 60 people working in them. Tomorrow, if the brigade size is reduced to 12 people as a result of expanding the mechanization of labor and raising productivity, many people will be released. Either it is necessary to develop other branches of agriculture, or it is necessary to put industrial units in the raion centers and villages. . . .
>
> We have a great natural population increase. In 1964 it was 2.5 times higher than the all-union natural increase. Therefore, it is necessary to build food enterprises and enterprises in light industry and non-metal-intensive machine-building. In 1963, 42 percent of the population was engaged in agriculture. Therefore, comrades, it seems to us incorrect to apply a single standard in making allocations to all the republics for housing and children's institutions.[132]

At the same Central Committee Plenum, the Kirgiz first secretary, Usubaliev, a propagandist who came to power in the purge of 1961, delivered an even more scathing indictment of the treatment received by the rural population of Kirgizia.

Authorities concerned with rural employment consistently argue that urgent steps must be taken to bring industry into the rural areas and smaller towns where the new jobs will be accessible to native people, who, as we have seen, are still relatively immobile. The key issue here is the location of light industry. In Uzbekistan (as in the other Central Asian republics), light industry—with the exception of cotton ginning—is distributed highly unevenly among the cities and towns. The lion's share is located in the Tashkent and Fergana regions, and only in these regions is there a good mixture of branches.[133] The arguments put forward in favor of shifting the locational pattern of light industry are both ideological and practical. The ideological arguments, which apply to the structure of industry, as well as its location within Uzbekistan, are built up from quotations from Marx, Engels, Lenin, and recent party programmatic statements.[134] The practical arguments start with a rejection of the rationale behind the prevailing location policy, namely that light industry should be located where there is an "appropriate raw material base and dense consumption." It is asserted, on the contrary, that other factors are—that is to say, should be—more decisive. The first is available labor: "The presence of labor resource reserves and the problem of their fuller and more rational utilization under conditions prevailing in Uzbekistan serve as determining factors in the location of light industry." A second, and related factor is the opportunity that industry located in the smaller towns provides to establish an economic metabolism between the urban economy and the surrounding countryside and to accelerate interaction between the two. And the third factor is the lower social overhead cost said to characterize development of light industry in smaller towns as compared with large urban agglomerations like Tashkent.[135] Before light industry can be developed anywhere, however, decisions on the *structure* and rate of industrial development must be taken.

The basic structural issues are the extent of desirable closure in the Central Asian economy, the degree of labor-intensive versus energy-intensive industry, and the closely related problem of light versus heavy industry. The general preference of Central Asian authorities for light industry is qualified by support for greater regional economic self-reliance. A good example of this point has been the attempt for many years to justify switching over to full-cycle production at Central Asia's steel mill, the Uzbek Metallurgical Factory located in Begovat. Another example has been support for more rapid development of the chemical industry. It is sometimes not appreciated in the West how significantly the discovery of vast quantities of natural gas in the Bukhara region transformed the economic *potential* of Central Asia, not only by expanding the region's fuel and power base, but also by providing the ideal raw material for developing the petrochemical industry—making possible great industrial diversification and a substantial reduction of manufactured imports.

An important argument for greater closure has been the high cost of interregional transportation—a cost frequently concealed by discriminatory freight rates and irrational wholesale prices. A crucial case in point has been the cost of shipping cotton. Through a subsidy system financed by cotton factories in Central Asia, the price for cotton paid by a textile plant in Moscow or Ivanovo is identical with that paid—for example—by the Tashkent Textile Combine to its next-door neighbor, the Tashkent Cotton Factory.[136] The role played by this remarkable example of plantation pricing in restricting Central Asia to primary processing of cotton should not be underestimated.

The case for expanding light industry more rapidly has been persuasively put for a number of years by the chairman of the Uzbek State Planning Commission, N. S. Ziiadulleav, supported by still more prominent officials such as the chairman of the Council of Ministers, Kurbanov.[137] In an article published in 1971, Ziiadullaev expressed his thoughts on light industry rather frankly:

> Uzbekistan produces 70 percent of all-union output of cotton lint, 38 percent of raw silk, and 90 percent of kenaf fiber. Yet only 2.8 percent of cotton cloth manufactured in the country, 2.7 percent of clothes and shoes, 2.6 percent of knitwear and 2.1 percent of stockings and socks are produced here, while the steadily growing share of the republic in the population of the U.S.S.R. reached 5 percent in 1970. By quantity of output per capita of light industry products, Uzbekistan occupies one of the last places in the Soviet Union. . . .
>
> Just in the past five-year plan, the average tempos of growth in output of light industry were 8.5 percent for the union as a whole, but 3.6 percent for Uzbekistan. . . .
>
> During the past 35 years, not a single cotton textile combine has been built in the Uzbek SSR. Up to now, there are no enterprises for manufacturing woolen fabrics and blankets. There are few knitwear, garment and shoe factories. . . .
>
> During the last five-year plan, the target for capital investment in light industry in the Uzbek SSR was fulfilled by about 75 percent, for starting up new capacity—by 35 percent. . . .
>
> In 1969–71, 15 new enterprises were supposed to be built and 8 existing enterprises reconstructed. In actual fact, only 3 are being built and 2 reconstructed. In 1971, 36 enterprises ought to have been designed, but in reality, only 5 are being designed.[138]

Ziiadullaev went on to argue that full capacity for the primary processing of cotton should be created immediately; that light industry capacity in Uzbekistan should be expanded to cover 80 percent of the republic's need for consumer goods; that "state economic protectionism" should be introduced to promote light-industry employment in the Khorezm, Surkhandar and Kashkadar *oblasts* and the Karakalpak ASSR; and that the preferential rate of light industry development set for Uzbekistan by the current five-year plan should continue as a "firm long-term tendency for the foreseeable future." In the article, he argumentatively observed that "The creation of a big textile industry in Uzbekistan is dictated by economic considerations and will not entail a restriction of textile production in the historically important centers of the country, inasmuch as it will proceed utilizing only part of the increased procurements of cotton and other raw materials. The Uzbek SSR will continue to supply, in expanding volumes, its traditional raw material to many union republics and friendly countries." [139]

Central Asia: A Plantation Economy?

Plantation economy and plantation society

In using the Plantation Economy model as a framework for analyzing problems of cotton mechanization in Soviet Central Asia, we are implicitly comparing this region with those studied by Beckford: primarily Caribbean, African, Southeast Asian and Oceanic areas capitalistically developed with immigrant indentured (or slave) black, Indian, or Chinese labor. If the "fit" of the model, despite all the obvious contrasts of circumstance, indicates a surprising structural congruence between Central Asia and other plantation regions, its measure of inapplicability points to aspects of the Central Asian case which deserve special attention.

It is apparent that the "plantation economy" features of Beckford's model more closely approximate the Central Asian experience than do the "plantation society" ones. The existence of private plots together with the semi-free market constitute an important exception to this generalization, and these phenomena indeed have had a continuing influence upon the operation of the system. Nevertheless, in terms of the general pattern of ownership, decision making, crop structure, production process, sales, financing, land control, primary processing and rural development, Soviet Central Asia fits the "plantation economy" model quite well. This pattern has not only kept the peasant sector in check, but—from the Central Asian standpoint—has been the source of much economic waste and human hardship. The basic *trends* characteristic of plantation economies have also appeared in Central Asia. Thus, we see an expansion of state-owned and "socially"-farmed irrigated acreage with a relative decline of the already small, yet highly productive private-plot land; and increase in mechanization; a continuing farm labor shortage *with* rising rural underemployment; and the building up of a large potential migrant wave. But these trends have *not* proven powerful enough by themselves to restructure the system from within. The official mechanization campaign has sought to rationalize production units without fundamentally altering the entire regional economy; it is eradicating one kind of hard physical labor without upsetting the "dynamic equilibrium of underdevelopment." As I have attempted to show the arguments advanced by local authorities and specialists against existing arrangements substantially parallel Beckford's critique of the costs associated with the "plantation economy." The specialists point out that labor is inefficiently utilized; farm labor productivity is low; great seasonalness persists; and there is increasing underemployment or unemployment. To put their arguments in Beckford's terms, they assert that the agricultural output mix is wrong, and that the monocrop emphasis supports a "segmental economy" which does not generate sufficient spread effects in the local economy, and does not create linkages which encourage the local development of labor-intensive industry. The prevailing vertical integration of the cotton industry shifts secondary processing to the metropolis, depriving Central Asia of employment opportunities and creating disadvantageous terms of trade. This primary processing role assigned to Central Asia is reinforced by politically decided discriminatory prices and freight rates.

On the other hand, Central Asia diverges significantly from the typical "plantation society." To be sure, there is a measure of congruence. The cotton farm—like all Soviet farms—has imported features characteristic of the "total institution": power relationships in it are highly stratified, its influence extends in principle to all its members' affairs, and it propagates a certain world view. Demographically, Central Asia has the high birthrates characteristic of "plantation societies." And politically it is controlled from the industrial metropolis of an alien ethnic group through a centralized bureaucratic hierarchy that enlists the collaboration of the upper native stratum. But in many respects Central Asia deviates from the "plantation society," and the deviations may have important implications for the future.

While Europeans *did* introduce cotton plantations in Central Asia which *have* been operated by nonwhite laborers, the latter are not immigrants but indigenous people working and living on their own historic ethnic territory. Although many cotton farms have workers who belong to various local national groups, there is no functional equivalent to the tripartite structure of blacks-Asians-Whites. The vast majority of supervisory personnel are natives, and race plays no role whatever as a mechanism of day-to-day social control. Hence, there is no social-psychological tension on the farm and no barrier preventing leaders at the farm level and higher from identifying with the labor force. Instead, the strong family tradition, Muslim culture, and general social cohesion undoubtedly encourage a certain ethnic solidarity between leaders and rural masses. Above the farm, Soviet policy has historically sought to assign large numbers of administrative jobs in the cotton complex to natives. Ethnically speaking, ultimate control at the top *has* been wielded by nonnatives, but administration has been mixed and substantially indirect. Secondary and higher education has by no means been rationed, with an intention of keeping the natives down. Deficiencies in the training and supply of native cadres appear to have arisen not by design, but rather as indirect consequences of the educational planning process and traditional native culture.

One may say, then, that the particular type of "plural society" envisaged by M. G. Smith has *not* existed in Central Asia. There has been no class-caste system of overt "institutional" differentation and sociopolitical stratification based on racial differences, rationalized in terms of a racist ideology. In *aggregate* terms the population of Central Asia has been stratified along urban-rural lines, which—until recently—*did* coincide with the division between Slavs and natives. Social integration between natives and nonnatives *has* largely taken place through common participation in the production and processing of cotton; not, however, because of *interpersonal* ethnic tensions (although these cannot be entirely absent) but because of the relative insulation so far of native and nonnative ethnic communities made possible by effective recruitment of a buffer layer of native officials. The type of "plural society" which *has* existed has been informal and partly covert, based upon the perpetuation of Muslim cultural traditions among ordinary natives and the maintenance or creation of unorthodox visions of the past, present, and future of the ethnic community by native thinkers.

Whither the future?

In contrast to the typical plantation situation, the original impetus for changing the Soviet "plantation economy"—through mechanization—came from the metropolitan controllers. Forced from the top down, mechanization has proceeded despite the "conservatism" of farm leaders and local agricultural officials, and despite the poor integration of eco nomic levers and bureaucratic malcoordination. Yet, the very success of regime's policy of mechanizing cotton growing, combined with the rapid rise in rates of natural increase among Central Asians, has now sharply posed the issue of altering the rest of the plantation economic matrix that has been present since collectivization. As we have indicated, economic trends by themselves have not shattered this matrix. The source of change, as Beckford insists, will only be found in *political* decisions and action. With the limited means at their disposal, some leaders and scholars in Central Asia have been attempting through technical but "non-political" argumentation to expand awareness by attentive publics of the nature of Central Asian economic problems and to swing policy toward greater closure of the economy. Until now Moscow has not come to grips with the broader problem but has simply sought to lower production costs and expand cotton output.

One possible explanation of this behavior is that the top leaders responsible for the strategic policy choices have not understood what they were doing. The circumstances surrounding innovations in policy suggest that swift ad hoc decisions arising out of occasional circuit tours of the Central Asian Republics by Politburo members (inspired by production shortfalls) have been an important feature of the decision-making process. In this atmosphere local leaders have probably not felt it prudent to persist in explaining to persons like Khrushchev or Brezhnev what has been wrong *in principle* with the leadership's policies of interregional specialization and industrial location; nor is it likely that central planners have filled this information gap. Other factors have made it comfortable for policy makers to drift along with the present system. Among them have undoubtedly been insistent, immediate cotton-supply needs, including those of Eastern Europe; the retarded development of the Soviet artificial-fiber industry; the lack of complete demographic evidence of a crisis prior to the 1970 Census; and, not least, competing demands for scarce investment funds.

Perhaps the deepest source of procrastination on the part of Soviet leaders, however, will turn out to be an unwillingness to face up to what appear to be the available long-run options. These are: (1) to grant Central Asia a well-rounded and labor-intensive pattern of industrial development; or (2) to pursue truncated industrial development (for example, stressing primary processing) combined with northern migration by natives; or (3) to attempt to find a structurally dependent pattern of development linking Central Asia to the rest of the Soviet Union, but also generating local employment. The first course of action might threaten to create unemployment in traditional Russia textile centers in the short term, or to play into the hands of Central Asian autonomist aspirations over the long term. The population balance in Central Asian cities is already beginning to swing in favor of the natives and the opportunity costs of maintaining effective European demographic reinsurance in a more closed economic setting will probably rise. It may also not prove as easy as it has been in the past to keep a solid Russian ballast among leading and technical cadres, given the success of the system itself in producing trained native personnel who meet the achievement and class criteria proclaimed in party cadres policy.

The second course of action is possible, but it would confound the expectations of most observers. As we have seen, one of the ways in which Central Asia does not fit the "plantation society" model is that the native population involved has lived for centuries in the region and is culturally rooted to the land. Despite Slavic immigration, it now seems unlikely that demographic forces will compel the natives to relinquish claim to Central Asia as their own. In any event, would the Soviet leaders want to create what John Armstrong has called an "internal proletariat" of Central Asians working at jobs in the Urals and Siberia? Would the Central Asians be technically equipped to fill skilled jobs for which specialized training is not available in Central Asia? And would the Central Asians be willing to leave their native lands for inhospitable regions from which Russians themselves are now migrating to Central Asia? There is little evidence to date that the answer would be yes to any of these questions.

Thus, the likeliest option would appear to be the third. But having one's cake and eating it too by combining employment with dependence may prove to be an elusive goal. The cost at which the optimum mix can be achieved may seem to be too high. The objective alone of locating many small industrial enterprises in overpopulated districts may founder on cost considerations, leading inevitably to a more rapid and less controlled migration of natives to existing big cities.[140] If the native urban population begins suddenly to swell without adequate employment opportunities and housing, the Soviet leaders will be confronted with an unpleasant situation. On the one hand, interpersonal ethnic tensions will probably rise, acquiring a mass base which may well not have existed heretofore. On the other hand, the new visibility of ethnic social problems, combined with increasing white-collar ethnic competition, will embolden native intellectuals and officials to agitate more openly against regime policies deemed to be unjust. Interaction between these two developments—especially in Uzbekistan—could lead to a more broadly based, self-conscious, and articulate nationalism than has existed in the past. It is not improbable that Soviet officials view the rioting between Uzbeks and Russians which occurred in Tashkent at the end of April, 1969 in the light of this possibility.[141]

Notes

I would like to express my appreciation to the following for their kind assistance: Azamat Altay, Columbia University; the library of Radio Liberty, Munich; Ralph Schultze of Auscott Pty. Ltd., Trangie N.S.W.; Harry Rigby, Paul Dibb, and Natalie Staples, of the Australian National University; the Foreign Agriculture Service of the U.S. Department of Agriculture; A. E. Dudko, chief of the Cotton-Growing Administration of the Ministry of Agriculture, Uzbek SSR; A. L. Kuznetsova, chief of the Planning-Economic Administration of the Ministry of Agriculture, Uzbek SSR; Kholmat Marozikov, chairman of the Karl Marx Kolkhoz, Akhunbabaev Raion, Fergana Oblast; David Montgomery, Brigham Young University; Jerry Hough, Duke University; and Liisa North, York University. Val Ogareff of the Australian National University deserves special recognition for help in collecting statistical data.

1. See James H. Street, *The New Revolution in the Cotton Economy: Mechanization and its Consequences* (Chapel Hill, 1957).

2. See David L. Cohn, *The Life and Times of King Cotton* (New York, 1956), 171–184 and Harland Padfield and William E. Martin, *Farmers, Workers and Machines: Technological and Social Change in Farm Industries of Arizona* (Tucson, 1965).

3. See Street, *The New Revolution in the Cotton Economy*, 107–134.

4. From the beginning, the production of an effective machine harvester was viewed with ambivalent feelings by persons concerned with its social consequences. The Rust brothers, who played a prominent role in inventing the machine, were themselves deeply troubled by its labor-releasing implications and for this reason sought to delay and control its commercial exploitation. (Street, *The New Revolution in the Cotton Economy*, 126.)

5. Thus, a Communist party theoretician, James S. Allen, rejected the argument of Browderist opponents that mechanization would be quickly introduced and would by accelerating the wartime migration of Negroes to the North, make it unrealistic to view the Negro question as one of incipient Black Belt nationhood:

> If cotton production is to be concentrated upon fewer and larger machine farms, this would mean the displacement not only of the croppers and tenants upon the plantations but also of many small producers no longer able to compete with mechanized production. The tenant-credit and landlord-rationing system, which is interwoven with the entire plantation-sharecropping economy and is the channel through which big capital penetrates and controls the semi-feudal sector, would also have to be eliminated.
>
> All this cannot take place in a vacuum. In the North the displacement of farm

producers by machines and the accompanying concentration of farm operations into larger units contributed the mainstream of labor for industry during recent years. In the South the main obstacle is the remnant of slavery in the form of sharecropping. Aside from this obdurate barrier, mechanization of agriculture must contend also with the limits placed upon industry in the South both by monopoly capital and by semi-feudalism. (James S. Allen, "Machines in Cotton," *Science and Society*, II, 2 [1948], 240–242.)

The debate within the American Communist party over the implications of mechanization for the "Negro question" is described by Joseph R. Starobin in *American Communism in Crisis, 1943–1957* (Cambridge, Mass., 1972), 130–135. Full mechanization was introduced least in the states of the Old Southland and progressively more moving west to California.

6. In 1953, for example, 3 percent of the crop was machine-harvested in Alabama, 34 percent in Louisiana, and 59 percent in California. (James H. Street, "Cotton Mechanization and Economic Development," *The American Economic Review*, XLV, 4 [September, 1958], 576.) Even in the regions of greatest mechanization, large numbers of rural laborers were dispensed with only gradually: "Whereas the growth of Cotton Belt agriculture was based historically upon chattel labor, the cotton industries of Arizona and the Southwest developed around mechanized technologies that alternated seasonally with massive labor populations not attached to the land." (Padfield and Martin, *Farmers, Workers and Machines: Technological and Social Change in Farm Industries of Arizona*, 88–90.)

An initial limiting technical factor, and one which inhibited the manufacture of mechanical harvesters, was that regional soil and climatic differences impose varying parameters upon the machines and may make their use difficult or even impossible under certain (e.g., muddy) conditions. The effectiveness of harvesters drops off rapidly if there are weeds in the fields, and they will not work at all unless the leaves have been removed from the cotton plants with chemical defoliants. Finally, strains of cotton must be available (suited to the specific local climatic and soil conditions) in which the bolls ripen more or less simultaneously; the machine—unlike hand pickers—cannot make unlimited passes over the field.

The most important financial factor restricting the introduction of harvesters in America has been the relatively high cost of machines, against labor. Capital investment costs for mechanical harvesting are high, and where a pool of low-paid workers has been available, there has been little incentive to mechanize. This consideration was especially true in humid regions where manual weed control was required; in order to keep the labor force needed for weeding on hand, it was necessary to provide harvesting jobs as well. Because machines miss some plants and knock the bolls off others, the yields (and hence the gross income) from machine-picked fields are lower than those received from hand-picked. There is also a loss of grade with machine-picked cotton: it is dirtier, wetter, and harder to process.

The fundamental socio-political factor slowing down mechanization was the existence of a plantation society; that is to say, social structures which generated a supply of low-cost labor—black and poor-white sharecropping and tenancy plus segregation and racial discrimination in the South, and migrant Mexican or reservation Indian labor in the Southwest. (See Street, "Cotton Mechanization and Economic Development," 573–75.) These structures are marked by what Street describes as the "demographic characteristics of a predominantly rural culture which has begun to be affected by technologically more advanced areas." Birth rates remain high, mortality rates drop, the population rapidly expands, and—if no outflow occurs—there is a tendency for the region "to oversupply itself with farm labor, leading to unemployment and substantial, though less apparent underemployment."

(*Ibid.*, p. 572.) In both the South and Southwest, planters fought to preserve these structures through political action. Other factors retarding mechanization included an unwillingness or inability of planters to acquire the specialized knowledge needed to operate a mechanized farm and a willingness on the part of some farm operators to phase mechanization in slowly in order to dampen unemployment and hardship among displaced pickers.

7. See Harry C. Dillingham and David F. Sly, "The Mechanical Cotton-Picker, Negro Migration, and the Integration Movement," *Human Organization*, XXV, 4 (Winter, 1966).

8. For the purposes of this paper Azerbaidzhan is grouped with the four other republics as belonging to Central Asia. Kazakhstan, which produces only a small amount of cotton, is not considered; nor are Armenia and the Ukraine, where some cotton used to be grown.

9. See Alec Nove and J. A. Newth, *The Soviet Middle East* (New York, 1967) and Charles K. Wilber, *The Soviet Model and Underdeveloped Countries* (Chapel Hill, 1969).

10. George L. Beckford, *Persistent Poverty: Underdevelopment in Plantation Economies of the Third World* (London, 1972).

11. Beckford justifies applying the notions of "export" to the produce of the American South and Brazilian Northeast in *ibid.*, 6–7.

12. See J. S. Furnivall, *Colonial Policy and Practice* (New York, 1956), and M. G. Smith, *The Plural Society in the British West Indies* (Berkeley and Los Angeles, 1965).

13. Beckford, *Persistent Poverty,* 216.

14. *Ibid.*

15. *Ibid.*, 86.

16. See Ian Matley, "Agricultural Development," in Edward Allworth, ed., *Central Asia: A Century of Russian Rule* (New York, 1967) and "The Golodnaya Steppe: A Russian Irrigation Venture in Central Asia," *The Geographical Review*, LX (July, 1970), 328–337; John Whitman, "Turkestan Cotton in Imperial Russia," *American Slavic and East European Review*, XV (1956), 190–205; Seymour Becker, *Russia's Protectorates in Central Asia: Bukhara and Khiva, 1865–1924* (Cambridge, Mass., 1968), 169–191; and Richard A. Pierce, *Russian Central Asia, 1867–1917* (Berkeley, 1960), 163–171.

17. See Alexander G. Park, *Bolshevism in Turkestan, 1917–1927* (New York, 1957), 311–316; Matley, "The Golodnaya Steppe . . . ," 339; and Arkadius Kahan, The Collective Farm System in Russia: Some Aspects of its Contribution to Soviet Economic Development," in Carl Eicher and Lawrence Witt, eds., *Agriculture in Economic Development* (New York, 1964), 262.

18. Cotton, the basic substance for satisfying these needs, was also a source of margarine, cooking oil, and livestock fodder, as well as an essential industrial raw material used in many different ways.

19. See John L. Sinclair, *The Production, Marketing and Consumption of Cotton* (New York, 1968), Chaps. 2–4.

20. The significant imports of long-staple cotton from Egypt since 1955 can be partly explained by political considerations but equally by the fact that climatic factors restrict the domestic production of long-staple cotton, with its desired technical properties, to Turkmenistan and Tadzhikistan—and these republics have been unable to satisfy Soviet demand. For Soviet-Egyptian cotton trade see Mohamed Youssef El-Sarki, *La monoculture du cotton en Egypte et le developpment economique* (Geneva, 1964), Chap. 3.

21. See the references by the USSR minister of agriculture, V. V. Matskevich, in *Materialy ob'edinennoi nauchnoi sessii po khlopkovodstva, sostoiavsheisia v. g. Tashkente 15–21 oktiabria 1957 g* (Tashkent, 1958), III, 228 and by the USSR Deputy minister of agriculture, D. R. Rasulov, in P. N. Besedin, ed., *Khlopkovodstvo v SSSR* (Moscow, 1958), 16.

22. See L. Grigor'ev and M. Aksentsova, "Sovetskaia tekstil'naia promyshlennost' i vneshnaia torgovlia tekstil'nymi tovarami i syr'em," *Vneshnaia Torgovlia*, 3 (1960), 46.

23. "Gradually most of the intermediate tasks were taken over by a new entrepreneurial class, partly Russian but chiefly native. This group organized buying, local transport, ginning, sorting, byproduct utilization, credit, etc., and the textile firms of the metropolis gradually retired from Turkestan, reverting to the position of purchasers of ginned fiber." (John Whitman, "Turkestan Cotton in Imperial Russia," 200.)

24. Theodore W. Shultz, *Transforming Traditional Agriculture* (New Haven, 1964), 123–128.

25. Albert O. Hirshman, *Exit, Voice and Loyalty* (Cambridge, Mass., 1970).

26. For the history of one important venture see Matley, "The Golodnaya Steppe. . . ."

27. For an historical review see A. M. Mamedov, *Irrigatsiia srednei azii* (Moscow, 1969).

28. In 1957 Mukhitdinov recalled that between 1942 and 1944 there had occurred "manifestations of localism and national narrow-mindedness in the leadership of cotton growing when all-state interests were neglected in favor of local tasks." Thus, in 1943 the production of cotton had been cut back by over three times what it had been in 1941, and yields dropped by over two and a half times. "This same mistake was committed also in 1947, when, to the detriment of all-state interests, material technical resources and part of the kolkhozniki assigned to cotton growing were diverted to other local goals." (*Materialy ob'edinennoi nauchnoi sessii po khlopkovodstva,* . . . 31.) See also B. A. Tulepbaev, *Osushchestvlenie leninskoi agrarnoi politiki partii v respublikakh srednei azii* [Moscow, 1967], 174–176.)

29. In 1967 the percent profitability of various crops in Tadzhik collective farms was as follows: fruits, 81.4; tobacco, 48.4; melons, 33.0; cotton, 29.4; potatoes, 4.2; oranges, 1.9; grapes, 1.2; vegetables, – 18.0 flax – 20.7; grains, – 31.2; fodder crops, – 50.5 (!). The profitability of livestock products (in 1966) was as follows: mutton, 60.6; beef, 14.6; fowl, 4.6; pigs, – 6.0; silk cocoons, – 7.0; milk, – 35.0; eggs, – 39.0. (E. I. Poliarush, "Rost urovnia selskokhoziaistvennogo proizvodstva i puti povysheniia ego effektivnosti," in R. K. Rakhimov, ed., *Problemy effektivnosti proizvodstva* [Dushanbe, 1970], I, 18, 27.) In 1968 only three out of eight basic branches of livestock raising in Turkmenistan were profitable: mutton, 38.5; wool, 9.6; and beef, 3.4. (*Turkmenskaia Iskra* [September 10, 1970].)

30. According to the *premii-nadbavok* system, collective farms received from 50 to 200 percent more than the procurement price for each centner per hectare above the planned amount established in the contractual agreement. The higher the planned target per hectare, and higher the above-plan delivery, the higher the premium.

31. This system established norms which determined how much grain, cottonseed cake, cooking oil, cotton cloth, tea, etc., would be provided directly by the state to the collective farm in return for given amounts of cotton. The collective farm paid wholesale prices for grain and cottonseed cake and retail prices for other

items. Thirty-five percent of these goods were issued on credit, and the rest upon procurement of the crop. Financial advances on the cotton crop have also been made by the procurement agencies to enable collective farms to pay out some income before the harvest. In recent years the short-term bank-borrowing capacity of the farms has been substantially increased. For a description of the *premii-nadbavok* and *vstrechnaia prodazha* systems, see S. D. Rodichev, "Ekonomicheskoe stimulirovanie khlopkovodstva v SSR," *Khloplovodstvo*, 4 (1967), 2–3.

32. For a dispassionate discussion of the problem, see "Regional Economic Policy in the Soviet Union: The Case of Central Asia," *Economic Bulletin for Europe* (Geneva, 1957), 69—71. For a critical account of current terms of trade, see I. Iskanderov, "O sovershenstvovanii optovykh tsen na promyshlennuiu produktsiiu," *Obshchestvennye nauki v uzbekistane,* 10 (1971), especially 18. Iskanderov presents data suggesting that the prices paid by the Central Asian republics for grain are among the highest in the Soviet Union.

33. There is no intention whatever of implying that any of the purges were exclusively connected with cotton growing.

34. See n. 28

35. Tulepbaev, *Osushchestvlenie leninskoi agrarnoi politiki partii v respublikakh srednei azii*, 189.

36. It was decreed that cotton production would expand between 55 and 65 percent by 1955 (actual increase—about 5 percent); that average yields would rise to between 26–27 centners per hectare, a level still not achieved by 1970, and that 60 to 70 percent of the harvest would be machine picked—a goal that might be achieved with exceptional luck by 1975.

37. The joint resolution of August 6, 1956 raised procurement prices from 34 to 73 percent above the 1949–55 level, depending upon grade and staple length. The republic councils of ministers were granted the power to make zonal price adjustments of up to 10 percent—a concession to the realities of economic rent, as was the alteration of the *premii-nadbavok* system. The resolution also reduced farm payments to the MTS, lowered fertilizer prices, eliminated kolkhoz payments to the state for irrigation water, and wrote off existing kolkhoz debts for water. See *Pravda Vostoka* (August 18, 1956).

38. In October 1957 the leading Central Asian political figure in cotton growing, Mukhitdinov, illuminated the background of the Seven-Year Plan when he told a major meeting of cotton specialists about consultations which had been taking place among the Central Asian first secretaries: "We consider that this task—to raise the production of cotton in the country from 9 to 10 million tons—can be successfully solved in 10 to 12 years [1967–69—G. H.]. I can inform the participants in this session that the leaders of the Party, the members of the Presidium of the CC CPSU fully support these proposals and consider it useful to hold an all-union meeting of representatives of cotton-sowing republics in Moscow, in the Kremlin." (*Materialy ob'edinennoi nauchnoi sessii po khlopkovodstvu*, 35.)

39. See N. S. Khrushchev, *Stroitel'stvo kommunizma v SSSR i razvitie sel'skogo khoziaistva* (Moscow, 1962), III, 37, 224–226, 237–239; *Plenum tsentral'nogo komiteta kommunisticheskoi partii sovetskogo soiuza 15–19 dekabria 1958 g., stenograficheskii otchet* (Moscow, 1958), 25–27, 77; *Plenum tsentral'nogo komiteta kommunisticheskoi partii sovetskogo soiuza, 22–25 dekrabia 1959, g., stenograficheskii otchet* (Moscow, 1960), 414–415, 419.

40. See *Plenum tsentral'nogo komiteta kommunisticheskoi partii sovetskogo soiuza 15–19 dekabria 1958, especially* 8, 23, 54, 62–66, 68–69, 72, and 79.

41. Whereas the state would invest 150 milliard rubles in agriculture during the

Seven-Year Plan, the kolkhozes would invest 345 milliard rubles of their own funds. This figure was over and above the debt saddled on the farms by the transfer of MTS machinery.

42. For an excellent analysis of the agricultural Seven-Year Plan, see Jerzy F. Karcz, "Seven Years on the Farm: Retrospect and Prospects," in *New Directions in the Soviet Economy*, U.S. Congress, Joint Economic Committee (Washington, 1966), Pt. II-B, 385–450.

43. *Plenum tsentral'nogo komiteta kommunisticheskoi partii sovetskogo soiuza, 10–18 ianvaria 1961 g., stenograficheskii otchet* (Moscow, 1961), 549. Tadzhikistan and Turkmenistan, in which no grain was procured in 1960, were asked to cover half their own needs in 1961.

44. "It is necessary to increase the production of meat and milk. But this must be done without detriment to the development of cotton growing. It is necessary to arrange crop rotations correctly so as not to decrease the area of cotton sowings. The maximum possible amount of land in the crop rotation must be sown to cotton. How the crop rotation should be arranged, what structure of sown areas should be adopted—these problems should be solved in each kolkhoz and sovkhoz on the basis of the specific conditions of the given farm." (*Stroitel'stvo kommunizma v SSSR i razvitie sel'skogo khoziaistva*, VI, 105.)

45. *Ibid.*, 103.

46. A summary of the resolution may be found in A. S. Pankratov, ed., *Zakonodatel'stvo o proizvodstve, zagotovkakh i zakupkakh sel'khozproduktov* (Moscow, 1967), 88–90. The significance of this decision as appraised by the chief Soviet procurement official for cotton, S. D. Rodichev, is indicated in "Novaia zabota partii i pravitel'stva o khlopkorobakh," *Khlopkovodstvo*, 5 (1963), 1–5.

47. The resolution of the Council of Ministers of August 5, 1965 may be found in Pankratov, ed., *Zakonodatel'stvo*, . . . 90–91.

48. See *ibid.*, 32–38.

49. The May 1966 Plenum of the Central Committee adopted a comprehensive plan for irrigation and reclamation over the entire USSR, which involved bringing millions of hectares of new land under cotton cultivation in Central Asia. See *ibid.*, 6–29. Serious thought also began to be given to channeling water from the great Siberian rivers through Central Asia.

50. See *Pravda Vostoka* (February 28, 1969).

51. The results have been attained entirely on irrigated land, which makes the comparative achievement less impressive than Soviet writers may realize.

52. "Regional Economic Policy in the Soviet Union: The Case of Central Asia." 60.

53. See Charles K. Wilber, "The Soviet Model of Economic Development: A Historical Approach with a Case Study of Soviet Central Asia," Ph.D.diss., (University of Maryland, 1966), 342.

54. For a fascinating analysis of earlier "sexual politics" in Central Asia, see Gregory J. Massell, "Law as an Instrument of Revolutionary Change in a Traditional Milieu," *Law and Society Review* (February, 1968), 179–228.

55. Khrushchev never beat around the bush in expressing his feelings about rural Central Asia. "Do the kolkhozniki go to the bathhouse?" he inquired in Turkmenistan. "And what did they call those villages, anyway . . . 'auls?' " (*Stroitel'stvo kommunizma v SSSR i razvitie sel'skogo khoziaistva*, VII, 179, 188.)

56. R. K. Kurbanov, *Razvitie material'no-tekhnicheskoi bazy sel'skogo khoziaistva uzbekistana* (Moscow, 1970), 73. See also Street, *The New Revolution in the Cotton Economy*, 128.

57. Kulichenkov, "O nekotorykh voprosakh kompleksnoi mekhanizatsii khlopkovodstva," *Pravda Vostoka* (January 26, 1955).

58. *Pravda* (January 16, 1953).

59. See *Soveshchanie rabotnikov khlopkovodstva respublik srednei azii, zakavkaz'ia i kazakhskoi SSR v tashkente 17–20 noiabria 1954* (Tashkent, 1954), 24, 65.

60. *Ibid.*, 155.

61. *Ibid.*, 34.

62. E. A. Koliasin, in *Materialy ob'edinennoi nauchnoi sessii po khlopkovodstvu*, 648.

63. *Ibid.*, 649.

64. Thus, for example, G. L. Volkov, the deputy minister of agriculture in Uzbekistan mentioned above, was serving in 1957 as chief of the Main Administration of Mechanization and Electrification of Agriculture of the USSR Ministry of Agriculture—a key assistant of the powerful minister, Matskevich.

65. See *Spravochnik partiinogo rabotnika* (Moscow, 1961), III, 203.

66. See Kurbanov, *Razvitie material'no-tekhnicheskoi bazy sel'skogo khoziaistva uzbekistana*, 74–76, 91.

67. Interview with A. E. Dudko, chief of the Main Administration of Cotton Growing of the Ministry of Agriculture of the Uzbek SSR (May 19, 1971).

68. The type of harvester most commonly used today in both the U.S. and the USSR has a complicated eggbeater-like head in which horizontally-mounted spindles, rotating upon one or more pairs of vertically revolving shafts, strip the cotton bolls off the plants as the self-propelled chassis moves down the rows. The pointed spindles are a hand's span long, made of high-grade steel, with precision-machined grooves and barbs which must be constantly lubricated to prevent gumming-up. There are dozens of spindles per head, and each must be replaced biannually. In brief, the harvester is a complex piece of equipment requiring frequent servicing and repair and a steady diet of spare parts. One of the largest and most modern cotton-growing companies in Australia, which the author visited in 1971, employed four skilled mechanics on a full-time, year-round basis to service its 50 harvesters.

69. For a typical account see *Kommunist Tadzhikistana* (August 25, 1970).

70. Kurbanov, *Razvitie material'no-tekhnicheskoi bazy sel'skogo khoziaistva uzbekistana*, 87.

71. *Turkmenskaia Iskra* (September 2, 1969).

72. *Sel'skoe khoziaistvo SSSR* (Moscow, 1971), 488–489.

73. For illustrative data on the rent problem, see A. Rakhmanov, "Vliianie prirodnykh razlichii na proizvoditel'nost i dokhodnost' v kolkhozakh chardzhouskogo oazisa TSSR," in S. Z. Martirosov, ed., *Uchenye zapiski (seriia obshchestvennykh nauk)*, (Chardzhou, 1965), IV, 26–62; A. Kh. Burnashev, *Zemel'naia renta i voprosy tsenoobrazovaniia v khlopkovodstve* (Tashkent, 1966), especially 69; and Poliarush, "Rost urovnia sel'skokhoziaistvennogo proizvodstva i puti povysheniia ego effektivnosti," 19–29.

74. See Wilber, "The Soviet Model of Economic Development: A Historical Approach with a Case Study of Soviet Central Asia," 344—345.

75. *XV s"ezd kommunisticheskoi partii uzbekistana, 10–12 fevralia 1960 goda, stenograficheskii otchet* (Tashkent, 1961), 258. Khanazarov also asserted that in 1960 20 percent of the labor force was completely redundant in some kolkhozes, while there was a labor shortage on farms in newly developed areas of the Golodnaia Steppe and Central Fergana.

76. *Khlopkovodstvo*, 7 (1960), 57.

77. *Ibid.*, 3 (1964), 7–9.

78. *Obshchestvennye nauki v uzbekistane,* 6 (1969), 37–38.

79. *Stroitel'stvo kommunizma v SSR i razvitie sel'skogo khoziaistva*, III, 31.

80. A. M. Airumov, "Nekotorye voprosy organizatsii obshchestvennogo truda v sel'skom khoziaistve," in A. M. Aminov, ed., *Razvitie i sovershenstvovanie proizvodstvennykh otnoshenii v period stroitel'stva kommunizma* (Tashkent, 1968), 15.

81. N. N. Shatskikh and A. G. Khadzhibaev, *Ispol'zovanie trudovykh resursov v sel'skom khoziaistve tadzhikistana* (Dushanbe, 1969), 48. The authors note that in 22 selected kolkhozes in 1964 the labor expenditure per hectare was one and a half to two times what it was in sovkhozes.

82. See Kh. Tursunkulov, "Chto tormozit uborku khlopka mashinami?" *Pravda Vostoka* (February 8, 1963).

83. The introduction of the "complex mechanization brigade" was supposed to be accompanied by a reconstruction of intrakolkhoz irrigation networks, at least some rearrangement and consolidation of dwellings, and the initiation of procedures for more precise accounting for the use of water. The introduction of crop rotation in the collective sector without an initial reduction of the area sown to cotton created immediate pressure to expand collective fields at the expense of private plots —pressure intensified by Khrushchev's anti-private-plot-and-livestock statements at the December 1958 Plenum of the CC CPSU.

84. Rodichev, "Novaia zabota partii i pravitel'stva o khlopkorobakh," 3.

85. Burnashev, *Zemel'naia renta i voprosy tsenoobrazovaniia v khlopkovodstve,* 85–86.

86. N. A. Abaev, *Razvitie khlopkovodstva sovetskogo turkmenistana* (Ashkhabad, 1963), 64.

87. Zhivaev, "Nedelimye fondy—ekonmicheskaia osnova razvitiia kolkhoznoi sobstvennosti," in Akademiia nauk uzbekskoi SSR, otdelenie obshchestvennykh nauk, *Nauchnye raboty i soobshchenniia* (Tashkent, 1961), 2, 33.

88. Shatskikh and Khadzhibaev, *Ispol'zovanie trudovykh resursov v sel'skom khoziaistve tadzhikistana*, 67–68.

89. In 1962, for example, 2 percent of kolkhoz money income and 4 per cent of the wage fund was overexpended because of the employment of outside laborers in Uzbekistan. The elimination of outsiders, it is said, would have raised the wage of the average able-bodied kolkhoznik by 50 rubles per year. (*Khlopkovodstvo*, 3 [1964], 9.) A higher figure is suggested by 1967 data for the Tursunkulov Kolkhoz of Iangiiul Raion, Uzbekistan, according to which 134,000 rubles were spent on wages for outside labor equal to that of 292 yearly workers. (*Obshchestvennye nauki v uzbekistane*, 6, [1969], 38.) In 1972 outside pickers received 5 kopecks per kilogram, or about 5 rubles per day for a top effort. (Hedrick Smith, "The Uzbeks Turn Out in Force to Serve King Cotton," *New York Times* [November 11, 1972].)

90. Visiting Bukhara in early November, 1972, Hedrick Smith discovered that "most of the faculty and a vast majority of the 7,000 students at the Bukhara Pedagogical Institute were away picking cotton. "Local residents, who reported that it closed about October 1, did not expect it to reopen until about November 20." (*Ibid.*)

91. In September, 1958, the *Pravda* correspondent for Uzbekistan, A. Ivakhnenko, revealed that in the spring of 1958 the Ministry of Agriculture, "with the knowledge of the Council of Ministers and the CC CPUz," issued a directive that permitted kolkhozes not to buy the SkhM-48. This action, he said, was equiv-

alent simply to writing the machinery off—which did in fact take place. Ivakhnenko also attacked the Bureau of the CC CPUz and the Council of Ministers for confirming the low target for machine harvesting in 1958 proposed by the Ministry of Agriculture. (*Pravda* [September 5, 1958].)

92. Tursunkulov, "Chto tormozit uborku khlopka mashinami?"

93. In 1963, for example, machine-harvested cotton was graded number two by the government agencies rather than number one, earning the kolkhoz 35 rubles per ton less—about a 10 percent loss. (*Ibid.*)

94. D. Erlich, "Ekonomicheskie problemy razvitiia sistemy mashin v khlopkovodstve," *Voprosy Ekonomiki*, 1 (1958), 51.

95. *Khlopkovodstvo,* 3 (1964), 6.

96. S. K. Ziiadullaev, *Promyshlennost' uzbekistana i osnovnye ekonomicheskie problemy ee razvitiia* (Tashkent, 1967), 208.

97. Shatskikh and Khadzhibaev, *Ispol'zovanie trudovykh resursov v sel'skom khoziaistve tadzhikistana*, 118.

98. D. Erlikh, in *Materialy ob'edinennoi nauchnoi sessii po khlopkovodstvu*, 539.

99. *Turkmenskaia Iskra* (September 2, 1969).

100. *Pravda* (February 12, 1954).

101. *Ibid.* (June 6, 1954).

102. *Pravda Vostoka* (January 18, 1959).

103. Ziiadullaev, *Promyshlennost' uzbekistana i osnovnye ekonomicheskie problemy ee razvitiia*, 213.

104. I was told in 1971 by a leading official in the Uzbek Ministry of Agriculture that housing was supplied gratis by the state to new settlers, that new farms received 20 percent more than the regular procurement price, and that settlers received a 30 percent wage bonus. (Interview with A. E. Dudko [May 19, 1971].) The chairman of a new kolkhoz in the Fergana Valley said that new settlers had been especially attracted by: (1) the wage differential; (2) the one-fifth of a hectare provided each family for its private plot and house; (3) anticipation that the kolkhoz would be wealthy in the future; and (4) the priority given to settlers in the queue for cars and motorcycles. (Interview with Kholmat Marozikov [May 23, 1971].)

105. *Sovetskaia kirgiziia* (February 2, 1969).

106. "A considerable amount of land [in Uzbekistan] is salinated and waterlogged (for example, up to 75 percent in Bukhara Oblast), and its reclamation condition is unsatisfactory, which lowers crop yields." (Ziiadullaev, *Promyshlennost' uzbekistana i osnovnye ekonomicheskie problemy ee razvitiia*, 176.)

107. *Ibid.*

108. A. Khamidov, "Material'noe stimulirovanie i povyshenie proizvoditel'nosti truda v khlopkovodstve," *Obshchestvennye nauki v uzbekistane*, 8 (1971), 23. Khamidov was referring to a joint resolution of the CC CPUz and the Uzbek Council of Ministers dated June 29, 1971 that raised the procurement price of fodder crops as a stimulus to crop rotation.

109. Potatoes, – 54 percent; vegetables, – 66 percent; melons, – 55 percent; fruits, – 89 percent. (Ziiadullaev, *Promyshlennost' uzbekistana i osnovnye ekonomicheskie problemy ee razvitiia*, 177.)

110. Nekhai, "Proizvodstvo prodovol'stvennykh tovarov i uroven udovletvoreniia v nikh naseleniia," 177.

111. Robert L. Burford, "The Federal Cotton Programs and Farm Labor Adjustments," *Southern Economic Journal*, XXXIII (October, 1966), 226.

112. *Sel'skoe khoziaistvo SSSR*, 572, 576.

113. Shatskikh and Khadzhibaev, *Ispol'zovanie trudovykh resursov v sel'skom khoziaistve tadzhikistana,* 111. A scathing critique of other rural employment opportunities is presented on 20–23.

114. *Ibid.*, 38–39.

115. N. N. Shatskikh and A. G. Khadzhibaev, "Migratsiia naseleniia i voprosy ispol'zovanie trudovykh resursov," in R. K. Rakhimov, ed., *Problemy effektivnosti proizvodstva* (Dushanbe, 1970), Tome I, 134.

116. L Bulochnikova, "Sel'skaia migratsüa i puti ee regulirovaniia;" *Planovoe khoziaistvo*, 8 (1969), 71.

117. See *Khlopkovodstvo,* 3, (1964), 7; also Shatskikh and Khadzhibaev, *Ispol'zovanie trudovykh resursov v sel'skom khoziaistve tadzhikistana,* 54, 67ff.

118. For example, by William M. Mandel in "Urban Ethnic Minorities in the Soviet Union," paper presented at the American Association for the Advancement of Slavic Studies (Dallas, March, 1972), 2.

119. In May, 1971 officials in the Uzbek Ministry of Agriculture emphatically stated to me that kolkhozniki released by mechanical harvesters strongly desired to migrate to the towns, irrespective of opportunities for alternative agricultural employment.

120. K. Popadiuk, "O sootnoshenii urovnei dokhodov i potrebleniia sotsial'nykh grupp naseleniia UzSSR," *Obshchestvennye nauki v uzbekistane*, 7 (1970), 20–27.

121. R. A. Ubaidullaeva, V. A. Gintovt, and A. A. Grigoriants, "O ratsional'nom ispol'zovanii trudovykh resursov v narodnom khoziaistve uzbekistana," *Obshchestvennye nauki v uzbekistane*, 5 (1968), 46.

122. A translation of the preliminary results may be found in *Current Digest of the Soviet Press*, XXIII, 16 (May 18, 1971), 14–18.

123. Shatskikh and Khadzhibaev, *Ispol'zovanie trudovykh resursov v sel'skom khoziaistve tadzhikistana,* 51.

124. A. A. Isupov, *Natsional'nyi sostav naseleniia SSR* (Moscow, 1964), 45.

125. *Materialy ob'edinennoi nauchnoi sessii po khlopkovodstva,* . . . 31.

126. See Shatskikh and Khadzhibaev, "Migratsiia naseleniia i voprosy ispol'zovannia trudovykh resursov," 127 and I. R. Mulliadzhanov, *Narodonaselenie uzbekskoi SSR* (Tashkent, 1967), 125. See also Ziiadullaev, *Promyshlennost' uzbekistana i osnovnye ekonomicheskie problemy ee razvitiia*, 207.

127. A resolution of the Council of Ministers of Uzbekistan (probably approved after 1964) is mentioned that forbade the recruiting of individuals living outside Tashkent for jobs in the city. See Mulliadzhanov, *Narodonaselenie uzbekskoi SSR*, 127.

128. *Obshchestvennye nauki v uzbekistane*, 7 (1967), 29.

129. Ziiadullaev, *Promyshlennost' uzbekistana i osnovnye ekonomicheskie problemy ee razvitiia*, 202.

130. *Kommunist Tadzhikistana* (October 4, 1969).

131. *Ibid.* (May 13, 1970).

132. *Plenum tsentral'nogo komiteta kommunisticheskoi partii sovetskogo soiuza 24–26 marta 1965 goda, stenograficheskii otchet*, 124–125.

133. See N. Ziiadullaev, "K voprosu o sovershenstvovanii razmeshcheniia legkoi promyshlennosti uzbekistana," *Obshchestvennye nauki v uzbekistane,* 6 (1967), 40–45. Elsewhere Ziiadullaev points out that the Tashkent Textile Combine alone produces 90 percent of the cotton cloth manufactured in Uzbekistan. (*Promyshlennost' uzbekistana i osnovyne ekonomicheskie problemy ee razitiia,*

220.) At this large enterprise, "almost 90 percent of the workers are persons who have come from other republics of the country." (A. Mutalov, "Problemy razmeshcheniia i vybora ratsional'nykh razmerov predpriiatii khlopchatobumazhnoi promyshlennosti UzSSR," *Obshchestvennye nauki v uzbekistane*, 5 [1969], 18.)

134. See Ziiadullaev, *Promyshlennost' uzbekistana i osnovnye ekonomicheskie problemy ee razvitiia*, 216–219.

135. T. R. Mirzaev and N. M. Faiziev, "K voprosu razmeshcheniia otraslei legkoi pramyshlennosti v malykh i srednei gorodakh." *Obshchestvennye nauki v uzbekistane*, 10 (1971), 11–15.

136. Railway shipping exepnses to the destination (e.g., to Ivanovo) are paid by the cotton factory. The cotton factory is then reimbursed out of a special fund administered for this purpose by "Soiuzglavlepromsyr'e." The fund, in turn, is generated from yearly payments into it by the cotton factories equivalent to 2 percent of their sales. The textile mill, wherever it is located, pays only the standard wholesale price for its cotton. (Iskanderov, "O sovershenstvovanii optovykh tsen na promyshlennuiu produktsiiu," 18–19.)

137. For example, see Kurbanov's speech at the 23rd Congress of the CPSU, in which he links the problem of providing full employment of the republic's "enormous labor resources" with rapid construction of new enterprises in the light, food, electronic, and radio-electronic industries. (*XXIII s'ezd kommunisticheskoi partii sovetskogo soiuza, stenograficheskii otchet* [Moscow, 1966], II, 221–222.)

138. N. S. Ziiadullaev, "Problemy optimizatsii razvitiia legkoi industrii uzbekistana v svete reshenii XXIV s'ezda KPSS, *Obshchestvennye nauki v uzbekistane*, 8 (1971), 7–13.

139. *Ibid.*, 10.

140. Sinclair's warning is apropos here: "The argument from [the textile industry's] value as an employer of unskilled, urban labor, is . . . of growing irrelevance as textiles production has become increasingly capital intensive. The textile industries of the main developing world producers/exporters have succeeded through their very modernity and high degree of automation rather than any special abundance of cheap unskilled labor." (Sinclair, *The Production, Marketing and Consumption of Cotton*, p. 59.)

141. See Peter Reddaway, ed., *Uncensored Russia* (London, 1972), 402.

CHAPTER 3

Women and Soviet Politics

Barbara Wolfe Jančar

In this, the age of Women's Lib, Soviet women are among the most fascinating enigmas. It is only recently that scholarly attention in the United States has been drawn toward research in this area;[1] but already it has shown that there seems to be a wide discrepancy between official Soviet claims regarding the emancipation of Soviet women and their actual social and political status. Article 122 of the Soviet Constitution grants Soviet women equal rights with men in "all spheres of economic, governmental, cultural, political and other public activity." According to the 1970 Census, women constitute 53.9 percent of the total population of the USSR and 51 percent of the working population. Forty-five and two-tenths percent of all women (as compared with 52.2 percent of all men) have completed higher or secondary education or have incomplete educations. General educational differences between the sexes among employed persons are said to have virtually disappeared.[2] By contrast, women comprise 22.6 percent of total CPSU membership[3] and only 14 women are full or candidate members of the CPSU Central Committee. Ekaterina A. Furtseva is the sole woman ever to have served on the all-powerful CPSU CC Politbureau, and she held full membership a bare three years.

We are confronted with a paradox. One of the central themes of Marx' *Communist Manifesto,* which carried over into the Russian Revolution, was the emancipation of women as the precondition of communism.[4] More women are active participants in the Soviet labor force than anywhere else in the world, with the possible exception of the People's Republic of China. The economic importance of women in the USSR has been exhaustively documented down to the mid-1960's by the economist Norton B. Dodge. No Western country can boast of as many women doctors, lawyers, or machine operators. With such a high rate of success in the education and training of women for a wide diversity of skilled jobs, how is it that, some 55 years after the Revolution, we find women in only token positions in the chief economic, cultural, and, most significantly, political decision-making bodies of the Soviet Union? As every aspect of Soviet life is subordinated to political considerations,[5] the modest participation of women in the CPSU becomes symptomatic of the wider situation. Membership in the party is virtually requisite for high-level decision-making positions. Hence, the low percentage of women party members (2.5 percent of the total female population) implies a low level of social mobility. Three million women constitute a relatively small leadership recruitment pool. Equality of participation in the work force is not synonymous with equality of status and power. While the former may be the precondition of the latter, it would seem impossible to speak realistically of full equality if equality in the vital sense of equal status and power is absent.[6]

It may be argued that the question of women achieving this type of equality is primarily a problem of postindustrial societies. An examination of Soviet data and research on the subject suggests this is not the case. In the past few years, Soviet sociologists have become increasingly concerned with the fact that women in the USSR are not equal to men in the sense I have identified above. The prevailing opinion in the Soviet studies is that women's failure to rise to leading positions is largely attributed to certain passivity towards involvement, despite encouragement on the part of the regime.

My research has indicated that this passivity does indeed exist. The reasons for it, however, cannot be sought in the behavior of Soviet women in isolation. In my opinion, passivity is part of the Soviet woman's response to the constraints imposed upon her by her socioeconomic, ideological-cultural, and political environments. The hypothesis of this study is that the failure of women to rise to positions of status and power in the Soviet Union is primarily the outgrowth of interaction between these three areas. Assuredly, policy making has intervened, but there has been no "revolution from above" where women are concerned. Instead, the ideas of the decision makers have been ambivalent, tending to be easily restructured by feedback from society. More bluntly, an essentially conservative environment has supported the regime in the maintenance of the primacy of the traditional female role.

The Socioeconomic Environment

Soviet policy toward the employment of women has been oriented around three central concerns: economic efficiency; the mobilization of women into the administrative structure; and, more recently, the demographic problem posed by World War II and a subsequent declining birthrate.

Economic efficiency

For a considerable part of Soviet history, the dominant economic theme has been industrialization. The first five-year plans required massive manual labor to offset the lack of technology. The entry of women into this force was an important regime target. The heroine of the period was the mannish shock worker, devoid of any embellishment and dedicated to building the new society.[7] As women were generally on a much lower educational level than men because education had been virtually denied them under Tsarism, they flooded the ranks of the unskilled labor force. Although they did make some gains in the skilled labor force during the 30's, their significant increase in this area came during the Second World War, when it was imperative that women replace men in skilled jobs.[8] Now that the pressures of technological backwardness and lack of manpower have subsided, Soviet sociologists have begun to consider the question of the placement of women not just in jobs, but in positions of status and power. An examination of the data indicates that if job choices are limited for Soviet men, Soviet women have an even narrower range of options open to them in every field.[9]

The chief means to a high-status position is, of course, education. While the Soviet Union may be termed highly successful in providing general education for its women,[10] bias seems to be a continuing feature of the selection of applicants to higher learning. Dodge's data show that the percentage of women studying in higher and specialized schools reached its peak of 41 percent during the war years but declined to 23 percent in 1956. According to recent statistics, it now stands at about 48 percent.[11] The toll wrought on the male population by the Second World War created an imbalance in the graduate schools, which the regime naturally sought to redress by giving preference to war veterans through lowering the entrance qualifications for them and through other measures. However, despite the improved male-female ratio in the population, the figures suggest that the present participation of women in higher education has leveled off by regime design, rather than by female preference. In recent years, the daily press has cited numerous instances of alleged discrimination against women in academia. Some professors have been more outspoken than others. One professor of pediatric surgery at Moscow University, for example, claimed that sex very definitely entered into the "rules of the game" as far as admission to medical school was concerned. Medical institutes made entrance requirements lower for men than for women, he said, because of "problems with women related to marriage, relocation difficulties, and career retirement."[12] On their part, women have also complained in the press of their difficulties in gaining admission to higher education.[13]

Another form of subtler discrimination occurs in the universities themselves. If a woman student becomes pregnant, she does not qualify for special benefits, nor does the time allotted for termination of graduate work change. Requests for time extensions can be made. When these are granted, the mother must leave graduate school until the child is born. Without special benefits, she must go to work to support herself. After she has given birth, and after having lost many months from graduate work, she may apply for readmission. When the requests are turned down, the expectant mother must choose either to finish her work in a hurry or else leave forever. The prevailing male attitude among responsible officials has been reported as hostile.[14]

This type of policy relates closely to another important factor, the attitude of the young Soviet woman towards having a family. Abortion is an option open to a student should she desire to stay in school. A decision to leave would suggest that the woman in question valued her traditional role over her new professional one. Official statistics show that Soviet women tend to marry at a younger age than men.[15] In addition, a recent Soviet survey published in *Voprosy ekonomiki* suggested that most women want to have at least one child. But the 1968 sampling of 22 Ukrainian factories found that only 3 percent of the pregnancies of women who had one child ended in birth. Women who already had two children invariably sought an abortion. Of those that did give birth, 70 percent did not return to their jobs for one year.[16] Such data give substance to the view that the family has priority over a professional career in the Soviet girl's eyes.

On its part, the regime has consistently laid a great emphasis on motherhood, both through its grants to mothers with large families and its awards for "heroine mother" and other similar medals.[17] When seen in this context, regime policy towards the sexes in the educational world would appear to exert a negative influence on the internalization by women of a strong professional identity. Thus, it should come as no surprise to learn that proportionately few Soviet women finish higher education compared with their total involvement in the educational process,[18]

TABLE 3–1 Average Degree of Education Held by Soviet Men and Women

Educational Level	Men	Women
Higher Education	31%	4%
Secondary Education	50	30
Elementary Education	19	66
	100%	100%

Source: Dr. M. Pavlova, *Literaturnaia gazeta* (September 22, 1971).

nor that the average difference in educational levels between men and women is reported as so marked.

A second area where options to women are limited is in career choice. A planned economy requires that somebody do the less desirable jobs and Table 3-2 shows that women fill that role in the Soviet Union. According to the table, the largest enrollment of women students is in public health and education programs. In each specialty, women tend to settle for less rather than for more education. As a result, we find women constituting 72 percent of all M.D.'s, but 93 percent of all medical workers. An analogous relationship exists between women pedagogues with Ph.D.'s (68 percent) and school teachers (84 percent).[19] It has been argued[20] that because of the educational time lag, there simply are not enough women available to put them in high-status economic positions. If such is the case, why is it that women constitute only 23 percent of the total number of secondary-school principals but 59 percent of all assistant principals of secondary schools and 54 percent of the primary-school principals? Clearly, the question here is not one of competence but is one of status.[21]

Table 3-3 underscores this low-status career pattern. Fifty-six percent of all employed women in the Soviet Union are found in three major work areas: health, education, and industry. In the case of industry, there is a further concentration of women in particular industrial branches and job categories. According to Dodge, in 1962, women comprised 76.6 percent of all employed workers in the textile industry and 97 percent of all spinners; 83.6 percent of all employees in the knitted-wear industry and 98 percent of all sewing-machine operators; 62.6 percent of employed workers in the food industry, and 82 percent of all employees in the leather and fur industry. In the metal-working industry, where they comprise 15 percent of the total employment, women constituted 73 percent of the drillers and 63 percent of the simple machine operators.[22] According to 1970 Census data, women workers in the machine and metal processing, textile, and food industries comprised 66 percent of all women employed in the industry.[23]

It should be noted that these areas where women tend to work are also the lowest paid. A beginning medical doctor receives two-thirds of the salary of a skilled worker, while the pay of a beginning engineer (a "manlier" profession) would equal that of a skilled worker. Moreover, the engineer would expect to increase his earnings by at least 50 percent over that of the worker.[24]

In agriculture, women are found mostly in occupations requiring physical labor, such as livestock and poultry raising or vegetable growing. Fifty-three percent of all collective farm workers are women, and Dodge estimates that women represent 50 percent of the total physical labor force of the Soviet Union. By contrast, they represent only 6 percent of all Soviet enterprise directors.[25]

Many more statistics could be given. But these are sufficient to demonstrate that women have only just begun to participate in the status revolution in the USSR. After 55 years of communism, they continue to dominate the lower-skilled white-collar and manual-labor jobs in specific fields apparently perceived as "woman's place." From a limited survey made of the attitudes of Soviet women, William Mandel found that Soviet women in general do not seem to "resent" their low-status positions. Indeed, many may not even be aware of the hidden discrimination.[26] These findings only serve to confirm my thesis that women accept themselves in an inferior economic role, in part because the nature of their involvement in the economy, as I have outlined it above, reinforces this self-concept.

In the first place, the late entry of women in large numbers into the educational world handicapped their chances to compete with men for higher positions. Discriminatory educational policies have contributed to the handicap. Second, the flow of women into certain work categories has resulted in the flight of men from them into higher-status positions. So massive, for instance, has been the influx of women into primary and secondary education that Soviet sociologists share the concern of some of their American counterparts of a possible adverse effect on the development of boys, particularly teenagers, who have no male teacher with whom to identify.[27] Finally, the year that women take time off to have a baby, as well as the time they have to invest in raising children, make them poor "ruble" risks for promotion, even though such time off is permitted by law. From another standpoint, competition for advancement automatically eliminates the woman who "drops out" from her career to

TABLE 3–2 Women Studying in Higher and Secondary Specialized Schools, 1927–1928—1969–1970
(in percentage of total, at beginning of academic year)

	1927–1928	1940–1941	1960–1961	1969–1970
Women as percentage of total student population of higher educational institutions, including those studying in the following types of Institutions:	28	58	43	48
Industry, construction, transport, and communications	13	40	30	37
Agriculture	17	46	27	29
Economics and law	21	49		60
Public health, physical culture, and sports	52	74	56	55
Education, art, and cinema	49	66	63	66
Women as percentage of total student population of secondary specialized educational institutions, including those studying in the following types of institution:	38	55	47	54
Industry, construction, transport, and communications	9	32	33	41
Agriculture	15	37	38	37
Economics and law	36	75	76	83
Public health, physical culture, and sports	89	83	84	87
Education, art, and cinema	53	60	76	81

Sources: Donald R. Brown, *The Role and Status of Women in the Soviet Union* (Stanford, 1968), 38 and *Zhenshchiny i deti v SSSR* (Moscow, 1969), 56; and "Zhenschchiny v SSSR: statisticheskie materialy," *Vestnik Statistiki,* 1 (1971), trans. in *Soviet Sociology* (*Summer,* 1972) 74.

take care of her family. With the equalization of the ratio between the male and female population, this competition will probably intensify sex bias as proportionately more men enter the market for prestigious jobs.

Employment in the administrative structure

Running parallel with the demands of economic efficiency has been the leadership's ambivalence on how to integrate women into Soviet society through their mobilization into the administrative structure. A major aim

TABLE 3–3 Breakdown of Women by Economic Branch as Percentage of Total Women Employed

	1928	1940	1950	1960	1969
Industry	41	37	37	35	34
Construction	2	3	4	6	4
Agriculture	14	6	7	10	9
Transport and communications	4	8	8	7	6
Trade, procurement, and public catering supplies	4	11	10	10	12
Housing and communal services	1	5	4	3	3
Health, education, science, and scientific services	24	33	23	24	25
Apparatus of government and economic administration and of cooperative and public organisations	8	6	5	3	3
Other	2	2	2	3	4

Sources: *Zhenshchiny i deti v SSSR*, 83 and *Zhenshchiny v SSSR*, 64–65.

of the Russian Revolution was the radical transformation of a primarily traditional society. The tempo and intensity of this transformation required that women move from the home into the public world as rapidly as possible. The situation was particularly acute in Central Asia, where the Soviet party especially wanted to hasten the process of modernization. The leadership thus made a special effort to attract Asian women into the Communist party, but it made no specific commitment about women sharing power and status once they had been recruited.

Anthropologists Stephen and Ethel Dunn concluded in 1967 that despite all their attempts, the Soviet leaders had failed to draw Central Asian women into industry.[28] Another study indicated that the low participation of women in the Central Asian Communist parties was a product of this failure. In Uzbekistan, one woman in 70 is a party member; in Tadzhikistan, one in 67; and in Kirghizia, one in 57.[29] As of 1971, there were not quite 13,000 women in the Turkmen party representing only 18.4 percent of the total membership. Of these women, 696 were reported as heading primary party organizations.[30] The Soviets appear to have credited the strength of traditional social values for the persistence of this negative situation. Even where women are employed in large numbers in industry and the administration, they have been criticized for not being a vocal or active force. According to *Kommunist Tadzhikistana,* 50 percent of the labor force in Tadzhikistan are women, while 50 percent of all women employed have completed secondary or higher education. Less than 5 percent are leaders in their communities.[31]

Those that do make it to the top are given considerable publicity. In a limited sense, the increased percentages of Central Asian women in the professions and more particularly the government administration do represent definite Soviet achievement. Women may now be found as mayors of large cities, and one is first secretary of the Central Committee of the Tadzhik Young Communist League.[32] But the reality of the situation is that even more than anywhere else in the Soviet Union, men (and Russian men at that, if one takes the effects of Russification into account) dominate the managerial and administrative jobs.[33]

The regime, of course, has been completely silent about one very important factor preventing the rise of more Central Asian women to positions of status and power: the advantage enjoyed by women of Slav nationality in the educational world. The extreme case is in Tadzhikistan, where the Slav nationalities comprise around 15 percent of the population and 55.2 percent of the women enrolled in higher education are of Slav origin. Nevertheless, the leadership evidently considers its failure of sufficient proportions to sponsor a series of resolutions on the part of the Central Asian party organizations "to increase women's activeness in communist construction." Among the tasks the parties have set themselves are, significantly, "new emphasis on the ideological upbringing of women" and the "promotion of women to leadership in party, state, trade union and the Komsomol agencies." [34]

At the all-union level, the leadership's success in mobilizing women into high-status positions in the administration can be deduced from the publicity it has given to increased percentages of women in the various state organs. The figures for female representation in the Soviets are given in Tables 3-4 and 3-5.

A comparison of the two tables indicates that the higher up the hierarchy one goes, even in these less politically strategic decision-making

TABLE 3–4 Percentage of Women in the Soviets at All Levels of Government, 1969

Level of Government	Percent Women of Total Deputies
Supreme Soviet USSR	30.5
Supreme Soviet Union Republics	34.8
Supreme Soviet Autonomous Republics	38.0
Local Soviets	45.8

TABLE 3–5 Breakdown of Women Participation in Soviets by Union Republics, 1969

Union Republics	Number	Percent of Total
Total	992,636	44.5
RSFSR	515,631	47.3
Ukrainian SSR	222,500	43.3
Belorussian SSR	36,259	45.0
Uzbek SSR	38,466	46.2
Kazakh SSR	50,284	45.0
Georgian SSR	22,623	46.3
Azerbaidzhan SSR	20,426	44.7
Lithuanian SSR	13,069	44.6
Moldavian SSR	15,961	47.7
Latvian SSR	11,566	48.2
Kirghiz SSR	11,020	44.8
Tadzhik SSR	9,531	45.1
Armenian SSR	11,804	46.4
Turkmen SSR	8,064	42.5
Estonian SSR	5,432	48.2
SOVIETS		
Krai (territory)	880	46.3
Oblast (province)	10,296	44.5
Autonomous oblast	505	43.6
National Okrug (region)	444	45.8
Raion (district)	104,235	45.4
City	115,495	45.8
Raion within Cities	43,839	45.7
Village	623,532	46.0
Settlement	93,410	45.9

Source: *Izvestiia* (March 22, 1969).

bodies, the fewer women one finds. At the top, there are just 27 women in the Council of Nationalities and 26 in the Council of the Union. The high figures in the 40 percents for total female participation in the soviets reflects the concentration of women in the lower echelons. The pattern is identical in the all-union and union-republic councils of ministers. In the 15 union-republic councils there are only 21 women out of a possible 538 members. Of these, only 9 are deputy chairmen of a council. At the all-union level, one woman holds a rather insignificant ministerial portfolio.

It must be made clear that the fact that women participate in larger numbers in the Soviet administrative structure than in almost every country in the world is inconsequential to my argument. I do not deny the great efforts made by the leadership to draw women into the Soviet state organs.[35] The point being made is that in terms of sharing of power and status in the USSR, the proportion of women *decreases* the more prestigious and politically important the administrative position.

A second factor to be considered is the evidence of tokenism in female recruitment into the Soviet administration. Table 3-5 suggests a conscious effort has been made to produce a suitable ratio of female to male deputies. Tokenism would seem to persist at the all-union level. In the Presidium of the Supreme Soviet there are three women members, none of whom is a member of the CPSU Central Committee. G. S. Orlova represents Armenia; Z. P. Pukhova, Moscow; and L. G. Tyrel, Leningrad. However, there are no women chairmen of the councils of ministers of the union republics and no women chairmen of the supreme soviets of the union republics. The distinctive pattern of this tokenism would indicate that both the regime *and* the average Soviet woman are inclined to consider high-status involvement in the administration primarily a man's job. Thus, participation of women in the administrative sphere parallels their participation in the economic sphere. In both, women are represented in large numbers, but always at the lower end of the status and power pyramid.

The demographic factor

A final consideration militating against the encouragement of women toward high-status jobs has been the declining birthrate, particularly in the RSFSR. *Voprosy ekonomiki* frankly stated that "women's increased involvement in social production during the past decade has been the main cause of a falling birth rate, which [would] have negative consequences, including economic ones."[36] The author cities urban employment as the chief culprit and Table 3-6 would seem to bear him out. According to the 1970 Census, the population growth was lowest in those republics which were most highly urbanized. However, this is not the whole picture. One of the most important facts of Soviet life in the last decade, in my opinion, has been the equalization of family size in the urban and rural areas. At the present time, the urban family averages one child, while the rural family averages one and one-half children.

TABLE 3–6 Natural Growth in Population by Union Republic per 1,000 People 1940–1970

Republic	1940	1950	1960	1970
USSR	13.2	17.0	17.8	9.2
RSFSR	12.4	16.8	15.8	5.9
Ukrainian SSR	13.0	14.3	13.5	6.3
Belorussian SSR	13.7	17.5	17.8	8.6
Uzbek SSR	20.4	22.1	33.9	28.0
Kazakh SSR	19.5	25.9	30.5	17.3
Georgian SSR	18.6	15.9	18.2	11.9
Azerbaidzhan SSR	14.7	21.6	35.9	22.5
Lithuanian SSR	10.0	11.6	14.7	8.7
Moldavian SSR	9.7	27.7	22.9	12.0
Latvian SSR	3.6	4.6	6.7	3.3
Kirghiz SSR	16.7	23.9	30.8	23.1
Tadzhik SSR	16.5	22.2	28.4	28.3
Armenian SSR	27.4	23.6	33.3	17.0
Turkmen SSR	17.4	28.0	35.9	28.6
Estonian SSR	– 0.9	4.0	6.1	4.7

Source: Tsentral'noe statisticheskoe upravlenie pri Sovete ministrov SSR, *Narodnoe khozaistvo SSSR v 1970* (Moscow, 1971), 50–51.

Even in the Moslem areas, the large family is disappearing.[37] In other words, the generally high level of female employment in the country as a whole would seem to exert a strong negative influence on the birth rate.

Another reason for the fall in the birthrate would be what Soviet sociologists have termed the results of the "growth of the material and spiritual needs of the population." [38] or just plain putting the desire for a television set before a child.[39] Finally, a less publicized but still important factor, mentioned mainly only in the scholarly Soviet journals, has been the negative effects of small living space on large families.[40]

So far, the Soviet leadership appears to be reluctant to accept the proposition that work and children are at variance with one another. Remedies are thought to lie in the reorganization of work time and in the improvement of work and home conditions offered women. Towards this end, the 24th Party Congress resolved to increase the material aid to families with children.[41] According to *Voprosy ekonomiki,* it now costs approximately 200 rubles monthly to maintain a family of four with two teenage children. One month's maintenance of a preschool child is estimated at 50 rubles. If the family receives a family allocation, the wages rise to 140.2 rubles a month. This sum is not sufficient to encourage women to have more than one child, Soviet sociologists argue.[42] The increased allowances provided in the party resolution would seem to meet the problem only half way.

Money is only a minor part of the problem. A study done in Tula showed that when both husband and wife work, the husband's working day is approximately 9 to 10 hours, while the wife's ranges from 11 to 12 hours. In addition, the husband has the weekend free, where the wife is kept busy doing household chores and caring for the children. The extra work that a woman generally performs daily has been dubbed "the second shift." Study after study by Soviet sociologists furnishes data that the wife and mother still is mainly responsible for keeping the home and feeding her family. More important, modern life has brought her a new burden, supervising the education of her children. Dr. Zoya Yankova of Moscow University's Institute for Concrete Social Research undertook a sampling of 427 working women in Moscow industries between 1965 and 1967. According to her findings, some 65 percent of her sample indicated that they alone were responsible for the upbringing of the children.[43] The survey was repeated with similar results in 1969–1970. To obtain a more accurate idea of the amount of time women spend in the home as a function of the number of children in the family, a study was made in Gorky in 1965 of some 8,000 women factory workers. Table 3-7 summarizes the findings.

Soviet sociologists have also undertaken studies of when women would prefer to work. Dr. Yankova found that because of the demands of home, 95 percent of her questionees preferred to work the first shift.[44] Newspapers published requests from women that a study be made of the advantages which might occur if a woman's work day in industry were reduced by one hour with a proportionate decrease in pay. It was hoped

TABLE 3–7 Expenditure of Nonworking Time (in Hours Per Week) by Women in Gorky Relative to the Number of Children

	Number of Children			
Type of work	*0*	*1*	*3*	*5 and over*
Work time	49.1	49.0	48.5	47.5
Time for sleep and meals	62.8	60.2	58.1	59.1
Time for sleep	50.0	47.0	44.3	45.4
Housework and cleaning	28.1	43.8	48.5	52.4
Leisure-time activities	11.4	5.6	3.9	4.3
Culture and education	16.6	9.4	8.0	4.7

Source: G. A. Slecarev, "Voprosy organizatsii truda i byta zhenshchin i rasshirennoe vosproizvodstvo naseleniia," *Sostial'nye issledovaniia* (Moscow, 1965), 159

hat women would then be able to do their housework within the confines of a normal eight-hour work day.[45] Such a suggestion would most certainly increase the time a woman could spend with her children, but it seems hardly likely to help her in her career. Any time off from work, without some safeguards, would lower a woman's ability to compete with her male peers for job advancement.

A third suggestion has been to increase kindergarten and nursery facilities. From 1960 to 1967, kindergarten attendance was reported to have increased from 3.1 to 9.2 million children. This increase takes care of less than 50 percent of the nation's 20.6 million youngsters below the age of five. Moreover, the bulk of children (over seven million) are enrolled in urban kindergartens, while only 1.8 million attend kindergarten in rural communities.[46] The pressure on the schools has been such[47] that there has simply not been enough room for the children demanding admission.[48] Even if space were available for every child whose parents would want it, the findings of Ms. Yankova's 1969–1970 survey suggest that there may be an association of kindergartens with low status. In this sample, the Soviet sociologist found that the more educated women *preferred* to take care of their children themselves rather than send them to nursery school.[49] On the other hand, their less-educated sisters felt ill-prepared to train a young child for modern life and thus turned to the educational institution. If such is the question, elite status in the minds of Soviet women would seem to retain its identity with the traditional rather than the newer professional female role.

Another of Dr. Yankova's findings from this 1970 study offers a new direction to the question of home versus work. Apparently, her survey found that there was a measurable relationship between a woman's professional and family life. The more educated woman spent less time on housework and was more likely to use mechanical conveniences. The Soviet sociologist stressed that home habits did not depend upon salary but upon educational level. The implication was that educated working women make better housemakers and mothers. Should these findings be further substantiated, the Soviet Union would have made progress towards reducing the strain that now exists for Soviet women between a family and a career. For such data reinforce both the traditional *and* professional self-image of the Soviet woman.

In summation, the structure of priorities presented to the Soviet leadership by its socioeconomic environment has generally argued against women getting into high level decision-making positions. The demands of industrialization brought women into the low-status jobs, a situation which in turn supported their traditional concept of inferiority vis-à-vi men. Women's entrance into and subsequent participation in the Sovie administrative system paralleled their experience in the economy. Finally by inferring precedence for the traditional female role, the post-World War II demographic problem further inhibited women from seeking equal status and power with the Soviet men.

The Ideological-Cultural Environment

The Soviet Union has done much to modify the highly patriarchic submissive concept of women inherited from Tsarist society.[50] However perhaps here more than anywhere else the regime has been influenced by behavior which it cannot completely check: the persistence of traditiona values regarding women in the home and antifeminism at work.

Traditional values at home

The communist ethic has a common tie with the puritan ethic in it outlook on sex and the family. While some early Russian revolutionaries preached free love, and there was much permissiveness in Soviet legisla- tion on marriage and divorce in the 1920's and 1930's,[51] the "glass of water" theory never won wide acceptance among the Soviet leaders. No less a person than Aleksandra Kollantai insisted that sheer physical at- traction unaccompanied by at least a "temporary passion" was unac- ceptable to communist morality.[52]

The question of sexual mores was resolved in the Stalin era in favor of traditional monogamy. Although a far cry from Marx' community of women, the liberation of women under socialism came to mean the equality of women with men *within* the marriage bond. This equality came piecemeal and in stages. The 1944 marriage legislation, for ex- ample, was highly prejudicial to women's interests in its essentially neg- ative position on divorce and particularly in its position on illegitimate children. The state's stance on abortion went the gamut from complete freedom to complete proscription in 1939 to freedom again in 1955. Each change in family law was seen as descriptive of a new stage of family relations. The adoption of the Principles on Marriage and the Family in 1968 reportedly reflected the new relations between the sexes as they had allegedly evolved since World War II. Just how new prevailing attitudes on sex were at the time may be seen by data compiled from a study evaluating attitudes towards premarital sex made at Leningrad University. (See Tables 3-8 and 3-9.) The sample included 500 students and faculty personnel. Table 3-10 reflects the survey findings of attitudes among 126 white and blue collar workers in the Leningrad area.

The tables suggest the continued existence of a double standard of sexual values for the highly educated and less-educated groups alike. In Table 3-8, it is interesting to note that both men and women were more traditional in their attitudes towards premarital sex than their profes-

TABLE 3–8 Sex Judgment of Students and Professional People of Leningrad University, 1968

Sex Judgment	Students		Professional People	
	Men	*Women*	*Men*	*Women*
Approve	53.0%	38.0%	62.0%	55.0%
Condemn	16.0	27.0	14.0	7.0
Indefinite	31.0	35.0	24.0	38.0
	100.0%	100.0%	100.0%	100.0%

TABLE 3–9 Age of Onset of Active Sex Life

	Men	Women
Before 16	10.3%	1.7%
16–18	42.2	12.8
19–21	32.8	50.4
22–24	13.1	27.3
Over 24	1.6	7.8
Total	100.0%	100.0%

TABLE 3–10 Approval of Premarital Sex for Self and Partner (percent)

	For Self		For Partner	
	with loved one	*with acquaintance*	*with loved one*	*with acquaintance*
Men	91.0	60.0	30.0	60.0
Women	81.0	14.0	48.0	41.0

Source: S. I. Golod, "Sociological Problems of Sexual Morality," publication of the Philosophical Faculty, Leningrad University (1968), trans. in *Soviet Review,* XI, 2 (Summer, 1970), 136–137.

sional peers, although the men tended to begin their active sex life considerably earlier than the women. In Table 3-10, women seemed to place higher value on emotional relationships than did the men.[53] They were also less likely to condemn their fiances for previous sexual experience. Men, on the other hand, were more likely to feel that sex with an acquaintance before marriage was permissible, but they still cherished dreams of virgin brides. It is dangerous to generalize from such a small sample. However, if these are prevailing attitudes in a large urban area like Leningrad, it may be inferred that attitudes in the smaller cities and the rural areas are even more conservative. It should be remembered that only one-fourth of today's urban population was born in the city.[54] A Victorian moral code would still seem to be part of the value structure for both Soviet men and women.

The regime, in my opinion, supports the image of the pure girl awaiting her true love in the bonds of matrimony. In the 1968 Principles on Marriage, the Soviet government introduced several modifications in marriage procedure, aimed at maintaining the stability of the family unit.[55]

Article 9 makes provision that marriages are to be performed in a ceremony. Prior to registration, a young couple must wait one month to think over the seriousness of the step they are about to take. Despite a great deal of popular pressure to relieve the injustices of the divorce procedure, Article 14 moved cautiously towards lifting the most serious obstacles to divorce, such as the high fees. But divorce proceedings must still take place in court, except in cases involving criminal conviction or where one of the parties has disappeared. Moreover, a husband may not institute divorce proceedings while his wife is pregnant or for one year after childbirth.[56] Annulment, however, can be granted "where there is no intention of establishing a family." Childbearing and marriage are thus closely linked together.

Perhaps the most important feature of the Principles in terms of strengthening the relationship between sex and the family is the ending of the "blank space" (Article 17). No longer does an illegitimate child have to go without a last name. The mother may now fill in the name of the father, her own name, or both on the birth certificate. Paternity may be determined voluntarily or by court decision. In either case, the father is required to pay alimony for the child. The provision does two things. It relieves unmarried mothers of the necessity of being the sole support for their children and thus was heralded as another "victory" in the emancipation of women.[57] More important, by designating male responsibility, the provision discourages the male partner's extramarital behavior which might lead to a child.[58]

These new provisions, together with the restatement of the obligation of mutual support for all family members[59] carried over from the 1944 law, make the 1968 Principles a strong legal prop of traditional values. Despite a certain flexibility in divorce, Soviet law generally supports the view that the family is the primary "social cell" in which "societal and personal interests are harmoniously combined."

There is no doubt that the Soviet Marriage Principles make a significant contribution to ensuring the legal equality of women *within* the home. At the same time, its emphasis on the family tends to support the identification of women with their traditional role. Values appear to be changing, but slowly. The classic image of the Russian mother was the all-suffering, all-compassionate woman with little book learning, whose self-sacrifice was worth all the education in the world.[60] The modern woman is less ready to fill that role.[61] Recently, *Izvestiia* chose to make an example of parental failure in assuming responsibility for a minor's conduct. A teenage girl had been seduced by an older man. A pregnancy was the result. When the case came before the court, the girl evidently felt unashamed of her behavior. The mother also seemed unconcerned, adopting the attitude that nothing could be done with young people nowadays. *Izvestiia* argued that a generation ago, no mother would have let her daughter get away with such behavior. "Can such eternal categories as a girl's honor and a woman's virtue have changed so swiftly?" the newspaper prudishly asked.[62]

The wording of the *Izvestiia* article is strongly conservative. Both the mother and daughter are censured for failing to play the stereotyped role. Why, for instance, was the father not mentioned? Why should the mother be charged with the responsibility of being the guardian of morality? Why not the father? The accent on stereotypes is not unique to this particular piece of commentary. It is present in major research. Even Ms. Yankova's study mentioned earlier, for all its attempt to counteract the mystique of the family-oriented woman, is defensive, enshrining the mother's role. To justify education, as Dr. Yankova does, on the ground of its contribution to motherhood is as irrelevant as to justify it on grounds of its contribution to fatherhood.

The problem is that Soviet men generally support the idea that women's place is in the home, and women tend to follow the male lead. A survey conducted in Kostroma by *Literaturnaia gazeta* found that Soviet men would prefer that their wives not work. Only 24 percent of the male respondents were enthusiastic about their wives working, while 64 percent of the female respondents said they felt that their jobs strengthened their home life.[63] Here again, a job is used as justification for domestic harmony.

Most Soviet women seem to retain the view that the man is the proper head of the household. In a survey of 595 working families in Leningrad, conducted in 1969–1970, Dr. A. L. Pimenova found that only 31 percent of the women questionees considered themselves as head of the family; the remaining 69 percent said their husband or some other male member was the family head. However, the number of women supporting male dominance tended to decrease the younger the couple, with couples over 50 years of age indicating the strongest patriarchal preference.[64] Traditional family patriarchalism in the Soviet Union may be on the way out. Nevertheless, if one turns to the top political and social echelons of Soviet society, he is at pains to cite a wife of a single major figure by name, let alone identify her as having made a noteworthy contribution to any aspect of Soviet life. With such a situation among the national elite, it is not surprising that the popular attitude which the regime has found least susceptible of change has been the male view that husbands should be waited on by their wives and exempt from housework.[65]

In the Moslem areas, the subordination of women to men in the family unit has also undergone some modification as religious ties have weakened. Many old customs, such as *kalym,* or bride money, are disappearing due both to proscription by law and to the fact that most Moslems today do not have the 50 head of sheep necessary to buy the bride. Collectivization effectively abolished private resources. Still, reports in the press of bigamy, bride kidnapping and systematic cruelty on the part of husbands towards their wives suggest that tradition persists. The Moslem wedding ceremony retains particular hold,[66] even over Central Asian Communists though the practice has been forbidden by law and can mean expulsion from the party for party members.[67] Since the Koran taught that women are inferior to men in the divine scheme of things (4:37),[68] there is a long history of male dominance that, despite Soviet efforts in changing attitudes towards women, has yet to be completely overcome.[69] As late as the 1950's, it was still common for fathers to take their girls out of school when they reached adolescence in order to give them a suitable husband.[70] Thus, the breakthrough of a woman like Iadgar Nasrridinova to her position as chairman of the Council of Nationalities and full member of the CPSU CC may well be considered exemplary of what Central Asian women can do once they have come to terms with tradition. But for the bulk of Central Asian women, life continues to be heavily husband and family oriented. Since large families are traditionally considered evidence of a Moslem male's virility,[71] the persistently higher birthrate in the Central Asian republics as compared with the Slav republics (see Table 3-6) suggests that most native women still comply with their husbands' expectations of them.

It would be unrealistic to locate responsibility for the survival of old attitudes towards the feminine role in the Soviet Union solely in the strength of traditional male preferences reinforced by official policy. Women have also made their contribution. Since World War II, it must be remembered, women have far outnumbered men in the USSR. It is only now that the balance between the sexes is reasserting itself. The 1970 Census revealed the following relationship between married persons and their age.

The toll wrought by the war years can be seen from the high percentage of men who are reported married in their 50's and 60's compared with the decreasing proportion of women.

Given such an adverse ratio of women to men, the primary concern of most Soviet women for the last 30 years has been to get and keep a man. To do so, she has had to behave as a man would want her to behave.[72] Institutes of beauty are flourishing in the larger cities of the "socialist" Soviet Union. One such in Moscow caters to some 35,000 women a year. The consumption of cosmetics has doubled over the past 10 years, as the regime has relaxed its strictures on "bourgeois" beauty aids.[73] The indication is that women set a high priority on their femininity, and femininity is closely associated with home and children in the Soviet male mind. The Soviet woman is thus encouraged to see herself as a woman primarily in the traditional role of wife and mother.

TABLE 3–11 Comparison of Percentage of Soviet Men and Women Married by Selected Age and Year

Age	Men		Women	
	1959	*1970*	*1959*	*1970*
20–25 years	27	29	50	56
25–29 years	80	77	76	83
30–34 years	92	88	78	85
35–39 years	95	93	73	84
50–54 years	96	95	47	60
60–69 years	91	92	36	37
70 years and over	75	79	17	20

Source: USSR Census, *Pravda* (April 17, 1971).

Antifeminism at work

Sexual discrimination against women on the job is little different from practices reported in the United States, with perhaps one exception. Soviet women are not considered freaks because they want to pursue a career. They are simply considered inferior, apt to be successful only in certain restricted areas. Soviet men think women incapable of learning to use heavy machines. Male collective farmers are reported as resistant to the idea of women being employed as tractor and machine operators.[74] Male attitudes downgrading a woman's strength are apparently more prevalent in traditionally male occupations than in the newer jobs. While there are virtually no women locomotive drivers, there are a high proportion of female permafrost scientists,[75] an occupation which requires a high degree of endurance but, it must be admitted, a rather low level of skill in using machinery. Again, male officials at the Ministry of Higher and Specialized Education have been quoted as asserting that female graduate students deliberately get themselves pregnant, and such "unprincipled" behavior should not be encouraged.[76] Soviet men like to start their weekends early so they see to it that women are appointed to the committees which meet Friday afternoons after work.[77]

In the Soviet press, there is considerable documentation available about the pattern of antifeminism displayed at Soviet work places. One popular male attitude which has been persistently noted is the theory that women have little initiative on the job and are less creative than men. Women are therefore less qualified by nature for high-level positions. A two-year, in-depth study completed in 1966, done on a team of 13 scientific workers from 30 or 40 years of age at the Siberian Scientific Center at Akademgorod, revealed some significant findings about worker attitudes towards superiors, inferiors, and equals.

TABLE 3–12 Worker Preference for Man or Woman as Manager, Colleague, or Subordinate

Work Role	*Man (%)*	*Woman (%)*
Manager	77	23
Colleague	59	41
Subordinate	50	50

Source: V. N. Shubkin and G. M. Kochetov, "'Rukovoditel', kollega, podchinennyi," *Sotsial'nye issledovaniia,* 2 (Moscow, 1968), 153.

Perceptions of the three roles mentioned were defined by a seven-point scale. It is interesting to note that colleagues were seen as ranking particularly high on scale 2 (work qualities such as ability to attract people, organizing ability, and so forth), 4 (moral qualities such as goodness, modesty, truthfulness and friendliness), and physical appearance. Subordinates ranked high only on scale 4. Neither group ranked high on intelligence, leadership, or aggressive qualities, which were seen primarily as executive characteristics.[78]

Admittedly, the size of the sample is small, but it has some relevance because the participants in the survey were highly trained individuals who were divided almost equally into men and women. Thus, the survey indicates that not only do men see women in the subordinate role but that women have been conditioned to see themselves also primarily as colleagues and subordinates. In other words, in both their family and professional lives, their self-image is one of inferiority.

If this case can be generalized, then we have found an important factor in the cultural environment which would inhibit women from competing for higher status positions. In fact, Soviet sociologists have demonstrated that women consistently choose the easier jobs and evince little desire to advance. In Dr. Yankova's survey sample of 200 women workers, 60 percent apparently had the same opportunities for advancement as men. Yet, in the evening courses considered by the factory management as obligatory for advancement, only 19 percent of the students were women. Other sociologists have made studies to demonstrate that there is little substantiation for the view that women do not make as good leaders. In a comparative sample of similar groups of men and women on the job, Dr. M. Pavlova found that in general women functioned on a much higher level in every job category than men.[79]

Dr. Pavlova offers two explanations of what she perceives to be a lack of motivation on the part of Soviet women to rise to high status and power positions. The first is the conflict experienced by women in delegating priorities. Women, she says, tend to look at promotion from more than one angle. They are most likely to choose a job on the basis of how it relates to their family. As a consequence, they are more readily satisfied by a position in the middle of the job hierarchy. While they would like to advance in terms of their career, home comes first. Second, Dr. Pavlova's own research found that women in authority are inclined to concentrate their attention, as she deftly put it, on "human relations" rather than on "purely administrative matters." In other words, the question of subordination and status vis-à-vis male colleagues was a *primary issue* for women in leadership positions. Dr. Pavlova suggested that the reason for this type of concern was centered on the fact that men in general were not accustomed to accepting a woman's authority on the job. Citing evidence from a Polish sociological study, she concluded that "women in authority constantly have to prove that they can work as well as men, since men are convinced that women are stupider than they."

The traditional value system regarding the woman's role which was outlined above is neither particularly Russian nor a product of Soviet communism. What is distinctive about the Soviet situation, of course, is the direct intervention of the leadership in the reshaping of attitudes, such as the 1968 Marriage Principles, the party's role in mobilizing Central Asian women, and the press critiques of the domineering husband. The data reviewed here seem to suggest that as in the economic sphere, the regime is sending out ambivalent signals. On the one hand, it seeks to strengthen marriage and the family by every sanction within its power. In this context, its view of the female role is highly conservative and supportive of non active involvement on the part of women at work. On the other, it is striving to modify the traditional image of women in the area where male resistance is highest, on the job; the regime's premise here is that inequality of career status ought not to exist under socialism. Women thus are urged towards high involvement both at home and at work. This combination of ideological stress on the woman's place at home and interaction between the sexes on the job has apparently provided insufficient motivation for women to break away from the traditional identification of themselves with the home.

The Political Environment

An examination of the data involving Soviet woman's participation in politics furnishes, I believe, some of the most important clues regarding women's failure to rise to positions of status and power in the Soviet Union.

The illustration below gives the graph of the percentage of female membership in the CPSU CC from 1919 to 1971. The Central Committee of the Soviet Communist party was chosen as the data basis rather than all the leading organs taken together, because membership in the Committee is generally indicative of access to political decision making. Second, the Central Committee has been a permanent feature of Soviet history, while the other organs have come in and out of existence according to policy directives at a given moment. While admittedly, the use of percentages may cause some concern, since the size of membership has changed so radically, it seemed to me to be a useful way to standardize for size.

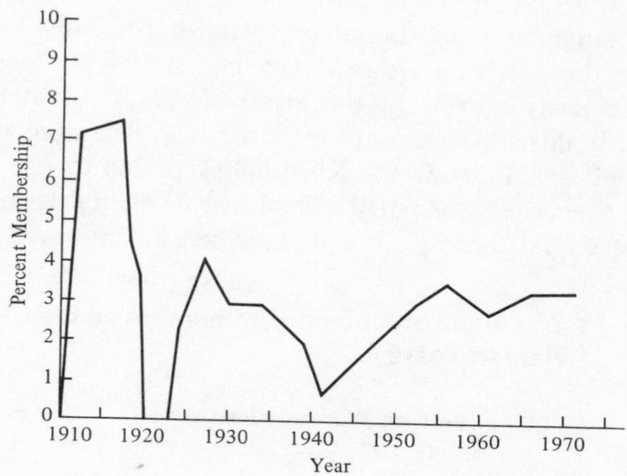

Percentage of Woman Membership in CPSU CC, 1910-1971

It is notable that female participation in the Central Committee was proportionately at its highest during the Revolution. It fell to 0.0 percent during the Civil War period, climbed again, suffered a drop starting in the mid-1930's, and reached another low point in 1941, when only one woman remained a member. Participation increased during the '50's, to decline once more in the early '60's when Khrushchev was ousted. It leveled off at around 3.3 percent at the 23rd and 24th party congresses.

Such a pattern suggests that female membership in the Soviet Central Committee varies inversely with the degree of political crisis experienced in the country. During periods where the survival of the regime is in mortal danger, such as the Civil War and the Second World War, women's participation drops to virtually zero. As the crisis eases, participation increases. One might argue that the Revolution was a period of crisis and thus atypical of the general trend, but membership in the Central Committee at that time was a function of pre-Revolutionary activities. Moreover, the real struggle to maintain Soviet power occurred during the Civil War.

Table 3-13 provides some substantiation of this theory in indicating a parallel vacillation over time in female membership in the CPSU as a whole. There were very few women communists during the Civil War period; their numbers increased until 1934 and then dropped to a new low percent in 1939, after the purges. During World War II, female membership remained proportionately low, rising to only 17 percent in 1945, despite the fact that women then constituted 41 percent of all recruits to the party outside of the armed forces.[80] Great efforts were made to remedy this situation right after the war. The percent of female membership fell again during the Khrushchev period to rise only slowly after that. So concerned was party officialdom to rectify the imbalance of women in the CPSU that in 1966 it launched an intensive recruitment

TABLE 3–13 Percentage of Women Membership on the CPSU, Selected Years

Year (Jan. 1)	Percent Women Members	Size of Party
1922	7.8%	410,430 Full 117,924 Cand.
1932	15.9	1,769,733 Full 1,347,477 Cand.
1934	16.5	1,826,751 Full 874,252 Cand.
1939	14.5	1,514,181 Full 792,792 Cand.
1941	14.9	2,515,481 Full 1,361,404 Cand.
1945	17.0	3,965,530 Full 1,794,839 Cand.
1950	20.7	6,300,000 Total
1952	19.2	6,013,259 Full 868,886 Full
1959	19.5	7,622,356 Full 616,775 Cand.
1962	20.2	8,872,576 Full 843,489 Cand.
1967	20.9	11,673,676 Full 797,403 Cand.
1971	22.6	14,109,000 Full 522,000 Cand.

Sources: Merle Fainsod, *How Russia is Ruled* (Cambridge, Mass., 1955), 212; *Party and Government Officials of the Soviet Union 1917–1967,* compiled by the Institute for the Study of the U.S.S.R., Munich, Germany, edited by Edward L. Crowley *et al.* (Metuchen, New Jersey, 1969), 1–92; and Thomas Howard Rigby, *Communist Party Membership in the U.S.S.R. 1917–1967* (Princeton: 1968), 361.

campaign. In 1971, party officials proudly announced that women constituted 29.2 percent of candidate members and in some places, such as Latvia, Kalinin, and Yaroslav, 40 to 50 percent.[81] These results cannot be considered highly successful as only in some areas was the percentage of women recruits beginning to reach the 1945 level.

It is evident that vacillations in the percentage of total female CPSU membership over time do not correspond exactly to the fluctuations in female participation in the ruling circles, nor do the latter coincide with the beginnings of a period of political crisis. A plausible hypothesis is a time lag between the time of political crisis and the reduced level of women members in the CPSU CC, and a second time lag between the reduction of female participation in the Central Committee and the lowered proportion of women in the party at large. As crises naturally cannot be predicted with 100 percent accuracy, their impact on membership change in both groups would likely be felt at differing points of time after the crises had occurred. It may be expected that the makeup of the Central Committee would be more immediately responsive to change in the political climate than would the makeup of the rank and file, and the data would seem intuitively to bear out this contention.

Tables 3-14 and 3-15 offer some explanation of this phenomenon. Most of the women elected to the Central Committee have no real political power: they are figureheads. The present female members are a case in point, with Furtseva and Nasriddinova perhaps the two exceptions. Moreover, an examination of the chart of all women participants in the leading Soviet decision-making bodies since 1917 (see the Appendix) reveals a high rate of turnover in female personnel. Few stay on more than the time between one congress. In 1971, half of the full CC members and three of the nine women candidate members were new. Of the others, only Furtseva and Lykova go back to the Stalin era; Nasriddinova and N. V. Popova were elected in 1956; Kolchina, in 1961; the rest, in 1966.

This pattern has held constant over the years. Those women who have remained longest or who have held really important party positions have been truly exceptional. The majority of these belong to the first generation of Bolsheviks. Elena Stasova was involved in pre-Revolutionary activity in St. Petersburg in Tsarist times and was partly secretary already at the Prague Conference in 1912. Aleksandra Artiukhina, a party member since 1910, was arrested and exiled many times. She was a leader in the Textile and Metal Workers Union in pre-Revolutionary St. Petersburg. Klavdiia Nikolaeva, another pre-Revolutionary Bolshevik, was

TABLE 3–14 Full and Candidate Women Members of the Central Committee by Occupation, 1971

Name	Position in Central Committee	Occupation
Biriukova, A. P.	candidate	Secretary, Moscow City Committee
Dement'eva, R. F.	candidate	Secretary, Moscow City Committee
Fominykh, A. M.	candidate	Brigade Leader in the pig-breeding section of the "Belovsky" state farm Altai krai
Furtseva, E. A.	full member	Minister of Culture; Deputy Soviet Supreme
Ivannikova, M. S.	full member	Brigade Leader, M. V. Frunze Cotton Factory, Moscow; Deputy, Supreme Soviet
Karpova, E. F.	candidate	Deputy Chairman, Council of Ministers, RSFSR
Kolchina, O. P.	candidate	Deputy Chairman, Council of Ministers, RSFSR
Lykova, L. P.	candidate	Deputy Chairman, Council of Ministers, RSFSR
Nasriddinova, Ia. S.	full member	Chairman, USSR Council of Nationalities, Supreme Soviet
Nikolaeva-Tereshkova, V. V.	full member	Pilot-Cosmonaut of the USSR Chairman, Committee of Soviet Women; Deputy, Supreme Soviet
Poberei, M. J.	candidate	First Secretary Leninsk Raion Committee, Volgograd oblast
Salnikova, E. A.	candidate	Machine operator in the contact department of the Beresnikovi Nitrogen Fertilizer Plant
Shevchenko, A. F.	candidate	Milkmaid on the "Buchansky" state farm, Kiev oblast
Popova, M. G.	full member	Presidium Chairman, Union of Soviet Societies for Friendship and Cultural Relations with Foreign Countries; Deputy, Supreme Soviet; Crane operator in Nahodkha

Source: *Supplement of the Bulletin of the Institute for the Study of USSR* (May, 1971).

editor of a woman's radical journal *Rabotnitsa.* Aleksandra Kollontai played a role in Bolshevik emigre circles and during the Revolution. Her usefulness was curtailed when she sided with the "Workers' Opposition" in the early '20's. Varvara Iakoleva was an old Bolskevik in the Moscow student movement. She was purged in the '30's for her "leftist" views.[82]

It is significant that no comparable women, again with the possible

TABLE 3–15 Selected Statistics on Woman Membership in the CPSU by Union Republic, 1971

Union Republic	Communist Party		Congress Delegates		Woman Membership in CP as Percent of Female Population
	Number of Women	Percent of Total	Number of Women	Percent of Total	
Armenia	unknown	unknown	175	28.3%	unknown
Azerbaidzhan	unknown	unknown	299	22.9	unknown
Belorussia	89,000[a]	20.0%	177	22.3	1.8%
Estonia	18,000	24.6	169	23.7	2.7
Georgia	68,665	23.2	235	23.2	2.8
Kazakhstan	110,000	19.1	407	26.7	1.7
Kirghizia	21,000	20.0	206	24.7	1.4
Latvia	42,313	33.9	180	27.2	3.2
Lithuania	unknown	unknown	219	27.5	unknown
Moldavia	unknown	unknown	220	26.4	unknown
Tadzhikistan	unknown	unknown	unknown	unknown	unknown
Turkmenistan	12,884	18.4	183	24.9	1.2
Ukraine	501,853	19.8	570	24.7	1.9
Uzbekistan	83,000	19.2	493	34.0	1.4
USSR	3,311,000	22.6	1,204	24.3	2.5

Source: Data for this table have been drawn from official USSR census report as published in the leading Russian-language newspapers of each union republic and the reports of the credentials commissions of the various union republic party congress held prior to the 24th CPSU Congress in 1971. These also were published in the leading Russian-language newspapers of each union republic. My thanks to Radio Liberty for its help in finding the data.

a. Approximated figure.

exception of Furtseva, more the typical apparatchik than these, or Nasriddinova, seem to have taken the older generation's place. Instead, tokenism has appeared. It is obvious from Table 3-15 that the proportion of female delegates to the union republic congress was predetermined. Further evidence of tokenism is that women were 30.9 percent *better* represented at the congress than their percent in total party membership merits. By contrast, women are *under*represented in the union republic parties vis-à vis the union republics' female population. As a general indicator, the ratio of women communists to the female population of the USSR is two-fifths that of the total CPSU membership to the population as a whole (2.5 percent as compared with 6.1 percent).

Party officials are concerned with percentages and proportions. The number of women secretaries in the primary party organizations increased from 30.4 percent to 33.4 percent in 1966, we are told.[83] But women secretaries are non-existent at the highest levels. It would seem as if women were easily accepted into low political positions, but pushed into high political posts, not from conviction, but because the party leadership wants it. Then, when conditions deteriorate, women are automatically less pressured into activity at the higher levels and either fall out or are dropped.

The conclusion which suggests itself is that there is something in the insecurity of the Soviet political system which does not allow women to become top executives of the political hierarchy. For all the "oppression" of the former Tsarist world, there were, percentagewise, more women actively engaged in the leadership of the Soviet Bolshevik party than after the Revolution, when the regime made such attempts to "liberate" them. It is significant that in the entire history of the CPSU as a ruling party, only 84 women have risen high enough to fill any of the approximately 4600 possible positions which have been available in the leading party organs since 1917. Only two women made it to the Orgbureau, the Secretariat, or the Politbureau; most only get as far as the Control or Auditing Commissions.

These findings, in my opinion, tell us something fundamental about the relation of women to the Soviet system. Men who have risen to the top of the Soviet power structure have devoted their lives to this goal or have been purged. It takes time to learn the skills necessary to survive in the Soviet political world, and a certain ruthlessness is essential if one wants to advance. If you are going to make it, politics is a full-time job. It is well-known that Stalin kept his officials on call 24 hours a day.

Khrushchev twice was the victim of political infighting when he was absent from Moscow. Once he managed to turn failure to success; the second time, he did not.

Another factor to be considered is the enormous demands made on the individual who seeks political success in the Soviet Union. Becoming a party member means giving up a good deal of your private life. The higher one rises, the more personal sacrifices have to be made at the cost of greater insecurity. Such demands are ill-suited to a woman with a family. Moreover, the devotion of a woman to her family may make her suspect as a less-reliable executor of commands from above. And with Soviet women, as we have seen, family loyalties come first.

In summation, the persistently low ratio of female membership in the CPSU as compared to the total Soviet female population; the small number of women in leading positions, their nonpower-based occupations, and their high rate of turnover in the higher posts all indicate why women have largely remained outside the power structure of the USSR. They further suggest that Soviet woman's acceptance of communism has been politically passive. The reason, in my opinion, derives from the very complexity of the situation presented so far. Both the economic and cultural environments have actively contributed to the continued internalization by Soviet women of a traditional self-concept. This self-concept would seem to set a too-high cost on involvement in an uncertain and ruthless political environment.

Conclusions

The characteristics of sex discrimination in the USSR have been examined in terms of the socioeconomic, ideological-cultural, and political environments of Soviet society. (1) In the economic sphere, the demands of industrialization have tended to bring women into the labor force where they can be most efficiently used, namely in the low-skilled, physical-labor categories. A persistently inferior educational level and the more recent demographic factor have contributed to women remaining by and large in the low-achievement, routinized jobs. (2) Official sanction has supported the survival of the traditional concept of the female role, as well as traditional male attitudes as regards women in the home and at work. (3) Soviet women have been only tangentially involved in the CPSU and have generally remained inactive as a political force. (4)

The continued internalization by Soviet women of their traditional role has left them essentially unaware of the nature of the problem they face.

The picture that emerges is one of a dual exploitation of women at home and at work. Soviet women cannot advance in career if the economic and social conditions for their advancement are not changed to permit the rearrangement of domestic priorities and if they fail to join or advance in the party. Women cannot overcome the traditional male image of them, when they in part internalize this image and thus retain low motivation to achieve in the political and economic world. And Soviet women cannot compete in the political arena if their economic and social status is inferior to men and if their capacity to improve their position is frustrated by male attitudes.

The future looks uncertain, precisely because discrimination against women in the USSR is so pervasive and subtle a part of the system. While the regime has been active in securing legal equality, it has tacitly supported the persistence of economic, cultural, and political inequalities, which in turn have reinforced the Soviet woman's traditional feelings of inferiority.[84] Thus, the leadership may be taking the initiative in finding solutions to the female conflict between home and job, but whatever solutions are found will probably be formulated in such a way that a projected birthrate or the family unit will not be endangered. The regime can make least modifications in the political sphere, any substantial change in which would risk its own power position. The essential arbitrariness of the political environment, in my opinion, imposes permanent restraints upon female involvement in high-risk, high-status careers.

For women to achieve equality of status and power in the USSR, a revolution of male attitudes is needed. The only way to achieve this goal would be for Soviet women to enter the political arena en masse and to compete actively for positions of power in the top party echelons. Yet, politics is the very sphere which has attracted women the least.

The changes wrought in the life-style of women in the USSR since the revolution cannot be denied. They have moved from nonparticipation to participation in large numbers in virtually every aspect of Soviet society, but always at the lower-status levels. Any rapid change in the Soviet woman's pattern of upward mobility in the near future would seem unlikely. Unless women overcome their political inactivism, an inactivism reinforced by their economic and cultural environments, what progress will be made can only come at the discretion of a male leadership that to date has considered the question of women's status and power of low priority in overall Soviet development.

Notes

1. The earliest and one of the best books written about Soviet women was Ella Winter, *Red Value: Human Relationships in the New Russia* (New York, 1933). More recent books are Norton B. Dodge, *Women in the Soviet Union: Their Role in Economic, Scientific and Technical Development* (Baltimore, 1966); Donald R. Brown, ed., *The Role and Status of Women in the Soviet Union,* 1968); and Bernice Madison, *Social Welfare in the Soviet Union* (Stanford, Calif., 1968). Most of the newest research has been published in the form of articles, many of which will be referred to in the course of the chapter. Among the many who have offered comments, I am particularly indebted to Jean Kirkpatrick, Judith Barwick, Ellen Mickiewicz, and Gayle Hollander for their criticisms of the original form of this manuscript and the help they gave me in revising it. My thanks also to Jane Shapiro and Robert Sharlet.

2. "Report of the USSR Councíl of Minister's Central Statistical Administration: The Population of Our Country," *Pravda* (April 17, 1971).

3. I. Kapitonov, "Some Questions of Party Buildings in the Light of the 24th Party Congress," *Kommunist,* 3 (February, 1972), 35.

4. Karl Marx, "The Communist Manifesto," *Marx & Engels Basic Writings on Politics and Philosophy*, ed. Lewis S. Feuer (Garden City, N. Y., 1959), 24ff.

5. See my discussion on the role of the "second function" in the Soviet system in Barbara Jančar, *Czechoslovakia and the Absolute Monopoly of Power* (New York, 1971), 19–21..

6. I am not suggesting here that identical roles with men are necessary for the realization by women of equality of status. In this context, I agree with Judith Bardwick that equality should mean a multiple choice of roles for women, not merely the assumption of the male roles. See Judith Bardwick, *Psychology of Women* (New York, 1971), the last chap.

7. For example, Taia in Nikolai Ostrovsky's *How the Steel Was Tempered* (Moscow, 1952).

8. For a discussion of this problem, see Dodge, *op. cit.*, Chap. 10, particularly 184–195.

9. Jean Kirkpatrick sees a four-point scale of range of role options: (1) Nobody has a choice of roles, including women; (2) Minimum choice of roles for men, but still more minimum for women; (3) Maximum choice for men but lower for women; and (4) all have maximum choice of roles. Women cannot have a maximum choice except under condition (4). Soviet women are, in fact, living under condition (2).

10. Since 1939, the number of women per 1,000 of the female population with a higher education has increased from 5 to 35 (or seven times) as against an increase of 11 to 48 per 1,000 for men. (*Pravda* [April 17, 1971].)

11. Dodge, *op. cit.*, 134–135 and "Zhenshchiny v SSSR: Statisticheskie materialy," *Vestnik statistiki,* 1 (1971), trans. in *Soviet Sociology* (Summer, 1972), 74.

12. *Komsomolskaia pravda* (December 22, 1970).

13. *Literaturnaia gazeta* (January 22, 1969).

14. *Izvestiia* (December 17, 1971). As benefits range from 40 to 60 rubles a month, the loss of one can mean a good deal. (Figures from *Pravda* [October 25, 1971].)

15. Fifty-six percent of Soviet women are married by the age of 24, as opposed to 29 percent of the men. See B. Ts. Urlanis, *Statistika naseleniia* (Moscow, 1971), 45.

16. A. K. "A Demographic Problem: Female Employment and the Birth Rate," research conducted by the Demographic Section of the Moscow House of Scientists, *Voprosy ekonomiki*, 5 (1969), trans. in *Soviet Review*, XI, 1 (Spring, 1970), 76–81.

17. USSR federal expenditures on grants to mothers of large families have increased from 123 million rubles in 1940 to 438 million rubles in 1969. Pregnancy and postnatal leave payments, as well as payments for layettes and feeding of infants have soared from 56 million rubles in 1940 to 788 million rubles in 1969. Between 1944 and 1949, the Soviet government awarded 31,000 "Heroine Mother" awards. The number of awards rose to 94,000 between 1950 and 1959. (*Zhenshchiny v SSSR, op. cit.*, 76 and 78.)

18. In 1917, there were no women Ph. D.'s in the Soviet sense of the word "doktor." in 1950, 7 percent of all "doktors" were women. In 1968, 12.5 percent of those with the advanced degree of Doctor of Science were women. In view of the fact that 58 per cent of all those in Soviet higher education are women, I do not consider these percentages very high. (Figures for 1950 and 1968 from William Mandel, "Soviet Women and Their Self Image," *Science and Society*, XXXV, 3 [Fall, 1971], 298. The 1969 figure is derived from *Zhenshchiny v SSSR, op. cit.*, 75.)

19. *Zhenshchiny i deti, op cit.*, 98 and 100.

20. Mandel takes this position. He argues that the number of female assistant professors, for example, is so low because there is a dearth of qualified women to fill the jobs. Yet, he points out that in 1968 alone, 17.6 percent of all "doktor" degrees and 31 percent of the candidate degrees went to women. It would thus seem that qualified women were available. (Mandel, *op. cit.*, 298.) How is it then, that official statistics for 1969 indicate that only 1,600 women hold the rank of full or corresponding academician, while 24,200 women are employed as junior research associates or assistants? (*Zhenshchiny v SSSR, op. cit.*, 75.)

21. *Zhenshchiny v SSSR, op. cit.*, 73.

22. The data which follow are taken from Dodge, *op. cit.*, 180–181 and *Zhenshchiny i deti, op. cit.*, 72–73 and 102.

23. *Zhenshchiny v SSSR, op. cit.*, 64–65 and 68.

24. Mandel, *op. cit.*, 294.

25. For a discussion of Soviet criticism of the prevalence of women in physical labor jobs, see Lotta Lennon, "Women in the USSR," *Problems of Communism* (July–August, 1971), 52–53. She notes that Article 68 of the 1970 USSR Labor Code, which specifically forbids the employment of women in heavy work, has not been strictly enforced.

26. Mandel, *op. cit.*, 296.

27. V. Golofast and O. Ivanov, "Manhood Starts with Boyhood," *Literaturnaia gazeta* (May 21, 1969).

28. Stephen P. Dunn and Ethel Dunn, "The Soviet Regime and Native Culture in Central Asia and Kazakhstan: The Major Peoples," *Cultural Anthropology* (June, 1967), 147–184.

29. See Gerald Sperling and Eliza Zurick, "The Social Composition of the Communist Parties of Central Asia," *Studies on the Soviet Union*, New Series, VIII, 1 (1969), 30–45.

30. Statistics from *Turkmenskaia iskra* (February 21, 1971).

31. *Kommunist Tadzhikistana* (Dushambe, August 21, 1971). The measures

the party has taken to overcome tradition in Central Asia have bordered on the romantic. In one account, a "reactionary" father was reported as swearing he would beat his two young daughters to death if they dared to continue their education after high school. Since the two were dedicated komsomols, they appealed to their local komsomol and party agencies. The CYL and party leaders, evidently delighted to play the role of Sir Galahad, "abducted" the girls in true cloak-and-dagger style and set them up in a university. (*Komsomolskaia pravda* [January 27, 1971].)

32. For an admittedly very positive account of the liberation of women in Central Asia, the reader is referred to the May, 1972, issue of *Soviet Life, passim.* Particular attention is devoted to the life and work of a female collective-farm director.

33. *Pravda* recently decried a situation in the Ministry of Trade in Azerbaidzhan where, of 2,000 women with secondary and higher education, only 54 were in managerial posts. (*Pravda* [April 8, 1970].) In Turkmenistan, party leaders revealed that most of the republic's agricultural teams were headed by men, while women were virtually nonexistent in store and office jobs. (*Ibid.* [March 7, 1970].)

34. Figures from Dodge, *op. cit.*, 120. See, for example, "The Resolution of the 19th Plenary Session of the Uzbek CPSU SS: On the Tasks of the Uzbek Party Organization in Further Increasing the Activeness of Women in Communist Construction," *Literaturnaia gazeta* (May 27, 1970).

35. Lenin incorporated a strong woman's plank in the 1919 Party Program and shortly thereafter instituted payment for women delegates to attract them into the soviets. (Mandel, *op. cit.*, 291.)

36. V. Perevedentsev, "The Problem of Population Migration and the Utilization of Labor Resources," *Voprosy ekonomiki,* 9 (September, 1970), 35.

37. Mandel, *op. cit.*, 295.

38. See B. Ts. Urlanis, "Our Social Biography," *Literaturnaia gazeta*, 18 (April 28, 1971). In the survey mentioned in the text, of the 22 Ukrainian factories, it is interesting to note that only 0.03 percent of the women had three or more children. Even in families where there were no children, 22 percent of the pregnancies ended in abortion. It will be recalled that where there was one child, 3 percent of the pregnancies ended in birth. The author considers such a high rate of abortion indicative of the effect of a higher socioeconomic status on women of childbearing age. ("A Demographic Problem," *op. cit.*, 78–79.)

39. In a public-opinion poll of 1,500 couples conducted by *Rabochaia gazeta*, only 15 percent of the couples considered children a source of happiness in marriage. Forty percent of those polled said they wanted only one child; 39 percent, two; 8 percent, three; 3 percent, four; 3 percent, five; and 1 percent, ten. Six percent wanted no children. (*Rabochaia gazeta,* [August 13, 1971], 3.)

40. G. A. Slesarev, "Voprosy organizatsii truda i byta i rasshirennoe vosproizvodstvo naseleniia," *Sotsial'nye issledovaniia* (Moscow, 1965), 159ff.

41. According to the resolution, the privileges of working women would be broadened and allowances for children would be introduced in families where the average income per person did not exceed 50 rubles a month.

42. *A Demographic Problem, op. cit.*, 77.

43. Z. A. Yankova, "O Semeino-bytovykh roliakh rabotaishchei zhenshchiny," *Sotsial'nye issledovaniia,* 4 (Moscow, 1970), 77 ff.

44. *Ibid.*, 81.

45. *Sovetskaia Rossiia* [September 17, 1971].

46. *Zhenshchiny v SSSR, op. cit.*, 81.

47. By 1967, it was estimated that each teacher was responsible for 14 children

for an entire working day. This figure was considered too high. ("A Demographic Problem," *op. cit.*, 80.)

48. From 1959 to 1969, the urban population increased by 36 percent (36 million) while the rural population declined by 2.8 percent. The number of residents of Soviet megapolises increased 4.6 times faster than was true of the small- and medium-sized cities. By 1970, 56 percent of all urban residents and 31 percent of the entire population lived in large and super-large cities, as compared with 6 percent in 1926. Needless to say, such a rapid increase would strain all public facilities, not to mention educational ones. (Perevedentsev, *op. cit.*).

49. The 1970 findings of Dr. Yankova were reported in *Nedelia*, 18 (April 24–30, 1972), 20.

50. For a description of the traditional patriarchal family in Russia, see H. Kent Geiger, *The Family in Soviet Russia* (Cambridge, Mass., 1968), 225–228. The best known Soviet study on the Soviet family is A. G. Kharchev, *Brak i semia v SSSR* (Moscow, 1964).

51. For a discussion of marriage and family legislation during this period, see John N. Hazard and Isaac Shapiro, *The Soviet Legal System*, Pt. III, *Legal Relations between Soviet Citizens* (Dobbs Ferry, N. Y., 1962), 99–135.

52. Kollontai did say, however, "Free sex must be regarded as the natural and legitimate manifestation of a healthy organism, like the satisfaction of hunger or thirst." As quoted in S. I. Golod, "Sociological Problems of Sexual Morality" (Philosophical Faculty, Leningrad University, 1968).

53. It is of interest to note that this finding supports Judith Bardwick's stress on the importance of emotional relationships for women in America. (See Judith M. Bardwick, *op. cit.*, Chaps. 3 and 8.)

54. Statistics calculated from the 1970 Census.

55. The full text of the Principles of Marriage and the Family may be found in *Izvestiia* (September 28, 1968).

56. Soviet citizens evidently interpreted the revised principles on divorce as liberal, for the number of divorces soared after 1968. For a Soviet legal interpretation of the changes in divorce procedure, see A Nechaeva, Kandidat juridicheskich nauk, "Rastorzhenie braka v sude," *Sovetskaia justitsiia*, 5 (March, 1970), 16–17.

57. For example, see V. Bilshai, candidate of jurisprudence, "Equality Before the Law," *Literaturnaia gazeta*, 19 (May 8, 1968). "How specifically," he asks, "is [an illegitimate child] the woman's sin, for which the man is not at all to blame." In terms of numbers, Mandel estimates that over 400,000 children a year are born to mothers out of wedlock. (Mandel, *op. cit.*, 305.)

58. It is interesting to note that in the discussion preceding the adoption of the Principles, men tended to be more opposed to this provision than women. Apparently, there was fear that the mother could cite anyone as the father of her child and thus create a scandal for those in high places. Women, of course, wholeheartedly endorsed the Article. For example, see the comments made by V. Kulikov, vice-chairman of the USSR Supreme Court, in *Izvestiia* (May 18, 1968), where he argues that it is difficult to establish paternity "unerringly on the events of the distant past." Another jurist, the assistant prosecutor of the Transcarpathian Province, also insisted that there was as yet no scientific way to establish paternity and abuses would occur. (*Izvestiia* [May 23, 1968].)

59. The husband is to support the wife, or the wife her husband, depending on who is ill. Similarly, children must support their parents or vice versa in the event of illness (Article 16). Moreover, no one person owns all the property in the family. All property acquired during a marriage is held in common or divided equally in the event of a divorce, *even if* the wife does not work (Article 12).

60. A poem by Nikolai Starshinov, for example, celebrates his mother in the conventional image:

"You did not finish any high schools,
Nor were you able to tell God from Priest.
You only bore children and rocked them . . .
So that each one of us be clean and fed . . .

You astounded everybody with your kindness,
With your most hopeless ignorance,
With your most luminous dream . . .
There are no saints.
But you were a saint."

(Nikolai Starshinov, "To My Mother," in *My Best Poems* [Moscow, 1961], trans. Vera Dunham, cited in Brown, ed., *The Role and Status of Women in the Soviet Union, op. cit.*, 66.)

61. The dedicated ideal mother still exists. In fact, a mother's dedication can go as far as crime, it appears. One highly placed mama in Uzbekistan, a director of a sewing-machine factory, no less, bribed the judges to have her son acquitted for stabbing. Using all her influence, she persuaded her son's best friend, a college dropout, to accept blame for the crime. (*Literaturnaia gazeta* [August 27, 1971].) Another mother, or rather grandmother, worked her whole life to support a grandson whose parents abandoned him. When the grandmother became ill, the grandson refused to let her live with his family. A court action finally forced him to assume responsibility for her support (*Pravda* [September 7, 1971].)

62. *Izvestiia* (November 13, 1968).

63. *Literaturnaia gazeta,* 39 (September 22, 1971). Betty Friedan's findings also suggest that the American nonworking woman makes a worse mother than her working sister. It is nice to have cross-cultural support. (Betty Friedan, *The Feminine Mystique* [New York, 1963], Chaps. 9 and 10.)

64. A. L. Pimenova, "Novyi byt i stanovlenie vnutrisemeinogo ravenstva," *Sotsial'nye issledovaniia,* 7 (Moscow, 1971), 38 ff.

65. The classic picture is where the husband comes home at the end of the day to watch television all evening, while his wife goes shopping, does the chores, and feeds the family, to fall exhausted into bed. Although some women have commented that men only get under foot if they try to help, the general feeling is that they should do their share of the housework. (*Sovetskaia Rossiia* [September 21, 1971].) An excellent short novel which deals with this theme is Natal'ia Baranskaia's "Nedelia kak nedelia," *Novy mir*, XLV, 11 (November, 1969), 23–56.

66. See Richard Pipes, "Assimilation and Muslims: A Case Study," *Soviet Society: A Book of Readings*, ed. Alex Inkeles and H. Kent Geiger (Boston, 1961), 588–607.

67. *Turkmenskaia iskra* (January 22, 1971). *Pravda vostoka* (February 12, 1971) condemns similar manifestations of survivals of Islam in Uzbekistan.

68. *The Koran*, trans. J. M. Rodwell (New York, 1963), 415. The typical Moslem view is presented in an excellent and sensitive novel centered on events during World War I in Baku by Kurban Said:

"A wise man does not court a woman. The woman is just an acre on which the man sows. Must the field love the farmer? . . . Never forget that a woman is just an acre."

"Then you believe she has no intelligence?"

"How can you ask? . . . Of course, she has not."

(Kurban Said, *Ali and Nino* [New York, 1971], 76.) Similar views are expressed on 80.

69. September, 1920, was the first time that Central Asian Moslem women appeared in numbers in public. The occasion was the Congress of the Peoples of the East in Baku. When their wives wanted to discard their veils, the Uzbek men fiercely protested. (Mandel, *op. cit.*, 292.)

70. *Central Asian Review*, I, 3 (1953), 47–53.

71. Golod, *op. cit.*, 79.

72. The appearance of the pantsuit created a minor scandal in the puritan Soviet-male eye. Some girls were fired for wearing them when they came to work in them the first time. (*Literaturnaia gazeta* [August 4, 1971].)

73. According to official statistics, Soviet women spend 830 million rubles a year on cosmetics and buy some 134 tons of lipstick annually. They also consume 147 million bottles of perfume weighing two and a half thousand tons each year. (Laura Velikanova, "Women, Stay Young," *Literaturnaia gazeta* [September 22, 1971].)

74. A leading article in *Pravda* reported that where women have qualified for a position of tractor driver, they have been passed over for men. The author pointed out that with a decreasing farm population, women should be encouraged to stay on the farms rather than be forced to leave to find jobs in the city. (*Pravda* [August 19, 1971].)

75. *Izvestiia* (March 7, 1970).

76. *Izvestiia* (December 17, 1971).

77. *Sovetskaia Rossiia* (September 21, 1971).

78. V. N. Shubkin and G. M. Kochetov, "Rukovoditel', kollega, podchinennyi," *Sotsial'nye issledovaniia*, 2 (Moscow, 1968), 143–155.

79. The following material on male attitudes towards women on the job has been taken from Dr. M. Pavlova, "Irena's Career," *Literaturnaia gazeta* (September 22, 1971).

80. M. Shamburg, "A Few Questions about Internal Party Work," *Partiinaia zhizn'*, 4 (February, 1946), 28.

81. I. Kapitonov, *Kommunist, op. cit.*, 35.

82. Information about the lives of these women has been drawn from the following sources:

Aleksandra V. Artiukhina: *Bol'shaia Sovetskaia entsiklopediia,* ed. O. Yu. Schmidt (Moscow, 1931) III, 516; *Bol'shaia Sovetskaia entsiklopediia,* ed. A. M. Prokharov (Moscow, 1970), II, 273–274.

Aleksandra M. Kollontai: *Bol'shaia Sovetskaia entsiklopediia,* ed. B. A. Vvedenskii (Moscow, 1953), XXII, 12.

Klavdiia I. Nikolaeva: *Bol'shaia Sovetskaia entsiklopediia,* ed Vvedenskii, XXX 4.

Elena D. Stasova: *Bol'shaia Sovetskaia entsiklopediia,* ed. Schmidt, LII, 731; *Bol'shaia Sovetskaia entsyklopediia,* ed. Vvedenskii, XL, 522–523.

Varvara N. Iakovleva: *Bol'shaia Sovetskaia entsiklopediia,* ed. Schmidt, LXV, 463. (She does not appear in the second edition.)

83. "Summary of the Accounts and Elections in the Primary Party Organization," *Partiinaia zhizn'*, 6 (March, 1972), 16.

84. I have as yet found no published evidence suggesting that Soviet women are conditioned by fear of success as a threat to their femininity. Fear of success is what Matina Horner suggests is a crucial factor in the nonmotivation of American women toward positions of status and power. (Matina S. Horner, "Femininity and Successful Achievement: A Basic Inconsistency," in Judith M. Bardwick *et al.*, *Feminine Personality and Conflict* [Belmont, Calif., 1970], 45–72.)

Appendix

Female Participation in the Leadership of the CPSU, 1912–1971

Year	*Name of Organ*	*Size of Membership*		*Name of Woman Member*	*Position Held*
1912	Central Committee	Full	10	Stasova, E. D.	candidate, CC
		Cand.	4		
1917	Central Committee	Full	9	x	x
		Cand.	5	x	x
	CC Secretariat		4	Stasova, E. D.	secretary
1917 (July)	Central Committee	Full	22	Kollontai, A. M.	full, CC
		Cand.	18	Stasova, E. D.	cand., CC
				Iakovleva, V. N.	cand., CC
	CC Secretariat		2	Stasova, E. D.	secretary
1918	Central Committee	Full	14	Stasova, E. D.	full, CC
		Cand.	8	x	x
	CC Secretariat		2	Stasova, E. D.	secretary
1919	Central Committee	Full	19	Stasova, E. D.	full, CC
		Cand.	8	x	x
	Politbureau		8	x	x
	Orgbureau		11	Stasova, E. D.	Orgbureau
	Secretariat		2	Stasova, E. D.	secretary
1920	Central Committee	Full	19	x	x
		Cand.	12	x	x
	Politbureau		8	x	x
	Orgbureau		5	x	x
	Secretariat		3	x	x
	Central Control Comm.		3	x	x
1921	Central Committee	Full	25	x	x
		Cand.	15	x	x
	Politbureau	Unknown			
	Central Control Comm.		10	x	x
	Secretariat		3	x	x
1922	Central Committee	Full	27	x	x
		Cand.	19	x	x
	Politbureau	Unknown			
	Secretariat		3	x	x
	Central Control Comm.	Full	5	Varentsova, O. A.	full, CCC
		Cand.	2	x	x
1923	Central Committee	Full	40	x	x
		Cand.	17	x	x
	Politbureau	Unknown			
	Secretariat		3	x	x
	Central Audit Comm.		3	x	x
	Central Control Comm.	Pres.	8 full	x	x
			5 cand.	x	x
	Party Board of CCC		7	x	x
	Central Control Comm.	Full	50	Sakharova, P. F.	full member, CCC
		Cand.	10	x	x
1924	Central Committee	Full	53	Nikolaeva, K. I.	full, CC
		Cand.	34	Artiukhina, A. V.	cand., CC
	Central Audit Comm.		3	x	x

Year	Name of Organ	Size of Membership		Name of Woman Member	Position Held
	CCC Presidium	Full	8	Krupskaia, H. K.	full member, Pres. CCC
		Cand.	13	x	x
	Party Board of CCC		7	x	x
	Central Control Comm.		151	Kirillova, E. E.	member, CCC
				Krupskaia, N. K.	" "
				Sakharova, P. F.	" "
				Vasil'eva, A. P.	" "
				Vishniakova, P. I.	" "
				Zasovina, N. K.	" "
	Politbureau	Full	7	x	x
		Cand.	6	x	x
	Orgbureau	Full	11	x	x
		Cand.	6	Nikolaeva, K. I.	member, Orgbureau
	Secretariat		6	x	x
1925	Central Committee	Full	63	Artiukhina, A. V.	full, CC
		Cand.	43	Kalygina, A. S.	cand., CC
				Nikolaeva, K. I.	cand., CC
	CCC Presidium	Full	22	x	x
		Cand.	9	Sakharova P. F.	cand., CCC
	CCC Secretariat	Full	5	x	x
		Cand.	3	x	x
	CCC Party Board	Full	5	Sakharova P. F.	full, Party Board
		Cand.	2	x	x
	Members, CCC	Full	73	Krupskaia, N. K.	member, CCC
				Sakharova P. F.	member, CCC
				Ul'anova, M. I.	member, CCC
				Vasil'eva, A. P.	member, CCC
	Members, CCC, on local assignments		35	Vishniakova, P. I.	local assignment
	Worker members, CCC		44	Belova, O. A.	worker member
				Goncharova, M. P.	worker member
				Medova, M. S.	worker member
	Peasant members, CCC		11	x	x
	Central Audit Comm.		7	x	x
	Politbureau	Full	4	x	x
		Cand.	10	x	x
	Secretariat	Full	5	x	x
		Cand.	2	Artiukhina, A. V.	Cand., Secretariat
	Orgbureau	Full	11	Artiukhina, A. V.	Full, Orgbureau
		Cand.	5	x	
1927	Central Committee	Full	71	Artiukhina, A. V.	Full, CC
				Krupskaia, N. K.	" "
		Cand.	50	Eliava, Sh. Z.	Cand., CC
				Kalygina, A. S.	" "
				Nikolaieva, K. I.	" "
	Central Audit Comm.		9	x	x
	Central Control Comm.		195	Alekseieva, F. Ia.	Member, CCC
				Barmasheva, S. F.	" "
				Bakhtina, E. Ia.	" "
				Gal'eva, M. I.	" "
				Grigor'eva, M. P.	" "
				Kuz'mina, A. P.	" "
				Lezhava, A. M.	" "

Year	Name of Organ	Size of Membership		Name of Woman Member	Position Held
				Moiseeva, N. E.	,, ,,
				Sakharova, P. F.	,, ,,
				Sakh'ianova, M. M.	,, ,,
				Ul'ianova, M. I.	,, ,,
				Vishniakova, P. I.	,, ,,
	Politbureau	Full	9	x	x
		Cand.	8	x	x
	Secretariat	Full	5	x	x
		Cand.	3	Artiukhina, A. V.	Cand., Secretariat
	Orgbureau	Full	13	Artiukhina, A. V.	Full, Orgbureau
		Cand.	7	x	x
	CCC Presidium	Full	23	x	x
		Cand.	10	x	x
	CCC Party Board		11	x	x
1930	Central Committee	Full	71	Krupskaia, N. K.	Full, CC
		Cand.	67	Eliava, Sh. Z.	Cand., CC
				Kalygina, A. S.	,, ,,
				Nikolaeva, K. I.	,, ,,
	Central Audit Comm.		13	x	x
	Central Audit Comm.		187	Artiukhina, A. V.	Member, CCC
				Chukenova, Zh.	,, ,,
				Goreva, Ye. G.	,, ,,
				Grigor'eva, M. P.	,, ,,
				Sakharova, P. F.	,, ,,
				Sakh'anova, M. M.	,, ,,
				Sokolovskaia, E. K.	,, ,,
				Stasova, E. D.	,, ,,
				Shaposhnikova, L. K.	,, ,,
				Ul'anova, M. I.	,, ,,
				Vasileva, S. V.	,, ,,
				Vasileva, E. O.	,, ,,
	CCC Presidium	Full	26	x	x
		Cand.	6	Artiukhina, A. V.	Cand., CCC Presidium
				Sakharova, P. F.	,, ,, ,,
	CCC Party Board		12	Sakharova, P. F.	Member, Party Board
				Stasova, E. D.	,, ,, ,,
	Politbureau	Full	10	x	x
		Cand.	5	x	x
	Secretariat	Full	5	x	x
		Cand.	2	x	x
	Orgbureau	Full	11	x	x
		Cand.	4	x	x
1934	Central Committee	Full	71	Krupskaia, N. K.	Full, CC
		Cand.	68	Nikolaeva, K. I.	Full, CC
		Cand.	68	Eliava, Sh. Z.	Cand., CC
				Nikolaeva, K. I.	Cand., CC
	Party Control Comm.		61	Sakharova, P. F.	Member, PCC
				Sakh'ianova, M. M.	Member, PCC
				Shaburova, M. A.	Member, PCC
	Soviet Control Comm.		70	Kozlovskaia, A. Ya.	,, SCC
				Ul'ianova, M. I.	,, ,,
				Vengerova, R. S.	,, ,,
	Central Audit Comm.		22	x	x

Year	*Name of Organ*	*Size of Membership*		*Name of Woman Member*	*Position Held*
	Politbureau	Full	10	x	x
		Cand.	5	x	x
	Secretariat		4	x	x
	Orgbureau	Full	10	x	x
		Cand.	2	x	x
	PCC Bureau		9	x	x
	PCC Party Board		3	x	x
1939	Central Committee	Full	71	Nikolaeva, K. I.	Full, CC
		Cand.	68	Zhemchuzhina, P. S.	Cand., CC
	Central Audit Comm.		51	Grekova, N. G.	Member, CAC
				Sadzhaia, A. N.	,, ,,
				Tsanova, L. F.	,, ,,
	Politbureau	Full	9	x	x
		Cand.	2	x	x
	Orgbureau		99	x	x
	Secretariat		4	x	x
1941	Central Committee	Cand.		Zhemchuzhina, P. S.	Expelled from Cand.
1952	Central Committee	Full	125	Kovrigina, M. D.	Full, CC.
				Pankratova, A. M.	,, ,,
		Cand.	111	Furtzeva, E. A.	Cand., CC
				Kuznetsova, K. S.	Cand., CC
				Lykova, L. P.	Cand., CC
				Stepanova, E. A.	Cand., CC
				Tumanova, Z. P.	Cand., CC
	Central Audit Comm.		37	Miranova, Z. F.	Member, CAC
				Tret'iakova, A. E.	,, CAC
	Presidium	Full	25	x	x
		Cand.	11	x	x
	Secretariat		10	x	x
1956	Central Committee	Full	133	Furtzeva, E. A.	Full, CC
				Kovrigina, M. D.	,, ,,
				Nasriddinova, Ia. S.	,, ,,
				Pankratova, A. M.	,, ,,
		Cand.	124	Andreeva, N. N.	Cand., CC
				Lykova, L. P.	,, ,,
				Nefiodova, O. I.	,, ,,
				Popova, N.V.	,, ,,
				Tumanova, Z. P.	,, ,,
	Central Audit Comm.		64	Boikova, A. P.	Member, CAC
				Miranova, Z. V.	,, ,,
				Murav'iova, N. A.	,, ,,
	Presidium	Full	11	x	x
		Cand.	6	Furtseva, E. A.	Cand., Presidium CC
	Secretariat		8	Furtseva, E. A.	Secretary
1957	Presidium	Full	15	Furtseva, E. A.[a]	Full, Presidium CC
1961	Central Committee	Full	175	Furtseva, E. A.	Full, CC
				Gaganova, V. I.	Full, CC
				Nasriddinova, Ia. S.	,, ,,
				Nikolaeva, T. N.	,, ,,
				Popova, N. V.	,, ,,

a. Furtseva was released from her duties as a secretary of the CC CPSU and member of the Presidium in connection with her appointment to the post of minister of culture of the USSR in May, 1960.

Year	*Name of Organ*	*Size of Membership*		*Name of Woman Member*	*Position Held*
		Cand.	155	Kolchina, O. P.	Cand., CC
				Lykova, L. P.	,, ,,
				Vorinina, P. A.	,, ,,
				Zhuravlyova, M. I.	,, ,,
	Central Audit Comm.		66	Boykova, A. P.	Member, CAC
				Burkatskaia, G. E.	,, ,,
				Dement'eva, R. F.	,, ,,
				Kulikova, M. V.	,, ,,
				Mironova, Z. V.	,, ,,
				Murav'oiva, N. A.	Chairman, CAC
	Presidium	Full	11	x	x
		Cand.	5	x	x
	Secretariat		9	x	x
	Bureau of RSFSR CC		11	x	x
1966	Central Committee	Full	195	Furtseva, E. A.	Full, CC
				Gaganova, V. I.	,, ,,
				Nasreddinnova, Ya. S.	,, ,,
				Nikolaeva, T. N.	,, ,,
				Popova, N. V.	,, ,,
		Cand.	165	Dement'eva, R. F.	Cand., CC
				Karpova, E. F.	,, ,,
				Kolchina, O. P.	,, ,,
				Lykova, L. P.	,, ,,
				Voronina, P. A.	,, ,,
				Zhuravliova, M. I.	,, ,,
	Central Audit Comm.		79	Komarova, D. P.	Member, CAC
				Kolbetskaia, M. A.	,, ,,
				Kruglova, Z. M.	,, ,,
				Murav'iova, N. A.	,, ,,
				Sal'nikova, E. A.	,, ,,
				Sysoeva, E. A.	,, ,,
				Yarushkovskaia, T. P.	,, ,,
	Politbureau	Full	11	x	x
		Cand.	8	x	x
	Secretariat		9	x	x
1971	Central Committee	Full	241	Furtseva, E. A.	Full, CC
				Ivannikova, M. S.	,, ,,
				Nikolaeva-Tereshkova, V. V.	,, ,,
				Popova, M. G.	,, ,,
				Popova, N. V.	,, ,,
		Cand.	156	Biriukova, A. P.	Cand., CC
				Dement'eva, R. F.	,, ,,
				Fominykh, A. M.	,, ,,
				Karpova, E. F.	,, ,,
				Kolchina, O. P.	,, ,,
				Lykova, L. P.	,, ,,
				Poberei, M. T.	,, ,,
				Sal'nikova, E. A.	,, ,,
				Shevchenka, A. F.	,, ,,
	Central Audit Comm.		81	Eliceeva, M. G.	Member, CAC
				Denisova, R. N.	,, ,,
				Komarova, D. P.	,, ,,
				Kruglova, Z. M.	,, ,,

Year	*Name of Organ*	*Size of Membership*		*Name of Woman Member*	*Position Held*
				Lotsmanova, G. P.	Member, CAC
				Mel'nikova, Z. V.	" "
				Petrova, L. A.	" "
				Sonygina, A. P.	" "
	Politbureau	Full	15	x	x
		Cand.	6	x	x
	Secretariat		9	x	x

Sources: *Party and Government Officials of the Soviet Union 1917–1967,* compiled by the Institute for the Study of the U.S.S.R., Munich, Germany, ed. by Edward L. Crawley et al. (Metuchen, N.J., 1969), 1–92; *Supplement of the Bulletin of the Institute for the Study of the USSR* (May, 1971), 16; and *XXIV S'ezd Kommunisticheskogo partii Sovetskogo Soiuza* (Moscow, 1972), II.

PART TWO

Politics, Society, and Welfare: Stability and Reform

CHAPTER 4

What Have Soviet Leaders Done about the Housing Crisis?

Henry W. Morton

The scope and persistence with which the housing problem is being solved is common knowledge. Almost 60 billion rubles have been spent for this purpose. More than 500,000,000 square meters of housing space were built during the [past] five years. This means that the equivalent of 50 large cities with a population of a million were built from scratch. . . . Most of the families that celebrated housewarmings moved into individual apartments with up-to-date conveniences.

Leonid I. Brezhnev at the 24th Party Congress (March, 1971)[1]

The tragedy of Soviet building is the repetitive and uninspired nature of its city and neighboring planning. The tragedy of the West is that it is impossible to mobilize building codes, trade union resources and production for the kind of coherent planning and problems solving that its sophisticated talents could provide.

Ada Louise Huxtable[2]

Determined to resolve a chronic housing shortage, Soviet builders, on orders of their political leaders, have constructed more housing units in a decade and a half than any other country in the world. Between 1956 and 1970, 34.1 million units of housing were built, and 126.5 million people, more than half of the country's population, moved into them. The rapid tempo of construction continues: more than 2.2 million housing units were completed in 1971 and 1972; and similar annual totals are expected for the last three years of the Ninth Five-Year Plan, which ends in 1975.[3]

The enormity of the Soviet achievement needs to be recognized and acknowledged—despite serious shortcomings in quality and design which Soviet planners, architects, and citizens are the first to criticize. "Soviet building now leaves much of the world behind," wrote the architectural critic, Ada Louise Huxtable. "While others talk of the need for a way to meet the fantastic building projection of the next fifty years, the Russians have developed the techniques."[4]

TABLE 4–1 Number of Persons Receiving Housing from the State, Cooperative, and Private Sectors, 1950–1970

	Individuals Moving into New Housing (in millions)	Number of Units Built (in millions)	Annual Average Number of Units Built (in millions)
1950–1970	153.0	41,318,000	1,967,524
1956–1970	126.5	34,193,000	2,279,533
1961–1970	84.4	22,901,000	2,290,100

Source: *Norodnoe khoziaistvo v SSSR v 1970 godu* (Moscow, 1971), 540, 545.

Our concerns in this chapter will be to seek answers to these questions:

1. To what measurable extent and satisfaction did the construction boom ease a severe housing shortage for the consumer?
2. What differences in housing comforts exist among the 15 republics, and why?
3. Why are Soviet leaders still dependent on private housing?
4. What lessons can be learned from the Soviet experience since its intensive construction program began?

To put Soviet housing in perspective, no nation—capitalist, socialist, or otherwise—has "solved" its housing problem by providing adequate shelter, however defined by a society, for its low-income groups, which comprise, in most industrialized countries, a sizable segment of the population, if not the majority.

In any society inadequate, dilapidated, overcrowded, or unsanitary housing conditions are produced by a rapid increase in the total need for shelter in relation to the available supply of housing units. Such conditions are caused by:

1. An inadequate housing base to start with. Historically, societies and their leaders have found it too expensive to provide decent housing for the masses without sacrificing other objectives which they considered more important.[5]
2. A rapid inflow of rural poor, crowding into urban areas, at a time when a country's population growth rate is accelerating.
3. The destruction of housing by wars, earthquakes, tornadoes, hurricanes, and other natural causes.
4. The rising level of expectation by a society in its evaluation of what constitutes "adequate" and "inadequate" housing.

In the USSR from the 1920's through the 1950's a family of four living in a one-room apartment plus kitchen would have considered itself very fortunate, because most families lived under far more stringent circumstances: two, three, and four families were commonly cramped into a single flat. At the present time, as the absolute level of housing improves, a family of four might consider two rooms adequate but one room inadequate, because its relative level of expectation has risen.

The willingness of a society to allocate sufficient sums from the public and private sectors for housing construction will depend not only in part on need as it is perceived, but also on the political organization of society, the ideological and actual commitment of its leaders to alleviate the housing shortage, the financial and technological means available in relation to competing political interests demanding satisfaction in such spheres as defense, heavy and light industry, education, public health, communications, and other vital areas. Such factors have been significant variables in determining Soviet housing policy over the years.

The USSR inherited a poorly developed housing fund from Tsarist Russia. Before 1917 most of the housing in towns and in the countryside consisted mainly of small, wooden, single-story, one-family homes almost completely lacking in utilities. As late as the First Five-Year Plan the great majority of Soviet cities resembled villages in their physical appearance.[6]

Under Soviet rule housing conditions worsened. During the 1918–1921 Civil War, which followed the Revolution, housing in cities fell into ruinous neglect. With no fuel deliveries from the countryside, workers, many of whom lived in partitioned apartments formerly belonging to the nobility and members of the bourgeoisie, ripped up and burned wooden floors and windows, and door frames in winter to stay alive. After the war most municipalities lacked the means to make adequate repairs, and even when they tried, building supplies were simply not available.[7]

The Urbanization of the Soviet Union

The Stalinist policy of rapid industrialization in conjunction with his forced collectivization of the countryside (begun in 1929) drove millions of peasants from their farmlands to new industrial sites and converted small towns into large cities almost overnight as the urban population more than doubled between December, 1926, and January, 1939. (See Table 4-2.) The mass migration into cities and towns and an increase in the natural growth rate added 109.7 million people to the urban sector

TABLE 4–2 The Urban-Rural Distribution of the Soviet Population (in millions)[a]

Census Dates	Urban	Rural	Total	Percent Urban
December, 1926	26.3	120.7	147.0	18.9
January, 1939	56.1	114.5	170.6	33.9
January, 1959	100.0	108.8	208.8	48.0
January, 1970	136.0	105.7	241.7	56

Source: *Narodnoe khoziaistvo SSSR v 1970 godu* (Moscow, 1971), 9.
a. Figures for 1926 and 1939 refer to USSR borders before September 17, 1939.

between 1926 and January, 1970—400 percent. (The rural population declined by only 15 million, or 12.4 percent, for that period.)[8]

The USSR in 1926 had just two cities with a population of over one million and a third with over 500,000 inhabitants. By 1970 there were 10 cities with over one million and 24 others with a population exceeding 500,000. Still another way of illustrating this phenomenon of urban growth is that Moscow's population since 1926 has grown by over five million, Leningrad's by two million, Kiev's, Tashkent's, and Novosibirsk's by over one million each. Nine cities added over 700,000 people each to their population, including Cheliabinsk, which expanded 15 times its size—growing from 59,000 in 1926 to 875,000 residents in 1970. All

TABLE 4–3 Population Growth of 15 Largest Soviet Cities, 1926–1970

	December 17, 1926	January 17, 1939	January 15, 1959	January 15, 1970	Percentage Increase 1926–1970	Percentage Increase 1959–1973
Moscow	2,029	4,537	6,009	7,061	248	17.5
Leningrad	1,731	3,103	2,985	3,513	103	17.7
Kiev	514	851	1,110	1,632	218	47.0
Tashkent	314	556	927	1,385	419	49.4
Baku	453	773	968	1,266	179	30.3
Kharkov	417	840	953	1,223	193	28.3
Gorky	222	644	941	1,170	427	24.3
Novosibirsk	120	404	885	1,161	868	31.2
Kuybishev	176	390	806	1,045	494	29.7
Sverdlovsk	140	423	779	1,025	632	31.6
Minsk	132	237	509	917	595	80.2
Odessa	162	599	664	892	451	34.3
Tbilisi	294	519	703	889	202	26.5
Donetsk	174	474	708	879	405	24.2
Cheliabinsk	59	273	689	875	1,383	27.0

Sources: *Narodnoe khoziaiastvo SSSR 1970 godu* (Moscow, 1970), 37–45 and *Strana soveta za 50 let* (Moscow, 1967), 21.

those people required shelter, as did their children, who eventually started families of their own. The great influx of people into towns and cities during the first three five-year plans, 1929–1941, greatly overburdened the already bursting housing facilities.[9] The First Five-Year Plan (1929–1932) had envisaged an increase of 33 percent in urban housing space, but only 16 percent was actually built. Housing production was sacrificed in favor of larger investments in heavy industry.

> Thus the urban population rose by much more than planned, housing space by much less, the overcrowding became worse than ever. Neglect of maintenance made conditions even less bearable. No Soviet citizen is likely to deny that lack of space, shared kitchens, the crowding of several families per apartment, often in sub-divided rooms, were the lot of the majority of the urban population over a generation, and that this was a source of a great deal of human misery.[10]

Investment Policy

Capital investment in housing for the 1930's was governed by two factors. To begin with, the total investment capacity of the USSR, a capital-poor nation, was severely limited and stretched to the breaking point by the unrealistically high goals set by Stalin. Secondly, within the confines of the capital investment structure, Stalin determined that housing construction (as all consumer-oriented industries) would receive low priority. Consequently, capital investment in housing from the public and private sectors averaged 15.0 percent of the total amount of capital invested for the first three five-year plans (1929–July, 1940).[11] (See Table 4-4)

The German invasion of the Soviet Union in June, 1941, made an already intolerable housing situation impossible. The war caused widespread destruction of housing in the European part of the USSR. According to Soviet figures, 1,710 cities, towns, and urban settlements were fully or partially destroyed, as were many thousands of villages. More than 25 million people were left homeless. Leningrad, Kiev, Minsk, Smolensk, Stalingrad, and other cities and towns had to be almost completely rebuilt from heaps of broken brick and rubble.[12]

Despite the war's devastation Stalin's low-priority treatment of housing continued and even intensified. Although 19.2 percent of the Fourth Five-Year Plan (1946–1950) was allocated for housing construction, only 36 percent of housing built during that period was constructed by

TABLE 4–4 Capital Investment in Housing Construction, 1918–1970 (in 1969 prices)

	Total Capital investment from Public and Private Sectors (in billions of rubles)	Capital Investment in Housing from Public or Private Sectors (in billions of rubles)	Housing as Percent of Total Investment	Percent of Square Meters of Housing Built by the State
1918–1970	985.6	185,430	18.8	48.6
1918–September 30, 1928	4.4	2,838	64.1	11.7
1929–1932 (First Five-Year Plan)	8.8	1,351	15.3	57.3
1933–1937 (Second Five-Year Plan)	19.9	2,526	12.7	55.2
1938–July, 1941 (part of Third Five-Year Plan)	20.6	3,481	16.9	55.1
July, 1941–1945	20.8	3,080	14.8	40.3
1946–1950 (Fourth Five-Year Plan)	48.1	9,233	19.2	36.0
1951–1955 (Fifth Five-Year Plan)	91.1	17,864	19.6	47.0
1956–1960 (Sixth Five-Year Plan)	170.5	39,614	23.2	47.2
1961–1965 (Seventh Five-Year Plan)	247.6	45,430	18.3	58.5
1966–1970 (Eighth Five-Year Plan)	353.8	60,013	17.0	61.5

Source: *Norodnoe khoziaistvo SSSR v 1970 godu* (Moscow, 1970), 482, 483, 538.

the state sector—the lowest percentage since the institution of the five-year plans.

Only after Stalin's death did a break-through in housing construction investment take place. Twenty-three and two-tenths percent of the country's capital investment (from the public and private sectors) for the Sixth Five-Year Plan (1956–1960) was earmarked for housing construction, the highest percentage figure for the entire five-year plan period. Moreover, the ruble investment more than doubled. Seventeen and nine-tenths billion rubles were invested, compared with 9.2 billion rubles during the previous plan period with the result that the number of square meters of housing built doubled. Since that time the ruble investment for housing has increased substantially for each of the succeeding five-year plans (although the percentage share of a growing capital investment total has actually declined) and the state sector has assumed an increasingly larger responsibility for building houses, 58.5 percent for the Seventh Five-Year Plan (1961–1965) and 61.5 percent for the Eighth Five-Year Plan (1966–1970).

The commitment by the post-Stalinist leadership, enunciated in a Central Committee CPSU and Council Ministers USSR resolution of July, 1957, to eliminate once and for all the intolerably crowded conditions under which the Soviet people lived, had manifest results.[13] A visitor to any Soviet city cannot fail to be impressed by the multiplicity of new housing districts that dominate its expanding perimeters and by the numerous high-rise housing developments that are being built.

However, despite the recent efforts to fulfill the housing needs of millions, the legacy of years of neglect, underinvestment, and war damage created a housing crisis of such proportions that it has not and cannot be easily or swiftly resolved.[14]

How Serious Is the Shortage?

The continuing housing need that exists can be evaluated by standards set by the Soviet leadership. Housing in the USSR is not measured by the number of people per room, but primarily in square meters of "living space" (*zhilaia ploshchad*) which an individual occupies. Living space encompasses bedrooms and living rooms but not kitchens, bathrooms, corridors and storage areas. Living and nonliving space according to Soviet specifications make up the aggregate "housing space" (*obshchaia ploshchad*) of a dwelling. Each of the 15 republics of the Soviet Union has determined by law the minimum standard, or "sanitary housing norm," for its citizens. For the Russian Republic, as well as for most of the others, it is nine square meters (sq. m.) of *living space,* which is approximately a room of 10 x 10 feet.[15]

The minimum housing norm of nine sq. m. of living space adopted by the Russian Republic in the 1920's and subsequently utilized by other republics proved to be unenforceable. In fact, the amount of per capita living space available in urban areas decreased from 5.7 sq. m. in 1926 to 4.5 sq. m. in 1940, for reasons which have already been indicated. It improved only slightly to 4.9 sq. m. by 1950, five and one-half years after the war's end.[16]

By the end of 1970, despite a vigorous construction program over the preceding 15 years, only Latvia and Estonia had achieved the minimum sanitary requirement of 9 sq. m. of living space for citizens residing in urban areas of each republic.[17] The Russian Republic, which contains 59.4 percent of the entire urban population of the USSR, averaged 7.7 sq. m. per urban dweller;[18] 7.7 sq. m. also happened to be the average for towns and cities in the USSR. Nine republics fell below the national average, with Uzbekistan recording the lowest per capita—5.7 sq. m. of living space.[19]

As the data in Table 4-5 demonstrates, the USSR can be divided into developed and underdeveloped republics in terms of urban housing. Thus, while all republics registered housing gains between 1958 and 1970, some did much better than others. Those living in Latvia, Estonia, and Georgia clearly benefited from the highest level of urban housing in the Soviet Union, which also reflected their generally high standard of living relative to other sections of the country. As a group the European republics (excluding Armenia and Azerbaidzhan) represented the most developed housing sector. In 1958 they averaged 6.6 sq. m. of per capita urban living space compared to 5.4 sq. m. for the five Central Asian republics, Armenia, and Azerbaidzhan. By 1970 the respective averages were 8.3 and 6.4 for each group, as the gap between the two widened. (See the top and bottom halves of Column III, Table 4-5.)

A primary cause for this situation is that the housing-poor republics had the highest increase in natural population growth in the USSR, which is reflected in the huge percentage increase of their urban populations between 1958–1970 (See Column V, Table 4-5).[20] Compared this to the three republics with the lowest urbanization rate—Latvia, Georgia, and Estonia—which maintained the highest urban housing standard, even though they ranked 13th, 6th, and 9th, respectively, in percentage increase of living space between 1958 and 1970. (See Columns IV and V, Table 4-5.) Other important factors are the per capita rates of capital investment in housing construction per republic, the number of housing units built per 1,000 inhabitants by each republic, as well as the number of sq. m. of housing space that was lost either due to razing or other causes, (See Appendices A, B, C, and D.)

TABLE 4–5 Per Capita Living Space in Urban Housing by Republics in Rank Order, 1958, 1965, 1970

I 1958		II 1965		III 1970		IV 1970			V 1970	
Per Capita Sq. M. of Living Space		*Per Capita Sq. M. of Living Space*		*Per Capita Sq. M. of Living Space*		*Percent and Real (Sq. M.) Increase of Per Capita Living Space 1958–1970*			*Percent of Per Capita Increase of Urban Population 1958–1970*	
USSR	5.8	USSR	6.9	USSR	7.7	USSR	32.8	(1.9)	USSR	39.1
Latvia	8.4	Latvia	8.9	Latvia	9.7	Russia	35.1	(1.9)	Moldavia	82.2
Estonia	7.6	Estonia	8.9	Estonia	9.6	Ukraine	29.7	(1.9)	Armenia	73.1
Georgia	6.7	Ukraine	7.6	Georgia	8.5	Belorussia	29.3	(1.7)	Tadzhikistan	72.3
Lithuania	6.6	Georgia	7.5	Ukraine	8.3	Moldavia	29.1	(1.6)	Kazakhstan	65.6
Ukraine	6.4	Lithuania	7.2	Lithuania	7.9	Kazakhstan	28.3	(2.3)	Belorussia	63.4
Belorussia	5.8	Russia	6.9	Russia	7.7	Georgia	26.9	(1.8)	Uzbekistan	62.6
Russia	5.7	Belorussia	6.7	Belorussia	7.5	Kirgizia	26.5	(1.3)	Kirgizia	62.5
Turkmenia	5.7	Moldavia	6.6	Moldavia	7.1	Armenia	26.4	(1.4)	Lithuania	55.5
Azerbaidzhan	5.7	Armenia	6.5	Turkmenia	6.9	Estonia	26.3	(2.0)	Turkmenia	51.9
Moldavia	5.5	Turkmenia	6.2	Kazakhstan	6.8	Turkmenia	21.1	(1.2)	Azerbaidzhan	48.5
Tadzhikistan	5.4	Kazakhstan	6.2	Armenia	6.7	Lithuania	19.7	(1.3)	Ukraine	37.3
Armenia	5.3	Azerbaidzhan	6.1	Azerbaidzhan	6.5	Azerbaidzhan	18.2	(0.8)	Russia	34.1
Kazakhstan	5.3	Tadzhikistan	5.7	Tadzhikistan	6.2	Latvia	15.5	(1.3)	Estonia	33.2
Uzbekistan	5.2	Uzbekistan	5.5	Kirgizia	6.2	Tadzhikistan	14.8	(0.8)	Georgia	33.0
Kirgizia	4.9	Kirgizia	5.3	Uzbekistan	5.7	Uzbekistan	9.6	(0.5)	Latvia	28.0

Sources: *Narodnoe khoziaistvo SSSR v 1960 godu* (Moscow, 1961), 613; *Narodnoe khoziaistvo SSSR v 1965 godu* (Moscow, 1966), 615; *Narodnoe khoziaistvo SSSR v 1970 godu* (Moscow, 1971), 10, 546.

By 1970 only 2 of the 15 largest cities of the USSR, Moscow and Donetsk, had realized the minimum housing standard. They provided their citizens with an average of 9.1 sq. m. each. Riga, the capital of Latvia, with 9.5 and Tallin, the capital of Estonia, with 9.4 sq. m. of living space per capita were the only other cities of substantial size to exceed that total. The inability of 13 of the 15 largest cities in the USSR to achieve the sanitary housing norm is another indication of how serious the housing shortage still is—even though cities with large industrial concentration are favored with capital investment in housing construction over small cities and towns. Proof of such priority is that the percent increase of living space of 12 of the 15 largest cities exceeded their population increase (some by very large margins) between 1958 and 1970. The exceptions were Tashkent, Minsk, and Odessa. Significantly, the reverse was true for all republics except the Russian; that is, their urban population grew much more rapidly than living space available. (See Columns IV and V, Table 4-5.) Most favored of all, as one might expect, was the nation's designated showplace, Moscow.[21] The capital's living space increased by 82 percent (and its per capita sq. m. of living space rose by 4.1) between 1958 and 1970, while its population grew by only 16.9 percent. (See Columns VI, VII, Table 4-6.)

The differences that exist between the per capita urban living space of European and Asiatic republics also apply to the comparative housing figures for the capital of each republic. The European capitals of the USSR (excluding Erevan and Baku) averaged 8.4 sq. m. of living space for their populace in 1970, while the capitals of the five Central Asian republics, Erevan, and Baku averaged only 6.5 sq. m.[22]

Thus, we have attempted to show, with the support of statistical evidence, that even though the Soviet government has made a serious and sustained effort since 1957 (perhaps more than any other in the world) to alleviate a serious housing shortage by launching an impressive building program, the results have been only a partial success. Although the Soviet housing situation has substantially improved, the fact remains that the great majority of the Soviet people living in urban areas have so far not yet achieved the minimum housing standard of nine sq. m. of living space set by the regime in the 1920's and that wide ranging differences in urban housing comfort exist among various republics—even when measured by only the single variable of space. Housing conditions in rural areas are worse where by observation the level of housing and amenities (gas, water supply, sewage disposal) is much lower. However, this is difficult to measure, since little data, perhaps for this reason, has been made available.

TABLE 4–6 Per Capita Housing and Living Space of 15 Largest Cities in USSR

	I 1939		II 1958		III 1960		IV 1970		V	VI	VII
	Housing Space	*Living Space*	*Housing Space*	*Living Space*	*Housing Space*	*Living Space*	*Housing Space*	*Living Space*	*Per Capita Urban Living Space of Corresponding Republic*	*Percent Increase of Space 1958–1970*	*Percent Population Increase January 15, 1959–January 15, 1970*
Moscow	6.7	4.3	8.6	5.0	10.2	7.1	13.6	9.1[a]	7.7	82.0	16.8
Leningrad	7.6	5.3	8.4	5.9	9.3	6.5	11.9	8.3	7.7	40.7	18.9
Kiev	7.9	5.5	8.0	5.6	10.3	7.2	12.6	8.8	8.3	57.1	47.0
Tashkent	7.3	5.1	5.8	4.0	8.0	5.6	8.0	5.6[b]	5.7	40.0	49.4
Baku	7.5	5.3	7.3	5.1	8.5	6.0	10.1	7.1	6.5	39.2	30.0
Kharkov	7.9	5.5	8.0	5.6	9.4	6.6	11.7	8.2	8.3	46.4	28.3
Gorky	6.6	4.6	7.3	5.1	8.4	5.9	10.7	7.5	7.7	47.0	24.3
Novosibirsk	6.0	4.1	6.1	4.3	8.2	5.7	10.5	7.4	7.7	72.1	31.2
Kuybishev	6.2	4.7	6.9	4.8	8.0	5.6	10.3	7.2	7.7	50.0	29.2
Sverdlovsk	6.5	4.8	7.6	5.3	9.0	6.3	11.2	7.8	7.7	47.2	31.7
Minsk	7.6	5.3	6.8	4.7	8.0	5.6	10.5	7.4	7.5	57.4	80.0
Odessa	9.5	6.3	8.6	6.0	9.7	6.8	11.1	7.8	7.7	33.3	34.3
Tbilisi	8.9	6.2	8.2	5.7	9.0	6.3	10.8	7.6	8.5	33.3	26.5
Donetsk	6.8	4.8	8.1	5.7	10.6	7.4	13.0	9.1	8.3	59.6	24.2
Cheliabinsk	6.3	4.4	7.0	4.9	9.0	6.3	11.3	7.9	7.7	61.2	30.3

Sources: *Narodnoe khoziaistvo SSSR v 1960 godu* (Moscow, 1961), 614; *Narodnoe khoziaistvo SSSR v 1963 godu* (Moscow, 1964) 516; and *Narodnoe khoziaistvo SSSR v 1970 godu* (Moscow, 1971), 37–45, 549.

a. Computing data from *Moskva v tsifrakh* (Moscow, 1972), 103, Moscow's per capita living space is 9.3 sq. meters.

b. Tashkent suffered a serious earthquake in 1966. Hence the zero increase between 1961 and 1970.

TABLE 4–7 Per Capita Living Space of Republic Capitals for 1970
(in sq. m. of living space)

Capital		Average	Capital		Average
Moscow, Russia	9.1		Tashkent, Uzbekistan	5.6	
Kiev, Ukraine	8.8		Baku, Azerbaidzhan	7.1	
Minsk, Belorussia	7.4		Erevan, Armenia	6.5	
Tbilisi, Georgia	7.6	8.4	Alma Ata, Kazakhstan	7.2	6.5
Riga, Latvia	9.5		Frunze, Kirgizia	7.4	
Tallin, Estonia	9.4		Dushanbe, Tadzhikistan	6.2	
Vilnius, Lithuania	8.1		Ashkhabad, Turkmenia	6.7	
Kishinev, Moldavia	7.1				

Source: *Narodnoe khoziaistvo SSSR v 1970 godu* (Moscow, 1971), 37–45, 549.

The Importance of Private and Cooperative Housing

The housing shortage in the USSR is part of a worldwide phenomenon about which we may make some general observations. In the socialist countries of Eastern Europe, state-sponsored housing construction has failed to provide adequate housing for the people because of the governments' inability (or unwillingness) to allocate sufficient resources to construct the requisite number of housing units.[23] Therefore, despite recurring misgivings on ideological grounds, they have consistently been forced to depend on the private, and lately, the cooperative sectors to help ease the housing shortage for the masses. The permanent presence of the private housing sector (of which the cooperative is a variant) has been, to a greater or lesser degree, accepted as a fact of life by Soviet and Eastern European leaders, depending upon which leaders are in power and their perception of the need for housing, a need which the public sector cannot fully satisfy.[24]

Conversely, in Western capitalist societies private enterprise has failed to provide adequate housing for the majority of its people, that is, for low-income groups and the poor. The political pressures resulting from this inescapable fact have forced their governments to become housing agents by allocating funds from the public sector to construct new housing, directly or by means of subsidy, and to assume, in many instances, the responsibility of administering their publicly supported housing. This circumstance and the ideological adjustment to it has been much more readily accomplished by Western European societies than by many groups and individuals in the United States.[25] Thus, paradoxically, it is in socialist societies where private housing is looked to as a means of alleviating a critical shortage and in capitalist societies where the demand is continually increasing for public housing.

The salience of private and cooperative housing in the Soviet Union today needs to be recognized and placed in the proper perspective; so far it has been relatively untreated by Soviet and Western analysts.

Simply stated, the majority of all Soviet housing in 1970, between 55 and 60 percent, was privately or cooperatively owned. This estimate is based on the following calculations. In 1970, 32.9 percent of all urban housing was privately (29.9 percent) or cooperatively (3.0 percent) owned. (See Table 4-8. Unfortunately Soviet statistics do not provide us with any data regarding the size of categories of ownership of the rural housing fund for the 104,873,000, or 43 percent, of the Soviet people who live in rurally designated areas. We do know that the vast majority of them, an estimated 90 to 95 percent, who are predominantly peasants live in their own prototypal, one-story huts, which are the prevailing observable houses that dot the Soviet countryside. By combining the known urban and the estimated rural housing fund in private and cooperative hands, the above estimate was made.[26]

Republican Differences

We can get a better appreciation of the relative weight of the private vis-à-vis the public sector of Soviet housing by examining the vast ranges of differences that exist among republics. As Table 4-8 reveals, in five republics (including the populous Ukraine) more than 40 percent of housing was privately owned. (Georgia led with 47.3 percent.) Six other republics were above 30 percent. Lowest in percentage figures were the three Baltic republics and Russia.

The reason for such wide-ranging differences can be variously but not conclusively explained. First, there is a strong correlation between the level of urbanization in a republic and the percentage of private urban housing. The three republics that are most urbanized, Estonia, Russia, and Latvia (63 to 66 percent), have the lowest percentage of private housing (22.0 to 24.4 percent).[27] Conversely three of the four republics which are the least urbanized, Moldavia, Uzbekistan, and Kirgizia (32 to 38 percent), have more than 40 percent of their urban housing in the

TABLE 4–8 Percent of Urban Housing Fund Owned Privately or by Cooperatives by Republics in 1970 in Rank Order
(based on sq. m. of housing space)

I		II		III		IV	
	Percent Private		*Percent Cooperative*		*Percent Private and Cooperative*		*Percent of Population Urban*
USSR	29.9	USSR	3.0[a]	USSR	32.9	USSR	57
Georgia	47.3	Lithuania	7.0	Georgia	50.2	Estonia	66
Kirgizia	44.5	Belorussia	4.8	Kirgizia	46.5	Russia	63
Uzbekistan	43.0	Moldavia	4.2	Moldavia	45.8	Latvia	63
Ukraine	42.0	Russia	3.3	Ukraine	44.5	Armenia	60
Moldavia	41.5	Estonia	3.3	Uzbekistan	44.4	Ukraine	55
Tadzhikistan	36.7	Latvia	2.9	Armenia	39.5	Lithuania	51
Armenia	36.7	Georgia	2.9	Belorussia	39.3	Kazakhstan	51
Kazakhstan	34.8	Armenia	2.8	Tadzhikistan	37.7	Azerbaidzhan	50
Belorussia	34.5	Ukraine	2.5	Kazakhstan	36.1	Georgia	48
Turkmenia	33.7	Kirgizia	2.0	Lithuania	35.3	Turkmenia	48
Azerbaidzhan	31.2	Uzbekistan	1.4	Turkmenia	33.7	Belorussia	45
Lithuania	28.3	Kazakhstan	1.2	Azerbaidzhan	32.3	Kirgizia	38
Estonia	24.4	Azerbaidzhan	1.2	Estonia	27.6	Tadzhikistan	37
Russia	23.9	Tadzhikistan	1.0	Russia	27.2	Uzbekistan	36
Latvia	22.0	Turkmenia	0.01	Latvia	24.9	Moldavia	32

Source: *Narodnoe khoziaistvo SSSR v 1970 godu* (Moscow, 1971), 545–547.

a. The data listing the cooperative housing fund are not given; the square meters of cooperative housing built since 1963, the year after cooperative housing construction was again encouraged on a large scale, is available. I have added the square meters of cooperative housing built between 1963 and 1970 for the USSR and for each republic and have used these totals for establishing the cooperative housing fund from which the percentage calculations were made. The total arrived at slightly underestimates the total square meters of cooperative housing. Some of the cooperative structures built in the 1920's and 1930's were not absorbed by the state sector in 1937 but have survived as cooperatives. Unfortunately their number is not given. (See John N. Hazard, *Soviet Housing Law* [New Haven, 1939], 18, 19.) Conversely the number of rural housing cooperatives built cannot be separated from the total; but on the basis of information available, it is statistically insignificant—consisting mainly of summer cottages (*dachas*).

private sector. The fourth, Tadzhikistan, is close behind with 36.7 percent. (See Columns I and IV, Table 4-8.)

Secondly, the rate of urbanization and government policy regarding private housing are closely related. All private-home building is restricted to one- or two-story structures with a maximum of 60 sq. m. of living space.[28]

In the post-1945 period the government for more than a decade depended more heavily on private building than on the state sector in urban areas to help ease a severe housing crisis in which two, three, four, or more families sharing an apartment was a common occurrence, and a family assigned to a single flat was a rare exception.

The government decree of 1948 and the joint party and government resolution of 1957 specifically encouraged private home building and ordered local government authorities and directors of state enterprises to help private builders in acquiring building sites, state home-building loans, and building materials—which were perennially in short supply.[29]

By 1962, however, the political climate turned against private-housing construction for several reasons. On ideological grounds it raised the specter of a private-property mentality at the time Soviet society, according to the new Party Program of 1961, was supposedly "constructing communism." In practice, private-home building led to speculative practices of building houses for rent or sale rather than for the personal use for which it was solely intended by law and to exceeding the imposed space limitation of 60 sq. m. of living space. Yet these factors, though in themselves significant, were superseded in importance by two other developments.

Soviet planners were forced to face up to the fact that good building sites were becoming scarce in large cities and towns. They were rapidly being taken up by low-rise, government-owned apartment buildings and by small private homes. This low-density population concentration necessitated the location of new building sites farther and farther on the outskirts. Construction of medium- and high-rise apartment buildings offered a far more rational utilization of space. With a higher population density the spiraling costs of expanding the transportation and utilities systems would also be significantly lowered (by keeping them shorter); fewer stores to service the consumer would need to be built and distributing goods to them would be easier and cheaper.[30] Lastly, by 1962 the housing construction industry had developed sufficiently to mass-produce prefabricated housing materials. It finally had the capacity to operate year-round, on-site assembly, principally in large cities.[31]

In the context of these developments Soviet leaders no longer felt dependent on private-home building in large urban centers to help ease the housing shortage. From the vantage point of their building strategy, private construction had, in fact, become an obstacle to progress.

It was for these reasons that a joint party and government resolution of June 1, 1962, ordered republics to prohibit the building of private homes in their capitals and to stop issuing credits to individual builders who lived there. As of January 1, 1964, individual private-home building in the Russian Republic became illegal in Moscow and in large province (*oblast*) territory (*krai*), autonomous republic centers and in industrial cities, as well as in resorts with a population of over 100,000.[32] At the same time citizens were greatly encouraged to invest their money in housing construction cooperatives which were organized to finance (with government support) the construction of multistory apartment buildings for their members. This offered those who could afford down-payments of 1,000 to 3,000 rubles (40 percent of the apartment's cost, depending on its size) the possibility of moving into newly constructed flats, hopefully within a few years of joining the cooperative, without having to wait their turn on the list for new government housing to become available—which might take many years longer.[33] The resolution, while recognizing the need for individual home building and credit support for it in cities with a population of less than 100,000, projected that this would gradually be replaced by housing cooperatives over the next few years.[34]

How did these measures affect the urban private-housing profile? It noticeably declined, not in absolute numbers but in proportion to a rapidly growing public sector.

As Table 4-9 indicates, the private urban sector grew much more rapidly between 1950 and 1960 than government-owned housing. But

TABLE 4–9 Percentage Increase of the Urban State, Private, and Cooperative Housing Funds

	Millions of Sq. M. of Housing Space		Percent Increase	Millions of Sq. M.	Percent Increase
	1950	1960	1950–60	1970	1960–70
State	340	583	71.5	1,025.2	75.8
Cooperative	—	—	—	46.8	—
Private	173	375	116.8	457	21.9

Source: *Narodhoe khoziaistvo SSSR v 1970 godu* (Moscow, 1971), 546, 547.

between 1960 and 1970 this tendency was dramatically reversed, with legal restrictions placed on private-housing construction in large cities and towns and with the razing of private housing in urban centers to make room for medium- and high-rise apartment buildings that were erected on an assembly-line basis.

Great differences in percentage increase of urban private housing were discernable among republics.

These differences were due to:

1. The relative level of urbanization. The less urban a republic, the greater the proportionate number of medium- and small-sized towns where private-home building was legal and encouraged, as in Moldavia.
2. A relatively low 1960 base figure for private housing in some republics. This was significantly augmented by 1970, as in the case of Estonia.
3. National traditions of some republics which slowed the advances of modernization. In these instances apartment buildings tended to

TABLE 4–10 Percent Increase in Private Urban Housing Fund by Republic in Rank Order (1960–1970, 1965–1970)

	1960	1965	1970	1960–70 Percent Increase	1965–70 Percent Increase
	(in million square meters of housing space)				
USSR	375	432	457	21.9	5.8
Estonia	2.0	2.7	3.0	50.0	11.1 (5)
Moldavia	3.3	4.4	4.9	48.5	11.4 (4)
Georgia	9.7	11.6	13.1	35.1	12.9 (2)
Kirgizia	3.3	4.0	4.4	33.3	10.0 (7)
Lithuania	4.0	4.6	5.2	30.0	13.0 (1)
Ukraine	101.8	120.4	131.6	29.3	9.3 (8)
Belorussia	11.7	13.5	15.0	28.2	11.1 (5)
Azerdaidzhan	6.0	6.9	7.6	26.7	10.1 (6)
Latvia	3.7	4.3	4.6	24.3	7.0 (9)
Kazakhstan	18.4	21.6	22.6	22.8	4.6 (11)
Tadzhikistan	3.0	3.2	3.6	20.0	12.5 (3)
Armenia	4.6	5.2	5.4	17.4	3.8 (12)
Russia	185.4	209.8	217.2	17.2	3.5 (13)
Turkmenia	3.0	3.2	3.4	13.3	6.3 (10)
Uzbekistan	15.1	16.1	15.6	3.3	−9.7 (14)[a]

Source: *Narodnoe khoziaistvo SSSR v 1970 godu* (Moscow, 1971), 547.
a. Earthquakes in Uzbekistan caused widespread destruction of housing in 1966.

undermine their life-styles. The Georgians (not in public statements but in practice) have been the most consistent adherents of private housing. (See Tables 4-8 and 4-10). The only people to live in a Mediterranean climate in the USSR, they are a nation of wine drinkers who prefer living in houses with small vineyards and pressing their home-grown grapes for wine.[35]

Whatever the reasons for variations, the increase in the urban private-housing funds for all republics slowed even more perceptably between 1965 and 1970 than they had during the previous five years. This was mainly due to the changing housing construction ratio with respect to the state, private, and cooperative sectors.

Yet from 1918 to 1970 the private and cooperative sectors built the majority, 51.3 percent, of all urban and rural housing in the USSR. This was an unexpected and quite an astonishing figure that emerged from our research. Upon reflection, however, it is not so surprising: the priority allocation made by the Soviet regime for housing has remained consistently low for the majority of years that it has been in power.[36]

Only in the 1950's did the state take an increasingly active role in housing construction, both in percentage and in absolute figures (see Table 4-11). But it was not until the Seventh Five-Year Plan, 1961–65, that the majority of all housing construction, 58.5 percent, was taken over by the government. This had occurred before, in the five-year plans of the 1930's, but now there was a significant quantitative difference. Between 1961 and 1965 the state sector built 2.8 times as many sq. m. of housing space as were built during the three five-year plans from 1928 to 1940. By 1970, 65 percent of all new housing was state constructed. Of this 82.7 percent was built in urban areas.[37]

Several facts emerge from Table 4-12. First, the urban sector's share of housing construction increased dramatically from 53.8 percent in 1960 to 67.2 percent in 1970—the direct result of an urban USSR benefiting from a developing industrialized housing production and assembly technology—while the total number of sq. m. of housing built remained relatively stable. Second, while the total percentage of state housing built increased only slightly, from 75.6 to 79.9 percent, the government did get its way in cutting back the number of private houses constructed. (This was becoming a major concern.) The building of small private homes in urban areas shrank to 9.3 percent by 1970 (from 24.4 percent in 1960). Its place was taken largely by site-saving, multidwelling units constructed for housing cooperatives which built 10.8 percent of all new urban housing in 1970.

TABLE 4–11 Housing Built by State, Cooperative, and Private Sectors, 1918–1970 (in million sq. m.)

	Housing Space Built (million sq. m.)	Built by State[a]	Percent State	Built by Coops	Percent Coops	Built Privately by Workers and Salaried Employees	Percent Privately	Built by Collective Farms, Collective Farmers, and Rural Intelligentsia	Percent Collective Farmers *et al.*
1918–1970	2,435.9	1,184.7	48.6	46.8	1.9	457.0	18.7	747.4	30.6
1918–1928	203.0	23.7	11.7	—	—	27.5	13.5	151.8	74.8
1929–1932	56.9	32.6	57.3	—	—	7.6	13.4	16.7	29.3
First Five-Year Plan 1933–37	67.3	37.2	55.2	—	—	7.1	10.5	23.0	34.2
Second Five-Year Plan 1938–July, '41	81.6	34.4	42.2	—	—	10.8	13.2	36.4	44.6
Third Five-Year Plan July, 1941–45	102.5	41.3	40.3	—	—	13.6	13.3	47.6	46.4
1946–50	200.9	72.4	36.0	—	—	44.7	22.2	83.8	41.7
Fourth Five-Year Plan 1951–55	240.5	113.0	47.0	—	—	65.1	27.1	62.4	25.9
Fifth Five-Year Plan 1956–60	474.1	224.0	47.2	—	—	113.8	24.0	136.3	28.7
Sixth Five-Year Plan 1961–65	490.6	287.2	58.5	13.1	2.7	94.0	19.1	96.2	19.6
Seventh Five-Year Plan 1966–70	518.5	319.0	61.5	33.7	6.5	72.8	14.0	93.2	18.0

Source: *Narodnoe khoziaistvo SSSR v 1970 godu* (Moscow, 1971) 538.

a. I deducted 46.8 million square meters of cooperative housing space built between 1963 and 1970 from the state sector (these two sets of data are combined in Soviet statistical tables) and placed the cooperative sector in a separate category.

TABLE 4–12 Urban Housing Built by State, Private, and Cooperative Sectors, 1960, 1965, 1970
(in million sq. m. of housing space)

	All urban and rural housing built	All urban housing built	Percent Urban	Urban Housing Built					
				State	*Per-cent*	*Pri-vate*	*Per-cent*	*Coop*	*Per-cent*
1960	109.6	59.0	53.8	44.6	75.6	14.4	24.4	—	—
1965	97.6	60.7	62.2	46.2	76.1	8.0	13.2	6.5	10.7
1970	106.0	71.3	67.2	57.0	79.9	6.6	9.3	7.7	10.8

Source: *Narodnoe khoziaistvo SSSR v 1970 godu* (Moscow, 1971), 539.

Republic Variations

Housing construction figures among different sectors varied greatly from republic to republic. In 1970, 35 percent of all housing was still constructed privately and by cooperatives. But in seven republics the majority of all housing space was built by these two sectors, with three other republics nearly reaching the 50 percent mark. Though these percentages are impressive, they do indicate a substantial drop in the private sector's contribution to housing construction when compared to previous decades. In 1960, 49.1 percent of all housing was privately built and 10 republics had the majority of their housing constructed by the private sector. In 1950, when only 40.4 million sq. m. of housing space was erected (compared to 109.6 in 1960 and 106.0 in 1970), the private sector predominated: 55.9 percent of all housing was built by it, and in 11 republics private housing was constructed at a higher rate than the national average; in these republics more than 80 percent of all housing was privately built. The Russian Republic's percentage for that year was 38.4; in 1970 it had declined to 17.8 percent. (See Appendix E for 1950 and 1960 construction figures.)

Table 4-13 reinforces our understanding of housing patterns previously described for house holdings of various republics. One expects the highly rural, less economically developed republics of Central Asia with a tradition-bound Muslim population to build a large proportion of their housing privately and mostly in the countryside. What is surprising is the highly retarded state of their cooperative sector. No republic of that area succeeded in erecting more than 2.7 percent of its housing in the cooperative sector (and the figures achieved by Turkmenia and Uzbekistan are

TABLE 4–13 Percentage of Housing Built by State, Private, and Cooperative Sectors in Rank Order, 1970

	Space (in thousands sq. m. of housing space)	Percent Private and Cooperative	Percent State		Percent Cooperative		Percent[a] Private		Percent[b] Collective Farms and Collective Farms	Percent Rural
USSR	106,000	35.0	65.0	USSR	7.3	USSR	12.3	USSR	15.4	43
Kirgizia	1,847	61.1	38.9	Lithuania	15.4	Georgia	24.7	Tadzhikistan	41.9	63
Moldavia	1,462	58.4	41.6	Georgia	10.4	Kirgizia	20.4	Kirgizia	37.3	62
Georgia	1,847	57.8	42.2	Belorussia	9.0	Belorussia	19.8	Turkmenia	36.7	52
Tadzhikistan	1,133	55.3	44.7	Latvia	8.7	Ukraine	18.9	Moldavia	36.1	68
Ukraine	18,764	50.3	49.7	Estonia	8.6	Uzbekistan	16.6	Uzbekistan	32.5	64
Uzbekistan	5,122	50.3	49.7	Russia	8.2	Moldavia	16.6	Azerbaidzhan	31.6	50
Lithuania	1,824	50.2	49.8	Ukraine	8.0	Azerbaidzhan	15.6	Ukraine	23.4	45
Azerbaidzhan	1,518	49.8	50.2	Moldavia	5.7	Armenia	15.2	Georgia	22.7	52
Belorussia	4,328	49.1	50.9	Armenia	3.9	Lithuania	14.5	Belorussia	20.3	55
Turkmenia	1,083	47.3	52.7	Kirgizia	3.4	Kazakhstan	12.4	Lithuania	20.3	49
Armenia	1,301	33.7	66.3	Tadzhikistan	2.7	Tadzhikistan	10.7	Armenia	14.5	40
Estonia	765	28.8	71.2	Azerbaidzhan	2.3	Turkmenia	10.2	Latvia	10.4	37
Latvia	965	26.6	73.6	Kazakhstan	1.9	Estonia	9.8	Estonia	10.3	34
Russia	58,611	26.1	73.8	Turkmenia	0.3	Russia	8.3	Russia	9.5	37
Kazakhstan	1,847	20.1	79.9	Uzbekistan	0.1	Latvia	7.4	Kazakhstan	5.7	49

Source: *Narodnoe khoziaistvo SSSR v 1970 godu* (Moscow, 1971), 10–11, 541–545.

a. Urban and rural housing built by workers and employees.

b. Collective farms are rural cooperatives. No breakdown is given for amount of housing built by collective farms, collective farmers, and rural intelligentsia.

statistically insignificant). Why could Moldavia more than double that percentage although it has the highest rural ratio of any republic? Perhaps, in addition to the rural factor, a combination of other factors—such as a small, modern-housing construction base in Central Asian cities, the Muslim influence producing large families, a low reservoir of individual savings, less specialized education, lower earning power, and a general inability to raise funds for the down-payment. At the other end of the spectrum is Lithuania, outdistancing all republics in cooperative housing construction. Yet, its standard of living is lower than Estonia's, Latvia's, and Georgia's. Is it because its housing technology is most advanced and aesthetically developed of all republics? Is it because its housing bureaucracy, less tied up in red tape, responds to the needs of housing cooperatives? These were my impressions in 1971 after interviews with Lithuanian architects and inspection of their new housing districts.

Why Kazakhstan should have the highest ratio of housing built by the state, 79.9 percent, and therefore the fewest homes erected privately (including cooperatives) not only in towns but also in the countryside (by collective farms and collective farmers) in somewhat easier to explain. Since the 1950's Kazakhstan has been the recipient of enormous capital investment to support the Virgin Lands project to which Khrushchev and Brezhnev were politically committed. Over 35 million hectares of marginal unused lands, much of it in Kazakhstan, were brought under cultivation—and area equivalent to the total farmland in use in Canada.[38] Most of the new cultivation was undertaken by state farms (*sovkhozy*) to attract workers to a high drought-risk area. (These were primarily Russians and Ukrainians and not Kazakhs.) Unlike collective farms (*kolkhozi*), which are agricultural cooperatives, state farms are owned and operated by the government and run like factories. They guarantee monthly wages and also assume responsibility for providing shelter. Ninety and seven-tenths percent of Kazakhstan's farmlands are worked by state farms, by far the highest incidence of any republic. Therefore, by far the greatest amount of rural housing was also built by the state.[39]

Two additional factors contributed to the hegemony of state housing construction in Kazakhstan. It is the only republic where the native population, the principal builders of private rural housing in Central Asia, is in the minority (32.4 percent). Russians (42.8 percent) and Ukrainians (7.2 percent) form a Slavic majority, consisting chiefly of laborers who migrated eastward to work on state farms and in industry. Also, it is the only republic east of the Ural Mountains which has the majority of its population, 51 percent, living in urban areas where government housing construction predominates.[40] Therefore, because Kazakhstan's ethnic and agricultural profiles have been transformed, its housing construction pattern closely resembles that of the Russian Republic, rather than those of its Central Asian neighbors.

The Future of the Private Sector

What will the future hold for private and cooperative housing in the USSR? The private sector will continue to be the mainstay of house holding and construction in rural areas. Whereas in large cities housing cooperatives have become a surrogate for private-home building in many republics, private housing in medium-sized and smaller urban centers will continue to perform essential functions of providing shelter for as much as half of the population. Seventy-two and two-tenths percent of the Soviet urban population in 1970 lived in towns of 500,000 and under; 42.2 percent lived in urban centers of 100,000 and less.[41] The smaller the urban concentration, the less likely that housing cooperatives will replace privately owned homes. The June, 1962, party and government resolution projected this, because the two types of housing are not necessarily interchangeable. Each sector services different clients who have different needs and who command unequal resources. This was explained by B. Svetlichny, writing for *Kommunist,* the authoritative theoretical journal of the Central Committee of the CPSU:

> The view is sometimes expressed that individual construction must be gradually curtailed in favor of expanded cooperatives. Those who join cooperatives today are mostly well-to-do city dwellers, specialists, highly skilled workers who wish to improve their housing conditions, live separately from grown children, move from an overcrowded communal apartment into a separate comfortable apartment in a modern building. The individual builder is often a man who has recently come from the country to the factory, is not yet highly skilled and is therefore interested not only in a dwelling but also in a personal subsidiary plot so that he can feed his family better. He and the members of his family participate in building the house and thereby save a great deal. And it will hardly be incorrect to say that most members of cooperatives are by no means attracted to the idea of an individual house in a suburban settlement, without plumbing, gas or bath; the individual builder frequently cannot, and sometimes does not wish to, pay thousands of rubles in order to move into a city apartment, say on the fifth floor. Therefore for the time being we still need both cooperative and individual construction.[42]

Subsequent official statements have reaffirmed the legitimacy of private-home ownership and its assured future in Soviet society—contrary to the conventional wisdom held by many local officials who give private housing lowest priority. *Izvestiia* of February 25, 1972, pointed a disapproving finger at these local bureaucrats who treat home owners in a high-handed, unfair, and insulting manner, denying them water lines, sewage systems, building materials, and other services which they are entitled to but do not receive because "we don't serve the private sector." In Kazan the department servicing the gas lines made private owners dig out pits along the pipes to permit safety inspections, whereas the agency did it for people living in state-owned housing. In a mining town of Kamensk-Shakhtinsky, miners living on one side of the street had water pipes installed in government housing; none were placed in private housing on the other side. In Krasnodar and Novosibirsk telephone applications from private-home owners were not accepted.

Such discriminatory treatment was deplored, as were chronic shortages of building materials needed for the maintenance of private housing. This was in violation of a Council of Ministers USSR resolution of August, 1967, requiring executive committees of city councils to expand the sale of local building materials to citizens for home repairs. It was suggested that if home owners could legally purchase such materials, then black market profiteering would decrease.

To remove some of the stigma from private-home ownership (on which the government is still dependent and which it encourages by providing low interest loans), *Izvestiia* emphasized that it was important not to confuse private property "with personal property of citizens in a socialist society. . . . There is really no 'watershed' between the needs of those living in their own home and those who occupy state housing."[43]

Concluding Remarks

"We build and build, and we still don't have enough," a Soviet housing official told me in 1964.[44] Eight years later *Literaturnaia gazeta* still voiced the same concern:

> The tremendous amount of apartment construction in the past 10 to 15 years has not been able to keep pace with the population's rising expectations and demands. This explains why the waiting lists for new or larger apartments are longer than ever and why officials of local Soviet executive committees, enterprises and institutions in charge of housing distribution have increasing difficulty determining who should have priority.[45]

Why does housing still remain such a crucial problem? Why has the directive of the party resolution of 1957 which called for "eliminating the country's housing shortage within the next ten to twelve years," not been realized?[46] A rising expectation accounts for part of the problem. Almost all my Soviet acquaintances and those officials whom I interviewed in 1971 told me that they lived in separate (*otdelnie*) apartments, usually in new housing districts in the outlying sections of cities. Ten to 15 years ago most of them lived in one room, sharing a communal apartment with several families. Yet, many are still not satisfied with the amount of space they occupy (aside from such considerations as quality of construction or distance from the metro station—a major concern for Muscovites particularly).

They would like to upgrade their living conditions further; to acquire a separate room for themselves or for their children to sleep in (other than the living room); or, in cases where two or even three adult generations of a family live together (which is common), to receive a separate apartment for the parents or for the children, particularly if the latter have married. The few who do get a separate apartment do so only after a lengthy struggle with the housing authorities, because there are still significant numbers who are less fortunate, living in shared apartments with other families (the prevailing Western image of Soviet housing conditions) or in barracks and hostel-type housing. According to law these less fortunate should get first preference. Little information has been made public regarding their number, except that by 1975 it is expected that only 25 percent will still be assigned to communal flats in state-owned urban housing, compared to 60 percent who lived under such circumstances in 1960.[47]

Therefore, the continuous backlog remains a basic problem to overcome. Although 31,273,000 housing units were built between January 1, 1959, and December 31, 1970, truly a remarkable achievement, this proved to be insufficient to take care of past and current expectations, because for the same period the Soviet population increased by 35.1 million people.[48] (See Appendices D and F.) The sharp decline in population growth of the Russian and other European republics has been directly attributed to the housing shortage, because of the reluctance of families to have more than one or at most two children, due to overcrowded conditions. In contrast a rapidly expanding population characterizes the Muslim areas of Central Asia and the Caucasus, where lack of adequate shelter appears not to be a deterring factor. The Russian Republic's 1970 growth rate of only 5.9 per 1,000 inhabitants has been particularly worrisome to Soviet officials. If the trend continues the Russian people will soon be a minority in the USSR.[49] (See Appendix B.)

During the Ninth Five-Year Plan (1971–1975) the USSR ambitiously has projected to build 12 million housing units with 580 million sq. m of housing space.[50] It is more likely, however, that Soviet construction brigades and private builders will achieve about 90 to 95 percent of that target figure, or approximately 11.5 million units with 520 million sq. m. of housing space (the results of the preceding five-year plan) because underfulfillment has been a consistent factor of Soviet housing construction, and one which has predictably been caustically criticized by Soviet officials. Churning out over 2.2 million units a year since 1957, an accomplishment perhaps unmatched by any other country in history, has been a considerable achievement and an implicit declaration by Soviet leaders that housing needs for the Soviet people rank with the highest domestic priorities.[51]

Compare this with the rhetoric of the U.S. Housing Act of 1968, which called for 26 million units of new and rehabilitated housing to be built in the United States over the next 10 years, including 6 million government subsidized dwellings designed specifically to meet the needs of the nation's "housing poor" families and match these goals against the record of accomplishments. Even before President Nixon's "temporary freeze" on federally subsidized housing in January, 1973, went into effect, the prospects for fulfilling the projected plan for federally subvention housing fell well below the 50 percent mark. This is in keeping with past federally supported housing programs. A previous congressional law, the Housing Act of 1949, announced the goal of "a decent home and a suitable living environment for every American family" and authorized the construction of 810,000 units of low-rent public housing to be completed by 1955. This total had not been reached 20 years after the bill was passed.[52]

In analyzing Soviet housing data it was evident that housing investment and construction policies varied markedly among republics. This raises more questions than it answers at this time. The most dramatic instance of change was Lithuania's quantum per capita investment jump from 21.5 rubles in 1960 to 65.7 rubles in 1970, while Azerbaidzhan's remained stagnant at 31.0, though all other republics increased theirs substantially. (See Appendix A.) What sections of *Gosplan* (the state planning committee), *Gosstroi* (the state construction committee), the Finance Ministry, and other bureaucracies on the USSR level determined these priorities. Or were they primarily ordered by their republic counterparts? And what role do departments of the Central Committee of the

CPSU and of the republics play in these decisions? In other words who governs the investment policies for the republics? Is not the process perhaps much less centrally coordinated than is generally perceived?

Lithuania, which so improved its investment ratio, did even better in per capita construction, moving from last to first place between 1960 and 1970, while Azerbaidzhan dropped from fourth place to last.[53] (See Appendix B.) These differences, which need closer study, highlight the rich diversity within the Soviet mosaic.

What can be learned from the Soviet experience? Socioeconomic problems of such magnitude as a national housing shortage are rarely solved by a society, no matter what system prevails. Sufficient sums of money, it seems, can never be allocated to "solve" the problem. Money, by itself, is not a guarantee of success—it only guarantees a swollen bureaucracy. If a nation's leadership sets its priorities to eliminate a serious social blight and creates the remedial machinery to implement the goals it sets, significant strides "in moving away from known social ills can be registered.[54] This the Soviet Union is certainly in the process of accomplishing in the sphere of housing.

Notes

1. *Pravda* (March 31, 1971).
2. *New York Times* (October 20, 1967).
3. *Pravda* (January 23, 1972), trans. in *Current Digest of the Soviet Press*, XXIV, 3 (February 16, 1972), 16 (hereafter *CDSP*) and *Pravda* (January 30, 1973).
4. *New York Times* (October 20, 1967).
5. See Anthony Downs, *Urban Problems and Prospects* (Chicago, 1970), 164–174.
6. Timothy Sosnovy, "Housing Conditions and Urban Development in the USSR," *New Directions in the Soviet Economy*, prepared for the Joint Economic Committee, Congress of the United States, 89th, 2nd Session (Washington, 1968), 534, 535 and Maurice F. Parkins, *City Planning in Soviet Russia* (Chicago, 1953), 1.
7. John N. Hazard, *Soviet Housing Law* (New Haven, 1939), 7.
8. The definition of urban has not remained constant over time and differs, sometimes sharply, by republic. In the 1926 Census the urban population included those living in officially designated town or city (*gorod*) and in a settlement of an urban type (*poselok gorodskogo tipa*) provided that it had not less than 500 inhabitants and that more than half of the labor force was engaged in nonagricultural pursuits. The 1939 Census (which was never fully published) held, in the main, to the criteria of the 1926 Census. In the 1959 and the 1970 Censuses an officially designated town or city varied in size from 12,000 to 5,000 by republic and urban settlements ranged from 3,000 to 1,000. See Robert A. Lewis and Richard H.

Rowland, "Urbanization in Russia and the USSR: 1897–1966," *Annals of the Association of American Geographers*, LIX, 4 (December, 1969), 778 and Maurice F. Parkins, *op. cit.*, 3–4.

9. The First Five-Year Plan was completed in four years and the Third was interrupted by the German invasion of the Soviet Union in 1941. Therefore, the first three five-year plans do not span a period of 15 years.

10. Alec Nove, *An Economic History of the USSR* (Baltimore, 1969), 198.

11. *Narodnoe khoziaistvo SSSR v 1970 godu* (Moscow, 1970), 482, 483 (hereafter *N.K.*). These percentages are based on 1960 prices. Problems of using later price index for an earlier period are discussed in Nove, *op. cit.*, 381–388.

12. Anatoly Shtylke, *Millions of New Apartments* (Moscow, n.d.), 30.

13. *Pravda* (August 2, 1957).

14. For an expanded treatment of this point see my concluding remarks.

15. For the Georgian Republic the minimum norm is 12 sq. m., and for the Ukraine it is 13.65 sq. m. of living space. (A. G. Vlasova, V. I. Zemiatiin and V. R. Skripko, *Zhilishchnoe zakonodatel'stvo*, 2nd ed. [Moscow, 1970], 60.)

16. Computed from *N.K. v 1960 godu* (Moscow, 1961), 641; *Narodnoe khoziaistvo SSSR* (Moscow, 1956), 17; and D. L. Broner, "Zhilishchnaia problema v trudykh i gosudarstvennoi deiatel'nosti V. I. Lenina," *Vestnik Statistika*, 3 (1970), 10. For the method used see n. 19.

17. Housing statistics released by the Soviet government have become more plentiful and sophisticated in recent years. Yet only certain categories have been published. Specifically omitted has been the housing-fund data for rural areas, for the USSR, and for the republics. Therefore, housing conditions for rural areas measured by such indices as sq. m. of housing or living space or number of units cannot be analyzed at this time; 104.9 million, or 43 percent, of the Soviet population resided in rural areas in 1970. (*N.K. v 1970 godu* [Moscow, 1971], 10, 11.)

18. The Russian Republic spans two continents. It would be first in territorial size and the fourth largest country in population in the world (130,697,000) were it not part of the USSR. The Russian Republic contains within its boundaries 16 autonomous republics, 10 national regions (*okrugi*), and 5 autonomous provinces (*oblasti*). These areas, populated by various nationality groups, are in different stages of economic development. So are its large urban centers of Moscow and Leningrad, when compared to smaller workers' settlements. Therefore, aggregate figures for the Russian Republic are less meaningful than those for other republics. These are smaller; ten republics have less people than the city of Moscow, and, therefore, data for them are more meaningful.

19. Soviet housing statistics are invariably reported in sq. m. of housing space and *not* in sq. m. of living space, which every Soviet citizen goes by. The reason for this, I suspect, is that since the minimum living space standard has not been achieved for most Soviet citizens, housing space figures, being larger, present a much more impressive total. To calculate living space from housing space figures I have used the correction factor of .7 as D. L. Broner suggests in his *Zhilishchnyi vopros i statistika* (Moscow, 1966) 8, cited in Donald D. Barry, "Housing in the USSR," *Problems of Communism*," XVIII, 3 (May–June, 1969), 2. Broner's correction factor results in a slight inflation of the real living-space figures, at least for Moscow, the only city or republic for which aggregate living space data is available. For seven years that have been reported: 1960, 1965–1970, the true correction factor has consistently been .67. See *Moskva v tsifrakh, 1966–1970* (Moscow, 1972), 103.

20. That is why Armenia and Azerbaidzhan have been grouped with the Asian republics. See also the natural growth rate of these republics per 1000 inhabitants in Appendix B.

21. In regard to Moscow, Leonid I. Brezhnev in his address to the 24th Party Congress said, "Moscow is cherished by all Soviet people as the capital of our homeland, as our most important center of industry, culture and science, as the symbol of our great socialist power. (Applause) Extensive work on housing construction, the provision of public services and amenities and improvement in the transport system will continue in Moscow. To make a model communist city, this is the honorable goal of the entire Soviet people. (Stormy applause)" (*Pravda* [April 7, 1971]; *CDSP*, XXII, 13 [April 27, 1971], 6–7.)

22. Even by excluding Tashkent, which had the lowest average of living space, 5.6 sq. m., the city suffered serious housing damage in the earthquakes of 1966, the sq. m. average for the remaining six capitals rises only by .4 sq. m. to 6.9. Erevan and Baku, capital cities of Armenia and Azerbaidzhan, respectively, were grouped with Asian capitals for reasons explained in n. 20.

23. Adequate means measured by the official standard of a society.

24. Article 10 of the Soviet Constitution states that, "the right of a citizen to own . . . a dwelling house is protected by law." However, the revised Rules of the Communist Party of the Soviet Union declared that "It is the duty of a Party member . . . to combat vigorously all remnants of a private property psychology . . ." (Adopted at the 22nd Congress of the Party [October, 1961].)

25. See Joseph P. Fried, *Housing Crisis USA* (New York, 1971), 63–65 for a brief comparative view. Early in the century the Massachusetts Homestead Commission in a study concluded that, "in no country has private enterprise been equal to the task of properly housing the inhabitants." (*Ibid.*, 65.)

26. By my calculations approximately 57.5 percent of the Soviet people still lived in privately or cooperatively owned housing in 1970. I arrived at this figure in the following manner: 32.9 percent of 139,873,000 urban dwellers equals 45,738,600 living in urban nonstate-owned housing. Ninety percent of 104,873,000 rural dwellers equals 94,385,700 living in rural private housing. The sum of the last two figures equals 140,124,300, or 57.5 percent of the population. *N.K. v 1970 godu*, 9–11. I fully realize that, although 32.9 percent of urban sq. m. of housing space are in the nonstate sector, this does not mean that 32.9 percent of the urban population lives in it. But it is the closest approximation that can be made from the data available.

27. Despite a low percentage (23.9 percent in 1970), the Russian Republic held 47.5 percent of all private housing in the USSR because it has 59.4 percent of the urban population. Computed from *ibid.*, 10, 547.

28. Land in the USSR is owned by the state and cannot be bought legally. Individuals wishing to build have to petition local government authorities to receive permission to build on a given site. For size limitations on private-home construction see Article 106, *Civil Code of the Russian Federated Socialist Republic*, trans. Whitmore Gray and Raymond Stults (Ann Arbor, 1965), 28 and "Edict of the Presidium of the Supreme Soviet of the USSR" (August 26, 1948), "On the Right of Citizens to Buy and Build Individual Dwelling Houses," V.E.D. SSSR, 36, (1948), 4, in Zigurds L. Zile, *Ideas and Forces in Soviet Legal History*, 2nd ed. (Madison, Wis., 1970), 254.

29. Ziles, *op. cit.*, 254 and *Pravda* (August 2, 1957).

30. A Soviet commentator in 1965 described the problem: "In such large cities as Gorky, Kuibyshev, Sverdlovsk, Cheliabinsk, etc., the average height of buildings is now only approximately one-and-a-half floors. One-floor and two-floor buildings constitute 60 percent to 80 percent of the area of all residential sections which makes it extremely difficult to provide them with utilities and services." (B. Svetlichny, *Kommunist*, 6 [April, 1965] and *CDSP*, XVII, 22 [June 23, 1965] 12.)

31. This differed from area to area. In 1962, 47.2 percent of Moscow's new housing consisted of prefabricated, large-panel construction. The percentage for the country, however, was only 15 percent. See Cattel, Chap. 6, n. 24 of this book.

32. Presumably similar restrictions went into effect in other republics. The joint resolution of the Central Committee CPSU and Council of Ministers USSR was discussed in *Pravda* (August 7, 1962); *CDSP*, XIV, 32 (September 5, 1962), 17. The decree of the Russian Republic limiting the building of private homes in large cities and towns was described in *Izvestiia* (September 20, 1963); *CDSP*, XV, 38 (October 16, 1963) 32.

33. The average monthly income for industrial workers, engineers, and employees in the USSR was as follows (in rubles):

	1960	*1965*	*1970*
industrial workers	89.9	101.7	130.6
engineers	135.7	148.4	178.0
employees	73.8	85.8	111.6

Source: *N.K. v 1970 godu*, 519.

34. Before 1962 the organizing of housing cooperatives was permitted, but, because prospective members had to have full payment in hand to join, few were formed. In several Eastern European countries cooperative housing plays an important role. In Poland, for example, between 1966 and 1970 residential urban construction by cooperatives increased from 36 to 64 percent, and between 1971 and 1975 the planned increase is 68 percent of all new urban residential construction. (*Zycie gospodarecze* [June 8, 1972], 8, noted in *ABSEES, Soviet and East European Abstract Series*, III, 3 [January, 1973], 227.) In Hungary, however, the government has supported private apartment building on a large scale. With a downpayment of 10 to 15 percent a worker can buy an apartment. In 1965, 59 percent or 32,209 of all new apartments completed were of this order. By 1971 the total had risen to 70.2 percent, or 52,831, of all apartment units constructed. (This information was reported in *Nepszava, Magyar Nemzet*, and *Magyar Hirlap* (January 19, 1973) and noted in Radio Free Europe *Hungarian Situation Report* 4 [January 30, 1973], 6.)

35. Georgians are notorious for exceeding, sometimes by large margins, the maximum legal limit of 60 sq. m. of living space permitted for a private home. *Pravda* (October 19, 1972) reported that hundreds of Georgians were involved in constructing or procuring palatial country homes which were in the majority of cases built at the expense of the state; 989 of them were in one area alone. These were not simply wooden cottages, as dachas around Moscow, but large "castles." See also *Pravda* (November 27, 1972); *Zaria Vostoka* (November 14, 1972); and *New York Times* (February 13, 1973). Such figures are, of course, not reflected in the official statistics; what is reflected, however, is that, true to their life-style, Georgians had the highest per capita average of living space per housing unit built in the USSR, 44.6 sq. m. in 1970, but ranked tenth in per capita average sq. m. of housing space constructed. This means that they built less but built larger units. Computed from *N.K. v. 1970 godu*, 9, 541.

36. Compare the percentage share of housing constructed by the state with housing investment figures in Table 4-4. Soviet statistics unfortunately did not separate urban and rural housing construction until the 1960's and then only for the USSR and not for the republics.

37. Computed from *N.K. v. 1970 godu*, 539.

38. Alec Nove, *op. cit.*, 331.

39. *N.K. v. 1970 godu*, 291. Uzbekistan with 56.4 percent and the Russian Republic with 53.5 percent were the only others to have the majority of their sown area cultivated by state farms. These figures are as of November 1, 1970.

40. *Ibid.*, 10, 11, 19. The Kirgiz, the largest ethnic group in their republic, are technically a minority with 43.8 percent. The Russians and Ukranians combined form 33.3 percent and the Uzbeki 11.3 percent.

41. *Ibid.*, 46.

42. B. Svetlichny, *op. cit.*, 13. His statement contradicted the intent of the party and government resolution promulgated three years earlier. See n. 32.

43. *Izvestiia* ASeptember 14, 1971); *CDSP, XXIII*, 37 (October 12, 1971), 18. The Council of Ministers USSR resolution was reported in *Izvestiia* (September 9, 1967).

44. Henry W. Morton, "The Leningrad District of Moscow—An Inside Look," *Soviet Studies*, XX, 2 (October, 1968), 218.

45. *Literaturnaia Gazeta* (July 12, 1972); *CDSP*, XXIV, 45 (December 12, 1972), 12.

46. *Pravda* (August 3, 1957).

47. N. Bobrovnikov, "Razvitie zhilishchnogo stroitel'stva v tekushchem piatiletii," *Voprosy Ekonomiki*, 5 (1972), 24. The *New York Times* estimated that 33 per cent of city dwellers still lived in communal apartments in 1972. (*New York Times* [December 10, 1972].)

48. *N.K. v 1959 godu* (Moscow, 1960), 568; *N.K. v 1970 godu*, 9, 540. Since 70.4 percent of the Soviet population in 1970 was under 50 years of age and 38 percent under 20, continued popular pressure for improved housing can be expected, *N.K. v 1970 godu*, 13.

49. In 1970 the Russian people made up 53.3 percent of the Soviet population. (*Ibid.*, 15.) On an economic level Soviet demographers "foresee an accelerating labor shortage unless steps are taken to increase births, especially among ethnic Russians, who have been traditionally the most mobile and industrially skilled among this country's many nationalities." (*New York Times* [December 10, 1972].)

50. *Pravda* (November 25, 1971); Moscow Radio (November 28, 1972).

51. Even with this sustained building effort Soviet writers concede that in providing housing comforts the USSR still lags behind the capitalist West. See Bobrovnikov, *op. cit.*, 26.

52. Fried, *op. cit.*, 59–61 and *New York Times* (February 4, 1973).

53. Considering relative population growth rates in assessing Azerbaidzhan's decline is only a partial answer, since Turkmenia and Kirgizia, which have a similar natural growth rate profile, did much better in housing. Another factor which undoubtedly contributed to the decline was the widespread corruption which was uncovered in Azerbaidzhan several years ago and led to the purge of that republic's party leadership.

54. David Braybrooke and Charles E. Lindbloom, *A Strategy of Decision* (New York, 1963), 71.

Appendix A

Per Capita Investment of Housing Construction by Republics from Public and Private Sectors for 1960, 1965, 1970, in Rank Order
(in millions of rubles, 1969 prices)

1960			1965			1970		
	Ruble Investment	*Per Capita*		*Ruble Investment*	*Per Capita*		*Ruble Investment*	*Per Capita*
USSR	9,456	43.7	USSR	9,638	41.5	USSR	13,439	55.1
Kazakhstan	667	64.2	Kazakhstan	733	61.6	Estonia	105	76.4
Russia	6,041	50.1	Armenia	112	50.0	Kazakhstan	900	68.9
Estonia	52	42.5	Russia	5,989	47.1	Lithuania	208	65.7
Turkmenia	61	37.5	Estonia	57	43.9	Russia	8,148	62.3
Armenia	69	36.5	Lithuania	107	35.8	Armenia	157	61.7
Ukraine	1,529	35.5	Latvia	81	35.5	Moldavia	143	57.5
Azerbaidzhan	123	30.9	Ukraine	1,448	31.8	Latvia	136	57.0
Latvia	65	30.3	Turkmenia	61	31.8	Turkmenia	120	54.0
Georgia	127	30.2	Belorussia	268	31.0	Belorussia	452	49.8
Kirgizia	67	30.1	Tadzhikistan	77	30.1	Uzbekistan	554	45.0
Moldavia	86	28.3	Kirgizia	78	29.8	Kirgizia	134	44.6
Belorussia	231	28.1	Georgia	132	29.3	Georgia	193	40.8
Tadzhikistan	56	26.6	Azerbaidzhan	125	26.9	Ukraine	1,892	39.8
Uzbekistan	222	25.6	Uzbekistan	267	25.3	Tadzhikistan	118	39.5
Lithuania	60	21.4	Moldavia	83	24.7	Azerbaidzhan	162	31.0

Sources: *Narodnoe khoziaistvo SSSR v 1960 godu* (Moscow, 1961), 8; and *Narodnoe khoziaistvo SSSR v 1970 godu* (Moscow, 1971), 9, 541.

Appendix B

Housing Units Built per 1,000 People by Republics from All Sectors in Rank Order and Population Increase Per 1,000 Inhabitants, 1960, 1965, 1970

1960				1965				1970			
	Units Built (in thousands)	*Units Built Per 1,000 People*	*Population Increase Per 1,000 People*		*Units Built (in thousands)*	*Units Built Per 1,000 People*	*Population Increase Per 1,000 People*		*Units Built (in thousands)*	*Units Built Per 1,000 People*	*Population Increase Per 1,000 People*
USSR	2,591.0	12.0	17.8	USSR	2,227.0	9.6	11.1	USSR	2,283.0	9.4	9.2
Kazakhstan	164.1	15.8	30.5	Armenia	26.8	12.0	23.3	Lithuania	38.1	12.0	8.7
Turkmenia	21.7	13.3	35.9	Kazakhstan	139.1	11.7	20.4	Estonia	15.3	11.1	4.7
Russia	1,554.0	12.9	15.8	Russia	1,296.3	10.3	8.2	Armenia	26.9	10.6	17.0
Azerbaidzhan	49.0	12.6	35.9	Estonia	12.0	9.3	4.2	Russia	1,317.0	10.1	5.9
Moldavia	38.0	12.5	22.9	Ukraine	403.3	8.9	7.7	Belorussia	89.7	9.9	8.6
Armenia	21.5	11.4	33.8	Azerbaidzhan	41.4	8.9	30.1	Kazakhstan	124.0	9.5	17.3
Ukraine	485.5	11.3	13.6	Tadzhikistan	21.7	8.5	30.1	Kirgizia	27.1	9.0	23.1
Kirgizia	23.2	10.4	30.8	Lithuania	25.3	8.5	10.2	Latvia	21.2	8.9	3.3
Tadzhikistan	19.9	9.5	28.4	Turkmenia	16.5	8.5	30.2	Turkmenia	19.4	8.7	28.6
Belorussia	76.3	9.3	17.8	Kirgizia	22.0	8.4	24.6	Ukraine	392.0	8.3	6.3
Uzbekistan	81.0	9.3	33.9	Belorussia	73.8	8.2	11.1	Moldavia	29.4	8.1	12.0
Estonia	11.1	9.1	6.1	Uzbekistan	78.3	7.4	28.9	Uzbekistan	95.1	7.7	28.0
Latvia	16.0	7.5	6.7	Moldavia	24.1	7.2	14.2	Tadzhikistan	22.8	7.6	28.3
Georgia	30.9	7.4	18.2	Latvia	16.0	7.0	3.8	Georgia	29.2	6.2	11.9
Lithuania	14.9	5.3	14.7	Georgia	28.1	6.2	14.1	Azerbaidzhan	32.4	6.2	22.5

Sources: *Narodnoe khoziaistvo SSSR v 1960 godu* (Moscow, 1961), 8; *Narodnoe khoziaistvo v 1965 godu* (Moscow, 1966), 46, 47; and *Narodnoe khoziaistvo SSSR v 1970 godu* (Moscow, 1971) 9,50, 51,540.

Appendix C

Per Capita Housing Space Built by Republics from Public and Private Sectors for 1960, 1965, 1968, 1970, in Rank Order
(based on square meters of housing space)

1960		1965		1968		1970	
USSR	.51	USSR	.42	USSR	.43	USSR	.43
Kazakhstan	.71	Armenia	.59	Lithuania	.48	Lithuania	.58
Turkmenia	.57	Kazakhstan	.52	Estonia	.48	Estonia	.56
Russia	.53	Russia	.43	Belorussia	.47	Armenia	.51
Moldavia	.53	Ukraine	.42	Kazakhstan	.47	Turkmenia	.49
Armenia	.49	Turkmenia	.42	Armenia	.44	Belorussia	.48
Ukraine	.48	Estonia	.41	Russia	.44	Russia	.45
Azerbaidzhan	.46	Kirgizia	.39	Kirgizia	.44	Kazakhstan	.45
Estonia	.44	Lithuania	.38	Uzbekistan	.44	Kirgizia	.44
Uzbekistan	.43	Belorussia	.38	Turkmenia	.43	Uzbekistan	.42
Georgia	.42	Tadzhikistan	.36	Ukraine	.40	Ukraine	.40
Kirgizia	.42	Azerbaidzhan	.35	Moldavia	.40	Moldavia	.40
Belorussia	.39	Uzbekistan	.34	Tadzhikistan	.38	Latvia	.40
Tadzhikistan	.38	Georgia	.34	Latvia	.38	Georgia	.39
Latvia	.35	Moldavia	.32	Azerbaidzhan	.36	Tadzhikistan	.38
Lithuania	.27	Latvia	.31	Georgia	.36	Azerbaidzhan	.29

Sources: *Narodnoe khoziaistvo SSSR v 1960 godu* (Moscow, 1961), 8; and *Norodnoe khoziaistvo SSSR v 1970 godu* (Moscow, 1971), 9, 541.

Appendix D

Loss of Urban Housing Compared to New Construction by Republics in Rank Order, 1960–1970
(in thousand square miles of housing space)

	New Construction	Loss of Housing due to Razing and Other Causes	Percent Loss
USSR	685,839	101,913	14.9
Uzbekistan	19,334	6,382	33.0
Turkmenia	5,041	935	18.5
Russia	416,716	66,720	16.0
Kazakhstan	34,088	5,445	16.0
Estonia	5,085	683	13.4
Tadzhikistan	4,318	526	12.2
Georgia	9,783	1,173	12.0
Azerbaidzhan	9,832	1,122	11.4
Armenia	7,683	859	11.2
Ukraine	127,367	13,818	10.8
Lithuania	8,884	854	9.6
Moldavia	5,595	538	9.6
Latvia	6,690	609	9.1
Belorussia	21,086	1,884	8.9
Kirgizia	4,337	365	8.4

USSR	New Construction	Loss of Housing due to Razing and Other Causes	Percent Loss
1960	59,030	5,833	9.9
1961	56,114	5,595	9.8
1962	58,858	6,519	11.1
1963	58,469	7,326	12.5
1964	57,459	9,470	16.9
1965	60,597	10,956	18.1
1966	63,400	14,040	22.1
1967	66,108	9,248	14.0
1968	66,039	9,679	14.7
1969	68,570	10,498	15.3
1970	71,195	12,749	17.9

Source: *Narodnoe khoziaistvo SSSR v 1970 godu* (Moscow, 1971), 548.

Appendix E

Percentage of Housing Built Privately and by the State

	1950				1960		
	Sq. M. of Housing Space (in thousands)	*Percent Private*	*Percent State*		*Sq. M. of Housing Space (in thousands)*	*Percent Private*	*Percent State*
USSR	40,400	55.9	44.1	USSR	109,600	49.1	50.9
Tadzhikistan	544	89.7	10.3	Moldavia	1,616	78.7	21.3
Kirgizia	477	86.0	14.0	Uzbekistan	3,740	70.2	29.8
Uzbekistan	1,708	85.7	14.3	Georgia	1,749	67.9	32.1
Belorussia	1,688	75.4	24.6	Kirgizia	930	64.8	35.2
Moldavia	280	74.3	25.7	Azerbaidzhan	1,837	64.4	35.6
Armenia	406	73.6	26.4	Belorussia	3,237	64.4	35.6
Turkmenia	560	71.1	28.9	Ukraine	20,838	60.4	39.4
Georgia	783	61.8	38.2	Armenia	924	59.6	40.4
Ukraine	7,688	60.5	39.5	Tadzhikistan	791	59.4	40.6
Kazakhstan	2,093	57.5	42.5	Turkmenia	932	58.0	42.0
Azerbaidzhan	659	60.0	40.0	Lithuania	753	49.1	50.9
Lithuania	180	56.1	43.9	Russia	63,553	42.3	57.7
Russia	23,041	48.4	51.6	Kazakhstan	7,379	40.8	59.2
Latvia	154	32.5	67.5	Estonia	537	33.7	66.3
Estonia	175	15.4	84.6	Latvia	741	32.8	67.2

Source: *Narodnoe khoziaistvo SSSR v 1970 godu* (Moscow, 1971), 9–11.

Appendix F

Population of Republics, 1959 and 1970
(in thousands)

					Urban			Rural		
	January 15, 1959	**December 31, 1970**	**Population Increase 1959–1970**	**Percent Increase 1959–1970**	*January 15, 1959*	*December 31, 1970*	*Population Increase 1959–1970*	*January 15, 1959*	*December 31, 1970*	*Population Increase 1959–1970*
USSR	208,827	243,896	35,069	16.8	99,978	139,023	39,045	108,849	104,873	3,976
Russia	117,534	130,697	13,163	11.2	61,611	82,576	20,465	55,923	48,121	—7,802
Ukraine	41,869	47,496	5,627	13.4	19,147	26,282	7,135	22,722	21,214	—1,508
Belorussia	8,056	9,074	1,018	12.6	2,481	4,054	1,573	5,575	5,020	— 555
Uzbekistan	8,261	12,305	4,044	49.0	2,759	4,487	1,728	5,502	7,818	2,316
Kazakhstan	9,153	13,068	3,915	42.8	4,037	6,685	2,648	5,116	6,383	1,267
Georgia	4,044	4,734	690	17.1	1,713	2,278	565	2,331	2,456	125
Azerbaidzhan	3,698	5,219	1,521	41.1	1,767	2,624	857	1,931	2,595	664
Lithuania	2,711	3,166	455	16.8	1,046	1,627	581	1,665	1,539	— 126
Moldavia	2,885	3,619	734	25.4	643	1,172	529	2,242	2,447	5
Latvia	2,093	2,386	293	14.0	1,174	1,503	329	919	883	— 36
Kirgizia	2,066	3,003	937	45.4	696	1,131	417	1,370	1,872	502
Tadzhikistan	1,981	2,987	1,006	50.8	646	1,113	467	1,335	1,874	539
Armenia	1,763	2,545	782	44.4	882	1,527	645	881	1,018	137
Turkmenia	1,516	2,223	707	46.6	700	1,063	363	816	1,160	344
Estonia	1,197	1,374	177	14.8	676	901	225	521	473	— 48

Source: *Narodnoe khoziaistvo SSSR v 1970 godu* (Moscow, 1971), 9–11.

CHAPTER 5

Crime and Its Study

Peter Juviler

Crime fighting remains a "major task" for Soviet leaders in their effort to "mold" a self-disciplined, productive "new man." [1] Khrushchev had reformed, popularized, and toughened law enforcement all at once. His successors continued this multiple approach. They added 30 new crimes to the codes in eight years. They extended coercion both against political crimes (probably hundreds of convictions annually) and so-called common crimes (probably close to a million convictions annually, as we shall see). Procedural short cuts and harsher penalties for existing crimes also characterized a series of anticrime drives from 1966 into the 1970's against dissidents, hooligans, disrupters, pilferers in production, and drunkards. They centralized and mobilized the militia under a restored MVD (Ministry of the Interior) and brought the courts under a restored Ministry of Justice.[2]

Stalin relied virtually exclusively on compulsion. He made no exception for common crimes—our topic here (except that common criminals fared best in the camps). Post-Stalin responses to crime have interpreted crime fighting more broadly. "Crime fighting" now includes both repression and "crime prevention": heading off lawbreaking before it becomes serious enough to bring to trial. Comrades' courts, people's police, and children's commissions (commissions on the affairs of juveniles) remain from the Khrushchev restorations. Crime prevention is gradually coming to mean a broad political, economic, social, and educational effort at engineered change in social behavior. Trial courts are prodded to send more effective "special findings to convicts' places of work concerning baneful influences there." [3] An unprecedented mass propagandization of law and "socialist legality" through print, courses, and lectures aims at getting people to internalize respect for law and order and those enforcing it.[4] The party reinstituted crime studies, in the belief that, to fight crime effectively, you had to know more about it than that it was a manifestation of inherited evil and a "lag of consciousness behind development." Unlike in Stalin's day, crime studies survived the new hard line on enforcement, simultaneously maintained with fluctuations since 1961.

Crime studies raise issues relating to the work of criminologists and to the work of other specialists on crime on whom criminologists depend for assistance in gathering data, administrative and professional support, and policy guidance. Issues treated here are among the more crucial ones facing all crime fighters and the regime guiding them: (1) How should the participation of experts be structured so as to contribute to policy making in a way compatible with the leading political and ideological role of the party? This is taken up in the section, *Consulting Experts.* (2) How is crime to be recorded and how much of the record divulged? This is taken up in the sections, *Measuring Crime* and *Juvenile Lawbreaking.* (3) How is crime to be accounted for in a way that will reaffirm party claims for the superiority of one-party socialism and yet give useful guidance for prevention programs? This is taken up in the section, *Explaining Crime.* (4) How are statistics and theories of crime to be applied to bring about the sort of policing and social changes which will prevent crime? This is taken up in the section, *Prediction and Planning.*

Issues of crime prevention touch two basic questions in all communist programs for development and social change: the mix of "red" and "expert" considerations and the place and rationale for coercion and alternatives to coercion.

Answers sought here are far from definitive. Rather, they are oversimplified first approximations in the complex matter of Soviet political responses to a problem of social change.

Consulting Experts

Criminological research, paralyzed under Stalin, resumed by 1955 as sample surveys of its labor-camp inmates by the MVD (Ministry of the Interior).[5] Attacks on scholarly dogmatism and the devastating influences of the "cult of personality" of Stalin at the 20th Party Congress (1956) and clear party encouragement to legal sciences, including criminology, encouraged the few criminologists surviving from the 1920's and 1930's, like A. A. Gertsenzon, B. S. Utevskii, and the late E. G. Shirvindt to promote as best they could the restoration of their shattered discipline.

By 1963 criminologists achieved a long-sought goal, the establishment of a national crime-study center, the All-Union Institute for the Study of and Developing Means of Preventing Crime—the Institute of Criminology, for short—under the USSR Procuracy.[6]

The Institute of Criminology absorbed the Procuracy's own Institute of Criminalistics, where crime studies had been under way. Also, it recruited researchers from IGPAN (The Institute of State and Law of the USSR Academy of Sciences) and from the USSR Council of Minister's All-Union Institute of Juridical Sciences (then renamed the All-Union Institute on Soviet Legislation). The Institute of Criminology has no monopoly. Crime study proceeds also in the law faculties and institutes of the Ministry of Higher and Specialized Secondary Education and even more prominently in the MVD, as we shall see. Studies relevant to crime prevention go on also wherever sociologists, educators, and psychiatrists explore problems of upbringing, the family, youth, labor, and deviance.[7]

Expertise on causes and statistics of crime centers, however, in the legal profession. That is the continental tradition. Politically, jurists' access to policy makers is unpromising; other law enforcers' access is generally not much better. Jurists no longer hold top party posts, as law-trained Lenin and Krestinskii did.[8] Iu. V. Andropov, head of the KGB (security police) since May, 1967, rose to be a full member of the ruling Politburo in 1973. But Andropov was not a jurist. And the extent of his responsibility for crime fighting was not clear. Nor are there any jurists among the top 25 Soviet leaders on the Politburo and Secretariat. Not even Andropov, let alone any jurist, has approached the influence A. Ia. Vyshinskii had in 1939. He was then Prosecutor General, director of the Institute of Law of the Academy of Sciences, full member of the Central Committee (CC), and editor of *Soviet State and Law* and *Socialist Legality*.[9] Given Vyshinskii's regimentation of the jurists, maybe the absence of a superexpert is just as well for the health of scientific development in criminal policy and prevention.

Prosecutor General R. A. Rudenko and USSR Minister of Internal Affairs N. A. Shchelokov (his responsibilities include regular police, visas and places of detention) were members of the CC. Chairman of the USSR Supreme Court (until 1972) A. F. Gorkin and USSR Minister of Justice V. I. Terebilov (administrator of the courts and mass legal propaganda) have been members of the less prestigious Central Auditing Committee of the Party.[10] Gorkin, Rudenko, and Shchelokov made up the tiny contingent representing law and justice in the USSR Supreme Soviet elected in 1970; they were outnumbered more than two to one by the delegation from the KGB.[11] Compare this figure of two jurists out of 1,517 deputies with the 20 percent of lawyers in the House of Commons and the 60 percent of lawyers in the U.S. Congress.[12] Another token of lawyers' influence, a national bar association, did not materialize in the USSR. Lawyers there had tried unsuccessfully to form an Association of Soviet Jurists in 1958–1959.[13]

But jurists are not as uninfluential as this slight access through political office makes them sound. Neither the Central Committee nor the Supreme Soviet in session spawn initiative, debate, or participation in policy making. The absence of a Soviet national bar association spares Soviet jurists the risk of the sort of centralized professional coercion brought against potential nonconformity by associations like the Union of Soviet Writers and Union of Soviet Artists. Gordon Skilling has pointed out that loose groupings of individuals are more likely to be active exponents of common attitudes and more likely to propose innovations to the leadership than are organized groups.[14]

Party approval is indispensible for any major step forward in studying and measuring crime.

> The Communist Party of the Soviet Union guides all sides of our social life. . . .
>
> A many-sided approach to perfecting social processes underlies the prevention of crime and other lawbreaking. . . .
>
> One of the conditions for a successful fight against crime and violations of public order is the ongoing coordination of the activities of all state organs and social organizations conducting the fight against crime. Party organizations provide that coordination. . . .
>
> The Communist Party defines the basic scope of action by State and social organizations include those agencies responsible for crime fighting.[15]

Sensing organ for the party is its CC Department of Administrative Organs, overseer of law enforcement and the legal profession,[16] since 1968 under N. I. Savinkin.[17] Savinkin and his party superiors supply political judgments, but the jurists inside and outside the CC provide the expertise. It is because of this expertise as scholars, practitioners and crime fighters that jurists have exerted a growing influence since Stalin. As a profession, jurists have outlived various abortive projects for the "withering away of the law" or law enforcement before and after Stalin,[18] growing from 15,000 in 1928 to 127,000 in 1970 (106,000 with higher legal education).[19]

Criminologists proper of all ranks probably number a fraction of a percent of all jurists, on whose support they must depend for publishing, conference organization, funds for research, and alliances in the bid for access. Their fellow jurists divide, approximately into 4 percent theorists (4,765); 45–55 percent officials or legal staffs of political agencies such as courts, procuracies, MVD, KGB, soviets, ministries, and trade unions; 41–51 percent attorneys: advocates in legal-aid offices under regional colleges of advocates (about 14,000), and the rest (37–47,000), jurisconsults, or legal counsels to institutions, enterprises, and farms.[20]

Jurists' post-Stalin expectations of greater participation in policy making through writing and consultation have been at least partly fulfilled. Soon after Stalin's demise the regime turned to the Ministry of Justice to draft reforms in criminal law.[21] Such piecemeal liberalization turned later into a major effort at liberalizing justice as part of an ongoing recodification in all law, from pension reforms in 1956 to environmental protection in 1972. Liberalizing justice developed a life of its own beyond ministerial confines through broad consultation and debate across the country among theorists, officials, and attorneys, in the pages of the press, in law faculty meetings, sessions at research institutes and agencies, regional law conferences on socialist legality, public discussions of crafts, and the detailed work of the last stages in the subcommissions of the Legislative Proposals Commissions of the USSR Supreme Soviet and republic supreme soviets.

The party may arbitrarily "turn off" advice or protest. Still, jurists, as other professionals, gained greater access to policy makers after Stalin.[22] As for criminologists, other crime fighters may not follow their advice and at times may inhibit it, but they do not ignore it, either. In fact, they and the party actively solicit it.[23] The Procuracy and MVD spend a lot of money on criminologists and their research, via the Institute of Criminology and the MVD's Higher School and research teams.

Neither crime fighters in general nor the jurists among them nor criminologists in particular are united on issues of crime and punishment. They form no single coherent "interest group," despite the sense of being in one profession that their training or legal calling may give them. Any potential effect due to crime fighters' professional access is necessarily reduced because they are no more in agreement, no less divided into cross-cutting opinion groupings than crime fighters are anywhere else. Only when professional crime fighters tried to head off Khrushchev's extremes in popularizing justice via antiparasite assemblies, comrades' courts and volunteer police did crime fighters come close to unanimity of opinion. They were defending their professional role, their administrative power, and their careers against being supplanted by amateurs and apparatchiki. Issues of how those roles might best be carried out were temporarily laid aside. Outside this muted confrontation with Khrushchev no one theory of crime or punishment, no single working, middle range, ideology or theory of crime causation prevails among jurists. Stalin's conformity was forced, more apparent and surface than real. Crime fighters today openly divide between reformists and hard-liners, between sociological and psychological explanations of crime. They disagree even within those groupings.[24]

Criminologists lean toward moderation and reformism. But as we shall see, they are sundered by unresolved conflicts dating back to the 1920's and before. Schisms limit the impact of expertise. They contribute to the piecemeal and contradictory nature of Soviet criminal policy. But they enliven the Soviet quest for law and order. Contrast the recent diversity of views with the apparent but imposed unity of Stalin's day. Jurists then knew they "must clearly reveal the advantages of the socialist state and the socialist social system" over capitalism and of "socialist law" over "bourgeois law." [25] After Stalin, jurists tried to shake off this imposed unity. Unbelievable though it was to the observer at a national law conference in 1958, most of the audience drowned out with foot stamping the speech of their top scholar-jurist, P. S. Romashkin, director of the Institute of State and Law, while a minority sat in stony silence. Romashkin had attacked some Soviet jurists for finding common ground between "bourgeois law" and "socialist law." Had they not heard of party strictures against "peaceful coexistence in ideology"? Much of that same audience, gathered in the classic auditorium of Moscow University's downtown campus, cheered when a young colleague went up to reproach Romashkin for "the polemics and methods of criticism I thought we had left behind us." [26]

Socialist chauvinism like Romashkin's survives the Stalinist past decades later. Soviet progress in measuring and explaining crime will depend in part on how rapidly and completely Stalinist ideological formulations about socialist social change lose their restrictive and obligatory force. It would be unwise to jump to conclusions that ideological survivals of Stalinism have crime study at a standstill. Contrary to the expectations of this writer, innovation and even some deideologization proceeded in crime studies even while the regime turned the clock back toward the Stalin era in its repression of political and cultural dissenters.

Measuring Crime

Party monitors of criminal policy, and crime fighters, seemed to recognize after the 20th Party Congress that criminology must be revived to help criminal law catch up with "the needs of life," [27] that criminology in turn would have to move from vignettes to statistics, and that to be of any use criminal statistics would have to be freed from the Stalinist plagues of amateurism and secrecy.[28] One cannot but deduce that the Central Statistical Administration—CSA—dragged its feet on criminal statistical reform.[29] Even without CSA's active cooperation, however, surviving statisticians like S. S. Ostroumov began efforts to modernize and standardize the gathering of crime data, with the assistance of the policy, Procuracy, and courts.[30] Meanwhile, national statistics came into print on sensitive areas like harvests, industrial production, birthrates, and divorces—despite unfavorable trends showing up in the data. Yet, years after Prosecutor General Rudenko demanded an end to secrecy and despite experts' later pleas for openness,[31] national crime statistics remain unpublished state secrets even harder to unravel than are the carefully screened Soviet military budgets. Optimistic crime-trend statements crop up from time to time, as in Ostroumov's *Soviet Criminal Statistics:*

> Thus criminal statistics reveal a continual increase in crime, reaching astronomical proportions, in all capitalist countries without exception, especially in the USA.
>
> It is fully understandable why we should see a diametrically opposite crime situation in our country, for crime and other afflictions of bourgeois society like unemployment, poverty and prostitution are alien to it because of its social and economic system. Let us turn again to statistics. If we take the number of persons convicted in 1928 in the USSR as 100, then in 1955 it went down to 63, although the population during that time grew from 147 to 200 mln. people, or by 30.5%. This diminution of crime continues today as clear from a comparison like this: the number of persons convicted in 1968 as compared with 1958, the year current criminal legislation was adopted, diminished by 35% while the population grew during that time from 208.8 to 238 mln. or by 14.4%.
>
> For the last 40 years the population of the USSR grew by almost 90 mln. people, but crime decreased almost 3.5 times. The number of persons convicted per 100 thousand population in 1967 fell nearly twice compared with 1940 and more than three times compared with 1928.[32]

Using earlier data and information like Ostroumov's one can piece together a series on criminal convictions since 1928, as in Table 5-1.

TABLE 5–1 Criminal Court Convictions, USSR, 1928, 1940, 1968; Trends in Convictions and Convictions Per Capita Population, 1959–1968
(approximate estimates)

Year	(1) Convictions		(2) Trends in Convictions (1959=100)	(3) Trend in Convictions Per Capita (1959=100)
1928	1,610,000			
1940	1,390,000			
1946	>1,220,000			
1955	1,015,000	Krushchev is first secretary		
1958	1,421,000			
1959	>1,130,000		100	100
1960	< 942,000		< 83	< 82
1961	825,000		73	70
1962	1,080,000		96	91
1963	905,000		80	75
1964	< 815,000		< 72	< 67
1965	755,000	Brezhnev is first secretary	67	61
1966	998,000		89	80
1967	> 835,000		> 74	> 68
1968	922,000		82	72

Sources: See Appendix A.
> = more than. < = less than.

Court convictions for crimes appear to run about 800,000 to one million annually. At least they are of that order of magnitude. Because of changes in criminal policy, police effectiveness, and types of crimes, I have added indices only for the most comparable, recent years, after the criminal law reforms of 1958. With registered divorce rates doubling and birthrates halving in the 1950's and 1960's, what is so wrong with the crime trends shown in Table 5-1? True, numbers of convictions were still substantial in 1968, as high as in 1960. But Brezhnev was even tougher on thugs than Khrushchev. Conviction rates dropped over the long run from Khrushchev to Brezhnev, even in absolute totals. During the same period in the United States, national crime indices soared. A soviet record to be proud of in a crime-ridden world, one would think. So, then, why the secrecy on absolute conviction rates and on other data such as reported crimes and arrests? I can only guess at several possible contributing factors, but I find none of these to be entirely convincing.

1. Conceivably, secrecy was removed from some social and demographic statistics because so many experts needed them that closed circulation of the data made no sense. On the other hand, at most two or three hundred crime researchers in all specialties should be needing national crime-rate statistics, judging from the consulting mentioned in the last section of this chapter. This is a tiny band compared with nearly half a million engineers with advanced degrees, 60,000 economists, 50,000 physicians and dentists, and so forth, according to the statistical handbook for 1970. There were only 4,765 legal scholars in all, 15th out of 17 down the listing of scientific workers by specialty. Even if a fifth of the legal scholars needed crime statistics (which I doubt since criminal law and procedure are only 2 of 12 branches of Soviet law), it would still be easy to keep those jurists supplied with statistics.

2. Inconsistent and unreliable statistics on crime[33] may be difficult to tabulate and interpret in the USSR, no less than they are in the United States.[34] Not so long ago the leading Soviet criminal statistician was urging his colleagues to learn from the high quality Tsarist data.[35] Add to these problems the difficulties of comparison created everywhere by changing criminal policy, legislation, and efficiency of enforcement over time.[36] Thus, it is hard to compare the conviction numbers in Table 5-1 meaningfully as indices of trends in real crime. Convictions rose after 1953, it is said, because the liberal 1953 amnesty released too many unreformed criminals. Convictions dropped in 1959–1961 because criminal punishment was de-emphasized and then rose because of the crackdowns in 1962 and 1966.[37] Of course, inconsistency alone does not bar statistics. Many policy changes lurked behind the ups and downs in Soviet divorce statistics of 1.1 per thousand inhabitants in 1940, 0.4 in 1950, 2.6 in 1970, and so forth.[38] Yet these statistics appeared. Reports on forecasting cited later confirm other evidence that there are Soviet statistics on "all registered crimes, persons charged with crimes, persons subjected to social influences, and persons convicted." [39] Other reports I

shall mention cast doubts on conviction statistics as reliable gauges of real crime. These difficulties may help inhibit publications. But it is hard to see how they alone would be decisive.

3. Perhaps crime data do not sufficiently prove that crime is alien to socialist society, "diminishing" and slated to disappear,[40] do not sufficiently obey Lenin's summons "to confirm the theoretical conclusions of Marxism and make them unassailable."[41] If this were the sole reason for nonpublication, it would betoken a remarkable ideological consistency, despite several leadership changes after Stalin.

4. Perhaps totals of reported crimes and arrests show less auspicious trends than convictions do, as in the only local trend data available to me.[42] The Russian Republic chief justice (later, in 1972 chief justice of the USSR) appraised conviction rate data as "superficial" measures of the "real state of crime and convictions," "frequently" contradicting it.[43] Behind the scenes high officials have been grimly determined to get to the "real state" of affairs. A special target of theirs has been that group of local police officials who "fix" crime figures to understate and "embellish" crime in their precincts. To cover up, they ignore reports of crime, list murder victims as missing persons, book suspects for crimes less serious than those actually committed, and improperly report crimes as less serious "administrative infractions." To make matters worse, prosecutors connive in this local whitewashing.[44]

Another reason for believing that the "real state of crime and convictions" is improving more slowly than conviction totals show is the fact that, because of the 1958 reforms, the share of all criminal cases based on private complaints sent to criminal investigation had dropped in 1967 to one-quarter of the share of cases based upon private complaint sent to investigation in 1958 before the criminal-law reforms. In constant terms, conviction totals should be raised 14 percent for this reason alone in 1967, if they are to be compared with convictions totals for 1958 and earlier postwar years.[45]

Whatever the Soviet motivations for statistical secrecy may be, Criminologists and other observers do not take lightly the "real state of crime," as it filters out from piecemeal reports in the Soviet press. Despite secrecy on national crime rates, these reports, as Walter Connor says, are "exceedingly informative and valuable in gauging the significance of problem of deviance in the USSR."[46] Take the state of affairs in Moscow. Virtually any New Yorker will find Moscow streets much safer than New York's. Professor Kuznetsova and her Moscow University law students have drawn the dramatic contrast between the disorderly and dangerous

Moscow of 1923 and the safe Moscow of 1968–1969.[47] Per capita convictions there have fallen several times over, especially so for the most dangerous crimes, like murder. Robbery by gangs of armed bandits is all but wiped out along with the once notoriously overdeveloped Moscow underworld of professional criminals. And all this has occurred despite the huge population increase since 1923.

Moscow, however, was always an extraordinary case, one way or the other. Moscow in 1923 as a major railroad hub was extraordinarily ravaged by transient vagrancy and child vagabondage in the aftermath of war and famine. Moscow in the years after World War II was extraordinarily controlled as to residence permits, population in-migration, and criminal deviance. Yet, even in contemporary Moscow thieves plague wealthier residents with well-planned burglaries. It is not uncommon for people living in an apartment house to have keys to the elevator, equip apartment doors with peepholes and double locks, chip in for someone to run the elevator, and lock and guard doors by one a.m.[48] And Moscow has not been spared worrisome juvenile violence, alluded to below.

Worst reports on crime come from the fastest growing, most rapidly industrializing parts of the USSR, the new industrial settlements and the provincial towns, such as Dzhambul, Kazakhstan. (Dzhambul's population tripled since 1939, while Moscow's increased 60 percent, and in 1971–1972, five percent, while Moscow's increased 1.5 percent.)[49] Citizens' lives in Dzhambul, Kazakhstan, have been turned upside down sometimes because of their widespread fear of violent crime in its streets. Apparently many crimes known to the authorities never enter crime registers. A visiting reporter found nine people recovering in hospitals from injuries inflicted by hooligans. *But not one of the incidents involved was reported in the log of the militia's headquarters, the city Department of Internal Affairs.*[50] Dzhambul, where people try to stay off the streets at night, is closer in atmosphere to many fear-ridden American cities than are most places foreign tourists reach in the USSR. Perhaps the average crime picture in the USSR lies somewhere in between James Reston's glowing depiction of a Moscow that is a "policeman's paradise"[51] and troubled Dzhambul, where sometimes one's wife or relative out late may not get home at all but end up in the clinic or the morgue.

Soviet car owners remove windshields from their machines except when driving in the rain. Citizens keep children off the streets as much as possible, especially after amnesties, such as the prisoner release in 1967. They carefully watch their baggage when traveling.[52] Gates on many a high garden fence carry a sign, *ZLAYA SOBAKA*, "Beware of the dog." Some homeowners go to the extent of sleeping outdoors with shotguns or stringing up electrified fences when their fruit and vegetables are temptingly ripe, sometimes with fatal results to unintended young victims.[53] Residents in factory barracks and distant collective-farm villages become accustomed to thieving, violence, and drunkenness among the young and not so young and try to protect themselves accordingly.[54]

Saratov is a Volga River manufacturing town of some 773,000 inhabitants; its population has more than doubled since 1939.[55] Researchers there asked a sample of 827 male blue- and white-collar workers in the mid-1960's about their experiences with crime. And they did get results published. One out of three respondents said they had been victims or witnesses of crime. Most crimes involved were serious: 45 percent hooliganism and violent crimes against individuals. The other 55 percent of crimes experienced or witnessed were those against socialist (state and cooperative) and personal property.[56]

National data such as listed in Table 5-2 show, roughly, the same high proportions of crime likely to be most felt by individual citizens or by persons responsible for guarding socialist property against theft.

According to these figures from the later 1960's, the largest number of convictions were for crimes most likely to be felt and feared by the general public: crimes associated with violence (39 percent) and against personal property (16 percent), or 55 percent in all. Most of the other crimes are "common crimes" (*obshcheugolovnye prestupleniia*) of general social concern.

Hooliganism, an age-old offense, persists as the leading cause of convictions, despite the period drives against it.[57] Hooliganism accounts for up to 40 percent of convictions in urban courts. Moonshining accounts for up to a third of court convictions in rural areas.[58] More often than not hooligans are males under 30, intoxicated, and with records of past disciplining for petty hooliganism.[59]

Levels of convictions for violent crimes like murder, aggravated assault, and rape stay high. Recent drops in convictions for these crimes seem to be more apparent than real.[60]

Serious state crimes like sabotage, espionage, and terrorism disappeared after the stormy years of the Great Patriotic War and its aftermath.[61] Crimes against state and cooperative property declined since the war years but remain frequent and widespread. According to a sample survey in the Lithuanian republic, 21–22 percent of public property thefts oc-

TABLE 5–2 Proportions of Crimes for Which Persons Were Convicted, USSR, c. 1967
(percent, estimated)

Hooliganism (rowdyism and assault breaching the peace)	24
Other crimes against public safety, order, health (including drug abuse)	over 9
Crimes against persons (murder, rape, assault, etc.)	15
Crimes against socialist (state and cooperative) property	16.5
Crimes against personal property (including larceny, burglary, fraud, blackmail, vandalism, arson)	11.2
Snatching (*grabezh*) and robbery (*razboi*)	4.8
Motor-vehicle crimes (negligence, joyriding, etc.)	5
Economic crimes (substandard production, speculation, moonshining, forging stamps and railroad tickets, poaching, violating veterinary and plant health rules, falsifying statistics, etc.)	5
Crimes against the administrative orders (slandering the Soviet system, public disorders, disobeying peace officers, violating rules governing passports, residence, military draft, etc.)	4
Malfeasance in office (abuses, carelessness, bribery, etc.)	2.3
Crimes against justice (by judicial personnel, inmates escaping, etc.)	1.5
Crimes against the political and labor rights of citizens	0.5
Crimes which are survivals of local customs (feuds, paying bride price, forcing women to marry or marrying a person under legal age, bigamy, polygamy—where said acts are survivals of local minority customs)	0.4
Other crimes (state crimes, military crimes)	less than 0.8

Sources: See Appendix B.

curred in factories, 9–15 percent in offices handling funds, 15–23 percent in construction organizations, 20–25 percent in state farms. Most of the thefts were by pilfering, embezzling, and misappropriation rather than by robbery or snatching (*grabezh*).[62] Taking public property is a crime likely to be understated in the percentages and higher than the 15–18 percent stated for recent years, because many people tolerate it or turn away when they see it, often because they steal themselves when they get the chance.[63] "Probably you know people," the USSR minister of justice has written, "to whom you would entrust the keys to your apartment with complete peace of mind knowing they would not take a pencil, but who have no inhibitions against 'helping themselves from production,' . . . rationalizing that the state won't miss it." [64]

Theft of personal property also has dropped since the World War II era. But it remains a frequent crime, and it is not going down everywhere. One in three of such crimes is particularly frightening, a robbery or snatching. There is a grim undertone of political repression in the USSR. But most lawbreaking there is nonpolitical. Criminal haunts, the old markets swarming with pickpockets, thieves, and child vagabonds—such adornments of Tsarist and Bolshevik Russia—have been all but eliminated in striking contrast to the failure in the U.S. to cope with the criminal underworld. The long-run trend in convictions has been down, as far as one can tell. But progress recently against serious crimes against persons and property has been at best mixed,[65] despite the many anticrime campaigns under Khrushchev and Brezhnev. To be fairer, one should compare Soviet results not with the optimistic official goal of "fully eliminating crime," but against the dismal failings of crime prevention in the U.S.

I shall not try to build a workable outsider's explanation for the persistence of crime in the USSR. This rash venture would take us far afield into theories of crime in modern societies. But I shall dwell for a moment on the no less striking persistence of countercultures opposed to official communist morality. There is the counterculture of white-collar crime among corrupt officials and speculators in everything from grave plots and college admissions to drugs, moonshine, foodstuffs, building materials, and neckties. There are the countercultures of drinking, about which more in a moment, and of the pilfering of state property, also widely tolerated among the public at large. There are remnants of an underworld of common criminals, as the statistics of the Institute of Criminology show. Of adult thieves 38 percent have no legitimate occupation and 72 percent are repeaters. Among the repeaters 53 percent have no legitimate occupation and 25 percent have no permanent place of residence but drift across the country at the edge of organized society. Only 20 percent of robberies and snatching are committed by criminals acting alone. Nearly 40 percent of the robberies and snatching are committed by permanently organized gangs or groups of at least two people. Recidivists make up 47 percent of all those convicted of robbery or snatching. Likely as not, these criminals began their careers in childhood or adolescence. For 60–70 percent of recidivists began their criminal careers before reaching the age of 18.[66]

Sovietskaia iustitsiia devoted part of three issues to reporting the trial of a criminal gang of 17 Georgians. The trial consolidated 60 cases and lasted six months. (Felony trials are usually over in a day or two.) Working in two's and three's, the crooks committed 67 known robberies and thefts in two years in more than a dozen cities, with takes running into thousands of rubles. They would gain a victim's confidence and then defraud him or, more often, rob him using a gun or knife or their favorite means, wine drugged with narcotic sleeping pills, from which three of their victims died through overdose. They used mistresses' flats as home bases and relied on the gullibility of victims and their readiness to drink. Hotels rented rooms to the crooks after seeing their forged passports or none at all. Private renters taking high payments failed to register them with the police, then regretted their failure when they discovered other tenants drugged and robbed. Savings banks honored stolen pass books on the basis of false identification to the tune of 170,000 rubles. The gang managed even to get a rather well-known writer to let them use his country retreat in the literary colony of Peredelkino.[67]

Statistics have brought out women's role in antilegal subcultures. Only 10 women get convicted for every 100 men. But women help mightily to swell the ranks of pilferers and shady dockside denizens. Women are 25 percent of persons convicted for stealing socialist property, 60 percent of persons convicted for speculation, and 70 percent of persons convicted for defrauding customers. The Institute of Criminology studied a sample of women inmates in two corrective labor colonies. Relatively few women had been convicted of murder, and among the murderers between a quarter and a third had committed infanticide. Over half the women were in for theft—38.1 percent for theft or misappropriation of socialist property. Most women inmates had been living in the cities. A negligible share of the inmates were peasants. Female thieves of personal property, mostly 18–25 year old, included a large number of single women without family ties—typically, professional thieves, vagabonds, or beggars. Former alcoholics, drug addicts and prostitutes abounded among them. As a rule, females serving time for stealing personal property had lived off sailors in port cities.[68]

Alcoholism is so rampant that it may be called a "subculture" only in that the rulers deplore and disapprove. They single it out as a "direct 'accomplice' of the convicted in a majority of cases."[69] Observers in America, with her nine million problem drinkers and 15 billion dollars annual social cost of alcohol abuse,[70] may wish to follow closely in coming years the results of an almost continual stream of punitive, therapeutic, and restrictive Soviet directives poured out by party, government, and courts between 1966 and 1972 to treat and prevent drunkenness.[71]

Soviet surveys associating drunkenness and crimes may not exactly tally, as Table 5-3 shows. But they show a consistently high rate of intoxication among persons when they committed crimes, especially crimes of violence. Curbing drunkenness is complicated not only by ignorance as to its social causes but also to public tolerance and social custom. In

TABLE 5–3 Percent of Persons in a State of Intoxication When They Committed Their Crimes, c. 1971, USSR and RSFSR

	Reporting Agencies	
	USSR Procuracy[a]	*RSFSR Min. of Justice RSFSR Supreme Court*[b]
All Crimes		53.3
All crimes and rowdyism	over 50	
Murder	68	73.9
Rape	69	73.4
Criminal hooliganism	over 85	90.9
Robbery and snatching	76	
Aggravated assault	75	

Sources: a. "Usilim bor'bu protiv p'ianstva i alkogolizma," *Sotsialisticheskaia zakonnost'*, 9 (1972), 9.
b. "Zadachi sudov v bor'be protiv p'ianstva i alkogolizm," *Sovetskaia iustitsiia*, 17 (1972), 5.

"no other case of deviance is the gap between official and unofficial or public attitudes so great as in that of drunkenness." [72]

Juvenile Lawbreaking

Alcohol abuse among juveniles (persons under 18) is for Soviet experts a particularly crucial symptom of a crime-breeding counterculture. Firstly, Soviet experts, as experts in the U.S., consider juvenile lawbreaking the number one key to bringing down rates of common crime generally.[73] Secondly, a majority of juveniles, too, commit crimes in states of intoxication,[74] or steal in order to get liquor.[75]

Heavily policed Red square, symbolic heart of the communist world, is an unlikely place for a rumble. But one took place there with the class overtones of "town and gown" conflict. Apparently a group of boys from 14 to 16 years old rode two hours to Moscow on the train from the factory town of Orekhovo-Zuevo. Arriving at Moscow's Kazan Station, they got into a fight with some Moscow lads and lost. Plotting revenge, the provincialites drank a lot of vodka, which they had no trouble buying. That evening, equipped with files and other sharp weapons, they went to Red Square. It was graduation night for secondary school students, which seniors traditionally celebrate by strolling and singing on Red Square, dressed in their best clothes. The boys from Orekhovo Zuevo attacked the celebrating students and in the ensuing melee one youth died and 17 were injured. Effective 1966, and evening curfew was placed in Moscow on youngsters under 16 unaccompanied by adults.[76] More than two years after the rumble *Izvestiia* ran a story of fatal conflict between groups of teenagers from different apartment houses.[77]

Another year later, I received some direct corroboration on teenage lawbreaking during a long conversation with a 20 year-old worker from northern Russia, a devoted member of the Komsomol (Young Communist League). Though aware of material difficulties, Tanya was still a true believer in the Communist future. I asked her whether there was any problem with juvenile lawbreaking in Archangel, an area off the tourists' beaten path (but from which we have some data; see Table 5-5). "Oh yes, the boys in our workers' dormitories carry knives." Why? "They don't trust one another. They are selfish. They live too much for themselves." Do they get into trouble with such attitudes? "Yes, you can go out in the provinces and you will see the labor camps are full—and predominantly with young people." How was the country to reach communism if young people felt like that? "Well, perhaps now they have nothing to do. They're bored. They get into trouble. But things are better now. Under Khrushchev, for example, the stores were empty. It was awful. Sometimes we could not buy bread. Now things are better."

Tanya and I spoke at the end of a decade during which the chances of being victimized by a juvenile criminal, one may guess, had risen about 80 percent, and the absolute number of juvenile crimes had just about doubled. The birthrate bulge after World War II had much to do with this.[78] No detailed national data exist on crimes committed by Soviet juveniles or their share in total crimes. But their stated share of criminal convictions runs from 3–4 to 9–10 percent, depending on the region.[79] About one-third to one-half of juvenile cases are dropped or handed over to children's commissions[80] (*Komissii po delam nesovershennoletnikh*). (These boards of volunteer local officials and public figures and their paid secretary, operating under local soviets, handle all cases of juvenile lawbreaking by children under 14, less serious crimes and other offenses of children 14 and 15 years old, and petty offenses of children 16 and 17 years old.)[81] The practical effect can be seen in Table 5-4.

Because of this channeling outside the courts, the juveniles' actual share in crimes may run closer to 5–15 percent. Apprehended juveniles are overwhelmingly males, as Table 5-4 shows. Among those sentenced by courts (for the more serious crimes) only some 2–5 percent are females. Serious juvenile crimes of violence are rarer than among adults, as a comparison of Tables 5-2 and 5-5 indicates. So do Soviet generalizations on the subject.[82]

TABLE 5–4 Age and Sex of Juveniles Convicted by Children's Commissions and Courts, USSR, c. 1962–67
(percent)

	Children's Commissions USSR[a]	Courts USSR[a]	Courts Lenin Borough Moscow[b]	
Males	90	95–98	93–96.5	
Females	10	2–5	3.5–7	
			1966	*1967*
Under 14	15–20	–	–	
14–15	40–45	15	13.1	–
16–17	35–45	85	86.9	100

Sources: a. *Kriminologiia,* 340–42.
b. D. S. Karev, ed., *Izuchenie i preduprezhdenie pravonarushenii sredi nesovershennoletnikh* (Moscow, 1970), 24–25.

Noncriminal juvenile offenses far outnumber crimes. In Moscow's Lenin Borough, 11.1 percent of lawbreaking was crimes, and 88.9 percent noncriminal infractions or juvenile status offenses. Unfortunately, the list of lawbreaking for which children were registered at children's rooms of police stations is incomplete, as often is the case with Soviet figures. We are told, then, that 11.1 percent of lawbreaking was in the form of crimes listed by the criminal code; 12.2 percent, petty hooliganism; 2.6 percent, petty stealing; 6.2 percent, running away from home, children's homes, and reform schools; 31.8 percent, malicious mischief (could include lesser forms of hooliganism—breaching the peace); 4.0 percent, violating traffic regulations; 1.1 percent, carelessness with fire; 0.6 percent, vagrancy and ticket scalping; and a large 30.4 percent, "for other violations." [83]

The children's commissions, as their legal authority indicates, handle cases mainly dealing with lesser crimes, infractions, and juvenile-status offenses, as listed, for example, in Table 5-6. Thieving and group violence seem to be the most frequent forms of juvenile lawbreaking. This conclusion from the information just considered is supported by other reports. A third of the inmates of juvenile labor colonies interviewed by the Komsomol's Institute of Public Opinion had been arrested when involved in fights. Much of the fighting came after sudden, unpremeditated bursts of hostility.

> "We had some drinks, then went out on the street. The guys had nothing to smoke. I went up to a fellow and asked for a cigarette. He did not give it to me, and that's how it began. . . ." "Sometimes I feel like

TABLE 5–5 Court Convictions for Juvenile Crimes, Selected Regions, USSR, 1962–1965
(percent)

	(1) Archangel Province 1963	(2) Leningrad (Sample) 1962	(3) Leningrad Moscow Borough 1962–1965
Murder	0.9	0.25	
Aggravated assault	2.9		
Inflicting bodily harm (including assault, rape, infecting with V.D.)		2.2	
Murder and inflicting bodily harm			2.8
Sex Crimes	8.7		
Hooliganism	6.8	30	
Stealing[a] (larceny, burglary)	32.0	35	
Snatching (*grabezh*)	12.7		
Robbery	7.2		
Unaccounted for	28.8	32.55	

Sources: (1) V. N. Kudriavtsev and N. A. Iakubovich, *Preduprezhdenie prestupnosti nesovershennoletnikh* (Moscow, 1965), 225.; (2) and (3) V. V. Orekhov, "K voprosu ob izuchenii prestuplenii nesovershennoletnikh protiv zhizni i telesnoi neprikosnovennosti," *Chelovek i obshchestvo,* II (1967) 139.

a. Column (1) target not specified; column (2) stealing socialist property.

TABLE 5–6 Lawbreaking (Crimes, Infractions, Juvenile-Status Offenses) of Juveniles Brought Before the Children's Commission, Krasnopresenskii Borough, Moscow, 1963
(percent)

Malicious mischief and hooliganism	26.3
Stealing (burglary, larceny, petty larceny)	37.5
Drunkenness	8.9
Joyriding	5.1
Making and carrying weapons	2.9
Sexual dissipation and debauchery	3.0
Running away from home	8.9
Other lawbreaking[a]	7.4
	100.0

Source: E. V. Boldyrev, *Mery preduprezhdeniia pravonarushenii nesovershennoletnikh v SSSR* (Moscow, 1964), 145.

a. Probably includes murder (if any), inflicting bodily harm, drug offenses (if any), etc.

> fighting." "Hostility springs up." "I was incensed when students sneered at my friends and me."
>
> Sometimes it is literally out of old testament antiquity—fist fights between boys from neighboring workers' settlements, ethnic districts, and streets. Your street is the beginning and end of the world. Beyond it lies alien soil and the people are enemies. Many inmates blamed their crimes on boredom and the lack of recreational facilities.[84]

Boredom anywhere may bring wanton violence, as in Tashkent, Uzbek Republic:

> On stoops and in alleyways one can often see idle, lounging, smoking teenagers. . . . In February on Figel Street, teenagers tied up drunken citizen R. Then one of the kids threw a cigarette butt on him. His clothes, soaked in a half litre, caught fire. Citizen R. died from severe burns he suffered. It was established that in the group of teenagers "amusing themselves" in this manner were pupils of various schools and ages: eighth grader from School No. 145 Nikolai Teplakov [school starts at age seven], sixth grade pupil from the same school Yuri Chikin, fifth grader Aleksandr Grishin, and second grader Aleksandr Metzlikin from School No. 52. Sergei Pesivtsev and Aleksandr Loshmakov in the group came also from the latter school. The oldest one was a tenth grade pupil Viktor Nekrasov from School No. 18.[85]

Note that the perpetrators were all in school and not indigenous Uzbeks, but apparently of Russian or other European nationality.

Soviet juvenile gangs seem smaller and less stable or organized than U.S. gangs are. Somewhere around 75 percent of juvenile stealing, robberies, and mayhem are committed in groups, however, and only 25 percent by solitary lawbreakers.[86]

Soviet secrecy about lawbreaking may have something to do with statistical difficulties, and even more to do with the persistent seriousness of crime. Recent drops in crime have been at best uneven; anticrime campaigns, no panacea. Stalin closed his eyes to this or reached for the cudgel. The party today turns also to criminology, or the study of crime and the development of ways to prevent it.

Explaining Crime

What causes crime in Soviet society? Answers to this question have reflected the *freedom and diversity* of studies in the 1920's, their pure *ideologization* by the mid-1930's, and the revival of research on crime under conditions of *partial secrecy and political tutelage* since the mid-1950's.[87] Here I shall trace some recent issues posed for crime studies not only by their own inner development but also by the efforts of the regime to keep social studies "red" while encouraging them to be "expert." By "red" I mean here ideologically orthodox, supportive of party legitimacy because supportive of the formulation that "the socialist system creates the preconditions for eliminating crime. Crime in inherent in capitalism but alien to socialism by its very nature." By expert I mean the empirical research on crime and development of "applied scientific means of social prophylaxis," [88] let the chips fall where they may. My thesis here is that gradually, and with setbacks, "expert" is gaining over "red" in the study of crime. Ideology does not hold progress in criminology quite to a standstill, as it is sometimes assumed.[89] I shall provide a few supporting bits of revealed evidence on this.

1. State funding of scientific research provides needed resources but adds operative (budgetary) rigidity in the USSR[90] as anywhere else. Likewise, state patronage over Soviet criminology through the research institutes and universities gives advantages of access to funds, agency cooperation, and crime data collected by the government. Among the disadvantages are the tutelage and secrecy that flow from the same patronage.

2. Khrushchev broke one ideological shackle in 1956 when he repudiated the class struggle basis of crime and increasing repression in the USSR.[91]

3. A second ideological shackle remained, the doctrine of "survivals." The party's "expert" mood since 1956 has been to encourage "concrete social research." The party's "red" mood leads it still in the 1970's to endorse from on high the thesis that crime is a "survival of the past." [92] "Survivals" was still part of official ideology (defining ideology as a stated set of beliefs and preferences oriented to evaluating, guiding, or justifying political action). The formulation persisted despite some withering of obligatory ideology in the USSR, because it supported the irreducible core of doctrine: the need for the party's leading role in society and the legitimizing purpose of that role: its "historic mission" to build the best society the world has seen. If crime is a stubborn survival of the previous social order, then its survival in the USSR does not blemish party achievements. Its survival does not belie the doctrine that only the guidance of a single "Marxist-Leninist" party and planned socialism can eliminate the evil side effects of industrialization.[93]

4. "Survivals" theory, however orthodox, left its users open to ridicule

in the Soviet Union.[94] They still felt it proper to include formulations attributing crime to "survivals of the past in the minds of certain people and the influence of the imperialist camp," but they have insisted that to say this alone about crime "means not to explain it at all." There was no question but that crime researchers could spell out "survivals" in terms of specific factors they found associated with crime and could go beyond human failings to cite deep-seated material problems of development.

> Research studies have drawn attention to such reasons for crime as trouble in the family, the absence of regular healthy influence of older people on the younger generation, shortcomings in schooling, difficulties in the job placement of youth, drunkenness, unfavorable housing conditions, material difficulties of the lower paid strata of the working people, deficiencies in recreational facilities for the working people, slipshod accounting of material goods in state and social organizations, badly organized protection of socialist property, shortcomings in the work of corrective labor institutions, etc.[95]

Because they define poverty as lack of bare necessities rather than relative deprivation, Soviet researchers rightly place poverty at the bottom of the list of factors causing crime.[96] "Non-antagonistic contradictions" between supply and demand, growing wants and low pay receive mention, but not "social stratification," or any more than passing glances at how crime-breeding disadvantages can be passed from generation to generation. Researchers have presented much evidence that criminal conviction rates go up sharply as one moves from samples of secondary school students to samples of trade school students, to samples of working youth and to samples of the unemployed. Juveniles' chances of ending up in a labor colony are said to be several times higher if they come from families with criminal, drunken, poorly educated, of divorced parents; if they have an abnormally low education for their age group and little interest in culture or socially "legitimate" forms of peer-group activity such as sports, political work, hobbies, and social outings.[97]

Because there is more stealing among lower-income groups and more violent crime among persons with lower educational attainments, it is widely assumed that stealing must automatically diminish as living standards rise and violent crimes must automatically diminish as educational attainments rise. Unpublished statistics, says Dr. A. Iakovlev, do not show this direct relationship.[98] His explanation is that living standards and education do not bring crime down as they go up. "The roots of criminal behavior," he says, "lie in the unwritten law and customs" of informal groups. People become lawbreakers when "socially beneficial" values lose out to "antisocial" values in the "conflict of norms (this is Sutherland's theory of differential association).[99] Crime may get worse, then, while life gets better, unless small-group influences are effectively controlled to support law and order.

5. Research on the connection between biological and psychological traits inherited by individuals faces the biggest barrier in criminology. Ironically, leading scholars who had the most to do with reviving criminology are the most adamantly opposed to biopsychological research.[100] Even reiterations of their opponents that, yes, "man is not born a criminal," not fatally programmed to obey or defy the laws as they stand, fail to open the door for biopsychological research on the causes of crime.[101] No matter how moderate their opponents' thesis may be, the social theorists reject biopsychological explanations for allegedly "begging the question of differences between socioeconomic systems, between capitalism and socialism," and in effect asserting that "the task of eradicating crime posed by Marxism on the basis of its analysis of social development is impossible." [102]

This dispute between advocates and opponents of research on genetic factors cuts across lines, dividing jurists. It is a rerun of similar disputes in the '20's and the sociological-biological debate in Western criminology. But the lopsided rerun favors the social theorists. As always in such disputes it is impossible to tell whether the attackers care only about doctrinal correctness or act also out of professional competitiveness, just as when they insist that criminology be centered in their discipline of criminal law, alone, of the social sciences, with the other social sciences like psychology and sociology being merely auxiliary. Social theorists have not yet been mollified by one of their main opponent's tries to assure them that biopsychological research will not displace sociology of law but will only "broaden the front" of crime prevention. Given the other movement in the discipline, perhaps the stalemate will end soon on the biological front.[103]

6. Although the regime seemed to favor social over biopsychological research on crime, the criminologists of the sociological school fared less well in their other major policy battle, the battle with the hard liners, as shown in the heavier penalties set in the '60's. They see no pressures to commit crime in the USSR that cannot be avoided and they blame crime on their perpetrators' lack of character.[104] Unlike in Stalin's day, however, the hawks win only partial victories; researchers keep their institutes and their access. Even during a hawkish crackdown it was possible for the criminologists to place a report in *Kommunist*, the theoretical journal of

the CC, saying that crime could not be eliminated by "some short-lived campaign" but only by "complex social, economic, ideological and legal measures" giving due weight to "prevention" as well as "coercion."[105] Instead of intensifying one approach, as Stalin did after the relative liberalism of NEP, leaders after Stalin have given something to both sides, intensifying both repression and prevention, to fight crime.

7. Even as repressions piled up, relative to the liberalization of the "thaw," criminology inched ahead. First came some strongly worded disclosures about slipshod and superficial methods in criminology and about the consequences of poor planning for heavy youth migration so that crime rates among in-migrants are several times crime rates among the indigenous population.[106]

Secondly, criminology recently entered another new, and maybe critical phase of rethinking, covering new ground untrod even in the ferment of research in the '20's. That criminology still seems to be moving forward, if slowly and with setbacks, can be appreciated perhaps if one compares new moves toward crime forecasting and future planning of prevention with efforts fruitfully to combine social engineering—general social prevention" indirectly reducing crime—with "special criminological prevention" aimed directly against crime. Antialcoholism drives, based on little other than crude numerical associations of drunkenness and crime, are one example of the simpler established approach. So is this blend of "general social prevention" and "special criminological prevention" from a textile region, perhaps Ivanovo-Voznesensk, which has suffered from a sexual imbalance:

> The region's chief industry, textiles, created a noticeable surplus of women due to its traditionally high concentration on female labor. Among the bad social consequences of this imbalance was the influx of various antisocial elements (drunkards, parasites, released convicts who did not want to do approved work, etc.), who had no trouble moving in with single women. As a result the region's moral climate deteriorated; rates of crime and other antisocial behavior went up. General social measures such as building large enterprises depending mainly on "men's work" were taken to correct this situation. And they were taken with the existing criminological situation in mind.[107]

8. Since the late 1960's, criminologists have moved toward implementing more complex planning against crime on a national and local scale and based on (1) long term forecasts of trends in crime (*kriminologicheskoe prognozirovanie*); (2) expanding measurement of antisocial behavior far beyond crime alone (still to come); (3) using feedback of

information about plan implementation and results as much as practicable to help improve forecasting and planning. A few words on forecasting and measurement are in order.

Here is an area where, safely behind institutional and conference doors, "expert" may be almost entirely replacing "red" in my sense of the terms. Winds of change, however unsteady, have been clearing some ground in industry for intensive retooling of management and planning on the basis of computer technology as fast as this can be modernized. There is no question that the drive for rationalization, conducted with no less fervor and maybe more permanence than an anticrime drive, has touched crime too.[108] Strong support for broad programs of crime prevention based on forecasts came from the Institute of Criminal Policy in the late 1960's.[109] Actual forecasting began about that time in the MVD. Whether forecasting linked with future planning will turn out to be a foundation for crime prevention or merely another episode in the fad for cybernetics—the art of steering processes through control and feedback—is too soon to say. But the commitment to making prognosis work could be a serious one.

Under its minister, N. A. Shchelokov, a former close associate of Brezhnev in the provinces before Brezhnev appointed him to the MVD, this ministry emerged as the first leading Soviet center for pioneering work in forecasting. An MVD jurist, A. G. Avanesov, headed this work in a Group for Forecasting and Long Term Planning within the Organization and Research Department of the MVD. It sponsored a ground-breaking national Seminar on Forecasting and Long Term Planning, May 14–18, 1970, an occasion for strong professional support for the idea of predicting to "gain time" and head off crime. An Expert Commission of eminent consultants was organized to meet at MVD headquarters periodically to discuss and evaluate its forecasting. By 1970, the MVD had produced a first long-term forecast, for 1971–1975, based on a combination of extrapolation, expert forecasting and a simulation model.

Note how they built this model. First they gave questionnaires to about 100 experts—jurists, psychologists, pedagogues, sociologists and economists—at a crime conference the MVD sponsored Ocober, 6–8, 1970, asking the experts what factors influenced crime rates, structure, and trends. Then, the MVD researchers questioned 150 criminologists on a nationwide scale, probably all the recognized criminologists in the USSR. What factors bred crime? Inhibited crime? How intensively did these factors influence the roles of various specific crimes? The answers formed matrices of 250 factors! Matrices then went out to 100 experts asked to anticipate whether each factor's influence would rise, drop, or stay the same over 5 years, 5 to 10 years, and later. On the basis of this expert opinion about factors, Avanesov and his team built and ran off "multi-factor forecasting models," compared the results with those from extrapolation and estimating, and drew up a final forecast for 1971–1975.

The forecast contained three parts: (1) a description of crime rates and trends in 1962–1970; (2) forecasts of relevant social, economic, and demographic changes in 1971–1975 (factor forecasts) and (3) forecasts in broad terms of specific and total crimes in 1971–1975, in minimum, maximum, and intermediate variants.[110] Unfortunately, these crime statistics and forecasts, of enormous comparative interest, remained state secrets, along with the many working documents and conference proceedings.

9. Forecasting has probably increased the influence and access of criminologists in planning decisions affecting crime prevention; that is, *assuming* there is enough appearance of success and enough state support for forecasting to continue. Dr. Kudriavtsev has urged his colleagues to turn their findings into broad programs of crime prevention.[111] Possibly there will be competing proposals from the MVD forecasters and the researchers of the Institute of Criminal Policy. In a country where published policy studies are virtually unknown, it is striking that Kudriavtsev has urged criminologists to study how decisions affecting crime prevention are made so as to be able to lobby more effectively for their proposals.[112] Among the several channels of access for criminologists are: (1) their professional chain of command though their institutes and consulting work for the MVD's Expert Commission and courts and up through ministers of the interior and justice and the procurator general to the government's planning and drafting bodies and (2) the party information chain through local committees to the Department of Administrative of the CC. Research institutes of the MVD, Procuracy, Academy of Sciences, and Central Statistical Administration have been cooperating to improve the quality of forecasting based on simulation models suggested by the Economic-Mathematical Institute of the Academy of Sciences.[113]

A. G. Avanesov's prestige and influence have probably been increased by the publication of his *Basic Principles of Criminological Forecasting,* hailed as the first work "in a new scientific direction." [114] A review of his second book, *The Theory and Methodology of Criminological Forecasting,* by one of the most astute Soviet criminologists showed some of the unresolved methodological problems to be surmounted and also casts new light on the gap I earlier mentioned between conviction figures and real crime rates in the USSR, as elsewhere. Prognosis is only as reliable as the statistics it uses. But on occasion, "criminal statistics may not show the growth" of real crime, "but may wrongly indicate a drop in crime," depending on law enforcement. Crime increases may be overstated relative to real crime or, on the contrary, "the so-called 'latent' (hidden, undiscovered) crime may be such a serious part of the 'iceberg' that its measured tip gives no realistic idea of the real national rates of crimes." Also, does one always know whether factors being forecasted are "positive" or "negative" 2. In addition, one runs into difficulties with demographic factors. They are closely linked with so many other social indicators.[115]

Accurate forecasting will depend on the political-administrative successes statisticians have in persuading the government to permit and fund a modernization of decrepit means of data gathering and a national center for standardizing and coordinating the operation. Another pressing plea of statisticians is to gather "moral statistics," as in the 1920's, on many types of deviant or personal behavior besides crime (such as alcoholism, drug addiction, parasitism, immorality, prostitution, suicides, abortions, and vagrancy). The USSR Supreme Court, Institute of Criminology, and Procuracy have joined forces to ask that data be gathered from nonjudicial agencies like the children's commissions, comrades' courts, and administrative commissions enforcing ordinances of the local soviets. Despite CSA approval, their requests were steadily refused in the early 1970's.[116]

The methological difficulties, the reasonable requests for better statistics and the subsequent unfathomable refusals, the juxtaposition of frankness and secrecy, the favoring of social over biopsychological research, the conflicts between "redness" and "expertness" add up to the picture of an effort at crime study and prevention which slowly lurches forward, and occasionally, backwards, impelled by state support and the enthusiasm with new methods from the "scientific and technical revolution" but inhibited by intraprofessional rivalries, difficulties of method, and survivals of Stalinism in the minds of men.

Work for this chapter yielded several surprises.

1. Tables of conviction rates based on Soviet statements and data show such relatively favorable long-term trends down, relative to, say, U.S. trends, that one wonders why Soviet authorities do not publish them themselves. I have tried to supply answers but do not feel sure all or any of them hit the mark.

2. Despite what I call "political tutelage" in crime studies, the mix in them of "red" and "expert" elements and the contradictory directions in some sectors point to a loose party reign giving play to professional interests and competition among the jurists which cut across the legal professions and other concerned disciplines.

3. Crime fighting has forked into two divergent trends: intensified prevention and study on the one hand, intensified deterrence and punishment on the other. The party "defines the basic scope of action by state and social organizations including those agencies responsible for crime fighting." But it seems to be hedging its bets on policy or maybe simply taking a middle course between moderate doves and the hawks.

4. Forecasting was the greatest surprise after Khrushchev. It became experimental. It now faces huge technical obstacles and no fewer political ones if the crime fighters ever get around to proposing elaborate and costly plans for social engineering in competition with established interest groupings in industry, agriculture, defense, health, education, and welfare. I reviewed a few of the obstacles in the path of forecasting. They show how far the Soviet growth is from the "organized, planned and scientifically based character" it is said to have under party guidance.[117] But other countries still dragging their feet in national crime prevention would do well to see how far even this experiment in forecasting has gone, as well as how far it still has to go. It remains to be seen whether political indifference and scattered priorities will not cancel out any advantages in the quality and diversity of crime study that certain crime-afflicted nonsocialist countries may gain from their relative lack of political tutelage over research.

5. Finally, one detects in Soviet responses to crime an erosion of ideology about crime and socialism but not necessarily the end of ideology, only the possible end of "red" ideology, and its replacement with an ideological impetus closer to the original spirit of Marxist hubris and rationalism, with its faith in man's ability to liberate himself through his command of nature and technology and thereby to end violence and crime.

Notes

I am grateful to Prof. Peter H. Solomon, Jr., for his many insights on Soviet criminology; to Prof. H. Kent Geiger for sending me his unpublished data on crime and delinquency in the USSR—this gave me a start in collecting conviction trend data; to Barnard College, Columbia University, for a faculty research travel grant;

to Profs. Jonathan Harris and Robert Sharlet for their comments on a draft of this chapter; and to Arthur Bregman for his devoted assistance at an earlier stage of this research. Of course, the responsibility for the contents is mine.

1. "Otchetnyi doklad Tsentral'nogo Komiteta KPSS s"ezdu Kommunisticheskoi partii Sovetskogo Soiuza. Doklad General'nogo sekretaria TsK tovarishcha L. I. Brezhneva," *Pravda* (March 31, 1971).

2. "Ot XXIII k XXIV s'ezdu KPSS," *Sovetskaia iustitsiia* (hereafter *Sov. iust.*), 6 (1971), 1–3. Harold J. Berman, *Justice in the USSR* (New York, 1963), 66–96 describes tendencies in post-Stalin legal reforms. For a good follow-up, see John N. Hazard, "Soviet Law and Justice," in John W. Strong, ed., *The Soviet System under Brezhnev and Kosygin* (New York, 1971), 93–114. See also my "Criminal Law and Social Control," in *The Post-Stalin Faces of Soviet Law*, ed. Donald Barry, William Butler, and George Ginsburgs (forthcoming).

3. "Preduprezhdenie prestuplenii—glavnoe napravlenie bor'by s prestupnost'iu na sovremennom etape," *Sov. iust.*, 6 (1972), 1–3 and "Effektivnost' chastnykh opredelenii po ugolovnym delam," *Sov. iust.*, 22 (1972), 1–2.

4. "Otchetnyi doklad . . ."; "Zasedanie Komissii zakonodatel'nykh predpolozhenii Soveta Soiuza i Soveta Natsional'nostei Verkhovnogo Soveta SSSR," *Vedomosti Verkhovnogo Soveta SSSR*, 39 (1972), 597; N. A. Shchelokov, "Pravovoe vospitanie na sovremennom etape," *Sovetskoe gosudarstvo i pravo* (hereafter *SGP*), 1 (1972), 11–19; B. Nifontov, "Deistvennost' raboty po pravomu vospitaniiu," *Sov. iust.*, 16 (1972), 18–19; and the monthly tabloid magazine published since January, 1972, *Chelovek i zakon*, with a *tirazh* (September, 1972) of 2,810,000 copies, together may give some evidence of the concern of Brezhnev and high officials and the immense scope of the campaign in legal education.

5. E. G. Shirvindt, "K istorii voprosa ob izuchenii prestupnosti i mer bor'by s nei," *SGP*, 5 (1958), 137–42.

6. A. A. Gertsenzon, "Ob izuchenii i preduprezhdenii prestupnosti," *SGP*, 7 (1960), 80–81 and Walter Connor, *Deviance in Soviet Society* (New York, 1972), 33–34.

7. N. Solov'ev *et al., Problemy byta, brake i sem'i* (Vilna, 1970); the periodical collections, *Chelovek i Obshchestvo*, published on the average twice yearly since 1967 under the auspices of Leningrad University and the Institute of Complex Social Research, USSR Academy of Sciences, in Leningrad; another publication issued annually since 1965 under the auspices of this institute, as well as the Soviet Sociological Association and the Scientific Council on Problems of Concrete Social Research, entitled *Sotsial'nye issledovaniia*; M. A. Alemashkin of the Institute of Psychology, USSR Academy of Pedagogical Sciences; "Problemy vospitaniia 'trudnykh' podorostkov," *Sovetskaia pedagogika* 10 (1966), 26–33; A. G. Kharchev, *Brak i sem'ia v SSSR* (Moscow, 1964); V. A. Iadov and V. I. Dobrynin, eds., *Molodezh i trud: Vsesoiuznaia Konferentsiia "Sotsializm i molodezh"* (Moscow, 1970); Arkadii Adamov, "Pozhnesh' sud'bu . . . : 'Trudnyi podrostok' i ego druz'ia," *Komsomolskaia pravda* (October 14, 1967), a report on a meeting on the upbringing of youth in which participated researchers and "practical workers" from the USSR Ministry for Public Order (Ministry of the Interior since 1968), which was the sponsor of the meeting, and criminologists, doctors, teachers, philosophers, sociologists, school principals, artists, party officials, and Komsomol officials (the meeting was devoted mainly to problems of juvenile lawbreaking; and "Nauchnaia zhizn': Problemy iskoreniia pravonarushenii v SSSR," *SGP*, 6 (1972), 134–40 and 7 (1972), 129–36 (summarizes a conference on eliminating crime in the USSR held at the end of 1971, organized by the Institute of State and Law of the USSR

Academy of Sciences, The All-Union Research Institute of Soviet Legislation, the Institute of Criminology, The All-Union Research Institute of the USSR MVD—the top research institutes in law—and attended by over 400 scholars and "practical workers" from many Soviet cities).

8. On Politburo member Krestinskii and his posts also in the Orgburo and Secretariat, see Merle Fainsod, *How Russia Is Ruled* (Cambridge, Mass., 1963), 178–80, 310.

9. Donald D. Barry, "Leaders of the Soviet Legal Profession: An Analysis of Biographical Data and Career Patterns," *Canadian-American Slavic Studies*, VI (Spring, 1972), 76, 78, 81–82.

10. *Pravda* (April 10, 1971).

11. Rudenko and Gorkin could be called jurists by occupation, though neither has a completed legal education and both officials were concerned with crime fighting and criminal policy. Iu. A. Andropov, his deputy, and seven chairmen of republic KGB's also sat in the Supreme Soviet. So did the new head of the Department of Administrative Organs, N. I. Savinkin, who received his degree from the Military-Political Academy. (*Deputaty Verkhovnogo Soveta SSSR. Vos'moi sozyv* [Moscow, 1970], 10, 23, 41, 55, 107, 142, 175, 220, 229, 313, 375, 380, 472, 499.) On earlier data see Donald D. Barry and Harold J. Berman, "The Jurists," in Gordon Skilling and Franklyn Griffiths, eds., *Interest Groups in Soviet Politics* (Princeton, 1971), 316.

12. Douglas V. Verney, *British Government and Politics: Life without a Declaration of Independence* (New York, 1971), 126; Louis W. Koenig, *et al.*, *American National Government: Policy and Politics* (Glenview, Ill., 1971), 221.

13. Barry and Berman, *op. cit.*, 296.

14. H. Gordon Skilling, "Groups in Soviet Politics: Some Hypotheses," Skilling and Griffiths, *op. cit.*, 30.

15. A. A. Gertsenzon, V. K. Zvirbul' *et al.*, "Vsesoiuznyi institut po izucheniiu prichin i razrabotke mer preduprezhdeniia prestupnosti," *Kriminologiia* (Moscow, 1968), 181–2, 185.

16. Barry and Berman, *op. cit.*, 315.

17. *Deputaty Verkhovnogo Soveta,* 380. *SSSR. Vos'moi* sozyv, *op. cit.*, 380.

18. Skilling, *op. cit.*, 34, 40–43; H. Gordon Skilling, "Group Conflict in Soviet Politics: Some Conclusions," Skilling and Griffiths, *op. cit.*, 381; Franklyn Griffiths, "A Tendency Analysis of Soviet Policy-Making," *Ibid.*, 373–75; Barry and Berman, *op. cit.*, 297–99.

19. *Narodnoe khoziaistvo SSSR v 1970 godu* (Moscow, 1971), 523.

20. *Ibid.*, 523, 657 and estimates in Barry and Berman, *op. cit.*, 301, 305–6, 308, 311.

21. Amnesty of March 23, 1953, Article 8, reprinted in *Sbornik zakonov SSSR i ukazov Prezidiuma Verkhovnogo Soveta SSSR 1938–1967* (Moscow, 1968), II, 628.

22. *Zasedaniia Verkhovnogo Soveta SSSR. Piatogo sozyva. Vtoraia sessiia (22–25 dekabria 1958 g.). Stenograficheskii otchet* (Moscow, 1959), 494–96; Harold J. Berman, "Law Reform in the Soviet Union," *The American Slavic and East European Review*, XV (April, 1956), 179–89; and Barry and Berman, *op. cit.*, 316–339.

23. V. Nikolaev, "Preodolenie nepravil'nykh teorii v ugolovnom prave—vazhnoe uslovie ukrepleniie sotsialisticheskoi zakonnosti," *Kommunist*, 14 (1956), 50.

24. On jurists as an "interest group," though with more emphasis on coherence than here, see Barry and Berman, *op. cit.*, 292ff.

25. "Obshchee sobranie Akademii Nauk SSSR: Iiun'skaia sessiia (4 iiunia 1949 goda)," *Vestnik Akademii Nauk SSSR*, 7 (1949), cited in Alexander Vucinic, *The Soviet Academy of Sciences* (Stanford, Calif., 1956), 67; P. F. Yudin, "Trud I. V. Stalina, 'Ekonomicheskie problemy sotsializma v SSSR'—osnova dal'neishego razvitiia obshchestvennykh nauk," *Vestnik*, 3 (1953), cited in Vucinic, *op. cit.*, 113.

26. Program of the conference, attended by this writer (November 17–21, 1958), was issued as *Mezhvuzovskoe nauchnoe soveshchanie na temu: dal'neishee razvitie sovetskoi demokratii i ukreplenie sotsialisticheskoi zakonnosti. Noiabr' 1958 g.* (Moscow, 1958).

27. Nikolaev, *op. cit.*, 50.

28. R. A. Rudenko, "Zadachi dal'neishego ukrepleniia sotsialisticheskoi zakonnosti v svete reshenii XX s'ezda KPSS," *SGP*, 3 (1956), 20–21; A. A. Gertsenzon, *Vvedenie v sovetskuiu kriminologiiu* (Moscow, 1965), 91, 95; S. S. Ostroumov, "Znachenie ugolovnoi statistiki dlia issledovaniia prestupnosti," *SGP*, 10 (1962), 88–95; V. Kudriavtsev, "Aktual'nye problemy sovetskoi kriminologii, *Sov. iust.*, 20 (1965), 6–9; S. S. Ostroumov, "Statisticheskie metody v kriminologii," *SGP*, 7 (1967), 68—75.

29. The CSA has acted publicly since Stalin as if the problem of criminal statistics did not exist. In the 1920's it actively published statistics on crime and related deviances.

30. S. S. Ostroumov, *Sovetskaia sudebnaia statistika* (Moscow, 1970), 4, 31–36, 49–50, 54–59, 67–77, 80–90.

31. See n. 28.

32. Ostroumov, *Sovetskaia sudebnaia statistika*, 246.

33. G. Bulatov, "Problemy sovershenstvovaniia sudebnoi statistiki," *Sov. iust.*, 11 (1971), 18.

34. Eugene Doleschal, "Criminal Statistics," in National Council on Crime and Delinquency, *Information Review on Crime and Delinquency*, 1 (August, 1969), 1–28.

35. S. S. Ostroumov, *Prestupnost' i ee prichiny v dorevoliutsionnoi Rossii* (Moscow, 1960), 4, 233.

36. Ostroumov, *Sovetskaia sudebnaia statistika*, 45–49.

37. *Kriminologiia*, 117, 170.

38. S. Ostroumov, S. Panchenko, and A. Shliapochnikov, "Uchet i statistika pravonarushenii v svete leninskikh ukazanii," *Sotsialisticheskaia zakonnost'* (hereafter *SZ*), 4 (1969), 13.

39. *Narodnoe khoziaistvo SSSR v 1970 g., 52.*

40. *Kriminologiia*, 15, 119, 181–82; *SZ*, 7 (1966), 27.

41. V. I. Lenin, *Polnoe sobranie sochinenii*, XVII, 119, quoted in Ostroumov, *Sovetskaia sudebnaia statistika*, 3.

42. N. N. Kondrashkov, "Analiz raionnoi statistiki prestupnosti," *Voprosy preduprezhdeniia prestupnosti*, 4 (1966), 39, states that in the Lida District of Belorussia reported crimes per capita increased to a peak of 186 in 1962, taking 1953 figures as 100, *while cases sent to court per capita increased only to 108* Table is reproduced in Connor, *op. cit.*, 160.

43. L. Smirnov, "XXII s'ezd KPSS i zadachi sudebnykh organov v bor'be s prestupnot'iu," *Sov. iust.*, 14 (1966), 1.

44. "Sovershenstvovat' organizatsiiu raboty Prokuratury v bor'be s prestupnost'iu," *SZ*, 11 (1968), 7, 9 and V. Tikunov, "Sniskhozhdeniia khuliganam ne budet," *Izvestiia* (April 21, 1966).

45. Only 4.6 percent of cases going to criminal investigation in 1967 originated in private citizens' complaints, as compared with 16.2 percent in 1958. (S. S. Ostroumov and S. N. Panchenko, "Aktual'nye zadachi ugolovnoi statistiki i preduprezhdenie prestupnosti," *SGP*, 8 [1968], 110.)

46. Connor, *op. cit.*, 34.

47. N. Kuznetsova, "Sravnitel'noe kriminologicheskoe issledovanie prestupnosti v Moskve (1923–1968/69 gg.)," *SZ*, 6 (1971), 22–27.

48. Bernard Gwertzman, "Soviet Awareness of Crime Problems Rising," *New York Times* (September 8, 1969).

49. *Narodnoe khoziaistvo SSSR v 1970 g.*, 35, 41.

50. A. Gramotkina, "Gorod khochet spokoistvo," *Komsomolskaia pravda* (September 12, 1971).

51. James Reston, *New York Times* (November 20, 1968).

52. V. Lyashenko, "Amnistiia—ostryi vopros," *Komsomolskaia pravda* (December 1, 1967). For text of amnesty see *Vedomosti Verkhovnogo Soveta SSSR*, 44 (1967), item 595.

53. Sergei Ostroumov, "Crime and Its Causes," *Soviet Life*, 4 (April, 1969), 60; Case of Alexander Bazhenov, heard by this writer (Moscow City Court, November 10, 1958). The proprietor of an orchard cited by Ostroumov used an electrified fence. Bazhenov stalked his trespassers with a shotgun and also more provocation.

54. S. Pulatkhodzhaev and A. Mikhailants, "Rabota sudov po preduprezhdeniiu prestuplenii," *SZ*, 8 (1971), 18; Andrei Amalrik, *Involuntary Journey to Siberia* (New York, 1967), 187, 190, 277; and conversation with Tanya described below.

55 *Narodnoe khoziaistvo SSSR v 1970 g.*, 43.

56. V. Kozak, "Chto znaiut grazhdane o neobkhodimoi oborone," *Sov. iust.*, 18 (1968), 12–13.

57. K. Cherniavskii and B. Kleiner, "Usilit' bor'by s khuliganstvom," *SZ*, 4 (1952), 36–38; Gablin, "Usilit' bor'bu s khuliganstvom," *SZ*, 8 (1952), 36–38; F. Kudrin, "Reshitel'no usilt' bor'by s khliganstvom," *SZ*, 10 (1952), 30–34; A. V. Kuznetsov, *Khuliganstvo i bor'ba s nim* (Moscow, 1962); and A. Sol'ts, "O khuliganstve," *SGP*, 10 (1937), 62–63.

58. Ostroumov, *Sovetskaia sudebnaia statistika*, 148.

59. *Kriminologiia*, 439–42.

60. "In 1967 the convictions for murder as compared with 1966 fell 8 percent, for aggravated assault 17.1 percent and for rape 7.4 percent. . . ." (Ostroumov, *Sovetskaia sudebnaia statistika*, 246.) But the drops seemed to be related to local whitewashing ("Sovershenstvovat' organizatsiiu, . . ." 3), and to ignoring other serious crimes because of the emphasis on hooliganism ("Sovmestnoe zasedanie kollegii Prokuratury SSSR i Ministerstva okhrany obshchestvennogo poriadka SSSR," *SZ*, 10 [1968], 28–30). "The number of murders, rapes and several other dangerous crimes increased in 1968," according to the RSFSR Supreme Court. ("V Prezidiuma Verkhovnogo Suda RSFSR," *Biulleten' Verkhovnogo Suda RSFSR*, 2 [1969], 1.)

61. *Kriminologiia*, 117–118.

62. Kondrashkov, *op. cit.*, 11; *Kriminologiia*, 118.

63. Connor, *op. cit.*, 151–52.

64. "Nash zakon i ego garantii: Na voprosy chitatelei 'Truda' otvechaet Ministr iustitsii SSSR Vladimir Ivanovich Terebiliv," *Trud* (March 2, 1970).

65. *Kriminologiia*, 118–119. Also, see n. 60.

66. *Ibid.*, 320, 428–31.

67. Natal'ia Kuznetsova, "Khishchniki," *Sov. iust.*, 9, 10, and 11 (1969), 30–31, 28–30, and 24–26, respectively.

68. V. A. Serebriakova, "Kriminologicheskaia kharakteristika zhenshchin-prestupnits (po materialam izucheniia lits soderzhashchikhsia v ITK," *Voprosy bor'by s prestupnost'iu*, 14 (1971), 3–16 and Ostroumov, *Sovetskaia sudebnaia statistika*, 254–55.

69. "Nash zakon. . . ."

70. Summary of report of National Institute on Alcohol Abuse and Alcoholism, in Harold M. Schmeck, Jr., "U.S. Report Says Top Drug Problem is Alcohol Abuse," *New York Times* (February 19, 1972).

71. Connor, *op. cit.*, 35–79; "Zadachi sudov . . ."; and "Usilim bor'bu. . . ."

72. Connors, *op. cit.*, 43.

73. See, for example, "Nash zakon. . . ."

74. *Kriminologiia*, 342–3.

75. S. S. Ostroumov and V. E. Chigunov, "Study of the Criminal Personality from the Materials of Criminological Research," trans. from *SGP*, 4 (1966), in Paul Hollander, ed., *American and Soviet Society: A Reader in Comparative Sociology and Perception* (Englewood Cliffs, 1969), 272.

76. *New York Times* (June 27, 1965), 16 and (January 1, 1966), 1, 2 and G. A. Aseev, "O pravilakh povedeniia detei v obshchestvennykh mestakh," *Vecherniaia Moskva* (December 28, 1965). Curfew hour was 9 P.M. schooldays and 10 P.M. Sundays and holidays, effective January 1, 1966.

77. Iu. Feofanov, "Nikolaev protiv Nikolaeva," *Izvestiia* (October 5, 1967).

78. A survey of juvenile criminals in Kurov and Ordzhonikidze Boroughs of Sverdlovsk conducted by a group of researchers from the Sverdlovsk Juridical Institute and officials of the courts, Procuracy, and militia in 1965, covering the years 1960–1964, found that more than half those convicted had been previously in trouble with the police of children's commissions or in children's educational colonies. The "overwhelming majority" were 16 and 17 years-old. The relative weight of this age group in the population went up 195 percent in 1960–1964. Criminality, measured in crimes per 1000 members of that age group, 16 and 17, diminished 5 percent during the same period. Hence the populace's chances of being victimized by juvenile crime increased roughly 195 × 0.95, or 185 percent. (Estimated from M. Kovalev, "Izuchenie prestupnosti nesovershennoletnikh i ee preduprezhdenie," *Sov. iust.*, 3 (1966), 15–16. The population of Sverdlovsk increased, roughly, 12 percent in 1961–1964. (*Narodnoe khoziaistvo SSSR v 1965 g.* [Moscow, 1966], 37.) If the boroughs studied followed this trend, then the total of juvenile convictions rose over 200 percent. The age group 14 through 17 years increased 78 percent in five years. Arkadii Adamov, "Poznesh' sud'bu . . . 'Trudnyi podrostok' i ego druz'ia," *Komsomolskaia pravda* (October 14, 1967).

79. *Kriminologiia*, 340.

80. *Ibid.*, 339.

81. V. S. Pronina, *Kommentarii k polozheniiam o komissiiakh po delam nesovershennoetnikh* (Moscow, 1968).

82. *Kriminologiia*, 340.

83. S. S. Ostroumov, "Nekotorye voprosy izucheniia pravonarushenii sredi

nesovershennoletnikh," in D. S. Karev, ed., *Izuchenie i preduprezhdenie pravonarushenni sredi nesovershennoletnikh: Sbornik statei* (Moscow, 1970), 50, 51.

84. T. Gromova and G. Ronina, "Chto privelo ikh na etu dorogu," *Iunost'*, 2 (1967), 84–90.

85. L. Zonnenberg, "Ulitsa i podrostok," *Pravda Vostoka* (July 9, 1965).

86. *Kriminologiia*, 343; Ostroumov, "Nekotorye voprosy, . . ." 44.

87. Iu. P. Kasatkin, "Ocherk istorii izuchenii prestupnosti v SSSR," *Problemy iskoreniia prestupnosti* (Moscow, 1965), 187–225; Walter Connor, *op, cit.*, 27–34, 93–113, 161–189; and *Kriminologiia*, 71–83.

88. Both quotations are from the paraphrase of a speech by Dr. V. M. Chkhikvadze, director of the Institute of State and Law, "Nauchnaia zhizn': Problemy iskoreniia pravonarushenii v SSSR," *SGP*, 6 (1972), 134.

89. Ivo Lapenna, *Soviet Penal Policy* (London, 1968), 143.

90. Mitchell Wilson writes of the Academic City science center in Siberia that its successes and existence "are possible only in a society that allows for ambitious and daring long-range planning, its failures too are due to precisely the same constricting forces that demanded its creation in the first place." ("The Siberian Jewel," *World* [February 27, 1973], 30.)

91. Nikita S. Khruschev, *The Crimes of the Stalin Era: Special Report to the 20th Congress of the Communist Party,* annot. by Boris I. Nicolaevsky (New York, n.d.), 24.

92. Shirvindt, 142; *SGP,* 4 (1956), 128; *SGP,* 5 (1964), 11–20; *Kommunist,* 16 (1963), 33–34; and see n. 94. Brezhnev did change his phraseology from "survivals of the past" (*perezhitki proshlogo*) in 1971 to "heritage of the past" (*unasledovanie ot proshlogo*) in 1972. ("O piatidesiatiletii Soiuza Sovetskikh Sotsialisticheskikh Respublik: Doklad General'nogo sekretaria TsK KPSS tovarishcha L. I. Brezhneva," *Pravda* [December 22, 1972]).

93. On the many meanings given "ideology" see Robert E. Lane, *Political Ideology: Why the American Common Man Believes What He Does* (New York, 1967), 13–16; and Willard A. Mullins, "On the Concept of Ideology in Political Science," *The American Political Science Review,* LXVI (June, 1972), 498–510. On the controversy mentioned see, e.g., Chaim I. Waxman, ed., *The End of Ideology Debate* (New York, 1968). On the USSR see Daniel Bell, "The End of Ideology in the Soviet Union," in *Marxist Ideology in the Contemporary World: Its Appeals and Paradoxes,* ed. Milorad M. Drachkovich (New York, 1966), 76–112; B. Mel'nikova, "Burzhuaznaia kriminologiia o vliianii eknonmicheskogo progressa na prestupnost' molodezhi," *SGP,* 5 (1967), 142–45; and F. M. Reshetnikov, *Sovremennaia amerikanskaia kriminologiia* (Moscow, 1965), 4–5, 95.

94. N. A. Struchkov, "Izuchenie obstoiatel'stv obuslovlivaiushchikh prestupnost' v SSSR," *SGP*, 12 (1971), 100.

95. A. A. Piontkovskii, "Puti ukrepleniia sotsialisticheskogo pravoporiadka," *SGP*, 1 (1967), 37.

96. *Kriminologiia,* 128; Alemaskin, 32; and Karev, 26–27.

97. "Bol'shoe vnimanie issledovaniiu lichnosti obviniaemogo," *Biulleten' Verkhovnogo Suda SSSR,* 3 (1969), 40; G. M. Min'kovskii, "Nekotorye prichiny prestupnosti nesovershennoletnikh v SSSR i mery ee preduprezhdeniia," *SGP,* 5 (1966), 87–90; and Gromova and Ronina, op. cit. 89.

98. A. Iakovlev, "Sotsiologiia pravonarushenii," *Sov. iust.* 22 (1972), 5–7.

99. Edwin H. Sutherland and Donald R. Cressey, *Principles of Criminology,* 7th ed. (Philadelphia and New York, 1966), 77–98.

100. Connor sums up the dispute well in op. cit., 176–82. See also A. A.

Gertsenzon, "Protiv biologicheskikh teorii prichin prestupnosti," *Voprosy preduprezhdeniia prestupnosti,* 4 (1966), 3–34 and *Voprosy bor'by s prestupnost'iu* (new title), 5 (1967), 3–53; Gertsenzon's attacks on the researches into x-y-y chromosomes' link with crime appear in "Novye popytki vozrozhdeniia lombrozianstvo v zarubezhnoi kriminologii," *SZ,* 8 (1970), 26–28; V. Kudriavtsev, "Dano li pri rozhdenii?"; and N. Struchkov and B. Utevskii (penologists believing in the need to consider biological causation), "Ne tak vse prosto," *Literaturnaia gazeta* (November 29, 1967); I. Karpets, V. Kudriavtsev, A. Leont'ev, and N. Felinskaia, "Priroda pravonarushenii," *Izvestiia* (July 8, 1968); O. E. Freierov, "O tak nazyvaemom biologicheskom aspekte problemy prestupnosti," *SGP,* 10 (1966), 108–113; and "Motivizatsiia obshchestvennogo opasnykh deistvii psikhicheski nepolnotsennykh lits," *SGP,* 4 (1969), 96–101; A. B. Sakharov, "Ob antisotsial'nykh chertakh lichnosti prestupnia," *SGP,* 10 (1970), 110–116.

101. N. A. Struchkov, *op. cit.,* 103–105.

102. *Kriminologiia,* 135.

103. N. A. Struchkov, *op. cit.,* 105 and see n. 100. A. A. Gertsenzon wants criminology kept in criminal law. (*Ugolovnoe pravo i sotsiologiia* [Moscow, 1970], 5–6 and 39–54.)

104. I. Kalmanovich, "O prostom slove 'nel'zia'," *Literaturnaia gazeta* (July 24, 1968).

105. "Teoreticheskaia konferentsiia. Antiobshchestvennye iavleniia, ikh prichiny i sredstva bor'by s nimi," *Kommunist,* 12 (1966), 58–68.

106. M. M. Babaev, "Kriminologicheskie issledovaniia problem migratsii naseleniia," *SGP,* 3 (1968), 86–90; M. Babaev, "Sotsiologicheskie issledovaniia i bor'ba s prestupnost'iu," *Sov. iust.,* 19 (1969), 10; M. M. Babaev, "Kriminologicheskaia otsenka sotsial'no-ekonomicheskikh i demograficheskikh faktorov," *SGP,* 6 (1972), 97–102.

107. A. B. Sakharov, "Sotsial'naia sistema preduprezhdeniia prestuplenii," *SGP,* 11 (1972), 69.

108. "Dostizheniia nauki—v praktiku bor'by s prestupnost'iu," *Sov. iust.,* 17 (1972), 1–2.

109. V. N. Kudriavtsev, "Struktura prestupnosti i sotsial'nye izmeneniia," *SGP,* 6 (1971), 108–109 and his *Prichinnost' v kriminologii* (Moscow, 1968), 151–170.

110. G. A. Avanesov, "Organizatsiia kriminologicheskogo prognozirovaniia i planirovaniia," *SGP,* 1 (1972), 110–114.

111. Kudriavtsev, "Struktura, ..." 109.

112. V. N. Kudriavtsev, "Sotsiologiia: pravo i kriminologiia," *SGP,* 2 (1969), 68.

113. L. Il'ina, "Seminar o prognozirovanii prestupnosti," *SZ,* 7 (1971), 66.

114. V. Kudriavtsev, "G. Avanesov, *Osnovy kriminologicheskogo prognozirovaniia.* M., izd. VSh MVD SSSR. 1970, 52 c.," *SZ,* 6 (1971), 95–96.

115. A. Iakovlev, "G. A. Avanesov, *Teoriia i metodologiia kriminologicheskogo prognozirovaniia* (izd-o "Iuridicheskaia literatura," 1972, 436 str.)," *Sov. iust.,* 15 (1972), 31.

116. S. Ostroumov, S. Panchenko, and N. Kondrashkov, "Neotlozhnye zadachi ugolovnoi statistiki," *SZ,* 5 (1972), 66–69.

117. From the preamble to the Rules of the CPSU.

Appendix A

SOURCES FOR TABLE 5-1

Source for Column (2): Column (2) is derived from the indices for 1928. In column (2) the base year is not taken as 1928, or 1955, because this would give a false sense of comparability of convictions. However, simply as a gauge of judicial conflict between state and offenders, changing policies and types of crimes not considered, here is the 1928 index series of convictions: *1928*—100, *1940*—86.3, *1946*—75.8, *1955*—63, *1958*—88.3, *1959*—>70.2, *1960*—<58.5, *1961*—51.2, *1962*—67, *1963*—56.2, *1964*—<50.6, *1965*—46.8, *1966*—62, *1967*—>51.9, *1968*—57.3. Sources for this 1928 series by years:

1940, 1963, 1964, 1965

"Analysis of court statistics for the country as a whole shows that the number of convictions is decreasing. For example, the number of convictions in 1965 was 7.6 percent less than in 1964, 16.7 less than in 1963. The number of convictions per 100,000 population in 1964 diminished in comparison with the prewar period (1940) more than twice, with 1928, more than 3 times. The number of convictions in 1963–1965 was the smallest in thirty years." (G. Z. Anashkin, chairman, Criminal Collegium, USSR Supreme Court, "O zadachakh i tendentsiiakh razvitiia sotsialisticheskogo pravosudiia," *Vestnik Moskovskogo Universiteta,* 4 [1966], 6–7.)

1958, 1962

"Numbers of convictions have decreased by 7.6 percent in 1965 as compared with 1964, by 30.3 as compared with 1962, and by 47 percent as compared with 1958." (V. Kulikov, first deputy chairman, USSR Supreme Court, "Za uprochenie sotsialisticheskoi zakonnosti," *Sov. iust.,* 7 [1966], 16.)

1959, 1960

The number of convictions was "nearly 20 percent less" in 1959 than it was in 1958; convictions in 1960 were "more than one-third less." (N. R. Mironov, head of the Department of Administrative Organs, Central Committee, CPSU, "O nekotorykh voprosakh preduprezhdeniia prestupnosti i drugikh antiobshchestvennykh iavlenii i bor'by s nimi v sovremennykh usloviiakh," *SGP,* 5 [1961], 4–5.)

1967

"During the last 40 years . . . crime has decreased more than 3.5 times. The number of persons convicted per 100 thousand population in 1967 decreased almost to a half, compared with 1940, and to less than a third, compared with 1928." (G. Anashkin, "Pravosudie. Nakazanie. Spravedlivost'," *Literaturnaia gazeta* [May 29, 1968]).

1946

"The number of persons per 100,000 inhabitants found to have committed crimes decreased more than two times in 1967 as compared to 1946." ("Vsesoyuznyi institut po izucheniyu prichin i razrabotke mer preduprezhdeniia prestupnosti," *Kriminologiia,* 116.) The average population of the USSR in 1946 I estimate at about 172 million.

1961

"Between 1961 and 1967, crime rates per capita decreased over 7 percent." (*Kriminologiia,* 117.)

1966

"Number of convictions in the USSR last year in comparison with those in 1968, when earlier criminal legislation was in effect, decreased as a whole by 29.8 percent." (A. Gorkin, chairman of the USSR Supreme Court, "Piatidesiatiletie sovetskoi vlasti i sotsialisticheskoe pravosudie," *SZ,* 11 [1967], 20.)

1955, 1968

"If the number of persons convicted in the USSR in 1928 is taken as 100, then in 1955 it declined to 63 . . . the number of persons convicted in 1968 as compared with 1958 fell by 35 percent. . . ." (S. S. Ostroumov, *Sovetskaia sudebnaia statistika,* 246.)

Sources for Column (1)

1928

Convictions per 1000 inhabitants, RSFSR, 1929 were 1363. (A Shliapochnikov, then director, Institute of Criminal Policy, "Likvidatsiia bezrabotnitsy v SSSR i prestupleniia," *Sovetskoe gosudarstvo,* 9, 10 [1932], 149.) For total convictions, RSFSR, 1929, derive population as follows: population of the RSFSR was 100,891,244 on December 17, 1926. (Frank Lorimer, *The Population of the Soviet Union: History and Prospects* [Geneva, 1946], 67.) Natural increase of population per 1000 in the USSR was 21 in 1928. (*Narodnoe khoziaistvo SSSR v 1968 g.* [Moscow, 1969], 36.) Population for the RSFSR midyear, then, is estimated at 106,200,000 for 1929, and convictions at 1,450,000 (106,200,000 × 0.01363). But these convictions were 131 percent higher than the convictions in 1928. (A. Shliapochnikov, "Prestupnost' i repressiia v SSSR [Kratkii obzor]," *Problemy ugolovnoi politiki,* I [1935], 78.) Convictions for 1928, RSFSR = 1,145,000/1.31 = 1,106,000. Convictions for the USSR in 1928, then, are estimated as 1,106,000 × (population of the USSR ÷ population of the RSFSR) = 1.45 × 1,106,000 = 1,610,000. A check exists on this important figure for the table: M. N. Gernet shows for *1927* 1,026,084 RSFSR convictions and 1,507,360 USSR convictions, for a ratio of 1:468 between convictions in the USSR and the RSFSR, meaning a difference of about one-half of one percent in the ratios. (*Prestupnost' za granitsei i v SSSR* [Moscow, 1931], 79.)

Sources for Column (3): Estimated midyear population figures for the USSR used here are in millions, 1928—150, 1940—195.6, 1955—194.4, 1958—204.9, 1959—210.6, 1960—214.3, 1961—218, 1962—221.5, 1963—224.8, 1964—227.9, 1965—231.1, 1966—233.2, 1967—235.6, 1968—238.4. See population for December 17, 1926 (147 million). (*Narodnoe khoziaistvo SSSR v 1958 godu* [Moscow, 1959], 7.) Populations for 1950–1968 are listed in *Narodnoe khoziaistvo SSSR v 1970 g.*, 7, and relevant natural increases for computing midyear populations in 1928 and 1940, approximately, are found in *Narodnoe khoziaistvo SSSR v 1967 g.* (Moscow, 1968), 36.

Appendix B

SOURCES FOR TABLE 5–2

The Structure of Crime Today

Types of Crimes	*Percent*
Stealing state and public property	17
Hooliganism	24
Crimes against personal property	16
Crimes against persons	17
Economic crimes	5
Malfeasance in office	4
Motor-vehicle crimes	5
Crimes against justice	1.5
Crimes against the administrative order	4
Others	6.5

Source: Ostroumov, *Sovetskaia sudebnaia statistica,* 248. Ostroumov attributes these data to *Kriminologiia,* 118–119. But data there are slightly different (and I estimate my Table 5-2 from both Ostroumov and *Kriminologiia*).

Types of Crimes	*Percent*
Persons convicted for crimes against socialist property "in recent years"	15–18
Persons convicted for crimes against personal property, 1967 (incl. about 30% snatching and robbery)	16
Persons convicted for crimes against persons "fluctuated at about 15% in recent years."	
Persons convicted for crimes against public safety, order, and health, of which the major share are persons convicted for hooliganism. . . . "more than one third."	
Persons convicted for malfeasance in office (1967)	2.3
Persons convicted for economic crimes	5.0
Persons convicted for crimes against political and labor right of citizens "currently"	0.5
Persons convicted for crimes against justice	1.5
Persons convicted for crimes that are survivals of the past	0.4

Source: *Kriminologiia,* 118–119.

CHAPTER 6

Comprehensive Consumer Welfare Planning in the USSR

David T. Cattell

Some Soviet Definitions of Welfare

Comprehensive welfare has always been the socialist ideal. The Soviet leadership had never ceased to proclaim that its highest goal and role is to provide the good life for the masses. In practice, however, welfare and welfare planning in the Soviet Union has had many meanings and directions beginning with the 1919 Program of the All-Russian Communist Party. Inspired by this idealistic program of communal living and goals, ideologists and scholars in the 1920's flooded the journals with proposals for model communities and comprehensive welfare. But freedom to dream about various paths to the socialist ideal was brought to an abrupt end in the early 1930's by Stalin, who suppressed these "utopian schemes" by purging the idealists and their works. Actually, little of practical value was lost by ending the dreams, because the first decade of Bolshevism was a struggle for survival and minimal recovery, and beyond a few experimental communities the Soviet Union lacked even the resources to draft plans.[1]

Although Stalin never actually repudiated the 1919 party program, welfare came to have a different definition and set of goals under his rule. The role of welfare was primarily to serve the drive for industrialization. Thus, under Stalin welfare meant keeping the population sufficiently fed, healthy, indoctrinated, and educated to perform the tasks of industrialization and prividing labor incentives. Beyond this the regime had little interest.

By 1952 Stalin had achieved his primary goals for Russia, making it into an industrial and great power second only to the United States. Tremendous sacrifices by the masses had made it possible and now the masses wanted their rewards. Consequently, Stalin and his successors proclaimed the Soviet Union had moved into the stage of transition to communism. It was time for a new definition of welfare. With all the fanfare leading up to the new party program in 1961, everyone expected it to provide the answer. Although it proclaimed mass welfare as a major goal, it did little more than repeat the Stalinist formulas stressing the goals of heavy industry and national security. It did nothing to establish consumer priorities or suggest how welfare would be expanded or organized. Even Khrushchev's idea that public participation in welfare programs would play a major role in the transition to communism found scant attention in the program. The party leaders were unwilling or unable to give form to Soviet welfare goals. In their theoretical statements the leaders have continued to be vague. Brezhnev in his report to the 24th Party Congress talked about increasing the well-being of the working people as the main task of the Ninth Five-Year Plan. He also declared that communism is impossible without a high level of culture, education, social consciousness, and inner maturity on the part of the people, just as it is impossible without the appropriate material and technical base. He gave no details.[2] Nevertheless, in practice, over the last two decades mass welfare has taken on various new meanings and goals. Not only has the definition of welfare goals been constantly shifting, but the instruments for planning and delivering welfare benefits have also developed and expanded. It is the latter which is the special focus of this chapter. After briefly reviewing the structure of welfare in the 1920's and under Stalin, this chapter will analyze the post-Stalin leadership's reorganization of housing construction and the distribution of consumer goods and services as two examples of comprehensive welfare planning in the USSR.

Welfare Organization in the 1920's and under Stalin

Soon after the Revolution it was obvious that the central authorities could not at the same time pursue the Civil War and provide for mass welfare. As a result providing for the masses had to be decentralized and made the responsibility of provincial authorities. Even after the Civil War, at best the commissars in Moscow could only handle some of the major issues of welfare. So, throughout the 1920's it was the expansion and concentration of party control at the provincial level which made it possible to control and coordinate services at the local level. With almost dictatorial powers the provincial party secretary and his bureau scrutinized and passed on the political, social, and all but a small part of the economic affairs of their domain. But with limited resources and skills the welfare needs they could provide were subsistence at best, and even in such great cities as Leningrad luxury services like gas did not begin to flow again until 1935. Although this early experience was hardly the ideal of socialism or modernization, nevertheless, it might have served as the basis for a comprehensive welfare system based on regional or provincial planning.

The launching of the five-year plans, however, put an end to provincial autonomy and coordination. The important sectors of the economy were centralized and, except for nominal control, local party officials lost all direction over major industries. Furthermore, in carrying out their remaining tasks of providing consumer goods and services, balanced planning was impossible. They were forced to ignore local needs in favor of special goals set for them by central authorities in support of industrialization. Finally, with decreasing resources and burgeoning populations, urban party and government organs were hard pressed and in many cases were helpless and incapable of providing food and basic consumer necessities. As a result, the regime began to look elsewhere for resources. In the case of some crucial services such as education, social security, and the police, Moscow itself assumed direct control. But the greatest responsibility for consumer services was passed on to industry, particularly in the new urban areas. Industrial managers needed consumer services and goods as incentives to attract workers and from their privileged position were able to command the scarce resources to provide them. In such new cities as Magnitogorsk they came to control about 90 percent of all housing.[3] Under these conditions comprehensive and developmental planning of consumer goods and services was out of the question. Even simple coordination was very difficult. The numerous decrees and resolutions from Moscow could not alter the situation. Only in the immediate postwar period did the separate parts of the system seem to overcome their isolation and work together toward the rapid reconstruction of cities. But once achieved they again went their separate ways.

Even though the irrationality of the Soviet system was nowhere more apparent than in the organization and lack of planning of consumer welfare, the actual level of some of the services was comparatively high, especially in those areas directed from the center, such as education, health, and social security (although in the last case the level of payments were low).[4] In contrast the services and goods provided by cities, such as housing, restaurants, consumer outlets, laundries, and utilities, were almost universally poor, and there were no immediate hopes of improving these services. Comprehensive planning was inoperative in this sector, the grandiose master plans of Moscow and Leningrad notwithstanding.

New Priorities and the Expansion of Welfare

Almost immediately on assuming power in 1953, the post-Stalin leadership announced new welfare priorities. In practice, however, the changes have been slow and marked by shift and tacks. Nevertheless, the gap between industrial production and consumer welfare gradually closed and a new pragmatic and comprehensive definition of Soviet welfare is emerging. Beginning with Malenkov's new course, the post-Stalin leaders have become more and more deeply committed to improving the standard of living of the masses.

On the one hand, it was relatively easy to expand those consumer welfare services, such as education, medical care, and social security, which under Stalin had developed a comprehensive and more or less autonomous infrastructure.[5] Some of the secondary effects, however, did create problems. For example, increasing pensions made it possible for older people to retire and this reduced the unskilled labor force on which the system still heavily depended. In addition the rapid expansion of social-security payments created inflationary pressures. It is also interesting to note that the expansion of these traditional services has not always been accompanied by a shift in priorities. For all the public debates on education, this field is still the most backward. While social security and medical benefits increasingly tend to be defined by the needs and wishes of the citizenry, the field of education remains tied primarily to the needs of the state. Continued educational quotas, the narrow curricula, and the programs to combine education and work all reflect a traditional Stalinist definition for the role of education.

On the other hand, were expansion of those consumer welfare services which were the responsibility of local governments and industry and had diffuse structures and required major reorganizations. Although initially it was possible to release and even expand the production of some consumer goods and services, with only the most rudimentary systems of production, distribution, and measurement of needs, capacities were limited. The new leadership was quick to recognize the shortcomings, but it has taken two decades to find some of the answers. Creating an integrated infrastructure for comprehensive welfare services proved to be a difficult task. Furthermore, the sudden demand for new resources on all the fronts, foreign and domestic, created shortages of capital and skilled labor, and highlighted the cumulative inefficiencies of the basic Soviet economy.

The initial optimism of the Soviet leaders, particularly Khrushchev, as well as the leaders attack on the problem of expanding consumer welfare, was typically Soviet. First, they chose one crucial area as the key and launched a campaign of major proportions. The central target they chose was housing. It was an area which had been sadly neglected and much in demand. Second, not trusting local authorities, they centralized control and planning. Third, while never sparing of energy in the form of resolutions, socialist campaigns, and competitions, the leaders held back on resources to force cost reductions and to squeeze local authorities. Fourth, the Soviet leadership in its conceit assumed it knew the desires of the population and that rationalization would be a simple process for the Soviet bureaucracy with its skills, discipline, and experience in planning. Grandiose city and regional plans began to emerge based on fundamental principles expounded by Soviet scientists. Engineers and geographers established the *microraion* as the true socialist unit for communal development.[6]

Two decades of experience have disabused the leadership of the notion that the goals of consumer welfare can be so easily attained. At the very minimum consumer welfare depends on developing adequate means of measurement, comparison, and integrated evaluation; in the command type of economy the only hope for efficiency is comprehensive planning. Successfully meeting the needs and expectations of the masses and predicting the responses of both the masses and bureaucracy requires input from below in the form of sociological surveys and broad consultation at all levels of the hierarchy. It comes down to the fundamental problem of how to organize and distribute the decision-making process. Traditional methods are inadequate. It is impossible for the central authorities to make the complex and numerous decisions of welfare planning. Nor do the perspectives of either the individual ministries and enterprises give them the capability to make comprehensive and beneficial welfare and communal decisions. The solution the Soviet leaders seem to be finding is in the direction of increased comprehensive, local decision making based on broad, functional representation. The answer is neither original nor even new to the Soviet Union. The next section will trace these developments in the first area of attack, housing.

Mobilizing for New Housing Construction

The first task in mobilizing resources for new housing was a fundamental reorganization of the construction industry. Beginning in 1954 the scattered housing construction organizations attached to local governments, all types of industries, and other units were taken away and formed into a single, centralized hierarchy. They were assembled under *glavki* (chief administrations), each controlling construction for a large city or a large geographical area.[7] Surprisingly this first and seemingly simple step took about eight years to accomplish. In part this was due to the fact that the reorganization was temporarily lost in the mass reshuffling of industry during Khrushchev's *sovnarkhoz* reforms of 1957, which attempted to reorganize the economy into 105 regional units. More important, however, was the resistance of the large, powerful industries which were in the habit of constructing and controlling their own housing. Only gradually was a compromise worked out. It was agreed that the bulk of new housing and civil construction would come under a central plan and be constructed by the trusts and *kombinaty* (large industrial units building primarily prefab housing) of the regional and city construction *glavki* but that the finished housing would still in large part be turned over to industry for their distribution and management.

Actually the slowness of the centralization process did not prevent the rapid expansion of housing construction, particularly around the large cities. Nor did it interfere with the drive to reduce costs in time, money, and resources. Initially there were many obvious ways to cut costs, beginning with the consolidation of very small construction organization, the standardization of designs and parts, the cutting of excess space by reducing the height of ceilings and the size of halls and stairs, and the building of five-storied walk-up apartments. Furthermore, as centralization proceeded, it was possible to introduce various techniques of mass production and automation, such as paneled and modular housing. Thus, speed and cheapness of construction improved throughout the 1950's and 1960's.[8] The one serious remaining drawback in the construction process was the very low standard of quality, a problem common to much of

Soviet industry and still to be solved. Although mechanization provided some upgrading of quality, shoddiness, often including serious structural defects, characterized the results. The regime continues to experiment in new controls and incentives to improve the quality of construction.[9]

It was outside the construction process that the most difficult problems developed. Although the Soviet leaders looked upon housing as a key to consumer welfare and poured in resources, the success of housing increasingly depended on comprehensive local planning. New housing tracts without transportation, roads, sewers, telephones, retail outlets, consumer services, day-care centers, schools, and so forth provided few advantages over the traditional overcrowded housing. Increasingly it was the inability of local authorities to supply the necessary services and the increasing costs of these services which were creating the stumbling blocks.[10] Reducing housing costs was of little value if hard-pressed local governments could not supply the services cheaply. As the housing tracts pushed indiscriminately farther out from the center of the city, the network of services became increasingly far flung and valuable farm land or prize industrial land was used up.

Khrushchev's grand reorganization scheme of 1957 was supposed to have the answers by providing comprehensive planning through a combination of central direction and rational local planning of both industry and consumer services. However, beyond stating the goals the reform accomplished little. It floundered for a few years and was gradually abandoned. For local governments it was almost a disaster. Their share of new housing also diminished.[11] By 1962 the experiment was virtually over and in that year housing construction was restored to tight central control. The regime returned to a more pragmatic approach in community planning.

From the 1920's Soviet planners have stressed that the first step in community planning is a long range urban master plan. By 1950, however, only Moscow and Leningrad had approved plans. Then after 1953, when it was decided to build housing on a grand scale, there was no time to draw up general plans. Furthermore, there were not enough architect-engineers to do the drafting, and these few were concentrated in Moscow and Leningrad.[12] And as an editorial in *Arkhitektura S.S.S.R.* complained, architect-engineers working at their desks in the capital were without sufficient knowledge of local conditions.[13] Even with sufficient personnel, however, it would have been impossible to plan even five years ahead, since predictions of future growth and welfare policies have been inadequate or unknown. Thus, for example, Dnepropetrovsk in the Ukraine planned on the basis of the population reaching 1,100,000 between 1985–1990, but more recent calculation show this figure being reached in 1972–1973.[14] Future calculations were also made unreliable because of the indecisiveness of the leadership on questions of restricting the population growth in large cities, on whether to mass-produce private cars, and on what new resources were likely to be made available to cities. Nevertheless, by the 1970's most large and medium cities had or were in the process of drafting long-range plans. Of course, they were in large part too late. Before even the first few had been approved the housing boom was in full swing and the amount of urban housing had more than doubled.

Approving a master plan is only the beginning. If long range planning is to do more than produce beautiful scale models on display in city halls, they must be enforced. Although in the Soviet Union master plans are passed into law, the record of enforcement has been poor. In the past even such prominent cities as Moscow and Leningrad were unable to stand up against the large economic ministries which in matters of locating industries were powers unto themselves. Not only were these giants able to ignore local planning, they have consistently got around central directives forbidding new industrial construction around Moscow, Leningrad, and Kiev, in favor of small cities. Typically such infractions are overlooked in favor of fulfilling productive goals. It was impossible to challenge these giants head on, particularly since the central planners in *Gosplan,* to which all agencies in the end must appeal for resources, have consistently favored the big industries. Nevertheless, in recent years it has proved possible to guide the expansion of industry along lines more consistent with long-range planning. First, local planners have established industrial parks near transportation and insist plant expansion must be confined to these areas. In this way it is possible to confine industry to particular areas, although the amount and type of new industry still depends on the whims of the central ministries and planners. Second, local governments have taken over the planning and construction of new housing and only release it to industry after it is completed. It is much easier to integrate development with the city's overall plan when the construction of new housing and consumer services is organized under one agency.

The city's master plan does not itself provide the basis for day-to-day decision making. The annual plans are the crucial link in giving reality to comprehensive planning. On the one hand, the direction and the allocation of resources to construction is centralized at the all-union and republic level. Housing and other civil construction are a part of the capital plans of the republics, which are in turn approved and supervised by *Gosplan* and *Gosstroi* (the State Committee on Construction). On the other hand, the actual supply of services, from roads to day-care centers, is for the most part a local concern. Consequently some means are needed (1) to finance not only new housing but additional services and (2) to integrate the central planning of construction with local city planning and the local supply of services.

Cost Analysis and Comprehensive Welfare Planning

The problem of financing both new housing and new services is a serious one. By Soviet figures each year about 15 percent of total capital investment has been put into housing construction, and its costs can be detailed, but it has been impossible to calculate secondary costs such as how much has gone into providing utilities and other services. The search for economies and an adequate cost analysis of housing construction has led to some basic changes not only in computing costs but in taking steps in the direction of more comprehensive planning.

Housing construction costs were traditionally figured on the basis of construction costs per square meter of living space, omitting the cost of service areas (halls, kitchens, closets, baths, and stairs), the cost of bringing services to the building and community, and the value of the land. The first change was to refigure cost based on all general usable space, including service areas. This shift helped to keep builders from economizing and cutting down on vital utilities and the size of kitchens, baths, and closets and to provide a more realistic cost analysis of construction. As mentioned earlier, figuring significant economies and new techniques on this limited basis had brought costs of construction way down. But without the inclusion of the cost of providing services, the real costs could not be determined. Sample investigations showed that the type of construction and the locality of a housing project had a significant effect on the cost of providing services. For example, purely from the construction point of view four- and five-storied walk-up flats were the least expensive. But, when the cost of supplying and maintaining the services is added in, large cities' buildings of 9 to 16 stories are often less costly.[15] It was obvious that costing of construction and services needed to be integrated, but since providing the services was the individual concern of each city, the task was not easy.

Still further investigation showed that the logical next step in cost analysis was to consider land values. Soviet theory holds that the land belongs to the state and all the people, and, therefore, there should be no change on its use.[16] The investigations, however, pointed up that some lands were significantly cheaper to build on than others. Furthermore, the development of long-range urban plans showed that certain areas are more desirable than others for industry. The value of land having been ignored in the past, much land along railroad rights of way, which is particularly useful for industrial purposes, had been built with housing. As a result, urban planners increasingly considered the comparative value of land in development and costing. Finally, in December, 1968, the Supreme Soviet ordered a land cadastre, including placing a value on all land in the USSR.[17] Thus, in the 1960's it became increasingly clear that further economies in construction depended on the integration of construction with local services into a comprehensive plan.

One way to integrate would have been again to disperse the civil-construction industry to local units. This was not seriously considered and probably would not have worked, judging by Stalin's experience in the 1930's and Khrushchev's *sovnarknoz* experiences. Except for a few large cities, local governments can neither command the resources nor the authority to carry forth a massive building program. Thus the solution adopted by Moscow was not to decentralize but rather to send out its agents to command and coordinate. The solution was not original but was in fact traditional for matters about which the leadership is concerned at the local level. The heads of the local militia, of primary and secondary education, and of the department of finance have from the early years of the regime been the agents and appointees of their central ministries at the republic or all-union level. At the same time, they are also members of the local-government executive committee and theoretically responsible to it. From this arrangement the agents of the central authorities are expected to get the cooperation of the local authorities to their needs and achieve maximum coordination. The new agent of Moscow for comprehensive planning of civil construction is the chief architect of the city.[18] He is the crucial link with the local executive committee. He heads the architect-planning department regulating new construction, and through the State Committee on Architecture he has important contracts with the ministries of construction, *Gosplan,* and *Gosstroi.* Although his authority over new industrial construction is restricted primarily to its location, all phases of housing and other civil construction are reviewed and authorized by his office. His role in local administration tends to differ from that of the heads of education and finance at the local level in that he cannot afford to remain aloof from local politics. His success depends not only on his authority and independence but on close cooperation with local officials in the comprehensive planning of a wide sector of local services in support of new construction. Furthermore, beginning in 1963 each city appointed under its executive committee a coordinating committee on construction composed of representatives of the local construction organizations, trade unions, the State Construction Bank (*Stroibank*), union of architects, fire department, and sanitary department, as well as other important local organizations (Resolution of Council of Ministers of the RSFSR, May 9, 1963).[19] The purpose of this commission is not only to coordinate planning among the interested parties but also to mobilize local notables behind the plan and to help lobby at higher echelons on behalf of the plan.

For local governments to play their role in supplying communal services, new sources of revenue had to be made available to them. As a result urban governments control over light industries has been restored and even increased, and they are able to benefit from the profits of these enterprises. Local executive committees also are able to insist that industries desiring new housing or utilities supply some of the capital.[20] Industries also can be required to turn over 5 percent of their capital investments intended for housing to the construction of trade and catering services.[21]

Once a focal point for comprehensive planning of urban development had been established, it was possible to expand the concept to introduce new factors such as (1) urban renewal and (2) sociological analysis:

1. It was the traditional approach in new construction to be concerned only with the desperate shortage of housing space, and therefore old structures were preserved regardless of their state, repaired and rarely torn down. There was plenty of vacant land for new construction. But the deterioration of most central urban areas, plus the more comprehensive evaluation of costs, have made urban renewal desirable. Beginning with Moscow more and more cities are adding to their long-range plans schedules for urban renewal.

2. Beginning in the 1960's the discipline of sociology was reborn in the Soviet Union. In 1966–67 it penetrated the housing field and was "discovered" by the architects. The first articles relating sociological data to housing appeared in 1966, and by 1967 it became a vogue.[22] As dramatic

as the introduction of sociology into civil planning appeared on the su face, it has a long way to go to having a meaningful impact. In 1967 ther were only 2,000 sociology workers for all the needs of the USSR, an there was not a single institute or department for training sociologists an no journal.[23] With demands for sociologists also increasing in industry few cities have as yet been able to have a staff of sociologists. Neverthe less, potentially it opens up a whole new dimension to comprehensiv planning at the local level.

The results of the reorganization of basic developmental planning i already evident. Even a casual survey indicates that in the large or well established cities the head architects and local executive committees ar making significant progress with their development plans. Although prob lems of controlling development still remain, it is clear that the majo cities are being transformed and basic living conditions are improving fo most inhabitants. Two serious difficulties still remain, however: (1 medium and small cities have barely felt the impact of comprehensiv planning and modernization, and (2) comprehensive local planning i not just a problem of new services and new construction; it is maintainin and improving the quality of the old.

The Problem of Small Cities

From the first reorganization of housing construction after Stalin' death, the small cities have lagged behind. Large cities with well-estab lished construction trusts and *kombinaty* fulfilled their goals and move on to new and better types of prefabricated housing, while the small poorly equipped construction trusts in small cities continued in thei traditional ways. Their reorganization into regional groups cannot over come their lack of skilled manpower and lack of mechanization. In the subsequent scramble for new resources, they cannot compete with the big cities.[24] At the same time, the small-city governments are too weak and ineffective to resist the continued domination over urban develop ment by industry. Finally, there are still not enough skilled architects and engineers to man the crucial posts in either the construction trusts or the architect-planning departments.[25] The decrees in 1968 and 1969 raising the salaries of construction workers, improving working conditions, and expanding training facilities are thus far the most significant steps toward improving the situation.[26] But the effects of these reforms at best will take at least a decade.

The Problem of Capital Repairs and Maintenance

From its core in new housing construction, comprehensive planning has been gradually expanding to include more and more facets of local government and welfare. One major problem closely related to housing which increasingly concerns urban and other planners is housing repair and maintenance. After all, in the long run the quality of the vast new fund is dependent on its maintenance. But no area of the economy is worse off or has suffered from more serious handicaps than housing maintenance and repairs. The difficulties derive from its financing, the very scope of the problem, and the nature of the task. The financial trouble is simply a question of not enough revenue from rents. The low rent schedules established in the 1920's and 1930's are not even sufficient to cover current expenses and provide nothing for capital repairs and depreciation. Furthermore, the old housing is getting increasingly costly to maintain and repair, the urban renewal is only beginning to eliminate some of the oldest structures. More important, new housing has tripled the fund to be maintained. Unfortunately the cost of maintaining this new housing is not much less than the old. The general poor quality of new construction makes repairs necessary almost from the beginning.[27] Furthermore, the additional services like elevators and plumbing facilities for every apartment are expensive to maintain. So the additional rent revenue from new housing does not nearly cover the additional costs. For local governments there is an additional burden, because the regime is pressuring industry to turn its housing over to local government to manage. Although this shift makes comprehensive local planning easier, frees industry from the burden of maintaining its own housing, and reduces overall costs by transferring housing to local governments (which are more efficient), it significantly increases the financial and managerial burden on local government. On top of all this is the expectation that through repairs the quality of old housing will be raised to the level of new housing.[28] The extent of the burden is indicated in the facts that investment in current and capital repairs in the 1960's was almost 40 percent of the investment in new housing[29] and that revenue from rents has covered only a small percentage of the investment. Furthermore, the burden is growing. In the case of the RSFSR expenditures by repair construction organizations went from 338 million rubles in 1960 to 904 millions in 1963 and is expected to reach 2–2.5 billion rubles in 1975.[30]

In the same eight years capital investment in new housing increased only slightly.

Thus, a comprehensive approach to maintenance has become necessary, creating a sound financial and organizational base and integrating its development with new housing and the general expansion of consumer services. Some steps have been taken, but progress is slow. Primary responsibility for dealing with these issues has been placed on the republic ministries on communal economy, and thus far they have not followed the pattern of new construction and centralized. The administration of maintenance has remained entirely in local hands. The republic ministries merely conduct research and issue directives for the cities to administer through their various service departments. Furthermore, the planning and operations in the maintenance sector have been kept completely separate from new construction even for capital repairs where there is extensive overlap. It would appear that the only real meeting place, if any, of the two systems is in the executive committee at the local level.[31] Only indirectly are the planners of new construction trying to help through urban renewal and by stressing the quality of new construction in order to reduce maintenance costs. Since analyses have shown that the cost of capital repairs on old buildings is often equal to an even more than new construction, the amount of old housing being demolished to make way for new has more than doubled in the last decade.[32]

As a control and economy measure, the first major reform of maintenance came in the late 1950's with the consolidation of the basic administrative units for urban management from an average of 9,600 square meters of housing to 23,800 square meters. This allegedly reduced administrative costs by 28 percent.[33] Industrial housing as it is being turned over to cities is being reorganized on the same pattern.[34] In respect to housing, these bureaus are the basic administrative units except for capital and some current repairs which are managed directly by the city governments. Furthermore, bureaus serve not only as basic units of housing management, they are the fundamental community-level unit for all social, recreational, and consumer-service outlets and political and adult educational activities. Thus they are a key unit in providing for consumer welfare and serve as a primary focal point around which comprehensive welfare planning needs to be built.

Beyond standardizing housing management and integrating them into local government, the central authorities have undertaken no real reforms in this sector. The institutes of the Academy of Communal Economy have been busy doing research seeking ways to mechanize maintenance and repairs and setting standards for work done, and the ministries of communal economy have been issuing numerous decrees incorporating the findings. The trouble is that the diversity in the kinds and types of services and housing do not lend themselves to standardization. Furthermore, without significant increases of investment, mechanization and automation of maintenance and repair are not possible.[35]

Except for a few cities such as Leningrad, which have a long tradition of handling their own affairs, comprehensive planning of maintenance and reconstruction will be possible only when the regime has found solutions to some basic problems. The first and most important is the lack of personnel. Maintenance and repair workers are, next to farmers, the poorest paid in the economy, and in prestige they are at the bottom of the urban social ladder. Only those who cannot fit in anywhere else stay in this sector.[36] This is even more true for competent executive personnel and planners. Although the gradual increase in minimum wages has improved the lot of the maintenance worker, it does not seem to have attracted more or better workers, only increased labor costs. The second problem is the lack of revenue. Without additional funds by doubling or tripling or rents, through central-government subsidies, or by new tax resources cities can only provide the barest minimum of maintenance and repairs.[37] Finally there is the problem of minimal capital investments in maintenance and repair organizations to provide modern equipment, spare parts, and other materials. Without capital support from the central government, local authorities cannot make a concerted attack on the problem of maintenance and cannot escape a decaying urban landscape, in spite of vast new modern housing projects.

Retail Trade and Services

While the problem of maintaining housing is assuming major proportions in the Soviet Union, the leadership has chosen to ignore the issue and emphasize still another sector of consumer welfare—retail trade and services. As a result the central focus of the Ninth Five-Year Plan (1971–75) is on the flow of goods and services to the population. Overall consumer turnover is scheduled to increase between 35 and 40 percent, compared to an increase in the rate of new housing construction by only slightly over 10 percent. As in the case of housing, traditional responsibilities in consumer goods and services have been diffused among various ministries, local governments, and individual enterprises. Both the production and distribution of retail goods and services lacked any logical pattern. Thus, for example, some 33 enterprises belonging to 10 different ministries have been producing washing machines, all of poor quality.[38] As in the case of housing, the first task will be to sort out this labyrinth, and it will take time, probably more than one five-year plan.

Currently the regime is giving attention to various elements of the problem: (1) the production of service equipment and the construction of a capital base; (2) the development of a comprehensive system of distribution and marketing; (3) research into methods of determining demand; (4) experimenting with quality controls; and (5) comprehensive planning.

1. An important auxiliary to the goal of the Ninth Five-Year Plan to increase overall consumer turnover by 40 percent is to build the capital base for improved services. This means the construction of many more warehouses, consumer outlets, and service centers. Also, special attention is being given to the production of automated and control equipment for light industry and distribution depots, packaging machines, self-service counters and vendors, and an adequate supply of spare parts for consumer items.[39]

2. Marketing even of industrial goods has never been a Soviet strong point, and in consumer goods it has been totally haphazard. Items produced by enterprises for national consumption have been distributed by a complicated system of general contracts between ministries and subcontracts between individual enterprises and/or supply organizations. But the largest part of consumer distribution, particularly food, has been considered a matter of local concern and local governments have organized supplies as best they could through a system of local contracts and limited distribution points and markets. The results were uneven from locality to locality, but overall it has meant generally poorly stocked stores, underequipped services, and local shortages. Beginning with the Ninth Five-Year Plan the distribution system is undergoing reorganization. On the one hand, the wholesale organizations have been enlarged to include both more goods and an increased number of wholesale depots. On the other hand, where the supplying of goods is over a long period and at a more or less constant volume, direct contacts between the manufacturers and retailers are being encouraged.[40] Finally, to help retailers know what goods are available, more trade fairs are being held.[41]

3. A major difficulty for retailers has not only been shortages but also shelves and stock rooms full of goods no one wants to buy. Even marking down prices does not always move the stock. It is not only a question of poor quality but no demand. As a result experiments are being conducted on the best way to provide feedback through the system as to what is or is likely to be the demand. These experiments include sociological surveys of the population, reporting by clerks as to what is selling and asked for, giving retail outlets authority to order only what they feel they can sell, and even allowing them in some cases to return unsold items.[42]

4. As with the rest of the economy, consumer production and services are plagued by low quality, for which there is no ready answer. Several means are being tried. The traditional right of wholesalers and retailers to sue for breach of contract is being stressed, but as a method of quality control it has not generally been successful.[43] In addition, retailers have been given more power to reject unwanted items, and consumers have been given more complete written guarantees. In a command economy, however, where the number of suppliers are few, these rights have limited effectiveness. The regime has also sought to shift the salary incentive and bonus system to reward not only the enterprise but individual shops and brigades for improved quality. More attention is also being given to quality inspections at various levels, and seals of quality are granted to products which meet exceptional standards. From the continued complaints it would appear none of these attempts have thus far succeeded in solving the problem.

5. Although upgrading the systems of marketing, demand measurement and quality will have some impact, in a command economy the key is comprehensive planning. Even more than in the case of housing construction comprehensive planning for consumer goods and services will necessitate a delicate balancing of the roles to be played by the central government, local governments, ministries, technicians, enterprises both as suppliers and consumers, and the masses. But no reorganization of the system or comprehensive planning is likely to succeed unless local authorities are given some discretion over prices and wages in order to allow them to dispose of surpluses, to encourage the production of scarce items and to create work incentives through commissions and bonuses.[44] Although no definite pattern has yet emerged, the leadership, based on its experience with housing, already seems sensitive to the complexity of the issues and is experimenting in several directions. The sociologists and some planners are arguing that, as the first step, long-range social devel-

opment plans—similar to the physical development plans for cities—are needed.[45] To this end they are beginning to study living patterns of the population and, as material demands are met and leisure hours are increased, projecting its needs over the next decade.[46] The architect-engineers are pushing for an extension of urban development planning to include all aspects of welfare planning into a single integrated plan.[47] The geographers, who have long been in the forefront of regionalization, are looking to the development of mathematical models for comprehensive regional and urban planning.[48]

Conclusions

From this brief survey of planning for consumer welfare in Soviet cities it is clear that the regime has moved slowly and assaulted the problem one by one at the three points in the system calculated to have the most dramatic payoff. Stalin began with social welfare including health, education and social security. During his drive for industrialization it provided minimal worker security and was used to convince the masses of the superiority of socialism. The second campaign, begun after Stalin's death, was for new housing, a sector he had long neglected. In 1952 urban dwellers on an average were crowded 2.6 occupants to a room, each with only 5.2 square meters of housing space. By the end of this decade the goal of every Soviet family having its own apartment will be in sight.[49] Beginning with the 24th Party Congress in 1971, a new campaign to improve retail trade and communal services was launched. In the cases of both Stalin's welfare programs and housing, organization and control were centralized while the actual administration was delegated to the local level and carried out by direct agents of the central government working with local officials. In addition the growing need for coordination and greater economic and administrative efficiency, particularly in housing, has led to efforts at comprehensive planning, both laterally and over time. Developments in consumer trade and services seem to be moving toward a similar pattern of control and planning. The record in all three sectors has been good, if slow in materializing. As a result the quality of life for urban citizens has been substantially raised. But the task is far from complete because in the long run to continue the progress, to make comprehensive planning in consumer welfare meaningful, to make controls effective, and to keep costs reasonable, the regime must face the consequences of its past mistakes, particularly in respect to the poor quality of most urban construction and the problem of maintaining and modernizing older services and housing. The rising costs in this area cannot be ignored for long. Not only can the Soviet Union not escape the problem of urban decay; in another decade it may well be overwhelmed by the problem.

Notes

1. Moscow, the capital and showplace of socialism, lacked a general developmental plan until 1935.

2. "Report of the CPSU Central Committee to the 24th Congress of the Communist Party of the Soviet Union by L. I. Brezhnev," *Pravda* (March 31, 1971), in *Current Digest of the Soviet Press,* XXIII, 14, 6 (1971).

3. *Gorodskoe khoziaistvo moskvy,* 3 (1964), 22. Even in the 1960's some 37 Soviet cities had no municipal housing fund and 284 had only insignificant amounts under their control. (E. I. Ianovskaia, *Khozraschet v zhilishchno khoziaistve i puti evo dal'neishego ukrepleniia* [Moscow, 1964], 2.)

4. In 1940 social-welfare payments represented 14.4 percent of national income and 24 rubles per capita. By 1950 this had increased to 17.6 percent of the national income and 72 rubles per capita. Social-welfare funds consist of that part of the national income which members of society receive as free goods and services. These include primarily medical care, education, pensions, and child-care centers. (*Izvestiia* [August 12, 1971], 5).

5. From 1950 to 1970 welfare payments increased from 72 rubles per capita to 262 rubles per capita. (*Ibid.*)

6. The *microraion* was developed as the basic planning and living urban unit. It varies from about 50 to 200 acres and for the inhabitants is supposed to include the following services: recreational areas, community rooms, nursery schools, creches, food stores, a housing office, cafeteria, some repair services, and a general-produce store.

7. L. P. Lukaev i N. A. Godlevskii, *Organizatsiia i planirovanie stroitel'stva* (Moscow, 1964), 12. The significance of this reform can be seen in the case of Moscow where it brought together 46 construction trusts and 190 departments. These 240 different organizations previously had been subordinate to 44 different ministeries and departments (*Zhilishchnoe stroitel'stvo,* 7 [1967], 8).

8. For example, one study of *Glavmosstroi* in Moscow showed that the introduction of mass-produced large-panel housing from 1954–1964 had reduced costs by 20 rubles per square meter of housing space or 13–15 percent and the amount of labor expended by 7–9 percent (*Ekonomika stroitel'stva,* 4 [1965], 15). Another study for Leningrad showed the average cost of construction of housing going from 178 rubles per square meter of living space in 1958 to 136 rubles in 1963. Subsequently there was a slight increase in cost due to the increased height of the average apartment building. (*Stroitel'stavo i arkhitektura Leningrada,* 4 [1966], 7).

9. See for example, *Pravda* (March 6, 1971), 8.

10. A study of plan fulfillment for Leningrad in the early 1960's indicated how serious the problem had become:

	New Nurseries and Creches			Store Outlets		
	Planned	*Fulfilled*	*Percentage*	*Planned*	*Fulfilled*	*Percentage*
1960	42	24	57%	25	2	8%
1961	30	13	43	19	6	31
1962 (6 mos.)	23	13	62	19	3	15

Source: *Voprosy proizvoditel'nosti truda i sebestoimosti v zhilishchnom stroitel'stve* (Leningrad, 1962), 90. See also report on Fifth All-Union Architects Congress in *Pravda* (October 22, 1970).

11. New housing constructed by local governments:

1960	14.6	million	square	meters	of	general	usable space
1961	12.4	"	"	"	"	"	"
1962	10.7	"	"	"	"	"	"

Source: *Ekonomika zhilishchno-kommunal'nogo khoziaistva* (Moscow, 1965), 54.

12. In 1959 in the USSR there were only 64 architects per million of population compared to 364 in England, 240 in Sweden, 130 in the United States, 312 in Bulgaria, 100 in Czechoslovakia, 129 in Poland, and 154 in Hungary. Furthermore, out of 10,462 Soviet architects in 1965, 3,640 were in Moscow and another 1,248 in Leningrad. The number of architects did not increase until after 1967 when the number and capacity of the architect-engineering training institutes were increased. By 1970 the institutes were producing 3,500 a year. (*Arkhitektura S.S.S.R.*, 9 [1969], 1.) But even in 1972 there were still complaints about the shortage. (*Izvestiia* [June 27, 1972], 2.)

13. *Arkhitektura S.S.S.R.*, 6 (1966), 2.

14. *Izvestiia* (August 27, 1968).

15. In a study of construction in Moscow it was found that the cost per square meter of usable housing space was:

Stories	*4*	*5*	*9*
	rubles	rubles	rubles
Basic cost of construction	121.70	117.20	122.40
Basic cost of engineering and roads	44.0	38.92	29.73
Cost of cultural and communal services	16.30	15.50	14.70
Connecting utilities	52.80	46.80	36.00
Total	234.80	218.82	202.83

Source: *Arkhitektura S.S.S.R.*, 1 (1965), 22.

16. Editorial in *Arkhitektura S.S.S.R.*, 1 [1966], 1 and L. N. Goltsman, *Ekonomika kommunal'nogo khoziaistva, uslugi, tarify* (Moscow, 1966), 147ff. tember 5, October 5, 10, and November 12, 1968).

17. For a general discussion of this problem see *Izvestiia* (August 26, Sep-

18. V. T. Bobotov, *Finansirovanie i kreditovanie zhilishchnogo stroitel'stva*, (Moscow, 1967), 15–16.

19. V. G. Vishniakov, *Uchastie deputatov mestnykh sovetov v raspredelenii zhilyi ploshchadi* (Moscow, 1964), 53.

20. *Izvestiia* (March 1, and August 24, 1972).

21. *Pravda* (January 30, 1972), 1.

22. See particularly the second issue of *Arkhitektura S.S.S.R.* for 1967.

23. *Voprosy filosofii*, 6 (1966), and *Komsomolskaia Pravda* (June 2, 1967).

24. Panel construction of urban housing in the public sector as percentage of total public construction:

	USSR	*Moscow*
1962	15.2%	47.2%
1964	25.0	51.0
1966	31.5	55.0
1968	32.0	61.0
1975 (Planned)	50.0	80.0

Source: Zhilishchnoe stroitel'stvo, 11 (1967), 15 and 1 (1969), 30 and *Arkhitektura S.S.S.R.*, 9 (1969), 1.

25. For example, in 1965 in the Perm Oblast, there were places for 33 chief architects but of those holding the posts only five had diplomas in architecture and in Bashkir of 63 posts only two had diplomas (*Arkhitektura S.S.S.R.*, 6 [1966], 1).

26. In February, 1968, the Central Committee and the USSR Council of Ministers passed a decree on improving the conditions and training of construction workers. Some two million skilled workers were ordered to be added to construction of all kinds from 1968 to 1970, including 834,000 trained in vocational and technical schools. Then, in June, 1969, the Council of Ministers of the USSR ordered the creation, during 1969–70, of 132 schools accommodating 51,800 pupils. These were to be vocational-technical schools with a three-year course of instruction. By 1973 these schools are to accommodate 100,000. Also at the beginning of 1969, the government raised the wages of construction workers on an average of 25 percent, and of workers in construction materials on an average of 23 percent. The increases began in the Far East on February 1 and then gradually were extended westward to cover all the Soviet Union by October 1.

27. One study of 609 apartment buildings in the 1960's showed that 64 percent needed roof repairs in four years, 90 percent in eight years and all in ten years, although the roofs were supposed to last 30 years. Another investigation in Leningrad in the same article reported that one series of new apartments after three or four years needed a capital repair expenditure of 9.9–14.2 rubles per square meter of housing space (*Arkhitektura S.S.S.R.*, 6 [1968], 22). Complaints and demands for more adequate quality controls have become perennial (*Pravda* [June 21, 1972], 3).

28. Capital repairs today usually entail completely remodeling old housing, tearing out walls and adding kitchens and baths for each apartment.

29. B. M. Kolotilkin, *Dolgovechnost' zhilykh zdanii* (Moscow, 1965), 110.

30. *Zhilishchnoe i kommunal'noe khoziaistvo*, 2 (1969), 21.

31. The author, in interviews with members of the housing-management departments and architect-planning department, was able to find almost no communication between the two offices.

32. Amount of urban housing demolished and withdrawn from housing fund in millions of square meters:

1960	5,833,000
1962	6,519,000
1964	9,470,000
1966	14,040,000
1968	9,679,000
1970	12,749,000

Source: *Narodnoe khoziaistvo S.S.S.R. v 1970g.*, 548.

33. A. K. Birkin i P. A. Petrov, *Finansovoe planirovanie i analiz deiatel'nosti zhilishchnykh organizatsii* (Moscow, 1965), 11–12.

34. *Izvestiia* (February 21, 1970), 5.

35. *Izvestiia* (June 10, and July 5, 1972).

36. *Izvestiia* (March 8, 1972), 2.

37. In 1962 one study concluded that the average deficit was about 1.50 rubles per square meter of usable housing space not covered by apartment rent and rent from nonliving space (B. I. Kolotilkin, *Dolgovechnost' zhilykh zdanii* [Moscow, 1965], 102–103.

38. *Sovetskaia torgovlia* (January 8, 1972), 3, in *Current Digest of the Press,* XXIV, (1972), 2, 2.

39. *Pravda* (January 30, 1972), 1.

40. *Izvestiia* (December 17, 1971), 3 and *Kommunist,* 8 (1972), 64ff.

41. *Pravda* (June 7, 1972), 3.

42. *Pravda* (June 18, 1972), 1 and (August 4, 1972), 3.

43. "Economic sanctions for contract violations do not have the necessary results, since they have no palpable influence on the size of the material incentives but instead are applied to the results of the economic operations of the enterprises." (*Izvestiia* [July 22, 1972].)

44. *Pravda* (November 4, 1971), 4 and *Literaturnaia gazeta,* 31 (1972), 10–11, in *Current Digest of the Soviet Press,* XXIV, 33, 1–2. It is, however, not just a matter of salary but the social status of workers in consumer services must be raised. (*Izvestiia* [December 1, 1971], 3.)

45. *Arkhitektura S.S.S.R.,* 5 (1971), 43 and *Pravda* (July 3, 1971), 3.

46. See for example *Arkhitektura S.S.S.R.,* 3 (1969), 14; no. 6, 33; and no. 9, 14ff and 62f.

47. *Arkhitektura S.S.S.R.,* 3 (1971), 15–19 and 27–33.

48. I. F. Zaytsev, "A Territorial Model of Productive Forces," *Voprosy Geografii* (1968), 64–83, in *Soviet Geography,* X, no. 9, 507ff. and B. S. Movchan, "Use of the Mathematical Method in the Solution of a Location Problem," *Izvestiia Vsesoyuznogo Geograficheskogo Obshchestva,* 6 (1969), 534–539, in *Soviet Geography,* XI, no. 8, 649–654.

49. For the city of Moscow alone it is promised that virtually every family will have its own apartment by 1980.

CHAPTER 7

Community Structure, Political Participation, and Soviet Local Government: The Case of Kutaisi

Theodore H. Friedgut

Introduction

Local government, the study of the structure and activity of government in individual communities, has in recent years become a subject of increasing interest to Soviet scholars seeking ways to develop institutions which will meet the policy goals and administrative needs of the Soviet government. The resulting discussions and the growing possibility of collecting data and observing governmental operations *in situ* have also attracted non-Soviet scholars to the study of local politics in the Soviet Union.

Within the USSR, the growth in activities of the local soviets is indicated by the increase in their budgets from 4.31 billion rubles in 1946 to 21.1 billion rubles in 1965, from 14 percent of the total USSR budget in 1946 to 20 percent in 1965.[1] The number of deputies elected to the local soviets has also grown rapidly over the last 15 years, from 1,549,777 in 1957 to 2,193,086 in 1973.[2] This growth in the funds and manpower allotted to local government has been underscored by a series of Communist party decrees, government legislation, and publications, all discussing the local soviets and ways of improving their effectiveness. A monthly journal devoted entirely to discussions of local government, *Sovety deputatov trudiashchikhsia,* appeared in mid-1957. Its predecessor, *Sovetskoe Stroitel'stvo,* founded in the mid-1920's, had ceased publication at the height of the Stalin purges in August of 1937.

The study of local Soviet politics by non-Soviet scholars has yielded a series of valuable works on the interaction of party and governmental bodies and the workings of local government. On the whole, these focus on the Communist party as the central wielder of power in the Soviet system.[3] Whether studying a broad range of party organs, as does Jerry Hough, or a single body, as does Philip Stewart, studies of this kind concentrate on the seat of power and its relation to policy adoption and implementation in the tradition of American studies of community power structure.[4] The questions asked are: "Who participates in decision making?" "Who gains and who loses from alternative possible outcomes?" "Who prevails in decision making?" [5] In short, "Who governs?"

The answers to such questions are fundamental to the understanding of any political system. However, another set of questions based on the how and why of government is equally important. What institutions serve to link the governors with the governed and what values underlie the policies adopted by the governors? These questions have generally led scholars into studies of political participation, in which the emphasis has been on the citizen's role as voter, as elected representative, or as active participant in electoral politics.[6] Only more recently, with the revival of interest in "community" and in "participatory democracy," have political scientists once more begun to examine the ways in which citizens may band together and affect the outcome of local politics—whether by assisting or resisting local authorities.[7] This new focus helps bring the study of political participation closer to what would appear to be the most fruitful areas for inquiry with relation to practice in the Soviet Union. Included in Soviet studies of this subject is the consideration of the essence of the Soviet conception of mass participation as the mobilization of all citizens into support for the institutions of public administration—particularly the local soviets as elected bodies allegedly representing the whole of Soviet society, through participation in trade unions, factory groups, and other public bodies.[8]

Non-Soviet studies of the citizen's role in communist politics have generally focused on the citizen as the object of mobilization and indoctrination and on Stalin's view of the soviets and other mass organizations as "transmission belts" carrying the Communist party's directives to the masses.[9] Relatively little attention has been given to the functions of mass participation beyond the legitimation of the regime, yet broad participation of citizens in political affairs is taken to be one of the hallmarks of a developed polity. Fred W. Riggs notes that both the democratization and the politization of the citizenry may be considered as processes of political development and that the one is not necessarily accompanied by the other.[10] This point is also forcefully made by James R. Townsend in his book *Political Participation in Communist China,*[11] where he links the creation of a modern nation-state in China with the politization of an apolitical population, stating that "with the victory of the Chinese Communist movement, however, mass participation became a source of governmental strength and stability. . . ." A modern industrial state has difficulty developing from a parochial population. In particular, where mobilized public support must be counted on to augment limited material resources and the weight of mass bodies is called upon in place of highly trained and efficient administrators, the mechanisms and operation of citizen involvement in government become an area of interest to the student of the political system.

At the local level of Soviet politics, and in particular at the urban district and rural district levels, normal contact between citizens and governmental institutions is intensified by the particular features of the Soviet political system. Not only is mobilized participation a basic value of Soviet politics, but government operation of activities which in non-Soviet-type systems might simply be subject to general licensing or supervision, brings citizen and regime into contact on many levels. The Soviet citizen who changes his residence, wants his boots resoled, or wants to buy new clothing will most likely have to deal with an agency of his local soviet. In fact, one of the major factors in the renewed attention paid to the local soviets by the Soviet authorities is the growing volume of consumer goods, housing, and social welfare expenditures in the Soviet budget. While consumer expenditures were minimal, they could be managed from the central ministries with the aid of local party committees, with little more than formal involvement of the soviets. With the simultaneous growth of production efforts and consumer welfare, some division of labor was indicated and a large part of this newly intensified activity was entrusted to the local soviets—from the *krai* and *oblast'* level down to the settlement and village.

The formal structure and competence of local soviets is similar throughout the USSR—with minimal variance between the activities prescribed for a city soviet in Lithuania or Uzbekistan. A little reflection, however, will lead to the thought that many local factors will almost inevitably influence the way in which the soviet succeeds in realizing its formal rights and the extent to which it succeeds in reaching its citizens and answering their needs. The administrative structure of the area, linking a local soviet to the republic level; the extent and nature of industrialization; existence of homogeneous local cultural and community traditions; the extent to which a local elite exists; circulation and rotation of leadership in the community; all of these are factors which will almost surely affect the workings of local institutions, whatever their formal structure.

It is within the framework of the above considerations that this chapter is written. It examines the institutions and activities of the local soviet of the Georgian city of Kutaisi and the manner in which the local leadership penetrates into the community, linking consideration of the structure and interrelation of the institutions of the local soviet with thoughts as to the influence of local conditions on the way and degree to which the soviet achieves its goals. In addition, examination of the personnel, institutions, and activities of the soviet of Kutaisi may give us some insights as to whether developments in the rights and duties of the local soviets, urged by central government and Communist party bodies, are reflected in local practice.

Materials on Kutaisi were gathered from three sources. During December, 1969, in the course of research dealing with citizen participation in local Soviet government, it was the writer's good fortune to spend some time in the city of Kutaisi, interviewing officials and studying the structure and operation of the local soviet. The visit was brief, one week in all. The surroundings were entirely new and unfamiliar. Notwithstanding the unreserved hospitality and cooperation of local officials, many key questions went unasked and some important aspects of the subject became clear to me only as a result of later readings and conversations with a number of people who had emigrated after living the greatest part of their lives in Kutaisi.[12] These two direct sources were supplemented by an examination of the Georgian Republic newspaper, *Zaria vostoka*[13] for references to activities of the Kutaisi soviet and indentification of its leadership, and by documents provided by the Organization and Instruction Department of the Kutaisi soviet.

The Development of Soviet Local Government, 1957–1972

The post-Stalin renaissance of the local soviets can, for convenience, be dated back to a resolution of the Central Committee of the CPSU issued early in 1957.[14] The complaints against the local soviets listed in this resolution give a picture of a moribund bureaucracy. Sessions of the soviets were held irregularly if at all; executive committees were co-opted rather than elected; executive committees neglected to report to their constituents. Nonfulfillment of their formal obligations by the representative and executive bodies of the Soviets forms a considerable part of this resolution, but the shortcomings of the administrative departments are not overlooked. "The facts show that the daily needs of the masses are ill-met not because the material resources and conditions are lacking in the local soviets, but because the soviets, who, having lost contact with the masses, do not see the living people through their papers." [15] The reader will quickly recognize this statement as a recurring theme in discussions of Soviet administration and one which was particularly emphasized by Khrushchev during his 1956–57 shake-up of the administrative organs.

One of the reasons for the lamentable state of the local soviets was their evident low priority in assignment of scarce manpower and resources. This may be inferred from the facts that the first postwar elections to the local soviets, to fill the many deputies' positions vacant because of war casualties and the passage of time since the 1939 elections, were held only in December of 1947—18 months after the cessation of hostilities and that the amalgamation of village soviets into large units began only in 1954—some four years after the corresponding reorganization of *kolhozy* had begun.[16] Following the 1957 resolution, attempts were made to recruit administrative manpower for the local soviets.[17] At the same time the numbers of elected deputies to the local soviets were increased by a quarter million, from 1,549,777 in 1957 to 1,801,663 in the 1959 elections, by far the largest increase in any two year period from 1936 to 1971.

The Soviet authorities had a number of reasons, both administrative and political, to revive the local soviets. As part of Khrushchev's campaign to get the Soviet system moving again, the soviets had important potential. They could symbolize regime legitimation at the grass-roots level, combining with it popular mass frameworks for mobilization and control of citizen participation. In addition, the soviets performed distributive functions, which, with growing production levels and an increasing emphasis on consumption and welfare, were taking on both political and economic importance. Other mass frameworks, such as the party and the trade unions, could have performed some part of these tasks, but each of these represented a particular segment of the public. Only the soviets combined all these aspects and could claim to represent all of Soviet society.

The question of increased responsibilities of local soviets is one which has caused considerable difficulty to Soviet planners and administrators over the years. While the authorities' goal in the late 1950's was to decentralize operative responsibility for local industry and consumption, the lack of trained personnel in the local soviets meant that disorganization and loss of production might result. A tug of war resulted in which the local industry departments of the soviets, given a portion of the responsibility for local industry when Khrushchev dispersed the central industrial ministries in 1957, quickly lost these rights to the *sovnarkhozy*.[18] The dispute over the local soviets' authority involved not so much a split between contending opinions within the central government, as the persistance of production-oriented values as the overriding imperative of Soviet society. Despite a decision in principle to strengthen local government, plan fulfillment dictated reliance on the *sovnarkhoz,* vitiating substantive changes in the local soviets' actual authority. Together with these powers, the lowest level soviets—towns and rural districts—lost a portion of their administrative staff, evidently taken to man similar posts in the *sovnarkhozy*. Despite the avowed trend to decentralization, administrative staffs on the all-union level grew by 26 percent, the union-republic level by 18 percent, and *oblast'* level by 18 percent, while the *raion* and urban soviets lost 13 percent of their staff—ostensibly because of "unjustified reorganizations."[19] It was only with the 1965 dissolution of the *sovnarkhozy* that the local soviets once again became the sole territorial units of government organizing production and distribution; they began to shoulder growing responsibility for consumer services, local industry, and trade.

While the responsibilities of the soviets grew, restrictions on overall administrative outlays in the apparatus of the soviets were maintained and even tightened. The percentage of government expenditure on administration began dropping steadily; it is decreasing even today, when it has reached just over one percent of all outlays. The resultant gap is expected to be filled by volunteers, for even though administration is recognized and respected as a science today and Khrushchev's enthusiastic efforts to replace professional administrators with the after-hours efforts of lathe operators and sales clerks has been largely abandoned, the deputies of the soviets, their volunteer *aktiv,* and numerous other public groups are still widely used to assist the administrators by checking the service in stores, maintaining the passport regime in housing and processing citizen applications and complaints.

The principal problem of the soviets, however, is still their impotence in the face of the overwhelming priorities of industrial growth and the continued central control of industry, with the concomitant funding of such matters as housing and services through the Union and Republic Ministries and the local enterprises subordinate to them. Despite the growth of local soviets' competence and activity over the years, a recent Central Committee resolution on the work of the soviets complained that close to two-thirds of the urban housing in the USSR is built and maintained by enterprises and institutions outside the control of the local soviets.[20]

The local soviets' control of housing varies considerably from one locality to another. In Moscow, the local soviets' control of housing has grown from two-thirds of the city's housing stock in 1965, to three-quarters in 1969.[21] At the same time, a local soviet in Kazakstan controlled only 999 square meters of housing while the local chemical plant administered 87,088 square meters. It was reasonable to expect that the soviets of relatively newly established "company towns," based largely on a single industry and lacking a stable and experienced corps of local administrators, would carry little weight against the "industrial notables" of the town and that the soviets of older and more economically diversified cities would have greater control of such important services as housing construction and management.

In this respect, the Kutaisi soviet appears relatively powerless, for of 100,000–120,000 square meters of housing scheduled to be built in the current five-year plan, the local soviet will construct only 16,565 square meters—between 13 and 14 percent.[22]

One of the reasons for the local soviets' weakness in the field of housing and services is the lack of a financial base for undertaking large-scale construction projects. The March, 1971, Communist party resolution noted above suggested that this be remedied by transferring a portion of the profits of centrally subordinated industrial enterprises to the budgets of the cities in which they were located—that is, a strengthening of the city's tax base.[23] The party resolution was closely followed by a resolution of the USSR Council of Ministers, "On Measures for Strengthening the Material and Financial Base of District and City Executive Committees," and a decree of the Supreme Soviet of the USSR, "On the Basic Rights and Duties of the City and Urban District Soviets."[24] Both of these emphasized the need to give the local soviets a larger role in the planning, financing and managing of housing and essential services.

These resolutions and decrees were followed at year's end by laws of the various Republic Supreme Soviets redefining the rights and duties of local soviets. The Georgian law on urban soviets does not, however, specify any right to levy taxes on industrial units located in the city but subordinate to a higher authority.[25] Nevertheless, the city budget which had been virtually stable for five years, growing from 13,706,600 rubles for 1966 to 13,927,700 for 1970, jumped to 15,108, 700 for 1972.[26]

All of the foregoing would suggest that Kutaisi is not a model or a leader in municipal government but shares the problems of a multitude of medium-sized industrial cities across the USSR.

When the Central Committee resolution of 1957 is compared to that of 1971, the areas of improvement of the local soviets become evident. Where previously the formal functioning of the soviet had been found sadly wanting, the current resolution points with pride to a situation in which:

> democratic principles in the activity of district and city soviets have been further developed. The importance of sessions of the soviets . . . . has grown. The deputies' ties with the voters have become stronger. Reports to the soviets and the public by the executive committees and their departments and administrations have become more regular.[27]

Whatever the weakness of content, the form of activities has been mastered. A framework has been created which, if given the wherewithall and the full backing of higher authorities would seem to be capable of fulfilling its role of *khozain goroda*—master of the city—not only with relation to its citizens' daily activities, but vis-à-vis its industries and services, as well.

The questions which will be pursued in the remainder of this essay deal with how Kutaisi's city council meets its problems and the effect of local conditions on its activities.

Local Government in Kutaisi

Kutaisi was chosen for this research as being typical of a large sector of Soviet urban localities. It is relatively far from Moscow, is of medium size, and is located in a non-Russian national area.

Kutaisi is the second largest city of Soviet Georgia, situated on the Rioni River, about 125 miles northwest of Tbilisi, the capital of Georgia. Its population growth in recent times has been rapid, from 78,000 in 1939 to 128,000 in 1959 and 164,000 in 1970.[28] The influx of population from the surrounding agricultural areas has created a shortage of housing and has strained the municipal services. At the same time the city appears well provided with medical services (one doctor for every 260 inhabitants, plus 1,600 paramedical workers), though its clinics and emergency service are badly in need of new quarters. The educational system, with 32 primary and secondary schools, two boarding schools, five *technicums*, a pedagogical institute, and a branch of the Tbilisi polytechnical institute, also appears effective and well provided for, with a municipal budgetary allocation of over 5,000,000 rubles annually, in addition to new construction.[29]

Kutaisi is an industrial city with 45 factories, ranging from the truck factory with several thousand workers, through chemical, textile, and electromechanical equipment plants to locally oriented enterprises producing beer, juice, and preserves. The growth of the main factories and the creation of ancillary shops overburdens the electric supply. The result is that electric power in some parts of the city fails almost daily for periods ranging from a few minutes to several hours. The limitations of municipal power give the city little chance to prevent or delay further locations of industry in Kutaisi, nor does the municipality have independent means of augmenting the power supply, since both these matters fall under the competence of all-union or union-republic authorities. The chairman of the local soviet must thus seek help of higher organs for solution to these problems, as well as to the incipient pollution problem caused by discharge of industrial waste into the Rioni and smoke emissions from heavy industry.

Development has brought problems to Kutaisi, but it has brought advantages, as well. The city's cultural institutions are well established. A large theater was built some years ago to house the hundred-year-old Kutaisi Dramatic Ensemble and a new, modern opera house has just been completed to house the local opera group. The Kutaisi Pedagogical Institute provides teachers for the school system, while the several technical schools in the city train skilled personnel for the factories. The result is a high level of self-sufficiency in the provision of cadres for development and government and ample employment opportunity for those who recieve academic or technical training. It would appear that in contrast to the development patterns in many areas of the USSR, Kutaisi has had a minimal influx of nonlocal people into the town, except for a small number of evacuees from the Ukraine during World War II. Local customs and relationships thus remain largely undisturbed.

The leadership of the city, both culturally and politically, is largely local and overwhelmingly Georgian; and the orientation of both leaders and citizens, while unhesitatingly Soviet, appears proudly and emphatically Georgian. With rare exceptions, the language on the streets is Georgian, and most shop signs are written only in Georgian. The working language of the soviet—both in speech and in print—is Georgian, and in referring to a decree of the Georgian Supreme Soviet, the report of the local council spoke simply of "the Supreme Soviet," as though there could be no doubt as to the institution referred to. In private conversation local officials repeatedly made reference to the antiquity of Georgian cultural traditions, comparing them favorably to other cultures. Of the 300 local deputies, 285 are Georgians (the remainder are 8 Jews, 5 Russians, and 2 Ukrainians). In the day session of the Polytechnical Institute, seven courses are offered in Georgian and only one in Russian, while all the evening courses are in Georgian.[30] All these separate items add up to a strong local patriotism, which gives the community as a whole a common base.

The combination of Georgian patriotism and Kutaisi localism is strengthened by the city's administrative position and relation with the capital. Kutaisi, though second among Georgian cities, is remote and provincial compared with Tbilisi's modernity and million plus population. Furthermore, Kutaisi has no intermediate administrative level between itself and the republic, so its elite either remains Kutaisi centered or leaves Kutaisi entirely for the capital. In cases in which an *oblast'*-level soviet intervenes between a city and republic, leading local officials may serve at *oblast'* level, but of the 13 Kutaisi deputies serving in the Supreme Soviet of Georgia in 1971, three are in fact ex-Kutaisians who were promoted to republic level and whose only remaining tie with the city is the constituency from which they are elected; one is the former chairman of the local soviet, now transferred to other work outside Kutaisi; seven are rank-and-file workers of plants in the city and, except for one, have no other known political position; one is the second secretary of the *gorkom,* a veteran party worker in Kutaisi; and one is the director of the city's largest plant, the Kutaisi Truck Factory. The latter is perhaps the city's foremost elite personality, for he is involved in every body of any importance locally, and many nationally. He is a member of the executive committee of the soviet and of the *gorkom,* a deputy to the Supreme Soviet of Georgia, and a candidate member of the Central Committee of the Communist Party of Georgia, and has served as a delegate to the Georgian Party Congress and the 24th Congress of the CPSU. The breadth of his activity overshadows even that of the city's first secretary.

In effect, the plant director's prominence symbolizes the predominance of the truck factory in Kutaisi, for the current director's predecessor had a similar range of posts and activities during his tenure.

In general, Kutaisi's political activists are not linked to the republic level. Only four are identifiable in the Georgian Central Committee—the *gorkom* first secretary and a widely publicized brigade leader from the truck factory as full members, and the truck factory's director and the rector of the Polytechnical Institute as candidate members. There is thus no extensive overlap of personnel between Kutaisi and the capital, a circumstance contributing to a certain isolation and self-containment in the leadership of the city. At the same time, this lends stability and continuity to the local leadership. For the average local leader, Kutaisi is the top, and he will finish his political and industrial career as a perennial secretary of the *gorkom* or a director of one of the city's lesser factories or institutions. The problem of an experienced cadre of decision makers and administrators is thus less in Kutaisi than in many other areas, and when a local leader makes the jump to a republic level, a locally known and experienced replacement is usually available.

Within the two leading political bodies of the city, the *gorkom* and the soviet, three groups are particularly well represented: factory directors, paid party functionaires, and paid staff of the soviet. Of 34 persons identified as having been in the *gorkom* between 1966 and 1972, 13 were from the party apparatus; 8 others were factory directors; and 4 were employees of the soviet.[31] Of the 300 deputies of the Soviet elected in 1969, 20 are Party or Komsomol functionaries, 28 are employees of the soviet; and 29 were classed as "directors and specialists in organizations and enterprises."

The Executive Committee is the heart of the Kutaisi soviet. Though nominally subordinate to the plenum of the soviet, it is the Executive Committee which defines priorities and guides the work of the deputies and the various bodies making up the paid and volunteer apparatus of the soviet. Sessions of the soviet deal only with matters brought by the Executive Committee, invariably ratifying them with minor, if any, amendments. The Executive Committee, as a link in the hierarchical system of soviets, generally defines its priorities in keeping with initiatives indicated in Moscow and Tbilisi. Thus, the report of the soviet dealing with its activities for the first part of 1969, had as its general reference points the decisions taken at the most recent CPSU congress and the plans for the then forthcoming Lenin centennial. On more specific issues, a speech by the first secretary of the Georgian Communist party and a decree of the Supreme Soviet of Georgia were cited.

This subordination is an explicit part of Soviet governmental structure. The recently adopted Georgian Republic law on urban and urban district soviets specifies that "urban and urban district soviets conform in their activities to [here follows a long list of institutions, beginning with the constitution of the USSR and decrees of the Supreme Soviet] decisions of superordinated soviets and their executive committees." [32]

In Kutaisi, the Executive Committee is made up of 15 members, of whom 14 are Communists and the other a Komsomol member. In addition to the committee chairman, two deputy chairmen, and the secretary, the Executive Committee's members are the directors of the five municipal administrations and two of the municipal departments, the first secretary of the city party committee, the commander of the local garrison, the director of the truck factory, and one worker.

The Executive Committee meets every two weeks and enjoys the assistance of the appropriate standing committees in preparing reports on particular areas of municipal activity for discussion. When a particular question is discussed, the standing committee and its *aktiv,* as well as central figures in the sector under discussion, will be invited to take part in the meeting. Places for 50 invitees had been prepared for a discussion of health services which took place just after the writer's departure.

Of the 15 members of the Executive Committee, 13 have higher education. Four are engineers, two are in economics and planning, and the remaining seven are listed as "other." The unspecified "others" are in all probability largely graduates of a party-school course in administration. These courses have been extensively promoted in recent years for the upgrading of executives and administrators of local soviets.[33]

The makeup of the Executive Committee illustrates clearly the dominance of the communist and administrative considerations in the work of the soviet. While communist dominance in the Executive Committees of local soviets is the rule, a complete monopoly is not. Party representation in the Executive Committees of soviets ranges from a low of 67.1 percent at the village level to 90.9 percent at the krai and *oblast'* levels, with 84.4 percent at the city level.[34] The orientation on party goals seems to be almost universal among officials interviewed and certainly is prominent in the consciousness of Executive Committee staff and deputies. Together with the participation of the first secretary of the city Party Committee in the Executive Committee and the soviet chairman's membership in the *gorkom,* this made it possible for the party (housed in the same building as the soviet) to maintain close supervision of municipal affairs, relying on shared values and interlocking personnel to avoid need for arbitrary imposition of party decisions on the Executive Committee.[35]

The chairman of the Executive Committee, though he is supposed to be the responsible authority in all local questions, appears to be occupied principally with the soviet's relations to the higher organs of authority, the republic and all-union ministries, which control most resource allocations and development plans. The two deputy chairmen deal primarily with functional areas, such as housing and industry. Local affairs, and in particular the guidance and coordination of the representative organs and citizen volunteer groups, are supervised by the secretary of the Executive Committee. She meets regularly with the chairmen of the standing committees and deputies' groups as well as with individual deputies.

Both the secretary and chairman use the Organization and Instruction Department of the soviet for information gathering, troubleshooting, and the supervising of deputies' activities in their constituencies. The department has grown in recent years and now consists of a director, a deputy director, and two instructors. A third full-time instructor is to be added very soon. While the director maintains overall control and contact with the Executive Committee, his deputy and the two instructors each take responsibility for the activities of the municipality in a particular area of the city. They also investigate and answer citizens' complaints directed to the Executive Committee, determining why they were not handled by the local neighborhood committee or deputies' group. The instructors also elicit from these groups regular reports to the Executive Committee and have the responsibility of providing the deputies with factual material for periodic reports to their constituents, as well as seeing that these reports are, in fact, made. The instructors of the department appear to be well-known in the city, drawing frequent greetings and nods from people in all walks of life.

The material for the deputies' reports is drawn up as a general report of the soviet's activities and carries a notation, "The deputy should supplement the above material with references to those measures carried out under his personal leadership." The department also prepares material for Executive Committee reports to the soviet and coordinates preparation of standing committees' reports to the Executive Committee or to the sessions of the soviet on the relatively infrequent occasions when such reports are made. The office of the Organization and Instruction Department is a center of constant comings and goings for consultation, as is the office of the Executive Committee Secretary.

The Deputies of the Soviet

The 300 deputies of the Kutaisi soviet are directly elected for a two-year term by universal suffrage of all citizens over 18 years of age. They include a majority who are not from among the political, administrative, and economic "notables" of Kutaisi mentioned above. From this, as well as testimony of the Soviet press and non-Soviet witnesses, we may understand that the deputies' primary functions are not in the field of legislative decision making.[36] However, in electing this large group of representatives, with one deputy for every 330 urban voters, the soviet strives not only to create the conditions for a deputy to be close to his constituents, but provides a mass of manpower for the standing committees and the other ancillary formations in which the bulk of the deputies' work is carried on.

In most respects the deputies of the Kutaisi City Soviet resemble the deputies of any other city soviet. There is the usual slight predominance of non-Party people (51.1 percent—exactly the same as the average for city soviets throughout the USSR); the same age distribution (10.1 percent under the age of 24 and a total of 53.3 percent under 40, as compared with 10.6 percent and 55.8 percent in the national average). Only in education do the Kutaisi deputies deviate from the national norm, with 42.7 percent listed as having higher education and the remaining 57.3 percent having a full secondary education, as against a national average for city soviet deputies of 26.4 percent with higher education and an additional 42 percent with secondary education.[37] Fifty-five percent of the deputies are classed as workers, thus adhering precisely to the national average for worker-deputies in city soviets.

With compact constituencies and educated, locally recruited leadership, it would be expected that the aim of having the deputies in close contact with their constituents would be easily achieved. All the conditions appear to exist for comparatively easy access to the deputies and for their serving to solve constituents' problems. It was therefore surprising that although the ex-citizens interviewed inevitably knew the name of the *gorkom* first secretary and the chairman of the soviet, not one of them knew by name the deputy in his constituency. All the interviewees had voted in the elections, and all had voted for the local candidates, but the best identification offered was of the deputy—"a fat man who had been a war hero." The unanimity of nonrecognition raises a question as to whether the origins of the interviewees are not a factor here, but attempts to question as to whether the same nonrecognition prevailed throughout Kutaisi were answered in such a way as to indicate that this was indeed a general phenomenon throughout the city.[38]

Two reasons for the anonymity of individual deputies can be advanced. One, which appears from the testimony of interviewees, is that in Kutaisi citizens do not turn to the deputy for solution of their individual problems, preferring to seek family or neighborly help. In cases in which contact with the authorities is inevitable, the contact was chiefly with the neighborhood committees (see below) or directly with the appropriate administrative departments, skipping the whole apparatus of deputies' groups and standing committees. Perhaps the most striking expression of this feeling is a statement regarding the deputies: "It's the higher-ups who need them to try and keep tabs on what we're doing."

The second reason for the anonymity of individual deputies may be the fact that the majority of their work with the public is carried out in groups rather than individually, with the citizen meeting the deputy, to the extent that such meetings occurred, as part of a committee. Such an arrangement is normal in local soviets. The rationale behind this collective work is that despite some tentative recent changes emphasizing prior experience in public affairs and knowledge of administrative procedures, deputies are still nominated either because they occupy positions to which the office of deputy is ascribed—for example, directors of principal enterprises, heads of the most important municipal departments and administrations, party officials—or they are chosen as outstanding production workers, people who are models of what the Soviet citizen should be.

The result is that some deputies are too burdened with other public duties to carry the full load of activities in the soviet which the ideal deputy should undertake, while others, less burdened, lack the required experience. In addition, though the accepted turnover of deputies is one-third each term, the turnover in the last election in Kutaisi was nearly twice that, and the organizing of the new deputies around the core of veterans is needed to maintain continuity. In Kutaisi, 196 deputies were classed as "new," although some had served in other soviet or earlier convocations of the Kutaisi soviet.

An added reason for the deputies' working within organized frameworks is supposedly the strengthening of their authority vis-à-vis the administrative organs of the soviet. The deputies' organizations, given formal legitimation through statutes by the executive committee and generally having among their numbers some of the notables of the city, have a collective influence which individual deputies lack.

Interviewed deputies varied widely in their perceptions of their work. When asked what they regarded as the deputy's basic task, their responses varied from: "I fulfill whatever duties the party gives me" to "I try to justify the voters' confidence in me by satisfying their urgent needs." This variety of outlooks was substantiated by the ways in which different deputies learned of their constituents' needs. One relied on lists of requests compiled by the Organization and Instruction Department, while another claimed that he met personally with his constituents on a regular basis. The particular aspect of a deputy's duties emphasized by each deputy interviewed varied somewhat with the load of other public and soviet tasks carried by the individual, as well as with his basic occupation. The factory director or school principal who was also chairman of a standing committee or other group tended naturally to focus on these duties and met the minimum requirement of one public report per year to constituents.

Deputies' Groups and Standing Committees

The 11 deputies' groups in the Kutaisi soviet include almost all the deputies of the soviet. These groups are organized territorially, with the city divided into 11 zones of varying size and population. The chairman of a deputies' group is usually a deputy of considerable experience and a man of standing in the city—prominent in a field other than the soviet. One chairman had accumulated a total of 12 years' seniority in the city soviet and a nearby rural district soviet. Another was the director of a factory and a man to whom the paid staff of the soviet quite visibly deferred.

Although the deputies' groups are supposed to meet monthly, they do not all do so. One group had met only twice between March and December. There had been, however, a division of functions at the first meeting, and the establishment of subcommittees among the 24 deputies making up the group. These subcommittees functioned more or less independently, submitting written reports of their activity to the chairman, who then took whatever action was necessary on the matters reported by the deputies. This was also the pattern in other deputies' groups in which the full group, ranging from 20 to 40 deputies, met infrequently, the chairman serving to maintain contact with the individual members and the subcommittees both personally and through written reports.[39]

One of the subcommittees in a deputies' group had surveyed the electrical services in its area and had written a report to the chairman. He, in turn, incorporated the report into a letter to the head of the electrical service sector of the Public Works Department, specifying the particular services and equipment which were the subject of citizens' complaints in various streets. The chairman stated that if he received a satisfactory report regarding arrangements by the municipality to overcome the deficiencies, he would report on it to the voters of the district, and if not, he would bring the matter before the Executive Committee. A similar report on the need for street repairs evoked an assurance that the requested repairs were part of the department's plan of work for the third quarter of 1969. The deputies' group had then reinspected the streets toward the end of the quarter to confirm that the repairs had, in fact, been carried out in full, and they had included this as a favorable item in their year end reports to their constituents. It should be noted that had this particular repair not been included in the work plan of the appropriate administrative department, the deputies' group could not have forced the department to respond to the citizens' needs. In such a case it could have only served the function of channeling citizen demands to the administration, thus assisting future planning. For the citizen, the deputies' group is an accessible body which can symbolize the government's concern and attention, even though it may not be able to solve the particular problem posed.

Where a legitimate request is being neglected or scheduled improvements are not implemented, the deputies' group may turn to the Executive Committee of the soviet for help. It is here that the personality and status of the chairman of the deputies' group become significant. In coming to the Executive Committee to complain of nonperformance by the departments and administrations of the soviet, the deputies' group chairman is coming before a body half of whose members are heads of such departments and administrations. Given the importance of plan fulfillment in career success of Soviet officials, it is understandable that such complaints are a last resort and that the emphasis of deputies' groups chairmen was on peaceful bargaining for inclusion of their constituents' needs within the work plans of various departments.

The deputies' group also takes an active part in the processing of citizens' requests and applications. Once or twice a week, four or five deputies are available for several hours at a central place in the group's area (a club or other cultural center), to meet with citizens and review their needs. If necessary, one of the deputies will check the documentary and factual basis of a request. If the request is considered legitimate and all the necessary papers have been properly filled out, it is passed on to the deputies' group chairman, who then brings it to the Executive Committee or to the appropriate department of the soviet for formal approval and implementation. If the request proves to be baseless, it is the deputy on the spot who must explain the deficiency to the citizen. To do this properly, the deputy must be informed as to the regulations concerning housing, pensions, and other matters, which may not be within the province of each deputy's knowledge. General requests for services from groups of citizens are generally easier to handle. If residents of a particular house or block request repairs or an improvement in some municipal service, the deputies' group can form an inspection team and make its recommendations.

Such inspections, and indeed any mass work which the deputies' groups undertake, will generally be shared with an *aktiv* of citizen volunteers from the area being inspected and particularly of persons active in the organized life of the community—for example, members of the neighborhood committees and comrades' courts, prominent workers, educators, or local clinic staff. In short, the effort is to activate the type of people who are likely prospects for eventual nomination as deputies or who have in the past served as deputies and are acquainted with the type of tasks to be undertaken.

In bringing Kutaisi's government to its citizens, the deputies' groups also serve to keep the citizens away from the government, channeling their access to the city administration through the intermediary stage of the unpaid deputies. As they perform these functions, new deputies are expected to grow in expertise, preparing themselves for even more responsibilities in subsequent terms of office.

The standing committees perform many of the same functions as the deputies' groups. They are, however, constituted on a functional rather than a territorial basis. At the height of Khrushchev's influence, there was a movement to have the standing committees handle the administrative work of Soviets, eliminating the need for paid administrators. The complex problems of modern administration have, however, taken away much of the enthusiasm for wholly volunteer administration. The Communist Party Program adopted at the 22nd Congress of the CPSU in October, 1961, suggests that deputies should be released periodically from their work for full-time committee service and that the standing committees should become decision-making bodies in administrative affairs.[40] Neither of these suggestions have as yet been implemented, despite the urging of some writers on the subject.

Formally, the standing committees are supposed to have power to oblige the administrative departments or economic enterprises to do whatever is necessary in support of decisions of the soviets. In fact, they have little real leverage with which to realize this right. Their main work is as gatherers of information for Executive Committee discussions and legislative proposals and the principal direction of their development in recent years has been advisory rather than supervisory.

An attempt is made to keep the standing committees independent and minimize possible conflict through statutory exclusion of the directors of municipal departments from the ranks of committees dealing with the same area of work. Though this is not the practice in every Soviet republic, it is in Georgia.[41] In Kutaisi, no head of a department or administration sits on a committee with which his department has dealings. The *aktiv* of the committees is another matter entirely. In general in the Soviet Union, the *aktiv* of a standing committee is recruited on the basis of expertise in the committee's field and contact with the administrative departments. The most extreme case is the important Standing Committee on Public Works (*Kommunalnoe khoziaistvo*) and Consumer Services (*Bytovoe Obsluzhivanie*). The 35 member committee, largest in the Kutaisi soviet, had an *aktiv* of 16, half of whom were employees of the Department of Public Works and the other half of the Administration of Consumer Services. The *aktiv* was thus totally professional in its concern for better works and services facilities and served as an efficient link between the standing committee and the administrators, though it must certainly have prevented the standing committee from serving as any sort of *kontrol* body over the administrative departments. Rather than consider this as a conflict of interest situation, the Soviet authorities, who reject any separation of powers theory, regard such a structure as realizing Lenin's idea that the soviets must at once make the laws, implement them, and audit the results.

As might be expected, the Committee on Public Works and Consumer Services prepares numerous suggestions for the Executive Committee to consider. These are often prepared by subcommittees working with the *aktiv*. The direction which such discussions take is often indicative of limitations on both the standing committees and the local soviets. The standing committees are explicitly precluded from any control over budgetary or material allocations and plan assignments.[42] The local soviet has very limited possibilities regarding any enterprises which do not come under its direct control. In Kutaisi, when the rapid growth of the city resulted in a water shortage, the Committee on Public Works and Consumer Services directed its principal efforts toward organizing water-saving campaigns among the citizens through slogans, lectures, and propaganda, rather than procedures involving regulation of industrial water use.

The Standing Committee on Education and Culture yields a somewhat different picture because of the nature of its work. Its 26 members were supplemented by an *aktiv* drawn from the militia and the comrades' courts and supplemented by personnel from the Organization and Instruction Department of the soviet. This is perhaps a reflection of concern with juvenile delinquency and breaches of public order in the city. A member of the committee, himself a pedagogue of long experience and high local standing, stated that his main work as a committee member was the organization of mass cultural work with youth. When pressed for specifics he stated that he often lectures on the harmful effects of narcotics. The question of narcotics had been a subject of a 1969 resolution of the Georgian Supreme Soviet and took up half a page of the annual report of the Kutaisi Soviet.[43]

In summary, the standing committees are functionally oriented and staffed in keeping with their areas of activity, acting primarily as ancillaries to the Executive Committee, providing legislative proposals and information for decision making, rather than acting in any independent capacity as a counterweight to industrial enterprises or administrative departments. Where the standing committees in Kutaisi do take action, it is likely to be oriented toward mobilization of the citizens into a current campaign.

The Mass Volunteer Bodies of the Soviet

Knowledge of the mood and needs of the citizens comes to the Executive Committee not only through the deputies' groups and standing committees but also directly from the chairmen of the 54 neighborhood committees of the city.[44] On the third Friday of each month they meet with the secretary of the Executive Committee to discuss neighborhood problems and hear about plans and activities of the soviet. Between these sessions, the chairmen are frequent visitors to the Organization and Instruction Department and to the secretary.

The chairmen of these committees, formally elected to two-year terms by neighborhood meetings, were described by the Executive Committee secretary as "all very reliable people—nearly all of them are Party members." Many of them are former deputies of the soviet, and many more are surely future deputies. The reliability of these neighborhood chairmen was considered a key factor in the functioning of the committees as "the voice of the Executive Committee in the neighborhoods." They are the equivalents of the block and precinct captains of American political machines—on the spot, actively aware of whatever happens in their neighborhood and concerned with a broad spectrum of social, economic, and political behavior in the neighborhood.

The neighborhood committees are compact, ranging from five to nine members. In addition to the elected chairman, each committee also has a deputy chairman and a secretary elected by the neighborhood meeting. These elected officials are subject to the ratification of the Executive Committee of the soviet. The remaining members of each committee are co-opted from among the active citizens of the neighborhood, with the assistance of the Organization and Instruction Department.

The neighborhood committee is more than just the voice of authority. It serves as the eyes, ears, and hands, as well. The neighborhood chairman has a list of all residents of the neighborhood and sees to the strict observance of the "passport regime." [45] The committees also serve to lighten the burdens of the administrative departments by performing such tasks as registration of preschool children for kindergartens and nurseries and the examination of requests for changes in documents and registration.

Of all the volunteer and representative organs attached to the local soviet, the neighborhood committees appear to have the most impact on the citizens, for the general impression of the emigrants interviewed was "They accomplish the things which are their business." The emphasis on their activities, in the citizens' eyes, however, is their functions of controlling the population. They know who works and who doesn't, carry out efficiently their supervision of the "passport regime" and generally live up to their reputation for "reliability."

One area in which the neighborhood committees apparently relax their vigilance is in the monthly cleanings in which all the citizens are supposed to participate. A chairman in one neighborhood said that this had become so routine that most families fulfilled their stint by sending their children to do their cleaning, while citizens reported that a few rubles bought either a substitute or a reprieve from participation.

While this system does not always maintain exemplary cleanliness in the city, it provides a mobilization potential capable of answering when called upon. In August of 1970, the outbreak of cholera in certain areas of European Russia brought sanitation questions to the fore and resulted in a scathing attack on the lack of cleanliness of the Kutaisi market, the sanitary conditions of its restaurants, and the disposal of sewage and garbage.[46] The accusations, made by a visiting reporter from the republic newspaper, appear to have been taken to heart, for within three weeks the head of the city's health services and the head of the construction and repair administrations responsible for the market facilities reported to a city party committee plenum on "improvement of medical services to the population and expansion of educational-prophylactic institutions," as well as "overfulfillment of construction and repair plans." [47] A week later, following further efforts, the chairman of the Executive Committee reported on mass cleanups of neighborhoods which had previously been in an unsanitary state. His report, which includes specific construction projects and decisions such as moving the city garbage dump, revolves around a continuing mass mobilization of the population for cleaning the city and maintaining a proper sanitary level in the 40 restaurants and food stores which were temporarily closed during the crisis.[48] Thus, the circle is closed. The first paragraph of the original report on Kutaisi spoke of the need for a campaign "in which the population of the city will be deeply involved." The chairman's report ends with the sentence, "The achievement of absolute cleanliness is possible only through the active participation of the entire population of the city, mobilized for that purpose." In this task, the neighborhood committees play a front line role.

In their day-to-day work, the committees vary. Meetings are generally supposed to be held at least once a month, but the frequency depends on the chairman. The frequency of neighborhood assemblies also depends both on the chairman and on the problems of the neighborhood and may vary from two to six a year. The size of the *aktiv* assisting the committee also varies from 10 to 50. In one district, the *aktiv* is elected at a neighborhood meeting. In another, the chairman, with the help of his committee and the Organization and Instruction Department, co-opts a few people from each street in the neighborhood.

One activity which appears to be common to all neighborhood committees is a weekly tour of the entire district by members of the committee, often accompanied by the local deputies. During these inspection tours, problems of utilities and services are given special attention and personal contacts are utilized to promote current campaigns such as the cleanup crisis. The presence of the deputies is generally sought during these tours to promote coordination between the neighborhood committee and deputies' group, but it appears that the committees, covering a smaller territory, are in no way dependent on the deputies and carry on their activity mainly through direct contact with the secretary of the Executive Committee without undue anxiety as to possible duplication of effort.

The individual needs of citizens also fall within the competence of the neighborhood committees, and in this they duplicate the work of the deputies' groups. In some cases, formal sessions of the entire committee are held in a neighborhood club to enable citizens to apply for *spravki* (certificates) directing them to one or another branch of the administration for work, housing, pensions, a solution to a family problem, or whatever may arise. Provided that a proper level of accessibility is maintained in the neighborhood, the arrangements for citizen applications appear to be entirely at the discretion of the chairman. One chairwoman, a housewife, simply let it to be known to the 700 voters in her neighborhood that she was available at home every day in the morning to consider requests. Estimates of the number of *spravki* handed out by the neighborhood committee chairman ranged from 50 to 120 a week.[49]

The neighborhood committees are only one of the mass volunteer groups which help keep the administration of Kutaisi going. In each neighborhood there is a comrades' court of five to seven people to try minor disputes and bring social influence to bear on unruly citizens. These courts appear to be of marginal significance in Kutaisi and are rarely resorted to. One neighborhood chairman reported only two trials in the previous year, while the others interviewed also noted that the courts had little to do. Mediation of family or neighborly disputes was frequently mentioned by deputies and neighborhood committee members as part of their jobs. One deputy noted that when a family in his constituency was known to be quarreling violently, a situation which in other locales might have resulted in a comrades' court trial, a delegation composed of himself, the neighborhood committee chairman, and the chairman of the local comrades' court visited the family and tried to put an end to the quarrel by a combination of arbitration and threats of public action against the warring couple. In discussion it was made clear that the mediation of prominent citizens outside a formal framework is preferred to the use of such institutions as the comrades' courts.

The local branch of the people's volunteer formations (*narodnye dobrovolnye druzhini*) numbers 3,000 members,[50] of whom 50 to 60 are on duty on any given day. The result is a tour of duty of once in seven or eight weeks. Their duties consist primarily of patrolling places of entertainment and outlying sectors of the city to see that there is no disturbance of the peace. Places serving wine and spirits are constantly patrolled in the evenings. Even when not on duty the Kutaisi *druzhini* are expected to be on the watch for hooliganism or antisocial behavior. One neighborhood committee chairman reported that he had 10 *druzhinniki* in each street in his neighborhood reporting constantly to him on wild or neglected children who might be potential delinquents.

Recruitment of *druzhinniki* is carefully controlled. Recruits are generally nominated by party and trade union groups and factory directorates and must be given the approval of the city party committee. The local *druzhini* unit is supervised by the second secretary of the city party committee as is the general case with *druzhini* formations throughout the USSR, with the head of the local DOSAAF (Society for the Support of the Army, Air Force, and Fleet) and the first secretary of the local trade union organization as deputy commanders. *Druzhinniki* who compile good records of service receive not only citations, but three days' extra vacation per year.[51]

As may be seen from the above, the ancillary bodies of the soviet maintain a high level of activity, and if the results are not always consonant with the avowed goals, neither are vital problems neglected. The soviet leadership not only goes through the prescribed rituals, but has effective machinery of information and control, as well as reserves to meet crises.

Nominally subordinated to the plenum of the soviet, but actually guided by the Executive Committee, a 15 man volunteer committee for the handling of citizens' suggestions and complaints keeps up-to-date on the flood of applications which comes to every soviet.[52] The committee, made up largely of pensioners, is headed by the rector of the Kutaisi Polytechnical Institute. It examines all citizens' requests directed to the Executive Committee, sending those which are routine to the appropriate administrative departments and rejecting those which are obviously unbased or improperly documented. It directs to the Organization and Instruction Department those letters which indicate a weakness or malfunctioning of the deputies' organizations and neighborhood committees which are supposed to act as the first line of review in such matters. The committee also receives from the chairman of deputies' groups requests which they have accepted from citizens and reviews them for approval by the Executive Committee or directs them to the appropriate department. In this way, the chairman and the deputy chairman of the Executive Committee are relieved of much of the burden of investigation of citizens' requests, expediting fulfillment of these requests. Since many of these applications have already passed a preliminary screening by a deputies' group or neighborhood committee, the volunteer committee acts as an additional screen, checking on the first.

Higher authorities judge the effectiveness of a local soviet in dealing with citizens' demands by the promptness with which it responds to these demands and the proportion of such demands sent up to higher instances by citizens for lack of local response. Elaborate auditing procedures have been established within the system of soviets for periodic review of the efficacy with which applications and complaints are handled. The work of the volunteer committee means that the ever-growing volume of demands can be more quickly channeled to the appropriate authority for decision and answer, eliminating as far as possible appeals to higher instances. Important, too, from the viewpoint of local as well as higher authorities is the fact that this additional capacity is gained without expenditure of funds for administrative salaries.

The principle of work "on a volunteer basis" is firmly enshrined in Soviet local administration.[53] In fact, a large part of the work described as being carried out by volunteers is incorporated into the volunteers' regular daily jobs. An example of this is the working of the Supervisory Commission of Juvenile Affairs. The commission has only one paid staff member, its secretary, who occupies a desk in the local soviet. The commission's other 16 members include a deputy chairman of the Executive Committee, the deputy director of the Municipal Department of Education, an assistant to the city procurator, and other persons working in the field of education, vocational problems, and employment.[54] All these were quite obviously involved in the problems of delinquents in the course of their everyday work. Certainly, membership on this commission obligated them to conferences and meetings after hours, but this is no more than persons at that level of responsibility undertake in any system. When we consider this feature of its structure, the size of the volunteer apparatus in Kutaisi, as well as in the USSR as a whole, takes on clearer perspective for us, as does its capability of meeting the problems with which such bodies are faced in their work. The aim of widespread public involvement in implementing policy in the field of juvenile affairs emerges clearly from the involvement of "practicals" (for example, personnel directors and youth leaders) as well as "theoreticals" in the commission's work.

The commission holds regular monthly meetings. Its main occupation is the work placement of juveniles who have left school and the supervision of their work conditions. In addition it supervises rehabilitation efforts with delinquents and difficult children. At its meetings the commission also performs a quasi-judicial function, hearing the cases of individual delinquents in the presence of their parents, their teachers, and their supervisors at their place of work if they are workers. Where the commission deems it necessary, volunteer educators are assigned to the children, overseeing their conduct and their progress at school and work, much in the spirit of the Big Brother movement in America. During 1969, the commission found employment for 812 children, handled the cases of 24 difficult juveniles, and assigned 11 volunteer educators.

As evidenced by the size of the commission and the positions held by its members, work with juveniles has high priority in Kutaisi. Issues raised by the commission regarding parental supervision of children and the barring of juveniles from evening film showings found expression in a half page of the five-page report of the soviet on its activities for the first half of 1969.[55]

Leaders and Citizens

It is not difficult to identify the economic and political notables of Kutaisi through their participation in the *gorkom* and/or the Executive Committee and plenum of the soviet. The more prominent of them are readily identified and remembered by the ex-Kutaisians interviewed, in distinct contrast to lack of knowledge regarding the deputies who are supposed to be the direct agency of mobilization in the city.

In similar fashion, the operation of such services as local clinics, schools, and trade outlets is thought by most of the excitizens interviewed to be the responsibility of the republic ministries in Tbilisi; and though there was a general expression of satisfaction with these services, it was not seen as an achievement of the local leadership. If the figures for housing construction are representative, then the citizens indeed have a realistic understanding of the relative powers of local and central ministerial authorities. A newspaper announcement that a large new hospital complex would be built in the auto workers residential district from funds of the auto factory[56] tends to strengthen the view that the Kutaisi soviet has as yet little power of initiative in its own city.

The top-level economic and political officials of Kutaisi are engaged—through both party and soviet channels—in ongoing bargaining with superior bodies to reconcile local interests and needs with the national plan. Such bargaining is one of the basic characteristics of communist urban politics. Michael Frolic has investigated the form and consequences of this process in some detail.[57] As the municipality raises only in the vicinity of 10 percent of its revenues from local sources, the ability of local leaders to influence the granting of additional budgets, the addition or deferment of new industrial plants or other republic-level decisions is crucial in any effort of local political notables to determine the pace and direction of their city's development.

In addition, however, the city's leaders—working in particular through the *gorkom*—will be judged according to their ability to solve industrial problems and meet production plans. "The *gorkom* usually concentrate their attention on the leading enterprises," notes one leading Soviet specialist in party organization, adding: "this is, of course, correct."[58] Thus, the first and tone-setting item in a discussion of the Kutaisi *gorkom's* work by the Georgian Central Committee was a favorable notation of the level of industrial production in the city.[59]

The direct mobilizers of citizen participation and activists within the various groups within and around the soviet appear to be a group apart, linked by personal association in Communist party endeavors. This appeared as a result of questions to members of the soviet and its administrators regarding their careers and those of their personal acquaintances. There seem to be common work places in the past experience of a whole chain of people in lower and middle posts. An instructor in the Organization and Instruction Department had been brought into the job by his former colleague in the Komsomol Committee of his institute. He in turn had recommended a friend who had worked with him in a factory committee for a job which was available. When a third instructor was needed in the department the director said: "Pick out someone you've worked with. Just be sure he's from the Komsomol so we know he's reliable."

The limited numbers of those who can be said to be the leadership of Kutaisi mean that the leaders—and those aspiring to be leaders—must take on many jobs simultaneously. The loading and overloading of tasks on the willing or reluctant shoulders of party members is a feature of Soviet life which is faithfully followed in Kutaisi. One energetic young man—apparently at the start of a public career—was a member of the bureau of his factory party committee and chairman of the people's control committee in his factory, as well as a key member of a standing committee who had prepared three questions for the Executive Committee and delivered a report to the soviet in the last year, while also taking an active part in the deputies' group to which he was assigned. Another prominent citizen was a volunteer lecturer for the city party committee's educational program as well as scientific secretary of the local branch of the Pedagogical Society. Among his previous tasks were membership in the city party committee and the chairmanship of the city's electoral commission. Such intensive levels of activity appear to be necessary in a public career.

There are, however, mitigating factors for the busy leadership. The factory director who was chairman of the Public Works and Consumer Services Committee met with members of his committee in his factory office in the course of a working day. Presumably, their work, too, was such that it could be adjusted to the committee's urgent needs—as was the work of the *aktiv*. The school principal who was chairman of a deputies' group had his files in the school office and his secretary there did the group's correspondence. The deputies' frameworks were thus able to maintain the necessary level of activity without causing the soviet any administrative outlay. In addition there were sinecures within the city (for example, management of a city park, an administrative post in a local sports organization, and so forth) whose incumbents had free time and the command of resources which could be mobilized to fulfill whatever tasks appeared—from supervising the election of the local committee of the Nature Preservation Society, to helping organize mass cleanups or meetings.

These second-echelon leaders, organizers, and controllers of mass participation may thus be considered "professional politicians" in the sense used by Robert Dahl, in that their participation is steady, and influenced only slightly by "cycles" in political life (elections, specific anniversary campaigns, and so forth).[60] As pointed out by Dahl, "probably the most important resource of the professional is his available labor time." [61] But unlike Dahl's professionals, the principal orientation of Kutaisi's subgroup of political professionals seems to be the mobilization of citizens, rather than the influencing of higher-level decisions.

The success of the "notables" in their tasks of bargaining and supervising is perhaps easier to assess than that of the second echelon in its mobilization activities. Without a larger and more representative sample of Kutaisi's citizenry, we can only suggest certain sensitive areas to which inquiry might profitably be directed.

Three prominent perceptions of the chance sample of citizens interviewed have already been mentioned: (1) They do not know their elected representatives. (2) They see the activity of the soviet's ancillaries more as control over them than as access to the political system and avoid contact with officialdom where possible. (3) They relate the operation of the city's services to higher rather than local authorities.

An additional insight into the soviet's operation was that economic corruption is ubiquitous in the life of the city. The citizen interviewees offered this spontaneously as an important factor in the understanding of local officials, no questions dealing with the subject having been originally included in the interviews. Nearly all of the interviewees had stories of how all levels of officialdom and all sectors of the community accepted bribes and shared in the profits of illicit trade. One interviewee, asked as to the most beneficial activity of the soviet, responded that it does not interfere in the "natural" economic life of the city. Bribery to obtain housing space and construction permits for private housing was taken for granted.[62] Given the severity of the housing shortage, which even Executive Committee members rated as their foremost problem, this might not be unexpected. Further probing into matters of economic corruption revealed that it was seen by the interviewees as pervading all economic activity. While pilferage and bribery may be found to various extents in all societies, Bert F. Hoselitz has noted that ascription of public office and appointment through personal influence—which we have noted as typifying Kutaisi's officials—are particularly open to corruption.[63] In the largely self-contained setting of Kutaisi, in which ties between individuals are of long standing, tolerance of corruption, as well as corruption itself, appears to be at least tacitly condoned, both among officials and between officials and citizenry. The illicit economy relieves pressures of shortage and provides satisfactions for the citizenry unattainable through licit channels.[64] When, as happens occasionally, a scandal of misappropriation breaks on the head of some high official, the result is said to be only his transfer to a new post until the storm blows over.[65]

Conclusion

Kutaisi is in many ways a reflection of Soviet values and difficulties. It grows on the basis of heavy industry whose managers are the backbone of its elite. The local leadership works diligently to maintain the city framework to sustain industrial growth. Although the competence and capabilities of the municipal government are circumscribed by the hierarchical determination of allotments and priorities, the institutions of the soviet, a dense and versatile network of functional and territorial organizations, provide a well-monitored apparatus for citizen mobilization, control of policy implementation, and crisis management.

The stability, homogeneity and generally high level of professional qualifications of the leadership was an advantage in meeting the needs of the city, while its developed educational system helped ensure that the growing population could be put to good use in the city's enterprises. Those leaders who were interviewed, while varying greatly in their approach to their work, expressed a uniform consciousness of being part of a system. Prominent in this was Communist party membership and intensive public activity. While the sample of deputies interviewed was clearly chosen by the authorities with a view to emphasizing *partiinost'* (party-mindedness) to me, random conversations and observation strengthened the impression that party membership was a key to all levels of elite standing and that the values and considerations put forward by the party were in fact accepted as guidelines by the city leaders. Thus, party values and goals appeared to outweigh both education and experience as factors in active political participation. At the same time, consciousness of Kutaisi as a specifically Georgian community with a longstanding local tradition was no less evident.

The citizens interviewed, while not sharing the party goals, accepted them as a fact of life and made their own way in the city in a state of conscious, but not resentful alienation from the leadership. They recognized the aims of the leaders, complied when necessary and pursued their own goals. While the citizens interviewed do not represent a representative or broadly based sample of Kutaisi's public, they are quite clearly consistent in their attitudes to the city's active leaders and their attitudes generally reflect conditions and problems which have been raised in other localities by observers of Soviet urban life.

As the standard of living of the USSR rises and the powers, capacities and experience of local government grow, relationships in Kutaisi may change. As nonlocal industry contributes more of its profits to the local soviet's activity, local officials and administrators may gain in authority and take on a more effective role in problem solving for local citizens, winning both their attention and their active allegiance. Although, at the time of writing, this process had not as yet had visible effect on the soviet's operations and its relations with the citizenry, this would appear to be a likely direction of development. While local Georgian characteristics of the culture of the city and its leadership will undoubtedly remain strong, the collective Soviet values may well spread from the leadership into broader circles of the citizenry, providing a better-socialized and more-responding matrix within which to carry on the mobilization of citizen participation.

The Formal Structure of the Kutaisi Soviet

The following chart indicates the formal subordinations in the structure of the Kutaisi City Soviet:

Soviet Plenum
300 Deputies
(11 Deputies' Groups of 20–40 members each)

Volunteer Committee
(15 members)
for review of citizens' complaints and suggestions

Standing Committees
(1) Mandate—9 members
(2) Budget—20 members
(3) Education and Culture—26
(4) Health and Social Welfare—26
(5) Trade—25
(6) Public Works and Consumer Services—35
(7) Youth, Sport and Physical Culture—34
(8) Law and Order and Socialist Legality—28

Executive Committee
(15 members)

Industrial Kombinat

Administrations
(1) Internal Affairs
(2) Trade
(3) Repair and Construction
(4) Consumer Services
(5) Housing

Departments
(1) Public Works
(2) Education
(3) Culture
(4) Health
(5) Social Welfare
(6) Finance
(7) Town Planning and Architecture
(8) Sport and Physical Culture
(9) Organization and Instruction
(10) General (secretarial)

Supervisory Commissions
(1) Juvenile Affairs
(2) Housing
(3) Labor Resources and Employment
(4) Socialist Legality
(5) Planning

Miscellaneous Services
(1) Bookkeeping
(2) Statistics Inspectorate
(3) Kommendatura
(4) Registry Office

Notes

1. K. F. Sheremet, *Povyshenie roli mestnykh sovetov v khoziaistvennom i sotsial'no-kulturnom stroitel'stve* (Moscow, 1967), 12.

2. The figures for 1973 are from *Izvestiia* (June 23, 1973). The figures for 1957 are from *Itogi vyborov i sostav deputatov trudiashchikhsia—1969* (Moscow, 1969), 217 (henceforth, *Itogi 1969*).

3. See, for instance, Jerry F. Hough, *The Soviet Prefects* (Cambridge, Mass., 1969) and Phillip D. Stewart, *Political Power in the Soviet Union* (New York, 1968); Merle Fainsod's *Smolensk Under Soviet Rule* (Cambridge, Mass., 1959) is a classic example. David Cattell, *Leningrad: A Case Study of Soviet Urban Government* (New York, 1968) and the much earlier E. D. Simon *et al., Moscow in the Making* (London, 1937) examine the problems of ruling the metropoli of the USSR; and Robert J. Osborn, *Soviet Social Policies* (Homewood, Ill., 1970) devotes considerable attention to the philosophy underlying the Soviet approach to urban communities. The material presented in this article is an offshoot of the author's work in preparation on political participation in the USSR.

4. The classic study is that of Robert and Helen Lynd, *Middletown* (New York, 1929). Other studies are Robert A. Dahl, *Who Governs*? (New Haven, 1961) and Nelson W. Polsby, *Community Power and Political Theory* (New Haven, 1963). The latter, an extensive critique of research on community structure, discusses details of several other major studies. An extensive review article of the subject is Douglas M. Fox, "Whither Community Power Studies?" *Polity* (Summer, 1971).

5. Polsby, *op. cit.*, 4.

6. See, for instance, Robert E. Lane, *Political Life* (New York, 1959) which focuses on the development of universal suffrage. A comprehensive survey of literature on citizen participation in noncommunist states is to be found in Lester W. Milbrath, *Political Participation* (Chicago, 1965).

7. See Hans B. C. Spiegel, *Citizen Participation in Urban Development* (Washington, D. C., 1968). This volume reflects the American scene, while Dilys M. Hill, *Participating in Local Affairs* (Harmondsworth, 1970) examines the community groups in the local politics of England.

8. For a discussion of boundaries of mass participation in Soviet society, see Iurii E. Volkov, *Tak rozhdaetsia kommunisticheskoe samoupravlenie* (Moscow, 1965), 13.

9. See, for instance, Merle Fainsod, *How Russia is Ruled*, rev. ed. (Cambridge, Mass., 1965), 383.

10. Fred W. Riggs, "Bureaucrats and Political Development," in Joseph La Palombara, ed., *Bureaucracy and Political Development* (Princeton, 1967), 139.

11. James R. Townsend, *Political Participation in Communist China* (Berkeley and Los Angeles, 1969), 211. Although the Soviet election system has been described recently by Max E. Mote in his *Soviet Local and Republican Elections* (Stanford, 1965), no comprehensive monograph on political participation in the USSR has yet been published.

12. The sample of former Kutaisi citizens interviewed was totally fortuitous in composition and neither scientifically selected nor representative. Of the 15 persons in the sample, none had higher education or executive position. The sample included a nurse, two tailors, three warehouse employees, a driver, an office worker,

two factory workers, two retail trade employees, a handicraft artisan, and two students. However, each was spoken to independently and the consistency of their attitudes and level of knowledge indicate that they are representative of a broad section of the population of Kutaisi.

13. As is the case with most local newspapers in the USSR, the Russian-language Kutaisi *Pravda* is not available abroad. Presumably it would carry a much more complete listing of local notables—e.g., full listings of the *gorkom* and local soviet membership and notice of by-elections to fill vacated deputies' positions.

14. CC, CPSU, "Ob uluchshenii deiatel'nosti mestnykh sovetov i usilenii ikh sviazi s massami," *Spravochnik partiinogo rabotnika* (1957), 450–458.

15. *Ibid.*, 458.

16. A detailed account of the problems of the local soviets in the immediate postwar period may be found in A. I. Lepeshkin, *Sovety vlast' naroda: 1936–1967* (Moscow, 1967), particularly 120–134.

17. See, for instance, the reference to transfer of party apparatus cadres to the local soviets in Dmitrii Polianskii, "Podbor i vospitanie kadrov," *Sovety deputatov trudiashchikhsia*, 2 (August, 1957), 19–24. See also the note in *ibid.*, 1 (July, 1957), 42 on recruitment of volunteer activists into the paid staff of the soviets' administration and their subsequent election as local deputies. It is of interest that at the same time that there was recruitment to the local soviets' apparatus, the party's paid apparatus was being reduced.

18. See A. V. Luzhin, "Vzaimootnoshenie mestnykh sovetov s sovnarkhozami i predpriiatami soiuznogo respublikanskogo podchineniia," *Sovetskoe gosudarstvo i pravo*, 4 (April, 1959), 43. For a detailed analysis of relations between the local soviets and the *sovnarkhozy*, see David Cattell, "Local Government and the *Sovnarkhoz* in the USSR 1957–1962," *Soviet Studies*, XV, 4 (1964), 430–442.

19. Iurii A. Tikhomirov, *Vlast' i upravlenie v sotsialisticheskom obshchestve* (Moscow, 1968), 46.

20. "O merakh po dalneishemu uluchsheniiu raboty raionnykh i gorodskikh sovetov deputatov trudiashchikhsia," *Pravda* (March 14, 1971). A full translation will be found in the *Current Digest of the Soviet Press* (henceforth, *CDSP*), XXIII, 11 (April 13, 1971), 1–5.

21. B. Michael Frolic, "Decision Making in Soviet Cities," a paper read at the annual meeting of the American Political Science Association (1970), 13.

22. *Zaria Vostoka* (Georgian Republic newspaper, henceforth, *Z. V.*) (March 24, 1972). No figures were available for the percentage of local housing administered by the city council.

23. *Pravda* (March 14, 1971).

24. *Izvestiia* (March 20, 1971), trans. in *CDSP*, XXIII, 11 (April 13, 1971), 5; and 13 (April 27, 1971), 27–30, 38.

25. For the full text see *Z. V.* (December 18, 1971). Article 13 deals with budgetary and financial rights and duties, while Article 14 defines the local soviet's relations with industrial enterprises.

26. The amount allotted to the city for its budget is published each year as part of the annual budget law of the Georgian Republic. For 1966, see *Z. V.* (December 25, 1965). For 1971, *Z. V.* (December 24, 1970). For 1972, *Z. V.* (December 24, 1971).

27. "O merakh, . . ." *Pravda* (March 14, 1971).

28. *Narodnoe khoziaistvo SSSR* (1970), 40.

29. "Materialy ob otchete Kutaiskogo soveta deputatov trudiashchikhsia" (henceforth, "Materialy, Kutaisi), typescript (Kutaisi, 1969), 3.

30. Announcement of the courses appears in *Z. V.* (June 30, 1971).

31. Except for three individuals known to have left the *gorkom* in the wake of reassignment by the party, there is no way of knowing how many of the 34 identified members were in the *gorkom* for the full six years. Nor do we have knowledge of the exact number of members of the *gorkom*. For a discussion of the size and composition of *gorkomy*, see Jerry Hough, *op. cit.*, 19–20, 330–331. Hough estimates the number of *gorkom* members at 50–70. A. Avtorkhanov, *The Communist Party Apparatus* (New York, 1968), deals with the *gorkom* in Chapter 8 of his work and gives a similar figure (144). An article by O. Bochoidze, first secretary of the Kutaisi Party Committee suggests about 40 members and candidate members in the Kutaisi *gorkom* (*Z. V.* [September 10, 1970], 2).

32. Zakon, *Z. V.* (December 18, 1971), Article 6. Article 27 empowers the city soviet to exercise leadership over village and settlement soviets within the territory of the municipality (a not infrequent situation in the rapidly urbanizing USSR), including ratification of their economic plans and the determining of their budget size—two vital points of local activities.

33. See, for instance, P. F. Pigalov, "Improving the Functioning of the Soviets," *Sovetskoe gosudarstvo i pravo*, 4 (1970), in *Soviet Law and Government*, IX, 3 (Winter, 1970–1971), 234–235. Brezhnev reported to the 24th Party Congress that 200,000 party and soviet workers had attended such training courses in the years 1966–1971. Regular announcements on the opening and completion of one month courses for party and soviet administrators appear in *Zaria Vostoka* throughout 1971.

34. *Itogi 1969*, 192–193.

35. At least five members of the Executive Committee of the soviet had seats in the *gorkom*, as well.

36. For instance, Lloyd G. Churchward, *Contemporary Soviet Government* (New York, 1968), 117 ff. Ghita Ionescu, *The Politics of European Communist States* (New York, 1967), 253 quotes a Czech deputy as noting that his work is principally in his constituency or in committees. The idea of adversary debate in council sessions is totally foreign to the Soviet system.

37. The statistics for Kutaisi were supplied by the local organization and instruction department. The general figures are from *Itogi 1969*, 114–120. Georgia ranked highest in the USSR for percentage of population with more than primary education, according to the 1970 Census—711 per thousand—with Armenia next at 697 per thousand. Among city soviet deputies, the Georgians lead with 81.6 percent having higher or complete secondary education, with Armenia again second with 79.3 percent. Lithuania scores lowest of the Soviet republics with 57.7 percent, while the Russian Republic has 65.5 percent.

38. For a case in which even the executive of a local soviet did not know a deputy's identity, see *Izvestiia* (September 22, 1965). A sociological study of Irkutsk also found only 10 percent of local citizens who could identify their deputy. See V. I. Pertsik, "Puti sovershenstvovaniia deiatel'nosti deputatov mestnykh sovetov," *Sovetskoe gosudarstvo i Pravo,* 7 (July, 1967), 16–21. Pertsik states, "Only some of the voters could name the deputy for whom they had voted. The deputies of urban and urban district soviets are better known than deputies of the Russian Republic Supreme Soviet." Later (n. 3) he states: "City-wide only 9.78 percent of the voters knew their urban district deputy."

39. For a general description of the origin and functioning of such groups, see R. A. Safarov, *Territorialnye deputatskie gruppy mestnykh sovetov* (Moscow, 1962). For a brief description of such a group at work see *Izvestiia* (January 13, 1967), or Safarov, 38.

40. Jan F. Triska, ed., *Soviet Communism: Programs and Rules* (San Francisco, 1962), 100.

41. V. I. Vasiliev, ed., *V pomoshch' deputatu mestnogo soveta* (Moscow, 1968), 91–92. The new law of the Georgian Republic on city soviets says only that members of the executive committee, procurators, and judges of people's courts do not serve on standing committees of the local soviets (*Z. V.* [December 18, 1971], Article 79). This would appear more as an effort to excuse busy officials from committee service than to attempt to avoid conflicts of interest.

42. See, for instance, the Moscow City Soviet resolution on the powers of standing committees in *Biulleten' ispolnitel'nogo komiteta Moskovskogo soveta deputatov trudiashchikhsia*, 10 (496) (June, 1962), 9.

43. *Materialy, Kutaisi*, 4–5. The report mentions cocaine and morphine, as well as hashish, and notes the particular danger to young people. The fight against narcotics was at the same time also the subject of a satirical bulletin board lampooning antisocial elements in Tbilisi.

44. These neighborhood committees are the approximate equivalent of village committees or house and street committees in larger urban centers.

45. A person settling in a Soviet city must be registered with the authorities as a legal resident at the address in his internal passport. Residence without registration is an offence.

46. *Z. V.* (August 29, 1970). I am most grateful to Professor Jerry Hough of Duke University for having originally called my attention to this incident. The leaking pipe in the market was already creating a mud puddle at the time of my visit in December, 1969.

47. *Ibid.* (September 17, 1970).

48. *Ibid.* (September 25, 1970).

49. Perhaps the chairmen were exaggerating their zeal. Fifty-four neighborhoods with only 50 *spravki* a week yield an annual total of 140,000 requests a year —considerably higher than figures for citizens' applications in other urban areas on which statistics have been published.

50. This number was supplied by the Organization and Instruction Department of the soviet in December of 1969. *Z. V.* (March 2, 1969), claims 4,000 *druzhinniki* and a staff of 41.

51. A similar incentive system was in operation in factories in Moscow.

52. For detailed studies of the scope and handling of this task by local soviets, see James Oliver, "Citizen Demands in the Soviet System," *American Political Science Review*, LXIII, 2 (June, 1969) and T. H. Friedgut, "Citizens and Soviets" unpublished paper presented at the Northeastern Slavic Conference of the American Association for the Advancement of Slavic Studies (Montreal, May 5–8, 1971).

53. Robert Wesson, "Volunteers and Soviets," *Soviet Studies*, XV, 3 (January, 1964) is an analysis of the use of volunteers in the local soviets during the Khrushchev period.

54. The full commission consisted of: the paid secretary; a deputy chairman of the Executive Committee; the deputy director of the Municipal Department of Education; an instructor from the City Party Committee; a factory director; two directors of municipal departments; an assistant to the city Procurator; a judge of the people's court; directors of personnel for two factories employing a large number of young people; a teacher who was deputy in the soviet; a school principal; a representative of the militia; the third secretary of the city Komsomol; the leader of the Pioneer group in an elementary school; and an official from a factory trade union committee.

55. *Materialy, Kutaisi,* 3.

56. *Z. V.* (July 8, 1971).

57. B. Michael Frolic, *Soviet Urban Politics* (Cambridge, Mass., 1972) and B. Michael Frolic, "Communist Models of Urban Development," prepared for the Comparative Administration Group of the American Society for Public Administration (New York City, CUNY, April 16, 1972). For details of the municipal budget planning process, see B. M. Frolic, "Decision Making in Soviet Cities," a paper delivered at the Annual Meeting of the American Political Science Association (Los Angeles, September 8–12, 1970), 3–8. William C. Taubman, *The Politics of Urban Development in the Soviet Union* (New York, 1973), also deals extensively with the bargaining between local and central authorities.

58. Lazar Slepov, *Vysshie i mestnye organy partii* (Moscow, 1958), 88, quoted in Jerry Hough, *op. cit.*, 30.

59. *Z. V.* (March 1, 1969).

60. Robert A. Dahl, *Who Governs?*, 301.

61. *Ibid.*, 306.

62. For similar scandals in another area of the USSR, see N. Utkin, "Housing Allocation Corruption," *Pravda* (March 7, 1972), 3.

63. Bert F. Hoselitz, "Levels of Economic Functions and Bureaucratic Structures," in J. La Palombara, ed., *Bureaucracy and Political Development*, 2nd ed. (Princeton, 1967), 193–195.

64. For an account of some Soviet attitudes to the allegedly ubiquitous practice of price-gouging and pilfering among Soviet retail employees, see George Feifer, *Justice in Moscow* (New York, 1964), 224–232. Steven J. Staats, "Corruption in the USSR," *Problems of Communism* (January–February, 1972), 40–48 is an attempt to analyze the role and importance of corruption in the functioning of Soviet society. For frank comments by Georgians on corruption in their republic, see Hedrick Smith, "Soviet Georgia: Poets and Purges," *New York Times* (October 21, 1972), 10.

65. Such was said to be the fate of a former first secretary of the Kutaisi Party Organization. K. Grishin, "O Trebovatel'nosti i distsipline," *Partiinaia Zhizn'*, 1 (1972), 21, devotes some space to denouncing these practices—with concrete illustrations of their existence.

PART THREE

The Soviet Example: Comparative Perspectives

CHAPTER 8

The Soviet Model: A Development Alternative for the Third World?

David E. Albright

Over the years since the Bolsheviks came to power in 1917, Soviet commentators have persistently held up Soviet experience as a model for the peoples of the "East" to emulate. During the Russian civil war, for instance, Stalin depicted "the revolution in Russia" as "the first to rouse the oppressed peoples of the East to fight imperialism," and he contended that "the Soviets in Persia, India, and China are a clear symptom that the age-long slumber of the workers and peasants of the East is becoming a thing of the past." [1] Not long after the end of World War II, a leading Soviet specialist on countries of the "East" maintained that "the victory attained by the Great October Socialist Revolution in Russia" was "the start of the crisis being experienced by the imperialist colonial system." He then suggested that the Bolshevik Revolution, by demonstrating "a new socialist method for resolving the national problem," had "inspired the oppressed colonial people and those of the dependent countries, awakened them and prompted them to action." [2] In the late 1950's, Nikita Khrushchev described "the great power of attraction of the example of the Soviet Union, which has established beacons of socialism in the East —the prosperous Soviet republics of Central Asia"—as an "inspiration to the peoples of the East in their fight for freedom and independency." [3]

With the rising assertiveness of the peoples of the "East"—or to use contemporary terminology, the Third World—since World War II, the question of their course of future development has become a highly important one, and the Soviet model obviously represents an alternative open to them. Consequently, a good deal of Western scholarship has now been devoted to the nature of the Soviet model and its potential relevance to the Third World as a path of political, social, and economic development.[4] By and large, however, these writings have tended to obscure the empirical fact that the actual influence of the Soviet model in Third World areas has declined significantly in recent years. Indeed, one can detect in revolutionary thinking there what might be described as a process of increasing "indigenization." This chapter will attempt to document the trend and to assess the potential for its reversal, as well as the prospects for its continuation.

The Model

At the outset, it is essential to clarify the meaning of the term "Soviet model" as it will be used here. Obviously, the essence of any aspect of Soviet experience can be distilled and labeled a "model." One can, for example, speak of the various measures that Moscow has employed in dealing with its nationality problems as a "model." The same is true with respect to such things as the Soviet approach to social security, the Soviet handling of the arts, the assigned role of the trade unions in the USSR, and so forth. But the Soviets themselves have portrayed the "Soviet model" to others as an integrated course of development involving the broad fundamentals, not partial elements, of Soviet experience. Thus, it seems imperative to adopt a similar perspective in the context of this discussion.

Defining these fundamentals, however, poses some difficulties. For instance, Soviet analyses have not necessarily perceived or interpreted them in the same manner as have outside observers; nor, in fact, has Moscow always based its counsel to the Third World wholly on them. For present purposes, it would appear crucial to construe them in light of what Soviet sources have said about them, for Third World elements have normally derived their understanding of the Soviet model in this fashion. At the same time, one must be careful to distinguish between advice which stems from these fundamentals and programmatic exhortations which reflect considerations other than Soviet experience.

Looked at from this general standpoint, the Soviet model consists of two basic components. Both are strategies for profound or revolutionary change. One has to do with the acquisition of political power; the other concerns the modernization of a relatively backward society.[5] The first, as Lenin expressed it in his writings and implemented it in Russia between 1903 (*What Is to Be Done*) and 1921 (the close of the civil war), entails first and foremost the creation of a militant, disciplined vanguard party.[6] This small committed band then endeavors to build up mass influence through agitation and propaganda to hasten the ultimate, "inevitable" revolutionary crisis. When the party leadership judges that the crisis is at hand, it gives the signal for an armed insurrection to seize power. Such a decision, however, can come only when the cohesion or loyalty of the military instruments of the existing state apparatus—namely, the armed forces and the police—has been undermined by factors like corruption, national military defeat in a war, and so forth, and when enough of the masses appear ready to follow the party to insure a reasonable chance of victory. Though regarded as legitimate at all times and crucial in the final hour, armed force in itself does not constitute a vital means of winning mass influence or of engendering the revolutionary crisis.[7]

The second, evolved by Lenin during the period of war communism and elaborated by Stalin during the years after his emergence as top leader in 1928, places primary emphasis on the foundation of a socialist state structure. This structure must be rooted in "a planned economy, systematically accumulating resources and properly distributing them among the different branches of the national economy." [8] Control of the structure has to be vested in a party "sufficiently solid and united to direct the efforts of all the best members of the working class to *one point* and sufficiently experienced to be unafraid of difficulties and to pursue systematically a correct, revolutionary . . . policy." In short, its guidance is to lie in the hands of a disciplined, vanguard party, highly committed to specifically defined socialist goals. To man the structure, there must be a body of technically skilled as well as revolutionary cadres capable of managing production and other complex tasks. Institutions within the overall structure, however, are to serve essentially as transmission belts, carrying the leadership's directives downward and mobilizing the masses to accomplish the assigned objectives. Though a somewhat more pluralistic concept of institutions underlay Lenin's New Economic Policy of 1921[9] and though Lenin might have considered permanent retention of that concept had he lived longer, the innovations of the 1921–1928 NEP period turned out to be only a brief digression from the basic Soviet approach to institutions. In the late 1950's and early 1960's, Krushchev did attempt to modify the transmission-belt institutions to at least ensure greater two-way communication between state and society than had prevailed under Stalin, but the effort failed miserably. Moreover, Krushchev's abandonment of Stalin's dedication to mass mobilization brought about what one observer has called "the final transformation of the party dictatorship into the role of a post-revolutionary, conservative bureaucracy." [10] This strategy, it should be underscored, involves two critical assumptions: (1) All genuine proponents of socialism subscribe to the same goals; conversely, there can be just one legitimate interpretation of socialist goals. (2) The masses must be mobilized to achieve socialist ends whether they approve of such ends or not. (If they do not, that deficiency merely reflects their lack of consciousness.)

While Soviet theorists have normally presented these two strategies as an integral package and while the two do have common elements—most notably, both attach great importance to a vanguard party—one does not necessarily depend on the other. It is logically conceivable, for example, that in a particular case revolutionaries might gain power by a route different from the Soviet road to power but then subsequently pursue the Soviet strategy for modernization. In fact, as we shall go into later, a number of Soviet commentators have proved willing to recognize this possibility as something more than hypothetical. Therefore, it is useful to break down the examination of trends in the influence of the Soviet model in the Third World and to look at trends in the influence of each of the strategies individually.

Strategy to Gain Power

With respect to the strategy for revolutionary takeover, there seem valid grounds for focusing our attention on the strategic outlooks and commitments of avowedly Marxist-Leninist parties. After all, the formation of a vanguard party lies at the heart of the Soviet strategy; indeed, such a party represents a sine qua non for the implementation of the strategy as a whole.

If one were to judge solely on the basis of the growing number of states and territories with Marxist-Leninist parties in what today constitute Third World areas, one might be inclined to conclude that the impact of the Soviet model has been on the upswing there.[11] Since the end of World War II, there has been roughly a 30 percent increase in the figure. In late 1945, it stood at 44.[12] By early 1959, it had risen to 54.[13] As of the fall of 1972, it had reached 62.[14] In several cases, to be sure, the parties maintain headquarters abroad and enjoy only the most tenuous links with their native lands; nevertheless, all the countries at least have parties which *seek* to operate locally.

But other evidence points in the opposite direction. The Marxist-Leninist left, for example, has undergone tremendous fragmentation during recent years.

At the conclusion of World War II, nearly all the existing Marxist-Leninist parties of the present-day Third World belonged to the international Communist movement under Moscow's direction; while a number of these parties essentially ran their own internal affairs and thus amounted to more than mere puppets, they universally tended to look to the USSR for revolutionary inspiration and guidance.[15] The chief maverick Marxist-Leninist organizations were the Trotskyite groups that had formed in a few countries, especially in Latin America, and their quarrel with Moscow was of a decidedly limited nature.[16] They contended that Stalin had betrayed the cause of world revolution by placing higher priority on "building socialism" in the USSR than on inciting and aiding international revolutionary forces. In short, they wanted to devote greater attention to revolutionary activity than Moscow had proved willing to do for some time, but they accepted the validity of early Soviet revolutionary experience.

These conditions continued to prevail until 1959, when things began to change radically. Over the ensuing years, fractionalism became rampant. Table 8-1 attempts to summarize the situations as of the fall of 1972 in all Third World countries with Marxist-Leninist parties. It indicates both the degree of organizational fragmentation and the dominant orientation of Marxist-Leninist elements in each land. I should emphasize that the kind of crude categorization that I have employed in compiling the latter information precludes any rendering of nuances, and one could cite minor differences of view among many of the parties to which I have attached the same label. Furthermore, the available data on the attitudes of several groups fall short of what one might ideally desire. Nonetheless, I believe that the broad picture that emerges here is precise and accurate enough to suffice for purposes of this discussion.

Primary interest, of course, lies in the aggregate figures. In just 13 of the 62 countries do staunchly pro-Moscow parties still retain an unchallenged position. Three other lands each have a single, pro-Soviet party; but two of these parties suffer from severe factionalism, and the remaining one incorporates only a minority faction of the local Communists, most of whom describe themselves as "national Communists" and belong to no organized Communist party. In the 35 cases where more than one Marxist-Leninist party exists, a pro-Soviet party is dominant in 22; a pro-Chinese party is dominant in two (one of these countries boasts two pro-

Chinese parties); an "independent" party is dominant in two; and there is some doubt about the dominant party in nine. Of the final 11 lands, four have stoutly pro-Chinese parties; however, in one of these the party represents only a minority of the local Communists, the bulk of whom class themselves as "national Communists." Two other countries have parties which are essentially pro-Chinese in outlook but have experienced strong factional conflict. In one land, the only party is an "independent" one. Three lands have pro-Vietnamese parties; one has a pro-Korean party. From the Soviet viewpoint, all these last four qualify as "independent."

TABLE 8–1 Marxist-Leninist Parties in Third-World Countries (October 31, 1972)

Country	*No. Parties*[a]	*Dominant Orientation*[b]
Afghanistan	2 main, but 5 altogether	Pro-Soviet
Algeria	1	Pro-Soviet
Argentinia	At least 4	Pro-Soviet
Australia	3	Independent
Bangla Desh	At least 4	In question
Bolivia	3	Pro-Soviet
Brazil	5	Pro-Soviet
Burma	2	Pro-Chinese
Cambodia	1	Pro-Vietnamese[c]
Ceylon (Sri Lanka)	7	In question
Chile	3	Pro-Soviet
Colombia	3	Pro-Soviet
Costa Rica	2	Pro-Soviet
Cyprus	1	Pro-Soviet
Dominican Republic	6	In question
Ecuador	At least 4	In question
Egypt	1	"National Communists"[d]
El Salvador	3	Pro-Soviet
Guadeloupe	2	Pro-Soviet
Guatemala	3	Pro-Soviet
Guyana	2	Pro-Soviet
Haiti	1	Pro-Soviet, but severe factionalism
Honduras	4	Pro-Soviet
India	3	In question[e]
Indonesia	1	Pro-Chinese, but severe factionalism
Iran	3	Pro-Soviet
Iraq	1	Pro-Soviet, but severe factionalism
Israel	2	In question
Jordan	2	In question

Country	No. Parties[a]	Dominant Orientation[b]
Korea, South	1	Pro-Korean[f]
Laos	1	Pro-Vietnamese[c]
Lebanon	3	Pro-Soviet
Lesotho	1	Pro-Soviet
Malagasay Republic	1	Pro-Soviet
Malaysia	1	Pro-Chinese
Malta	1	Pro-Soviet
Martinique	1	Pro-Soviet
Mauritius	1	Pro-Soviet
Mexico	1 main plus multiple minor[g]	Pro-Soviet
Morocco	1	Pro-Soviet
Nepal	2	Pro-Chinese[h]
New Zealand	3	In question
Nicaragua	3	In question
Nigeria	1	Pro-Soviet
Pakistan	1	Pro-Chinese, but severe factionalism
Panama	2	Pro-Soviet
Paraguay	2	Pro-Soviet
Peru	6	Pro-Soviet
Philippines	2	Pro-Soviet
Réunion	1	Independent
Saudi Arabia	1	Pro-Soviet
Senegal	1	Pro-Soviet
Singapore	1	Pro-Chinese
South Africa	1	Pro-Soviet
Sudan	1	"National Communists"[d]
Syria	2	Pro-Soviet
Thailand	1	Pro-Chinese
Tunisia	1	Pro-Soviet
Turkey	1 main plus multiple minor	Pro-Soviet
Uruguay	6	Pro-Soviet
Venezuela	3 main and 1 minor	Independent
Vietnam, South	1	Pro-Vietnamese[c]

a. Some of the groups or "movements" included in this listing (notably those of pro-Cuban persuasion) shun the traditional "party" label, but they have many ideological and organizational characteristics in common with the acknowledged Marxist-Leninist parties. Hence, they properly fall within the realm of consideration.

b. This breakdown indicates the general outlook of the dominant party (in terms of membership) in each country. "In question" means that the dominant party is in doubt. The reasons for such a situation vary. In some countries, there are multiple parties, none of which encompasses a majority of local Marxist-Leninists within its ranks; in other countries, there are two parties of roughly equal size.

The classifications themselves reflect party attitudes on a broad range of matters—intraparty democracy, interparty relations, the road to power, "peaceful coexistence" with "imperialism," and so forth—and not just a single issue. For example, the chief Mexican party has chastised the Communist party of the Soviet Union for the USSR's 1968 invasion of Czechoslovakia and for Moscow's promulgation of the Brezhnev Doctrine to justify this interference in the internal affairs of another Communist party-state, but on most questions the Mexican party's views coincide with those of the CPSU. Hence, the "dominant orientation" given here for Mexico is "pro-Soviet."

c. This party adheres essentially to the perspectives of Hanoi, which differ at least to some degree from those of Moscow, Peking, and Havana and therefore constitute a distinct category.

d. While an underground party exists here, the bulk of the local Marxist-Leninists do not belong to it. Instead, they designate themselves "national Communists" and participate as individuals in the local ruling party, which is not only a heterogeneous body but also the only political organization in the country allowed to function openly.

e. There is even considerable disagreement among sources about the relative sizes of the two chief parties. *Cf.*, Bureau of Intelligence and Research, U.S. Department of State, *World Strength of the Communist Party Organizations,* 24th Annual Report (Washington, D.C., June, 1972), 95; and Bhabani Sen Gupta, "Indian Communism and the Peasantry," *Problems of Communism*, XXI, 1 (January–February, 1972), 1.

f. This party adheres essentially to the perspectives of Pyongyang, which differ at least to some degree from those of Moscow, Peking, and Havana and therefore constitute a distinct category.

g. Excluding the pro-Marxist but "independent" Popular Socialist party, which has attributes incompatible with a true Marxist-Leninist party—most importantly, a large non-Communist membership.

h. Though the professedly pro-Chinese group maintains close ties with the pro-Soviet Communist Party of India.

Sources: Bureau of Intelligence and Research, U.S. Department of State, *op. cit.*; Richard F. Starr, ed., *Yearbook on International Communist Affairs 1972* (Stanford, Calif., 1972); *New York Times* (January 1–October 31, 1972); and *World Marxist Review* (Toronto, January–October, 1972).

What matters about this fragmentation from the standpoint of present concerns is why it has occurred. Unquestionably, quarrels among the communist states since 1959 have entered into the situation, and factors such as ethnic or regional affinity with one of the non-Soviet states have in turn played a role in shaping the orientations of many parties. For example, the pro-Chinese outlooks of the Malaysian, Thai, and Singapore parties patently owe something to the essentially Chinese makeup of these parties; similarly, the pro-Cuban perspectives of the Sandinista National Liberation Front (FSLN) in Nicaragua and the Armed Forces of National Liberation (FALN) in Venezuela stem in part from a "Latin American" identification with Cuba. Nevertheless, a key, and usually decisive, element in most cases has been dissatisfaction with various aspects of the Soviet strategy for attaining power in light of the internal conditions that confront the individual parties. For instance, the pro-Chinese entities—in keeping with Maoist doctrine—advocate protracted armed struggle, waged from rural bases, as a means of undermining extant governments and precipitating revolutionary crises.[17] The pro-Cuban groups—in accordance with the teachings of Fidel Castro and Ernesto (Ché) Guevara—likewise favor protracted armed struggle with particular attention to the countryside, but they place less emphasis on the construction of a political infrastructure in rural areas, as well as more emphasis on the organization of rural guerrilla bands, than the pro-Chinese parties do.[18] The "independent" bodies propound courses with distinctive wrinkles too. For example, the main Australian party stresses the vital nature of "intraparty democracy" in winning support and has discarded "democratic centralism" as an operative principle; moreover, it has abandoned the concept of "working-class" leadership of the socialist revolution and speaks of a "coalition of the left" at the revolutionary helm.[19] By the same token, one of the two largest Indian parties has devised a road which combines militant parliamentarianism with peasant struggles of "controlled militancy" (short of guerrilla warfare).[20] These illustrations in no sense exhaust the diversity of strategies now articulated and pursued, but they will suffice to establish the basic point.

Another sign of the declining influence of the Soviet model of political takeover has been the change over the last 15 years or so in the attitudes of many of the pro-Soviet parties toward armed force as a method of obtaining power. Table 8-2 sets forth the public views of the individual bodies on this issue as of the fall of 1972. Of the 50 extant pro-Moscow parties, 42 now endorse "peaceful" means of gaining authority,[21] although three of these have factions that persist in championing armed efforts.

This statistic, to be sure, must be approached with great caution, for endorsement of the "peaceful" road to socialism does not necessarily mean either a deviation from the Soviet model of acquiring power or increased attention to local political conditions. Virtually none of the 42 parties that uphold "peaceful" means of capturing authority have explicitly forsaken armed struggle under any and all circumstances. Hence, advocacy of the "peaceful" road could represent expediency rather than a basic departure from the Soviet precedent. That is, the parties, recognizing their weaknesses of the moment, could merely have decided to bide their time until more propitious conditions loom on the horizon and then intend to reverse themselves and take up arms to seize control of their countries. Furthermore, Moscow, for reasons which we will discuss later, has in recent years counseled Third World Marxist-Leninists to employ "peaceful" techniques. Therefore, the stances of the parties could merely reflect adherence to the present Soviet line.

TABLE 8–2 Pro-Soviet Parties and the "Peaceful" Acquisition of Power (October 31, 1972)

Country of Party	Attitude on "Peaceful" Acquisition of Power	Political System of Country[a]	Party's Access to Parliamentary or Governmental Institutions	Party's Share of Last National Vote[b] (in percent)
Afghanistan	For	Quasi-representative	Some[c]	?[c]
Algeria	For	Nonrepresentative	None	n.a.
Argentina	For	Nonrepresentative[d]	None	n.a.
Australia	For	Representative	Some	Less than .08[e]
Bangla Desh	For	Quasi-representative	Some[f]	n.a.[f]
Bolivia	For	Nonrepresentative	None	n.a.
Brazil	For	Quasi-representative	None	n.a.
Ceylon (Sri Lanka)	For	Representative	Some[g]	3.4
Chile	For	Representative	Some[g]	16.9
Colombia	Against	Representative	Some	.4
Costa Rica	For	Representative	Some[h]	Less than 5.0[h]
Cyprus	For	Representative	Some	39.7
Dominican Republic	Against	Representative	None	n.a.
Ecuador	For	Nonrepresentative	None	n.a.
El Salvador	For (though factions against)	Representative	None	n.a.
Guadeloupe	For	Representative	Some	38.74
Guatemala	Against	Representative	None	n.a.
Guyana	For	Representative	Some	36.9
Haiti	Against	Nonrepresentative	None	n.a.
Honduras	For	Representative	None	n.a.
India	For	Representative	Some	4.8
Iran	For	Quasi-representative	None	n.a.
Iraq	For (though factions against)	Nonrepresentative	Some[i]	n.a.[i]
Israel	For	Representative	Some	2.84
Jordan	Against[j]	Nonrepresentative	None	n.a.
Lebanon	For	Representative	Some[k]	n.a.[k]
Lesotho	For	Nonrepresentative	None	n.a.
Malagasay Republic	For	Quasi-representative	Some	3.0
Malta	For	Representative	Some[l]	Nil[l]

Country of Party	Attitude on "Peaceful" Acquisition of Power	Political System of Country[a]	Party's Access to Parliamentary or Governmental Institutions	Party's Share of Last National Vote[b] (in percent)
Martinique	For	Representative	Some	16.86
Mauritius	For	Representative	Some	Negligible
Mexico	For	Representative	Some[m]	n.a.[m]
Morocco	For	Nonrepresentative	None	n.a.
Nepal	For	Quasi-representative	Some[n]	?[n]
New Zealand	For	Representative	Some	Less than .01[o]
Nicaragua	For	Quasi-representative	None	n.a.
Nigeria	For	Nonrepresentative	None	n.a.
Panama	For	Nonrepresentative	None	n.a.
Paraguay	For	Nonrepresentative	None	n.a.
Peru	For	Nonrepresentative	None	n.a.
Philippines	For	Nonrepresentative	None	n.a.
Saudi Arabia	Against[p]	Nonrepresentative	None	n.a.
Senegal	For	Quasi-representative	None	n.a.
South Africa	Against	Quasi-representative	None	n.a.
Sudan	Against	Quasi-representative	None[q]	n.a.
Syria	For (though factions against)	Nonrepresentative	Some[r]	n.a.[r]
Tunisia	For	Quasi-representative	None	n.a.
Turkey	For	Quasi-representative	None	n.a.
Uruguay	For	Representative	Some	6.6[s]
Venezuela	For	Representative	Some	2.8[t]

a. Three types of political systems are distinguished here—representative, quasi-representative, and nonrepresentative. In a representative system, the leadership positions in political institutions are filled essentially on the basis of universal popular elections; in a nonrepresentative system, the general populace has no role in the selection process, A quasi-representative system falls between these two types. It has some institutions with elected officials, but it does not qualify as representative for one of several reasons—the elective institutions have limited power, the right to vote is heavily restricted, party competition or competition between candidates of a single party is prohibited, and so on.

The classifications in this breakdown are meant to provide only a rough indication of the political contexts in which the various parties operate hence, considerable diversity exists among the political systems of the countries listed in the same category here. For example, the representative institutions in, say, Australia, the Dominican Republic, Honduras, Israel, and Lebanon differ appreciably in vitality, as well as in precise characteristics. Similarly, the situations in countries with quasi-representative political systems vary widely. A few cases will suffice for purposes of illustration. Afghanistan has a parliament made up of a lower house in which all members are elected and an upper house in which a third of them are elected. Under the current constitution, however, this body enjoys only limited powers. In Nepal, there is an indirectly elected National Assembly, but it may only debate bills approved by the king. The king thus possesses virtually complete authority to govern. In Senegal, both the president and the parliament are elected, yet only one party is allowed to present candidates. South Africa boasts a parliamentary government; however, the majority black-African population does not have the franchise.

b. Where applicable. Here n.a. stands for "not applicable."

c. While the Afghanistan party does not have legal status, party members have been permitted to participate as individuals in the nonpartisan elections to parliament, which was established in 1964. In view of the nonpartisan nature of the elections thus far, it is impossible to determine the percentage of the vote that the party has gathered.

d. However, national elections to prepare the way for a return to representative government are scheduled for March, 1973.

e. The figure .08 percent encompasses all Communist votes—i.e., those for all Communist parties.

f. Since Bangla Desh acquired its independence in the wake of the 1971 Indo-Pakistani war, the party has become legal and has opened a headquarters in Dacca, but it has not yet had an opportunity to take part in any elections. The last elections held in the country were the Pakistan elections of December, 1970, which resulted in a resounding victory for Sheikh Mujibur Rahman's Awami League and helped precipitate the civil war that split Pakistan into two sovereign nations.

g. This party belongs to a government coalition.

h. Though the Costa Rican party is proscribed, it has been allowed to run candidates for office on the slate of the leftist Socialist Action Party. In the 1970 legislative elections, the SAP slate, only a portion of whom were Communists, received 5.0 percent of the votes.

i. After the signing of a Soviet-Iraqi treaty of friendship and cooperation in April, 1972, the Iraq Communist party agreed to join with the Ba'ath party in a national front, though the former still remains officially illegal.

j. The Jordanian party has its own organization of Palestinian guerrillas, but this group has proved leery of actual military operations and consequently is highly suspect among the activist *fedayeen* bodies.

k. Since the Lebanese party only acquired legal status in 1970, it did not have a chance to participate in the 1968 national elections.

l. The Malta party, though in existence since 1970 and free to operate openly, did not field a list of candidates in the 1971 national elections.

m. While the party is not proscribed, its membership is not sufficient to meet Mexico's election-law requirements for national registration.

n. The Nepal party is formally outlawed; however, party members are permitted to run as individuals in the indirect elections to the National Assembly. Although roughly 10–15 percent of those occupying seats in the Assembly are reputed to be Communists or sympathizers, many of these persons probably do not belong to the pro-Soviet party.

o. The figure .01 percent covers all Communist votes—i.e., those for all Communist parties.

p. Presumably, though information about the party's attitude is sketchy.

q. The Sudan partly is outlawed, and only "national Communists" have been allowed to participate in any fashion in the elections that have taken place in the country under the present government of General Jaafar Numeiri. These "national Communists" eschew affiliation with an organized Marxist-Leninist body and seek to work as individuals within the single legal party, the Sudanese Socialist Union.

r. Through Syria has no representative institutions and the party itself is officially proscribed, members of the party do hold two positions in the national cabinet.

s. This figure represents the actual share of the vote that the Uruguayan party won in the 1971 elections; however, the party participated as an element of the *Frente Amplio,* a broad popular-front coalition of left-of-center organizations. The *Frente* altogether received 18.6 percent of the vote.

t. This figure is for the 1968 congressional elections in Venezuela, and since then, the party has undergone a major split. Indeed, the rump body retains the allegiance of only a minority of the members of the former unified party. However, its electoral strength has yet to be tested in a national ballot.

Sources: Data on party attitudes come from Bureau of Intelligence and Research, U.S. Department of State, *World Strength of the Communist Party Organizations,* 23rd Annual Report (Washington, D.C., May, 1971), and *World Strength of the Communist Party Organizations,* 24th Annual Report (Washington, D.C., June, 1972); Richard F. Starr, ed., *Yearbook on International Communist Affairs 1972* (Stanford, Calif., 1972); *The World Marxist Review* (Toronto, 1958–72); and the *New York Times* (January 1–October 31, 1972). The classifications of national political systems are based on information derived from Richard P. Stebbins and Alba Amoia, eds., *Political Handbook and Atlas of the World, 1970* (New York, 1970), and *The World This Year 1972, Supplement to Political Handbook and Atlas of the World, 1970* (New York: Simon and Schuster for the Council on Foreign Relations, 1972); and the *New York Times* (January 1–October 31, 1972). Data on party access to parliamentary or governmental institutions and party shares of the last national votes are drawn from *World Strength of the Communist Party Organizations,* 23rd Annual Report, and *World Strength of the Communist Party Organizations,* 24th Annual Report; *Yearbook on International Communist Affairs 1972;* George Lenczowski, *Soviet Advances in the Middle East* (Washington, D.C., February, 1972); Paul E. Sigmund, "Chile: Two Years of 'Popular Unity,'" *Problems of Communism,* XXI, 6 (November–December, 1972), 38–51; and the *New York Times* (January 1–October 31, 1972).

Scrutiny of Table 8-2 leads one to conclude that such considerations probably underlie the positions of a number of the parties. For example, of the 42 parties favoring the "peaceful" path, 18 do not enjoy even limited chances to participate in the normal political life of their lands. In eight of these cases, it is true, the political contexts in which the parties operate afford them some ground to hope for a possible redress of this state of affairs. At least quasi-representative systems exist in the countries where seven of the parties function, and in the native land of one other a representative system is supposed to be restored in early 1973. Nevertheless, there is a strong basis for presuming that all the 18 parties have adopted their positions for tactical reasons and largely at Soviet urging. Such a presumption is bolstered by the fact that most of these parties, as we shall see in a moment, have only tiny followings and consequently must depend heavily on the USSR for moral and financial support.

However, the circumstances of the other 24 parties suggest not only that most feel a deep commitment to the pursuit of power by "peaceful" methods, but also that their stances mirror their own calculations more than Soviet advice. Altogether, 21 of them operate within political systems of at least a partially representative nature, and several of the 21 exert appreciable leverage within their individual political environments. Indeed, two—those in Ceylon and Chile—belong to ruling coalitions. The one in India likewise enjoys a measure of influence on the current government, especially at the state level.[22] Of the remaining three parties, two have some access to governmental institutions but work within non-representative political systems; the other remains illegal but functions within a representative system. There is thus substantial room for debate by these parties about the wisdom of the "peaceful" road, and all three have experienced factional discord on the subject.

Further reinforcement for the contention that assessments of local conditions have constituted the primary factor behind the attitudes of many of the parties comes from an examination of the situations of the parties that still argue for the employment of armed force. Of the eight parties involved, seven lack any opportunity whatsoever to engage in open political activities in their lands, and while the remaining one—that in Colombia—does have a chance to do so, parties of every political persuasion in the nation have traditionally maintained their own military arms.

The foregoing data, of course, contain an element of bias, for using countries or parties as the basic units of calculation entails an implicit assumption that all countries and all parties are of equal weight—a proposition which the varying importance and size of the countries and parties render indefensible. It would obviously be more accurate, therefore, to cast the analysis in terms of trends in the attitudes and outlooks of Marxist-Leninist party members. Unfortunately, available statistics on the memberships of Marxist-Leninist parties—let alone on the perspectives of their individual adherents—are sketchy and incomplete,[23] so one cannot produce a detailed breakdown of this sort. Nevertheless, enough information does exist to afford some notion of what such a breakdown would show. This information tends to confirm the general picture that has already been sketched.

In the late 1950's the U.S. State Department's Bureau of Intelligence and Research began publishing unclassified annual estimates of the strength of Marxist-Leninist parties around the world. While the authors of this series have not employed as intellectually rigorous a concept in carrying out their estimates of membership as one might wish,[24] the series does embody the most systematic and in-depth work undertaken on the subject to date. According to it, at the beginning of 1959 Marxist-Leninist party members in what are now Third World areas numbered 1,543,325. By the opening of 1972, that figure had dropped to 534,830 —primarily as a result of the decimation of the Indonesian Communist party, the Third World's biggest, after the abortive coup of 1965.[25]

Though there is evidence that a few Marxist-Leninist parties in the Third World had conducted internal debates on local revolutionary strategy prior to 1959,[26] the great bulk of Third World Marxist-Leninists seem not to have questioned the merit of the Soviet road to power as a model up to that point. Furthermore, the attitudes toward the Soviet path of the participants in the debates that had taken place remain obscure. These debates for the most part centered on the viability of a particular revolutionary tack at a specific juncture in time. That is, they did not revolve around the validity of the Soviet strategy for revolutionary takeover; they focused on the issue of what tactical line should be pursued in the existing context. The absence of any significant organizational fragmentation up to 1959 suggests that most of those who advocated a course unlike the Soviet road to power did not reject the Soviet model outright, but merely sought to modify it to fit the circumstances that currently confronted their parties.

Subsequent years, however, witnessed a dramatic alteration in the situation. Parties splintered on a grand scale, and as of the first of 1972, an estimated 182,410 Third World Marxist-Leninists (34 percent of the total) belonged to bodies not aligned with Moscow. (Table 8-3 breaks down this sum by country. It ought to be noted that the figures listed for the Indonesian and Pakistani parties cover the entire memberships. Since each party has a minority of unknown size oriented toward Moscow, the figures given slightly overstate the number of local Marxist-Leninists who have spurned the Soviet revolutionary model, though virtually all the Indonesian Communists do at least appear to favor protracted armed struggle.) Moreover, only 12,820 of the remainder were associated with parties which still retained a clear-cut commitment to armed methods of attaining power.[27] This number, to be sure, does not include the opponents of the "peaceful" path among the 4,100 adherents of the three pro-Soviet parties in which there had been major strife over the merits of that path.[28] But even if one adds in them and the 77,450 members of parties which, while having verbally embraced the "peaceful" road to socialism, are barred from participation in the normal political processes of their countries and hence probably lack any true dedication to such a course,[29] one still comes up with a sum of less than 95,000. Thus, roughly 260,000 Marxist-Leninists belonged to pro-Soviet parties which had departed in a major way from the Soviet model for the assumption of authority.

TABLE 8–3 Membership of Marxist–Leninist Parties in the Third World

Country of Party or Parties	January 1, 1959		January 1, 1964		January 1, 1972		National Population January 1, 1972
	Pro-Soviet[a]	*Others*[a]	*Pro-Soviet*	*Others*	*Pro-Soviet*[b]	*Others*[b]	*(in millions*
Afghanistan	—	—	—	—	250	150	18.000
Algeria	7,500	—	5,000	—	400	—	14.422
Argentina	75,000	—	45,000	—	52,250	6,750	23.832
Australia	5,500	—	6,000	1,000	900	3,000	12.947
Bangla Desh[c]	—	—	—	—	200	800	62.192
Bolivia	6,000	No estim.	4,500	2,500	1,500	1,275	4.832
Brazil	50,000	—	30,000	1,000	13,000	3,000	96.818
Burma	12,000	—	—	5,000[e]	—	5,000	28.517
Cambodia	1,000	—	—	1,000	—	15,000	7.075
Ceylon (Sri Lanka)	3,950	2,150	3,000	2,000	3,000	5,000[f]	12.937
Chile	22,500	—	27,500	—	90,000	1,000	9.124
Colombia	5,000	—	11,000[e]	Unknown	10,000	1,100	22.913
Costa Rica	300	—	300	—	1,000	100	1.820
Cyprus	5,000	—	10,000	—	13,000	—	.653
Dominican Republic	No estim.	—	Unknown	Unknown	470	935	4.259
Ecuador	1,000	—	2,500[e]	—	500	800	6.414
Egypt	No estim.	—	1,000	—	—	900[g]	34.616
El Salvador	500	—	500	—	100	50	3.741
Guadeloupe	1,000	—	1,000	—	2,000	100	.337
Guatemala	1,000	—	1,300[e]	—	750	200	5.497
Guyana	6,000[h]	—	11,000[h]	—	20,000[h]	100	.745
Haiti	No estim.	—	Unknown	—	500[i]	—	5.020
Honduras	500	—	2,400[e]	—	300	100	2.719
India	250,000	—	120,000[e]	—	90,000[j]	72,000[j]	556.193
Indonesia	1,000,000	—	1,900,000[k]	Neglig.	—	5,000[e]	123.979
Iran	1,500	—	1,500	—	500	200	29.912
Iraq	1,000	—	15,000[e]	—	2,000[e]	—	9.814
Israel	2,000	—	2,000	Unknown	1,000	1,000	3.006
Jordan	250	—	200	—	250	250	2.443
Korea, South	No estim.	—	—	Neglig.	—	Neglig.	32.219
Laos	100	—	—	100	—	13,000	3.069
Lebanon	4,000[m]	—	3,500	—	1,000	500	2.918
Lesotho	—	—	100	—	Neglig.	—	.926
Malagasay	No estim.	—	—	100	Neglig.	—	6.982

Country of Party or Parties	January 1, 1959 *Pro-Soviet*[a]	*Others*[a]	January 1, 1964 *Pro-Soviet*	*Others*	January 1, 1972 *Pro-Soviet*[b]	*Others*[b]	National Population, January 1, 1972 (*in millions*)
Republic							
Malaysia[n]	5,000	—	—	2,000	—	2,000	10.912
Malta	—	—	—	—	100	—	.323
Martinique	2,500	—	700	—	1,000	—	.347
Mauritius	—	—	—	—	Neglig.	—	.855
Mexico	5,000	—	3,100[e]	5,200	5,000	1,000	51.633
Morocco	1,250	—	1,250	—	300	—	16.324
Nepal	3,250	—	3,500[e]	—	4,000	6,000	11.343
New Zealand	400	—	—	500	100	250	2.908
Nicaragua	200	—	250	Unknown	100	100	2.071
Nigeria	—	—	100	—	1,000	—	57.000
Pakistan[o]	3,500	—	—	2,900[e]	—	750	55.635[p]
Panama	150[q]	—	400	Unknown	250	150	1.497
Paraguay	500	—	3,500[e]	—	3,000	1,500	2.498
Peru	6,000	—	8,500[e]	Unknown	2,000	1,800	14.233[r]
Philippines	1,500	—	1,750	400	1,000	850	38.931
Réunion	—	—	No estim.	—	—	500	.461
audi Arabia	—	—	—	—	Neglig.	—	5.500
enegal	No estim.	—	Unknown	—	Neglig.	—	4.029
Singapore[s]	No estim.	—	—	—	—	200	2.127
South Africa	1,500	—	800	—	100		22.118
Sudan	750	—	1,500[e]	—	750[t]	1,000[t]	16.289
Syria	4,000[m]	—	4,500[e]	—	2,000	1,000	6.557
Thailand	5,200	—	—	Unknown	—	1,000	35.774
Tunisia	375	—	1,000	—	100	—	5.325
Turkey	250	—	1,000	—	1,250	Unknown	36.765
Uruguay	3,000	—	10,000[e]	Unknown	22,000	2,000	2.938
Venezuela	32,500	—	30,000	Unknown	3,500	5,000	10.972[u]
Vietnam, South	1,750	—	—	20,000	—	20,000[v]	19.054
Totals	1,541,175	2,150	2,276,150	43,500	352,420	182,410	
Percent of grand sum of party members	99.9%	0.1%	98.1%	1.9%	65.9%	34.1%	

a. This breakdown, though the best one can produce, has some notable deficiencies, for the 1959 *World Strength of Communist Party Organizations* fails to give estimates for the membership of a number of the minor Marxist-Leninist parties, most of which were either pro-Soviet or Trotskyite in orientation. It should also be underscored that the classifications of parties here miss some important nuances. For example, the Cambodian, Laotian, and South Vietnamese parties all looked primarily to Hanoi for revolutionary inspiration, and the South Korean party took its revolutionary cues fundamentally from Pyongyang. At the beginning of 1959, however, both North Vietnam and North Korea were adhering to a pro-Moscow line and were not yet propounding distinctive revolutionary models based on their own experiences.

Wherever the *World Strength of Communist Party Organizations* estimate involves a range between two amounts, the two have been averaged to arrive at a single figure. This same procedure has also been employed in compiling the estimates in other sections of the table.

b. The membership figures here are derived essentially from the 1972 *World Strength of the Communist Party Organizations*. In some cases, however, this source provides an estimate which does not afford a breakdown of the memberships of individual parties and/or does not cover certain minor parties. Wherever possible, the *Yearbook on International Communist Affairs 1972* has been used to supplement, interpret, and adjust the estimates in question, but the data in it are not always sufficient for the purpose. In such instances, the supplementations, interpretations, and adjustments have been carried out in light of the descriptive discussions that accompany the estimates in the basic source.

c. Until after the 1971 Indo-Pakistani war, Bangla Desh was a part of Pakistan; therefore, estimates of the size of its Communist organization in 1959 and 1964 are reflected in the total estimates for Pakistan for these years.

d. This figure is an unofficial estimate based on a breakdown of the official total for East and West Pakistan combined (117,827,000) in terms of the proportions of the projected January 1, 1972, estimates for Bangla Desh and Pakistan (formerly West Pakistan).

e.) However, the party contained an undetermined number of dissidents of one kind or another.

f. This estimate draws upon figures in Charles S. Blackton, "Sri Lanka's Marxists," *Problems of Communism,* XII, I (January–February, 1973), 32, as well as those in the 1972 *World Strength of Communist Party Organizations.*

g. This figure encompasses the "national Communists" who belonged to no formal Marxist-Leninist party but operated as individuals within the country's sole legal party, a "national-front" body.

h. The People's Progressive Party of Guyana did not openly proclaim itself a Marxist-Leninist party until 1969. Consequently, its membership in the preceding years included a number of non-Communists who identified with it because of its anticolonial stance or, particularly by the mid-1960's, its predominantly East Indian makeup. Many of these individuals remained faithful to the party on racial grounds even after the leadership declared the party officially Marxist-Leninist. The hard-core Marxist-Leninist element as of January 1, 1972, probably amounted to no more than about 100 members.

i. The estimate here comes from the *Yearbook on International Communist Affairs 1972,* for the 1972 *World Strength of Communist Party Organizations* does not give a concrete estimate for Haiti. It should be pointed out, too, that the party contained an undetermined number of dissidents with basically a pro-Cuban orientation.

j. Estimates of the sizes of the three Indian parties vary radically from source to source. For example, some observers maintain that the Communist party of India (Marxist), the independent party, had more members at the beginning of 1972 than did the pro-Soviet Communist party of India; others contend the opposite. To preserve as much consistency in the estimates as possible, the figures used here are those in the 1972 *World Strength of Communist Party Organizations.*

k. The Indonesian Communist party had been lending increasing support to the Chinese Communist party against attacks by the Communist party of the Soviet Union and its allies at international Communist gatherings, but the Indonesian party's internal stategy and the general outlook of the majority of its members reflected much more of a pro-Moscow than a pro-Peking orientation.

l. This figure applies to the population within the country's pre-June, 1967, borders.

m. The 1959 *World Strength of Communist Party Organizations* gives the total membership for the Lebanese and Syrian Communist parties af 8,000. The breakdown here is based on the discussion that accompanies the estimate.

n. Over the years, the borders of Malaysia have changed, and the estimates listed here for Malaysia take in different territories. The 1959 figure covers only Malaya, Singapore, Sabah, and Sarawak; that for 1972 encompasses just Malaya, Sabah, and Sarawak.

o. The estimates for 1969 and 1964 include both East and West Pakistan. By 1972, of course, East Pakistan had become independent as Bangla Desh, and that development accounts to a great extent for the apparent drop in membership of the Pakistan party.

p. This figure is an unofficial estimate arrived at by subtracting the 62,192,000 estimate for East Pakistan (Bangla Desh) from the 117,827,000 estimate by the Bureau of Economic Analyses, U.S. Department of Commerce, for West and East Pakistan combined.

q. The 1950 *World Strength of Communist Party Organizations* offers no estimate for Panama, but later volumes in the series, including that for 1964, suggest that the membership around 1959 was 150.

r. Excluding the Indian jungle population, which was estimated at 101,000 in 1961.

s. In 1964, Singapore was part of Malaysia, so the estimate of the membership of the Singapore Communist organization for that year is reflected in the figure for Malaysia.

t. The *Yearbook of International Communist Affairs 1972* indicates that there may have been as many as 2,000–3,000 additional pro-Soviet Communists in jail. It should also be noted that the "Others" figure encompasses the "national Communists" who belonged to no formal Marxist-Leninist party but operated as individuals within the country's sole legal party, a "national-front" body.

u. Excluding the Indian jungle population, which was estimated at 32,000 in 1961.

v. The 1972 *World Strength of Communist Party Organizations* provides no membership total whatsoever for cadres of the People's Revolutionary Party, the South Vietnam branch of the Lao Dong (Workers' Party), but it does suggest that the body's native South Vietnamese component had diminished recently. Since the volume for the preceding year contained an estimate of roughly 40,000 indigenous southerners in the Communist military apparatus (see Bureau of Intelligence and Research, U.S. Department of State, *World Strength of the Communist Party Organizations,* 23rd Annual Report [Washington, D.C., May, 1971], 124), the 1972 figure in the table seems to be reasonably conservative—especially in light of the fact that the *Yearbook on International Communist Affairs 1972* places the PRP's membership at 75,000–100,000.

Sources: The estimates of party membership are derived from Bureau of Intelligence and Research, U.S. Department of State, *World Strength of the Communist Party Organizations,* Intelligence Report, No. 4489 R–11 (Washington, D.C., January, 1959); Bureau of Intelligence and Research, U.S. Department of State,

World Strength of the Communist Party Organizations, 16th Annual Report (Washington, D.C., January, 1964); Bureau of Intelligence and Research, U.S. Department of State, *World Strength of the Communist Party Organizations,* 24th Annual Report (Washington, D.C., June, 1972); and Richard F. Starr, ed., *Yearbook on International Communist Affairs 1972* (Stanford, Calif., 1972). The figures for national population in 1972 are official U.S. estimates prepared by the Bureau of Economic Analyses, Department of Commerce.

Strategy for Modernization

In turning now to trends in the influence of the Soviet strategy of modernization in Third World areas, we need to widen the scope of our considerations. Though an ideologically dedicated vanguard party is an essential component of the Soviet model for modernization, only that model's historical link with the Soviet strategy for revolutionary takeover would require a specific scenario for the formation of such a party. Over the last 20 years, with the emergence of independent nations in much of the Third World and with the widespread eagerness there to promote social and economic development, Moscow has tended to ignore that link. That is, it has projected its modernization experience as a model for emulation by all those who desire rapid social and economic progress, whether they currently happen to be Marxist-Leninists or not. As one Soviet commentator put things several years ago,

> Two paths of development, socialist and capitalist, are open to the former colonies after their liberation. Which is more likely to facilitate rapid economic progress and higher living standards?
>
> Imperialist propaganda is trying to convince Asians and Africans of the advantages of capitalism, the system prevailing in the so-called free world. . . .
>
> Now, as the Soviet Union enters its forty-second year, socialism is seen by the people everywhere as a powerful and invincible force to which the future belongs. It has become the symbol of peace and progress, liberation and fraternity, prosperity and culture.
>
> Socialist ideas are steadily gaining ground in the East, where the competition between the two systems is closely watched.[30]

In practical terms, of course, the non-Marxist-Leninist elements of the Third World with the greatest potential susceptibility to the appeals of the model have been the so-called radicals or revolutionaries, who usually function within more or less like-minded governments/ruling parties or opposition parties. Therefore, our analysis must take into account the attitudes of these "radical" governments and parties, as well as those of the straightforward Marxist-Leninist parties.

Let us, however, deal with the Marxist-Leninist parties first. On the whole, the Third World Marxist-Leninist parties and their members have been preoccupied with the problem of winning power throughout the post-World War II era. Only in a few isolated instances have any of them had a chance to implement, or to help implement, modernization programs in their countries; and most of them have not attempted to formulate elaborate blueprints for the post-takeover period. In fact, some of them have deliberately avoided drawing up precise schemes on the ground that doing so might cause splits in the revolutionary forces and prolong the revolutionary struggle. Consequently, appraisals of the attitudes of the majority of the parties toward the Soviet model across the years have to be based on piecemeal information about their outlooks. Nonetheless, the available evidence permits us to draw some tentative conclusions on the subject.

Hand in hand with the fragmentation of the Marxist-Leninist left that has taken place since the late 1950's has gone a pronounced drop-off of support for the Soviet modernization strategy among Third World Marxist-Leninists. It is not possible to measure this drift except in terms of the data on fragmentation already presented, and even these rough figures may be subject to a fairly substantial margin of error as indicators because some of the "splinter" elements have chosen to remain vague about their programs. Yet, the general evidence pointing to a decline of major dimensions is compelling. As I have already argued, a key reason for the fragmentation has been discontent with the Soviet strategy for acquiring power because of a perceived lack of suitability of various of its features to local situations, and the parties and individuals unhappy with this strategy have by and large not distinguished between it and the Soviet strategy for modernization. Rather, they have rejected both simultaneously.

In seeking more amenable modernization strategies, these parties and individuals have followed diverse courses. On the whole, for example, the pro-Chinese and pro-Cuban elements have tended to embrace the Chinese and Cuban strategies without qualifications, and these strategies have distinctive characteristics which set them apart from the Soviet strategy. For example, Mao Tse-tung has maintained that modernization brings with it functional differentiation and specialization which can result in ideological differentiation within a vanguard party; therefore, the Chinese leadership has conducted extensive campaigns aimed at "remolding" the thinking of cadres along "proper" lines. In the process, moreover, it has attached greater weight to ideological consistency than to economic performance and progress.[31] Mao has also held that modernization requires a healthy mixture of both "revolution from below" and "revolution from above." He has repeatedly stressed the basic creativity of the masses, and he has commanded those in positions of responsibility to "learn from the masses" rather than to treat them as mere objects of mobilization. In fact, this idea infused the original design for the Great Proletarian Cultural Revolution of the late 1960's.[32] The Cuban strategy, as it has evolved as a distinctive phenomenon, de-emphasizes the role of the vanguard party and relies heavily on the armed forces and the military organizational apparatus as the instrument of mobilization. It likewise assigns principal importance to moral, as opposed to material, incentives as means of mobilization.[33]

Other elements have seemed to want to combine features of different strategies—for example, Yugoslavia's economic decentralization through the establishment of worker' councils and China's emphasis on "remolding" the thought of cadres—and still others have groped toward original strategies of their own. The latter group consists of the "independent" parties and "national Communists." Among those parties which have proceeded farthest along such a road is the Communist party of Australia—no doubt because Australia, instead of being a fairly backward country, boasts many attributes of a modernized society. Since the mid-1960's, the party has acknowledged Australia's strong democratic tradition by adopting reforms aimed at doing away with "democratic centralism" within the party and by evincing a willingness to contemplate the continuation of parliamentary struggle for the implementation of "programs of basic social reform" even after the triumph of a "coalition of the left." [34] The Communist party of India (Marxist) in 1972 elaborated a concept of a "people's democratic state" which also takes into account India's present commitment to the democratic process by allowing for the preservation of representative institutions even after the party attains power.[35] As one top official has explicitly stated, "We realize that we can learn very little from the experience of the Soviet and Chinese revolutions. In the peculiar objective realities in India, we have to rely on ourselves to formulate the strategies and tactics of our revolution." [36] Since breaking away from the old-line Communist party of Venezuela in December, 1970, the Movement to Socialism (MAS)—of which Teodoro Petkoff, an outspoken critic of the USSR, is one of the principal guiding forces—has failed to chart a clear political line, but the whole rationale for its foundation was a rejection of the Soviet Union as a model for the development of socialism in Venezuela.[37] The list of parties could be expanded, but these citations will do for illustrative purposes.

A similar waning of enthusiasm about the Soviet strategy for modernization, and corresponding search for strategies of greater social relevance, has occurred among "radical" governments and parties of the Third World. Some evidence, it is true, would appear to suggest otherwise. For instance, the number of "radical" parties that have been attending the congresses of the Communist party of the Soviet Union since the late 1950's and the number of governments that Moscow has classed as "socialist" in orientation over the years has been on the rise. In 1961, three ruling parties of the Third World sent delegations to the 22nd CPSU Congress; in 1971, 12 Third World governments or ruling parties (if one counts the delegations from the two components of Tanzania—Tanganyika and Zanzibar—as separate entities) and five nonruling parties had representatives present at the 24th CPSU Congress.[38] During the first half of the 1960's, the Soviets bestowed praise on five and sometimes six "radial" Third World governments for their "socialist" aspirations.[39] As of November, 1972, the figure stands at nine.[40] But these statistics reveal more about shifting Soviet policies and standards of evaluation than about anything else, and they veil currents of a much more negative character.

To enable us to examine such currents in a coherent, meaningful fashion, we need to define the concept of "radical" or "revolutionary" governments and parties operationally and to establish a precise basepoint in time from which to make comparisons. In approaching the first task, it is imperative to distinguish between "rebellious nationalists" and "revolutionary nationalists." [41] This distinction applies most directly to elements in countries under colonial rule or some other form of outside domination. Rebellious nationalists seek merely to remove the alien rule or domination and have no commitment to reordering their societies in basic ways. Revolutionary nationalists, in contrast, propose to undertake major systematic changes in their lands. In countries which have already gained their sovereignty—whether recently or in the distant past—the application becomes somewhat more complex. Rebellious nationalists there want to steer a national course free from foreign interference but do not intend to carry out extensive internal reforms. Revolutionary nationalists, on the other hand, go a step farther and advocate a large-scale revamping of their societies. Jomo Kenyatta and the other leaders of the Kenya African National Union in Kenya qualify as "rebellious nationalists"; Sékou Touré and the rest of the hierarchy of the Parti Démocratique de Guinée in Guinea fall into the category of "revolutionary nationalists." The importance of the distinction lies in the fact that only for the "revolutionary nationalists" would the Soviet strategy for modernization logically have much appeal. Therefore, in the context of this paper, it appears justifiable to restrict the concept of "radical" or "revolutionary" governments and parties to those at least verbally dedicated to a thorough restructuring of their native societies.

A further refinement would also seem desirable—namely, to exclude those governments and parties which do not endorse the construction of a "socialist" society. Proponents of socialism, it is true, differ greatly in their understandings of that ultimate goal. Nevertheless, the distinction between "Socialists" and "nonsocialists" does serve a useful purpose here in that it significantly narrows the range of governments and groups whose attitudes toward the Soviet modernization model we must appraise in some detail. Not all Third World "radicals" or "revolutionaries" have accepted or do accept socialism of any variety as their objective, yet the potential attractiveness of the Soviet modernization model to persons without any inclination whatsoever to embrace socialism would appear highly dubious. Therefore, we shall concentrate our attention on governments and parties formally committed to major societal changes in their countries and, at minimum, vaguely oriented toward socialism.

Fixing a date from which to begin our analysis plainly involves a certain degree of arbitrariness, but late 1962 would seem to represent the best choice in light of a couple of considerations. In the first place, the base line cannot come before the close of the 1950's, for it was only then that Moscow commenced recommending the Soviet strategy for modernization as a model to non-Marxist-Leninist forces of the Third World who wanted to bring about rapid social and economic development of their lands. Second, the flood of Third World countries rushing towards independence did not crest—especially in Africa—until the early 1960's, and it took a while for most new states to chart precise courses since many of the movements that had waged the struggles for independence embraced widely heterogeneous elements. By late 1962 all except a few of the colonial territories had won their sovereignty; moreover, one could discern an emerging political spectrum.

As of late 1962, seven independent governments and six nonruling parties of substantial consequence in their countries qualified as "radical" or "revolutionary" according to the criteria that we have just laid down. The governments included those of Algeria, Burma, Ghana, Guinea, Indonesia, Mali, and the United Arab Republic (Egypt). Among the nonruling parties were the national "commands" of the Ba'ath party in Syria and Iraq; the Movimento popular para a Libertaçao de Angola (MPLA) in Angola, the Partido Africano de Independençia a de Guiné "portuguesa" e das Ilhas de cabo Verde (PAIGC) in Portuguese Guinea (now called Guinea-Bissau), the Barisan Socialis in Singapore, and the Socialist party in Chile.[42] While one could add a number of small and relatively ephemeral groups to this last list, it would appear adequate for our purposes here to confine the discussion to those bodies of some genuine significance.

Of the total, one government and four nonruling parties evidently paid little heed to the Soviet model of modernization. President Sukarno of Indonesia voiced mounting praise for "scientific socialism," but his virulently "anti-imperialist" international line tended to turn his eyes toward Peking rather than toward Moscow.[43] The preoccupations of the nonruling parties were with pursuing the battle for power; furthermore, their orientations, like Sukarno's, did not lie in the USSR's direction. Both the Iraqi and Syrian branches of the Ba'ath party maintained staunchly independent positions.[44] The Barisan Socialis looked to the Chinese mainland for revolutionary instructions and guidance.[45] During the last part of the 1950's, the Chilean Socialist party had labeled itself "Titoist" in outlook, but after 1960 it had become increasingly fascinated with "Castroism" (which, while still highly amorphous at this early stage, already embodied the seeds of a somewhat different approach to modernization than the Soviet strategy entailed.)[46]

The remaining governments and parties, however, did accord the Soviet model for modernization a degree of weight in their calculations.[47] Discerning the actuality of this influence is far easier than characterizing or measuring it. In the case of the governments concerned, it rested basically on the perceptions of the heads of these regimes that their countries were engaged in a common enterprise with the USSR, the "building of socialism." This perception manifested itself in a number of ways. For instance, several rulers—notably Modibo Keita of Mali and Kwame Nkrumah of Ghana—were now expressing an intention to construct "scientific socialism;" others followed suit within a matter of months. Many, too, already permitted avowed Marxist-Leninists to operate within party or governmental institutions, and the rest soon did likewise. In fact, professed Marxist-Leninists sometimes occupied important posts as counselors or advisers to the top leaders. Yet none of the rulers in question here treated the Soviet strategy as a sacrosanct blueprint to be applied *in toto*. To the contrary, they by and large stressed the peculiarities of their own society and politics. Gamal Abdel Nasser, for example, accepted the proposition that the creation of a "socialist" order required the foundation of a party of cadres dedicated to this end, but when he set up the Arab Socialist Union in 1963, he endowed it with mass features which he deemed to be more in keeping with the Egyptian context than a Soviet-type vanguard party would be. In short, the leaders of these governments regarded the Soviet model of modernization as a prime source of ideas about how to handle the problems that confronted them; at the same time, they saw themselves as blazing new "socialist" trails of their own.

In the nonruling parties, the influence was somewhat more nebulous since the parties were devoting most of their energies to the advancement of their "liberation" struggles; nevertheless, the general perspectives just outlined prevailed there as well. The leaders of the two parties associated themselves with the broad international movement of "builders of socialism," and they appeared to foresee some relevance of the Soviet strategy of modernization to the post-"liberation" situations in their lands. But they by no means thought it provided exact policy prescriptions; indeed, they insisted on mapping their own distinctive courses.[48]

As of the fall of 1972, 15 governments and four nonruling parties of major significance in their countries fall into the "radical" or "revolutionary" category. Only four of the governments from the 1962 list remain—Algeria, Burma, Egypt, and Guinea. The newcomers include Ceylon (or Sri Lanka since its name change early in 1972), Chile, the People's Republic of the Congo (Brazzaville), Iraq, Libya, Peru, Somalia, Sudan, Syria, Tanzania, and the People's Democratic Republic of Yemen (Aden). Of the nonruling parties, there are three repeaters from the 1962 group—the Barisan Socialis, the MPLA, and the PAIGC. The fourth is the Frente de Libertaçao de Moçambique (FRELIMO) in Mozambique.

Despite the general increase in the total number of governments and parties, the Soviet stategy for modernization exerts less influence among them now than it did in 1962. Perhaps the only two governments whose leaders display any true feeling that they share a common endeavor with the USSR in "building socialism" are those of Chile and Ceylon. While both follow idiosyncratic strategies of modernization designed to take account of local circumstances and traditions,[49] each is a coalition regime composed of several political parties, including the pro-Soviet

Marxist-Leninists as a subordinate element. The outlooks of the rest of the governments vary considerably, but all reject the Soviet model for modernization and look elsewhere for their revolutionary inspiration. Marien Ngouabi's government in the Congo (Brazzaville) has formally declared the state a "people's republic" and proclaimed its intention to implement measures of "scientific socialism," yet the domination of the Congolese Labor Party by pro-Chinese politicians tends to orient the government toward Peking rather than Moscow.[50] The professedly Marxist-Leninist regime in the People's Democratic Republic of Yemen also leans toward Peking, though its overall revolutionary perspectives bear closest resemblance to those of Castro during his early years of power.[51] All the remainder favor approaches to modernization which they regard as fundamentally indigenous responses to indigenous conditions. The comments of Tanzania's Julius Nyerere to an interviewer early in 1972 are illustrative:

> Since 1962, the period when I used the expression "African socialism," there have been so many definitions that today I avoid this expression. Now we speak in Tanzania of "ujamaa" (solidarity) rather than of "African socialism" because of this multiplicity of definitions.
>
> But I am not saying that what we are trying to build in Tanzania is in opposition to all aspects of Marxism. It is in opposition to certain aspects only. For example, Marxism as it was conceived in the 19th century, starts from the supposition that one is dealing with a highly capitalistic society. This is the very basis of this kind of socialism. It starts from the concepts of capitalism and a proletariat [which is] fully developed. A Marxist socialism cannot be conceived of without a fully developed proletariat. It is not possible. It stands to reason, consequently, if we want to build socialism in an essentially rural economy, we will discover that certain aspects of Marxism are not adaptable to it, and in reality Marxists, including Lenin, thought exactly the same thing. . . . The other aspect, perhaps even more important from the point of view of our differences, is that to be Marxist or Communist, one must be an atheist obligatorily. . . . A position must be taken on religious matters. We do not do so. In our party we have atheists, Moslems, Christians, and people you call pagans, if you will. . . . Finally, Marxism—communism—has now become a kind of religion. It possesses a theology. Its debates are now theological. One asks: What did Marx say? And one finds the citation. . . . All this is very difficult for us to accept. Society evolves, and, in reality, we should interpret socialist thought in terms of society's progress. We cannot say: Marx said this, and therefore we will do it. There are, thus, aspects of Marxism we do not accept and others we do accept. To be sure, Marxists try to construct a classless society based on joint ownership of the means of production. That we accept.[52]

As for the nonruling parties, there has been little change in the impact of the model among them. Singapore's Barisan Socialis continue to be pro-Chinese in its outlook. The leaders of both the MPLA and PAIGC still evince a feeling that they and the Soviets possess a common purpose in bringing about the construction of socialism—a feeling no doubt bolstered by the fact that Moscow has been a major source of aid for their "liberation" struggles. FRELIMO's leadership exhibits a similar belief, probably equally reinforced by the help the USSR has extended to it.[53]

Contributing Factors

Incontestably, then, the influence of the Soviet model of development in the Third World has gone down enormously during recent years, and many Third World revolutionaries have been casting about for alternatives more in tune with local circumstances than they feel the Soviet model is. But a crucial question remains. Will this situation prove lasting, or might the future bring a dramatic reversal of it. To attempt to answer this question rationally, if tentatively, one must ponder the reasons for the decline of the Soviet model's impact to date to see what clues they may offer about the prospects for the years ahead.

It would doubtless be possible to draw up a lengthy list of factors which have had a bearing on the model's diminishing influence in the Third World, but six stand out as critical. First of all, Moscow's counsel to Third World Marxist-Leninists since the late 1950's has from time to time departed significantly from the Soviet model of development and thus implicitly acknowledged the model's limited relevance to Third World conditions. In 1959–60, for example, Moscow, convinced that revolutionary opportunities existed in Third World areas despite the weakness of Marxist-Leninist forces in most countries, devised a new strategy of takeover which would permit the local Marxist-Leninists to capitalize on these perceived opportunities. This strategy—summarized in the phrase, "the formation of states of national democracy"—combined features of "alliance and struggle" with the extant non-Marxist-Leninist leaders, particularly in the independent nations. Marxist-Leninist forces would establish or maintain functioning "united fronts" with the ruling "national-bourgeois" elements in favor of "progressive" reforms, but they would also endeavor to enhance their own positions within the fronts by pushing for more radical measures with supposed appeal to the general populace. After gradually accumulating greater and greater authority, they would finally assert their control over the state machinery, in which they would already play a major role. Wherever a separate Marxist-Leninist party was to be found, Moscow evidently contemplated that it would serve as the vanguard for the implementation of the strategy, but where none existed, Moscow apparently did not always see a necessity for organizing one. Indeed, it was sometimes clearly prepared to rely on a rather loose amalgamation of leftist elements within a broad, united front party —for example, in Guinea, Ghana, and Mali—as the requisite vanguard.[54]

Later, after the Soviets became fairly pessimistic about immediate revolutionary prospects except in those few places where radicalization actually seemed to be occurring, the predominant elements in the Soviet leadership (there was controversy on the issue from the very outset) endorsed still another road to power as legitimate, for the radicalization was resulting from shifts in the views of the more "progressive" Third World rulers rather than from the increasing sway of avowed Marxist-Leninists, who by and large remained virtually impotent in the nations concerned. Moscow suggested that these "radical" rulers, or "revolutionary democrats," might be persuaded to embrace "scientific socialism" enthusiastically, to transform their existing mass parties into vanguard parties, and to carry out wholesale social and economic reconstruction in their countries. Moreover, it urged professed Marxist-Leninists to operate within the ruling parties as "socialist" counsellors while it fashioned close ties with the parties to assist with the "educational" process, and it even went so far as to sanction the dissolution of organized Marxist-Leninist parties if that proved necessary for individual Marxist-Leninists to improve their access to the wielders of power.

Though in operational terms the USSR had discarded both these strategies by the late 1960's, the mere fact that it had embraced them as creative applications of Marxist-Leninist thought undermined the claim that the Soviet model of development possessed universal validity. So too did the aura of legitimacy that even carefully qualified Soviet praise of the programs of so-called national democracies and revolutionary democracies bestowed on these states' modernization strategies, which differed in many respects from the Soviet model. Thus, many Third World revolutionaries concluded that their own insights into the situations that faced them were at least equal, if not superior, to those of the Soviet ideologues.

Second, the USSR has adopted over the last decade less of a revolutionary and more of a power-politics approach to the outside world than it had pursued during the early post-World War II era. With its growing military and economic strength and enhanced global prestige, it has acquired a certain stake in global stability. Thus, the USSR has evinced a mounting desire to keep outbursts of violence at low levels of intensity to avoid great-power confrontations, especially with the United States. Considerations of this kind have led the Soviet leaders to urge Third World Marxist-Leninists to pursue a "peaceful" road to socialism; they have also underlain the efforts that the Soviet Union has devoted to preventing big escalations of Third World confrontations in which the USSR has become directly involved—for example, the Arab-Israeli conflict. Such policies, of course, have been anathema to large numbers of Third World revolutionaries, non-Marxist-Leninists as well as Marxist-Leninists. These revolutionaries' belief that Moscow has betrayed them and forsaken revolution, in turn, has produced highly negative attitudes toward the Soviet model among them and prompted them to hunt for alternatives to it.

Third, while the Soviet economy has not fulfilled Nikita Krushchev's 1959 prediction that "the time is not far off when the Soviet Union will catch up with the United States in per capita reproduction of major types of output" and "will have the highest living standards and the shortest working day in the world," [55] it has performed sufficiently well to transform the USSR from a "developing" country into a "developed" one. In many senses, indeed, the USSR has entered a postindustrialization phase. Whereas the economy recorded an annual rate of economic growth of about 7 percent in 1950–58, that figure fell to roughly 5 percent in 1959–65.[56] In 1966–70, it stayed at about the same level.[57] The termination of the Seven-Year Plan in 1965, in effect, marked the close of a long historical period when economic growth could be achieved by "extensive" measures such as massive inputs of capital and labor and ushered in a new stage where growth would have to depend on "intensive" development based on increased efficiency. It was recognition of this fact by the Soviet rulers that sparked their announcement in 1965 of a program of economic reforms intended to improve productivity, though the subsequent implementation of these was checkered at best and they have new been abandoned in their original form.[58]

This shift in the Soviet internal situation has tended to erode the pragmatic basis upon which many Third World revolutionaries identified with the Soviet Union, for to them the USSR has now joined the ranks of the "advanced" countries. Consequently, they have come to regard Soviet policies and experience as of little use to them in dealing with their own immediate problems. For most non-Marxist-Leninists, the feeling of a new alien quality about the USSR has been reinforced by the chariness with which Moscow has extended economic aid to non-Communist governments in the Third World since the mid-1960's. Because of shortfalls in production and other difficulties encountered during the period of the Seven-Year Plan (1959-65), the Soviet leaders bluntly informed the Third World in October, 1965, that "the peoples of the socialist countries are concentrating their main efforts on the building of socialism and communism in their own countries." [59] Since then, despite improvements in the state of the Soviet economy and insistent complaints from Third World countries, Moscow has adamantly declared that it has insufficient resources to furnish more than modest amounts of credits to the Third World.[60]

Fourth, the diverse quarrels between and among Communist states since the late 1950's have resulted in the articulation and projection to the Third World of revolutionary alternatives to the Soviet model of development. Peking has proved the most energetic and vociferous publicizer of its particular model, but others—like Havana—have demonstrated nearly the same diligence even if they have not created as much clamor. What has rendered the appearance of the alternative models especially important in the present context has been the vigorous competition that their proponents have waged with Moscow and each other to win support in the Third World for the models. This competition has forced most Third World revolutionaries to make some sort of response, and in the process of working out their responses, many have relied on their evaluations of local circumstances as their governing criteria. A substantial number of these elements have found the Soviet model wanting from such a standpoint.

Fifth, internal conditions in individual countries of the Third World have compelled the revolutionaries there to reexamine the roads that they have been pursuing. Perhaps the classic example has been the Indonesian army's onslaught against the Indonesian Communist party after the abortive coup in the fall of 1965. In a "self-criticism" of past policy, the remnants of the party Central Committee attributed the party's virtual destruction to an excessive reliance on legality and elite alliances under the leadership of D. N. Aidit. His unwillingness to organize peasant unrest and to prepare for "counterrevolutionary" violence, the document declared, had left the party defenseless. The only true road to power, it went on, was to set up a "revolutionary united front" under Communist leadership and to pursue an armed agrarian struggle in the same manner as the

Chinese had done in the 1930's and 1940's.[61] While none of the other instances has involved such dramatic circumstances, their total would amount to a fairly sizable figure.

Sixth, the Third World governments that have displayed the most enthusiasm for the Soviet model of development have registered poor records of performance. In fact, several of the regimes most notably, Ahmed Ben Bella's in Algeria, Kwame Nkrumah's in Ghana, and Mobido Keita's in Mali—have now fallen.[62] The rest have all experienced major difficulties. Such records have produced negative reactions to the Soviet model on the part of an appreciable body of Third World revolutionaries. The prevailing judgment among this group seems to be that the governments concerned have depended too heavily on alien inspiration and paid too little heed to the domestic realities confronting them.

Some General Conclusions

All the foregoing factors would appear likely to have permanent effects on the attitudes and outlooks of Third World revolutionaries, and it is their attitudes and outlooks which in the final analysis count decisively in our discussion here.[63] Moscow cannot blot out from the pages of history its experimentation with strategies of development different from the Soviet model in critical respects; nor can it change the fact that the Soviet economy has become an industrialized one, though a modification of present Soviet reluctance to furnish economic aid to the Third World might serve to mitigate the impact of this transformation. While the USSR could conceivably abandon the internal posture that it has assumed over recent years and revert to a more revolutionary stance, such a move would probably not restore the faith of many Third World revolutionaries in the Soviet Union's steadfastness as a revolutionary ally. Moreover, Moscow's adoption of such a course could well jeopardize many of the gains it has made in world politics, and the current leadership has given every sign that it feels the costs involved in this kind of step would far outweigh the benefits to be derived. The rifts between Communist states remain, and competition for support for their individual revolutionary paths persists. To be sure, some potential does exist for a reduction of tensions among them. For example, China might seek some form of rapprochement with the USSR after Mao passes from the political scene, and Cuba's economic dependence on the Soviet Union could compel it to become even more responsive to Moscow than has been the case since Soviet-Cuban relations warmed somewhat at the end of the 1960's. But even the restoration of the degree of formal communist unity that existed in early 1963 does not seem likely. Memories of local events and experiences that have turned a number of Third World revolutionaries away from the Soviet model may fade in significance as the current generation of leaders gives way to younger elements, yet it is most improbable that these events and experiences will be wholly forgotten—especially in instances where they have been as traumatic as in Indonesia. The same holds true for the performances of the governments that have been most intimately associated with the Soviet model in the past.

An examination of the causes of the decreasing interest of Third World revolutionaries in the Soviet model of development and their mounting preoccupation with finding what they deem to be better alternatives suggest that the changes of a reversal of the trend are remote. Indeed, it indicates that the trend will probably continue in the foreseeable future, though perhaps at a slightly reduced rate. If so, of course, the outcome will no doubt be further diversification of the revolutionary models espoused in Third World areas.

However, one cannot entirely rule out the possibility that Third World revolutionaries who have turned their back on the Soviet model of development might reevaluate its merits and change their attitudes toward it, for conditions in the Third World may in actuality severely limit the range of viable strategies that the local revolutionaries can adopt. Several scholars have at least implied that the goals of industrialization and modernization, particularly rapid industrialization and modernization, greatly restrict the roads that those pursuing them can take. For example, Barrington Moore, Jr., argues, on the basis of a major historical investigation, that there are only three principal routes from the preindustrial to the industrial, modern world—the bourgeois revolution (like that in Britain, France, and the United States), the conservative revolution (like that in Germany and Japan), and the communist revolution (like that in Russia and China)—and he contends that all inevitably involve high levels of violence and massive coercion.[64] Richard Lowenthal advances a less deterministic view, but he does maintain that the political systems most likely to succeed in carrying out the tasks of politically forced development are those that "combine strong governmental powers, severely limiting the representation of independent interests and the expression of independent opinions, with a modernizing ideology that legitimates these powers by invoking the urgency of material and national progress and the will of the people."[65] Other writers could be cited as well.

Unfortunately, one has no sound basis at the moment for either supporting or refuting such judgments, for there is not yet any body of scholarly work which systematically assesses present Third World situations and seeks to clarify the options inherent in them for would-be modernizers.[66] In light of the variety of models propounded by those Communists who have risen to power in their native lands essentially as a result of their own resourcefulness, I am inclined to suspect that the range of choice may be considerably wider than the above-mentioned observers seem to think, but a single piece of evidence hardly constitutes sufficient grounds for venturing a definitive conclusion on the matter. Therefore, until the issue can be resolved, prognostications about the future of the Soviet model in the Third World will have to be hedged accordingly.

Notes

1. *Zhizn' natsional'nostei,* 3 (November 24, 1918), 1, quoted in Xenia Juokoff Eudin and Robert C. North, *Soviet Russia and the East, 1920–1927: A Documentary Survey* (Stanford, 1957), 156.

2. I. I. Potekhin, "Stalinskaia teoriia kolonial'noi revolutsii i natsional'no-osvoboditel'noe dvizhenie v Tropicheskoi i Iuzhnoi Afrike," *Sovetskaia etnografiia,* 1 (1950). This paper was presented at a session of the Institute of Ethnography in 1949 to mark the 70th anniversary of Stalin's birth.

3. Report to the Supreme Soviet, November 6, 1957, in *New Times,* 46 (November 14, 1957), Documents Supplement, 26.

4. For example, Alex Inkeles, "The Soviet Union: Model for Asia?—The Social System," *Problems of Communism,* VIII, 6 (November–December, 1959), 30–38; Oleg Hoeffding, "The Soviet Union: Model for Asia?—State Planning and Forced Industrialization," *ibid.,* 38–46; Francis Seton, "Planning and Economic Growth: Asia, Africa and the Soviet Model," *Soviet Survey,* XXXI (January–March, 1960), 38–50; Alec Nove, "The Soviet Model and Underdeveloped Countries," *International Affairs* (London), XXXVII, 1 (January, 1961), 29–38; John M. Montias, "The Soviet Economic Model and the Underdeveloped Countries," in Nicolas Spulber, ed., *Study of the Soviet Economy,* Russian and Eastern European Series, XXV (Bloomington, Ind., 1961), 57–82; W. Donald Bowles, "Soviet Russia As a Model for Underdeveloped Areas," *World Politics,* XIV, 3 (April, 1962), 483–504; Alfred Zauberman, "Soviet and Chinese Strategy for Economic Growth," *International Affairs* (London), XXXVIII, 3 (July, 1962), 339–352; Kenneth W. Grundy, "Marxism-Leninism and African Underdevelopment," *International Journal,* XVII (Summer, 1962), 300–304; John H. Kautsky, ed., *Political Change in Underdeveloped Countries: Nationalism and Communism* (New York, 1962); Nicolas Spulber, "Contrasting Economic Patterns: Chinese and Soviet Development Strategies," *Soviet Studies,* XV, 1 (July, 1963), 1–16, and *Soviet Strategy for Economic Growth* (Bloomington, Ind., 1964); S. Swianiewicz, *Forced Labor and Economic Development: An Enquiry into the Experience*

of Soviet Industrialization (London, 1965); Charles K. Wilber, *The Soviet Model and Underdeveloped Countries* (Chapel Hill, 1969).

5. For a similar definition, see Zvi Gitelman, "Beyond Leninism: Political Development in Eastern Europe," *Newsletter on Comparative Studies of Communism,* V, 3 (May, 1972), 20–25.

6. Lest there be any misunderstanding about the ensuing characterization of Lenin's strategy, let me state explicitly that I am stressing its features of universal applicability. Lenin himself recognized that the differences in the situations of Russia and the "Eastern" lands would necessitate some differences in approach to the acquisition of power in the "East." For example, while the "main enemy" of the Bolsheviks had been "capitalism" and "bourgeois democracy," that of "Eastern" revolutionaries was "imperialism and colonialism;" hence, the forces with which "Eastern" revolutionaries could potentially ally themselves against the "main enemy" varied from those in the Bolshevik case. Nonetheless, Lenin did believe, as the "Theses on National and Colonial Questions" he submitted to the Second Congress of the Communist International attest, in the Bolshevik path's general validity for other countries. See his *Selected Works,* X (New York, 1938), 231–238.

7. On this aspect of the Soviet model, see Richard Lowenthal, "Soviet and Chinese Communist World Views," in Donald W. Treadgold, ed., *Soviet and Chinese Communism: Similarities and Differences* (Seattle, 1967), 383–384.

8. The quotations in this paragraph come from a speech that Stalin delivered at the First All-Union Conference of Leading Personnel of Socialist Industry on February 4, 1931. In the course of his remarks, he set forth six requisites for modernization, and the key ones are cited here. See J. V. Stalin, "The Tasks of Business Executives," *Works* XIII (Moscow, 1949), 31–44. Emphasis in the original.

9. Lenin contemplated that structure would proliferate but would coexist on a noncompetitive basis. For example, he indicated that the trade union would be "not a state organization, nor designed for coercion, but for education. It is an organization designed to draw in and to train; it is, in fact a school; a school of administration, a school of economic management, a school of communism. . . . The trade unions are a *link* between the vanguard and the masses, and by their daily work bring conviction to the masses." See his *Collected Works,* XXXII (Moscow, 1965), 20.

10. Richard Lowenthal, "Development vs. Utopia in Communist Policy," in Chalmers Johnson, ed., *Change in Communist Systems* (Stanford, 1970), 96.

11. The analysis in the next few paragraphs draws upon Walter Z. Laqueur, *Communism and Nationalism in the Middle East* (New York, 1956); Robert J. Alexander, *Communism in Latin America* (New Brunswick, N.J., 1957); A. Doak Barnett, *Communist China and Asia: A Challenge to American Policy* (New York, 1960); Alastair Davidson, *The Communist Party of Australia* (Stanford, 1969); Kevin Devlin, "Interparty Relations: Limits of 'Normalization,'" *Problems of Communism,* XX, 4 (July–August, 1971), 22–35; Colin Legum, "Africa's Contending Revolutionaries," *ibid.,* XXI, 2 (March–April, 1972), pp. 2–15; Richard F. Starr, ed., *Yearbook on International Communist Affairs 1972* (Stanford, 1972); and Bureau of Intelligence and Research, U.S. Department of State, *World Strength of the Communist Party Organizations,* 24th Annual Report (Washington, D.C., June, 1972).

12. Algeria, Argentina, Australia, Bolivia, Brazil, Burma, Ceylon, Chile, Colombia, Costa Rica, Cyprus, the Dominican Republic, Ecuador, Egypt, El Salvador, Guatemala, Haiti, Honduras, India, Indonesia, Iran, Iraq, Korea,

Lebanon, Malaya, Mexico, Morocco, New Zealand, Nicaragua, Palestine, Panama, Paraguay, Peru, the Philippines, Singapore, South Africa, Sudan, Syria, Thailand, Turkey, Tunisia, Uruguay, Venezuela, and Vietnam. In delimiting "the Third World" for purposes of this chapter, I have adopted the boundaries that most Soviet analysts seem to have in mind when they employ the term as a synonym for "the national liberation movement." These boundaries embrace Oceania but not Japan.

13. In two instances, the growth resulted from the breakup of a colonial territory at the time of independence—India into India and Pakistan, Palestine into Israel and (a portion of) Jordan—and an accompanying split in what had originally been a single party; in three other cases—Guadeloupe, Madagascar (later Malagasay Republic), and Martinique—it reflected a transformation of local branches of the French Communist party into autonomous entities. Entirely new parties appeared in Cambodia, British Guiana (later Guyana), Laos, Nepal, and Senegal. (The People's Progressive Party of British Guiana came into being in 1950, but it remained publicly ambiguous about its ideological position until 1969, when the leadership declared the body to be Marxist-Leninist in character. This long period of ambiguity enabled it to attract many non-Communists into its ranks. The Parti Africain de l'Indépendence of Senegal was founded in 1957; while it from the outset claimed to be Marxist-Leninst in nature, it did not receive formal recognition of its claim from Moscow until 1962.) The division of Korea and Vietnam into communist and noncommunist states did not produce new parties, for in both instances the party of the communist state continued to exercise fundamental control over Communists throughout what it held to be the national patrimony.

14. Here again, the increase to a certain extent mirrored processes other than the establishment of a new party. With the separation of Bangla Desh from Pakistan, the party elements in what had previously been the two sections of Pakistan emerged as independent units; and the local branch of the French Communist party in Réunion acquired autonomous status. Wholly new parties came into being in Afghanistan, Lesotho, Malta, Mauritius, Nigeria, and Saudi Arabia.

I ought to point out that the figure in the text counts Malaysia (the enlarged Malaya) as a single entity even though the Communist apparatuses on the Malay peninsula and in Sarawak apparently are relatively independent of each other. It also excludes states or territories which have at least a Marxist-Leninist cell if no formal party. Ten countries fall into this category—Angola, the People's Republic of the Congo (Brazzaville), Ethiopia, Guinea, Guinea-Bissau, Mali, Mozambique, Somalia, Yemen, and the People's Democratic Republic of Yemen (Aden).

15. The closest things to exceptions may have been the parties in Malaya, Singapore, and Thailand, all composed basically of overseas Chinese. It seems highly unlikely, however, that these parties took their cues on revolutionary strategy solely or even principally from the Chinese Communists. The Malayan party, for example, launched an insurrection in 1948 only after Moscow had given the green light for such undertakings, though the Malayans had been preparing for such a venture since the war days. Moreover, once the insurgency had failed, the party conducted negotiations with government officials in the mid-1950's about the possibility of laying down its arms and coming out of the jungle in return for legalization. In neither Singapore nor Thailand did the parties visibly attempt to build up guerrilla bands during the 1940's or 1950's. See Barnett, *op. cit.*, 485–491.

16. The Trotskyite movement in Third World countries has received only spotty scholarly attention. For some of the more important work done on the subject, see Alexander, *op. cit., passim,* and Robert J. Alexander,, "El Trotskismo

en la América Latina," *Problemas Internacionales,* XIX, 3 (Washington, D.C., May–June, 1972), 15–31; George J. Lerski, *Origins of Trotskyism in Ceylon: A Documentary History of the Lanka Sama Samaja Party, 1935–1942* (Stanford, 1968). Only in Bolivia and Ceylon did the Trotskyite parties enjoy any substantial political following in the mid-1940's. See Alexander, *Communism in Latin America,* 20–21.

17. On this fundamental tenet of Maoist thought, see Lowenthal, "Soviet and Chinese Communist World Views," *op. cit.,* 384–386.

18. For a good explication of the Cuban strategy for revolutionary takeover, see Ernesto F. Betancourt, "Exporting the Revolution to Latin America," in Carmelo Mesa-Lago, ed., *Revolutionary Change in Cuba* (Pittsburgh, 1971), 113–117.

19. See Davidson, *op. cit.* 169-172; Devlin, op. cit., 28–29; and *Australian Left Review* (Sydney, 1970–1972.)

20. See Bhabani Sen Gupta, "Indian Communism and the Peasantry," *Problems of Communism,* XXV, 1 (January–February, 1972), 1–17.

21. It should be underscored that the term "peaceful" here does not exclude the use of violence in ways short of a resort to arms. Strikes, demonstrations, and the like fall within the purview of acceptable methods, and they can often take on dimensions that go well beyond normal definitions of "peaceful." The modification in positions, in short, is a matter of degree and not kind. Nonetheless, the shift has considerable importance from the standpoint of faithfulness to the Soviet model of obtaining power, for that model entails an ultimate armed showdown to wrest the reins of authority from the extant "bourgeois" government.

22. Bhabani Sen Gupta, "India's Rival Communist Models," *Problems of Communism,* XXII, 1 (January–February, 1973), 1–15.

23. Even when local parties or international Communist sources have published membership claims, these claims have in most cases run vastly higher than the most alarmist of non-Communist estimates. Consequently, one has to rely by and large on the educated guesses of knowledgeable persons.

24. For instance, the estimates sometimes list figures for each individual party in a specific country; sometimes, for all parties collectively; sometimes, for just the major parties; and so forth.

25. The latter total differs somewhat from the sum of the figures for Asia and Oceania, the Near East and South Asia, Latin America, and Africa given on p. viii of the 1972 edition of *World Strength of the Communist Party Organizations,* for I have adjusted the amount to take care of two factors. First, the figures for Asia and Oceania and for the Near East and South Asia include the members of the Japanese and Greek parties, respectively; and none of the regional totals cover the adherents of the party in Malta. Second, some of the country estimates, especially for Latin American nations, do not incorporate the members of certain parties not oriented toward Moscow. (For an explanation of the manner in which the adjustment for the second factor was carried out, see footnote *b* in Table 8–3.)

26. Those within the Communist party of India had probably been the most extensive. For details, see John H. Kautsky, *Moscow and the Communist Party of India* (Cambridge, Mass., 1956); Gene D. Overstreet and Marshall Windmiller, *Communism in India* (Berkeley, 1959).

27. This amount constitutes the sum for the pro-Soviet parties in Colombia, the Dominican Republic, Guatemala, Haiti, Jordan, Saudi Arabia, South Africa, and Sudan.

28. The total is for the parties in El Salvador, Iraq, and Syria.

29. This figure covers the pro-Soviet parties in Algeria, Argentina, Bolivia, Brazil, Ecuador, Honduras, Iran, Lesotho, Morocco, Nicaragua, Nigeria, Panama,

Paraguay, Peru, the Philippines, Senegal, Tunisia, and Turkey.

30. K. Brutents, "The Regenerated East," *New Times,* 45 (November, 1958), 5–7.

31. See, for instance, Mao's February, 1957, speech "On the Correct Resolution of Contradictions Among the People" (New China News Agency, June 18, 1957); H. F. Schurmann, "Organizational Principles of the Chinese Communists," *The China Quarterly* (London), 2 (April–June, 1960), 47–58, and *Ideology and Organization in Communist China* (Berkeley, 1966); Lowenthal, "Soviet and Chinese Communist World Views," *op. cit.,* 387–389; Tang Tsou, "The Cultural Revolution and the Chinese Political System," *The China Quarterly,* 38 (April–June, 1969), 63–91.

32. For further discussion, see Tang Tsou, *op. cit.*; Maurice Meisner, "Leninism and Maoism: Some Populist Perspectives on Marxism-Leninism in China," *The China Quarterly,* 45 (January–March, 1971), 2–36.

33. For relevant analysis, see James M. Malloy, "Generation of Political Support and Allocation of Costs," in Mesa-Lago, *op. cit.,* 25–42; Edward Gonzales, "Castro: The Limits of Charisma," *Problems of Communism,* XX, 4 (July–August, 1970), 12–24.

34. The new organizational system within the party permits factions to operate, renders all national executive decisions subject to the scrutiny and approval of the rank-and-file members, and replaces the old Central Committee, Political Committee, and Secretariat with a National Committee, which has a secretary. For these details and other aspects of the party's modernization strategy, see Davidson, *op. cit.,* 167–172, *and Australian Left Review* (1970–72).

35. See Sen Gupta, "India's Rival Communist Models," *op. cit.*

36. Quoted in Sen Gupta, "Communism and the Indian Peasantry," *op. cit.,* 2.

37. For brief descriptions of the MAS's origins and recent behavior, see Bureau of Intelligence and Research, U.S. Department of State, *World Strength of the Communist Party Organizations,* 23rd Annual Report (Washington, D.C., May, 1971), 246–248; the 1972 volume of the same series, *op. cit.,* 158–159; Devlin, *op. cit.,* 31; and Starr, *op. cit.,* 445–450.

38. Those parties with delegations at the 22nd Congress were the Convention People's Party, of Ghana; the Parti Démocratique de Guinée, of Guinea; and the Union Soudanaise, of Mali. The governments and ruling parties at the 24th Congress included the Chilean Socialist Party; the Congolese Labor Party, of the Congo (Brazzaville); the Arab Socialist Union, of Egypt; the PDG, of Guinea; the Ba'ath Party of Iraq; the Parti du Peuple Mauritanien, of Mauritania; the Supreme Revolutionary Council of the Somali Republic; the Revolutionary Council of the Sudan; the Ba'ath Party of Syria; the Tanganyika African National Union, of Tanzania; the Afro-Shirazi Party (Zanzibar), of Tanzania; and the National Front of the People's Democratic Republic of Yemen (Aden). (At that time, two delegations—those from the Sudan and the Somali Republic—came from governments because these regimes had not yet established formal parties as foundations for their rule. This situation has since changed in the Sudan.) Among the nonruling parties were the Movimento Popular para a Libertaçao de Angola, of Angola, the Partido Africano de Independençia a de Guiné "portuguesa" e das Ilhas de Cabo Verde, of Guinea-Bissau; the Democratic Party of Kurdistan; the Frente de Libertaçao de Moçambique, of Mozambique; and the African National Congress, of South Africa. See *Pravda* (October 25 and 26, 1961, and March 31, 1971). For some comparative analysis of the 22nd, 23rd, and 24th Congresses, see Christian Duevel, "Balance Sheet of Foreign Parties Attending 24th CPSU Congress," *Radio Liberty Research* (Munich, March 31, 1971).

39. The group encompassed Algeria, Burma, Ghana, Mali, the U.A.R. (Egypt), and sometimes Guinea. For a typical example, see "Soiuz sil sotsializma i natsional'no-osvoboditel'nogo dvizheniia," *Kommunist,* 8 (May, 1964), 7–8.

40. Algeria, Burma, the People's Republic of the Congo (Brazzaville), Egypt, Guinea, Iraq, Somalia, Syria, and Tanzania. For the most authoritative recent listing—by the deputy chairman of the International Section of the Central Committee Secretariat—see R. Ul'ianovskii, "Sotsial'no-ekonomicheskie problemy osvobodivshikhsia stran," *ibid.,* 8 (May, 1972), 89.

41. For a similar distinction, see Robert D. Crane, "Revolutionary Nationalism: An Instrument of Systematic Change in the Third World," Hudson Institute Discussion Paper (January 22, 1968).

42. Although the Ba'ath party had an "international command" in accordance with its claims to embrace the entire Arab world, the various "national commands" in the final analysis constituted its most important elements; the strength of the party in these terms lay principally in Iraq and Syria. The MPLA was both the oldest and one of the two main "national-liberation" groups in Angola. The PAIGC dominated the "national-liberation" movement in Portuguese Guinea. The Barisan Socialis posed a severe challenge to Lee Kuan Yew's ruling People's Action Party in Singapore. Chile's Socialist Party was one of the country's leading opposition groups; its candidate for president in the 1959 election had nearly bested his more conservative rivals.

43. For relevant analysis, see Guy J. Pauker, "Indonesia: Internal Development or External Expansion?" *Asian Survey,* III (February, 1963), 69–75; Arnold C. Brackman, "The Malay World and China: Partner or Barrier?" in A. M. Halpern, ed., *Policies Toward China: Views from Six Continents* (New York, 1965), 280–288.

44. See, for example, Kamel S. Abu Jaber, *The Arab Ba'ath Socialist Party* (Syracuse, 1966); George Lenczowski, *Soviet Advances in the Middle East* (Washington, D.C., 1972), Chaps. 6 and 7.

45. On this general subject, see Alex Joseph, "The Struggle for Singapore," *Far Eastern Economic Review,* XXXIV, 5 (1961), 263–265; and "Singapore's Extreme Left Wing," *ibid,.* XXXVIII (December 6, 1962), 525–529.

46. See, for instance, Ernst Halperin, *Nationalism and Communism in Chile* (Cambridge, Mass., 1965), 137–155.

47. The ensuing judgments derive from an exploration of a wide body of literature dealing with "socialism" and "socialist" forces in the Third World. A representative sampling would include Malcolm Kerr, "The Emergence of a Socialist Ideology in Egypt," *Middle East Journal,* XVI, 2 (Spring, 1962), 127–144; Manfred Halpern, *The Politics of Social Change in the Middle East and North Africa* (Princeton, 1963); Fred R. von der Mehden, "The Burmese Way to Socialism," *Asian Survey,* III, 3 (March, 1963), 129–135; William H. Friedland and Carl G. Rosberg, Jr., *African Socialism* (Stanford, 1964), especially Chaps. VII–X; Colin Legum, "What Kind of Radicalism for Africa?" *Foreign Affairs,* XLIII, 2 (January, 1965), 237–250; Waldemar A. Nielsen, *African Battleline* (New York, 1965); Charles Issawi, "The Arab World's Heavy Legacy," *Foreign Affairs,* XLIII, 3 (April, 1965), 501–512; Jaber, *op. cit.;* P. J. Vatikiotis, ed., *Egypt Since the Revolution* (New York, 1968); Robert Legvold, *Soviet Policy in West Africa* (Cambridge, Mass., 1970); David and Marina Ottaway, *Algeria: The Politics of a Socialist Revolution* (Berkeley, 1970); Mya Maung, "The Burmese Way to Socialism Beyond the Welfare State," *Asian Survey,* X (June, 1970), 533–551; Lawrence D. Stifel, "Burmese Socialism: Economic Problems of the First Decade," *Pacific Affairs,* XLV, 1 (Spring, 1972), 60–74.

48. In this connection, it is worth recording that one astute Western observer has described Amilcar Cabral, the late head of the PAIGC, as among the Third World's most important revolutionary thinkers. See Colin Legum, "Africa's Contending Revolutionaries," 11.

49. For example, Socialist Salvador Allende, winner of the 1970 presidential election in Chile, told the country at his inauguration in November, 1970: "We Chileans are proud of having managed to choose the political path instead of violence. . . . We have always preferred to solve social conflicts with the resources of persuasion, with political action. We Chileans reject in the deepest part of our conscience fratricidal struggles, but without ever renouncing the duty to secure the rights of the people. . . . My government will respond to this confidence [the popular will] by keeping the democratic tradition of our people true and solid." (Radio Santiago broadcast, November 5, 1970.)

50. See, for instance, Arthur H. House, "Brazzaville: Revolution or Rhetoric?" *Africa Report,* XVI, 4 (April, 1971), 18–21.

51. For a brief evalution, see D. C. Watt, "The Persian Gulf—Cradle of Conflict?" *Problems of Communism,* XXI, 3 (May–June, 1972), 32–40.

52. Interview by Peter Enahoro, *Jeune Afrique* (Tunis, January 15, 1972). In addition to the more recent items cited in n. 47, see Josef Silverstein, "Political Dialogue in Burma: A New Turn on the Road to Socialism?" *Asian Survey,* X, 2 (February, 1970), 133–141; C. P. Cook, "Burma: The Era of Ne Win," *The World Today,* XXVI, 6 (June, 1970), 255–266; Jane and Idrian Resnick, "Tanzania Educates for a New Society," *Africa Report,* XVI, 1 (January, 1971), 26–29; John Badgley, "The Union of Burma: Age Twenty Two," *Asian Survey,* XI, 2 (February, 1971), 149–157; Marcel Niedergang, "Revolutionary Nationalism in Peru," *Foreign Affairs,* XLIX, 3 (April, 1971), 454–463; Peter Mansfield, "Egypt after Nasser," *The World Today,* XXVII, 7 (July, 1971), 302–309; Colin Legum, "Sudan's 'Three-day Revolution,'" *Africa Report,* XVI, 7 (October, 1971), 12–15; Lenczowski, *op cit.;* Robert Stephen's interview with President Muammar al-Qaddafi of Libya, *The Observer* (London, January 30, 1972); John Badgley, "Burma: The Army Vows Legitimacy," *Asian Survey,* XII, 2 (February, 1972), 177–181; Jim Hoagland, "Iraq's Oil Crisis: A Battle of Wills with High Stakes," *Washington Post* (July 23, 1972). During the period 1966–70, when the left wing of the Syrian Ba'athists held power, the line between Ba'ath and Soviet strategies of modernization got rather blurred, but with the restoration of a more moderate Ba'ath leadership in Damascus in 1970, the distinction sharpened once again.

The modifications in the attitudes of the four governments that had shown some interest in the Soviet model of modernization in 1962 flowed from several causes. In Algeria, Houari Boumedienne overthrew President Ahmed Ben Bella in 1965, and Boumedienne proved less radical than his predecessor. Egypt had already begun to disassociate its Arab socialism from any connection with the Soviet model before Nasser's death in 1970, because the Soviets had waxed more critical of the Egyptian version of socialism than they had once been, but the succession of the more moderate Anwar Sadat to the presidency ensured the completion of the process. In Burma and Guinea, largely internal problems and pressures impelled the existing rulers to revise their thinking.

53. See Legum, "Africa's Contending Revolutionaries," 10–12.

54. For more extensive discussion of the points in this paragraph and the next one, see my "The Soviet Union, Communist China, and Ghana, 1955–1966," unpublished Ph.D. dissertation, Columbia University (1971), especially Chaps. II, IV, and VI. For other treatments of the same topics, see Legvold, *op. cit.;* Richard

Lowenthal, "On 'National Democracy': I. Its Function in Communist Policy," *Survey,* 47 (April, 1963), 119–134, and "Russia, the One-Party System, and the Third World," in *ibid.,* 58 (January, 1966), 43–58; Uri Ra'anan, "Moscow and the Third World," *Problems of Communism,* XIV, 1 (January–February, 1965), 22–37; Donald S. Zagoria, "Russia, China and the New States," in *Soviet and Chinese Communism: Similarities and Differences,* 405–425. My own interpretations, however, differ in some respects from the ones in these.

55. *Pravda* (November 15, 1958).

56. Stanley H. Cohn, *Economic Development in the Soviet Union* (Lexington, Mass., 1970), 61.

57. Douglas Diamond, "Principal Targets and Central Themes of the Ninth Five-Year Plan," in Norton T. Dodge, ed., *Analysis of the USSR's 24th Party Congress and 9th Five-Year Plan* (Mechanicsville, Md., 1971), 48.

58. For a good analysis, see Gertrude E. Schroeder, "Soviet Economic Reform at an Impasse," *Problems of Communism,* XX, 4 (July–August, 1971), 36–46.

59. *Pravda* (October 27, 1965). For discussion of the general situation facing Soviet leaders, see R. A. Yellon, "The Winds of Change," *Mizan,* IX, 2 (London, March–April, 1967), 51–57, and 4 (July–August, 1967), 155–173.

60. For a particularly emphatic statement, see Lev Stepanov's article on the subject in *Mirovaia ekonomika i mezhdunarodnye otnosheniia,* 6 (June, 1968), 64–71.

61. *Indonesian Tribune,* as quoted in *Peking Review* (July 21, 1967), 14–15, 20.

62. For details, see my "The Soviet Union, Communist China, and Ghana, 1955–1966," Chap. VI; Legvold, *op. cit.,* Chap. VII and VIII; Ottaway and Ottaway, Chap. IX.

63. Human purpose, I believe, has figured far too little in the theoretical writings on political change in recent years. It is true, as Chalmers Johnson has pointed out, that whether or not revolutionaries succeed depends upon instabilities or "dysfunctionalities" in the social systems in which they operate. (See his *Revolution and the Social System* [Stanford, 1964] and *Revolutionary Change* [Boston, 1966].) But, as he recognizes, imperatives in the system do not necessarily predetermine how the revolutionaries will manage to come to power, what kind of change they will try to accomplish, and how they will seek to bring it about. To put the point in a positive way, much of political change "is fashioned by men who can exercise a choice between multiple cases of evolution," and "it is the social scientist's function to ascertain the margin of human choice and to clarify the choices in that margin." (See Danquart Rustow, "Communism and Change," in Chalmers Johnson, ed., *Change in Communist Systems* [Stanford, 1970], 358.)

64. *Social Origins of Dictatorships and Democracy: Lord and Peasant in the Making of the Modern World* (Boston, 1966).

65. "Development vs. Utopia in Communist Policy," 38–39.

66. Samuel P. Huntington offers some suggestive insights in his "Social and Institutional Dynamics of One-Party Systems," in Samuel P. Huntington and Clement H. Moore, eds., *Authoritarian Politics in Modern Society* (New York, 1970), 3–47. However, his focus here is quite narrow—the formation and functioning of one-party systems.

CHAPTER 9

Eastern Europe and the Soviet Union: Convergence and Divergence in Historical Perspective

Paul Shoup

The growth of comparative communist studies has opened a new perspective in our understanding of the political process in the Soviet Union and the countries of Eastern Europe. Scholars making comparisons have nevertheless been slow to address themselves to the problem of similarities and differences between the Soviet Union and Eastern Europe and whether, within the boundaries of the communist world in Europe, there is a pattern of convergence or divergence between the political, social, and economic institutions and structures of the two areas.[1]

There are a number of reasons for the reluctance to discuss Eastern Europe and the Soviet Union as comparable areas. One is the existence of great differences in respect to the social and cultural traditions, levels of development, and, in the case of Yugoslavia, political institutions, within Eastern Europe itself. A second consideration—quite different from the first—is the similarity between the governmental and political systems of the Soviet Union and the Eastern European countries under Soviet influence. A third factor which has worked to discourage methodical comparisons of Eastern Europe and the Soviet Union is the assumption that it is the differences, rather than the similarities between the two areas which require emphasis, and that those similarities which do exist are the result of Soviet military and political controls over the Eastern European communist states. The point was emphasized several years ago by Ghita Ionescu in his pioneering work on comparative political institutions in Eastern Europe. In essence, Ionescu took the position that the political culture of Eastern Europe is Western; that it rests on a *Bewusst-*

sein, a sometimes suppressed but never completely extinguished respect for pluralistic forms of social and political life, as well as for the institutions which express that pluralism.[2]

This chapter will explore certain aspects of the problem of making comparisons between Eastern Europe and the Soviet Union, focusing on developmental problems, the changing social structures of the two areas, and the cultural and economic differences which have both separated Eastern Europe from the Soviet Union and divided the Eastern Europeans among themselves. Our hope is to show that the two areas have had much in common in the past, in respect to the modernization experience and its political consequences, and that after World War II they have been deeply influenced by a common social system, while older, prewar, cultural and economic differences have been reduced. At the same time we are concerned with pointing out the differences that continue to exist between the two areas, and suggesting the reasons why the process of economic development in the postwar period has tended to follow somewhat divergent paths in Eastern Europe and the Soviet Union, rather than showing signs of growing convergence. The political dimension of these problems will be alluded to in the course of the discussion and examined separately in the concluding remarks of the essay.

Because the essay is concerned with implications of the modernization process, there is a temptation to focus on theoretical models, and in so doing to impute a "teleological nexus" to the analysis. An attempt is made to avoid this pitfall by focusing on historical trends and referring wherever possible to empirical data which permit comparisons between the Soviet Union and Eastern Europe. Nevertheless, it must be realized that certain assumptions concerning the nature of modernization do play a role in the discussion. As used here, the term modernization refers primarily to the process of economic development. At the same time, we are concerned with modernization in a broader sense: as a type of basic change involving the transformation of society as a result of rising living standards, greater social mobility, improved health and education, and the diminishing influence of traditional forms of social behavior. Thus the term modernization as used in this chapter is not limited simply to problems of economic growth, or industrialization, but refers to those types of changes which are today associated with the "development experience," [3] and include, as part of one process, interrelated social, economic, and cultural factors.

One further distinction must be made before proceeding with the discussion, that between the terms "backwardness," and "modernization."

Broadly speaking, the two concepts focus on different aspects of the same problem, and no sharp distinctions will be made between the situations to which each will apply. Nevertheless, the importance of backwardness in the Soviet and Eastern European cases lies in certain special qualities which are associated with that term: first, its relative nature (in this case, the generally inferior position of Eastern Europe and the Soviet Union vis-à-vis Western Europe); secondly, the suggestion that it reflects a state of awareness in a society of its own relative lack of development; and thirdly, the fact that backwardness is often associated with a transitional stage of development associated with rural overpopulation and the early stages of industrialization. It is these factors, therefore, which will be stressed when the problems of backwardness are analyzed. As was true in the case of modernization, the problem of backwardness will be considered in the pages to follow as a social and cultural problem, as well as an economic one.

Eastern Europe and Russia Prior to World War II

From an examination of the literature dealing with Eastern Europe and Russia prior to World War II, it will be found that comparisons involving the two regions dealt to a far greater degree than today with underlying differences that were thought to exist—quite independently of political frontiers—between the societies and political systems with a Western tradition and those of the East. As Professor Seton Watson has pointed out in a recent essay, the dividing line between East and West was not thought to lie between Russia and Eastern Europe, but within Eastern Europe, itself, either along a line approximating the cultural and political boundary between the Western empires of Austro-Hungary and Germany on the one hand and Russia and Turkey on the other, or in accordance with an economic division between the more prosperous and advanced West and the more backward East.[4]

This idea of an Eastern Europe divided into two zones, one Eastern and one Western, became deeply embedded in the thinking of many Eastern Europeans, who saw themselves and their nations as outposts of Western civilization and who, as a consequence, often viewed their Eastern neighbors, as well as the Russians, as representatives of Eastern primitivism. While this view lent itself to great exaggeration, even among Western scholars, it is interesting to note that data gathered before World War II supported the notion of increasing backwardness, the further one moved eastward. Statistics on birthrates, child mortality, the relative size of the agricultural population, and the amount of surplus labor in rural areas showed an unmistakable spatial dimension. As one moved east (and south), indices of births and child mortality rose; the percentage of the population employed in agriculture increased, the degree of overpopulation employed in agriculture increased, and the degree of overpopulation of the countryside became greater. In a word, backwardness grew more pronounced.[5]

The change about which we are speaking was not recognizable only along a west-east axis, however. Rather the phenomenon of backwardness was one which could be represented pictorially as a series of concentric rings spreading outward from Great Britain and northwestern Europe, and therefore involving a north-south element, as well as a west-east one. The existence of a north-south problem could also be seen within certain areas of the Eastern European countries of the interwar period; Transylvania was more advanced that Wallachia; northern Bulgaria had a lower birthrate than portions of the country lying to the south, and, of course, northwestern Yugoslavia was profoundly separated by cultural and economic differences from the backward southeastern parts of the country. There were exceptions, of course. Poland and Hungary both had poorer regions in the northern portions of their respective countries (but were also divided along the west-east axis). In Russia proper the distinction between west and east did not relate to the country's economic problems. Siberia, for example, although lacking in industry, was never a backward area but rather a frontier. Backwardness was most pronounced in the Black Earth regions of central Russia, in Central Asia, and the portions of White Russia and the Ukraine. In purely cultural terms the west-east axis had a certain logic, however, for the vast spaces of the country did cut off the interior from Western influences.

If Eastern Europe and the Soviet Union are examined over time, and in terms of the problem of development, a different picture emerges from that we just presented. Now west-east differences essentially disappear, and Russia (and following her, the Soviet Union), appear closely linked to the Eastern European experience. Neither convergence or divergence seem to explain this phenomenon, but rather a parallelism in which both regions find themselves faced with common problems of overcoming backwardness. Until the great turning point marked by the collectivization of agriculture in the Soviet Union (and even, to a certain extent, after this event), the countries of Eastern Europe and the Soviet Union pursue not dissimilar programs in seeking solutions to their difficulties.

In the interwar period up to 1928, the parallelism has definite elements of a pattern of modernization which is neither east nor west, but is that of the group of newly emerging nations, latecomers to the industrialization process.

This shared set of experiences can be traced back to the initially slow penetration of industrialization into Eastern Europe and Russia, the impact of the demographic revolution, which resulted in growing pressures on the land, and the active intervention of the state in fostering economic development. The results were, of course, not the same in the case of each individual country, and it would be presumptuous to try to summarize such a complicated phenomenon in a region with such great contrasts.[6] Nevertheless, prior to World War I, the modernization process in Eastern Europe and Russia held out hopes for balanced growth. It is interesting to observe, in this connection, the beginnings of a spontaneous modernization process emerging in a parallel fashion in Eastern Europe and Russia around the turn of the century, notwithstanding increased population pressures, the growth of government bureaucracies, and the intensification of nationalistic currents. In both areas there is the hint of a new era of sustained economic growth, the spread of political tolerance, the emergence of a modern party system, and last but perhaps most important, the appearance of a more diversified society anchored in a newly educated urban middle class. Gerschenkron describes the economic expansion of the period 1906–1914 in Russia as one in which the peasant is freed to move to the towns, the quantity of bread grains available for domestic consumption rises, and entrepreneurial attitudes begin to develop. "The industrialization between 1906 and 1914," in his words, "no longer offers a picture of a race against time, and of a progressive exhaustion in physical and mental terms of the population's power to suffer and endure." [7] In Hungary during the same time, as Alexander Eckstein has shown, there was a period of balanced growth (that is, an increase in output in both the agricultural and industrial sectors) which has not been equalled since.[8] In Bulgaria, T. Tchitchovsky spoke of the period of Bulgarian politics prior to World War I as a time "of organic growth and consolidation [when] a spirit of tolerance and courtesy gradually permeated the relations between political parties and coalition governments became possible." [9]

Following World War I, this fragile modernization process along Western European lines broke down. At the same time, the politics of Eastern Europe and the Soviet Union began to diverge sharply. Eastern Europe witnessed a period of national consolidation following the redrawing of political boundaries, a process which was essentially conservative, but allowed a great deal of freedom for social and political forces to confront one another, while giving the East European peoples at least a rudimentary experience in parliamentary government. The Bolshevik revolution marked a radicalization of Russian politics and the wedding of the traditions of Russian despotism to the techniques of one party rule. While the one-party system in the Soviet Union encouraged a trend toward greater social and political mobilization of the masses as a means of strengthening the new regime against the traditional but at the same time more educated and in many ways more Western elements in Russian society, the political situation in Eastern Europe encouraged a reverse trend, in which the "mobilization" of popular feelings by the multi-party system was gradually curtailed for the sake of political stability. In both areas, however, political development was marked by the growing role of the state, heightened national tensions (partially as a consequence of social mobilization and partly as the result of the international situation), and an increasing gap between the city and the countryside. In preserving a modicum of democracy is was undoubtedly true that the countries of Eastern Europe were showing a greater affinity for and understanding of Western political styles. But both the Soviet Union and the countries of Eastern Europe faced a common set of pressures shaped by their rather similar social and economic problems, which in turn reflected the fact that they were at approximately the same stage of economic development.

This point becomes clearer when certain parallels between the developmental process in the Soviet Union and Eastern Europe between the two world wars are noted. One was the appearance, in both countries, of the peasant as a significant social and political force in the 1920's, followed by the return to totally urban-based politics in the 1930's. In Eastern Europe this phenomenon was closely associated with the broadening of the franchise and the introduction of the multiparty system. The peasant, in these overwhelmingly agrarian societies, at once became the object of intense political interest. The strong traditions of the peasantry and the radical trends after World War I broke, for a time, the hold of the urban middle classes over the political party structure and made possible the emergence of independent peasant parties. In the Soviet Union many of the same forces were at work. The peasantry gained possession of the land after the revolution and were a strong enough force to compel the Bolsheviks to adopt a "face to the countryside" policy during the mid-1920's. Although the growth of peasant incomes in the Soviet Union lagged behind that of the workers, the peasants were able slowly to regain prewar levels of production by 1928.[10] At the same time, the question of the willingness of the peasant to provide the cities with grain played an important role in the economic deliberations of the Bolsheviks until 1928 and the termination of NEP.

The peasant revolution in Eastern Europe and the Soviet Union lost momentum as the urban elites reestablished their control over the countryside. In both areas the drive to industrialize became the dominant theme. This expansion was financed at the expense of the peasantry, not only in the Soviet Union, but in Eastern Europe, as well. In Hungary this was reflected in a process of disinvestment which took place in the agricultural sector during the interwar period, the price of the "billion pengo plan" aimed at building up Hungarian defense industries and promoting industralization.[11]

The period between the two world wars also saw the Soviet Union and the countries of Eastern Europe take steps to improve social services. While it is difficult to compare the two areas in respect to programs in such fields as education and health,[12] one can suggest that both the Soviet Union and the Eastern European states in the interwar period were engaged in a two-fold task of improving human capital while encouraging economic expansion. To the extent that this was the case, developments in the area anticipated an approach to the modernization process which was to become common in the third world after the war, and which differed, in certain respects, from the style of development characteristic of Western Europe in the nineteenth century.[13]

Collectivization of the land in the Soviet Union ended the period of what we have called parallel problems and parallel responses to modernization in Eastern Europe and the Soviet Union. Such a step was impossible to envisage under the conditions that prevailed in Eastern Europe prior to the Communists' seizure of power. Not only was the apparatus with which to carry out such a policy lacking, but strong populist currents among the peasantry and a segment of the intellectuals[14] and the interests of the conservative regimes in preserving the status quo made such draconian measures unthinkable. At the same time, there were still, in the 1930's, important parallels between the Soviet Union and the Eastern European states. Although the social systems of the Soviet Union and Eastern Europe were shaped by radically different principles, the main groups in both societies (the bureaucracy, intellectuals, workers, and peasants) were the same and displayed may similar attributes. In both areas, life in the countryside was little affected by modernization,[15] while the sacrifices of the collectivization period in the Soviet Union had a parallel in the sufferings of the Eastern European peasantry during the depression. As we have seen, furthermore, a number of the schemes for industrialization launched in Eastern Europe in the 1930's were motivated by the same considerations which guided the policy of forced industrialization in the Soviet Union.

It should be noted, finally, that in the extended controversy over economic development that went on in the interwar period in Eastern Europe, the Soviet experiment did not receive the kind of blanket condemnation that one might have anticipated. Collectivization was not necessarily criticized on the grounds for which it is attacked today, namely, that it laid the basis for a command economy which was inherently inefficient and could not compete with the industrial nations of the West. As a solution to the problems of backwardness, the Soviet approach was seen as workable, but involving sacrifices of a type which the Eastern Europeans were not ready to accept. This view was well expressed by the Rumanian economist Mihail Manoilesco, a champion of industrialization as the solution to the problems of southeastern Europe:

> If domestic consumption, as in the Soviet Union, could be markedly reduced, that is, to approximately one quarter, in the countryside, and one third in the cities, then Rumania could, with greater exports of foodstuffs, realize a surplus of imports of industrial investments of 22 billion lei and triple its present investments in the course of three years. . . . This example shows how great in an agrarian country are the sources of national income in comparison to invested capital, and to what degree a centralized and ruthless economic leadership can shorten the stages of natural industrialization at the expense of the standard of living of the people. This explains the great possibilities of the "Soviet phenomenon" in the southeast European framework. . . .[16]

Manoilesco rejected this solution to the problem of southeastern Europe on the grounds that the costs would be too great and would exhaust the physical and spiritual resources of the peoples. On the other hand, he predicted that Rumania could become the "Japan of Europe" if she followed the Soviet course:

> The reduction in prices of industrial products produced in southeastern [Europe] can go so far in certain sectors that it is possible to think of an industrial offensive, that is, an energetic, forced, dumping-type of exporting. In particular the Rumanians could, thanks to cheap labor and their incredibly diverse sources of energy, take over the role of a European Japan and flood Europe with certain industrial products at dirt-cheap prices.[17]

In one sense Manoilesco's views were prophetic, for he anticipated elements of the developmental strategy which were to be used in Rumania in the 1960's. On the other hand, his analysis overlooked the fact that the system of planning introduced in the Soviet Union was extremely crude and concealed a command-type economy; that the Soviet system did not promote economic efficiency and still less the creation of an industrial sector which could compete on foreign markets (which was in any case not the Soviet intention); and that if Eastern Europe were to adopt the Soviet model of economic development, the small size and lack of resources of the Eastern European countries would have extremely serious effects on the ability of these countries to maintain economic growth over longer periods of time. These were crucial considerations for the development of Eastern Europe in the 1950's and 1960's; they were not, however, as clearly seen in the 1930's, when state interference in the economy, "planning," and economic nationalism were looked upon by a great many of the governments as perhaps the only way for Eastern Europe to succeed in overcoming the problems of economic backwardness which prevailed at the time.[18]

Eastern Europe and the Soviet Union in the Postwar Period

The process of Sovietization of Eastern Europe after World War II will not concern us in this essay. The impact of this experience on the Eastern European attitudes is nevertheless important for our account of the postwar period and will be briefly reviewed.

It may be noted first that the Soviet conquest of Eastern Europe not only altered the military and political map of Europe, but set on motion a process by which Soviet political beliefs and Russian cultural values were diffused over a wide area stretching from the center of divided Germany to the Balkan states. These values and outlooks were rejected by a majority of the Eastern European people. There was a minority, all the same, that for political, personal, or national reasons, felt sympathy toward the Soviet Union. As a result of this situation there arose a new kind of division in Eastern Europe, one which saw the vast majority rejecting Soviet influence but a significant minority in some countries sympathetic to Soviet views, and deeply influenced by them.[19]

Meanwhile, Soviet attempts over the past two decades to create a new type of society and culture, cut off from Western traditions, have served to accentuate Eastern Europe's position as a bridgehead to the West, and, with the passage of time, to project Eastern Europe into the role of a transmitter of Western ideas eastward.[20] (One is reminded, in this connection, of how the more Western women's magazines and other journals from the Eastern European countries are available in the Soviet Union in limited quantities, while Western publications are still kept out of the country.) The west-east continuum, characterized by decreasing penetration of Western values as the distance from Western Europe increases, also survived in respect to certain artifacts of modern culture which have a spatial dimension: Western television and radio, for example, penetrate only a certain distance eastward into Eastern Europe and the Soviet Union, while the impact of tourism is greatest in Eastern Europe, where both Western Europeans and Soviet citizens are able to mingle.

Prewar notions of an Eastern Europe divided along East-West lines are nevertheless far less relevant today than 50 years ago. Over two decades of industrialization, combined with the relocation of the Soviet and Eastern European borders after World War II, have fundamentally altered the old economic dividing lines between east and west (although not eliminating them completely). The more backward regions of White Russia, Galicia, the Carpatho-Ukraine, and Bessarabia are now part of the Soviet Union. The vast relocation of the population of Poland after the war resulted in persons from eastern, more backward areas, being settled in the newly acquired territories in the west. Rather than being transformed into a backward area as the result of this migration, the newly acquired territories in Poland became a frontier region characterized by a relatively sparse population, rapid industrial growth, and growing cities with a large peasant population.[21] (In a complete reversal of the usual pattern, the rate of natural increase of the population in the cities of the Western territories of Poland was often greater than in the surrounding rural areas. In 1951, the rate of natural increase of the population in Szczecin reached 37 per thousand, a record for postwar Poland.)[22]

The frontier spirit has also come to prevail in other regions of Eastern Europe where rapid industrial growth has occurred in very backward, or relatively sparsely populated, areas. Macedonia, notwithstanding its oriental flavor, has such a quality; Skoplje, because of its open and sometimes violent style of life, has been called a new "Wild West" in Yugoslav newspapers.[23] Northern Moldavia, where factories have been built in the open countryside, is characteristic of the new type of rural industrialization which has broken down old distinctions between backward and advanced regions in Eastern Europe.[24] Slovenia and Dalmatia, thanks to tourism, are now prosperous regions which have assimilated many aspects of the mass-consumption culture of the West.

These changes have been paralleled by a growing diversity in patterns of regional growth in the Soviet Union.[25] As a result, problems of regional development in Eastern Europe and the Soviet Union have greater similarities than in the past. At the same time, the rapid economic development of Moldavia and Belorussia in recent years has tended to reduce the importance of these regions as zones of backwardness separating the Soviet Union from the rest of Europe. The effect of these changes has been to reduce greatly the significance of any East-West measure of economic development, not only within Eastern Europe, but in respect to the Soviet Union and Eastern Europe taken as a whole.[26]

A comparison of the economic policies pursued by the Soviet Union and the countries of Eastern Europe after the war tends to confirm, in part, the picture of greater diversity and the breakdown of East-West patterns of development just alluded to. Despite a high degree of commitment to the Soviet pattern of growth in Eastern Europe, the actual extent to which the Soviet model has been adopted has varied from country to country and in different periods.[27] Yugoslavia and Poland, as we know, rejected collectivization at an early stage in their development, at a time when they were still committed to other aspects of the Soviet developmental strategy. Until 1961, the existence of an escape route to the West through Berlin prevented the application of the Soviet model in all its particulars to East Germany, while the events of 1956 in Hungary set that country on a course of improving living standards which eventually culminated in the introduction of the New Economic Model in 1968. In both these cases, political factors dictated a modification of the former stress on heavy industry, and the share of the consumption in total income was kept fairly high in comparison to other countries in the area.[28]

The picture assumes a somewhat different aspect, however, when we examine the economic behavior of Eastern Europe as a whole, and compare it to that of the Soviet Union. The near collapse of the Eastern European governments in the 1950's under the strain of the early stages of forced industrialization, followed by the economic recession of the early 1960's, demonstrated the vulnerability of all of the countries of Eastern Europe to the limitations inherent in the Soviet developmental stategy. Yugoslavia, although it replaced the mechanisms of the command economy with a system of decentralized decision making, continued to adhere to other aspects of the Soviet developmental model through the early

1960's, when the economy suffered a serious slowdown. It was not until 1965, when Yugoslavia geared her economy to trade with Western Europe, that a complete break with the Soviet model was accomplished. Rumania, in the early 1960's, succeeded in achieving economic growth along the lines suggested by Manoilesco; by exporting raw materials and agricultural produce to the West in the early 1960's, the country was able to import capital goods and thus increase her already rapid rate of economic growth. By the mid-1960's, however, this development strategy began to falter. Agricultural produce was needed for the country's new industries which, contrary to Manoilesco's prognosis, found few markets in the West. The effects of this problem were felt in the late 1960's, when the rate of growth of the Rumanian economy was maintained, to an ever greater extent, at the expense of the standard of living of the Rumanian people. The difficulties in applying the Soviet model to a highly developed economy were illustrated by the economic recession in 1963 in Czechoslovakia, the sharpest in all of Eastern Europe.

The effects of rapid economic development and the strains it induced in Eastern Europe have been discussed on many occasions; we may note simply at this point that these changes have moved the Eastern European nations measurably down the road to the point where backwardness, in the sense in which this was understood in the prewar period, is no longer the major obstacle to growth. On the other hand, the effect of following the Soviet developmental strategy has been to promote a new kind of backwardness, while not entirely eliminating the old. This new type of backwardness is the consequence of technological lag with the West, poor planning, and the neglect of agriculture and consumer goods production, all problems traceable to the workings of the command economy and the distorted priorities that this system has encouraged. The more advanced the country in Eastern Europe, the more profound the economic crisis that has resulted, generally speaking. This is not only because of the complexity of the economies in question, the explanation that is most often put forward, but has also been the consequence of labor shortages, the importance of trade for the more developed economies, and because of the fact that the problem of technological lag has been more evident in the advanced than in the less advanced countries of Eastern Europe. East Germany and Czechoslovakia, the two advanced countries in the region began, after the war, with technologies equal to those in Western Europe. Twenty years later these countries found themselves far behind.[29]

The Soviet economy suffered from many of the same problems as the economies of Eastern Europe in the 1960's. Soviet economic growth was somewhat less than that of the underdeveloped countries of Eastern Europe, and her technological lag in many areas perhaps more severe than that experienced by Eastern Europe. But in the 1950's and 1960's, at any rate, fluctuations in the rate of economic growth in the Soviet Union were less sharp than in Eastern Europe.[30] As the result of her higher and more steady rate of growth,[31] the Soviet Union not only increased the absolute size of her economy vis-à-vis those of Eastern Europe at a very rapid rate,[32] but also improved her rank among the communist nations in terms of per capita production, rising from fifth in per capita gross domestic product in 1950 to third in 1967.[33]

The success of the Soviet economy was only relative to that of the countries of Eastern Europe and did not mean that the underlying problems of economic organization were any less severe in the Soviet Union than in the other communist countries. The ability of the Soviet Union to sustain rapid growth for a longer period of time than countries at her level of development in Eastern Europe and with fewer concessions to the principles of the developmental model adopted in the 1930's was nevertheless indisputable. This not only had far reaching consequences for Eastern Europe—by making the Soviet Union unwilling to reform her own economy and therefore reluctant to encourage economic reforms in other communist countries—but served to highlight the basic differences in size, endowment with raw materials and labor, and effectiveness of political controls, which distinguished Eastern Europe from the Soviet Union and at the same time made sustained growth in the latter country possible.[34] Paradoxically, considerations such as these had played far less of a role in the economic growth of Eastern Europe and Russia during the early stages of development of these regions prior to World War I. In certain respects, therefore, the introduction of a Soviet model of development in Eastern Europe after World War II increased, rather than decreased, differences between the two regions, for in this way the focus of the problem of growth shifted to those factors which the Soviet Union possessed—especially size, and an ample supply of raw materials—and which the countries of Eastern Europe lacked.

The implications of these developments will be explored further in our concluding section. First, however, it is necessary to consider briefly those changes in society which were associated with rapid economic growth in Eastern Europe after the war, and alterations in the class structure of the Eastern European societies which took place following the Communist seizure of power. We shall see that in this instance the societies of Eastern Europe, while undergoing profound transformations, experienced fewer dislocations that did the Soviet Union at an equivalent stage of growth.

The initial stage of the transformation of East European society, lasting from the war until the mid-1950's, was a period marked by the destruction of traditional property relationships, mass population movements, and the hardships associated with reconstruction and the initial phase of the drive for industrialization. While these changes broke the bonds that linked the peoples of Eastern Europe to the societies of the prewar era, many of the features of the semideveloped agrarian way of life of that earlier time survived relatively intact.[35] The impact of the immediate postwar period on the Eastern Europeans was in fact similar to that of the first five year plans on the Soviet people, although the duration and scope of the upheavals were considerably smaller.

By the mid-1950's, a more normal pattern of social change began to manifest itself in Eastern Europe, marked by massive shifts of the population from agrarian to nonagrarian occupations, rapid urbanization, and an overall rise in the standard of living. Notwithstanding the neglect of agriculture during this time, it was the peasant whose income rose most rapidly and whose position, in comparison to the prewar period, showed the greatest change.[36] In Poland and Yugoslavia, where the peasant retained ownership of the land, the occupation of peasant-worker provided an important means of supplementing income for the persons whose plots were too small to farm profitably. This in turn provided an outlet for pressures on the land in densely populated and backward areas—in Polish Galicia, for example, or the underdeveloped republics in Yugoslavia.

The class structure in postwar Eastern Europe was shaped by the revolutionary nature of the communist regimes and the far-reaching changes accompanying industrialization. The first decade after the war witnessed unprecedented upward social mobility on the part of the workers and the peasants. (This was, however, largely intergenerational mobility rather than a shift in the class status of individual workers and peasants.)[37] Differences in incomes between the manual and nonmanual classes were sharply reduced as part of a campaign to do away with the privileged position of the white-collar classes.[38] These changes were effective in encouraging the rapid emergence of a new type of society oriented toward industrialization and factory life, just as was the case in the Soviet Union 20 years earlier. At the same time, these societies were far from being egalitarian, and in this respect they also resembled the Soviet system. A sharp line could be drawn between the privileged elite, made up of the political leadership and a small group of prestigious intellectuals, on the one hand, and the rest of the population on the other.[39] The white-collar class (or at least its upper strata), although paid little more than skilled workers, was usually able to find better housing and enjoyed a higher standard of living than persons in blue-collar occupations.[40] Great differences also existed within the working class after the war, both in respect to pay and housing. The difference between skilled and unskilled workers was especially noticeable in some countries as a result of the fact that a high percentage of unskilled labor consisted of peasant-workers who commuted from the village to the factory and therefore did not constitute an integral part of the labor force.[41]

Economic development in the 1960's mitigated some of the class differences which appeared after the war;[42] in this respect the modernization process in Eastern Europe followed the path of other developing countries in which social differences have grown initially and then lessened at a higher stage of development. This was particularly true in respect to differences between urban and rural living standards, as we have already noted. In Yugoslavia and Hungary economic reform accelerated the process of equalization between urban and rural incomes in the late 1960's with the result that by 1972, the income of the collective-farm worker in Hungary approached that of the urban worker.[43] The other side of the picture of development during the 1960's was urban discontent, created in part out of the absence of a rise in disposable income (as contrasted to income provided in the form of services),[44] and the persistent shortage of consumer goods, housing, and services. In addition, the policy of wage equalization between the manual and nonmanual classes in Eastern Europe, while it enhanced the social status of the worker, had the effect of discouraging upward social mobility in the blue-collar class and helped to set the emerging middle class of white-collar workers and professional persons against the workers.[45] The great paradox of modernization during the communist period in Eastern Europe, and one of the great differences with the Soviet Union, was the manner in which rural living standards rose as rapidly, and sometimes more rapidly, than those in urban areas. In Eastern Europe the agrarian discontent of the prewar period was transformed into urban discontent under Communist rule and disguised unemployment in agriculture reappeared in the form of disguised unemployment in the nonagrarian sector of the labor force.[46]

Developments in Yugoslavia and Hungary in recent years suggest how the change to a consumer-oriented society may exacerbate the tensions of this modernization process. In Yugoslavia, the development of a society oriented toward consumption has gone forward at a dizzying pace since the mid-1960's,[47] well before the development process has had the opportunitiy to equalize differences among classes or among the developed and underdeveloped regions of the country. While it has proven impossible to determine to what extent this has resulted in an increase in differences in incomes,[48] the conspicuous consumption of the newly emerging middle classes in Yugoslavia has created social tensions which have been played upon by rival political factions within the country. In Hungary the workers have demonstrated their hostility not only towards the middle class, but toward the newly prosperous peasantry as well.[49] In both cases, affluence has been welcomed by the great majority, but has also offended the deeply ingrained yearning for equality created in the revolutionary period after the war.

The early stages of the development process in the Soviet Union were marked by a more prolonged and intense period of turmoil than in Eastern Europe, accompanied by a sharp decline in living standards, especially among the peasantry, in the early 1930's.[50] This ordeal, followed by the terrible losses of World War II and the privations of the postwar reconstruction period, make it difficult to speak of the Soviet experience as development in the usual sense. Many social indicators illustrate the distortion of the normal modernization process in the Soviet Union after 1928: the massive and sometimes misleading growth of the city population in the 1930's (entire areas classified as urban were in fact forced labor camps);[51] the precipitous drop in birthrates, which for a certain time were virtually identical in rural and urban areas;[52] and the "feminization," not only of entire occupations, as was frequent in Eastern Europe, but also of whole industries and towns.[53]

The society which emerged in the USSR after World War II was less developed and contained greater differences in incomes (both within the urban labor force and between the agricultural and nonagricultural population) than in Eastern Europe. It is also generally assumed that social mobility was less after the war in the Soviet Union than in the younger and still more revolutionary Eastern European societies.[54] Because of a lack of data, it is nevertheless difficult to make explicit comparisons between the two areas for the postwar period. Data on social mobility suggest that both Eastern Europe and the Soviet Union have experienced a high degree of upward social mobility, although the upper ranks of the intelligentsia and white-collar class tend to be self-recruiting in both societies.[55] While differences in incomes among persons receiving salaries and wages were undoubtedly greater in the Soviet Union than in Eastern Europe up to 1956, after that time there was a considerable leveling of incomes in the Soviet Union;[56] this may explain the findings of a recent study on income distribution, which presents data indicating that wages and salaries are more equal in the Soviet Union than in Poland.[57]

Notwithstanding the lack of comparable data, one can point to convergence between Eastern Europe and the Soviet Union as the latter country emerged from the turmoil of the Stalinist period. We have just alluded to the reduction of differences in incomes among the nonagricultural population of the Soviet Union after 1956. Note must also be taken of the progress that was made in the 1960's in reducing the great differences that existed between the living standards of the peasantry and the urban population, thus bringing the Soviet union much closer to conditions that prevailed in Eastern Europe.[58] The growth of "mixed income" families in rural areas in the Soviet Union[59] points to the breaking down of the distinction between the peasantry and other classes which could be seen in Eastern Europe in the 1960's, and Soviet literature now speaks of the growing importance in the Soviet Union of persons in rural areas who live in the village and work in the cities—like the peasant-worker of Eastern Europe.[60] In a general sense, one may suggest that the last decade of growth in the Soviet Union has been characterized by a more normal pattern of social change than in earlier years, not vastly dissimilar from that taking place in Eastern Europe. In turn, these developments seem linked to the gradual fading of the hierarchical society—the *Standegesellschaft* as Boris Meissner called it—of the 1950's.[61] In its place there has emerged a still very rigid and closed society—by Eastern European as well as Western standards—but one nevertheless more modern than a decade ago.

A thorough comparison of Soviet and East European societies must, of course, consider many other matters in addition to those just discussed. Great differences still exist between the social systems of the two areas, especially in respect to the sharply defined character of the privileged elites in the Soviet Union and the influence these elites exercise over the rest of society. A second distinguishing feature lies, as we have already suggested, in the greater penetration of Western styles and fashions into Eastern Europe. Both these matters will be examined in the conclusions to follow.

In addition, one must take into consideration differences in the standard of living between the two areas. The conviction of the Eastern Europeans that they enjoy a higher standard of living than persons in the Soviet Union is partially borne out by data on consumption patterns in Eastern Europe and the USSR, although the general level of economic development of the countries being compared is clearly an important factor in determining consumption levels.[62] Many of the factors which most impress East Europeans (and Westerners) in this regard—for example, the lack of variety of consumer goods in the Soviet Union or the lines in front of stores—unfortunately cannot be taken into consideration when making comparisons between the two areas, although they undoubtedly reflect real differences in the quality of consumer goods and the efficiency of the distribution networks in Eastern Europe and the Soviet Union.

Conclusions

The discussion of Eastern Europe and the Soviet Union has raised a number of points to which we would now like to return. The first of these concerns differences between East and West and the manner in which such differences have been reflected in the distinctions made between Eastern Europe and the Soviet Union.

It has been suggested how, thanks to economic development and modernization, many aspects of the East-West distinction have been rendered less important, if not altogether obsolete. Eastern Europe is now a more homogeneous area, while modernization in the Soviet Union has had the effect of reducing social differences among classes and lessening the contrasts between the city and countryside which characterized the initial stages of industrialization. These changes have produced a society in the Soviet Union which is in a number of respects more like that of Eastern Europe than was the case a decade ago.

Furthermore, we have seen that, despite great differences regarding size, political traditions, and cultural backgrounds, Eastern Europe and the Soviet Union have faced similar problems in the economic sphere. It has been argued that the developmental experiences of Russia and Eastern Europe have had much in common from the beginning. They were neither Eastern nor Western, but were deeply influenced by the backward nature of both areas, their proximity to Europe, and, after World War II, the concrete problems of maintaining sustained economic growth within the restraints imposed by the Soviet developmental model.

It must be noted, nevertheless, that in tracing out the effects of economic development and modernization in Eastern Europe and the Soviet Union, we have not gone into detail into the many differences that continue to separate the two societies and political systems. Brief mention shall be made of two which are of importance for our analysis: (1) the attitude of the East Europeans toward Europe, and (2) the problem of political and social stability in the two systems.

In our account we alluded to the fact that Eastern Europeans have been divided between those who continue to have feelings of loyalty to the Soviet Union and those who look upon themselves as European. It nevertheless remains true that the impact of economic development and modernization in Eastern Europe has been to increase the sentiment among Eastern Europeans that they belong to a European community of nations and to decrease the feeling of identity with the Soviet Union.[63] Eastern Europeans are extremely conscious of their Westernness, in fact, and not uncommonly express shock at the conditions they find when visiting the Soviet Union.[64]

Contrasts that exist in respect to political and social stability have also led to differences between the two systems which promise to grow greater with time. The portion of the ruling elite in Eastern Europe dedicated to maintaining communist rule is far smaller and less secure that that in the Soviet Union, and the communist regimes of Eastern Europe have failed, after many years of effort, to acquire real legitimacy in the eyes of their people.[65] Partly as a result of this fact, the Eastern European systems have tended to show a susceptibility to group pressures and social unrest. In certain cases, these societies are also marked by a fairly high degree of friction among classes and groups in society.[66] The Soviet system, on the other hand, has displayed a high degree of stability up to the present time, notwithstanding the presence of alienated groups on the fringe of society. While there is active opposition to the Soviet regime, it is restricted largely to the privileged strata, very much in the tradition of the "counterelites" of prerevolutionary Russia.

These trends do not, we would argue, negate the significance of the common features of societies of the two areas nor the importance of the growing number of ties that exist among Eastern Europeans and the Soviet Union at the economic, scientific, and professional levels. One must emphasize, in this respect, the extent to which the countries of Eastern Europe and the Soviet Union are involved in an increasingly complex system of interaction, one which extends beyond formal relationships maintained among the states in question or their political parties. Yugoslavia is part of this system, and it is the virtue of the recent monograph of Professor Gitelman on the diffusion of political innovation in Eastern Europe and the Soviet Union to recognize this fact.[67]

These considerations lead us to a final point concerning the economic problems of Eastern Europe and the Soviet Union and the prospects for a new period of growth characterized by the parallel development of both systems into a higher economic stage. The fact is that both the Soviet Union and Eastern Europe appear to be on the brink of a new period of economic development. On the basis of existing trends in economic growth, it has been predicted that the gross domestic product of the Soviet Union and Eastern Europe combined will reach approximately 2,000 dollars per capita by 1980, a level about equal to that presently enjoyed by most developed Western European countries.[68] This could mean a substantial change in living standards in the communist countries, and, inevitably, a change in the developmental policy inherited from the days of primitive industrialization in the 1930's. It would mark, for both the Soviet Union and Eastern Europe, the transition from an industrializing society to a society more concerned with raising the standard of living and enjoying the benefits to be derived from an advanced state of development.

If such changes take place, it may be argued, they will not initially involve reforms of the command economy system such as occurred in Yugoslavia in the 1950's or Hungary in 1968. Basing our analysis on present trends in the bloc, it seems likely that both the Soviet Union and the East European states are more apt to seek changes in the pattern of investments and in foreign trade practices along the lines now being followed in Poland, rather than to introduce some modified type of market socialism. This would signify a gradual departure from the policy of production for production's sake, and the stress on economic autarchy, which characterized the developmental model of the 1930's and which caused the Eastern European economies such great difficulties after the war. If successful, it would introduce a period of evolutionary change and steadier growth than took place in the 1960's.

The extreme complexity of the economic problems facing Eastern Europe and the Soviet Union make any prediction concerning future growth hazardous. The growing problems of the more advanced states in Eastern Europe, and the difficulties that have accompanied the application of the mechanisms of the command economy to Eastern Europe nevertheless cast doubt on the likelihood of a smooth transition to a new developmental model which would permit present rates of growth—or slightly lower ones—to be maintained. Rather that anticipating the parallel development of Eastern Europe and the Soviet Union in the decade ahead, we might envisage a pattern of development marked by severe economic crises in Eastern Europe. Such an eventuality suggests that the campaign for reform in Eastern Europe may continue to grow, kept in check by the reluctance of the Soviet Union to permit radical experimentation as long as the advantages which she derives from her size and the great supply of raw materials at her command allow her to maintain her present rate of growth.

The situation which we have just described may, of course, be altered by many factors, including a more lenient attitude on the part of the Soviet Union toward economic experimentation in Eastern Europe or a serious drop in the growth rate of the Soviet economy itself. It may be that new configurations of states will appear on the basis of the degree to which economic reforms and Western influences are permitted to take root, or as a result of growing differences between the more advanced, and in many respects more rigid and authoritarian systems (East Germany, Czechoslovakia, and the Soviet Union) and the developing states of Eastern Europe. At the same time, the more realistic view would be to expect differences between Eastern Europe and the Soviet Union to continue along present lines. This would suggest a division between the communist states of Eastern Europe and the Soviet Union on the basis of differences in the degree of stability of their political and social systems and in respect to their attitudes toward the larger political community of European nations. These states will nevertheless be closely linked in their political and social development by virtue of common social and economic problems, the growing similarities between their societies and, of course, the many parallels in the modernizing experience of the two areas.

Notes

1. The exception to this lack of comparisons between the two areas can be found chiefly in the field of economics. Note in this connection the recent work of Paul Gregory, *Socialist and Nonsocialist Industrialization Patterns: A Comparative Appraisal* (New York, 1970). A new approach along these lines among Eastern European publications in which empirical data on the labor force in the Soviet Union and Poland is discussed in a comparative fashion is the joint work of Polish and Soviet social scientists, G. W. Osipow and J. Szczepanski, eds., *Spoleczne problemy pracy i produkcji* (Warsaw, 1970).

2. Ghita Ionescu, *The Politics of the European Communist States* (New York, 1967).

3. United Nations Research Institute for Social Development, *Research Notes*, 1 (June, 1968), 8.

4. Hugh Seton-Watson, "Is There an East Central Europe?" in Sylva Sinanian, Istvan Deak and Peter Ludz, eds., *Eastern Europe in the 1970's* (New York, 1972), 3–12.

5. The demographic data may be found in Dudley Kirk, *Europe's Population in the Interwar Years* (New York, 1946), 44. One of the most thoughtful attempts at distinguishing between the Eastern and Western portions of Eastern Europe in terms of levels of economic development was made by Harriet Wanklyn. She drew a line down the center of Eastern Europe based on what was, in the interwar period, probably the most basic component of backwardness; the method of farming. The "Wanklyn line" divided Poland along the pre-World War I frontier between Germany and Russia, Czechoslovakia along the border of Slovakia and the Czech lands, and Hungary along the Danube. To the West of this line, agriculture was pursued in what she called a pastoral fashion, essentially capital intensive and comparable to that in Western Europe. To the East, the peasant had to contend with an inefficient, backward agriculture characterized by a high degree of disguised unemployment and subsistence farming. Although differences of degree were involved, there was also a clear suggestion that Eastern Europe to the east of this line was caught up in the vicious circle of backwardness for which no easy solution was possible, while the regions to the west had, thanks to development in the agricultural sector, made significant progress in modernizing along Western lines. See Wanklyn's *Czechoslovakia* (New York, 1954), 219, and her earlier suggestion of how this difference can be viewed in Hungary, "The Role of Peasant Hungary in Europe," *The Geographical Journal*, XCVII, 1 (January, 1941), 18–35.

6. Many areas in both Russia and Eastern Europe were untouched by the first surge of development; others, such as Congress Poland, experienced early growth but then a decline by the turn of the century. Rumania, although expanding her economy rapidly, did so in a totally unbalanced fashion, increasing grain production by pressure on the peasants rather than by improving agricultural techniques. In the 1890's, Witte's economic policies drove Russia into forced economic growth, but at the price of peasant exhaustion and economic depression. On the growth of the Eastern European economies in this period, see Nicholas Spulber, *The State and Economic Development in Eastern Europe* (New York, 1966). Russian economic policy in the 1890's is described in Theodore Von Laue's contribution to Cyril Black, ed., *The Transformation of Russian Society* (Cambridge, Mass., 1960), 209–225.

7. Alexander Gerschenkron, *Economic Backwardness in Historical Perspective* (Cambridge, Mass., 1962), 137.

8. Alexander Eckstein, "National Income and Capital Transformation in Hungary, 1900–1950," *Income and Wealth*, Series V (London, 1955), 167.

9. "Political and Social Aspects of Modern Bulgaria," *The Slavonic Review*, VII (1928–1929), 283.

10. By 1928 the peasant still had not quite achieved the living standards he enjoyed in 1913, however. Maurice Dobb, *Russian Economic Development Since the Revolution*, 2nd ed. (London, 1929), 395, and Gertrude E. Schroeder, "Consumption in the USSR: A Survey," *Studies in the Soviet Union*, X, 4 (1970), 3–4.

11. PEP, *Economic Development in SE Europe* (London, 1943), 102. For this period, see also Charles Gati, "Modernization and Communist Power in Hungary," *East European Quarterly*, V, 3 (September, 1971), 325–59.

12. The Eastern European states made great strides in reducing illiteracy in the interwar period. This was also a time when many welfare programs were introduced for the urban population, and health services were greatly expanded. A great deal of investment went into urban housing. At the same time these countries spent approximately 2 to 3 percent of estimated national income on education, and 2 percent or less on social services. (PEP, *op. cit.*, 106.) While the demographic trends were positive in Eastern Europe in the interwar period, indicating the impact

of education and health measures, the rate of decline in infant mortality was not much greater than in Western Europe during the same time. Mortality rates hardly fell at all in Rumania between the two world wars. (Jean-Claude Chasteland, "La Population des Democraties Populaires d'Europe," *Population*, XIII, 1 [January–March, 1958], 79–100.) Data on these problems for the Soviet Union in the interwar period is difficult to obtain. An extraordinary jump in literacy—from 24 percent in 1897 to 51 percent in 1926 and over 75 percent in 1939 is recorded in official data, but definitions of literacy became much more lenient during the period of Soviet rule. (See Nicholas De Witt, *Education and Professional Employment in the USSR* [Washington, D.C., 1961], 72.) In respect to infant mortality, Dudley Kirk shows death rates higher in the USSR than in Eastern Europe, even higher than Rumania, in 1926. The Soviet infant mortality rate per thousand in 1926 was given as 181, as compared to 159 for Yugoslavia (1930–31), 178 for Rumania, and 121 for Poland. (*Europe's Population in the Interwar Year* [Princeton, 1946], 263–76.) Gertrude Schroeder, in writing of this period, has commented that in terms of communal service, the Soviet people were better supplied than before World War 1, noting rising expenditures for health and education, but adds that "the data on this element of consumer welfare during this early period still awaits compilation and analysis." (Schroeder, *op. cit.*, 4.)

13. United Nations, *Report on the World Social Situation with Special Reference to the Problem of Balanced Social and Economic Development* (New York, 1961), 45.

14. This attitude was well expressed in a Yugoslav volume, *Svjetska kriza i urbanizacija naroda*, which appeared in 1936. Its author, M. Martinis, attacked the growth of cities in Yugoslavia, the rapid expansion of higher education, and the increase in the size of the urban bureaucracy. His proposed solution to this problem was a novel one: disurbanization. Under this scheme modern technology—TV and radio—would be brought to the service of decentralization and disurbanization, allowing the break-up of parasitical urban society and the spread of culture to the villages. The plan was also urged as a way of protecting the country from bombing raids in case of war. For the idea of a "garden Hungary," advocated by the Populists in Hungary, see Gati, *op. cit.*, 347.

15. In the words of Seton-Watson, "the river Dniestr was the boundary between an allegedly socialist state and a semicapitalist, semifeudal bureaucratic state. But the peasants working on each side of it were far more like one another than were the Rumanian peasants to the polished Europeans who ruled in Bucharest." (Sinanian *et al., Eastern Europe*, 8.)

16. "Probleme des Industrialisierungsprozesses in Südosteuropa," *Weltwirtschaftliches Archiv*, LXI, 1, 8.

17. *Ibid.*, 11.

18. For a direct rebuttal of Manoilesco, meanwhile, note the observations of Antonin Basch, made during the war, that "If it should be suggested that these countries could accumulate the capital needed to meet the great demand for investments of various kinds by indirect compulsory savings arising from a forced reduction in national consumption, as was done in Russia, then this is a fallacy. It must be remembered that Russia was able to obtain most of the necessary raw materials at home in ample quantities; this does not apply to this region even if regarded as a unit, and much less to the separate small states. Further, Russia's vast resources made it possible for her to take the chance of great waste in carrying out her program of industrialization. Finally, there is the general question of whether the people, freed after the war and expecting improved living conditions,

will be willing to bear sacrifices similar to those borne by the Russians in carrying out their industrial programs." (*The Danube Basin and the German Economic Sphere* [London, 1944], 242–43.)

19. On this point, note the interesting results of a poll reported in *Nedeljne Informativne Novine* (hereafter, NIN) (October 1, 1972), 31–34 on the statesman admired most by citizens of Belgrade. Indira Gandhi received the greatest amount of support, but Brezhnev was chosen by 12 percent of those polled. The methods by which these results were obtained were not revealed in the article.

20. Note in this connection the work of Zvi Gitelman, "The Diffusion of Political Innovation: From Eastern Europe to the Soviet Union," *Comparative Politics Series*, Sage Professional Paper, III, 1972.

21. And also considerable violence. For an account which deals with the problem of crime and disorder in the Western Territories, see Hans Koerber, "Sozialpolitische Probleme Polens in den Deutschen Ostgebieten," in Werner Market, ed., *Osteuropa Handbuch: Polen* (Cologne, 1959), 314–326.

22. Piotr Zaremba, "The Spatial Development of Szczecin in 1945–1961," *Polish Western Affairs*, III, 1 (1962), 191.

23. *Nedeljne Informativne Novine* (March 26, 1972), 21. The term "Wild West" was also used—in a strongly perjorative sense—to describe the violence of the Western Territories. See Andrzej Kwilecki, "Polish Western Territories in Sociological Research and Theory," *Polish Sociological Bulletin*, 2 (1968), 61–68.

24. Andre Blanc, "Problèms de Géographie urbaine en Roumanie," *Revue Géographique de L'Est*, III, 3 (July–September, 1963), 307—331.

25. We may speak of at least four or five different regional patterns in the case of the Soviet Union: (1) older urban or industrialized areas such as the Donbas, the Urals, or the Moscow coal basin, which experienced rapid industrialization in the 1930's but have now ceased to grow rapidly; (2) the Central Asian pattern of growth, characterized by high rates of increase for both the urban and the rural populations; (3) the pattern of development taking place in widely scattered areas of the Soviet Union, including Moldavia, White Russia, the Baltic states, and the Black Earth region, characterized by low rates of population growth, rapid urbanization, and a sharp decline in the size of the agricultural population; (4) underdeveloped ethnic regions, which are now being favored with industry, as in the autonomous republics in the Volga-Vyatka region; (5) neglected areas with little industry, marginal agricultural potential, and peripheral location, such as Transcarpathia, the Karelian ASSR, the Chita Oblast, and the Sakhalin Oblast. An excellent source for an understanding of these problems is Chauncy D. Harris, "Urbanization and Population Growth in the Soviet Union," *Geographical Review*, LI, 1 (January, 1971), 102–24.

26. For an excellent introduction to problems of regional development in Eastern Europe, see Kosta Mihailovic, *Regionalni razvoj socialistickih zemalja* (Belgrade, 1972).

27. The question arises as to what, precisely, constitutes the Soviet model. Our discussion has stressed first, the command economy and second, the developmental model of forced industrialization. After Fallenbuchl, we may describe the latter in terms of (1) economic growth through import substitution (what we have rather loosely referred to as economic autarchy); (2) high investment rates; and (3) a greater rate of growth of producers goods than consumer goods. (Z. M. Fallenbuchl, "The Communist Pattern of Industrialization," *Soviet Studies*, XXI, 4 [April, 1970], 458–84.)

28. Maurice Ernst, "Postwar Economic Growth in Eastern Europe," in Joint

Economic Committee, *New Directions in the Soviet Economy*, Part IV (Washington, D. C., 1966), 885–86.

29. Edwin M. Snell, "Economic Efficiency in Eastern Europe," in *Economic Developments in the Countries of Eastern Europe* (Washington, D. C., 1970), 240–96.

30. This was true notwithstanding the fact that the USSR also suffered a recession in 1963. On this point see the discussion of Soviet and Eastern European growth in the 1960's in United Nations *Economic Bulletin for Europe*, XVIII, 1 (November, 1966), 31–32, which deals with the period 1950–1965. In comparing growth rates between free market and planned economies for the period 1950–1960, George Staller found the lowest fluctuations in the total output to have occurred in the Soviet Union and Norway (and the highest in Yugoslavia and Turkey). ("Fluctuations in Economic Activity: Planned and Free Market Economies, 1950–1960," *American Economic Review*, LIV, 4 [June, 1964], 388. For further discussions of the problem, see Roland Granier, *Rythmes de Croissance et Inégalités Internationales de Développement* [Paris, 1968], 71–73.)

31. The annual rate of growth of gross domestic product in the years 1950–1967 was 7.6 percent in the Soviet Union and 5.9 percent for Eastern Europe. (Economic Commission for Europe, *Economic Survey of Europe in 1969*, Part I [New York, 1970], 9, Table 2.3.)

32. In 1950, the difference between the GDP (Gross Domestic Product) of the Soviet Union and Eastern Europe was approximately 35 billion dollars (in 1963 prices); in 1967, over 150 billion. (*Ibid.*)

33. *Ibid.*

34. See the *Economic Bulletin for Europe, supra* for comments that fluctuations in growth in Eastern Europe were to be explained by the fact that "the possibility of directly applying the Soviet planning experience is . . . limited because they are . . . much smaller in size, much more densely populated and—in spite of the per capita national income gap in the area—mostly also at different stages of economic development and industrialization. In addition, their relative poverty in fuel and raw-material resources makes them incomparably more foreign-supply dependent than the Soviet Union." (p. 32).

35. In Yugoslavia and Poland, the first wave of migrations in this period involved the movement of peasants from one agricultural region to another. Elsewhere, rural urban migration was important from the start. Nevertheless, urbanization was not terribly rapid in this period in most of the Eastern European countries. Those who were recruited for the construction of new industrial plants, although they helped to swell the ranks of the nonagricultural labor force, were often peasants who subsequently returned to their villages. The collectivization drives of the early 1950's led to a flight of labor from the land. Still, differences between the cities and the countryside remained very great. For a partial description of the changes of this period, see Thomas Schreiber, "Die Umwandlung der Sozialstruktur in den Ländern Osteuropas," *Europa Archiv*, XVII, 1 (January 10, 1962), 13–20; Institut drustvenih nauka, *Migracija stanovnistva Jugoslavije* (Belgrade, 1971), *passim*; and Mikolaj Latuch, *Migracje wewnetrzne w Polsce na tle industrializacji (1950–1960),* (Warsaw, 1970), Chap. 2.

36. UN Economic Commission for Europe, *Incomes in Postwar Europe* (Geneva, 1967), 27. It should be added that the flight from the land in the early 1950's and disinvestment by peasants fearing collectivization contributed to the rise in peasant incomes. The period of the "thaw" in the mid-1950's, meanwhile, was marked by concessions to the urban population in Eastern Europe. In Hungary,

incomes of peasants on the one hand, and workers and employees on the other, were about the same until 1957–58, when urban incomes rose faster than agricultural incomes. (Varga, "Changes in the Social and Economic Status of Hungary's Peasantry," *The New Hungarian Quarterly*, VI, 20 [Winter, 1965], 36.)

37. Reliable data on this point is of course scarce. But see Zbigniew Sufin, "Procesy ruchliwosci spolecznej," in Wlodzimierz Wesolowski, ed., *Struktura i dynamika spoleczenstwa polskiego* (Warsaw, 1970), 93–130, for a summary of the studies that have been made of social mobility in Poland, and the very important contribution of Vojin Milic on Yugoslavia, "General Trends in Social Mobility In Yugoslavia," *Acta Sociologica*, IX (1965), 116–36.

38. On the basis of sample surveys carried out in Poland, differences in income between the unskilled worker and the upper elements of the white-collar class (engineers, doctors) in the early 1960's were found to be approximately in the range of 1:2. This was several years after a policy of encouraging high salaries for the intelligentsia had been in effect. The studies were described in Wlodzimierz Wesolowski, "Przemiany strukturalne we wspolezesnym socjalizme," *Studia Socjologiczne*, 2 (1969), 55. Data based on labor statistics for manual and non-manual laborers can be found in Antoni Rajkiewicz, *Zatrudnienie w Polsce Ludowej w latach 1950–1970* (Warsaw, 1965), 189–90. Both sources are excellent in pointing to the pitfalls in making such comparisons. According to data provided by Helmut Klock on Hungary, the income of an office worker and workers in industry were about the same in the mid-1950's and only about 70 percent less than the technical intelligentsia. "Wandlungen der Sozialstruktur im Europäischen Vorfeld der Sowjetunion seit 1945," *Osteuropa,* IX, 12 (December, 1959), 795. In Yugoslavia in 1953 civil servants, who had been the best paid salaried officials before the war, were receiving 15 percent less than office employees in industry, and only 4 percent more in wages than the average worker. ("Differentiation of Personnel Incomes," *Yugoslav Survey*, X, 1 [February, 1969], 81.) The reader is reminded that this data does not include bonuses, premiums or other additional income, that distinctions between various occupational groups were often very arbitrary after the war, and that many office workers in the immediate postwar years were extremely poorly educated, some having had only an elementary education.

39. The privileges of the political elite were especially noticeable in Yugoslavia, of the technical and scientific elite, in East Germany. Frank Grätz, "Wirtschaftsführer in Ost und West," *Deutschland Archiv*, IV, 10 (October, 1971), 1035, gives the example of Professor Nelles, director of the Bunawerk, who was receiving a salary of over 10,000 marks a month in the 1950's. Such high wages ceased to be paid in the GDR after 1961. The best general treatment of these much discussed elite groups remains Petru Dumitriu, "The Two Classes," *East Europe*, X, 9 (September, 1961), 3–6 and 30–33.

40. In studies carried out in Szcheczin and Koszalin in the early 1960's cited by Wesolowski, it was found that while the size of apartments of the intellectuals and workers was about the same, 50 percent of the apartments of the intellectuals had amenities—gas, bath, central heating—but only 9 percent of the apartments of the unskilled workers ("Przemiany strukturalne," *op. cit.*, 56.)

41. Note the findings that nearly half the unskilled workers in Yugoslavia live in the villages. (Milic, *op. cit.*, 116.)

42. Data on this development is not easy to find, but with the end of the extreme scarcities of the postwar period, greater access to housing, and so on, it appears likely that differences among classes based on certain privileges tended to lessen. The very high salaries of the technical personnel in the GDR are a thing of

the past. On the other hand, differences in salaries between workers and nonmanual laborers did grow somewhat in the 1960's.

43. See Radio Free Europe, *Research*, Hungary/1 (February 25, 1972). In Czechoslovakia and East Germany, peasant incomes were also close to those of the urban worker. For a discussion of peasant incomes vis-à-vis other classes, see Mihailovic, *op. cit.*, 89. It should be borne in mind that most studies of conditions in the village have shown a level of living still under that of the urban population when factors such as housing, quality of diets, and education are taken into account.

44. This problem has been most often discussed in connection with Poland, where real disposable incomes rose slightly, if at all, during the late 1960's. See Andrzej Karpinski, *Polityka uprzemyslowienia Polski w latach 1958–1968* (Warsaw, 1969), 26–28.

45. Daniel Kubat, "Social Mobility in Czechoslovakia," *American Sociological Review*, XXVIII, 1 (February, 1963), 206.

46. The fact that disguised agricultural unemployment could become "disguised industrial unemployment" is a sensitive issue in Eastern Europe, notwithstanding frequent discussions of the problem of overutilization of labor in achieving economic growth. Kosta Mihailovic uses the term "disguised unemployment" in reference to industrial labor in his excellent work on underdevelopment in Yugoslavia, *Razvoj i zivotni standard regiona Jugoslavije* (Belgrade, 1970), 76.

47. In 1956, 17.2 percent of Yugoslav families had a radio, in 1971, 65 percent. In 1956, 0.2 percent had refrigerators, in 1971, 44.5 percent. In 1956, 0.3 percent had autos; in 1971, 16.2 percent, and so on. ("Dosije o standardu," *NIN*, 119 [June 18, 1972], 39–41.)

48. The problem lies in the fact that in Yugoslavia there are great differences in incomes among branches of industry, among individual enterprises, and within each enterprise. Berislav Sefer, *Socijalni razvoj u samoupravnom drustvu* (Belgrade, 1971), 140, reports a pronounced tendency toward a *reduction* in the number of enterprises with a great range of salary differences. These enterprises with differences no larger than 1:1.9 tripled from 1964 to 1970, while those with a range of salaries and wages of 1:5 dropped by one half. The widespread assumption is that there are more opportunities today for earning extra income from rent, land speculation, premiums, and outside work, and that this explains the wealth of the new "middle class." There is no data, however, to prove this point, and while income difference may have risen over the past decade, it is also true that the greater availability of consumer durables makes existing income differences more noticeable.

49. Radio Free Europe, *Research*, Hungary/13 (June 11, 1971).

50. Maria Elisabeth Ruban, *Die Entwicklung des Lebensstandards in der Sowjetunion* (Berlin, 1965), 22–27.

51. David J. Dallin and Boris I. Nicolaevsky, *Forced Labor in Soviet Russia* (New Haven, 1947), 50–51.

52. Warren Eason, "Population Changes," in Allen Kassof, ed, *Prospects for Soviet Society* (New York, 1968), 219.

53. See the *New York Times* (March 24, 1971) for an account of the textile city of Tchaikovsky.

54. Frank Parkin, "Changing Social Structure," in George Schopflin, ed., *The Soviet Union and Eastern Europe: A Handbook* (London, 1970), 401.

55. Eastern European writings on social mobility have been cited above. For the Soviet Union, see Janina Markiewicz-Lagneau, "Les Problèms de Mobilité

Sociale en U.R.S.S.," *Cahiers du Monde Russ et Sovietique*, VII, 1 (January–March, 1966), 161–88, and the Rutkevich volume referred to below.

56. Murray Yanowitch, "The Soviet Income Revolution," *Slavic Review*, XXII, 4 (December, 1963), 683–97.

57. P. J. D. Wiles and Stefan Morawski, "Income Distribution Under Communism and Capitalism," Part 2, *Soviet Studies*, XXII, 4 (April, 1971), 505.

58. David W. Bronson and Constance B. Krueger, "The Revolution in Soviet Farm Household Income," in James Miller, ed., *The Soviet Rural Community* (Urbana, 1971), 214.

59. Karl-Eugen Wädekin, "Nicht-Agrarische Beschäftigte in Sowjetischen Dörfern," *Südosteuropa Wirtschaft*, 3 (1968), 183–203.

60. An account of such persons in the Ural region is contained in M. N. Rutkevich and F. R. Filippov, *Sotsial'nie peremeshcheniia* (Moscow, 1970), 96–97. According to data provided in this account, in 1968, 9.3 percent of the employed rural population in Sverdlovsk province worked in enterprises or institutions located in cities or settlements of an urban type; in 1969, 10.2 percent. See also Wädekin, "Nicht-Agrarische Beschäftigte in Sowjetischen Dörfern," 184.

61. *Sowjetgesellschaft im Wandel* (Stuttgart, 1966), 47.

62. Comecon data on consumption of food products (which does not include Rumania or Yugoslavia) show the following *per capita* levels of consumption of meat and meat by-products: Mongolia—105.8 kilograms; Czechoslovakia—69.2 kilograms; GDR—65.0 kilograms; Poland—61 kilograms; Hungary—55 kilograms; USSR—47 kilograms; Bulgaria—44.8 kilograms. (Sovet Ekonomicheskoi Vzaimopomoshchi, *Statisticheskii ezhegodnik* [Moscow, 1970], 50–51.) Kotkovskii has calculated the consumption fund of the East European countries and the Soviet Union for 1963, with the USSR as 100, as: GDR—150; Czechoslovakia—138; Hungary—110; Poland—106; Bulgaria—99. (*Sopostavlenie urovney ekonomicheskogo razvitiia sotsialisticheskikh stran* [Moscow, 1965], 207.) National income comparisons between Eastern European countries and the Soviet Union have been made by Comecon, as well as by the UN. The figures arrived at by the Economic Commission for Europe, for 1965, based on the USSR as 100, gave the following comparisons for the total consumption fund of the Eastern European states: GDR—146; Czechoslovakia—143; Hungary–109; Poland—99; Bulgaria—87; Yugoslavia—73. (*Economic Survey of Europe in 1969*, Part I, 144.) Per capita living space in 1966–1967 in the Soviet Union was approximately two-thirds that of Czechoslovakia, and about the same as Hungary. (Schroeder, *op. cit.*, 22.) These figures conceal differences in the quality of housing and the availability of services, however. The 1960 housing census showed that 62 percent of all urban housing units in the Soviet Union lacked running water. (Vladimir Treml and John P. Hardt, eds., *Soviet Economic Statistics* [Durham, 1972], 340.)

63. In the poll from the Yugoslav magazine NIN cited earlier, Brezhnev was chosen the most popular foreign leader most frequently by those in the 40–55 age bracket. He was least popular among the experts and the youth. Some further statistical evidence of the Western outlook of the Eastern Europeans can be found in Audience and Public Opinion Research Department, Radio Free Europe, *Attitudes Toward Key Political Concepts in Eastern Europe* (Munich, December, 1969).

64. See, for example, the account in the *New York Times* by James Feron (August 25, 1972), entitled, "Nowadays, When in Moscow, the East European Feels as Foreign as Many Western Visitors Do."

65. The problem is discussed by Alfred Meyer in his contribution to Sylvia Sinanian *et al.*, *Eastern Europe in the 1970's*, 45–67, and in the commentary on the Meyer article by Oskar Anweiler, Rudolf Tőkés, and others.

66. These aspects of the Eastern European systems are of course greatly conditioned by circumstances in each individual country. The notion of a "conflict" society has become widespread among Yugoslav social scientists. See Mihailo Popovic, "Neuskladjenosti i suprotnosti u procesu transformacije jugoslovenskog drustva i njegove strukture," *Sociologija*, XXI, 2 (1970), 161–77.

67. See n. 18.

68. *Economic Survey of Europe in 1969*, 43.

CHAPTER 10

The Change to Change in Communist Systems: Modernization, Postmodernization, and Soviet Politics

William Taubman

Prologue

At a recent international conference a Soviet sociologist smilingly informed an American about a piece of scholarly work underway in Moscow. Its revelation was that most works of American Sovietology reveal more about their authors than about the USSR. That there is more than a grain of truth in this hardly reflects a conspiracy. To purge scholarly work of the researcher's values would be impossible. To recognize their existence and to profit from conscious contrasting of various points of view are enterprises which it is the purpose of this chapter to endorse.

The Change to Change

"The Change to Change." The phrase is Samuel Huntington's, coined to describe the shift by American political scientists in the 1950's and 1960's from "the study of given conditions" to the examination of political change.[1] Borrowing from sociology (the latter "rich with works on the theory of social change") comparative politics began its "renaissance" with a "concern with modernization and the comparison of modern and traditional political systems." But meanwhile, sociologists were having second thoughts about "modernization," in particular about a tendency among analysts to equate modern with Western and to project for developing nations a future patterned on the past of the developed. Such doubts led, by the late 1960's, to a "small-scale corrective reaction" which Huntington calls "modernization revisionism," then on, he reports, to "broader efforts to generate more general theories of political change." [2]

A change to change has been taking place in the study of Communist systems as well. Considering the origins of the field in the study of revolution, the need for such a shift seems surprising. "The study of Communism by non-Communist scholars," wrote Dankwart Rustow, "developed in relative isolation from . . . trends in twentieth century sociology and political science." [3] But given Huntington's testimony about political science, one might have thought such isolation an advantage. Instead, Rustow continues, "the Western literature on Communism remained exegetic, polemical or descriptive and at a relatively low level of abstraction." [4] "Until the post-war period," adds Roger E. Kanet, "there existed no mature, systematic account of the Soviet political system." [5] And when such an account arrived, it came in the form of the "totalitarian model"—brilliant in its conception, full of insights concerning Stalinism, yet ill-suited, numerous scholars have concluded, to illuminating the nature of politics and the direction of change in post-Stalinist and in particular post-Khrushchevian Russia.

In 1968, the American Council of Learned Societies convened a Planning Group on the Comparative Study of Communism. Participants agreed, reported R. V. Burks, that "the totalitarian model so much concentrates on the mechanism of control that no internal change within the system seems possible, only its destruction from the outside by superior forces." [6] "Within the confines of the so-called 'totalitarian model,'" added Chalmers Johnson, "it is hard enough to conceptualize 'development' and its consequences—that is, to say at what rate a Communist regime is moving toward achieving some or all of its self-proclaimed . . . goals. It is even harder to conceptualize the resulting unintended changes in the social structure and the consequences of those changes." [7]

Even before 1968 it had become clear to many that, as Johnson put it, "scholarship on the various Communist systems was not adequately exploiting the new social science concepts of change, development and 'modernization.'" [8] By 1967, the scholarly journals rang with calls for new approaches.[9] Soon, enough new approaches had appeared to fill at least two collections on communist studies and the behavioral sciences.[10] And in 1970, the ACLS Planning Group published its own work, *Change in Communist Systems,* a series of attempts to view Communist systems as modernizing systems, or as most of the contributors preferred, "mobilization systems" moving into or through a "post-mobilization phase."[11]

With this burst of scholarship, with *Change in Communist Systems* in particular, communist studies caught up with the change to change in political science—at precisely the juncture, described by Huntington, when modernization, the theoretical concept which had powered the shift, was itself being reappraised. The proliferation and resulting confusion of terms risks obscuring the moment's significance. Concluding the ACLS volume, Dankwart Rustow argues that "the theory of modernization (as we have seen) measured change by generations or centuries, and could not with the help of much intermediate conceptualization be applied to regimes that originated as recently as 1917 or 1949."[12] But contributors to *Change in Communist Systems* apply it anyway. David Apter's concept of a "mobilization system" is, according to Rustow, a potentially disorienting neologism. But ACLS contributors employ that, too. " 'Post-modern' theorizing emerged," Huntington reports, in the late 1960's, concerning not "the transition from tradition to modernity," but rather "the impact of technology on modern society." But even more than modernization theorists, such futurists as Daniel Bell (on "postindustrial society") and Zbigniew Brzezinski (on the "technetronic era") have been criticized for an overly optimistic and Western-oriented approach.[13]

Have the new social-science concepts made new sense of communism? Or have efforts to apply such concepts to communist systems tended to buttress doubts about the theories themselves? In the late-developing "Soviet field," the change to change is telescoped. Even as modernization and postmodernization theory are being applied to the USSR, there has appeared a species of revisionism, a "corrective reaction" to the effect that the Soviet Union may be developing a non-Western but nonetheless viable road to modernity and beyond. Which leads, however, to further theoretical complications. For if the USSR may be finding its own way while, as at least some scholars suggest, the United States is losing its, then what is modernity anyway? Can there be any objective, scientific standard? Given the values any social scientist brings to his work, how can he (or she) speak of "the requirements of modernity"? And given the difficulties of so speaking, how can Soviet specialists continue to produce in good conscience what has been a favorite product in recent years—the grand, Olympian assessment of the past, present, and future of communist systems?

This chapter will attempt a guided tour through the change to change in communist systems. To the fundamental questions just posed, it will offer no ultimate answers—only a modest suggestion of how to make the most of the confusion.

The Short Road to Theory

According to those who have applied them, modernization and post-modernization theory are something new under the Sovietological sun. In fact, they are reminiscent of an older and much-maligned approach—old fashioned, optimistic convergence theory.

The main outlines of convergence theory are well-known.[14] It was developed in the 1950's—most notably by Isaac Deutscher—but its adherents are still heard from. It was popularized in the West but has found new converts among dissenting Soviet intellectuals like Andrei Sakharov. It included a hope—that the Soviet Union would open itself to democratic pluralism, while the United States mustered the will and the skill to plan and to allocate its resources in service of human needs. But the hope was based on an argument—that industrialization makes for an increasingly complex society, that social pluralism provides the basis for political pluralism, that affluence weakens the fiber of totalitarian rule, while education prepares its subjects to participate in a democratic process.

Is the wish for convergence not father to the theory? Perhaps the strongest of many arguments to that effect was made by Brzezinski and Huntington. At its core, they said, convergence theory amounted to "anti-Soviet Marxism: the forces of production will shape the social context of production, which in turn will determine the political superstructure." [15] Brzezinski and Huntington pointed, as Andrei Amalrik was to do, to formidable obstacles in the path of democratic evolution—the Communist party, anxious and able to oppose it; the lack of traditions favorable to it among the Soviet masses. They pointed as well to the system's special potential in an age of science and technology; they quoted Peter Wiles to the effect that "because of its introduction of computers, linear programming and the various modern techniques usually associated with the concept of 'economic rationality and maturity,' 'central planning or, better, the so-called command economy can now be rationally conducted.' " [16]

"A multiplicity of expertises (inherent in any modern society) is not the same thing as social-political pluralism based on group autonomy (inherent in a particular form of development)." [17] This Brzezinski and Huntington dictum can still stand as a warning against equating modernity with its Anglo-American variant, which makes it all the more surprising that within three years, Brzezinski was moving toward a view in many ways similar to that of his former targets.

Brzezinski's article, "The Soviet Political System: Transformation or Degeneration," set the tone for a whole round of Sovietological speculation.[18] It described the Soviet "socio-economic setting" as "far more developed and stable, far less *malleable* and atomized" than in the past. The post-Khrushchev leadership (labeled "clerks") had been "attempting a compromise solution—in effect, a policy of 'muddling through.'" But the system required more—not only were "institutional reforms" needed to "revitalize the national economy," but they "are just as badly needed—and even more overdue—in the political sector." [19] Warned Brzezinski: "The effort to maintain a doctrinaire dictatorship over an increasingly modern and industrial society has already contributed to a reopening of the gap that existed in pre-revolutionary Russia between the political system and society, thereby posing the threat of degeneration of the Soviet system." [20] In the long run, "perhaps the ultimate contribution to Soviet political and social development that the CPSU can make is to adjust gracefully to the desirability, and perhaps even the inevitability of its own gradual withering away. In the meantime, the progressive transformation of the bureaucratic Communist dictatorship into a more pluralistic and institutionalized system—even though still a system of one-party rule—seems essential if its degeneration is to be avoided." [21]

What aspects of "modern and industrial society" made the party's prospects so bleak? In 1970 Brzezinski offered a full-dress answer—the imperatives of "the technetronic era." [22] At first glance, Brzezinski's 1970 analysis seemed to hold out more hope for the USSR; instead of two, the system had five options. But of these, two were varieties of degeneration ("oligarchic petrifaction" and "political disintegration"), two amounted to transformation ("pluralism evolution" and "militant fundamentalism") and only one ("technological adaptation") could be considered a more or less incremental extension of the present system. To be sure, Brzezinski's own prediction was "fusion of the first (oligarchic petrifaction) and the third (technological adaptation) variants, in an attempt to construct a novel kind of 'technetronic communism.'" [23] But such a fusion could hardly be expected to last. For "barring an upheaval resulting from internal paralysis . . . the more probable pattern for the 1980's is a marginal shift toward the combination of the second (pluralist evolution) and the third (technological adaptation) variants. . . ." [24]

Brzezinski rejected the notion of inevitability. He cautioned that "unintended consequences of economic-technological adjustments will not suffice to bring about significant political change," but rather that "as in Yugoslavia or pre-1968 Czechoslovakia, at some point the political elite must decide to embark upon deliberate political reforms." [25] And yet, if his analysis is correct, the elite will have little choice. For while:

> Yugoslavia leads all communist states in economic reform, in the openness of its society, and in ideological moderation, . . . similar trends are slowly developing elsewhere. To be sure, they are opposed by entrenched bureaucrats, but in the long run the reactionaries are fighting a losing battle. Social forces are against them everywhere. It is doubtful that they can reverse, though they certainly can delay, the trend toward a more open, humanistic, and less ideological society.[26]

If convergence theory constitutes "anti-Soviet Marxism" then what is one to think of Brzezinski's approach? To political theorist George Kateb, who concentrates his attention on Brzezinski's discussion of the American condition, it is reminiscent of none other than Marx, it is "another version of scientific historicism . . . this time . . . based on the trends of technology in the advanced countries of the world, especially the United States." [27] To the author of *Utopia and Its Enemies,* Brzezinski's writing represents not so much an "attack on utopian thought" as "a continuation of it." For "if Marx saw in class violence the method by which historical rationality is brought into the world, Brzezinski sees in the conscious application of technical-scientific rationality by an intellectual elite the method by which the ambiguous promises of modern knowledge are to be made good." [28]

Brzezinski was ahead of his time in communist studies. But not for long. Like him, the authors of *Change in Communist Systems* were aware of methodoligical dangers. "They reject," noted Dankwart Rustow, "a widespread simplistic notion of social change," the assumption that "the pattern of economic evolution is unilinear," and that "political evolution is a surface reflection of underlying economic and social change." [29]

Or do they? According to Chalmers Johnson, the weakness of the totalitarian model is that it does not allow for certain "fundamental kinds of change that are occurring or seem about to occur in the Communist world." Among these are (1) "changes in the structure of the political system, generally from a one-party system . . . toward a party-dominated national front"; and (2) "changes in the structure of the economic system, generally from a centralized command economy . . . toward market socialism." [30] In the mobilization phase, writes Johnson, the regime uses totalitarian means to mobilize resources (economic, political, social) for a few overriding goals, prime among them industrial development. But "however much totalitarian mobilization may contribute to modernization, it can never *complete* the modernization process." [31]

> The various official bureaucracies, territorial party unit and pre-emptive organizations are all part of the structure that *must* be dismantled when the regime's unbalanced mobilization effort begins to produce diminishing returns. [Italics added.][32]

> An *inescapable* concomitant of economic modernization—what might be called a 'built-in boomerang'—is increased functional differentiation and societal complexity. [Italics added.][33]

> Why do functional differentiation and complexity *force* the leadership to relax controls? There are many reasons. [Italics added.][34]

> No Communist system has as yet successfully passed through the post-mobilization phase; accordingly . . . all such systems face a choice between isolationism (with economic stagnation) and revolution unless a political leadership capable of managing reform comes to the fore.[35]

According to this analysis, there would seem to be two separate gauntlets which communist systems must run—first from totalitarian mobilization into a postmobilization phase, then through the latter stage. Johnson himself is not clear on this, but Richard Lowenthal makes the distinction explicit (although, to confuse matters more, without using the same terms) and in each case awards victory in a competition labeled "Development vs. Utopia" to (Could there be any doubt?) development.[36]

Modernization, as understood by Lowenthal, subjects communist systems to the Perils of Pauline; they escape from one developmental dilemma only to fall onto the horns of another. Lowenthal's major emphasis is on the conflict in the years of "totalitarian communism" between "the elite of revolutionary veterans identified with the utopian orientation and the new technocratic elite," between "the long-term egalitarian ideals of Communism and the need to raise productivity." Stalin's new managers become party members; Khrushchev's plan for making manual labor compulsory falls by the wayside; Stalin rejects egalitarianism; Khrushchev's departure means the end of "utopian social engineering." "The victory of modernization over utopianism!" [37] But then a further dilemma:

"If a Communist regime tends to lose revolutionary momentum characteristic of the totalitarian political systems as it approaches the level of industrial society, how are we to describe the new political forms of its post-revolutionary and therefore potentially post-totalitarian phase?" [38] Lowenthal's answer is avowedly Marxist, and hardly pro-Soviet.

> The basic relation between the political system and the development of society has been reversed. Formerly the political system was in command. . . . Now the political system *has to* respond to pressures generated by an increasingly advanced society. Formerly the Communist political superstructure was concerned with forcibly transforming the system's economic and social basis. . . . Now, the economic and social basis of the countries under Communist rule, having reached a state of development comparable to that of the modern West, is beginning to transform the political superstructure in the familiar manner described by the Marxist interpretation of history. [Italics added.][39]

Lowenthal refers to a "persistent contradiction" during the post-revolutionary or postmobilization phase, between "the requirements of legitimizing Party dictatorship and the growth conditions of industrial society." [40] Let us next examine those "growth conditions," as described by other writers, more closely.

The first is none other than the great hope of convergence theory, social differentiation. According to Amitai Etzioni, differentiation is "the main sociological characteristic of modernization." [41] For Talcott Parsons, to whom the new wave in communist studies owes much, "the basic argument for considering democratic association a universal . . . is that, the larger and more complex society becomes, the more important is effective political organization." Political effectiveness, in turn, "includes both the scale and operative flexibility of the organization of power. Power . . . depends overwhelmingly on a consensual element," and "no institutional form basically different from the democratic association can . . . mediate consensus at high levels of structural differentiation in the society itself and in the governmental system." [42]

Parsons is precisely the kind of major theorist of change whose absence Huntington noted in the ranks of political science. Yet he is also one whose work was criticized for ethnocentric bias as early as the 1950's. "The ideology underlying Parsons' political theory," wrote Andrew Hacker in 1961, is the "liberalism of the eighteenth and nineteenth centuries." [43] Is liberal faith anywhere more apparent than in Parsons' own statement of the "transformation or degeneration" dilemma—that "Communist totalitarian organization will probably not fully 'match' democracy in political and integrative capacity in the long run," that such organization "will prove to be unstable and will either make adjustments in the general direction of electoral democracy and a plural party system, or 'regress' into generally less advanced and politically less effective forms of organization"? [44]

A second "growth condition" is economic. "In early stages of economic development," writes Alexander Eckstein, "a command economy and polity may be quite functional as a model for rapid industrialization." [45] As industrialization proceeds, however, "a command economy with its centralized network of direct controls becomes more and more difficult to manage." "At our present state of computer and economic management technology," Eckstein continues, "theoretically three alternative paths might be pursued." The first (recalling the Peter Wiles notion which Brzezinski and Huntington gave credence in 1964) is "computopia," under which "central planners would retain complete control while simulating the behavior of a decentralized market system." Such a system could "assure retention of centralized political control without loss of economic efficiency." Its only flaw, reports Eckstein, is that "in the present state of our theory and computer technology this is not a feasible or practical solution." [46]

Second and third options are two varieties of decentralization. "Under the first, decision-making powers are retained by the governmental authorities but are decentralized with the governmental apparatus." The difficulty is that "judging by the experience of Communist regimes thus far, [bureaucratic decentralization] solves very few of the problems of a large system and creates many new ones." [47] That leaves market decentralization transferring decision-making powers "from the polity . . . to the market." Such a change would "foster autonomous centers of power," something that Communist leaders are naturally reluctant to do.[48]

All of which leads back to the warning that communist societies face "contradictory demands of centralized political control on the one hand and economic efficiency on the other." [49] Eckstein, too, rejects any suggestion of a "unilinear pattern of development or an inevitable line of progression." His argument is not "that economic changes are bound to produce political changes," but that the maintenance of "certain political arrangements and practices . . . entails growing economic costs," that "in the case of Czechoslovakia, for instance, a highly centralized command system could be maintained in a complex, highly industrialized, and strongly foreign-trade oriented economy only at a serious sacrifice in efficiency and growth." [50]

What's good for Czechoslovakia may or may not be the fate of quite different communist systems. And yet two other "growth conditions" have been launched toward the status of "universals" with an important lift from the Czech experience.

"In an advanced socialist country such as Czechoslovakia," wrote Rodovan Richta and a research team, "the main barrier in approaching the scientific and technological revolution is provided by some elements of immaturity in the economic structure. . . . Consequently, full implementation of fundamental measures underlying a new system of economic management is the main step in a decisive turn to intensive growth of the productive forces and the precondition for an approach to the scientific and technological revolution." [51]

Writing in 1967, Radovan Richta and company had to put the matter circumspectly. In 1970, R. V. Burks was more direct: "The basic obstacle to technological innovation in Communist countries is the inability of the Stalinist central planning to provide automatic institutional responses to new situations." [52] The answer? Not merely scientific and technical reforms, but economic reforms, as well. Like Eckstein, Burks noted two kinds. "Type B" is bureaucratic decentralization. In the short run, "any country, regardless of its stage of development, is probably better off with a type B reform than without it." But "except for the most backward countries—Rumania, Bulgaria, and Albania—type B reform promises at best only a temporary gain in efficiency, not a real solution. . . ." [53] It was not surprising to Burks that the Soviet leadership had opted for type B (since then largely discarded), but it was "difficult to foresee whether the gains from this limited, in-system reform will be sufficient to permit the continued postponement of structural change." [54] Or, as another Western observer, Gertrude Schroeder, put it: "The Soviet Technological Lag: System vs. Progress." [55]

Finally, political pluralism, itself. For some it is a derivative phenomenon, flowing, that is, from prior imperatives of economic or technological change. For Zvi Gitelman, however, "the need for intensive economic development seems . . . to be paralleled by a need for 'intensive political development.' . . . Just as the economy stagnates when the command economy is maintained after having outlived its usefulness, so too, the political system becomes less effective—though it is difficult to measure this—as its political formula becomes increasingly irrelevant." [56]

"The further development of Communist systems," declares Gitelman, "depends on their ability to go beyond Leninism." [57] Needed, he argues, are three kinds of reforms: (1) a new mechanism for leadership succession so that "change of leadership in Communist systems" will no longer be "both dramatic and traumatic, producing bureaucratic and personal insecurity"; (2) "a mechanism for the reliable transmission of public opinion"—if not freely contested elections, then frank and honest public opinion polls; if not an entirely open political process, then new scope for experts and interest groups; and (3) new possibilities for "authentic," as opposed to "spurious" citizen participation, participation characterized by "efficacy, voluntarism and responsiveness, none of which are typical of Communist systems." [58]

To be sure, Gitelman distinguishes between the changes communist systems need and those they (particularly the Soviet Union) will get. His analysis of the former draws heavily on the writing of Czechoslovak reformers. But of the four "schemes of political development" which have been "bruited about in Eastern Europe for at least a decade," only one, the "socialist pluralist" fits the Czech reform prescription. Gitelman admits that "the socialist pluralist developmental prescription comes closest to the Western notions of political development, at least for the post-modernization stage." [59] But of the Soviet regime he writes that it "probably enjoys more authority than most Communist regimes owing to such distinctive features as sheer duration of its rule, which has enabled it to effectively socialize several generations, its position as a global power, and the scientific, economic, and domestic and foreign political successes it had achieved." [60] What is likely for the short run, then, is change within the system. But in the long run familiar handwriting is on the wall:

> If Communist systems are arrested at their present stage of development they will inevitably decay, for 'not to advance is to recede.' The decay of the Communist political system will make it as a phenomenon of the modernization-mobilization stage, incapable of generating from within itself the capacity to persist by changing. Like the dinosaur, Communism may become extinct as a result of its failure to adapt to its changing environment. While it behooves us to remember that the age of the dinosaur lasted for millions of years, we must also be aware of the fact that environments change infinitely more rapidly in the twentieth century than in the Jurassic period.[61]

Revisionism

The beauty of the transformation-or-degeneration doctrine is that it is impossible to disprove. What would constitute transformation is fairly clear, but how is one to know when degeneration has set in? Furthermore, the time scale is open-ended. Is a communist system still somehow muddling through? Well, then—can the day of reckoning be far behind?

In the years since Khrushchev's ouster, the Soviet political system has neither transformed itself nor, it would seem, degenerated. Leadership succession has been neither dramatic nor traumatic: rule by oligarchy lasted longer than had been expected, then appeared to erode to the benefit of Leonid Brezhnev without the anticipated turmoil. Nor, conventional wisdom to the contrary, has leadership by "clerks" produced stagnation—unless stagnation is defined as the absence of transformation. True there have been persistent problems and examples of irresolution and indecisiveness, but few would deny that the post-Khrushchev leadership has managed, in Richard Lowenthal's words, "to improve the Soviet Union's position as a world power, by edging closer to the United States military strength. . . . and by extending areas under predominant Soviet influence."[62] Lowenthal, of course, draws the line at the water's edge, saying, "We are watching the successful outward expansion of an internally declining regime." But others, like Jerry Hough, find internal dynamism, as well—including "increased vitality of public debate" and "some major steps toward greater egalitarianism—steps that amount to a veritable war on poverty affecting millions of low-income citizens."[63]

One could, indeed many have, argued that the USSR is particularly suited, by special circumstances of size and tradition, to finesse the dilemma of postmobilization change. The scope and power of the Soviet economy may permit continued experimentation—further rounds of bureaucratic decentralization or regionalization instead of structural reform. In the Soviet Union, as compared with Eastern Europe, nationalism tends to support communism instead of undermining it—at least among Great Russians who despite a declining share of the population still play a disproportionate role in national political life. For some analysts, the prospect that the USSR may be a temporary exception proves the rule. But for others, the fact that the largest and most important communist system may not be archtypal but is instead to be explained by special circumstances only goes to show that the interesting elements of the equation are the special circumstances and not the rule.[64]

I am calling those doubters, on the Huntington model, modernization or postmodernization revisionists. At the risk of oversimplification, they stand in relation to the others considered above as follows: Isaac Deutscher predicted that the Soviet Union *would* change fundamentally. Brzezinski and Huntington wrote in 1964 that it *would not*. Later, Brzezinski and the postmobilization analysts concluded that the Soviet system *had to* change, but that at great cost to itself *might not*. According to revisionists, the system *need not* change to survive as an effective governmental process.

It is perhaps not surprising that Samuel Huntington should be counted among revisionists. As early as 1965, he differentiated between political modernization defined primarily in terms of participation, and political development which Huntington urged be understood as "the institutionalization of political organizations and procedures." [65] What distinguished "modern, developed, civic polities" were "high levels of both mobilization and institutionalization," both of which the Soviet Union had achieved. The Soviet Communist party was no obstacle to progress. Rather "the public interest of the Soviet Union is approximated by the institutional interests of the top organs of the Communist party: 'What's good for the Presidium is good for the Soviet Union' . . . . Just as a strong Presidency is in the American public interest, so also a strong Party is in the Soviet public interest." [66]

If some people (as the Soviets would say) are to be described as "anti-Soviet Marxist," then Huntington's 1965 analysis is an example of "anti-Soviet Leninism." [67] Which would explain Zvi Gitelman's "Beyond Leninism" charge that "Huntington consistently over-rates the ability of Communist systems to create new political institutions," that he fails to see that in the post-mobilization phase "Communist systems seem to have lost the capacity to continue to create political institutions which are 'adaptable, complex, autonomous and coherent' enough to deal effectively with social and economic transformations that they were so successful in bringing about." [68]

The basis for a Huntington reply to Gitelman appears in the former's essay on the "Social and Institutional Dynamics of One-Party systems." [69] Here, Huntington accepts several postmodernization arguments about what he chooses to call "the adaptive phase." "As a result of modernization and economic development, the society and the economy *are* more complex." [Italics added.] The party must *indeed* deal with "legal-rational challenges to its authority which are, in large part, the product of its earlier successes." Prime among these challenges *is* the rise of a new technical-managerial class, for it is true enough that "the innovators are not the reds but the experts." And yet the challenge to the party is not, as Brzezinski put it, "to adjust gracefully to the desirability and perhaps even the inevitability of its own gradual withering away." "What is required," according to Huntington, "is no longer a general staff directing the fundamental change from one type of society and economy to another but rather a coordinating staff relating to each other the various initiatives taking place within the society." The innovators may be experts; "the party apparatus, on the other hand, becomes a gyroscope rather than a motor." [70]

Like his former collaborator, Huntington takes his stand on the "requirements" of advanced industrial society—except that in his scheme of things modern, the party has an important place:

> The conflict between political generalist and managerial specialist is built into modern society, much as the conflict between church and state was built into medieval society. This conflict is inherent but limited. A complex society requires both increased functional autonomy for managerial specialists *and* increased political authority for the central political leadership. Meeting this latter need is the principal function of the party *apparat*. It is as essential to the system as the expert bureaucracy.
>
> In such a system the conflict between the political generalists and the managerial specialists continues, but it is a conflict between complements, the existence of each of which is necessary for the existence of the other.[71]

Is the CPSU *willing* and *able* to play the role of gyroscope? (Both subjective and objective dimensions are important.) According to Frederic Fleron, Jr., and Jerry Hough, among others, the party may well be. Dissatisfied with the equation, modern = pluralist, Fleron has proposed two alternative models. One, he calls an "adaptive-monocratic system"—in which a political elite which lacks skills needed to govern a complex, industrialized society obtains them either by retaining its cadres or by recruiting new ones. The second is a "co-optation system"—in which the political elites acquire needed skills by co-opting members of "various specialized elites in society, thus giving them direct access to the policymaking process." [72] Fleron's own research indicates, he reports, that "both the recruitment and co-optative mechanisms of adaptation have been employed by the Soviet political and party elites, resulting in the fact that those elites themselves possess the skills necessary to take an active part in the administration of industrialized society." [73]

Hough approaches the question through a study of local party organs in action. These do indeed play the role of a "coordinating staff relating to each other the various initiatives taking place within the society." According to Hough, party secretaries do not emerge as "men with 'an ideological form of political calculation and analysis' and a 'rigid and closed . . . set of rules of conduct spelled out by the ideology.' Rather they emerge . . . as men 'increasingly rational, analytical and empirical in their political action,' men with a 'pragmatic instrumental style' and 'the open, bargaining attitudes associated with full secularization.' " [74] Hough's conclusion, then, is that there may be "a variety of political systems with a large component of 'rational' and 'instrumental' behavior—including a number of political systems based on values quite offensive to our own," that "we may have to abandon the language of 'political development' with its inevitable images of lineal movement . . . or perhaps incorporate a more cyclical type of analysis," and that "the type of 'modern' but still quite authoritarian system into which the Soviet Union has evolved will prove quite durable," such that it, too, can "serve as the basis for a model of one possible 'modern' political system." [75]

How more fully and precisely to describe the Soviet model of modernity? That is the difficult question. Fleron's alternate "systems" deal with an important but limited problem—the nature and training of the political elite. Similarly, George Fischer, having mentioned "the monist model," which "holds that some mechanisms other than social autonomy can serve to pull together a vastly complex society," continues: "We know little about how such alternate mechanisms might look or work. Their study, theoretical as well as empirical, lies ahead." And so Fischer, too, "take[s] up only one such mechanism, centered on a society's ruling group and its top political executives." [76] Jerry Hough uses evidence of continuity and change in Soviet society to test three models—and arrives at ironic results which are worth considering at some length.[77]

Hough's first model is the "Directed society": the party still remoulding the system in accordance with established ideology. This he rejects as "hardly appropriate to the Soviet Union of the last seven years." Another model (borrowed from Brzezinski) is labeled "oligarchic petrification," a condition said to be characterized by "immobilism." The third involves "incrementalism," progress, even if slow, toward the healthy state of "institutional pluralism." [78]

Why choose pluralism as the touchstone of health? At first Hough seems unaware of the irony. He attempts to demonstrate that the Soviet polity has been evolving in the direction of institutional pluralism. But then there arises a problem. How to reply to a counterargument—that "the pace of change is so slow compared with societal requirements that the system must be called immobilized"? This objection could come, Hough knows, from those who say "the party has played out 'its historical role' and that the present state of technological development of Soviet society dictates evolution toward constitutional democracy and market socialism. . . ." [79] One way to counter would be to argue that according to tests often applied to the USSR (amount of innovation in domestic policy; age of leadership) the United States "is also afflicted with immobilism." But that could invite the riposte that "the Soviet system is so anachronistic that it requires more radical change that the American, or that the Soviet leadership must be more innovative to compensate for the weakness of innovative forces in the social and economic systems." [80]

On this train of thought, Hough approaches a disturbing conclusion—the time-honored Sovietological practice of predicting the Soviet future may be but a polemical guessing game backed by no verifiable standards. The comparison with the United States is suggestive, but "a comparative perspective—particularly one based on a two-country comparison—provides no final standard for judging petrification." [81] The question of what "society requires" is "not susceptible of a definitive answer, except perhaps by a future historian who will have the advantage of knowing what has occurred during the rest of this century." [82] How to differentiate between immobilism and incrementalism?

> In trying . . . we are essentially making a judgment as to whether changes are or are not "important" or "significant." As the debate over the New Left's charge of immobilism in the American political system demonstrates, however, any evaluation of this type rests essentially upon a subjective value judgment and/or on an unprovable assumption about what is "required" at a particular stage of history. In practice, there is a real tendency for such judgments to vary according to one's view of the status quo. If the status quo is considered fundamentally unjust then no change short of the most drastic transformation of the system will be considered significant. If, on the other hand, the status quo is considered more or less tolerable (given the inevitable imperfections in man and society), then incremental change seems much more important—and, in fact, desirable. Judgments of this type must remain basically "non-scientific" in nature.[83]

With this passage—perhaps unique in the annals of Sovietology—Hough arrives at the problem of ideology. Not ideology as it has been often discussed in communist studies; not Brzezinski and Huntington's definition ("a set of political ideas that are overt, systematic, dogmatic, and embodied in a set of institutions,") which frees the authors to declare that American political beliefs lack "the coherence and concreteness to qualify as an ideology." [84] But rather ideology of which, Andrew Hacker has written, "social scientists whether they acknowledge it or not, cannot help being bearers"; ideology which may be "purportedly normative, composed of philosophcial propositions which are actually rationalizations for preserving the status quo or attaining a new set of social arrangements," but which may also be "purportedly scientific: an unintentionally distorted picture of social reality, the distortion arising because the observer sees what he wants to see." [85]

The trouble, of course, comes in getting agreement on which constitutes "social reality." Many social scientists would agree with Hacker that "any theory which combines fact and norm, whether by accident or design, runs the risk of forcing descriptive reality into the Procrustean bed of ideology." But how many would plead guilty themselves? Hacker's conclusion is that "the real test is not whether fact or norm is tainted with ideology, but whether the ideology itself is a viable one." [86] William I. Connolly's answer is to call for "responsible ideology," in which "a serious and continuing effort is made to elucidate publicly all of the factors involved in its formulation and in which a similar effort is made to test the position at strategic points by all available means." [87] Granting that Hough is indeed on target, what remedy should communist studies resort to?

Revisionism Extended: Toward Bureaucratic Pluralism

One remedy, and a worthwhile strategy under any circumstances, would be to spend more time investigating the standards by which various groups in Soviet society gauge the effectiveness of their own system, and less time judging it by our own. One would no doubt find official Soviet handouts to be predictable. But scholarly journals might offer more interesting material as would, of course, the writing of dissenters.

But the basic challenge to students of communist societies is to work toward a set of criteria for modernity which would encompass both communist systems and those of the West. Ideally, the task would be to oppose a full-fledged counterthesis to the modernization and postmodernization theories criticized above. Instead, this article argues for a more limited goal: for greater awareness of the limits of orthodox approaches and for efforts to try other avenues—not in spite of their obvious ideological underpinnings, but rather precisely because those underlying assumptions have the effect of illuminating aspects of Soviet reality which other ideological lenses tend to filter out.

Connolly chides pluralist analysts of American society for defining pluralism with the aid of a less than challenging "contrast-model"—for example, the very model of monolithic totalitarianism about which so many Sovietologists now have such doubts. The trouble with such black and white comparisons is that they "fail to emphasize problems and dislocations we share with these other systems; they fail to dramatize future possibilities here which are not in practice somewhere else." [88]

Of course, the change to change in communist systems was undertaken precisely to avoid that pitfall. In contrast to the totalitarian-democratic comparison, the conception of the Soviet Union as a modernizing or an advanced industrial system *does* bring out features common to non-Communist societies, as well. And yet despite the similarities—"the nature of contemporary technology; the system of mass education; the key role of modern cities; the highly developed transportation and communication facilities, the dominant position of scientific undertakings; a certain commitment to rational procedure in the organization of production and the utilization of human resources" [89]—the Soviet system is said to be not fully modern.

Nor do the revisionist alternatives go far enough. Theirs is a plea for diversity: although different from the West, the Soviet Union may be no less modern. But suppose one questions the Western model itself? What happens to the Soviet-American comparison when one considers the arguments, by radical and not-so-radical critics, that the American system is itself ill-suited in important regards for the postmodern world?

Let me summarize, at the risk of oversimplification, two major critical arguments concerning American pluralism. The first, more moderate, warns of a surfeit of pluralism. The more radical critique emphasizes limits of pluralism in American politics. These are not necessarily contradictory. Combined, they add up to the worst of two worlds—a tendency toward stalemate on the issues which are openly debated, but at the same time a built-in bias against the raising and championing of other important causes.

The first criticism may be illustrated with a discussion of technology and political change in America. Emmanuel G. Mesthene was director of the Harvard University Program on Technology and Society established in 1964 by the IBM Corporation. Mesthene's argument is that the result of our attachment to individualism and pluralist decision making has been an "inability to adjust our decision-making structures to the realities of technology so as to take maximum advantage of the opportunities it offers, so that we can act to contain its potential ill effects before they become so pervasive and urgent as to seem uncontrollable." [90] What is required, Mesthene believes, is a new role for government, no longer "the simple arbiter of conflicting interests between business, labor, farmers or whatever," but as "social pioneer and leader of a team." "Allowing political change to come gradually and of its own accord may no longer be viable strategy for contemporary society." We, no less than the Soviets, face a need for transformation, for "deliberately restructuring our political institutions and decision-making mechanisms—including the system of economic decision-making—to make them adequate to the enhanced role of the public sphere." [91]

The second argument—made by many but summarized here by William Connolly—contains a number of points: (1) that "the prevailing system inhibits some segments of society from efficacious involvement while bestowing cumulative advantages on others"; (2) that the "process of interest aggregation ignores some concerns explicitly shared by many citizens because persistent, active and legitimate 'groups' fail to define these concerns as high priority interests"; (3) that "many *latent concerns* —those that might well interest wide segments of society if they were publicly articulated as issues—are not identified or sharply defined by the prevailing system of issue formation." What this adds up to is the very dilemma which post-modernization analysis sees confronting the USSR—that while "a rapidly expanding technology promotes equally rapid social change, ideological and institutional constraints in the political system inhibit efforts to cope with the accompanying dislocations." [92]

What are the implications for an understanding of the Soviet system of these critical evaluations of the American? Consider as an object lesson Frederic Fleron's reaction to Robert Paul Wolff's judgment that "the pluralist system of social groups is an obstacle to the general good!" If Wolff were to be proven right, Fleron continues, then the "social and political character of Western industrialized society will have progressed through phases essentially individualistic, pluralistic and collectivistic," to the point where " 'modern' political systems would be those characterized by such a collectivist approach." That in turn would necessitate an "embarrassing revision of current theories" with the result that "systems would be viewed as developing toward this postpluralist higher stage or facing decay and destruction." Which would imply, Fleron concludes, that "perhaps the Soviet Union is again 'skipping historical stages' since it has been guided by a collectivist ideology for several decades." [93]

Fleron's speculation is overly schematic. His notion of a "transform-or-decay" imperative is particularly unfortunate. But the idea of skipping stages is fascinating. For may it not be the case that a collectivist or monist governmental process which was functional for rapid industrialization but may indeed be less than conducive to technological innovation could in a modified from become useful to contain technology's potential ill effects?

With such a statement of the case, critics of American pluralism might be expected to agree. Instead, they argue that communist systems have ironically managed to match or even exceed industrial capitalism's shortcomings. In sum, they offer a different notion of modernity and a different conception of convergence—and in doing so direct our attention to some often-neglected features of the Soviet system. Consider Galbraith. His view of America is that science and technology have given power to the "industrial system"—economics and politics organized in service of the system's goals ("the expansion of output, the increase in consumption, technological advance and the public images that sustain it"), other goals (a peaceful foreign policy, urban planning, environmental reform) getting short shrift. When Galbraith looks at the USSR he finds another industrial system in the saddle. There, too, a "technostructure" operates to increase its autonomy; there a conflict exists "between those for whom the needs of government, including above all its needs as economic planner and producer of goods, are pre-eminent, and those who assert the high but inconvenient claims of uninhibited intellectual and artistic expression." [94]

Or take Robert Heilbroner. He continues to believe that socialism is "the expression of a collective hope for mankind, its idealization of what it conceives itself to be." [95] But it is also his view that both the Soviet Union and the United States have shown themselves "ill-adapted to the problem of our age," and that "both will have to improvise and experiment to make their social systems operate effectively in a world in which technology and bureaucracy present overwhelming challenges for which we have discovered no adequate responses as yet." [96]

In the time-honored tradition of discourse on socialism, Heilbroner stands other commentators (this time Brzezinski and Burks) on their heads. Rather than setting the imperatives with which Soviet society must come to terms, technology, to Heilbroner, threatens two kinds of disaster. That a new elitism may be "inherent in a society dominated by technology," that a "highly trained research elite . . . has all the attributes of a potential ruling class," is Heilbroner's first warning. His second is that "the problem of maintaining ecological balance, the very viability of the earth itself" poses to socialism the enormous challenge of imposing "stringent limitations . . . not alone on the productive apparatus of society" (which in the Soviet Union has for so long been favored), "but very possibly on its consumptive patterns," which are beginning to burst forth after being repressed.[97]

Are Galbraith and Heilbroner right and Brzezinski and Burks wrong? That is, I submit, the wrong way to put the question. Neither approach is "scientifically objective." Both have ideological content in the sense that I have defined ideology. Different perspectives produce different angles of vision on the Soviet system. Galbraith and Heilbroner bring to mind James Burnham's argument that the "Managerial Revolution" had triumphed in both East and West.[98] Which most practicing Sovietologists would probably describe as putting the managerial cart before the party horse; to which Soviet experts would counterpose Jeremy Azrael's conclusion that while:

> both American and Soviet societies have industrial executives and in both societies economic leadership entails political influence, . . . for the purposes of political analysis, this similarity may be *less significant* than the fact that group activities of the Soviet managerial elite have never been accorded political legitimacy; that members of the group have occupied bureaucratic positions within a centralized state system; that recruitment into the managerial elite has been governed by political criteria. [Italics added.][99]

In part such a difference concerning the power of industrialists may reflect a terminological confusion as to who is included in the category of managers. But the more important question, and the key point for our purposes, is what is to be considered more or less significant? True enough that on important issues Soviet industrial managers have not won their way. Is that more or less significant than the fact that the system has given first priority to industrial growth at the expense of other important goals —to the point that Jerry Hough could argue that "surely the dominant forces of recent decades" have been those, including managers *and* party apparatchiki, which "emphasize priority for industrial growth over other interests"? [100]

To those who are less fearful of technical elitism or take a less apocalyptic view of environmental decay, Heilbroner's warnings may ring hollow. And yet his and Galbraith's approach does jibe with certain evidence that fits neither Brzezinski's nor Huntington's account. Both the latter agree that "the innovators are not the reds but the experts." Such a rule is overly general, but grant for the sake of argument that it holds true for technical or economic issues. It is decidedly not the case, however, as far as other postmodern issues, for example, urban and environmental reform are concerned. In these areas managerial technocrats are not necessarily innovators, but often vigorous opponents of change which would challenge power positions built up in the years of all-out industrialization. On these issues, the much-maligned party apparatchik is indeed needed, as Huntington inferred, to rein in managerial specialists. Yet ironically, supposedly powerful party secretaries are far from powerful enough to dictate to entrenched industrialists.[101]

Which brings us back to political pluralism. According to Gordon Skilling, Soviet pluralism cannot be described as "genuine." [102] To quote Andrew McFarland, it is "spurious" because "one could say that the administrators make unimportant routine decisions whereas the Party makes the important critical decisions," spurious in contrast to American politics "where there is more bargaining by more people over more important more critical policy decisions." [103]

Such a comparison does have a point, as even critics of American pluralism admit. Writes one critic: "The [American] mass media, although definitely biased, present a significantly wider range of information and opinion"; "freedoms of association, assembly and speech are comparatively well protected here . . . even after one has corrected for the gap between official rhetoric and established practice." [104] Furthermore, whereas only a few critics accept the simplistic notion that an identifiable power elite conspires to produce the bias of American pluralism, the limits on Soviet dissent are established and maintained by an entirely visible hand. But consider the issues on which Soviet debate *is* permitted. Consider the fact, reported by Hough, that in recent years "on all but the most central questions, Party policy is less and less incorporated into a clear-cut undebatable ideology," with the result that "there has, in fact, been virtually no conceivable proposal for incremental change in Party policy in the last five years that has not been aired in the Soviet press." [105] Many of these issues *are* fought through in a pluralist political competition which is inadequately described by the term "spurious." And at the same time, there is observable a "mobilization of bias" which far from deriving from the party's "monopoly of power," rather reflects the ability of vested bureaucratic interests—the military-heavy industrial complex, for example—to resist the central leadership's efforts to encourage change.[106] Both the presence and these limits of Soviet pluralism reflect the hierarchical nature of the Soviet political system. The fact of centralization is real. But it is also the case that the Soviet policies, and lack of policies, mirror the clashes and compromises of bureaucratic agencies and their representatives, and that Soviet governmental behavior reflects not only the Politburo's deliberate political purpose but also the mode of operation of complex large-scale organizations that even a powerful central leadership cannot always and everywhere control.[107]

In short, Soviet pluralism is neither genuine nor spurious, but rather different (and yet not so different) because of its bureaucratic nature.

Compared to the dark days of Stalinism, the increased scope for politics surely represents a gain. How the degree of pluralism correlates with the "amount of modernity" is, however, as the saying goes, another question.

Notes

1. Samuel P. Huntington, "The Change to Change: Modernization, Development and Politics," *Comparative Politics*, III, 3 (April, 1971), 283–322. The term, "the study of given conditions" is quoted by Huntington from David Easton, *The Political System* (New York, 1953), 42.

2. Huntington, "The Change to Change," 285.

3. Dankwart A. Rustow, "Communism and Change," in Chalmers Johnson, ed., *Change in Communist Systems* (Stanford, 1970), 347.

4. *Ibid.*

5. Roger E. Kanet, ed., *The Behavioral Revolution and Communist Studies* (New York, 1971), 4.

6. R. V. Burks, "The ACLS, Summer 1968 Workshop on the Comparative Study of Communism: A Report," *Newsletter on Comparative Studies of Communism*, II, 2 (June, 1969), 2.

7. Chalmers Johnson, "Comparing Communist Nations," in Johnson, ed., *Change in Communist Systems*, 2.

8. *Ibid.*, 1.

9. See, for example, "Symposium," *Slavic Review*, XXVI, 1 (March, 1967), 3–28. For later discussion see John N. Hazard, "What Future for Communist Area Studies?" *Newsletter on Comparative Studies of Communism*, IV, 2 (February, 1971), 3–10; and Gabriel A. Almond, "Toward a Comparative Politics of Eastern Europe," *Studies in Comparative Communism*, IV, 2 (April, 1971), 71–78.

10. See Kanet, ed., *The Behavioral Revolution and Communist Studies* and Frederic J. Fleron, Jr., ed., *Communist Studies and The Social Sciences* (Chicago, 1969).

11. See Johnson, ed., *Change in Communist Systems*.

12. Rustow, "Communism and Change," 350.

13. See Huntington, "The Change to Change," 293, n. 17. That, in Huntington's words, "political scientists have yet to probe very deeply the political implications of the new historical transition," makes particularly pertinent an examination of the "post-modern" approach to Soviet politics.

14. For two recent surveys, see Alfred G. Meyer, "Theories of Convergence," in Johnson, ed., *Change in Communist Systems*, 313–314 and John S. Nelson, "Theories of Convergence," *Newsletter on the Comparative Study of Communism*, IV, 2 (February, 1971), 11–28. I am not entirely in agreement, however, with classifications employed in these articles, for example, Professor Meyer's placing in the same category of W. W. Rostow and J. Kenneth Galbraith who have very different notions of where the two systems stand and what's right or wrong with them.

15. Zbigniew K. Brzezinski and Samuel P. Huntington, *Political Power USA/USSR* (New York, 1963), 10.

16. *Ibid.*, 423.

17. *Ibid.*, 424.

18. Zbigniew Brzezinski, "The Soviet Political System: Transformation or Degeneration," *Problems of Communism*, XV, 1 (January–February, 1966), 1–15.

19. *Ibid.*, 11–12.

20. *Ibid.*, 14.

21. *Ibid.*, 15.

22. Zbigniew Brzezinski, *Between Two Ages: America's Role in the Technetronic Era* (New York, 1970).

23. *Ibid.*, 170.

24. *Ibid.*, 172.

25. *Ibid.*, 174.

26. *Ibid.*, 301–302.

27. George Kateb, ed., *Utopia* (New York, 1971), 20. See his *Utopia and Its Enemies* (New York, 1972).

28. *Ibid.*, 21.

29. Rustow, "Communism and Change," 353.

30. Johnson, "Comparing Communist Systems," 3.

31. *Ibid.*, 12.

32. *Ibid.*, 20.

33. *Ibid.*, 22.

34. *Ibid.*, 24.

35. *Ibid.*, 25.

36. Richard Lowenthal, "Development vs. Utopia in Communist Policy," in Johnson, ed., *Change in Communist Systems*, 33–116.

37. *Ibid.*, 54.

38. *Ibid.*, 110.

39. *Ibid.*, 112.

40. *Ibid.*, 116.

41. Amitai Etzioni, *Modern Organizations* (Englewood Cliffs, N.J., 1964), 106.

42. Talcott Parsons, "Evolutionary Universals in Society," *American Sociological Review*, XXXIX, 3 (June, 1964), 355–356.

43. Andrew Hacker, "Sociology and Ideology," in Max Black, ed., *The Social Theories of Talcott Parsons* (Englewood Cliffs, N.J., 1961), 309.

44. Parsons, "Evolutionary Universals," 356.

45. Alexander Eckstein, "Economic Development and Political Change in Communist Systems," *World Politics*, XXII, 4 (July, 1970), 490.

46. *Ibid.*, 493.

47. *Ibid.*, 492.

48. *Ibid.*, 493.

49. *Ibid.*, 494.

50. *Ibid.*, 475–476.

51. From Epilogue of *Civilization at the Crossroads: Social and Human Implications of the Scientific and Technological Revolution*, II, by Radovan Richta and a research team (Prague, 1967), as excerpted in Robin Alison Remington, ed., *Winter in Prague* (Cambridge, Mass., 1969), 9.

52. R. V. Burks, "Technology and Political Change," in Johnson, ed., *Change in Communist Systems*, 288.

53. *Ibid.*, 292–293.

54. *Ibid.*, 311.

55. Gertrude Schroeder, "The Soviet Technological Lag: System vs. progress," *Problems of Communism*, XIX, 5 (September–October, 1970), 19–29.

56. Zvi Y. Gitelman, "Power and Authority in Eastern Europe," in Johnson, ed., *Change in Communist Systems*, 240.

57. Zvi Y. Gitelman, "Beyond Leninism: Political Development in Eastern Europe," *Newsletter on Comparative Studies of Communism*, V, 3 (May, 1972), 28.

58. *Ibid.*, 31.

59. *Ibid.*, 41.

60. Gitelman, "Power and Authority," 258.

61. Gitelman, "Beyond Leninism," 43.

62. Richard Lowenthal, "Changing Soviet Policies and Interests," in *Adelphi Papers*, 66 (March, 1970), 11.

63. Jerry Hough, "The Soviet System: Petrification or Pluralism?" *Problems of Communism*, 2 (March–April, 1972), 37, 39.

64. For a discussion in parallel terms of the notion that the United States is the archtypal example of capitalism, see Robert L. Heilbroner, "Phase II of the Capitalist System," *New York Times Magazine* (November 28, 1971), 87.

65. Samuel P. Huntington, "Political Development and Political Decay," *World Politics*, XVII, 3 (April, 1965), 393.

66. *Ibid.*, 413–414.

67. How else to describe an argument which (1) sees the mark of a successful polity as political stability and control; (2) endorses "the Bolshevik concept" of political development because it "provides a conscious and explicit answer to the problem of mobilization vs. institutionalization"; and (3) describes Communists as "the most energetic and intense contemporary students" of de Tocqueville's "art of associating together"?

68. Gitelman, "Beyond Leninism," 20.

69. Samuel P. Huntington, "Social and Institutional Dynamics of One-Party Systems," in Samuel P. Huntington and Clement H. Moore, eds., *Authoritarian Politics in Modern Society* (New York, 1970), 3–47.

70. *Ibid.*, 32–33.

71. *Ibid.*, 33.

72. Frederic J. Fleron, Jr., "Toward a Reconceptualization of Political Change in the Soviet Union: The Political Leadership System," in Fleron, ed., *Communist Studies and the Social Sciences*, especially 231–234.

73. Frederic J. Fleron, Jr., "Co-optation as a Mechanism of Adaptation to Change: The Soviet Political Leadership System," in Kanet, ed., *The Behavioral Revolution and Communist Studies*, 133–134.

74. Jerry F. Hough, *The Soviet Prefects* (Cambridge, Mass., 1969), 312. The quotes within quotes are from Gabriel A. Almond and G. Bingham Powell, Jr., *Comparative Politics: A Developmental Approach* (Boston, 1966).

75. Hough, *The Soviet Prefects*, 317.

76. George Fischer, *The Soviet System and Modern Society* (New York, 1968) 14.

77. I refer to Hough, "The Soviet System: Petrification or Pluralism?"

78. *Ibid.*, 25–29.

79. *Ibid.*, 37.

80. *Ibid.*, 41.

81. *Ibid.*, 40.

82. *Ibid.*, 41.

83. *Ibid.*, 36.

84. Brzezinski and Huntington, *Political Power*, 19–20.

85. Hacker, "Sociology and Ideology," 298.

86. *Ibid.*

87. William I. Connolly, *Political Science and Ideology* (New York, 1967), 152–153.

88. William I. Connolly, "The Challenge to Pluralist Theory," in Connolly, ed., *The Bias of Pluralism* (New York, 1969), 23.

89. Allen Kassof, "The Future of Soviet Society," in Kassof, ed., *Prospects for Soviet Society* (New York, 1968), 504–505.

90. Emmanuel G. Mesthene, *Technological Change* (Cambridge, Mass., 1970), 44.

91. *Ibid.*, 69

92. Connolly, "The Challenge to Pluralist Theory," 18–19.

93. Fleron, "Co-optation as a Mechanism of Adaptation to Change," 142. Wolff's statement appears in "Beyond Tolerance," in Wolff, Barrington Moore, Jr., and Herbert Marcuse, *A Critique of Pure Tolerance* (Boston, 1965), 51.

94. J. Kenneth Galbraith, *The New Industrial State* (New York, 1967), 404.

95. Robert L. Heilbroner, "Socialism and the Future," *Commentary*, XLVIII, 9 (December, 1969), 45.

96. Heilbroner, "Phase II of the Capitalist System," 90.

97. Heilbroner, "Socialism and the Future," 41, 42.

98. See James Burnham, *The Managerial Revolution* (New York, 1941), especially Chaps. 6, 7, and 14.

99. Jeremy Azrael, "The Managers," in R. Barry Farrell, ed., *Political Leadership in Eastern Europe and the Soviet Union* (Chicago, 1970), 247.

100. Hough, "The Soviet System: Petrification or Pluralism?" 38.

101. On environmental issues, see David E. Powell, "The Social Costs of Modernization: Ecological Problems in the USSR," *World Politics*, XXIII, 4 (July, 1971), 618–634. On political change in Soviet cities, see William Taubman, *Governing Soviet Cities: Bureaucratic Politics and Urban Development in the USSR* (New York, 1973).

102. H. Gordon Skilling, "Interest Groups and Communist Politics: An Introduction," in Skilling and Franklyn Griffiths, eds., *Interest Groups in Soviet Politics* (Princeton, 1971), 17.

103. Andrew S. McFarland, *Power and Leadership in Pluralist Systems* (Stanford, 1969), 88–89.

104. Connolly, "The Challenge to Pluralist Theory," 13.

105. Hough, "The Soviet System: Petrification or Pluralism?" 31.

106. See, for example, Gertrude Schroeder, "Soviet Economic Reforms at an Impasse," *Problems of Communism*, XX, 4 (July–August, 1971), 36–46.

107. For a bureaucratic politics framework worth applying to Soviet politics, see Graham T. Allison, *Essence of Decision* (Boston, 1971).

Index